The Literature of Cinema

THE LITERATURE OF CINEMA presents a comprehensive selection from the multitude of writings about cinema, rediscovering materials on its origins, history, theoretical principles and techniques, aesthetics, economics, and effects on societies and individuals. Included are works of inherent, lasting merit and others of primarily historical significance. These provide essential resources for serious study and critical enjoyment of the "magic shadows" that became one of the decisive cultural forces of modern times.

The Cinema

*Its Present Position
and Future Possibilities*

National Council of Public Morals

ARNO PRESS & THE NEW YORK TIMES

New York • 1970

Reprint Edition 1970 by Arno Press Inc.
Library of Congress Catalog Card Number: 78-124002
ISBN 0-405-01608-5
ISBN for complete set: 0-405-01600-X
Manufactured in the United States of America

THE CINEMA

THE CINEMA

ITS PRESENT POSITION AND FUTURE POSSIBILITIES

BEING THE

REPORT OF AND CHIEF EVIDENCE

TAKEN BY THE

CINEMA COMMISSION OF INQUIRY

INSTITUTED BY THE

NATIONAL COUNCIL OF PUBLIC MORALS

LONDON

WILLIAMS AND NORGATE

1917

Printed in Great Britain by
Richard Clay & Sons, Limited,
Brunswick St., Stamford St., S.E. 1,
and Bungay Suffolk.

INTRODUCTION

IT is necessary to a right understanding of the objects of the Commission that we should briefly explain why it was initiated by the National Council of Public Morals. The Council had published in June 1916 the report of the National Birth-Rate Commission giving the results of its three years' inquiry into the causes and effects of the declining birth-rate, and had presented it to the Government. The Rt. Hon. W. H. Long, M.P., President of the Local Government Board, in receiving the Commission said—

" My first duty, and a very great privilege it is, is, on behalf of the Government and on behalf—may I for a moment voice something much wider and much larger than the Government ?—on behalf of society in the country, to thank your Commission for the splendid work which you have done. The last speaker referred to the financial cost of this work. I venture to say, although I do not for a moment doubt that the burden in this respect was a heavy one, that the good which you have done by your inquiries and by your report cannot by any possibility be measured in terms of money.

" I am confident that, if you have done nothing else, and I think you have done a great deal more, you have stirred the minds and the hearts of men in so profound a way that even the most careless, the most indifferent, cannot be deaf to your entreaties or regardless of your suggestions."

Many leading articles and reviews appeared in the Press of the United Kingdom and America on this Report, from which two extracts may be given.

Church Times : " A Royal Commission was demanded. An even more characteristically English method, however, has been preferred. The National Council of Public Morals, one of those unofficial organisations which are the pride of English endeavour, undertook the work; the offer was welcomed by the Government, officials of which were instructed unofficially to lend all possible aid."

New Statesman (Dr. Sidney Webb) : " The National Council of Public Morals has done a great public service. The Commission has produced the most candid, the most outspoken, and the most impartial statement that this country has yet had as to the extent, the nature, and the ethical character of the voluntary regulation of the marriage state which now prevails over the greater part of the civilised world.''

The Council, as that Commission more fully disclosed, is a composite body of religious, scientific and educational leaders, and its objects are felicitously expressed in the words of H.M. King George V which form its motto—

" The Foundations of National Glory are set in the homes of the people. They will only remain unshaken while the family life of our race and nation is strong, simple and pure.''

Amongst the various branches of the Council's work it has for some years been deeply concerned with the influence of the cinematograph, especially upon young people, with the possibilities of its development and with its adaptation to national educational purposes. The Bishop of Birmingham, the President of the Council, took a leading part, together with the Rev. F. B. Meyer, D.D., the Chairman of its Executive in the first Cinematograph Congress at the Olympia in 1913.

It is well that we should again recall the principles, as set out in its reports, upon which the Council conducts its operations. We have striven in and out of season to remove the emphasis from rescue to prevention and from prevention to construction. We have sought, not to come out into the streets and with clamouring to strike the evil on the head, for the effect of this policy has been, whilst appearing to clear the evil away in one place, to drive it to take deeper root underground and to spring up again with tenfold more vigour elsewhere. We have rather set ourselves to undermine the evil, to get at the deeper causes in character, low ideals, ignorance, and false prudery. And in so doing we have expressly desired to win the sympathy of the men and women who are writing our books, are catering for public amusement, edit or own our newspapers, and have under their control the vast machinery for instantly and effectively reaching millions of people. We have seen the folly of making enemies of those who control these great and potent agencies by indiscriminate denunciation, by standing upon a lofty pedestal and playing the superior part, censoring, denouncing, imprisoning. The law must be enforced and constantly pressed up to the level of public opinion, and we have all along taken our share in doing that work. But our deepest concern has been to help all those whose enterprises are calculated, when run on a low level, to foster the merely animal nature, especially of the young, to raise the whole tone and character of their industries, as well as to get rid of the obviously indecent thing, which is by no means the greatest danger we have to fear.

Acting on these principles, we resolved to lose no opportunity of dealing fully with the cinematograph. Our previous work had prepared the way of approach. Although known to be stern enemies of the evils we all deplore, we have happily been known to be as earnestly desirous of encouraging the better thing, and dealing fairly and honestly with all men. Our record, especially our Commission on the Birth-Rate, and our principles brought the leaders of the cinematograph trade to seek our help. Here is a great invention with as yet unrealised possibilities for the healthy amusement and education of the people, which is influencing the lives of the overwhelming majority of the inhabitants of every city, town, and remote hamlet in the United Kingdom : why should we stand aside, or merely denounce and alienate the men who run it, and only call upon the police to censor it ?

Much more than this was required of us. We were invited to meet representatives of the whole trade, and to discuss frankly the best means of getting rid of whatever evil elements existed, and of meeting the demands of the best public opinion for a higher-class programme, for more suitable exhibitions for children, for the suppression of certain evils which had thrown themselves on the cinema halls as they had on other places, and which the war had accentuated, and also for the establishment of a censorship which would give legitimate freedom for the proper development of the cinematograph whilst rigorously cutting out undesirable films. We met the trade, and fully and openly discussed these proposals. We carefully studied the whole subject and situation, discussing them with Government and educational authorities, and we met many times to confer upon them. We saw that we all ought to know much more about the character, extent, and the influences of the cinematograph. There was clearly a strong case for thorough and impartial inquiry. This the leaders of the trade saw and heartily welcomed as the best means of obtaining the results we all desire. But the Council resolved not to propose the matter themselves, but to wait until the various sections of the trade should themselves ask us to establish such an inquiry. And in due course we received the following letter—

" 199 Piccadilly, London, W.
" *November* 24, 1916.

" At a meeting yesterday of the Cinematograph Trade Council, representing the Cinematograph Exhibitors' Association of Great Britain and Ireland, Ltd., the Incorporated Association of Kinematograph Manufacturers, Ltd., and the Kinematograph Renters' Society of Great Britain and Ireland, Ltd.,

" It was Resolved :

" That the National Council of Public Morals be requested to institute an independent inquiry into the physical, social, moral, and educational influence of the cinema, with special reference to young people.

" (*Signed*) A. E. NEWBOULD."

On receiving this the Council met, and resolved to accept the invitation, subject to certain conditions, one being that our inquiry should not be used in any way whatever to interfere with the proposals [1] for a Home Office censorship, and that it was perfectly distinct from that question. That condition was accepted by the trade, and has been loyally observed. We also made it known at the Home Office when we mentioned the matter of the proposed inquiry, together with the draft terms of reference and suggested names of the Commissioners, and invited them to appoint a representative. This was done some time before the matter was finally decided and before any notice had appeared in the Press. When it was also mentioned to the Home Secretary, Mr. Herbert Samuel, M.P., at a private interview on Friday, October 27, 1916, he expressed his pleasure that the inquiry was to be undertaken. At subsequent meetings our Council decided upon the persons who should form the Commission, upon the exact terms of reference, and arranged all its details. We did not invite any member of the trade to our Council meetings. Our action was taken independently of them, and the Commission was appointed solely by the Council, and its report has been presented to and is here published by the Council. The Council undertook the whole financial responsibility, and has not asked for nor received any financial help from the trade.

MEMBERS OF THE COMMISSION

The following are the Members of the Commission appointed to undertake the Inquiry. It should be noticed that we included three members of the trade, nominated, at our request, by the Trade Council.

The LORD BISHOP OF BIRMINGHAM (President).

Rev. PRINCIPAL ALFRED E. GARVIE, M.A., D.D. (Vice-President).

Lt.-General Sir R. S. S. BADEN-POWELL, K.C.V.O., K.C.B., LL.D.

Sir W. F. BARRETT, F.R.S.

Rev. CAREY BONNER (General Secretary, representing The Sunday School Union).

Sir EDWARD W. BRABROOK, C.B. (President, Child Study Society, London).

Right Rev. MONSIGNOR CANON W. F. BROWN.

Mrs. BURGWIN (late Superintendent Special Schools).

Mr. C. W. CROOK, B.A., B.Sc. (President, National Union of Teachers).

Commissioner ADELAIDE COX (representing the Salvation Army).

Mr. A. P. GRAVES, M.A. (representing and Chairman of the Representative Managers of L.C.C. Elementary Schools).

The Rabbi PROFESSOR H. GOLLANCZ, M.A., D.LIT. (representing the Jewish Community on the National Council).

Dr. C. W. KIMMINS, M.A. (Chief Inspector under the Education Committee of the London County Council).

[1] We now know that these proposals had been virtually abandoned before the Commission began its sittings.

Mr. W. GAVAZZI KING (Secretary, Cinematograph Exhibitors' Association).

Sir JOHN KIRK, J.P. (Director of Ragged School Union).

Mr. SIDNEY LAMERT (Director, London Film Company, Ltd.).

Rev. F. B. MEYER, B.A., D.D., ⎱ representing the National Free
Rev. F. C. SPURR. ⎰ Church Council.

Mr. A. E. NEWBOULD (Chairman, Cinematograph Exhibitors' Association; Director, Provincial Cinematograph Theatres, Ltd.).

Mr. T. P. O'CONNOR, M.P. (Chief Censor).

Dr. C. W. SALEEBY, F.R.S., Ed.

Dr. MARIE STOPES, ⎱ representing the Incorporated Society
Mr. EDGAR JEPSON, M.A. ⎰ of Authors, Playwrights and Composers.

Rev. W. E. SOOTHILL, M.A. (representing the Young Men's Christian Association).

Rev. JAMES MARCHANT, F.R.A.S., F.L.S., F.R.S., Ed. (Secretary).

TERMS OF REFERENCE

The Terms of Reference to the Commission were as follows—

1. To institute an inquiry into the physical, social, educational, and moral influences of the cinema, with special reference to young people; and into

2. The present position and future development of the cinematograph, with special reference to its social and educational value and possibilities.

3. To investigate the nature and extent of the complaints which have been made against cinematograph exhibitions.

4. To report to the National Council the evidence taken, together with its findings and recommendations, which the Council will publish.

ACKNOWLEDGMENT AND THANKS

The National Council desires to tender grateful thanks to the witnesses, some of whom travelled long distances to give evidence, and all of whom most willingly accepted the invitation of the Commission to attend, and in some cases prepared elaborate précis of their proposed evidence for the convenience of the Commissioners. It is to be regretted that owing to the great shortage of paper it has not been possible to publish all these précis in their entirety.

The Council desires to express its appreciation of the kindness of His Majesty's Foreign Office and of the Commissioners of H.M.'s Dominions in obtaining for their use the Regulations of the Cinematograph Censorship in force in other countries; of the Chief Constables of the United Kingdom whose valuable memoranda appear in Appendix III; and of the London County Council for allowing its Chief Inspector, Dr. C. W. Kimmins, M.A., to serve on the Commission, and for sending a representative of its Licensing Committee to give evidence before the Commission.

The Council wishes to offer its warmest thanks to the National Review Board of New York for undertaking an inquiry on their behalf into the effect of Cinematograph Exhibitions upon Juvenile Delinquency in the United States, and for offering to send a representative to England to confer with the Commission.

The Cinematograph Trades Council has rendered every assistance in its power, has produced all documents and films necessary to the inquiry, has freely answered every request for information, and its officials have willingly submitted to extensive cross-examination. For this assistance the Council desires to offer its best thanks; and in particular to Mr. A. E. Newbould, Chairman of the Exhibitors' Association, who has rendered conspicuous public service in working for the highest interest of the industry and the country.

The cordial thanks of the National Council are tendered to the Council of the Institute of Civil Engineers for their generosity in placing their excellent Council Chamber at the disposal of the Commission for its sittings; and to Mr. J. D. Tippett for the use of his private theatre for the inspection of films and posters kindly collected at considerable trouble by Mr. F. R. Goodwin. The Rev. T. M. Thornton has gladly and freely assisted the Commission in many ways, for which the Commission and Council are very thankful.

Finally, the National Council would respectfully beg to be allowed to express its profound gratitude to the President the Lord Bishop of Birmingham; to the Vice-President the Rev. Principal A. E. Garvie, M.A., D.D., and to every Member of the Commission for their eminent services whole-heartedly given to this extensive and difficult investigation, the value of which we believe will be gladly acknowledged by the whole nation.[1]

On behalf of the National Council,

JAMES MARCHANT,
Director and Secretary.

20 *Bedford Square, W.C.*
July 16, 1917.

---

[1] It has been decided to keep the Commission in being for the purpose of furthering its recommendations and co-operating with the Censor with respect to the Advisory Council.—J. M.

LIST OF WITNESSES

CONTENTS

PART I

THE REPORT OF THE COMMISSION

SECTION I

MORAL AND SOCIAL ASPECTS OF THE CINEMA

ADDENDUM

SECTION II

THE CINEMA IN ITS RELATION TO THE EDUCATION OF CHILDREN

PART II

MINUTES OF EVIDENCE

Witnesses:

MR. F. R. GOODWIN

Chairman of the Cinematograph Exhibitors' Association
(London Branch)

CONTENTS

CONTENTS

CONTENTS

b

CONTENTS

PART I

THE REPORT OF THE COMMISSION

WHILE no one to-day would venture the suggestion, so commonly made a few years back, that the popularity of the cinema is no more than ephemeral, it may be doubted if there is even yet sufficient realisation of the strong and permanent grip which the picture palace has taken upon the people of this country. All other forms of recreation appeal only to a section of the community, but the lure of the pictures is universal; while the cheapness and accessibility of the houses make it possible for the masses to indulge in this enjoyment almost to an unlimited extent. In the course of our inquiry we have been much impressed by the evidence brought before us that moving pictures are having a profound influence upon the mental and moral outlook of millions of our young people—an' influence the more subtle in that it is subconsciously exercised—and we leave our labours with the deep conviction that no social problem of the day demands more earnest attention. The cinema, under wise guidance, may be made a powerful influence for good; if neglected, if its abuse is unchecked, its potentialities for evil are manifold.

The figures presented to us in relation to the industry are bewildering in their immensity. Carefully tabulated returns of attendances have been kept, and these show that in this country there are no fewer than 1,075,875,000 attendances at picture shows in the course of a single year. In the British Isles there are approximately 4500 theatres with a mean seating capacity which affords accommodation for one in every thirty-seven of the population. On the basis of these figures the entire population of the United Kingdom visits picture shows approximately once each fortnight. About 5000 new " subjects " are issued each year, and some 70,000,000 feet of film are running through the projectors of the country each week. From 80,000 to 100,000 persons are directly engaged in the various branches of the trade

The cinematograph industry has been aptly likened to an international circulating library business of which each country forms a branch station. The films which are exhibited in our houses go the rounds of the world, literally from China to Peru. In considering the literary and artistic qualities of the pictures, it is necessary to bear in mind that they are produced to meet the taste of the great mass of the people.

The functions of the cinema are broadly three—recreative, educational and propagandist. Of these the recreative is at present the most prominent, but to this aspect of the cinema we have not exclusively directed our attention in this inquiry. We recognise quite clearly that it would be a mistake to throw on an industry commercially conducted for private profit the onus of leading public opinion, and indeed no claim is made that the leaders of the industry desire or are competent to undertake this work. Accordingly, educational and other authorities in the country might well consider how far they can assist in raising the whole status of the cinema, and to assist them in this endeavour has been a main object of our inquiry.

In accordance with the terms of reference from The National Council of Public Morals, the Cinema Commission of Inquiry began its work on January 8, 1917, and finished July 9, 1917. It has examined forty-three witnesses, representing all the different interests involved in the inquiry, as well as a number of boys and girls. In addition to the weekly sittings for hearing witnesses, the Commission has held a number of other sittings at a private theatre for the inspection of the films complained of. It also appointed Committees to visit various cinema halls, and, as the evidence shows, caused many other inquiries to be made on its behalf amongst Chief Constables, Clerks to the Justices of the Peace, and among School and Y.M.C.A. workers. It has received numerous communications from the general public in almost every part of the United Kingdom, and as far as possible has given attention to every complaint made. It is to be regretted that a few of those who have most prominently identified themselves with the attacks on the picture house, which were the immediate occasion of the inquiry, have refused to give evidence so that their charges might have been thoroughly investigated, and their validity or otherwise have been established. While the representatives of the trade have offered every facility, the inquiry has been absolutely independent and impartial; and we, the members of the Commission signing this Report, submit it with the conclusions and recommendations we have reached, in full confidence that it will receive the unprejudiced consideration which we believe that by its character it deserves, and which in the moral, social, educational and religious interests of the nation it is desirable should be given to it.

As of primary importance, we first of all report on the moral and social aspects of our subject, dealing with the accusations brought against the picture house. As connected with this, the use made of the cinema by religious agencies and other movements is briefly referred to. Next, with a view to indicating its possibilities, we report on the educational aspects, and in this connection also with the music in the picture house. This may be treated from two points of view: the educational, as a means of cultivating popular taste; and the physical, as a relief from eye-strain. We are thus led to the consideration of the conditions under which the films may be viewed without injury to the eyes. The amount of the light in the building has a bearing on the moral aspect of the subject as well, since darkness may be used for evil purposes; in this way we have found the different parts of our inquiry closely related. We then at the close of our Report deal with the ideal conditions and offer our recommendations.

SECTION I

MORAL AND SOCIAL ASPECTS OF THE CINEMA

THE STANDARD OF JUDGMENT

IN stating the results of our inquiry in regard to the influence of the picture house on the morals of the people, and on society generally, it is necessary to discriminate between what is ideal and what is practicable. While in public amusements there should be constant endeavour to raise the standard, and the possibility of elevating popular taste by the kind of amusement provided must be recognised; yet, on the other hand, the action of public authority cannot go very far ahead of the common moral judgment. While manifest evil must be repressed, what approves itself to the highest moral sentiment cannot always be enforced. It is this distinction that we have kept before ourselves in dealing with the question.

SPECIAL CONSIDERATIONS REGARDING THE CINEMA AS A PLACE OF AMUSEMENT

The picture house is the cheapest, the most accessible, and the most widely enjoyed form of public entertainment; it is most popular in the poorest districts, and is attended by a very large number of children and young people.[1] Owing to the variety of the pictures shown, it is impossible for any person entering to be quite sure as to the quality of the entertainment which will be provided for him.[2] In a programme for the most part unobjectionable, one film of a very objectionable character may be shown.[3] This uncertainty must be taken into account in dealing with the moral influence of the moving pictures. For these reasons the conclusion seems justified that a rather more rigid standard of judgment should be applied than to the theatre or the music hall, where the programme is known beforehand, and the attendance of children is almost negligible.

[1] pp. 1–6.　　　[2] p. 149[24].　　　[3] p. 17[104]; p. 211[6].

I.—THE CHARGE OF INDECENT CONDUCT

A distinction must be made between moral evils *incidental* to the picture house and those *consequential* on the kind of film shown. The charge has been brought against the picture house that the darkness encourages indecency, especially where there are boxes, though this is the case in a very few houses;[1] and that the promenade or the standing room at the back of the building, where such exists, affords opportunities for improper conduct.[2] In 1915 there were only two prosecutions for indecency in connection with the cinema brought under the notice of the London Branch of the Exhibitors' Association.[3] A probation officer of twenty-five years' experience stated that he had known of only one indecent assault in a cinema,[4] and another that during four years one charge of indecent assault had been made, and that there were far more charges of indecency taking place in open spaces.[5] A social worker in East London stated that she had " seen the boys behave in a very nasty manner towards the girls," and gave a specific instance of a gross act she had herself observed.[6] Sir Robert Wallace reported that a number of cases of indecent assault had come before him, and that there was reason to believe that many women, shrinking from the publicity involved, did not make the complaint they might have made. He had had a number of letters from fathers of girls telling of horrible things, for which the standing room at the back had afforded opportunity. He strongly objected to any promenade or any unnecessary moving from seat to seat.[7] This unwillingness on the part of the public to make complaint in such cases shows that the number of charges cannot be taken as absolutely indicating the extent of the evil.

THE MORAL DANGER OF DARKNESS

The insufficient light in some picture houses has been represented as involving this grave moral danger. The Chief Constable of Edinburgh, who in his statement dealt only with the indecency or suggestiveness of films, when cross-examined replied that he did not think it possible for immorality to take place within the buildings, " but he had had one or two complaints of indecent assaults having been committed," and "other chief constables had had similar complaints." He had no doubt that this was "due largely to the fact that the cinema is carried on in a state of darkness more or less,"[8] and agreed that "the darkness, com-

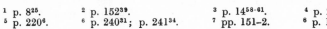

---

[1] p. 8[25].   [2] p. 152[39].   [3] p. 14[58-61].   [4] p. 208[20].
[5] p. 220[6].   [6] p. 240[31]; p. 241[34].   [7] pp. 151–2.   [8] p. 178[14].

bined with the low standard of morality of the individual," led to indecency.[1] The Chief Constable of Dundee stated his belief that " were due attention paid to the construction of the premises, and the highest degree of light consistent with the proper working of the lantern insisted on, cause of complaint in this respect would be removed." [2]

Similar opinions have been expressed by the Chief Constables of Guildford,[3] Hull,[4] and Margate.[5] The Directors of Education of Liverpool [6] and Manchester [7] concurred in desiring better lighting for the same reason, and the latter expressed the opinion that not only would eye-strain be relieved, but the value of the pictures would not suffer.[8] Other evidence to the same effect has been given.[9] In the Report of the Special Inquiry submitted by the Rev. Carey Bonner, the following statistics were given : 70 per cent. of the replies reported lighting good; 20 per cent. of the replies reported lighting insufficient or bad, and 10 per cent. as only fair.[10] Our conclusion from this evidence is that the degree of lighting has a large bearing upon the decent or moral conduct in the theatre. Cases are not unknown where misuse of the premises is entirely traceable to the dim character of the lighting. Given adequate illumination, this misuse disappears.

ACTION OF THE LONDON COUNTY COUNCIL

In 1916 the London County Council, moved thereto by " some very terrible although somewhat ambiguous charges " regarding " the molestation of children," [11] took action. At first the County Council proposed that seats from which all adults should be excluded should be reserved for children unaccompanied by adults.[12] When the exhibitors pointed out the difficulties this would involve, the County Council waived the proposal, and accepted the suggestion of the trade that in every hall there should be an attendant, bearing a distinguishing badge, whose sole duty during the time the premises were open to the public should be to look after the children attending the hall.[13] A suggestion from the Chief Commissioner of Police to the Home Office also led the London County Council to add the regulation that the lights should go up after every picture.[14]

ACTION OF THE HOME OFFICE

The Chief Commissioner of Police arranged with the National Union of Women Workers of Great Britain that a systematic

---

[1] p. 179[16].　　[2] p. 179.[15]　　[3] p. 352.　　[4] p. 356.　　[5] p. 360.
[6] p. 42[127].　　[7] p. 165[10].　　[8] p. 170[38].　　[9] p. 134[26]; p. 156[56]; p. 240[30].
[10] p. 307.　　[11] p. 8[27].　　[12] p. 9[28].　　[13] p. 9[28].　　[14] p. 11[30].

visitation of all the picture palaces should be made. The 248 halls in London were visited.[1] In sixty-six a special children's attendant was seen.[2] In eighty-three separate accommodation for children unaccompanied by adults was provided. In sixty-six cases the darkness would have made it difficult to discover cases of indecency. In thirty-nine cases the structure, viz. dark corners, boxes, use of curtains, etc., might afford opportunity for indecency.[3] While in the West End halls few children were seen, in the suburban halls there were many, even children in arms, especially on Saturdays and Sundays. The halls seemed to the visitors for the most part unnecessarily dark; in a few cases also the ventilation was bad, and the buildings dirty. " No instance of any act of indecency is described by the lady visitors." " The general conclusions," says the Chief Commissioner, " at which I have arrived are that it is very desirable that the regulations as to children's attendants and children's seats should be strictly enforced and that consideration should be given to the question of better lighting, ventilation, the prohibition of expectoration, the exclusion of children in arms, and finally, that steps should be taken to institute an efficient censorship so as to prevent the exhibition of films calculated to familiarise the young with ideas of violence, crime and immorality." [4]

Rebutting Evidence

Mr. Goodwin, representing the Exhibitors of London, asserted that in many cases the charge should never have been made. " When investigation is made it is usually found that the alleged misconduct is nothing more than the privileged manifestation of affection between the sexes." [5] He maintained that the danger of indecency was no greater in the cinema than other places of public resort.[6] In reference to the kindred evil of solicitation, he stated that steps were taken to eject any woman who used the standing room or moved from seat to seat for any such purpose, even although there was in case of mistake the risk of heavy damages.[7] He also expressed the opinion that more light would give more opportunity to women for solicitation,[8] and that there was the danger of spoiling the picture.[9] He stated that the London Branch of the Exhibitors' Association had approached the Home

[1] Although in this Report other matters are referred to besides the question immediately before us, we have thought it best to summarise the Report as a whole.

[2] In some of the high-class West End houses no children's attendant would be found for the reason that they do not cater for children, and no child unaccompanied by an adult is admitted (p. 10).

[3] Cf. pp. 178–9[14-16].   [4] pp. 10, 11[30].   [5] p. 83.   [6] p. 14[63].

[7] p. 87[27-30]; p. 26[7].   [8] p. 8[22-4]; p. 19[135-6]   [9] pp. 21–2[161-4].

Secretary with suggestions for dealing wit the evil,[1] and he assured us that the trade is endeavouring to prevent the misuse of the picture house for any evil purposes, as it is in the interest of the exhibitor to maintain the good reputation of his house, and nothing could be worse for him than that it should get a bad name.[2] It is anxious to do all in its power to comply with the present regulations, and to accept any new regulations, if necessary, to abate the evil as far as possible.[3] Last year it issued to all the members of its organisation an urgent recommendation that there should be immediately installed, " (a) a separate light in each box; and (b) a glass panel in the door of each box." In very few of the theatres are there boxes, and it might be desirable that these should be altogether prohibited, a course that the authorities concerned are said to be contemplating, if by the means suggested the evil is not removed.

Mr. Cecil Hepworth, a representative of the trade, urged a number of technical objections to the increase of light beyond a certain point in the lighting of the halls. He maintained that the analogy with a scientific lecture hall was not complete, and mentioned as an increase of the difficulty the smoking in the halls. He agreed that some places might be better lighted without any injury to the distinctness and brilliance of the picture.[4] Mr. Newbould also pressed this objection,[5] and maintained that the prevention of indecency required only light sufficient to allow of adequate supervision; and he explained that by adequate supervision he did not mean that an inspector should be able to survey the whole building at once, but that an attendant walking down the aisles should be able to see the end of the seats fed by that aisle.[6] With some hesitation he also mentioned the increase of cost that would be involved.[7] The question of lighting in its scientific aspects is further discussed in another section of this report.[8]

The Means of Dealing with the Evil

While this is an evil which is not easy of proof; that it does exist in both forms of indecent assault and solicitation, there is no doubt, although the charge has been exaggerated. But there is no evidence that it is more prevalent in the picture house than in other places of popular resort. This is not an evil inherent in the picture house. It is evident that where it exists it can be restrained by more adequate supervision and lighting, the provision of a seat

---

[1] pp. 83–5.   [2] pp. 18–19[120-22].
[3] pp. 19–20[138-9, 149-52].
[4] pp. 74–5[179-81]; cf. p. 21–2[161-4].   [5] p. 267[5].   [6] pp. 263 and 267[5].
[7] pp. 264 and 267[5].   [8] See pp. lxxvi ff.

for every person admitted, the abolition of standing room and boxes where they exist, and the provision of a special attendant to look after the children. When there are boxes, adequate lighting beyond the control of the occupant should be insisted on. It is generally agreed that sufficient light to secure adequate supervision can be provided without interfering unduly with the distinctness and brilliance of the picture.[1] Even if the picture has to suffer a little, we think that adequate lighting must be insisted on. It is only fair to add that by the withdrawal for the army of so many men who had been trained for the delicate task of supervision, the difficulty of control has been greatly increased,[2] and that in some picture houses frequented by soldiers and women of bad character the necessity for it has at the same time become greater. The difficulty of turning out any undesirable persons must be recognised, as in case of mistake a heavy penalty might be incurred. While women are doing excellent work as ushers, we are of opinion that there should be at least one male attendant in every picture house to deal with matters for which women are obviously unsuited. It is for the local authority to enforce such regulations as will prevent these dangers, which, however, as far as we have been able to ascertain do not appear as widespread as is often assumed. We strongly urge that the public, however disagreeable a task it be, in the general interest should help the authorities by at once calling their attention to any house where these exist, if on appeal the management of the house has refused to act, as it was stated that such information would be gratefully received and treated as confidential by the local authority.[3]

II.—THE CHARACTER OF THE FILMS

A still more difficult problem presents itself in the moral influence of the films displayed. It is often asserted that the films are vulgar and silly; in reference to these two charges it is impossible to set up a rigid standard of judgment. As regards vulgarity not only do individual tastes differ, but the conventions of different classes vary. Indecency or obscenity can be repressed by public authority; vulgarity can be got rid of only by the elevation of popular taste. Worthy people find silly what they have not enough sense of humour or of the ridiculous to appreciate; and are offended by the joke which they themselves fail to see. It must be remembered that the picture house is a place of amusement, and if it makes people laugh, it cannot be condemned on that account. It is much easier to define and therefore to deal

[1] p. 267.   [2] p. 267.   [3] p. 296[25]

with indecency or obscenity; and that this evil should be rigorously excluded from the cinema all our witnesses who expressed
an opinion were agreed. Several witnesses did give specific instances of films that they themselves regarded as coming under
this condemnation. But even where indecency or obscenity, as
the law would define it, may be avoided, there often is a suggestiveness in dealing with " sex " relations which for the large number
of youthful spectators attending picture houses must be regarded
as objectionable.[1] A committee which in the city of Worcester
has been investigating the question reports that " some at least
of the cinema exhibits—for instance, in ' Society Dramas,' and the
like—are helping to lower the standard of reverence for women,
and familiarising the minds of our young people with loose ideas
of the relations of the sexes." [2] This statement was entirely en-
dorsed by the Dean of Worcester.[3] As far as possible, when any
film was specially mentioned as objectionable, some members of
the Commission saw it. One film which had been condemned
by several local authorities was seen by some of the members of
the Commission in order that they might form an independent
judgment of it for themselves. They needed to see only a part
of it to be convinced that from beginning to end it offensively
obtruded sensuality. Other films condemned without reservation by one of the witnesses were also carefully examined; while
in some respects objectionable, they were not felt to be so bad that
public opinion generally would support their entire prohibition.
It is to be regretted that in drama and novel as well as film the
" sex " interest is often made so dominant, unmodified by other
interests as it is in actual life. To exclude it altogether must be
confessed practically impossible in the present condition of public
opinion. But at least such reserve may be insisted on as will
prevent a film being a stimulus to sensual desire, not in the sexually
morbid, whom it would be impossible always to keep in view, but
in the normally constituted youth and maiden.

NEED OF A STRICTER CENSORSHIP

While the evidence as a whole could not justify a charge that
many films, objectionable on this account, are exhibited, and
while we recognise that the previous Censor and his examiners
discharged their difficult duties with the desire to protect the
public, yet the evidence before us shows that there is a need for
a stricter censorship than has been exercised in the past. It
would be in the long run in the interests of the trade itself that it

[1] p. 134[27]; p. 240[30].   [2] p. 143.   [3] p. 147[10].

should free itself from any ground of reproach,[1] and we have evidence before us that a stricter censorship is now being exercised.[2]

Evidence was submitted to prove that the posters advertising the films are often much more objectionable than the films themselves,[3] when they emphasise the sensational or sensual aspects. At present the Trade Censorship does not touch these at all, and the Billposters' Association controls only the posters that go on the public hoardings. And, therefore, posters on the front of the hall itself are altogether uncensored, but steps are being taken to deal with this evil.[4]

DIFFICULTIES IN THE WAY OF IMPROVEMENT

It is well in conclusion to state the practical difficulties which have to be met in bringing about an improvement, so as to avoid unreasonable advice or hasty action which would imperil the continuance of the picture house as a cheap and popular form of amusement.

1. It has been insisted again and again by representatives of the trade that exhibitors can only provide profitably what the public will take. They state, for instance, that the public does not to any extent want the educational film. This contention cannot be allowed absolutely; the danger of the position of the purveyor of public amusements is that it inclines him to rate both the intelligence and the conscience of his patrons lower than they actually are, or at least can possibly be made.[5] But the education can be only gradual, and time must be allowed for it.

2. The following consideration has been pressed upon us.

As more than 90 per cent. of the films being now shown in British picture houses are American,[6] and as the British market is only a negligible fraction of the market of the American producer both at home and throughout the whole world,[7] a raising of the standard here without a corresponding rise there, would mean that the picture houses might be deprived of the supply they need for the constant change of programme twice a week. It is not at all likely that the American producer would take the trouble to make special provision unless at a greatly enhanced price for a market so small as the British is, if it so differed in its standard from the American as to make any considerable portion of the American output unacceptable. It is just as

---

[1] p. 63[44-6].   [2] pp. 244–6.
[3] p. 18[112-18]; p. 24[198]; p. 29; p. 85[1-3]; p. 135[28]; p. 208[19].
[4] pp. 221–5.   [5] p. 5; p. 67[82-8].   [6] p. 15[72-80].
[7] pp. 195–6[2-9]. There are 30,000 cinemas in the United States as compared with 4500 approximately here.

unlikely that for many years to come it would be at all possible
for the British manufacturer to supply more than a small proportion
of the total number of films constantly required.

Mr. Newbould, who gave evidence on behalf of the trade, did
not admit without qualification the suggested improbability of a
sufficient supply of British films for many years to come. " There
is a big public demand for British films, but it is not articulate,
and British manufacturers are working under serious commercial
difficulties as against the American manufacturer, inasmuch as
they have great difficulty in selling their productions in America.
A joint advertising campaign urging the public to insist on seeing
British productions, together with the setting up of an efficient
sales organisation for the handling of British-made films in America,
would, in my opinion, quickly result in at least 50 per cent. of
the films shown in this country being of British origin, while the
development of the American sales of such films would enable the
British manufacturer to expend more money on his productions." [1]
Mr. Seddon, the organising secretary of the Exhibitors' Association,
was asked the question : " Seeing that the vast majority of the films
that come into the country are American, how are they to be made
to conform to the standards that we should like here ? " and answered, " Well, I should say the best means would be to cultivate
home production." When the objection was urged : " We are told
that the home manufacturer is struggling against this competition
and that he does not see his way to crush it ? " he took up the
challenge in the words : " The proposition is that we, as an
Association, are out to make the business reputable and respectable,
and we are anxious for censorship so that the public and the trade
will have confidence in the man who has been appointed as Censor
because of his experience." [2]   As regards the improbability of the
American producers making special provision for the British film
market, one suggestion may be offered. The closer relation between
this country and the United States, a result of the calamity of the
war, from which we expect not a little good in the future, lead us
to hope that we on this side of the Atlantic may be able by closer
co-operation with those on the other side who are equally interested
in the morals of the people, to raise the standard in the production of films there even as here. The same expectation may be
cherished as regards our Allies, France and Italy. This is as probable at least as the assumption that so utterly impracticable a
standard of censorship will be set up in Great Britain as would
exclude so large a proportion of American films that British producers would be quite incapable of making up for the shortage,

[1] p. 266.   [2] p. 293[22-3].

and picture houses would need to close for lack of films to show. Our proposals, while insisting on the elevation of the standard, recognise the practical difficulties of any too hurried change.

3. A third difficulty which deserves passing notice is this : that the exhibitor cannot in most cases see the films for his house before they reach him, but must depend on others for the selection of them. " Each of the trade journals (three in number) print reports on all important films, and most of the others ; but even of the unreported films (unreported because of lack of space) there is a synopsis." [1] We have been informed that the Cinematograph Exhibitors' Association issues weekly to its members a list of films which have been carefully viewed, and this list contains only films which could be shown to persons of any age. Besides this agency, two classes of viewers are employed. " In many instances exhibitors engage the services of individuals òr a staff whose sole work is that of viewing and passing judgment on films." [2] Those exhibitors who cannot afford to maintain such a staff employ " the free-lance viewer." " There are a number of viewers, both male and female, who spend their time in viewing films for many theatre proprietors, and whose reports can be purchased by any exhibitor who wishes to subscribe to such service." [3] While the viewer's main concern is commercial, *i. e.* to choose the films which will be most attractive to the kind of spectators the picture house is catering for, it is not exclusively so. " He will tell you whether it is sensational, and whether it is bordering on the immoral. All the viewers in the trade are looked upon as censors." [4]

III.—THE SPECIAL CLAIMS OF CHILDREN

As the picture palace is attended by a larger number of children than any other form of public amusement, their interests must be more fully considered here than elsewhere. While it would be impossible to require that all exhibitions should be determined by exclusive regard for children, yet care must be taken to protect them from what would be morally injurious to them. Many of the public authorities are realising their duty in this respect, although they have been prevented by legal difficulties from giving full effect to their good intentions.

SPECIAL INQUIRY REGARDING THE INFLUENCE OF THE PICTURE
HOUSE ON CHILDREN

A special inquiry was made on behalf of the Commission by the Rev. Carey Bonner, General Secretary of The Sunday School

[1] p. 194.   [2] p. 193.   [3] p. 194.   [4] p. 197[14].

c

Union, among Sunday-school teachers and others interested in the welfare of the young. In respect to the character of the films he states : " The reports are characterised by impartiality, and even where some objection is taken to certain films, due admiration for the good ones is expressed. In dealing with the ' crook ' films the observer noted the enthusiasm of the youngsters when the wrong-doer was brought to book. Many testify to the greater care now exercised by proprietors in showing better-class films. Seventy-five per cent. replied that in the pictures seen there was nothing they deemed injurious to children. Another $7\frac{1}{2}$ per cent. replied similarly, but with a slight modification, such as ' for the most part,' or ' many were silly ' or ' inane,' but not harmful; or ' out of twenty-eight films viewed, only two were objectionable.' The remaining $17\frac{1}{2}$ per cent. considered that the pictures they saw were (for the most part, at any rate) objectionable, or were, in their judgment, likely to be harmful to young people. In the more general answers under this heading, several visitors strongly objected to details of crime being shown; others objected to ultra sensationalism or the exhibition of impossible or dangerous feats of daring; and others to the ' innuendo and suggestiveness ' of several of the situations in sex problem films." [1] One film which was specially objected to was seen at a children's matinée.[2] The result of this inquiry is, on the whole, reassuring as regards the kind of entertainment provided. This report also refers to another charge against the cinema, to which we must next give fuller attention.

Juvenile Crime

It is very strongly alleged and widely believed, that the picture house is responsible for the increase in juvenile crime, and that boys are often led to imitate crimes (larceny or burglary) which they have seen in the pictures, or to steal money that they may pay for admission. Here we must again distinguish between the incidental and the consequential.

(a) Thefts to pay for Admission

There is nothing so peculiar to the cinema that only by its attraction are children led to pilfer that they may be able to pay for admission. Children steal to buy sweets, or " penny dreadfuls," or any object on which their hearts are set. Even a picture house quite unobjectionable in every respect might exercise such an attraction. The only way to obviate this evil would be to abolish the picture house altogether, or to banish children from it, or to

----

[1] p. 308. Cf. p. 143.   [2] p. 17[104].

make admission free, or to make it so " deadly dull " that no child would want to go there.   But is the charge true, or true as generally as it is represented ?   One probation officer declares that the statements of children as to why they stole are not to be taken too seriously, as sometimes these are suggested to them by others, and they are only too ready to accept any excuse that they think will secure for them more lenient treatment.   " Sweets, cigarettes, tram rides, music halls as well as picture palaces are the reasons frequently given for stealing." [1]   Another probation officer says :   " As soon as these thefts have been effected, the confectioner's shop is the first place visited.   Then sometimes the picture show, or, if the money stolen was sufficient, the first houses of the music halls are commonly patronised." [2]   Sir Robert Wallace, however, takes the charge much more seriously.   " The boy goes there day by day, and the result is that he exhausts his own money first, and then arises that which has been so frequently the case, he then takes his employer's money to go, and he is starting that criminal career." [3]

But can the cinema as such be held responsible for the evil, assuming even that it exists more widely than the evidence before us has given us any reason to believe ?   On the one hand, the miserable conditions at home and in the streets in which many of these children live account for the irresistible attraction of the picture house, which brings some brightness into a very drab lot.   On the other, the lack of parental control and other elevating moral influences explain how some yield so very easily to the temptation.

(b) IMITATIVE CRIME

To the other charge against the picture house we now turn : that it is what the boy sees there that suggests, and even stimulates crimes, such as larceny or burglary.   It is admitted that the young mind is very responsive to suggestion, and ready for imitation.[4]   Risk, danger, adventure, boldness appeal to the boy. Sir Robert Wallace gives two cases from his own experience of such imitative adventurous crime.   In the one case a youth of seventeen years had committed six burglaries, in which he had stolen watches and jewellery to the value of £80 or £90, of which he had not realised a single penny.   His circumstances were such, the witness alleged, as to exclude any other motive than the impulse to do himself what he had seen done in the picture houses, which he visited almost daily.   In the other case two

[1] pp. 218–19.   Cf. p. 41[119-23]; p. 120[7]; p. 130[34].
[2] p. 205.   [3] p. 154[40].   Cf. p. 212[7-8].   [4] p. 120[4]; p. 141[62]; p. 309.

youths, seventeen or eighteen years of age armed with a stage
pistol, entered a shop, and under the threat, " Your money or
your life," made the owner hand over the contents of his till.
There, too, the only reason that the witness could assign was
the wish to do themselves what in the films they had seen done.[1]
Such cases must, however, be regarded as exceptional; although
their possibility does afford a good reason for the rule now adopted
by the Censor 'of Films, that no film shall be exhibited in which
the method of a crime is presented, nor any in which crime is
the dominant and not merely a subordinate interest.[2]   A probation
officer expresses himself very moderately on the question : " So
far as films depicting burglaries, robberies, and other infringements of the law are concerned, I have this to say—where a good
home influence is wanting, then I think quite possibly such films
may have a pernicious effect on the young.   It must be borne
in mind that children who are looking at these pictures are at
the impressionable period.   Their home life does not provide
for the inculcation of the cardinal virtues, and in a large number
of cases they are children of unhealthy body and mind.   In such
cases films of this type may give a wrong impetus to the imagination of the child.   These films, though possibly harmless to adults
and not providing any practical information even to the children,
may in some cases stimulate the imagination in an undesirable
way.   Even in these films it is necessary to point out that the
moral lesson is always satisfactory.   It is always demonstrated
that vice brings its own penalty in suffering, both for body and
mind.   I have never seen any film in which the contrary result
was illustrated, and undoubtedly this spectacle of inevitable
retribution must tend to offset the fictitious glamour of wrong-
doing." [3]   Another probation officer does not even admit the
connection between the cinema and crime to the same extent :
" The films chiefly complained of, crime and ' crook ' films, have,
in my opinion, little if anything to do with the increase in juvenile
crime.   Let any keen observer attend a cinema when a ' crook '
film and detective story is shown and listen to the children's
cheers when the crook has been run to earth and punished.   To
my mind' the effect is neutral, if anything, and almost forgotten
in the pictures that follow.[4]   The children of this district could
learn little, if anything, about crime from such films.   They see
and hear very much more in their miserable so-called homes,

[1] pp. 152–3[40].   [2] p. 245; pp. 249–50[16]; p. 251[25].   [3] p. 205.
[4] Evidence submitted by Dr. Kimmins shows, however, how retentive
the memories of the children are, p. 275. The sensational and romantic
parts are said to be longer remembered than the comic, (p. 129[19]).

and sometimes in the places of detention. They recount to one another their exploits." [1]

Causes of the Increase of Juvenile Crime

One of the witnesses indicates as one of the greatest causes of juvenile crime and of the increase of it the receiver of stolen property.[2] A reason given for the recent increase of juvenile crime may be mentioned : " The main cause is the absence of the fathers, and I want to say that history is only repeating itself. During the South African War for two years I had boys under my control whose fathers, being reservists, had been called up for service." When asked if at that time there were no cinemas, the witness added : " I do not remember any. In a number of cases I also find that the mothers go out to work, and I have known cases where families of nine and ten children have been left entirely to the care of a girl of twelve or thirteen years of age, and even, in some cases, these children are left at night." [3] There are other economic and social changes due to the war, which must be recognised as factors in the increase of juvenile crime.[4] There has really been an increase of juvenile crime, but not so great as the numbers of delinquents would indicate ; for on the one hand children are now brought before the courts for offences which cannot be called crimes, and on the other a greater number of persons is now engaged in keeping the young in the right way, sometimes with too great zeal. "There has been a tendency in recent years to increase the *variety* of offences with which children may be charged. For instance, children are now charged with wandering, with being without proper guardian-ship, with being beyond proper control. Our streets are now more rigidly supervised than ever before. There is a large and increasing number of officials whose duty it is to watch over child life. In many cases the zeal of these officers was not always tempered adequately by humanity and expediency." [5] The problem is far too complex to be solved by laying stress on only one factor, and that probably a subordinate one, among all the contributing conditions.[6] Many well-meaning persons who bring such charges have neither the knowledge nor the skill for difficult social investigations. Even in those cases where a crime can be shown to be imitative of what has been seen in the pictures, the whole blame must not be cast on the cinema. On the negative side we must take account of the absence of the restraining moral

[1] p. 219.   [2] p. 220[2].
[3] pp. 207–8[13-15].   Cf. p. 180[19]; p. 184; p. 242[2].
[4] p. 204.   [5] pp. 204–5.   [6] p. 37[62-3].

principles which a good home and wise training would supply, and which in so many cases are altogether lacking. On the positive side we must recognise the superfluous energy of youth, and its spirit of adventure, which are often deprived of lawful and useful outlets. The cinema suggests the form of the activity rather than provides the impulse to it. That same impulse, unless rightly restrained and wisely directed, in other circumstances would find some other form. There is genuine insight in the remark of a probation officer : " From my personal experience with these cases I am of the opinion that generally the evil of certain pictures has not been so much the cause of the crime as an indication of a line of action to some children who, by neglect and adverse environment, are already inclined to lawlessness." Our conclusion then must be, that while a connection between the cinema and crime has to a limited extent in special cases been shown, yet it certainly has not been proved that the increase of juvenile crime generally has been consequent on the cinema, or has been independent of other factors more conducive to wrongdoing.

Conflict of Evidence

The foregoing conclusion may be confirmed by showing how conflicting is the evidence which has been brought under our notice by witnesses, or has been secured by the special inquiries we have made through correspondence.

No Connection discovered between Cinemas and Juvenile Crime

The Director of Education for Newcastle-upon-Tyne, Mr. Sharp, whose duty it is to inquire carefully into all the cases of children committed to Industrial Schools, is most definite in asserting that he has, in his own experience, not met with any such connection between the cinema and juvenile crime.   " I have not during the last three years of investigation (covering 186 cases of committal) had a single case brought to my notice in respect of which it is alleged, or even suggested by police, school-attendance officer or head teacher that the genesis of the wrongdoing was to be found in the cinema show, either immediately or remotely. I have mentioned the period of three years because that covers the period of my work in Newcastle, up to date. I may add, however, that I do not recall a single such instance in the preceding ten years, during which I acted in a similar capacity in a Lancashire county borough of 100,000 population. I have gone further, and examined the records of my predecessors, which have been preserved in this office, of 76 other cases from this city area now being maintained in Industrial Schools, and I cannot find any trace of a single child whose wrong-doing has been attributed, either directly or by inference, to the influence of the cinema show." [1]

A Close Connection

In 1916 in Liverpool a report on Juvenile Crime was issued by a Joint Committee of justices and members of the Education Committee. About the picture house it makes this statement : " Nearly all the witnesses were agreed that constant attendance at cinematograph theatres has an injurious effect upon juvenile mind and character. Not only are children frequently induced to steal in order to obtain admission (it is quite a common excuse in theft or begging cases that the money was wanted for ' the pictures '), but what is perhaps of even greater importance is that in very many cases the intellectual morale of the child is injured, and its powers of concentration are weakened by a too frequent attendance at such places. It is suggested that, where desirable, the magistrates should introduce by way of a condition in Probation Orders, restrictions as to the attendance of the probationer at cinema exhibitions. The evidence adduced has also impressed on the Committee the urgent necessity for continued strict supervision of the theatres and illustrative posters, with insistence upon the observance by licensees of the Justices' Rules and Regulations regarding films, and the attendance of children." [2]

The Connection not so Certain

Mr. John Kay, head master of a school in Liverpool, gave evidence regarding an inquiry conducted by the Lancs. Teachers' Association. Regarding the charge that children steal in order to get to the pictures, he says : " Teachers recognise that it is most difficult to establish cause and effect, and that in many cases the theft would probably have occurred in any case. The picture shows only afford a ready means of disposing of part of the booty. But two facts clearly emerge. In the first place, children of criminal tendency in a school are found among the most regular frequenters of the shows. Secondly, the ' street-trading ' class in large centres, already beset by many handicaps, are frequent attenders at the ' second house ' when their papers or other wares are sold." [3]

Difficulty of estimating Influence of a Film

Mr. Spurley Hey, Director of Education, Manchester, in a paper on " Juvenile Crime," considers the influence of the cinema.

[1] p. 284.   [2] p. 29.   [3] p. 119.

" It is clear that a categoric condemnation of the picture house, even as organised at present, is impossible; further, it would appear that the use of films might be made an educative instrument of a high order. The limits and character of subconscious suggestions cannot be measured and defined; and whereas certain imitative criminal acts committed by boys have undoubtedly been traced to a suggestive film, it is more difficult to trace the impress on other boys who have witnessed the same film, and who have been influenced more by the abstract courage or endurance portrayed by a character than by the concrete acts he performed : yet suggestion and the imitative faculty should be considered as operative in these cases also. But it is possible to produce films for boys which would be at once striking in action and manly in tone, and from which, therefore, no criminal imitative action could accrue." [1]

A SPECIAL INQUIRY REGARDING JUVENILE CRIME : THE REPLIES OF CHIEF CONSTABLES

A special inquiry was made of the chief constables of the United Kingdom : extracts from some of their letters are given in Appendix III.[2] The statement made by the Chief Constable of Edinburgh, in which the Chief Constables of Dundee and Aberdeen concurred, was submitted to them for their comment. In this statement the chief points were these : (1) " That the cinemas as a rule have proved to those who patronise them an educative, morally-healthy, and pleasure-giving entertainment." (2) " That the picture houses have been instrumental in reducing intemperance in the city." (3) That no case had come to his knowledge of boys being incited to crime in the desire to imitate what they had seen on the films, although he considered that there was grave danger in such representations, and was opposed to their being shown to the young. (4) That he had been " unable to find a single case where any juvenile set out to steal " for the purpose of going to the picture house, although the proceeds of several thefts had been so spent. (5) That sexually suggestive films are sometimes shown, and should be eliminated; [3] and (6) that in some cases where a charge of indecency, or suggestiveness in the

---

[1] p. 159. Cf. pp. 166–7[16].   [2] pp. 333–72.

[3] " Such films which contain suggestions of the kind ought, in my opinion, to be eliminated from the cinema. It must be remembered that of the great number of people patronising the picture house many are girls and youths of impressionable age, and while such exhibitions may, on the majority of persons, leave no impression, there is always the fear that in some instances these exhibitions suggesting immoral conduct may have a deleterious effect " (p. 176).

character of a film had been made, it was found on investigation that the representation could not be regarded as indecent within the scope of the criminal law.[1] In this statement thirty-eight chief constables concurred without any further comment. Of the seventy-seven others who stated their own views in more or less detail the majority were in general agreement with the above statement. A considerable number, however, affirmed that cases had come under their own observation both of theft to gain the means of admission to the picture house and of imitation of crimes seen in the pictures. The crime film in general, but especially any exhibition of the methods of crime, was very generally condemned. The difficulty of bringing a film within the scope of the criminal law for indecency was by many recognised. The most common complaint against the cinema was the suggestiveness of many " sex " films ; their evil effect on youth and even children was in many of the replies deplored. The need of a rigid censorship was in general insisted on in order to prevent any attempts in the stress of competition to obtain patronage by pandering to vicious or prurient minds.

(c) WRONG IDEAS OF LIFE AND CONDUCT

Apart from the stimulus to vice and the incitement to crime with which the picture house has been charged, a more general accusation may be made of generally unwholesome influence on the young. " Nearer to the charge of inducing criminal conduct," says Mr. Leeson,[2] " in children, is the criticism—and it appears well founded—that the pictures give to children quite wrong ideas of life and conduct. The villain is often ' lionised '; he does wrong things in a humorous way, he does ' smart ' things—things the youngsters wish they had thought of doing. At the same time, the reception of pictures such as these convinces us that the attractive thing to the child is not the wrongness of the act, but the humour or the cleverness of it. The cinema villain who is villain and nothing else invariably gains a satisfactory measure of execration from the audience ! Clearly, it is not good to present to a young child wickedness in the guise of humour, but our chief objection to the films is that they make children, whose thoughts should be happy and wholesome, familiar with ideas of death

---

[1] pp. 175–7. In answer to a question the witness stated that he did not think it possible for immorality to take place in the building, but that he had had one or two complaints of indecent assaults, as had other chief constables, and this he held to be due be the state of darkness more or less, (p. 178[14]).

[2] *The Child and the War.* A pamphlet put in as part of his evidence. See pp. 188–91.

by exhibiting shootings, stabbings and the like. Nor are these
death-scenes merely brief incidents in the stories, for when a
character is represented to be mortally wounded the story pauses
while the children are shown an enlarged view of the victim's
features during the death agony. Owing to this deliberate
emphasis of the repulsiveness of such situations it is difficult to
see how the child's nerves can maintain their tone; we should
look for a want of balance in children subjected repeatedly to these
ordeals,[1] and delinquency would not be unlikely. At any rate,
such exhibitions are highly objectionable for children, whether
they lead to delinquency or not." [2] The practice of showing the
enlarged view of the face so that the expression of hate, lust, pain,
grief may be emphasised seems an undesirable one. Children who
were examined by us, for the most part expressed their dislike of
tragedies, and a few admitted that they afterwards dreamed of
the pictures they had seen.[3] For younger children, at least, such
films cannot be regarded as desirable. A counterpart to the
above statement is found in the words of a probation officer:
" I very frequently take my probationers to picture shows with
beneficial results, and the general phases of life there shown are,
in the main, what I should wish them to be for such a purpose—
that is to say, they give a faithful representation of city life in
which both the failings and virtues of humanity are thrown up in
bold relief. From my point of view I should not wish to give my
probationers a view of life which was too widely different from the
actual conditions they would themselves later have to encounter." [4]

When men engaged in the same kind of work reach so diverse
conclusions, it is evident how difficult it would be to lay down
rigid rules as to what films should be shown except in those cases
where stimulus to sensuality or inducement to crime is patent.

SPECIAL PROVISION FOR THE YOUNG

As we are specially concerned with the influence of the cinema
on the young, the previous discussion compels us to raise the
issue whether any, and if so what, separate provision should be
made for them. The special entertainment for children in its
educational aspect is treated in another part of the Report; here
we are concerned only with the moral aspect. Several of our
witnesses strongly favoured the greater provision of special

---

[1] The frequency with which some children attend the cinemas—several
times a week (p. 129[20])—is an important factor in their influence. Evidence
was submitted to us that the maximum attendance that could be approved
would be once a week (p. 103[26]), or twice in three weeks (p. 43[143-7]).
[2] Cf. p. 129[16].   [3] p. 202[24-32]. Cf. p. 260.   [4] p. 206.

entertainments for the young; and the suggestion found some favour that films distinctly suitable for the young should be marked C, just as at present films for universal use are marked U, and those suitable for adults only A. One witness very emphatically expressed his dissent from the proposal of special exhibitions for adults from which children should be excluded. " I view with distaste," says Mr. Sharp, " proposals for differentiating between exhibitions for adults only and those for children. The child mind is intensely inquisitive, and when such distinctions are established, the juvenile boy is very anxious indeed to see what his big brothers may see from which he himself is excluded. It predisposes the mind of the child to look forward with a nasty expectancy to those exhibitions which he is for the time denied. It is, I think, unfortunate to recognise as an expedient thing forms of entertainment for adults not fit for the sight of children." [1] If the provision of a special class of films and a special kind of entertainment for children involved as a consequence a lowering of the standard of censorship for the films for adult exhibition it would certainly be undesirable to press any such proposal. If it were possible to secure that no film would be passed for general exhibition that was not entirely suitable for children to see, such a proposal would not be necessary. But would adult audiences, in the present state of public opinion, be prepared to accept the restriction that they should be allowed only to see on the films what it was suitable to show to children? In literature, drama, and art do we not recognise a distinction between the adult and the juvenile mind, so that what might with moral propriety be known by the one should be kept from the knowledge of the other? [2] It has been several times stated by representatives of the trade that special exhibitions for the young, at which only films approved for them should be shown, are " not a commercial proposition," and that a business carried on for profit could not, therefore, be expected to provide them.[3] If this need is to be met, it was urged, it must be by philanthropic effort or by public authority.[4] We urge that the question should be reconsidered in consultation with such societies or such authorities as may be specially interested in the youth of the country, in order to discover, if at all possible, some practicable means of supplying an urgent demand.[5] Otherwise it would seem to be necessary either to have more regard to the interests of the young in arranging the programmes for the general exhibitions,

[1] p. 285.
[2] pp. 189–90[11].
[3] p. 190[20-21]; p. 262[12]; p. 264.
[4] pp. 261–2[10-16].
[5] A boys' organisation in Newcastle has its own private cinema (p.191[32]).

or to discourage the attendance of young people under twelve or
thirteen unless accompanied by their parents, upon whom must
fall the responsibility of their presence at what might prove
an unsuitable form of entertainment.[1]

IV.—THE VALUE OF THE PICTURE HOUSE

We are convinced that the picture house means so much happiness not only to children but even to adults living and working
under adverse conditions, that any attempt at suppression would
be a grievous social loss, and that, accordingly, every effort should
be made to make all picture houses, as places of public amusement for old and young, clean and safe morally without sacrificing
their interest and attraction.   The testimony of one whose work
for many years has been among the poor must be given.   "In my
judgment," says Mr. Massey, "it would be a great blow to my
neighbourhood if the cinemas were suppressed or closed against
the children.   Just imagine what the cinemas mean to tens of
thousands of poor kiddies herded together in one room—to families
living in one house, six or eight families under the same roof.
For a few hours at the picture house at the corner, they can find
breathing space, warmth, music (the more the better) and the
pictures, where they can have a real laugh, a cheer and sometimes
a shout.   Who can measure the effect on their spirits and body?
To be able to make the poor, pinched-faced, half-clad and half-
nourished boys and girls in the crowded slums in cities forget their
pain and misery and their sad lot is a great thing, and the pictures
do it."[2]   There is also the relief to the mother.   "My knowledge,"
says the Rev. T. Horne, "is of tired-out mothers working hard
during the greater part of the day.   They are only too glad to
know that their children are able to go to an interesting entertainment such as the cinema, and that they are enjoying themselves out of the dangers and risks of the street."[3]

Another social worker, less favourable to the cinemas on the
whole, recognises that it is better for the children in her district
to be in the picture house than even in their homes or in the
street.[4]   This is a form of amusement that reaches a poorer class
than any other, and it is, therefore, incumbent on those more
favourably placed, while doing all possible to improve it, not to do
anything that would rob shadowed lives of the little brightness
that comes to them.

[1] See p. 233[8].   [2] p. 219.   [3] p. 184.   [4] p. 239.

The Alternatives to the Picture House

We must recognise that the picture house fulfils a useful and needful function amid social conditions which press very hard not only on the very poor, but even on the bulk of the working classes. So unsatisfactory is housing both in town and country, that there are few homes in which the leisure hours can be spent in quiet comfort and enjoyment. Not only are the slums and mean streets physically injurious, but they are beset with moral perils; the sights seen and the sounds heard are potent factors in the deterioration of the morals and the manners of youth. For many months, owing to our climate, the parks and open spaces cannot supply a refuge from the house or the street. Apart from the picture house the only resort that is offered to the teeming masses above the prohibited ages is the public-house, with its constant temptation of strong drink and its no less polluted moral atmosphere.

The Influence of the Picture House in Decreasing Hooliganism

Evidence has been submitted to us that the picture house has had some influence in reducing hooliganism, and in withdrawing custom from public-houses. " In my opinion," says Mr. Barnett, " the closing of the picture houses, or their prohibition to children, would have most unbeneficial results. In many cases the cinemas are the only form of healthy recreation available, and this is particularly the case during the long winter months. The children in question have neither the taste nor the facilities for indulging in any sport, and if the cinemas were closed to them, so far from the condition of the streets being improved, I am convinced there would be an immediate and immense increase in hooliganism, shoplifting and similar street misdemeanours. Fifteen years ago street hooligan gangs were a real menace and problem. Now such gangs are quite unknown in my district." [1] This opinion is confirmed by other evidence submitted to us.[2]

The Cinema as a Counter-attraction to the Public-House

The same witness declares : " I think it is obvious that the cinemas are a strong counter-attraction to the public-house." [3] All the witnesses questioned agreed with this opinion.[4]

" The public-house proprietors," says Mr. Massey, " have made

[1] p. 205.   [2] p. 167[17].   [3] p. 206.
[4] p. 34[24]; p. 89[50]; p. 176; p. 179[17]; p. 183; p. 208[18]; p. 226[29].

a complaint that the picture palaces have interfered with the takings, and one man told me that he lost from £15 to £20 a week."[1] It must be observed that no picture house has a licence to sell intoxicating drinks, and no pass-out checks are given as in the theatre.[2] It reveals a deplorable condition in many districts that in the opinion of some social workers even the least desirable picture house is a better place for the children than their homes or the streets, and that no thoroughly wholesome entertainment is being provided for them, especially in winter. While we have had sufficient evidence to show that there is need of much improvement as regards many picture houses, yet it is cheering to find that in the judgment of some of our witnesses there has been a marked improvement. The Rev. T. Horne, who has known the industry from its very commencement, is confident that there has been a great improvement, and that there will be a still greater. He, in answer to a question, also expressed his conviction that the organised trades of the cinema industry " will in reasonable time deal with anything that is undesirable.[3] This view is confirmed by the Rev. A. Tildsley, who has watched the growth of the industry from its beginning, and rejoices in the improvement that has been made.

FINDINGS

1. While we recognise that there are difficulties in securing the necessary improvement, we do not admit that these are insuperable. Improvement is imperative.

2. While the charges of indecency have been greatly exaggerated and the evil is not nearly as widespread as is often assumed, yet that it does exist must be admitted, but not to any greater extent than in any other places of popular resort; and the regulations in force in London to suppress it should be made of general application.

3. Not only should the local authority enforce existing regulations, and regulations which after due inquiry and conference may be added, but the public should assist the local authority by calling attention to any disregard of them, or any acts of indecency.

4. A much stricter censorship than at one period prevailed is necessary. Steps have now been taken to effect this improvement. The censorship should include not only films, but also the posters advertising the films.

5. Owing to the large number of children visiting the picture

---

[1] p. 220[4].   [2] p. 19[123-8].   [3] pp. 183-5.

houses, special care is necessary to protect them from what would be morally, as well as mentally or physically, injurious to them.

6. The charge that the children are induced to steal in order to pay for admission cannot be regarded as a condemnation of the picture house itself, for (*a*) the same objection might be, and has been, offered to any object of desire or form of pleasure that powerfully affected the child; (*b*) even if the money stolen is spent in the picture house, it must not be concluded that the money was stolen for that purpose, and it is found that such money is used for other enjoyments; (*c*) it must also be recognised that the picture house is often used as an excuse, when it is not the reason for the theft.

7. Regarding the connection of the cinema with imitative juvenile crime, there was presented to us conflicting evidence— some asserting as emphatically as others denied any general connection. Our conclusion is that such a connection does exist, though to a limited extent. It is not, however, a necessary connection, and not exclusive of many other factors too often ignored, because less obvious to the untrained observer of social phenomena.

8. Apart from " sex " and " crime " films, an injurious effect is produced on young minds by the excessive sensationalism and frightfulness of some of the films shown, and the wrong ideas of life and conduct often suggested.

9. It is evident that additional provision should be made for the young, both as regards arranging special exhibitions for them and securing suitable films to be there exhibited.

10. Despite the practical difficulties in making such provision, we urge that educational authorities and societies interested in the welfare of youth should co-operate in the endeavour to meet the need.

11. Compelled as we were in our inquiry to give special attention to the alleged defects in the picture house, we have been convinced by the amount of testimony offered in its favour of its value as a cheap amusement for the masses, for parents as well as children, especially as regards its influence in decreasing hooliganism and as a counter-attraction to the public-house.

12. The abolition of the picture house, as advocated by some, is impossible, even if it were desirable, as in our judgment it is not. On the other hand, we are strongly of opinion that not only is improvement practicable, but also of great national importance.

ADDENDUM

THE USE OF THE CINEMA IN RELIGIOUS AND SOCIAL WORK

ONE matter which was brought under our notice in evidence submitted to us, although it was not one of the subjects which we set before ourselves for inquiry, was the possibility of the use of the cinema in connection with religious and social work. In reporting that evidence we do not offer any opinion whether directly religious teaching can be suitably given by this means. The Rev. T. Horne favoured the use to a large extent, but added : " I might point out that some years ago I wanted to get the picture of the Life of Christ, but the price put upon it was prohibitive." [1]

THE TESTIMONY OF THE Y.M.C.A.

The Y.M.C.A. includes cinema entertainments amid its varied beneficent activities for the army during this war. The experience of three of their workers may be given, even though it must be recognised that the conditions are quite abnormal. The first, " C," says : " The so-called religious film is a very doubtful quantity. It leaves room for tremendous improvement, and seems to be received generally as a caricature. On the other hand, films of national events from which lessons may be drawn are of undoubted value, and I think that some of the " booked " films also lend themselves to a good story-teller as a very great aid indeed in matters religious." The second, " O," is much more favourable : " To an unlimited extent many an empty church might be filled if it were equipped with a cinema or other means of ocular demonstration for the purpose of illustrating the speaker's remarks, and in my opinion every church should have one." The third, " M," enters into further details : " It is important, however, to let the men know definitely what they are to expect, i. e. a religious service at the end of the cinema picture. From experience it has been found that the men do not go out after the picture is finished, but that they all stay, with few exceptions, to the religious meeting. On the other hand, suitable films can be procured which lend themselves as a suitable subject for a lecture or a distinctly religious address actually given whilst the film is being shown. Existing films treating biblical subjects are not recommended ; but films adapted from the works of well-known authors of fiction are procurable. These pictures are always popular, and result in a large demand by the men for books from the Y.M.C.A. library of the same title as

[1] p. 185.

the film. The moral of the pictures is good, I believe, and leaves a good impression on the men." [1]

Mr. McCowen, the head of the Y.M.C.A. work in France, gave this testimony to the influence of the cinema : " We have noticed that the cinema in France makes a very remarkable contribution to the behaviour and the *moral* of the troops. I have repeatedly had testimony from town majors and men in charge of the discipline of the various places, that the opening of one of these cinemas in a town has meant an immediate diminution, amounting in some cases to 50 per cent., in drunkenness and crime. In one town at the northern end of our line we opened a cinema; the 'drunks' there had been at a hundred a night, and the town major told me that the night we opened they went down to sixteen, and they have not gone up to twenty-five. In another town, not twenty miles from that, the town major said it meant an immediate diminution of crime to the extent of 50 per cent. In our large reinforcement camps, where the men are sometimes for three weeks or a month with nothing to do, it is the greatest boon in the world for them to get in and have a good real laugh, and spend a pleasant hour without the drink." [2]

The testimony of Mr. Yapp is most favourable : " If properly run a good cinema is helpful in town or city, as it occupies time and attention that might be spent in worse ways. Its influence may be positive and altogether helpful. For large out-of-the-way camps, particularly in Flanders, France, Egypt and Mesopotamia, we have found our cinema a perfect godsend." [3]

The conditions in which and the supervision under which these entertainments are being given are admittedly exceptional; but the experience of the Y.M.C.A. is worth recording as an encouragement to similar efforts elsewhere. It is not suggested for a moment that the picture house run for profit can or ought to be used for religious teaching. All that can there be required is that there shall be nothing morally injurious.

USE IN A CHURCH

The Rev. Carey Bonner in the course of his evidence submitted a statement by the Rev. A. Tildsley of the Poplar and Bromley Tabernacle, who for seventeen years, from the beginning of September to the middle of July, has conducted a Pleasant Thursday Evening for the People, at which he has used the cinematograph with assured success. His testimony is : " Speaking for my own church and district only, I can honestly say that the cinemato-

[1] pp. 229–30.   [2] pp. 226–7.   [3] p. 228.

d

graph entertainments have been a great help to my work, and real enjoyment to the people. I have had testimonies from the police that Thursday evening was one of the quiet times, because so many people were at the Tabernacle. The local librarian has given me the same testimony. Each Thursday at 5.30 p.m. the children of the district come in good numbers and pay a penny. . . . I have seen to every programme and every detail myself, and I honestly state that I do not know of one solitary case where these pictures have had a detrimental effect on child-life in my district."

PROPAGANDA BY THE FILMS

There can be no doubt that in the films there is offered to social, moral and religious movements an effective means of popular propaganda. Films dealing with moral and social problems have recently been prepared. While very great care will need to be exercised so as to avoid any danger of making known to the ignorant the evil which is being exposed for condemnation, yet with due safeguards, not only as regards the quality of the film, but also the kind of person to whom it is shown, this agency may be recommended. The usual exhibition at the picture house would not in some cases be suitable for this purpose.[1] This consideration offers a suitable transition to the educational aspects of the subject.

[1] The Government has made extensive use of moving pictures in connection with the various national efforts during the war.

SECTION II

THE CINEMA IN ITS RELATION TO THE EDUCATION OF CHILDREN

INTRODUCTION

THE cinema industry is a commercial undertaking conducted for private profit, and does not make any claim for the picture house as an instrument of direct education. The main purpose of the industry is to provide a healthy form of amusement and recreation of such a nature as to prove attractive to a large number of people, and thus ensure a profitable return for the vast amount of capital invested in the trade. The cinema appeals to a much larger public than any other form of public entertainment by reason of its continuous programme and the low prices charged for admission, ranging under normal conditions from 1d. to 2s. 6d., and varying with the position of the cinema theatre. A large mass of the poorer population has thus for the first time within its reach an opportunity of attending places of amusement, which was previously impossible in consequence of the comparatively high prices charged for admission.

Although the picture house makes no special claim to be of direct value for educational purposes, the fact that in thickly populated areas about 90 per cent. of the elementary school population from eight to fourteen years of age frequent this form of entertainment, to a greater or less extent, makes it imperative that the Commission should take into serious consideration not only the effect the cinema is at present producing on the school child, but also the possibilities of utilising it in the future to the greatest advantage. At present the cinema is undoubtedly having an enormous effect for good or evil on young children, and is affecting the work of the elementary schools to a considerable degree. The cinema, moreover, has undoubtedly come to stay, and will exert a powerful effect on the moral, mental and social development of young children for generations to come.

We have interviewed during our inquiry many witnesses, and

li

many views for and against the cinema as affecting school children have been expressed. On two points, however, there has been general agreement—

1. It is better for the child to be in the cinema than in the streets.

2. The cinema provides a better type of entertainment for the child than the music hall.

The Effect of the Cinema in regard to the Physical and Mental Condition of the School Child

The witnesses who have given evidence before us with reference to the effect of the cinema upon the educability of the child in school, complain that children who are habitual frequenters of cinema theatres suffer physically in consequence of abnormal excitement and late hours consequent on attendance at these places of amusement, and in some cases also from bad ventilation and excessive eye-strain, and thus to some extent the cinema frustrates the efforts of the teachers. They also complain that the interest which has been created by exciting films, in which through the excessive peptonisation of the material presented there is a consequent absence of much necessity for mental effort, renders the child a more difficult subject for instruction in which concentration and hard work are the necessary conditions of successful teaching. There was such general agreement on these points among educational experts, many of whom were by no means hostile to the cinema, that we must regard such complaints as being well founded. The development of anti-social ideas by the cinema has been dealt with in the previous section of the report.

The Evidence of Experts with regard to the Value of the Cinema for Educational Purposes

The variety of opinions expressed by acknowledged experts in educational matters is shown by the following selections from their evidence—

Dr. Lyttelton, formerly Head Master of Eton, says—

1. " I think the influence of cinemas on adults is not good, but on children it is positively bad." [1]

2. In answer to the question, " I gather from your evidence that you are dealing with the educational value of the cinema as at present put before us, that really education has nothing to

[1] p. 138[66].

do at present, or only accidentally, with the cinema ? " he replied :
" I am afraid I can go further and say, from the nature of the
case it is bound to be bad education." [1]

3. In answer to the question, " Do I understand that you want
all young people up to the age of eighteen to be excluded from the
cinema as now conducted ? " he replied : " I think so." This
statement was somewhat modified on further examination.[2]

On the other hand, BISHOP WELLDON, formerly Head Master of
Harrow, states : " I am quite sure the cinematograph show is
the most valuable of all educational agencies. Teaching through
the eye is the most effective kind of teaching in the education
of the young. If I may take the films which display the proceedings of the great Durbar, Delhi, it is not too much to say that
any person who saw those films saw more of the Durbar than he
would have seen if he had been at Delhi himself. Further, I
cannot imagine that teachers will be so foolish as to make a general
attack on cinematograph shows. I hope that the shows will
be more and more used in education, and I believe they are capable
of giving teaching which it is impossible to give with equal effect
by any other means." [3]

MR. J. G. LEGGE, Director of Education in Liverpool, gave
evidence to the following effect—
" There is some educational value in films of such subjects as—

1. Scenes in foreign lands.
2. Historical incidents.
3. Travel and adventure.
4. Nature study.
5. Pictured plays and novels.
6. Industrial and agricultural life.
7. Noteworthy events of the day.

But this educational value can easily be exaggerated, granted
the most careful selection of films. The residuum of history
left after reading an historical novel is small, still less is that left
after witnessing a film. The use of the cinema for definite teaching
purposes, particularly with regard to nature study and science,
is of far more value in the case of older students who have some
conception of abstract ideas of space and time, and whose impressions are not too confused by the bewildering rush of a film across
the field of vision. Much more might be done than is done at
present to present films which inculcate high qualities, such as
courage, self-sacrifice and generosity." [4]

[1] p. 140[75].   [2] p. 142[86,92].   [3] 242.   [4] pp. 29–30.

Mr. Spurley Hey, Director of Education in Manchester, states that films of travel, natural history and passing events, have intellectual value as they are informative, recreative, and arouse intelligent interest in everyday affairs. He maintains in this connection that children are less apt to form wrong ideas from moving pictures than from the verbal or written descriptions. He also says : " I have taken a deep interest in this aspect of children's welfare and education, and have endeavoured to pre-serve an open mind in considering the effects of the films on children. When in Newcastle-on-Tyne I inaugurated a trial scheme where-by children in elementary schools were taken in drafts to a certain school hall at which films were shown which had been chosen by a committee of educational experts. In Manchester I have frequently encouraged teachers to send drafts of children during school hours to cinema houses showing approved films." [1]

Mr. Percival Sharp, Director of Education in Newcastle-on-Tyne, in referring to the cinema as an instrument of education, says : " The subjects in respect of which claims have been made for the educational value of the cinema are history, geography and nature study. One recognises the value of good pictures, whether kinetic or static, as an aid to the formation of mental pictures of scenes geographical or historical; but to claim more than that would be, in my judgment, confession of a very inadequate concept of the true meaning of the study of either subject. A much more insidious claim can be made for the cinema as an educational aid to nature study. No doubt many very interesting processes can be brought to the intellectual door, but I feel strongly that the effective study of science must be based on personal observations, comparisons, measurements and de-ductions." [2]

Mr. John Kay, formerly President of the National Association of Head Teachers, is of opinion that " There does not appear to be a large place for the cinema in primary school work. In the essentials of instruction it can be of no service. As an in-teresting and attractive aid, purely illustrative, to the teaching of a small group of subjects—industrial geography, travel, con-temporary history, natural history and the like—there is a small field for it. Used in conjunction with lecture and letterpress it can give much colour to fact and terminology, but the cost would have to be small to justify its employment." [3]

[1] p. 164.   [2] p. 285-6.   [3] pp. 119-20.

MR. J. W. BUNN, member of the Executive of the National Union of Teachers, states: "I do not think that there is any educational value in the films worth mentioning at present. Some houses, in deference to the clamour for improving the mind, put in films showing manufacturing processes and natural phenomena, but I believe these only bore the audience and are tolerated in silence until the real entertainment commences again. I think that in poor neighbourhoods where the children need more change and variety in school work than among the well-to-do, it would not be a bad plan to have a cinematograph lesson once a week. It could be done by arranging for children from three or four schools to go for an hour to a suitable cinema, and the education authority could pay proprietors a penny per head, exactly as they do now for visits to the baths. I should arrange for the programme to be selected by the teachers, and for one of the teachers to explain the films in a few suitable words as the exhibition proceeded. The film proprietors have hundreds of beautiful films illustrating mountain, river and forest scenery, the manufacture of common articles, etc., which they are ready to loan at any time, and there will be no difficulty in getting the managers of local halls to admit school children during school hours at a penny each." [1]

MR. GRANT RAMSAY, Principal of the Institute of Hygiene, who has given much attention to the educational value of the cinema, says—

1. " The development of the cinema on educational lines can hardly be said to have come up to anticipations, but this is not altogether surprising. Messrs. Pathé Frères and other makers have devoted much time and money to the production of scientific and educational films, but at a great loss. The reason is simple : school books would not be popular on bookstalls, and before educational films can be in any demand there must be facilities for showing them. Further development rests largely with the educational authorities." [2]

2. " Children deserve and require very special consideration in regard to cinema pictures. They are more readily influenced than adults, and their nerves are more delicate and more easily exhausted. I do not think they should ever be taken to a cinema at night, as it affects their sleep and development. I am altogether in favour, however, of cinema pictures for children under proper conditions. They might, with advantage, have special theatres

[1] p. 127. [2] p. 235.

and pictures devoted to them. I have received many proofs
that children prefer interesting and instructive pictures, such
as those shown at the Institute, to the weary dramas and other
pictures usually shown at the popular theatres." [1]

The memory of visual impressions received at the cinema was
referred to in the evidence of DR. KIMMINS, who made an investigation as to the films which proved most attractive to a large number
(6701) of school children. He says : " The most striking result
that emerges from the investigation is that the older children
have a remarkable power of giving good accounts of films they
have only seen once. This is not merely a passing interest. In
one of the schools about thirty girls had promised their teacher
in 1914 not to go to the cinema during the war. In spite of this,
girls who had kept the promise were, with one exception, able
to give good accounts of films they had seen more than two years
before. This would seem to open up possibilities of great educational
developments if films could be produced which, in addition to
being of value from the educational point of view, were of sufficient
general interest to command the concentrated attention which is
evidently given to popular cinema films." [2]

MISS MARGERY FOX, head mistress of the County School for
Girls, Gravesend, who is much opposed to the cinema, admitted
the permanence of impressions received, as is shown by the
following extracts from her examination—

1. " Now, have you ever tested children after a time to see what
they remember of things they have seen at the cinema? "—
" Yes."

" Do you find they have a very vivid memory? Much more
than by reading a book? "—" Yes. I remember an intelligent
sixth form going to see ' A Tale of Two Cities,' but it ended quite
wrong, and I do not think I ever succeeded in making that form
realise what the real end of the novel was."

2. " You referred to the extraordinarily vivid impression a
cinema has on a child, and you have given an illustration of a
child remembering something you did not wish it to remember.
Is there any reason why the cinema should not give an extraordinarily vivid impression of something you would like the child
to remember? "—" It certainly would."

" If a film projected on to a screen can give an extraordinarily
vivid impression for evil it can also give a vivid impression for
good? "—" Yes." [3]

[1] pp. 235-6.   [2] p. 275-6.   [3] pp. 137-8[55 59].

MR. A. P. GRAVES, formerly one of His Majesty's Inspectors of schools, Chairman of the Educational Cinematograph Association, gave the Commission suggestions for the use of the cinema in schools—

1. " As regards the elementary schools the question of apparatus and installation arises first.   In my opinion the teaching by cinematograph should be both by the larger instrument and the pathescope used side by side with the magic lantern, perhaps in an apparatus combining static and dynamic teaching."

2. " The lantern slide should be used as the first illustrations in lessons of from twenty minutes to three-quarters of an hour according to the ages of the children.   They should be followed by a cinematograph film which would summarise the illustrations given by the magic lantern."

3. " The films might be inflammable or non-inflammable. The inflammable films cannot be presented upon the screen for more than a couple of minutes, if that, but their pictures are much more telling, and if by screening or some other device they can be maintained upon the screen for a little longer, they would be most suitable for teaching purposes, the more so as danger from fire has been guarded against in a manner which now makes them safe for schools.   The non-inflammable films do not last as long and do not project as good an image, but the image can be kept longer on the screen, and if their material could be improved they might furnish the best means of teaching.   They are specially adapted at present to daylight screens, which have the advantage of enabling students or scholars to take notes with the illustrations before them." [1]

With such a variety of opinion among experts as to the use of the cinema in relation to the education of children, we are of opinion that a good case has been made out for a thorough examination of the subject by a competent and authoritative committee.

SHOULD CHILDREN ATTEND THE CINEMA?

The fact that in densely crowded areas some 90 per cent. of the children in the senior departments of elementary schools frequent cinema theatres, more or less regularly, is sufficient evidence that this type of entertainment makes a very strong appeal to the school child.   The exclusion of school children under present conditions of housing in poor districts, and of inadequate provision of means of recreation for children out of school hours, would be a hardship.   The alternative for a large

[1] p. 303.

proportion of the children would be the street, and the witnesses we have interviewed were almost unanimously of the opinion, which we share, that whatever faults may be found with the cinema as it exists at present, it is better for the child than the street. A limit of time at which children should be admitted to, or allowed to remain in, the cinema, more especially if unaccompanied by parents or guardians, is very necessary. We understand that the trade would not resist a regulation for the exclusion of children after a certain hour.[1] From every point of view it is undesirable that the young child should remain in the cinema (or in any other place of amusement) to a later hour than nine o'clock. Effective regulations, which should be of universal application, with regard to this, would to some extent meet the natural complaints of teachers that children who remain in cinemas witnessing exciting films till late at night are less fit subjects for instruction in morning school.

The lighting of cinema theatres, which is discussed in another section of the report, is of special interest in considering the ill effect of the cinema on young children. With a higher standard of illumination in the theatre, the physical and moral evils would be considerably reduced. Too great difference between the illumination of the screen and the auditorium is productive of eye-strain and headache. Further, the more exciting scenes of the film story produce far less injurious effects when the auditorium is sufficiently lighted. Darkness tends to exaggerate the emotional effect to a marked degree.

Should there be Separate Performances for Children?

Opinions are much divided on this subject. The evidence we have received with regard to Saturday afternoon programmes for children has not been conclusive. In some cases where great interest is taken in the matter, satisfactory results appear to have been obtained, but it is stated that, as a rule, the programme does not differ materially from that of the evening performance, except by the inclusion of one or more educational films. Moreover, the education authorities have no control over the children out of school, and if a child prefers an evening performance to that of the afternoon, he will probably go to the former.

Some of the children whom we interviewed said that they would not pay to go to the cinema if they knew the films were to be mainly

---

[1] Mr. Goodwin stated that the trade would not resist a regulation for the exclusion of children after eight o'clock, but pointed out that the exclusion of children in arms would inflict a hardship on poor mothers, who must bring their babies with them, or stay away themselves, p. 17[106].

educational. The object of the child in going to the cinema is to obtain amusement and recreation, not education. Some of the children said, moreover, that they would welcome the educational films at the school, but not in the cinema theatre. The child evidently thinks he is being defrauded if, having paid for admission to a cinema theatre, he is shown films which have no other than an educational interest. On the other hand, when the educational interest is subordinated—as, for example, when a dramatic story is unfolded among beautiful surroundings—there is evidence that the scenic effects make their appropriate appeal to the child. This was clearly shown in essays on moving pictures, by young children, some of which were read to the Commission.

THE EDUCATIONAL FILM

Although, as already stated, the cinema is to be regarded primarily as a means of amusement and recreation, many praiseworthy attempts have been made by some producers of films to deal with natural phenomena from the educational standpoint, and films have been prepared in which the educational interest is predominant. Films of natural history, geographical and historical interest, have been prepared with marked ability and at great cost, but it must be admitted that these films have not proved sufficiently attractive to the general public to warrant the expenditure involved in their production. The reasons for the failure of the mainly educational films are many. The most important are the following—

1. The public to which the cinema appeals has not sufficient general knowledge of science, natural history, geography or history to form that connection between previous experience and the subject matter of the film which is so essential to vivid interest.

2. The atmosphere in which such films are introduced is highly antagonistic to their favourable reception and to their educational value. A film, however beautiful, of the life-history of a plant or insect sandwiched between a Charlie Chaplin film and a thrilling episode of the Exploits of Elaine has little chance of survival. The interest—if ever it has been aroused—is soon switched off, and a feeling of boredom results. To be effective in such surroundings the film must have interests other than the purely educational.

3. To make an educational film of real value there must be preliminary preparation by work in the school, or the running comment of a lecturer. The valuable film of the making of the Panama Canal would have lost its educational value without the accompanying lecture.

Teachers and children who have appeared before the Commission had little to say in favour of the educational film as it is at present shown in a mixed programme, though some mentioned the possibility of such films proving of educational value under favourable conditions and in close association with the work of the school.

We were also told by representatives of the trade that the public would not tolerate a greater admixture of educational films than 10 per cent. in a mixed programme. From statistics of an investigation of the interests of children in different classes of films, it appeared that the total number who preferred educational films was almost negligible. The small percentage of children who liked this type of film more than any other was, however, markedly greater among those with good home surroundings than among those from very poor districts. Such films were also shown to be more popular among girls than among boys, but even among girls from good homes only about 3 to 4 per cent. declared a preference for educational films.

The Commission is thus driven to the conclusion that under existing conditions the educational film has failed to make an appropriate appeal to the school child.

FILMS OF EDUCATIONAL VALUE IN WHICH THE INTEREST IS NOT PREDOMINANTLY EDUCATIONAL

The evidence presented to the Commission with regard to the purely educational film proves conclusively, as has been previously stated, that the conditions of its appearance in a mixed programme are fatal to its success. On the other hand, films of great educational value in which other interests of a more general character are involved are popular, and are able to compete successfully with films for which no educational value can be claimed. The official war pictures, for example, which have proved to be of intense interest to the public, have an undoubted value from the educational standpoint for children and adults. The popularity of such films with children was clearly shown by an investigation of the interest of school children in different types of film. About 7000 children were asked which moving picture they liked the most of all they had seen in cinema theatres. Of these more than 10 per cent. selected the war pictures, and the excellent descriptions of such films demonstrated clearly that the children had fully appreciated the main points and had derived great benefit in thus being able to obtain the best kind of evidence of what is going on at the Western Front. The child, after seeing such films as the battle of the Somme and the battle of the Ancre, would naturally be able to form a far more intelligent conception of the nature of warfare than would be possible by means of reading or class instruction. The same would apply to naval scenes and films of polar expeditions.

It would appear to the Commission that, in the exhibition of films which combine matters of general with great educational interest, and which from their nature are not capable of direct observation by children, the cinema may prove a valuable adjunct to the school. This function of the cinema should, however, be clearly distinguished from that of its use as a means of direct education and as a part of the apparatus of the school. The confusion of the two functions has led to much misunderstanding. In the opinion of the Commission, no film of purely educational interest, and which for its successful employment needs preparatory work in the school, can serve any useful purpose in a mixed programme for adults and children.

The Film Story

Abundant evidence has been presented to the Commission that there is room for much improvement in many of the film stories. The continual harping on incidents of marital infidelity in films, mainly of American origin, is unworthy of the magnificent opportunity offered of introducing dramatic stories of real merit. Such films give school children and adolescents an entirely wrong ideal of married life, and tend to give the impression that in the upper strata of society a standard of morality exists which is deplorable to the last degree. Drastic reform of this type of film is sorely needed.

The cowboy and Indian films, which are immensely popular with school children, have merits peculiarly their own. They are crude, but they represent a lower standard of civilisation, and appeal so directly to the primitive instincts and emotions that their position is secure. They lend themselves, moreover, very readily to vigorous action and rapid movement, and they introduce a variety of experience so new and attractive to the city child that, provided they are shorn of incidents of unnecessary brutality and cruelty, this type of film may serve a distinctly useful purpose and should be welcomed. It is natural, also, that films of a melodramatic type should be popular with a large section of the public for which the cinema caters.

The good detective story will always be popular with the normal schoolboy, but the typical American " crook " films, dealing exclusively with crime, do not meet the demand in a satisfactory way. They deal too much with the sordid elements of the story, the machinery of the police department, and the sufferings of detectives and criminals. There is generally no interest apart from the crook interest, and there is little or no comic relief. Wilkie Collins and Sir Arthur Conan Doyle have shown that in fiction the detective story need not be of the " penny dreadful " type, and there seems to be no reason why this class of story should not be produced on the screen so as to interest and attract without being objectionable.

The comic film, in spite of its occasional vulgarity, is mainly innocuous, and amply serves the primary purpose of providing great amusement. Its moral standard, moreover, compares very favourably with that of some of the theatrical and music-hall farces. The great success of this type of film is to a large extent due to the ability and popularity of a famous film comedian. The complaint of some teachers, however, that boys imitate the actions of the film artist, and that their ideal of humour becomes that of the low comedian, is probably well founded.

The output of film stories each year has reached such enormous proportions [1] that inevitably much that is produced is of very poor quality. The first suggestion which occurs to any one interested in the improvement of the picture house programme is that more of the best stories and plays of the world's literature should be filmed in place of the silly and sordid melodrama which is much too frequently seen. This is, however, not a practical suggestion, because nearly all such works have already been dealt with, and in many instances their repetition, even where most desirable, may be barred by tangles of copyright or trade rivalry.

The future of the film story appears to depend on an adequate supply of scenarios of the right type, and it is greatly to be hoped that producing firms will recognise more fully their grave responsibility in this matter.

THE SCHOOL AND THE CINEMA

The evidence of witnesses with regard to the educational value of the cinema has been somewhat conflicting. The general opinion, however, appears to be that it may render assistance in the teaching of such subjects as nature study, geography, and to a less extent in the teaching of history in the elementary and secondary schools, and that it may be of especial value in advanced scientific and technical work. In this connection our attention has been drawn to the successful use of the cinema in the Science course at Oundle School.

As practical work in any scientific instruction is the most

---

[1] See Mr. Tippett's evidence, pp. 56-8.

essential portion of the teaching, so for the cinema might be devised a corresponding use in schools which would give it the maximum educational value. Already a comparatively simple apparatus is obtainable with which an amateur can take a short film himself. This is used for recording experiments or operations in some university departments or, where the conditions are favourable, in a school. Children could collaborate with the teacher in arranging an experiment such as growing plants, or breeding dragon-flies, etc., and then be present while one or two of their number assisted the teacher to take the film. If this were done only once or twice by each class, their interest in and understanding of all other films shown to them would be greatly enhanced. In the course of a year, for instance, each class, might prepare the experiments for one film which when complete could be seen by all the other classes. In this way a school could get a series of carefully arranged experiments and moving objects filmed in just the way adapted to the classroom, and these could accumulate for intermittent use at suitable times as lantern slides accumulate usefully now. An exceptionally good film could be printed off and either exchanged with, or sold to, other schools.

In some such way a teacher could get films really suitable for schools, scholars would have an acuter interest both in their school experiments and in all pleasure picture shows they saw, and a great deal of valuable scientific instruction in light, chemistry, etc., could be not only imparted incidentally, but added on to something the children know to be a part of the " real life " outside the schoolroom.

No really serious investigation on an adequate scale has, however, been made in this country to test the value of the cinema as an instrument of direct education. The attempts so far have been almost entirely confined to the production of films to serve the dual purpose of being of interest to the general public and of educational value to children. As previously stated, the praiseworthy attempts in this direction have not been hitherto successful, and it cannot be claimed that what are termed educational films have achieved such popularity as would warrant further experiment in this direction. In our opinion the failure is due to the attempt to make the film combine two functions which are incompatible. The films produced fail in arousing sufficient general interest, and at the same time fail to form a useful part of the normal curriculum of the school.

The solution of the problem appears to lie in the separation of the two functions. In the public cinema performance healthy amusement and recreation should be the main function. A film which fails to be interesting to the general public should have no place in a mixed programme. It may be tolerated, but it serves no useful purpose. Nevertheless the really good programme must have a considerable value educationally. The school child may acquire useful information at such performances. He is introduced to scenes and representations of natural phenomena which open up a new world to him. Dramatic films, too, may foster conceptions of courage, endurance and self-sacrifice which may be of the highest value in the formation of character.

In this indirect way the cinema may prove, under suitable conditions, a useful supplement to the school. The educational value of the official war films and films of polar exploration cannot be denied, yet their main interest is outside the school curriculum. If education, however, were entirely confined to what goes on within the walls of the school, a very poor type of citizen would result. The child goes, and will continue to go, to the cinema theatre, and no efforts should be spared to make the programme wholesome and elevating, so that he may derive from it the maximum benefit without in any way interfering with the function of the cinema as a means of recreation and amusement.

The function of the cinema as a possible means of direct education is a matter which requires the most careful consideration. Much expert and exhaustive investigation will be necessary in order to reach a satisfactory and authoritative solution. In France this matter is receiving the attention of a strong commission appointed by the Minister of Public Instruction. In England, in our opinion, a similar commission, appointed preferably by the Minister of Education, should be formed. Failing this, a committee of teachers, psychologists and other experts in education, together with representative members of the trade, should be appointed by this Commission. Visual methods of instruction in schools have made great progress of recent years, and the time is ripe for an adequate investigation to be made in order to demonstrate the part the cinema can play in this modern development.

Possibilities of the Use of the Cinema in Education

Without prejudging in any way the work of any committee to be appointed to conduct a thorough investigation into the possible use of the cinema in education, it should be stated that though comparatively little work of a really scientific character has been carried on in this country, much has been done in America, France and Germany. One of the witnesses has handed in some of the literature on the subject, much of which expresses views highly favourable to the use of the cinema for direct educational purposes.

ANALYSIS OF EXPERT INVESTIGATIONS

Those investigators who are favourably impressed with the educational value of the cinema, claim for it the following advantages in addition to its primary object of providing healthy amusement and recreation.

Range of Information.—On the average, where other conditions are equal, the fund of general knowledge possessed by children who frequent the pictures is far wider and far richer than that possessed by those who do not. Much of the knowledge acquired may be trivial and superficial. Much of it is not. Essays set to children upon useful information learnt at the picture house reveal a long list of items of educational interest. Facts of geography, history, literature, natural science, industrial processes, social life, and current events are detailed in great variety.

Ten minutes' demonstration with the cinematograph would impart more knowledge of some subjects in a more effective and more interesting manner than an oral lesson which lasts for an hour. In a few seconds the child can see the caterpillar spin its cocoon and break it again and the butterfly unfold its wings, the seed germinate, the plant spring up out of the ground and put forth buds, the bud expand into blossom, the blossom fade and give way to ripening fruit.

No class of information interests the child so much as that which deals with human personalities. Perhaps no form of knowledge is more universally required. It is true that the social conflicts are crudely drawn and over-simplified. But simplification is inevitable even in the highest form of art. And the crudity may disappear when the producer learns that his public has a higher æsthetic standard than himself.

Accuracy of Ideas.—Often the ideas formed from a moving picture are demonstrably more accurate than those which children had previously acquired from a verbal or printed description. Those who have dealt with young university students know only too well how extensively the knowledge acquired at school is based primarily on textbooks, sentences and phrases, rather than on first-hand observation of the objects and processes themselves. With a concrete or material subject a moving photograph plainly gets far nearer to reality than a textbook statement, and it becomes possible to give a knowledge not only of the static object, but of the dynamic process.

Visual Presentation most Natural to the Child.—The information

e

is acquired through the channel which is most appropriate, not only to the subject matter, but to children of school age—namely, through the eye. The majority of human beings are visualisers, and those in whom, owing to book learning, the power to visualise has atrophied, do not cease to regret it. Childhood is pre-eminently the time of vision. The educational importance of concrete visual illustration is now an admitted principle. Many schools have their optical lantern. The addition of motion to the picture trebles the amount of realism thus gained, and the amount of interest is, at the same time, enormously enhanced.

Since the eye provides a natural channel for the acquisition of knowledge during childhood, it follows that information thus gained can be acquired without undue mental strain. The strain and fatigue that are reported by the children are physical in origin and can be eliminated by the enforcement of simple hygienic requirements.

Necessity of Preparation for Cinema Work.—Undoubtedly information is more effectively gained if two channels and two media are employed—eye and ear, pictures and words. The moving and pictorial representation should supplement, or be supplemented by, description or explanation in words, if not at the time, then before or after the visit. In the children's essays the items most frequently reproduced, and the points most clearly and accurately expounded, are those where the information has been learned first from a picture and then from the teacher or book, or first from the school and then from the cinema. The vivid, concrete imagery derived from the picture palace at once illuminates and can be expressed in the nomenclature and formulæ derived from lessons or from print.

Many of the psychological disadvantages of the cinematograph could be eliminated, and its benefits many times enhanced, by correlating the subjects chosen with written and oral work.

Mental Activity.—The mental passivity of the spectator is only relative. The moving picture does not of itself depress all mental activity. The particular pictures at present shown presuppose merely an exercise of the mind which is comparatively feeble. If the incidents are made so extremely obvious or familiar that their comprehension calls forth no effort, boredom rather than passivity is likely to result. This is actually the complaint of many intelligent children. Even at present, however, many of the films are by no means easy to follow unless the spectator brings with him a habit of alert watchfulness. The occasional visitor is amazed at the rapidity with which juvenile frequenters pick up the thread of the story and identify the various characters, while he himself misses point after point and confuses one face with another.

Training in Observation.—Children who habitually frequent the cinema undoubtedly develop a remarkable power of observation, at least for incidents depicted on the screen. This is repeatedly demonstrated by comparing the remarks made by such children either during the performance or in an essay subsequently composed, with the remarks of children, equal or superior in intelligence, who are visiting the cinema almost for the first time. The occasional spectator commonly finds that the changes and movements take place too quickly to be grasped, or occur when his eyes are directed to a different part of the screen, or when his attention is busy with his thoughts and reflections instead of with his retinal impressions. But with half a dozen visits even he can trace within himself the gradual development of a capacity for rapid observation.

Cultivation of the Imagination.—Imagination, especially visual imagination, is, if not trained, at least saved from atrophy by attendance at the cinema. The cinema picture provides a rich variety of experience for recall, and constructive as well as reproductive imagination seems often to be encouraged. There is much to be said for the possibility of filling the mind by means of the cinematograph with a store of healthy mental imagery.

The Moving Picture as a Form of Amusement.—Of all forms of popular amusement the cinematograph undoubtedly contributes the greatest measure to the greatest number. For many it is almost the sole haven of refuge from a sordid round of misery and dulness, the only glimpse of a brighter, more variegated and more thrilling life. This point appears and reappears with great persistence in the essays, debates and in the replies of the children themselves. For the child the cinema means primarily recreation, play, not work. But this must not depreciate our estimate of its educational capacity. The two functions are not incompatible. Recreation does not exclude instruction. Education through play is now acknowledged as a valuable principle, both in appealing to the intellect and in developing the character.

Cultivation of Moral and Æsthetic Appreciation.—It must be observed that the emotions excited at the cinematograph are not merely those of sympathy, but those of moral approbation and æsthetic enjoyment. We not only weep and rejoice with the heroine. We also admire the hero and get angry with the villain and appreciate the beauty of the scenery or the magnificence of the dresses. There could be no more potent instrument for the education of æsthetic taste among the general public than an artistically constructed series of cinematograph films. Passage after passage in the children's essays show, not only by mere statement but also by picturesque phraseology, how genuine an appreciation of natural scenery has been elicited by what they have seen.

Summary

According to these investigations there appear to be great possibilities for the cinema in education. The dangers, both physical and psychological, have already been reduced. Those that survive seem chiefly a consequence of the picture palace as at present arranged and the moving picture as at present produced. Both are universally acknowledged to be imperfect. Superior lighting, seating, ventilation, control of the admission of children, and, above all, a higher standard in the production of films considered as works of art, should largely remove the dangers that remain. Any mental damage done is thus incidental to the cinema and not essential, not an indissoluble characteristic of the moving picture as a specific form of art. The moving picture is intensely exciting, intensely realistic, and can cover an amazingly wide field of information. But these very characteristics, which may make it such a powerful instrument for evil, guarantee its future possibilities as a potent instrument of culture.

FINDINGS

1. The witnesses interviewed were almost unanimously of opinion that the cinema as at present conducted is better for the child than the street.

2. There was general agreement that the cinema theatre is better for the child than the music-hall.

3. The great variety of opinions expressed by educational experts as to the value of the cinema in education points to the need of an exhaustive inquiry into the subject by an expert commission or committee.

4. The Educational film, with no interest other than the educational, has been given a fair trial in the picture house and has not proved to be of sufficient general interest to prove a success in the ordinary programme of the cinema.

5. The reasons for this comparative failure are—

> (a) The position in a mixed programme with films of far more general interest.
> (b) The need of preparation in the school or the running comments of an experienced lecturer.

6. The Educational films have been prepared with great care and at great expense, and they reflect much credit on the enterprising firms who have produced them. If correlated with the work of the school, they might prove of value for direct educational purposes.

7. There appears to be an extensive field of usefulness in the indirect rather than the direct method of education by the cinema.

8. The subjects which lend themselves most successfully to direct educational treatment appear to be nature study, geography (including popular scenes of foreign travel), and, to a less extent, history. In advanced science work much use is already being made of the cinema, as e. g. in the course of science instruction at Oundle School and in many institutions of university rank.

9. We have been impressed by the popularity of films of war and naval scenes and those of polar and other explorations, the educational value of which cannot be denied.

10. The cinema can bring within the range of the child's experience a fund of valuable information which it would not be possible to obtain by other means.

11. Evidence has been given to us of the vividness and permanence of the visual impressions given by the cinema to the older school children.

12. There is much evidence to show that good scenery and appropriate setting of film stories make a strong appeal to children.

13. We have received abundant testimony as to the great popularity of the cinema with school children.

14. Complaints have been made to us that ill effects, physical and moral, follow excessive attendance at picture houses, owing to the exciting nature and continuous strain of the performances, and that in cases where the houses are open to children until late hours those who attend after nine o'clock are less fit to receive school instruction on the following day.

15. It appears that much can be done by hygienic improvements in the direction of better lighting, ventilation and seating where necessary, and the limitation of hours of attendance, to remove some of the objections at present made to the cinema performance.

16. We are impressed by the necessity of a definite regulation of universal application being made with regard to the attendance of children under fourteen years of age at cinemas beyond the hour of nine o'clock.

17. There is diversity of opinion as to the value of separate exhibitions for school children. If sufficient interest and care are

taken in the arrangement of the programme such exhibitions might prove a valuable adjunct to the school.

18. A great improvement in the nature of the film story is urgently needed in the interests of children. This might be accomplished without decreasing in any way the attractiveness of the cinema programme.

19. Drastic reform is needed in the treatment of stories dealing with "sex" questions, and such films should never be shown at exhibitions specially intended for children.

20. We regard the adequate filming of stories of acknowledged literary merit to be a matter of primary importance in the interests of both children and adults.

21. We consider that amusements and recreation can exert a powerful influence educationally. The universally admitted principle of the educative value of play can with confidence be applied to wholesome performances in the cinema theatre.

22. The moving picture is intensely exciting, intensely realistic, and can cover an amazingly wide field of information. But these very characteristics, which may make it such a powerful instrument for evil, guarantee its future possibilities as a potent instrument of culture.

ADDENDUM

THE PLACE OF MUSIC IN THE PICTURE HOUSE

THE Commission heard the evidence of a competent and experienced musician, and also heard the opinions of other witnesses.

The music heard in picture palaces is certainly an attraction to the public. Its quality constantly tends to rise, and, within the experience of members of the Commission, the supreme pages of musical literature, such as the Overture of the " Magic Flute " and the B Minor Symphony of Schubert, are frequently to be heard at the best houses.

The educational value of such music would be much enhanced if all houses adopted the practice of printing on the programme the chief musical items to accompany given films where this is possible.

The conditions of the work are quite satisfactory in representative cases, comparing favourably with those of work in theatre and music-hall orchestras, and in restaurants. Though so near the screen the musicians rarely look at it, so that their eyes are not injured. There is no reason to think the work unsuitable for women. The hours are such that records of musicians' cramp are not, so far as we are aware, more numerous than elsewhere.

The showing of pictures to musical accompaniment brings into use a second sense concurrently with vision, and answers the highly doctrinaire objection to the use of one sense at a time advanced by certain witnesses against the cinema—an objection equally applicable to reading or to hearing music.[1]

Musical *entr'actes* of various kinds are very popular, being commonly received with rounds of hearty applause. Many licensing authorities object to them,[2] or to certain types of them. One bars all singers, but admits violinists; another ineptly asks a symphony orchestra to come without its brass instruments. The evidence of oculists and others strongly suggests the very great desirability of such *entr'actes* in relieving the tendency to ocular strain. The Commission is of opinion that the interpolation of musical items, whether vocal or instrumental, is highly desirable on this ground, especially for the eyes of children,[3] and would deprecate the continuance of the policy which discountenances them and for which no comprehensible motive, if not jealousy on the part of other places of entertainment or offence to local interests, can be found,[4] unless it be a general objection to anything that makes the cinema more attractive.

The possibilities of the cinema as a means of musical education and of executive employment for musicians would appear to be very considerable, and as yet only in their infancy. The moving picture is quite remarkable as a test of the genuine emotional content of music, as many musicians, amateur and other, have noticed. Conversely, the more genuine and significant the drama, the more inadequate is any but the best music to accompany it. The musician long familiar with such works as the " Hebrides " overture of Mendelssohn or the " Flying Dutchman " overture of Wagner receives new impressions of their beauty and significance when he hears them accompanied by pictures of serene and stormy seas respectively, and therefore better realises the inadequacy of second-rate music to accompany the authentic movements of Nature herself. It is evident that very much could be done in teaching the emotional as distinguished from the technical appreciation of music by such visual accompaniments. Further, there is the teaching of evolution and period and folk tune involved in the use of eighteenth-century music for costume plays, minuets of Lully or Gluck for minuets of their periods in

---

[1] p. 136[35,8]; p. 137[44].　　[2] p. 38[75-7].　　[3] p. 169[32].　　[4] p. 170[43]; pp. 171-2.

the picture, Irish tunes for an Irish story, Scottish tunes for, say, Mr. Hepworth's film " Annie Laurie," sea-songs for sailor stories and naval films, and so on. In all these and similar instances the cause of musical education and appreciation would be enhanced by some means of letting the audience know what is being played, with the name and date of composer. Good music well played by competent musicians is much to be desired, but where the provision of this is economically impossible mechanical records of the best music offer a substitute for much of the inferior music now heard in too many of the smaller halls.

SECTION III

LIGHTING AND EYE-STRAIN

THE question of the lighting of the auditorium, or, as it might be more properly called, the spectaculum of cinemas during an exhibition is a matter of very great importance, both from a moral and from a hygienic point of view. Much attention has already been paid to this matter, but more needs to be done both by the exhibitors and the authorities, especially since there is much error as to the amount of darkness essential for the proper exhibition of the film. The subject of adequate lighting for the spectators, and the need of this, have therefore received considerable attention by the Commission, and much evidence bearing on the question has been obtained.

EYE-STRAIN AND OTHER ILL EFFECTS DUE TO THE DARKNESS OF THE HALLS

The report of the Investigating Committee in the City of Worcester speaks emphatically of the serious effects of eye-strain, headache, etc., resulting from the conditions under which the films are shown.[1]

The most important expert evidence on this point was given by Mr. Bishop Harman, F.R.C.S., senior ophthalmic surgeon to the West London Hospital, and ophthalmic surgeon to the Belgrave Hospital for Children, etc. Mr. Bishop Harman stated that—

" The unpleasant effects associated with the cinematograph exhibition so far as they affect the eyes may be set out as follows—

1. Glare.
2. Flicker.
3. Rapidity of motion.
4. Concentration of attention.
5. Duration of exhibition.

[1] p. 144.

lxxiii

Some of these effects are peculiar to the cinematograph, others are found in the same or some degree in other optical exhibitions." [1]

Concerning the results of these unpleasant effects on eyesight, Mr. Bishop Harman said : " Children may be taken to fall into the class of the more impressionable adults, owing to their lesser power of resistance and readier experience of fatigue." [2]

As regards glare and its injurious effect on the eyes in cinema exhibitions, Mr. Harman reported as follows—

" To enhance the effect of the show the room is made as dark as possible, the light of the lantern as bright as possible, and the transparency as strong as possible. The light from the lantern is projected on to the whitest possible screen, and therefrom it is reflected directly into the eyes of the observer. All these necessary conditions of the show are the worst possible conditions for the eyes, they all tend to produce the maximum of fatigue. . . . Glare cannot be dissociated from the shows. It can be reduced by providing a sufficient illumination of those parts of the room or hall removed from the immediate region of the screen; by attention to ordinary details connected with the use of fixed slides, and by care in the degree of illumination of the hall during the interval." [3]

Flicker, Mr. Harman explained, is largely due to bad films, is most evident in coloured films and is affected by the rate of motion of the film; in all these points great improvement has been made in recent years in the best cinemas. The rate of movement as seen on the screen should be as near as possible to that of the motion of the object depicted. [4]

Concentration of attention is required in a greater degree in a cinema show than in any other kind of exhibition. This creates fatigue, and is especially injurious to children. The eye really sees clearly only one point in the object looked at, and rapid but unconscious motion of the eye is necessary to take in the whole moving picture; the effort to avoid blinking the eyes is an indication of the effort of concentration required to follow the pictures.

The duration of the exhibition Mr. Harman stated should be much shorter, especially for children. " If the attention can be forced by the thrill of the picture show, for a longer period than is natural, the nervous effect is increased out of all proportion

[1] p. 98.   [2] p. 97.   [3] p. 98.   [4] p. 99.

. . . with the length of the show." The evidence that children's eyes do suffer from the picture shows " cannot be presented by figures and percentages," but it exists in some cases. " Fortunately the effects are temporary, and unless the indulgence be frequent, it is easily recovered from." [1]

There is, however, in Mr. Harman's opinion some evidence to show that permanent aggravation of defective eyesight may be caused in children by frequent attendance at lengthy cinema shows. Mr. Harman's recommendations are as follows—

" So far as eyes are concerned the best protection for the child will be secured by the following provisions : (1) The reasonable illumination of all parts of the hall not directly beside the screen. (2) The improvement of the movement of the film so as to reduce flicker; and the withdrawal of films immediately they are damaged. (3) The improvement in taking the picture so as to bring the rate of motion of the objects depicted more nearly to the natural. (4) The increase in the number of intervals to the show, and the interposition of exhibitions other than that of the optical lantern. (5) The limitation of shows for children to one hour, and the prohibition of ' repeats.' (6) The reservation of the children's seats to the ' optimum ' position in the hall." [2]

In reply to a question from the Chairman whether the more light that is given to the auditorium the less danger to the eyes of children in looking upon the films, Mr. Harman replied : " There is no doubt about that; that is my experience with the cinematograph and with optical lanterns and for medical lectures. We find these are quite satisfactory even if the room is fairly light, provided there is a dark part round the screen and the rest of the room is quite light enough to take down notes and so forth." [3]

Mr. Harman, in the course of his examination, emphasised the points in his recommendations that the hall should be moderately lighted; that the duration of the show should be short—an hour being ample for the children, and that, as children " hang on " to the very end of a cinema show, special seats in the best position to avoid eye-strain should be provided for them; that there should be a variety in the per ormance, such as intervals of music, so that the sight may be rested.[4]

On the other hand, the evidence of an examiner of films under

[1] p. 100.   [2] p. 101.   [3] p. 101.   [4] pp. 102–6.

the censor modifies this conclusion as to the harmful effect on the sight of viewing films. The evidence on this point is as follows—

83. "MR. T. P. O'CONNOR. How many hours a day do the examiners work?—We go at ten o'clock and we work until six o'clock, and if necessary, if the boats are late from America, we stay until the work is done.

84. "DR. SALEEBY. Five days a week?—Yes.

85. "Seeing the pictures all the time?—Yes; when I joined this Censorship Board I read a letter from an eminent authority, an oculist, warning the public not to allow their children to attend cinema shows, as any child there for one and a half hours would be running the risk of having its eyesight impaired for life. I have been there four years, and my eyesight is not stronger than it was at childhood. I am bound to say that my eyesight is not affected. That, I think, is one point for the cinema trade.

86. "MR. T. P. O'CONNOR. Is that the experience of your colleagues?—Well, they have made no complaints, but one of them adopted the precaution of wearing green-tinted glasses." [1]

There can be no doubt that the rapid passing from one picture to another, if the strain of attention is unrelieved by intervals when the sight is rested, is the cause of much headache and eye-strain in those who frequent the cinema.

SCIENTIFIC EVIDENCE AS TO THE LIGHTING OF CINEMA THEATRES

Mr. Leon Gaster, honorary secretary to the Illuminating Engineering Society, and editor of the *Illuminating Engineer,* gave important evidence bearing on this subject. His suggestions cannot well be summarised, and are therefore given in full.

Mr. Gaster says—

"The following matters appear to deserve special consideration:—1. "In the darkened condition of cinema theatres the eye is very sensitive to glare from bright sources. It is therefore suggested that no source brighter than the screen should fall within the angle of vision of the audience, when looking towards the picture. Also that any lamps used to indicate exits or for general lighting in the theatre should be properly shaded.

[1] p. 115.

2. " An excessive contrast between the bright screen and the dark surroundings is trying to the eyes. The walls and ceilings of the theatre might therefore preferably be fairly light in tint; this would also assist the effect of any permanent artificial lighting.

3. " With a view to the proper display of pictures the lantern should be capable of giving an illumination on the screen of not less than one foot-candle before the film is interposed. The operator could then adjust his light according to the nature of the film.

4. " In order to meet the views of authorities as regards propriety, and to diminish the objectionable contrast between the brightness of screen and surroundings, and also as a measure of safety, a small amount of permanent general artificial illumination, maintained while the display is in progress, appears desirable. A minimum of value of $\frac{1}{10}$ foot-candle [1] is suggested. The running cost of providing such an illumination would be small, probably within 5 to 10 per cent. of the cost of the electricity provided for the lantern and other illumination in the theatre building. By careful direction of light it should be possible to provide such an illumination without prejudice to the image on the screen. Stairs, both within and without the theatre should be lighted to the minimum value specified above, and the edges should preferably be white so as to be easily seen. The full lighting should be provided between performances, but the lights should be gradually raised or lowered by " dimmers " (resistances gradually inserted in the lighting circuit), so as to avoid the shock to the eye of sudden transition from darkness to brightness or *vice versa*. In order to prepare the eye for the conditions within the theatre the illumination in vestibules, corridors, etc., should have a value intermediate between that prevailing in the theatre and outside, and all lights should be effectually screened.

5. " It is common knowledge that observation of the screen at close quarters is productive of eye-strain. The distance should be such that the angle subtended by the screen at the eye does not exceed forty-five degrees, and the angle of obliquity at which the screen is viewed should not exceed thirty degrees. Children should not occupy seats which do not comply with these requirements. In view of the irregularities produced by screens giving a certain amount

---

[1] A " foot-candle " is the illumination produced by a source of light equivalent to one candle, at a distance of one foot.

of polished reflection (*e. g.* powdered aluminium) a screen of dead white material is to be preferred.

6. " Due regard should be paid to the vision of lantern operators. A window provided with glass of suitable opacity and of a nature to absorb ultra-violet rays should be provided for observation of the arc, and the eyes of the operator should be screened from direct light as far as possible. I desire to refer also to lighting conditions in rooms where film preparation goes on. The industry should take steps to secure that the conditions are hygienic on the lines adopted in dealing with lighting of the theatrical stage."

Mr. Gaster, in answer to questions, agreed that it would be a good thing if a committee of his society met and advised the Commission on the subject of lighting; insisted on the physical injury resulting from too great a contrast between the bright screen and the dark surroundings; and urged that the Commission's Report should recommend reduced lighting outside cinemas as a measure of economy.[1]

A paper read before the Royal Society of Arts on February 20, 1917, by Dr. James Kerr of the Public Health Department of the L.C.C., fully corroborated Mr. Gaster's views. In the discussion which followed the reading of Dr. Kerr's paper at the Society of Arts, one of the highest authorities on vision, Dr. F. W. Edridge Green, said : " That for the past twenty-five years he had considered it a fundamental principle of lighting that in order to see well with the centre of the retina the periphery must be stimulated. It was absolutely necessary that this physiological principle should be complied with in the cinema theatre, and therefore that there should be a reasonable amount of illumination in the auditorium without interfering with the picture on the screen." [2]

FINDINGS

1. We recommend the adequate illumination of the picture houses whilst the films are being shown.

2. The best relative illumination of the screen and hall should be determined by a special committee consisting of a few members of the Commission, together with representatives of the Illuminating Engineering Society and technical advisers from the trade. The

[1] p. 299. The arrangement of lamps to provide such an illumination could be determined beforehand, and in case of dispute the illumination could be readily measured and verified with an illumination photometer.
[2] pp. 297-9.

recommendation by the Secretary of the Illuminating Engineering Society that the illumination of the hall whilst the display is in progress should be one-tenth of a foot-candle appears to be reasonable.

3. The continuous display of films extending over some hours is extremely injurious, especially to the young and those with defective eyesight. Hence we recommend that frequent intervals of music, song, or other form of entertainment, should be encouraged to relieve the constant strain on the eyes.

4. We recommend that the front seats should be removed to at least twenty feet from the screen.

SECTION IV

TRADE CENSORSHIP AND ORGANISATION

HISTORY OF THE CENSORSHIP

A BRIEF summary of the history of the Trade Censorship of films may properly lead to an estimate of the present position. Owing to the objectionable character of some of the imported films, the question of establishing an independent censorship was discussed towards the end of 1911, and in October 1912, with the approval of Mr. McKenna, then Home Secretary, the Board of Censors was established. Soon after Mr. Redford was appointed President of the Board, and the details of administration were accepted as satisfactory by the Home Office. Four examiners were appointed by Mr. Redford, and the work was begun on January 1, 1913. Entire independence and impartiality were assured to, and have been maintained by the Board of Censors. As the scheme was voluntary, it was intended to issue a Certificate to the Exhibitors who showed only censored films, but the proposal proved ineffective. The local authorities were approached, and between forty and fifty have agreed to allow only films passed by the Board to be exhibited in halls under their jurisdiction. Two certificates are issued, one "U" for films to be shown to any audience, and one "A" for films suitable for adults only. The measure of public confidence enjoyed by the Board is shown by the request of the War Office in 1915 that all films intended for export should be submitted to and sealed by the Board.[1] This Board passes about 97 per cent. of all the films exhibited.[2] It has been found by experience that to show a film condemned by the Board does not pay the exhibitor.

WORKING OF THE CENSORSHIP

When Mr. Redford entered on his duties, he laid down only two rules, viz. : "that the living figure of Christ should not be permitted and that nudity should be in no circumstances passed."

[1] pp. 213–14; pp. 257–8[66].　　　[2] p. 216.

The Examiners have been guided in their judging of the films by the broad principle that nothing should be passed by them which in their honest opinion was calculated to demoralise an audience or any section of it. Guided by experience, this broad principle has found application in forty-three reasons for refusing to pass a film.[1] But it is still held that each film must be judged on its merits, and that it is impossible to aim at strictly logical decisions.[2] The greatest difficulty has been experienced with " sex " and " crime " films.[3] The procedure in examining the films is that two examiners, who are never working together for more than a week at a time, are looking at each film; whenever any part of the film seems doubtful, they consult the other two, and only when the four agree is the film passed without being brought under the notice of the President of the Board of Censors. In case of any disagreement a report as to the objection is submitted to him, and he decides whether he will grant or withhold the certificate, or suggest to the producer the changes necessary to make it acceptable.[4] Any attempt to exhibit the film in its unaltered form, when the changes had been insisted on as a condition of securing the certificate, would be treated as so flagrant a breach of honour that the Board would refuse to look at any other products from the same firm, and the certificate would be withdrawn; but there has been no occasion to take such action.[5] One of the examiners stated in his evidence that " very occasionally it happened that Mr. Redford took what I would call a broader view of the matter than we did," and so passed a film to which the examiners had taken exception; and that " our present president has shown a disposition to make the meshes a little smaller." [6]

THE INTENTIONS OF THE PRESENT CENSOR

Mr. T. P. O'Connor, who entered on his duties as President of the Board of Film Censors in January of this year, stated in evidence that he " was surprised and pleased to find that the censorship had been conducted with remarkable assiduity, usually with great success ";[7] and called special attention to a decision of his predecessor as showing the scrupulous care with which he exercised his functions. " When complaint was made to him of films founded on certain books he made the decision that though the films in these cases might in themselves be quite innocuous, yet, owing to the lurid repute of the books, audiences might be tempted to go and see them on false grounds, and, therefore, that

[1] pp. 254–5. [2] p. 104. [3] pp. 105–6. [4] pp. 106[2], 107[3], 109[25].
[5] pp. 108[19], 109[24]. [6] pp. 114–15[78–80]. [7] p. 244.

f

in future it was inexpedient to allow the production of the innocent
film of a book with a lurid reputation." As regards his own
standard he stated : " The chief difficulty arises from the number
of what may be called ' crook ' films which come mainly from
America and which have been brought partly into existence by
the popularity of the detective story. On these films the examiners had already laid down some severe restrictions, as for
instance, that none of the methods by which thieves can carry
out their purposes should be exhibited. I have somewhat
extended these restrictions, and I have sent out a circular . . .
urging the trade to give as few films of this character as possible;
and I think there is already a steady diminution in that form of
film." He expressed himself as desirous of having the assistance
of an advisory committee [1] and also of closer co-operation with
the Home Office and local authorities. "The Home Office should
have the right of veto of the appointment of the President . . .
and the President, if accepted by the Home Office, should have
the co-operation of the Home Office in having his decisions supported," [2] so that the 300 licensing authorities should be induced
to accept his censorship.

The Present Position

It must be pointed out, however, that time must be allowed
for the intended improvement to take effect. " It would take
Mr. O'Connor some months," we have been informed, " before
he could have any effect on our screens, and then years before
he could fulfil the object of getting the old films replaced by
fresh ones. It is a very slow thing. Most of the things that
are showing now were published perhaps a year or eighteen
months ago, and many of the films recently passed will not see
daylight for another six months." While the appointment of
Mr. O'Connor was under consideration, negotiations were going
on with the Home Office regarding a State Censorship, but these
were brought to an end on January 24, 1917; and Mr. O'Connor's
appointment did not, as was hoped, receive the endorsement of
the Home Office.

Negotiations with the Home Office

Of the abortive negotiations between the Home Office and the
trade a summary account was submitted to us by Mr. Newbould, who conducted these negotiations on behalf of the trade.
" Briefly, the proposals were : (1) A voluntary censorship under

[1] p. 245.   [2] p. 246.

the control of the Home Office for which the trade was to pay a sum of not less than £6000 a year.[1] As the Home Office had no legal power either to enforce such a censorship as final throughout the kingdom, or to compel renters and manufacturers to submit their films for censorship, or to prohibit exhibitors showing films which had not passed the censorship, these proposals offered no improvement on existing conditions. (2) The Chief Censor and Examiners were to be selected and appointed by the Home Office. (3) There was to be ' a strong Advisory Committee appointed by the Secretary of State, including representatives of local authorities (including educational authorities), well-known members of the general public, authors of standing not connected with cinemas, with a representative of the manufacturers and a representative of the exhibitors. One member at least should be a woman.' The trade was asked to make observations on these proposals, and the objections the trade raised were as follows : (1) That a Government Censorship must be compulsory, universal in its application, and final in its decisions. (2) That the Chief Censor should either be selected or appointed by the Advisory Board or the Home Office in agreement with the trade, and that one Examiner should be appointed by the trade. (3) The trade asked for a better representation on the Advisory Board. After very considerable delay, the Home Office had to admit : (1) That it was unable, without legislation (which was out of the question), to make the censorship compulsory, universal or final. (2) The Home Secretary [2] adhered to his decision that all the appointments should be made by him, although the salaries would be paid by the trade. (3) The Home Secretary intimated his willingness to concede three representatives on the Advisory Committee instead of two." [3] As the Cinematograph Trade Council could not come to an agreement with the Home Office, the Home Secretary [4] did not proceed with the scheme, but postponed it till it could be dealt with by legislation, and intimated that he would advise local licensing authorities " to exercise to the full extent the powers of control which they possess under the Cinematograph Act."

The Attitude of the Trade

A circular issued by the Cinematograph Exhibitors' Association to its members in connection with these negotiations, was put in in evidence; as one of the sentences it contains (" The trade

[1] The total cost of the present Board of Censorship, including the salary of the President, the Examiners, and all office expenses is, we are informed, about £5000.
[2] Then Mr. Herbert Samuel.   [3] pp. 264–5.   [4] Now Sir George Cave.

is in immediate danger from a most drastic Government Censorship which will have the effect of depriving you of 75 per cent. of the films which are most popular with your patrons "), has been widely used to the prejudice of the inquiry on which we have been engaged, Mr. W. Gavazzi King, the Secretary, was thoroughly cross-examined about the meaning of it; and stated that when the circular was issued, he and others were under the distinct impression, from the interviews that they had had with Home Office officials, that the censorship was intended to exclude all films that were regarded as in any way unsuitable for children, from a standpoint that most people anxious to purify and elevate the picture house would themselves regard as extreme in its rigour.[1] He and the Chairman of the Association, Mr. Newbould, have assured us of their desire to have an effective censorship of films that would meet reasonable requirements; and the latter expressed his opinion that " to the present organisation should be added an Advisory and Appeal Committee, which should be appointed by some such body as the National Council of Public Morals in consultation with the Home Office." [2] As regards the regulations imposed as a condition of licence by local authorities, the same witness suggested " that a Committee should be set up consisting of representatives of (1) The trade, (2) the local authorities and Home Office, and (3) this Commission, with a Chairman appointed by the Home Office to consider these regulations and draw up a model set, which should then be issued by the Home Office for use throughout the entire kingdom." [3] With these two proposals we deal in our recommendations.

THE REORGANISATION OF THE TRADE

The defect of the voluntary censorship in the past has been that it could not be enforced on the whole trade. Of the 4500 picture houses in the country, until the reorganisation, only a little over half the number was in the Exhibitors' Association. In London the conditions were better, as 200 out of 248 were in the local branch.[4] The best houses, however, are in the Association. The members appear to have been loyal in carrying out suggestions for improvement pressed upon them. In case of disregard a member could be turned out, and this would involve the loss of some benefits which co-operation can secure. The Exhibitors' Association has recently transformed itself into the National Union in order (1) to secure that all exhibitors shall become members of it : (2) and to enforce such discipline on the members as will protect the trade as a whole from the disrepute

---

[1] pp. 299–300.   [2] p. 265.   [3] p. 266.   [4] p. 23.

and charges that a badly-conducted picture house can bring upon it. Mr. Seddon, equipped with his long experience of Trade Unionism, has been appointed Organising Secretary to bring about this tightening up of the organisation. In regard to the first object, he stated in his evidence that the Union hoped " by peaceful persuasion and other methods known as trades-union activity to bring them into line at no distant date." Asked to define the methods more fully, he said, " If they did not belong to the Union, it would be extremely difficult for them to get hold of the things they want to show." He admitted that this power would depend on the Union securing the great majority of exhibitors as members. " If 90 per cent. are in the organisation, then the manufacturers would want the custom of that 90 per cent. rather than the custom of the 10 per cent." [1] In order that local authorities and the public may know what houses are in the Association, and accept its censorship, a card of membership for display in the picture house is being issued, and also there is to be a white list of picture houses enrolled in the Union as well as of films passed by the Censor.[2] If any house showed films of " a detrimental character," the Association, explained Mr. Newbould, would oppose its being licensed.[3]

The Defects of Local Censorship and Regulations

One of the strongest motives of the present endeavour to organise the trade throughout the country generally is the difficulty imposed upon it by the lack of uniformity in the requirement of the local authorities both as regards the character of the films shown, and other regulations imposed.[4] The conditions under which the films are changed twice a week, and have to be moved with all possible speed from place to place, make it very difficult to comply with a local censorship.[5] With this complaint we have some sympathy; and believe that the necessity for insisting on the local censorship might be removed by a central censorship that secured because it deserved full confidence. We offer a recommendation to this end. We regret, however, that the trade seems to regard as impracticable the requirement that for children's performances a suitable programme should be provided; and we do not regard the description, " the milk-and-water " variety, as altogether just to those who rightly recognise the importance of protecting the young life of the nation against any possible moral injury.[6] Some of the regulations mentioned to us, do seem to go beyond what a public

[1] p. 291[1,6]. Cf. pp. 255–6[44]; pp. 258–9[72-3]. [2] p. 292[13, 16-17].
[3] p. 293[24-5]. [4] Cf. p. 22[165 7]; p. 287[9, 16]. [5] p. 194. [6] p. 22[165].

authority should impose.[1] It would be a distinct advantage, as the trade desires, to have legislation that would secure some uniformity in the requirements made. Two special grounds of complaint as regards local censorship mentioned in evidence are (1) the influence of " cranks " and " faddists," and (2) the entrusting of this delicate and difficult task to the police superintendent.[2] While until the central censorship has gained the assured position which we hope that as improved it will secure, the local authority cannot be asked to accept without question all censored films, yet it is not unreasonable to ask that local authorities should assist the trade in its efforts at improvement by making a condition of licence that only films passed by the Board of Censors should be shown in picture houses.[3] We have already communicated with a considerable number of local authorities, almost all of whom have expressed their willingness to enforce this condition, and we trust that all will agree when the censorship under the new conditions has justified itself.

The Censorship of Posters

The censorship so far spoken of refers only to films, not posters. The Billposters' Association in 1891 appointed a Censorship Committee on which the Billposters, Poster Printers and Theatrical Interests were represented. In spite of some opposition it has obtained control over practically all the public hoardings, and no poster which has not been passed by it can be exhibited on one of these. The principles of the censorship seem rigid enough to prevent anything objectionable appearing.[4] Over posters which are put up on the picture houses themselves the Association has no control. Although representations may be made to the exhibitor, these may be disregarded. The proposal has also been made that the Cinema Trade Censorship should deal with the posters as well as with the films.[5] As the Billposters' Association, however, would not accept this censorship for posters to be put on public hoardings, but would insist on exercising its own censorship, this would involve a double censorship.[6] The cinema trade were invited to appoint representatives on the Censorship Committee of the Billposters' Association, in the same way as the theatrical interests are represented.[7] The negotiations have not been concluded; but in our judgment it is desirable that there should be no avoidable delay, and that as soon as possible a censorship of posters, in some respects even more necessary than of films, should be firmly established.

[1] p. 27[237-9].   [2] p. 271[56-9].   [3] p. 27[244]; p. 213.   [4] pp. 221–2.
[5] p. 18[112-17].   [6] pp. 224–5[12].   [7] p. 224[8].

SECTION V

CONCLUSIONS AND RECOMMENDATIONS

THE ultimate problems presented by the rapid evolution of the picture house are many and complex, but fortunately one may define within simple terms the immediate objects of wise legislation on the subject. They are to ensure that suitable pictures shall be shown in suitable conditions.

I. SUITABLE CONDITIONS

As regards these conditions, the Commission has heard a great mass of evidence from which certain desiderata have emerged with clearness. It may help if we begin by constructing an ideal, and then see how far we can go towards reaching that ideal.

The evidence we have taken leads chiefly to these conclusions—

A. The picture house should be commodious and well constructed, thoroughly ventilated and scrupulously clean.

B. Seating accommodation should be ample to avoid the obvious evils of overcrowding.

C. Children should be seated in the optimum position, which is the centre of the hall, at a distance from the screen not less than one and a half times its own height.

D. The body of the hall should be lighted sufficiently by means of screened lights during the showing of the picture to ensure—

1. That no objectionable practices shall be possible in the auditorium, and
2. That the eye-strain imposed by the necessity of constantly watching a brilliantly illuminated object from a dark or nearly dark locus shall be reduced to a minimum.

E. Capable and experienced attendants should be present in the hall to look after the welfare of the children.

F. The projection of the pictures should be in the hands of a highly skilled operator.[1]

[1] It has so far escaped attention that bad projection resulting in pictures being shown out of focus is an immediate cause of eye-strain. Owing to the

G. Our ideal standard would call for a new copy of each film at every performance, or, at least, at frequent intervals; perhaps it will suffice if we make a proviso that the copy shall be in good sound condition.

H. The titles should be projected on to the screen for a sufficient length of time to enable children to read the text without any strain.

I. Between the showing of the different films in the programme there should be short intervals, in which the theatre should be suffused with light. This serves a double purpose: the tension of the child's mind is relaxed and indecorous behaviour in the auditorium is greatly discouraged. The programme might be advantageously broken up by having musical items interspersed between the films.

J. The children should visit the theatre at such an hour as will ensure that their night's rest is not encroached on; indeed, they should be allowed some considerable interval after leaving the picture house before retiring to rest, so that they may not carry straight to bed the exciting incidents which they have just seen.

K. Their attendance at the picture house should not be too frequent; one witness suggested three times in a fortnight as the maximum. But the idiosyncrasies of the child must be taken into consideration, and it may well prove that in certain cases even three times in a fortnight may prove too much.

L. As the picture-house performance is frequently " continuous," means should be provided to prevent children from staying too long at any one visit.

M. The pictures which the children ought to see should be exhilarating without leading to undue mental strain. They should be rendered attractive by the beauty of the settings, the novelty of the incidents depicted or the interest of the scenes, and, speaking broadly, the aim should be to enlarge the mental horizon, and whenever possible to excite the finer emotions. The educational value of the picture-house film will always depend on the extent to which improving thoughts are unconsciously conveyed to the child.

N. The film which is designedly educational—that is to say, the film which is meant to teach a lesson—must either

---

impossibility of getting mechanical repairs done in war time, many projecting machines are at present sadly out of gear, with the result that projection suffers. Moreover, the scarcity of both men and women is leading to young and incapable operators being too frequently employed.

be explained as it proceeds by a capable lecturer, or should be prepared for by an antecedent course of teaching in the school. If shown in the picture house great care should be taken not to spoil its effect by too rapid transition to pictures of an exciting or comic type.

O. The vestibule of the picture house may easily become a danger point, especially in the case of young girls. Strict supervision should be exercised to prevent loitering and the possibility of children being accosted.

Now it is quite possible for Parliament to frame laws to carry out all these objects so far as it is within the power of the picture-house proprietor to give effect to them. Some of the reforms which are most desirable are, comparatively speaking, inexpensive, but others may prove so costly in their practical application that it will be impossible for the picture house to continue to provide popular entertainment as cheaply as heretofore. It would not be difficult to draft regulations which would appear perfectly reasonable, but which in practical application would close half the picture houses in poorer districts. We are all agreed that cheapness is the foundation of success of the picture house, and legislation which had the effect of placing this form of entertainment beyond the reach of the million should be very slowly undertaken.

Accordingly, we recommend that, to secure uniformity of regulations in regard to the suitable conditions which are practicable, there should be a conference of representatives of the Home Office, local authorities, the trade, and a small number of persons who have shown special interest in the picture house to draw up a list of model regulations; and that these be made statutory.

II. Suitable Films

The Reasons for a State Censorship

In regard to the censorship, we cannot help feeling that to some extent this matter is intensified in its difficulty because of the excellent way in which the present President of the Board of Censors has done his work. Mr. T. P. O'Connor has taken such pains, and has shown such initiative, that we hesitate to make any suggestions which would imply that there was necessity for improvement, and we should view with great anxiety any one else in his position until he has been enabled to turn what we may call his sketch of the position of censor into a finished picture.

Our judgment is in favour of a State censorship. The cinema is now the most important of the entertainments provided for the public in this country. Millions of people are amongst its patrons, and its influence is very far-reaching. It appeals to every class of society, and to people of all ages. It is certainly the most democratic of the means of enjoyment at the disposal of our populace. For its own protection as well as for the ensuring of its continued suitability to the nation, it should have the support and the official countenance of the State.

We want to place it in a position of real dignity. We want it to be something more than a trade; in fact, we wish it to be one of the assets of our national entertainment and recreation.

We are anxious that the cinema should be beyond all suspicion in the mind of the average member of the public.

We deeply regret that the negotiations between the Home Office and the trade proved abortive, and we do not think that fault attaches to the trade because of the failure of these negotiations.

While local authorities are justly jealous of their right in accordance with local sentiment to control the public places of amusement, there are difficulties and disadvantages for the trade in local censorship of films which we have been led by evidence submitted to us to recognise, and many of these authorities would be glad to be relieved of a duty for which they do not possess the appropriate machinery. Accordingly it is in the interests of the trade itself, as well as for the advantage of the local authorities, that the central censorship shall command such a measure of public confidence that the exercise of the right of local censorship will become increasingly unnecessary.

The Objections to a State Censorship

We recognise that a State censorship may be objected to on the following grounds—

1. The censorship of plays by the Lord Chamberlain has not proved satisfactory, but objection has been made to it as on the one hand preventing the serious discussion of moral and social problems in the acted drama, and on the other allowing much altogether objectionable matter in the way of some reviews, farces and musical comedies, to be presented on the stage.

2. The tendency of a Government department is towards an official rigidity, out of close touch with and not quickly responsive to public opinion.

3. It is more in accord with the distinctive characteristics of the nation to encourage voluntary self-regulation rather than compulsory State control, unless the latter alone could achieve what the former failed to do.

THE CONDITIONS OF A STATE CENSORSHIP

Should a State censorship be decided upon we recommend that, in order as far as possible to meet these objections, it should be constituted under the following conditions—

1. One censor should be appointed for the United Kingdom, not by a State department, but by His Majesty in Council, and the person so appointed should not necessarily be a civil servant, but one who will bring to the discharge of his duties adequate knowledge and generous appreciation of the people whose interests are primarily to be considered.

2. An Advisory Council, representative of public interests,[1] should be appointed, to whom the censor may apply in matters of doubt and difficulty.

3. While the appointment of the examiners should be in the hands of the censor, the Advisory Council should be consulted, and out of the Advisory Council a small executive should be chosen, with whom the censor should be in constant touch.

4. The expense of the censorship should be charged on the Parliamentary estimates.

5. This censorship should be made final and supersede all local censorships.

CONTINUANCE OF THE PRESENT CENSORSHIP

Pending such an appointment we recommend the continuance of the present censorship, with some modifications.

1. There is a growing recognition by the trade that in its own interests, apart even from higher considerations to which the leaders of the industry, we are assured, are not indifferent, such reproach as can be brought against the character of the films shown should be removed as speedily as possible.

2. The hands of the censor in giving effect to his decisions are strengthened by local authorities when they make a condition of licensing a picture house that it should show only films on the white list, issued by the trade, and also by the public if they refuse to enter a house which does not restrict itself to films on this list.

3. An Advisory Council, as previously described, should be appointed as soon as possible by mutual agreement of the censor and the Commission.

4. The trade censorship should apply only to films exhibited for public entertainment and recreation. Any film for social, moral or religious propaganda, to be shown under such conditions

[1] Such as Religion, Morals, Education and Literature.

as may be specified by the promoting society, should not be subject to such censorship, but should be exhibited on the entire responsibility of the reputable public society the objects of which it is used to serve. Where the exhibition of such a film in a picture house is desired, the trade Censor shall consult the Advisory Council regarding such exhibition. A similar consideration should be shown by him to any film, submitted by a producer not connected with the trade, which has a serious educational, literary or artistic intention.[1]

H. R. BIRMINGHAM (*President*).
ALFRED E. GARVIE (*Vice-President*).
M. C. STOPES.
ADELAIDE COX.
HERMANN GOLLANCZ.
EDWARD BRABROOK.
ROBERT BADEN-POWELL.
JOHN KIRK.
W. F. BROWN.
C. W. SALEEBY.
CAREY BONNER.
W. GAVAZZI KING.
ALFRED PERCEVAL GRAVES.
EDGAR JEPSON.
A. E. NEWBOULD.
SIDNEY LAMERT.
CHAS. W. CROOK.
FREDERIC C. SPURR.
W. E. SOOTHILL.
C. W. KIMMINS.
E. M. BURGWIN.
F. B. MEYER.
W. F. BARRETT.
JAMES MARCHANT (*Secretary*).

N.B.—Mr. T. P. O'Connor, M.P., owing to his absence on an important political mission in America, was away from the later meetings of the Commission when the Report was being prepared, and it has been found impracticable to communicate with him in order to obtain his signature.

[1] The detailed recommendations which we have made in connection with the separate sections of our Report will be found in the following places—
Moral and Social Aspects, pp. xlvi–vii.
Educational Aspects, pp. lxviii–ix.
Lighting and Eye-strain, pp. lxxviii–ix.

NOTE OF RESERVATION

The three representatives of the cinema industry sitting on the Commission, in giving their support to the findings generally, desire to make it clear that they are supporting the principle of State censorship on the lines indicated by the Commission as an ideal to be worked for. They must expressly reserve for the industry the right to oppose any attempt to set up this form of censorship without the provision of adequate safeguards against its many possible disadvantages and dangers.

A. E. NEWBOULD.
SIDNEY LAMERT.
W. GAVAZZI KING.

PART II

MINUTES OF EVIDENCE [1]

FIRST DAY

Monday, January 8, 1917,

Westminster, S.W.

The BISHOP OF BIRMINGHAM (President) in the chair.

STATEMENT OF MR. F. R. GOODWIN

PRÉCIS

THE present inquiry into the status of the cinematograph industry is sincerely welcomed by those connected with the business on its exhibiting side. We can face with serenity the most drastic investigation. But we feel that it would have been desirable that such an inquiry should have been held either before or after the war, as conditions are for the moment abnormal and unrepresentative. The business is one by its very nature particularly susceptible to any change in public conditions. It lives by catering for and reflecting the popular mood, and these moods have been profoundly affected by the war. There has been a change in the type of film demanded by audiences. Films which in pre-war days were thought interesting and amusing are no longer welcome; the tendency is to favour films which would provide distraction from the stress of war conditions. The quiet film, the placid story, does not appeal at the moment to people whose nerves are jangled and strained by worry and loss. They seek distraction with an avidity and a feverishness which is quite natural but not normal. In considering the types of films which find most favour at the present moment, this qualifying factor of abnormal conditions must be borne in mind.

In other ways, too, the war has caused disturbances. The whole development of the industry, which was proceeding at a phenomenal rate, was abruptly checked. Schemes of improvement and expansion had to be deferred owing to the virtual impossibility of securing new capital. So far as the development and expansion of the industry is concerned, we stand in no better position than in August 1914. In some ways we are actually worse off.

[1] The witnesses have corrected and passed the proofs of their evidence as here printed.

B

We have remarked on the phenomenally rapid growth of the business. About 1908 a few men began to recognise that, in spite of the constant predictions of impending collapse, the business was steadily advancing. Far from showing signs of satiety, audiences were increasing in number and in keenness. The day of the picture " palaces " dawned. A glance at the record of companies registered since the beginning of 1908— which may roughly be taken as the beginning of the moving picture boom. The figures are as follows—

Year.	Companies.	Capital. £
1908	12	167,000
1909	78	708,000
1910	231	2,183,700
1911	254	1,214,400
1912	400	1,627,400
1913	544	2,954,700
1914	314	2,449,300
1915	244	1,035,469
1916 (incomplete)	208	899,926
TOTAL	2,285	£13,239,895

These show a steady and rapid increase in the number of new companies formed up to 1914. For over two years the normal expansion of the business has been suspended; nevertheless, the figures indicating the present position of the business are not unimposing and may fittingly be referred to here.

The Inland Board of Revenue accepted the following figures as representative of the position at December 13, 1914—

Number of Companies registered to December 31, 1914	1,833
Combined capital	£11,304,500
Number of Liquidations to December 31, 1914	271
Combined capital	£2,347,700
Net capital	£8,956,800

These figures refer to Public Companies, and the following additions must be made.

Combined capital of private enterprises	£2,000,000	
Mortgages and Debentures	£4,500,000	
		£6,500,000
Total, as at December 31, 1914		£15,456,800

The New Companies registered during 1915 and 1916 totalled 452, representing a capital of £1,935,395.

The number of liquidations during 1915 and 1916 was 114, and the total combined capital may be taken at £650,000. By bringing the 1914 figures up to the present date we have a total capital of about seventeen and a half millions invested in the business.

In the British Isles there are approximately 4500 cinematograph theatres. The seating capacity varies from 100 to three or even four thousand, according to the district. Based on carefully tabulated returns the average attendance per day per cinematograph theatre throughout the country may very conservatively be placed at 750. The total number of patrons per day on this basis is 3,375,000, which gives a gross attendance for the year, for week-days only, of 1,056,375,000. The number of theatres open on Sunday is relatively small and has steadily decreased. The large majority of such houses are to be found in the London area, and assuming a total of 500 theatres, with 750 patrons each Sunday, we have an additional 375,000 patrons per Sunday, or 19,500,000 per year. The gross total of visitors during the year thus becomes 1,075,875,000.

Since these returns were secured, a small number of theatres have been closed down, owing to the war; but the number of these closures have not, it appears, exceeded 6 per cent. of the total, and the houses affected have been almost exclusively the smaller isolated ones. Moreover, it by no means follows that a reduction of 6 per cent. in the number of theatres involves a corresponding diminution in the number of patrons.

Fully one-half of these visitors occupied seats to the value of threepence or less, the analysed figures being as follows—

ANALYSIS OF SEATS OCCUPIED IN THE COURSE OF A YEAR (WEEK-DAYS).

Value of Seat.	No. occupied.	Per cent. of total.
1d.	78,250,000	7·4
2d.	58,844,000	5·6
3d.	400,640,000	38·0
4d.	186,235,000	17·6
6d.	195,468,500	18·5
9d.	97,812,500	9·2
1s.	39,125,000	3·7
Total	1,056,375,000	100·0

It is interesting to attempt to realise what these huge figures mean. They represent a visit to the cinema on the part of every living inhabitant of the British Isles practically twenty-four times a year. Roughly speaking, half the entire population, men, women and children, visit a cinematograph theatre once every week.

The distribution of these theatres roughly corresponds to the distribution of the population. In the city of Leeds, for instance, there are fifty-seven cinematograph licences in force and forty-nine picture houses actually open, with a total seating capacity of 35,036. This represents one seat for every thirteen of the population. Assuming each seat to be filled twice a day, it will be seen that these figures represent a seat for every man, woman and child of the population for one visit per week. The figures for remote provincial districts are of course much higher, but on an average it may be said that there is a seat in a picture house for every thirty-five of the total population.

The number of persons engaged in the manufacture, exhibition and distribution of films in the British Isles may be estimated at from 80,000 to 100,000.

Something has already been said of the type of buildings. After the first novelty of moving pictures had worn off, audiences were no longer sufficiently attracted by animated pictures to be content to put up with discomfort while watching them. There began then a race to provide suitable theatres, and the modern picture " palaces " have been the result. Drastic regulations were quickly enforced, and it may safely be said that upon no other public buildings has so much careful attention been given to the questions of ventilation, heating, safety and comfort. Many of these modern " palaces " have cost over £100,000 to build; the seating arrangements are the most luxurious in any public type of building; elaborate plants are installed to ensure the washing, drying, heating and circulation of the air; they are provided with ample emergency exits; stringent precautions are taken against fire, and in the main the buildings are staffed by an adequate number of respectable attendants. Latterly, the proprietor has found it to his advantage to provide luxurious cafés and lounges, and it is to be noted that the general tendency is to increase the type of house which offers this high-class accommodation.

Assertions as to the way in which these theatres have been managed would be out of place here, for that is essentially a matter of evidence. But we must make two comments. The first is that there has been a gratifying tendency on the part of audiences for some years past to hold the business to strict accountability. The average patron is neither timid nor inarticulate in his criticism : a dull picture or a slow operator, both alike have been relentlessly drawn to the manager's attention with an imperative demand for a remedy. This democratic outspokenness of the picture audiences, is a fact that cannot be too steadily borne in mind when sweeping charges are levelled against the business.

The second comment is that the necessity of working in sincere co-operation with the local authorities has been constantly emphasised by the responsible leaders of the trade. Even when the powers claimed by the local authorities have been doubtfully legal, they have been acquiesced in, and on this point we believe you will find a significant amount of evidence.

The legal control of the business has not yet been placed on a satisfactory footing. Irritating and needless regulations of doubtful legality have in some instances been made by local authorities concerning programmes, particulars of films, substitutes, and synopses, etc., and lately there have been ingenious attempts to drive the children out of the theatres by imposing conditions regarding children's performances with which the exhibitor cannot possibly conform. There seems to be no uniformity possible save an inclination to hamper and throttle the industry. Regulations which are really necessary for the children should obviously be imposed by Parliament after due discussion, and should be part of the law of the land.

The trade in 1912, realising the desirability of a censorship of films, appointed a film censor, who was given very extensive powers. In a great many cases, the right of censorship was claimed also by the local authorities, while recently there has been a proposal on the part of the Home Office department to appoint another censor.

We have said something about the early character of the films. The subjects were very short, sometimes only forty or fifty feet in length, and were very crude both in production and photography. Even so recently as seven years ago, we find an imposing subject completed in a film of 450 feet in length, its presentation occupying only seven to eight minutes ! The average comedy of the period ran from 100 to 250 feet in length, and took from two to five minutes to project.

How far the business has travelled since those days is easily appreciated when one considers such subjects as " The Birth of a Nation," " Cabiria," " Quo Vadis," " Les Misérables," and a host of other similar films on which many thousands of pounds were expended, which occupied anything from two to four hours in exhibition, and were produced on a scale of magnificence and costliness beside which the ordinary stage productions are insignificant. As a matter of fact, the early crudities are no longer to be met with anywhere.

The number of films turned out yearly has reached a colossal figure. During 1915 no fewer than 4767 new subjects were issued. The total footage of new films, both " exclusive " and " open market," provided for the exhibitors' selection is well over 6,000,000 feet per year, and over 70,000,000 feet of film are running through the projectors of the country each week in the year.

The question of the selection of the films which constitute the weekly programmes is one of considerable interest in so far as it involves the responsibility of the exhibiting trade for the type and character of the programme shown. It cannot be too strongly emphasised that it is not in the power of the trade or of individual exhibitors to force upon audiences subjects which they do not find attractive. It is the business of every manager to ascertain and supply the type of film which appeals to his particular audience. A good deal of complaint has been made in some quarters of the infrequency with which films of an educational nature are shown. When the absence of educational and instructive subjects is commented on, it must be remembered that if there was a serious demand for or appreciation of this type of film, the exhibitor would be eager to meet it. In the main, particularly as regards what we may term incidental subjects, it may be taken for granted that the films being shown are strictly those for which the majority in the respective audiences shows a preference. It is obvious that the tastes of an audience cannot be coerced.

The cheapness of this form of amusement has created what is really a new type of audience. Over a half of the visitors to the picture theatres occupy seats to the value of threepence or less. In the main, the vast majority of picture house patrons were not in the habit of attending any other places of amusement. The picture house is emphatically the poor man's theatre, and it must always be remembered, is the only organisation which *systematically* provides amusement for children.

There has been a general consensus of opinion that the development of picture houses has produced a marked improvement in the streets. The cinematograph theatres have proved a powerful counter-attraction to the public-houses, and the Board of Control has shown a very practical recognition of this fact by installing a cinematograph in some of their latest houses. Moreover, the picture theatres have provided a centre of social intercourse for thousands who previously spent their evenings drifting idly about the streets, and the Chief Constables have reported a noticeable diminution in the number of street offences. There has been a decrease in the amount of drunkenness among those who from sheer lack of occupation at night gravitated to the public-house; and this is, of course, of particular importance in connection with the youth of both sexes. In their case, there can be no comparison between idle lounging about the streets and sitting in a clean, well-ventilated, comfortable theatre among decent, well-behaved people.

MINUTES OF EVIDENCE

THE SECRETARY. I have to announce that the witnesses to-day are Mr. Goodwin and Mr. Hepworth.

MR. F. R. GOODWIN.[1] *Examined.*

THE SECRETARY. I think it is understood that we take the printed evidence of the witness as read.

1. THE CHAIRMAN. I think you are Chairman of the London Branch of the Cinematograph Exhibitors' Association of Great Britain and Ireland? You are also Managing Director of the Central Metropolitan Theatres, Limited? And the United Kingdom Picture Theatres, Limited? And of houses at Wolverhampton, Crouch End, Ealing, Maida Vale, Kilburn, and Stamford Hill?—Yes.

2. Now, your evidence has been put in and we will ask questions upon anything that may arise therefrom. I notice you begin by rather taking exception at the time this Inquiry was held on account of the abnormality of things?—Just that much exception, that is all; the time is not quite right.

3. Thereby you mean that some of the films now being exhibited are not the kind of things that they possibly would have been in past times?—I rather inferred that the general character of the trade has not, perhaps, improved with such rapidity during the last two years as before the war. We, in common with all, have suffered in our attempts at advancement.

4. On the other hand you have had the opportunity of stirring up our patriotism?—Yes; much work has been done that way.

5. At the present time what films find most favour? What kind, for instance, do you think is the most favourable?—Just

1 See also pp. 81–91.

now I think the most popular kind is the standard works : such as the novelists' books and Dickens characters. As a matter of fact, the type of film desired just now is the right sort.

6. I notice the numbers of theatres open on Sunday is small and has steadily decreased : can you give any reason?—Yes, there has been opposition in various parts of the country—at Lincoln in particular. They permitted entertainments until eight o'clock, but now they have taken away the privilege altogether, and that means that four or five halls have lost the Sunday evening. That was the case, too, in Middlesex about two years ago. You may take it that London, Brighton, Blackpool, St. Helens and a few more towns, still have their Sunday evenings, but on the whole there is no increase.

7. Might I ask whether the theatrical authorities have set themselves against the opening of cinemas on Sunday?—I have no knowledge of that.

8. Can you tell me any reason why a different law should apply to the cinema on Sunday as compared with the theatre ? Well, if there were arguments to be advanced as distinguishing between the two trades, it would be on the ground that such a small amount of labour is required for the pictures as against the theatres, and, say, the music halls. Picture performances can be run by an operator and assistant with just a few ushers to seat the people properly, whereas in the other case, you have the whole of the players, which, perhaps, is a matter of ten to a hundred people.

9. Tell me, if you can, why the smaller isolated cinemas would be likely to fail?—They are unable to give that measure of enjoyment that the large places are able to offer. Their ventilation is not right, their seats are not comfortable, they have inferior furniture, bad carpets, bad machinery, in fact, everything is old.

10. I notice you say that apparently every one in the British Isles practically goes twenty-four times a year to the cinema?— That is so as it seems from the figures.

11. Whatever happens you are not likely to do much better than you are doing now?—Yes, we are always hoping. The business man, by that I mean the showman, would be rather dissatisfied if some people came only twenty-five times a year. You see there is scope for advancement there.

12. You say there is a seat in a picture house for one in every thirty-five of the total population?—Yes.

13. As to the great improvements, I might almost say the luxury of your buildings, has that been forced upon you by the authorities, or has it been that you have had really good business?—Good business.

14. And the better the kind of place you have your exhibitions in, the more attractive it is ?—Yes, without doubt.

15. And the association of lounges and cafés all helps?—They all help.

16. In all these places can you go to the café without going in to the performance ?—Yes.

17. And that is a good deal done; I mean you get many people who go merely for their afternoon tea without going into the performance ?—Yes, that is so; the café is nicely laid out and sometimes there is a little band, things they don't get at other places.

18. So you are even competing with the cafés ?—Yes.

19. In the latter part of your evidence you rather give the impression to me that there is some organised opposition other than I ever considered there was ?—There is much more.

20. Would you say that that is by a large number of people or a smaller number of people who are very determined ?—The latter.

21. And of what nature ?—The complaints are addressed to three things : there is the character of the film and its influence on the children; there is the other question of children, the molestation of children that has been made a lot of this last year; and the other thing is the undesirable character of visitors or indecency.

22. With regard to the last mentioned, the indecency: that, of course, is assisted by the fact that the building has to be kept in darkness during the performance ?—We are not very much afraid of that. We have had occasion to point out just recently to the authorities in London that it is possible, purely from the point of view of undesirable characters frequenting the hall, that too much light is not a benefit. We have complained that if you overstep the mark and give too much illumination, you rather help the very undesirable people in their undesirable calling.

23. You mean they would change their seats ?—It gives them the opportunity of accosting.

24. Changing from seat to seat to get near some people they might accost ?—Yes, that is what we pointed out to the Home Secretary recently.

25. And in some places there are private boxes ?—Yes, but not very many.

26. Are they as visible to the audience directly the light is turned on as practically any other part of the building ?—Yes, all that are in my knowledge are, and I know most of them.

27. With regard to the molestation of children ?—In 1916 some very terrible, although somewhat ambiguous, charges were made. It was stated that unmentionable evils were going on in many cinemas and more often arranged for in the cinemas and carried out in private houses. " It is impossible to describe these evils in public print," but, wrote a Sociologist in his magazine, " our readers will understand that we quote a certain passage of Scripture: ' Giving themselves over to fornication and going after strange flesh,' " (Jude).

28. Does that apply to children ?—I want rather to get at this sort or this kind of evidence or knowledge with regard to children being molested I presume, by adults, at cinemas. " From the information received from eye-witnesses "—the reference already quoted goes on—" the amount of criminal vice carried on in most of these places is appalling, and utterly unknown to

the generality of respectable people. The Criminal Law Amend-
ment Act passed for the protection of young girls has been too
often entirely ignored. The convictions have been apparently
few. Worse than this, to evade the law the offence has been reversed and, horrible to relate, both boys and girls have been
taught to commit the offence and solicit money so that the real
culprits have escaped the law. Further evils lead to an alarming
amount of blackmailing, which has now become very prevalent
in large towns." Well, that statement was taken to the London
County Council and to the Home Office and the London County
Council consulted my association on the matter. The London
County Council reported on this matter under date December 15,
1916 : " In regard to the number of cases which have taken place
during the present year of children who have been molested by
men in cinematograph halls. In two of the cases it appeared
from the licensee's statements that it was due to the action of
the manager of the hall that the police were called in and the
men arrested. We have considered whether in order to prevent
as far as possible the recurrence of such cases the licensees should
be required to reserve special accommodation for children unaccompanied by adults and to prohibit any adult occupying any
of the seats so reserved. A deputation from the Cinematograph
Exhibitors' Association has pointed out to us that in the majority
of cases the men would bring the children to the hall, having
made their acquaintance outside, and that such cases would not
be met by reserving special accommodation for children unaccompanied by adults. The deputation further stated that the suggestion, if adopted, would inflict hardship on many exhibitors,
especially in the case of the smaller halls, as on those occasions
when children attended in great numbers they did not attend
and leave at the same time, and consequently, proprietors might
have to refuse admission to adults while having many vacant
seats. It would also result in the worst seats being always reserved
for children. They state that in their opinion the best safeguard
would be to have in every hall an attendant whose special duty
it would be to look after the children attending the hall."

29. Has that been done?—That was done and the regulation
of the London County Council, which we drafted between us,
stipulated that : " Such attendant shall bear a distinguishing
badge, shall be on duty during the whole time the premises are
open to the public, and during such time shall have no other
duty than the care of the children in the hall." That, sir, was
the action of the London County Council. The action of the
Home Office is related in the letter from the Chief Commissioner
of Police to the Home Office under date July 28, 1916 : " I have
to acquaint you, for the information of the Secretary of State,
that in consequence of complaints received that indecency takes
place at cinematograph picture halls, I deemed it advisable to
cause a systematic inspection of these places to be made, and
accordingly, with the Secretary of State's authority, I arranged
with the National Union of Woman Workers of Great Britain

and Ireland to undertake this work. The County of London was divided into convenient districts and in the course of three weeks 248 halls were visited." I break off there, if I may, to say that the 248 halls represents the entire operative picture theatres of London. There are 350 cinematograph licences issued, but a lot of these are to places which do not come under the category of cinematograph halls. To continue : " The attention of the lady visitors was directed to the following questions : (1) Is there a children's attendant with a badge or a distinguishing mark ? (2) Are children unaccompanied by adults seated separately from the remainder of the audience [these two points were included as they formed the subject of recent regulations made by the London County Council]. (3) Is the darkness such as to make it difficult or impossible to detect indecency should any take place ? (4) Is the structure such as to facilitate indecency, that is, are there specially dark corners or galleries, boxes or other secluded places ? (5) Is any particular age, sex, or class of spectator noticeable ? (6) Any observations which appear to bear on the subject. If, say, a film of a kind likely to produce a pernicious impression on children is seen, its name and character should be given.

" The following is a summary of the results of the observations kept—

" Question 1.—Sixty-six instances reported in which a special children's attendant was seen." May I break off to say that in some of the theatres children are not allowed in alone, whereas in other cases children are not allowed in unaccompanied by adults ? that is to say, in some of the high-class West End theatres you would not find a children's attendant there because they don't cater for the children.

30. What do you call a child ?—We call a child a child up to fourteen years of age.

" Question 2.—Eighty-three instances where children unaccompanied by adults were seated separately from the rest of the audience.

" Question 3.—Sixty-six cases quoted where darkness made it difficult to detect indecency should any have taken place.

" Question 4.—Thirty-nine cases of opportunities for indecency through the structure, viz. dark corners, boxes and the use of curtains, etc.

" Question 5.—In the West End halls scarcely any children were noticed, but in the suburban halls many children were seen, especially on Saturdays and Sundays. Also many children in arms were noticed.

" Question 6.—It is the general opinion of the Patrols that the halls are unnecessarily dark, especially in the intervals between the exhibition of the films, and that improvement could well be made in this respect, without impairing the clearness of the pictures. Comment is made as to bad ventilation, particularly in the poorer districts, and, in a few cases the dirty condition of the halls is the subject of remark.

" It is also thought undesirable to exclude all adults from the children's matinees and that mothers at least should be admitted on these occasions. It is suggested that no boxes should be permitted unless they are illuminated and that a regulation should be made as to the age of children allowed in cinemas. It is reported that in several halls of the poorer districts many babies in arms have been seen during the later hours of the evening.

" The prevalent offensive habit of spitting is very noticeable and it is suggested that some regulation should be made with regard to it.

" It is considered by one of the ladies that the women attendants are in many cases too young to be fitted for such an occupation, as.they would be useless on any occasions involving panic.

" One lady suggests that children should not be seated close to the screen as the extra strain on the eyes at such close quarters must be very detrimental to the sight.

" The opinion generally expressed is that films depicting crimes should be censored. It is thought that the exhibition of films of this character is most unwise and may lead children to the commission of similar acts. The ' Charlie Chaplin ' films are also commented on by one visitor as being vulgar and suggestive to evil. No instance of any act of indecency is described by the lady visitors.

" The general conclusions at which I have arrived at are that it is very desirable that the regulations as to children's attendants and children's seats should be strictly enforced and that consideration should be given to the questions of better lighting, ventilation, the prohibition of expectoration, the exclusion of children in arms, and, finally, that steps should be taken to institute an efficient censorship so as to prevent the exhibition of films calculated to familiarise the young with ideas of violence, crime and immorality."

The effect of this report was, that the London County Council noted in particular the suggestion that the lights should go up after every picture, and that is now an order of the Council.

31. Has that letter been considered by your Association?—Yes.

32. And have you found anything very much you could not agree with there?—No, I think there is nothing at all. We should not go so far as to say that " Charlie Chaplin " was conducive to evil.

33. MONSIGNOR BROWN. Might I ask a question which would save a great deal of time? Can you give any idea of the number of halls not controlled by your Association?—Yes, our membership is 200 out of 248.

34. Then 200 of them are under you?—Two hundred of them are in our combination. Now a very dreadful allegation has recently been made against the cinemas.

35. THE SECRETARY. You refer to this : " That in fact, one of our own secret agents "—quoting the person making the

charge—" was asked by the agent at one hall if he should place him amongst the boys or the girls "?—That is so.

36. You suggest that he was asked to go amongst the girls to commit immorality?—Yes, or whether he would rather have a boy.

37. THE CHAIRMAN. The hall has not been named?—No, we had hoped it would be.

38. You still feel that the accusations made against the cinema are made by the smallest number of people and are of a determined character—we won't say anything more than determined —I will say this of the terms of the reference of the National Union of Woman Workers : " We have received complaints that indecency takes place." Does it take place?—No, it does not take place. We have not seen it at all, but what we do get is a lot of expectoration. Well, expectoration in the East End of London is general and also there are some circumstances which would facilitate indecency if any one went there for that purpose.

39. And for all that your Association would deal?—Yes; if a light was wanted in each box, it would be there, it is not at all unreasonable.

40. Now that deals with your statement as to the sweeping charges levelled against your business. The necessity of working in sincere co-operation with the local authority has been emphasised by your trade, has it not?—Yes.

41. In regard to the general management of your house and so on; is it desirable that the power should be left with the local authority or should it not come from the central authority?—It should come from the central authority.

42. That is your strong feeling?—Yes.

43. But at present you are doing all you can to get into friendly relationship with the local authority?—Yes.

44. There was a great deal of anxiety and nervousness, I think, with regard to the possibility of fire being a danger in these halls, was there not? People had a very strong feeling about that at one time?—Yes.

45. And that has now been safeguarded against?—It is a thing of the past, this question of inflammable material. Supposing this room were a hall, the inflammable material is outside the hall. You must show through a brick wall intervening, and in London they make you fill up the aperture with a thick glass. In fact, the operating room is a room apart. It is not an enclosure within the hall, that is not allowed.

46. You say that certain conditions are imposed with regard to the performance for children with which the exhibitor cannot possibly conform. Can you tell me what those are?—It would be impossible to impose the condition that a child shall not see a comic picture or a drama. The request then would be that the performance should be specially selected for children only, and while that is possible for a special performance for children, it is not possible for the ordinary course of the business.

47. I see you say that a censor was appointed by the trade to

whom was given extensive powers.   Can you tell me those powers ?
—They were the fullest possible powers for every film that was
presented to him.

48. Recently there has been a proposal on the part of the
Home Office department to appoint another censor.   Do you
object to that appointment if that means a censor for the whole
country ?   Yes, we do object unless we can have some voice in the
thing, such as in the way of an Advisory Committee, so that we
can examine the standards being set up by the censor, from our
knowledge of what we, the exhibitors, want and of what the
manufacturers want.   We are afraid, if it becomes purely a Government matter, that certain hard and fast acts and trying conditions
will be imposed, such as that a film which a child of nine can
view is the kind we shall have to show the adults.

49. You referred to your high-class and highly developed films.
Do you find that these attract the less educated parts of a town ?
—Yes.

50. Just as acceptable as the others ?—Yes, absolutely, and
I think I see the trend of your inquiry.   The finest films shown
in the West End of London in their turn go to the poorest halls
in the East of London.   It is only a question of the age of a
film.   There are no bad films which are made for the East End
and good films which are made for the West End.   Take the
films " Quo Vadis ? " and " Les Misérables ; " they went to the
East End in their turn.

51. Now, take that celebrated Italian film " Cabiria."   That
is really a very high-class production.   Would you unhesitatingly
take that to Whitechapel ?—Not " Cabiria."   That did not go
to ordinary places because it took some three hours to see it
through ; but there is no reason why a showman should not show
it.

52. And do you say that the West End would sit four hours to
see one film ?—No, very occasionally.

53. MR. CROOK.   Was " Nero and Poppæa " a very long film,
would you consider that a suitable thing to show to children ?—
.Yes, I think so.

54. The case of a woman trying to lure Nero ?—Well, I do not
think the children would follow that particularly.   They would
follow and like the marching and all that.

55. THE CHAIRMAN.   You would argue, I presume, that it is
perfectly legitimate to have that on the film—the things which
appear at the theatre, say, sensual dramas ?—No, I would not
say that, because something can be said on the stage, but nothing
can be said in the film, and while you can hint on the stage what
adults know, you must not illustrate.

56. In order to make the thing real to the people who have only
their eyes to help them, you have to put much more detail in the
pictures than you have in the theatre ?—You would have to.

57. And, therefore, there is a greater danger in the sensual
details in the film than there would be in a play ?—It is impossible
to put it on the film.

58. Sir R. Baden-Powell. Can you tell me whether there is any record of the number of cases of indecency?—Yes; in the year that I was dealing with there were two cases in picture halls, and these came under my personal notice. In one case a man was given into charge at once, and was eventually found guilty. He was an old offender and was given six months' hard labour. The second case was a young man of twenty-one, who was found to be an imbecile and was put away.

59. What period does that cover?—That was in the year 1915.

60. Monsignor Brown. You have no records for 1916?—No.

61. There were some prosecutions I know, because there was one near me.—Yes, we got that.

62. Sir R. Baden-Powell. How do you judge the popularity of a film?—By the way it is spoken of; by the patrons and the knowledge we get when it comes from the reviewers. Many of us have a suggestion box in the vestibule and little notes are dropped in that by our patrons who, perhaps, will say they don't like a certain film, or they do like it.

63. Mr. T. P. O'Connor. I suppose that there is no more danger of the abuse of the cinema theatre than there is in other large congregations of human beings?—No. I should say there is less chance of real indecency taking place in a cinema than in any other form of amusement, for the reason that there are repeated interruptions during the whole of the entertainment. After every reel—which holds 1000 feet and takes about twenty-six minutes to show—there is an interruption of the performance. People are coming in or going out every few minutes. They don't all arrive when the door opens and sit down for two hours; they are being interrupted every minute of the time.

64. With regard to the censorship and this question we have just been discussing, I suppose you regard this as two separate problems?—Yes.

65. The censorship, as I understand it, is engaged simply with the question of whether a certain film is or is not a good film for the public to see?—Yes.

66. And the other matter is a question for the police?—Yes.

67. Do I understand you to say that the Association which you represent has expressed its entire desire and determination to make no changes mentioned in either the construction or management of the theatres that may prevent the possibilities of immorality, such as with reference to boxes, for instance?—No, we are not opposing; on the contrary, where boxes are separate and not lit, we welcome the suggestion.

68. Are there any such boxes now not lit?—Yes, there are boxes which are not lit except by the general light of the theatre.

69. That you propose to change?—Yes.

70. The Secretary. Are there many theatres with boxes like this?—There are a few.

71. Mr. T. P. O'Connor. What is the number of boxes, separate boxes, unlit at the present moment?—The London County Council, or, I should say, the Fire Brigade, says : " Boxes are now quite a feature in cinematograph theatres, and plans showing the provision of such boxes in existing theatres have been approved in perhaps half a dozen cases within the past year. Regard is had to the adequate illumination of boxes in reports of the general lighting of the hall. It is doubtful, however, whether the arrangement of the lighting hitherto accepted in boxes, etc., is sufficient for increased supervision as indicated in the police report. If increased lighting is desired in these spaces slight revision or rearrangement, e. g. a provision of secret switches and inaccessible or enclosed lamps, would perhaps be necessary. Comparatively secluded spaces are also formed by the draught curtains, which are in many instances hung so as partially to enclose several rows at the rear of the seating. If considered necessary, the lighting in these could be increased by the provision of additional fittings." That is the report of the Fire Brigade, who usually deal with this question of lighting arrangements, to the Committee.

72. On the question of the supply of films, can you give me some idea of the proportion between British and American films? —I would put it at 90 per cent. American.

73. I assume, therefore, that 90 per cent. of the films are engaged rather in the description of American than British life?— Yes, that is so, except that we are very glad to see that the Americans are now taking films of English subjects and English novelists.

74. And I assume also that there are films from America which deal with scenes in Egypt and the Scriptures?—Yes; you know they sent us " The Eternal City," where most of the scenes were taken in Rome.

75. Then we get from America many of the films founded upon the crook?—Yes, they are very fond of that. You get the sheriff in a Western drama or else the crook working in New York, but in that connection the Americans are at least as wise as our English manufacturer, as there is always the most severe punishment at the end for the crook or a great scene of reform. I have never seen a crime unpunished on a film.

76. I may take it that a respectable exhibitor would not accept in England a crook playing where there was no adequate justice done to the crook?—No.

77. Don't you think it would be desirable to diminish the villainy which represents the lawless and the revolver-shooting life of the wilder parts of America?—I do not think so. It is a turn that we call stirring, or a thrilling Western drama just now and again.

78. Yes, you must have wild life described.—That, we think, is to an extent educational; it shows the life in these parts.

79. Like Buffalo Bill's Wild West Show?—Yes.

80. Still, you would regard that as rather an infrequent than a constant dish for the cinema theatre?—Yes.

81. Have you looked into the question of the educational possibilities of the cinema?—No, not more than as it comes before my business, you know.

82. Have you had any films like natural history?—Yes, we usually have one of those. I have this week's " Films Released " in my pocket, and they are always about. For the first half of the week there are four dramas which are good films; they have passed the censor and earned their six marks in our combination. There are four comedies and two interest or travel pictures. The first interest picture is " Insect Oddities." That is made by an English firm, and the other is a Pathé " Our Troops in South Africa." For the second half of the week we get five dramas, four comedies, and two interest and travel pictures; one is " From the Ostrich Egg to the Feather Boa," and the other is " Views of Ilfracombe and Clovelly." So you will see the relation is two to nine and two to eight in number.

83. MONSIGNOR BROWN. Not in duration?—No; the drama is about 1200 feet and takes about twenty-five minutes, the troops 1000 feet, and the " Insect Oddities " is about 450 feet; and the same during the other half.

84. MR. T. P. O'CONNOR. Do you find the travel pictures very attractive?—Yes, in their turn, but it would not do to put on an hour of it.

85. Have you seen " The Advance to Gorizia " by the Italians? —Yes.

86. A picture like that is quite popular?—Yes.

87. That, I take, is the kind of picture which as the industry advances it would be able more and more to produce?—Yes, I should say that that is the easiest picture to produce.

88. THE SECRETARY. The cheapest, you mean?—No, the easiest. It is so easy to take current events. They are there, and you have no brain work, no constructive work.

89. SIR EDWARD BRABROOK. I should like to understand these statistics of yours. I see that you have a thousand million visitors in one single year?—Yes.

90. And that a little more than half of them paid less than threepence?—Yes.

91. I take it that those who paid more, so far as they were children, would be accompanied by older children?—Yes.

92. You have no statistics or numbers of children who would be in those different classes?—No, I have not.

93. I take it that the money value of the whole amount is very nearly twenty millions. Is it possible that twenty millions has been earned by the cinema shows? That is what I make it out to be.—That is the gross takings, not earnings; for, you see, there are little items such as wages and that kind of thing.

94. I have seen some excellent scientific films showing the changes in the life of insects and other scientific subjects like that. Are they at all popular in the shows?—You usually find one in a well-selected programme.

95. You don't think much more can be done? Do you see

your way to admit the popularity of really scientific and instructive films?—I should be very happy to try it, but I fear if I
gave up more than a quarter of an hour of my two hours entertainment I should bore many people and get many complaints.

96. DR. KIMMINS. Who arranges the programme of the film;
what choice have you of the kind of film you get down?—There
is an enormous choice.

97. And the proprietor draws up his own programme, does
he?—Yes, there is absolutely a free market in this country.

98. Just one other point : how is it seen whether the regulations of the Council are carried out at the different houses?—By
a very diligent and efficient system of inspection, the older Fire
Brigade men, selected for marked intelligence and discretion, are
put on to evening inspection work. They visit every theatre in
London once or twice every week, and make confidential reports
of what they see to the Chief Fire Brigade Officer, who passes out
the complaints to the various Departments, whether lighting, or
misconduct, or whatever the complaint may be. These inspectors
only report on films, questions of misconduct, immorality or the
like, if complaint has been received by the Council, and if special
instructions are given to the Fire Department to place certain
matters under special observation.

99. The inspection is entirely under the Fire Brigade?—Yes.

100. MR. CROOK. The gross takings come to twenty millions.
Do you consider the industry is worth that to the country?—
Twenty millions for amusement?—Yes.

101. Against the beer bill and the streets?—Yes, twice the
money.

102. What proportion of children attend the cinema?—Well,
I do not believe during the week-days there is more than 10
per cent.

103. What do you mean by the week-days?—In many parts
of the country there is a special Saturday afternoon performance
for the children, and where in the ordinary way they would have
to pay threepence, at this performance they pay a penny. This
performance usually starts at one o'clock and is over by three
o'clock, when the adults' performance commences.

104. That is where I saw " Nero and Poppæa," at a special
Saturday afternoon performance for children?—Yes.

105. Have you thought of fixing a time for children to leave
in the evening?—No.

106. Don't you think it is a wise thing? Do you think it is
wise for children of twelve to be out after eight o'clock at night
in the cinema?—I do not think we should resist such a regulation if it were demanded. You see, there is some difficulty about
such a matter as that. I submit if the babies are nursed in
their mothers' arms it is just as well whether they are out or not
as long as they are asleep. You must bear in mind that some of
these people only live in one room, and perhaps they find it
cheaper to take a short time at the pictures. You see, it means
they have not got to light a fire at home, and that would be

c

cheaper for them. Again, mothers are at work all day in some of the poorer districts, and they could not go out at all unless they took the child with them.

107. I understand that the evidence of the Woman Workers was that the babies were taken to the cinema and were crawling about the floor?—That is so in the Whitechapel district.

108. That does not bear out your remark?—Well, I do not conceive of a theatre where it is allowed.

109. We find that children come to school frequently too tired because they have been out to the pictures the night before?—Are you sure they were not more tired before the pictures came?

110. I find them more tired now. I have been a master some time before the pictures came?—Were they not more tired then?

111. I take it if the Government fix the time at half-past seven or eight o'clock each night, after which no children would be allowed in the cinema, you would not oppose such a regulation?—We should not oppose it.

112. Has your body ever considered, not the nature of the film itself, but the nature of the advertisement of the film?—Yes.

113. Does the censor touch these?—No.

114. Who does?—The Billposters Association. They are an extremely powerful and well-organised body, and no bill can go on to the hoardings unless it is sanctioned by them. We welcome that.

THE CHAIRMAN. The Billposters Association has no authority as to the bill which is on the private house, I mean on the actual cinema palace itself.

115. MR. CROOK. That is what I am aiming at.—We are in accord with the Billposters Association, and there is only one thing left for us to do, and that is for us to control the posters which are put on to our own members' front halls.

116. I mean these coloured monstrosities, those shady pictures where the revolver is very prominent and the woman always looking very tragic?—Do you ever see such posters?

117. Yes, the other day.—Then the billposters are not looking after their work. The tendency of these posters now is only to illustrate the star of the performance. The posters of this year are nearly always a photograph of the leading lady or the leading gentleman. They are getting so well known that their photographs are used.

I mean those coloured posters of perhaps one incident in the drama which is very highly coloured.

118. MR. T. P. O'CONNOR. Is it not proposed that these posters to which allusion has been made shall come under the censor like the rest of the things?—Yes; we have been negotiating with the Board of Films censors, whether they can take over the censorship of the bills as well, and we are getting to a point where that can come about.

119. MR. LAMERT. These 1,056,000,000 people — can you classify them, are they of the lower order?—No, every class.

120. In certain theatres it has been the case in the past that there has been catering for a certain class of people who are

undesirable; I don't mean loose women only, but there have been a certain class of people going to that theatre. Now, would that pay any cinema proprietor?—No, the worst possible thing that would be.

121. I take it that if the cinema proprietor or manager wants to do his duty he wants to put that down?—It is his greatest anxiety.

122. It would never pay him to have it known that his hall was the place where loose men and women went?—Quite so.

123. All these buildings practically are teetotal?—Yes.

124. Absolutely teetotal; because drink and the other thing have gone together. There are none of them licensed?—All are teetotal.

125. Now, in theatres they have pass-out checks so that people can go out and get a drink?—That is not done in any cinema theatre I know of.

126. You don't have that business?—There is no re-admission under any circumstances whatever.

127. And you say they are a very sober population?—Yes.

128. They are a particularly sober class; I mean, have you had complaints of drunkenness?—No.

129. Now, with regard to this question of indecency. You gave us a good deal of one criticism, and we disposed of that. Is there any other general accusation?—The most striking accusation of the year was that of Sir Robert Wallace when he said we were the curse of London.

130. You mean the magistrate?—Yes.

131. Is there any specific complaint beyond what one man says in the Mile End Road about indecency which we have already dealt with? Is there anybody that has brought forward definite statements that: " We know children are being molested." Is there anything definite?—No.

132. Have you had any definite complaints that can be investigated?—No; I can give you nothing closer than the printed stuff of Mr. ——.

133. If there were any complaints would they come under your notice?—Yes, any complaint we have is very carefully gone into. We very carefully watch the Press and everything said is brought before us.

134. And these are practically the only ones you have had to deal with?—Yes, to pin down.

135. There is the point about the darkness. You rather made the point that if there was more light it would give more opportunities for women to do anything they wanted to do?—That is what we fear.

136. If at the present time a man sat down by a woman it would be pure chance?—She could not select her place.

137. There is the dangerous point at the vestibules, in the halls. Have they all vestibules?—Yes.

138. Can it occur in the vestibules?—It would not be allowed to occur. The vestibule of a picture house is more guarded than the vestibule of a theatre.

139. Whom by?—By the proprietor, by the manager; there is always a doorman in charge whose duty it is to cry the goods.

140. Now, with regard to the question of the children. Suppose the rule was made that the children should go out at 8.30, how would you get them out, would you ring a gong or sound a whistle?—I suppose we should deal with it. It would be an interruption of the programme.

141. You would not oppose it?—We could not successfully oppose it.

142. MR. GRAVES. Is much injury to sight caused by the flickering of the films and the use of worn-out films? I understand that injury has been done to the sight by that. I understand that in Liverpool people are not allowed to sit nearer than fifteen feet from the films. Would you recommend any regulation of that sort?—It is not a regulation, but in most of the theatres in London the distance is very considerably over fifteen feet before you come to the seats.

143. There is no doubt that children will remain in the cinematographs. You don't turn them out, and they may sit as long as they choose?—Yes.

144. As a matter of fact, they will sit two hours and go out in rather a dazed condition. There is no means, therefore, of moving children on; they can stay, you might say, for two hours and more. Now, do you think that is a good thing?—I do not know whether it is good for children.

145. Now there is another question, the question of the diffusion of light; is it not a fact that light is sometimes equally diffused through a house, and is it not a fact that that would not lead to any immorality? I notice that is the case in Liverpool?—Yes, but their standard is not any higher than London.

146. I am asking whether that does not happen in Liverpool, and whether they do not do it with an object. Your suggestion is that if you darken the hall there is less likely to be immorality than if the hall was light?—No, that is not quite what I wanted you to gather. I say if you get the light beyond a certain amount you assist the undesirable women by giving them the opportunity to accost, and that is a fact.

147. My point is that a man who brings a woman to a place with evil intent would prefer darkness to light?—Yes.

148. You have got cafés apparently, have you not?—Yes.

149. In these cafés are women of undesirable character likely to go, and use them as a promenade?—No, not if they are known.

150. You know that the music hall people by public regulation lately have really turned a great number of the people out of the promenades, and these people have unfortunately gone to your shows?—They are trying to get in.

151. Have you any means of turning them out?—Yes.

152. Your only means is by noticing their behaviour, or when you have reason to know from the police that they are women of that sort?—No, we should detect the woman changing her seat twice or three times. If we saw her change her seat we

should keep a watch upon her, and if she changed it again we should eject her.

153. One question on the educational side of affairs. Apparently the only educational authority that regulates films is the Customs? —Yes, they have to decide whether the entertainment is educational or not.

154. I take it with an educational entertainment there are decreased fees?—Not to my knowledge.

155. When it is entirely educational. Therefore you do not know that the Customs are the authority which decides whether the film is educational or not. I believe they refer it to the Board of Education?—You are dealing with the import tax on films coming from abroad.

THE CHAIRMAN. No, the amusement tax.

156. MR. GRAVES. There is the entertainment tax?—Yes.

157. And in the case of an entertainment which is purely educational there is no tax, and the Customs regulate that tax and decide whether that film is educational or not?—That is so.

158. Then how would you yourself decide whether a film is educational or not in putting it upon your screen? Have you an educational department connected with your firms, or how do you manage it?—We have nothing in that way, but surely it does not want any examination to detect what is an educational film.

159. It depends upon how you use the film. Should you suggest it is education to put upon a film the sudden growth from an egg to a chicken, or other cases of animal movement? You put these things before the city child who knows nothing about them, and you give no explanation?—Yes, before that rapid photographing is gone through there is a statement on the screen that the eggs will take so many days to hatch, and so forth.

160. Still, in spite of that you do not leave the statement long enough on the screen, and therefore the child, seeing the thing, would be much more likely to think it saw what really happened? —Yes.

161. SIR W. BARRETT. Dealing with the question of light in the cinema theatres, are you aware that in all theatres where there is a screen, I mean educational theatres, the class is not left in darkness? The place can be perfectly well illuminated so that they can take their notes, and yet the screen is kept in perfect darkness?—Yes, but your halls are very small compared with the modern cinematograph theatres.

162. Is it not a fact that the films can be perfectly well shown while the audiences are comparatively well illuminated by shaded lamps which are put to avoid the light falling upon the screen?— Yes, perfectly shaded lights. But there must be no lights in the centre of the hall. They can be at the side.

163. I have been lecturing for nearly forty years showing lantern and microscopic slides, and I have found it is not necessary for the class to be in darkness. They can take notes of my

lectures.—Because your class-room or lecture hall was of such a small size compared with the modern cinematograph theatre. There is one hall in London I have in mind where the distance from the lantern to the screen is 215 feet, which is the longest throw in London. The picture there to be seen is thirty feet by twenty-four feet. It is a tremendous area, and that hall will hold 2000 people. Half of them would be men, and half of them, again—that is 500 people—would be smoking. These are things you have to consider, and while there is no difficulty in lighting the sides of the hall, I see a very great difficulty in carrying on a commercial enterprise with a fully lighted hall all over.

164. Would the audience fall off if there was more light in the auditorium?—Not unless it came to the point that we had spoilt the picture. If we spoilt the picture the audience would fall off very rapidly. The only test is, can we show the picture?

165. Sir W. Barrett. You say the local authorities impose irritating regulations with regard to children?—You see, there is an attempt to ask us to provide full programmes of the milk-and-water variety for the duration of about two hours, and we simply cannot do that.

166. You object altogether to the local authorities?—Yes.

167. But are they not much more likely to know what is suitable and unsuitable than any central authorities as regards their immediate population?—Not in the least likely. They are more likely to be local, and being local are possibly bigoted in their ideas, more so than a central authority which would fight out and settle this question on a national basis.

168. I presume picture palaces pay local rates?—Yes.

169. Why, then, do the local authorities try to hamper and throttle them?—I do not know. We pay the rates just the same, you know.

170. Does your Association extend to Scotland and Ireland?— Yes.

171. You are aware of the case in the Dublin Police Court some little time ago concerning one of the large and fashionable picture palaces in which it was alleged that a film prejudicial to morality was shown?—No.

Monsignor Brown. This gentleman said he had mainly to do with London.

172. Sir W. Barrett. I ask what security have the public that no portion of the film may be cut out by the exhibitor before the case came before the Court, as was alleged in this case?—I do not think there would be any security, but that would not stop the responsibility, as you would find from the manufacturer whether it was originally in the film, and it could then be held that it had been suppressed if the complainant could describe in detail what the part was.

173. Professor H. Gollancz. I understand there is a suggestion of a special attendant to move about among the children who were unaccompanied by any adult. If the molestation is supposed to take place and does take place in the body of the

hall, how can that attendant have any power at all?—This girl or woman in charge of the children unaccompanied by adults would attend to the children as far as possible, attend to their little wants and keep them in order.

174. That would not remove the risk of molestation in other parts?—It would not remove the risk of molestation if a man brought the child in with him.

175. The question of the light has been dealt with, and you speak about the question commercially. I should like to know whether, scientifically speaking, the performance could not be equally good if there was light, not only side lights, but full lights in the body of the hall?—If you say full lights I say that it is impossible.

176. At all events, such light as to make indecency or molestation absolutely impossible?—You can have enough light to make indecency almost impossible, but there is a great difference between us if you mean the full, or practically full, light of a room like this.

177. Is it scientifically impossible?—Scientifically impossible. It is a question of standard. If this is the standard (the lighting of the Committee Room), a picture could not be shown here.

178. MONSIGNOR BROWN. I should like to ask a few questions about this Association of yours. It covers England, Ireland, Scotland and Wales?—Yes.

179. What is the total number of exhibitors in those areas?—We have got something in the neighbourhood of 4500.

180. How many of these halls are affiliated or belong to your Association?—Slightly over one-half.

181. The remainder, are they federated or gathered into any kind of Association?—No.

182. Are those belonging to your Association mainly the larger and more popular halls?—They are the best, of course.

183. Will you say all the high-class halls are in it?—Yes.

184. Then, after you have got your membership those outside it are mainly the smaller or cheaper class of hall?—Yes.

185. Therefore you cannot speak for them at all?—No, except what I know about London. Of the 248 in London I have 200.

186. Questions have been asked this afternoon which not only deal with London, but range over the whole area, and I beg leave to suggest, with all due respect to you, that some of your questions have been answered without any personal knowledge. I don't mean to say you have done so wittingly. The questions have been addressed to you as if you know every question about every hall in England, Ireland, Scotland and Wales?—I do not know them all.

187. You specially represent London, and by that you mean the Administrative County of London?—Yes.

188. In London, you say, you have 248 licensed halls?—Yes.

189. And you have 200 of them in your Association?—Yes.

190. Can you speak of the forty-eight outside from personal

knowledge of how they are conducted?—Yes, I have knowledge of those halls which are not in our group.

191. How did you gain that knowledge?—I know the methods under which they work and their regulations.

192. Have you visited them all?—No.

Therefore it is more or less hearsay and not practical personal knowledge.

193. THE CHAIRMAN. Have you visited all your own 200?—No, but I have seen most of the proprietors from time to time.

194. MONSIGNOR BROWN. When you make use of an expression that such a thing never occurred, you mean that it has not come under your knowledge, for, you see, the fact that it has not come under your knowledge does not mean that it has not occurred?—Which question do you mean?

Cases of immorality.

195. THE SECRETARY. You mean you have not heard of these things from any of the persons who came in contact with you?—I think I am bound to hear of them if there is any question of a prosecution.

196. MONSIGNOR BROWN. How are you bound to hear of prosecutions in any hall which is not yours?—We cannot take notice of any alleged complaint of immorality.

197. I am asking, how would you know this : A mother comes to me and says : " My child was in a hall last Saturday afternoon and some bigger boy touched her indecently." There is no means of knowing that?—No, unless she had gone to the manager.

198. I live almost opposite a cinema, and I have an opportunity of seeing the picture palace people. I also have an opportunity of seeing the bills which are posted up outside. I have seen one this morning of a girl in a certain kind of dress, and round about are quite a number of men's heads floating in the air, and nearly all are engaged in looking up at this girl's feet. It is called " The Cup of " something.—It is so nice to get something definite. I would propose, if you would allow me, to have a copy of this poster sent to you—(hear, hear)—because there are such different aspects of these things.

THE CHAIRMAN. It is on the building?

MONSIGNOR BROWN. It is on their display board.

199. THE SECRETARY. Then we understand you will produce it, Mr. Goodwin?—Yes.

200. MR. T. P. O'CONNOR. Is it not a fact, Mr. Goodwin, that if any of these facts are brought before your Association you do what you can to point out the danger?—Yes, we exist for that purpose.

201. In that way I understand you bring certain pressure to bear on these halls outside your Association?—Yes.

202. MONSIGNOR BROWN. It does not follow, I think Mr. Goodwin will admit, that every parent whose child was molested would like the publicity of police court proceedings?—I wish they would.

203. At this hall I am speaking of there was a prosecution

brought against a man with reference to three little girls. He bought them seats, and he was afterwards prosecuted at Westminster Police Court?—Yes, these monsters do exist.

204. There was evidence, you seem to suggest, that the prosecution had been at the instigation of the proprietors?—I said that the London County Council said——

205. What the London County Council said is not necessarily true?—It is said and printed in this very report.

206. Now as to films. Would it be your opinion that even if the public did like scientific, landscape or other films which are mainly short and not of the romantic character, there would not be time enough for them, as the programme is limited on account of the drama and other films, which are mainly longer?—No, I do not think that is so.

207. To put it simply, do you think they are crowded out?—No.

208. How is the programme arranged? Is it a matter of the selection of the exhibitor?—Yes.

209. It is the exhibitor, then, who deliberately in making up the programme says: " I cannot give more than twenty minutes of short stuff "?—I do not think that is the way he looks at it. When I am making up a programme, if there is a scientific picture, a picture of interest, or a picture of travel, and it is over ten minutes in length, I view it with some suspicion as to whether it is the class of thing I want.

210. What do you mean by " I want "? What you would like to see, or what you think the public will have?—I speak for my public.

211. As a caterer, don't you feel the public pulse and give them just as much of that as they will stand?—Yes.

212. And you think they won't stand any more than they are getting now?—I think about one-eighth.

213. Now, have your Association ever been urged to take off undesirable films?—No.

214. Have any theatrical exhibitors been attacked for undesirable films?—Yes.

215. Have they, as the result of that, taken them off?—Yes.

216. Would you tell me why they waited to be attacked?—Some exhibitors would not appreciate the point of view that was being taken exception to. There is a case in my mind of " ——— ———," and another, " —— ———." " —— ——— " is no doubt known to all the members of this Committee. Now, the film as a film was absolutely unobjectionable, with the exception of one rather prolonged embrace of the two leading characters. The exhibition aroused, perhaps, in some people's minds the expectation that they were going to see the objectionable incidents of the novel on the picture, all outlined and describing the sensual stuff, and certain licensing authorities said that the film should not be shown.

217. There was, in fact, litigation over it?—Yes.

218. I think that the eye is one of the quickest avenues of mind?—Yes.

219. Is it not one of the most dangerous avenues ?—Yes.

220. Can you tell me why the exhibitors selected such a doubtful book as a subject for a film, even if they did not put all the details in it ?—Well, the film was made in America.

221. Are we obliged to have everything made in America ?—It was not taken up generally in this country by the exhibitors.

222. Mr. T. P. O'Connor.   I should just like to ask this point with regard to " —————— ."   Where you had an objectionable book and an objectionable film, did that not lead to a rule being made that no film should be produced from an objectionable book ?—My Association waited upon the British Board of Film Censors, and as a result it was made a rule that no novel of an objectionable reputation should be filmed, even though the films may be innocuous, and Mr. Redford obtained a list of books from Scotland Yard and from Mudie's and other libraries, to see that no more of these films should be brought out.

223. Monsignor Brown.   Would you consider it desirable to have a film, say, arousing sympathy in the minds of the audience with a discarded mistress, making her the attractive figure or subject of the film ?   Would you consider that desirable ?   There is such a film in existence ; it deals with Oriental scenery.   There is a film in which that is the main theme, if I may call it so.

224. The Secretary.   Can we have the name of the film ?

225. Monsignor Brown.   I will get it for you.   (To witness.) What do you say ?—Am I not to show a discarded mistress ?

226. No, my point is, are you to depict scenes in life that would excite sympathy with people who have been living immoral lives ?   There is justice, you say, with the crook.   He is punished at the end of his career.   But this mistress is discarded under all the circumstances of pathos, and the feeling of the audience is that she is the person who should be sympathised with ?—Jane Shore was a discarded mistress.

227. I am asking your opinion ?—So much depends upon the treatment of what you want to bring out.   If it were necessary that the discarded mistress should be employed to impress certain lessons, or to show a certain phase of life which ought to be avoided, then use the discarded mistress by all means.

228. Dr. Saleeby.   Do you try to get licences for intoxicants for the cinema ?—No.

229. You don't complain if you don't have any ?—No.

230. Don't you think if the people who are responsible for education or science took an interest in those sort of films that you might put in more than one-eighth in your programme ?—Yes.

231. In a country like Scotland, where there is some interest in education, it might be that some of these educational films might be found attractive ?—Yes, I think so.

232. Mr. Newbould.   The Cinematograph Act deals only with public safety, but any exhibitor showing any immoral film could be prosecuted under common law ?—In the ordinary way, yes.

233. And would probably lose his licence ?—Yes, that would follow.

234. Is it not a fact that the main objection which the exhibitors have to the various regulations in use by the local authorities is because of the lack of uniformity of these regulations?—Yes.

235. And it is the object of your Association to procure legislation to unify the regulations?—Yes.

236. In regard to the Home Office or so-called official censorship, I believe that the objection was not to the principle, but to the proposals in detail?—Yes.

237. THE SECRETARY. I have here some written questions which have been submitted by Dr. Garvie, and I will put them. What does Mr. Goodwin mean by the needless restrictions he has alluded to?—That one may not, if one wants to, give a bag of lollipops to a child; that one may not, even if one wants to, give free passes to a certain number of people in payment for the fact that they have shown bills in certain shop windows.

238. The giving of lollipops is an unfair attraction for the children to come?—I do not know why they should make such a rule.

239. It would probably have the effect that it would bring children there to get the lollipops rather than see the show. Why should local feeling and opinion not be recognised in the regulations instead of treating the country as a whole?—We say again that the whole country should have one Act.

240. Is the trade not responsible for withholding certain films that might be hurtful, or do you simply follow the demand?—Well, there is always the censorship. We have no control over the matter, but our Association would see that a certain picture was not desirable, and therefore we should see that it was not shown in any hall we hold.

THE CHAIRMAN inquired whether it would be possible for the Commission to see the films " ―― ―――― " and " ―――― ―――― ."

241. MR. T. P. O'CONNOR (to witness). Is " ―――― ―――― " out of existence?—I do not think so. You know it could not be played at all in forty of the towns.

242. I understand that a certain number of firms are in the Association of which you are Chairman?—Yes.

243. And are subject more or less to the instructions and resolutions of that Association?—Yes.

244. The principles of your Association, therefore, apply to all the theatres represented in your Association, and one of them is that a film should not be exhibited unless passed by the Board of Censors?—That is so. We were strongly in accord with the resolution, and the London County Council agreed with me that they would place on the licence that no film should be shown in London unless passed by the British Board. But when it came to the Council a member opposed it because he said the London County Council should not take any line from a body over which they had no control. So that was lost; but I applied again recently, and I am told, as nearly as one can have permission without the Council endorsing it, that the licences in London are going to be re-endorsed for next year with the condition.

245. May I take it that the desire of your Association is that all the theatres and all the firms should be brought into your Association ?—Yes.

246. Have you reason to hope that will result ?—Yes, I have. It is coming along; every day now we are taking certain steps.

SECOND DAY

Monday, January 15, 1917,

THE BISHOP OF BIRMINGHAM in the chair.

STATEMENT OF MR. J. G. LEGGE,

Director of Education in Liverpool

PRÉCIS

THE number of licensed houses in the City in the present year of 1917 is forty-nine. The figure in 1914 was thirty-eight. The Justices' Rules governing the attendance of children at cinema houses are as follows—

" Children under fourteen years of age shall not be allowed to enter or be in the licensed premises after the hour of 6.30 p.m. unaccompanied by their parents or guardians.

" If any afternoon exhibition is held in the licensed premises to which the minimum price of admission for children is twopence or less, such exhibition shall be deemed to be an exhibition for children within the meaning of these rules, and there shall be shown at such exhibition only such films as are by their nature specially suitable for exhibition to children. A printed programme giving the name and, when practicable, a sufficient synopsis of each film intended to be exhibited shall be sent to the Superintendent of Police for the Division in which the licensed premises are situated, not less than twenty-four hours before such exhibition is held.

" At exhibitions for children no child shall be allowed to view the exhibition from a distance of less than fifteen feet from the screen on which the pictures are shown."

There are, in addition, rules prohibiting the exhibition of anything that is objectionable or indecent, etc., etc., and for the exclusion of children in the case of infectious diseases in a neighbouring school.

The difficulty in the way of regulations such as these, which was raised by the Halifax decision, Theatre de Luxe (Halifax), Ltd. *v.* Gledhill, has been met in Liverpool by attaching them to a music licence. This the Justices have power to do in virtue of provisions of the Liverpool Corporation Act, 1889.

These regulations are good, and it is not easy to suggest anything much more drastic, if they could be carried out; but, as a matter of fact, children under fourteen, unaccompanied by their parents or guardians, are often smuggled in by strangers to whom they give their penny or twopence. The principal of a Liverpool school found that of the children in his school who attended evening performances in a single week in 1916, 40 per cent. were thus smuggled in.

The total number of children in average attendance in Liverpool Elementary Schools is 120,399. Unfortunately there has been no census taken by the police of the attendance of children at cinema houses since the Great War, but two school censuses were taken in 1912 and 1914 giving the numbers of children in attendance at the matinee on Saturday afternoon as follows—

November 23, 1912,   *June* 13, 1914,
13,232.   11,379.[1]

In 1916 a Joint Committee of Justices and members of the Education Committee was formed to consider the question of Juvenile Crime. This Committee issued its report in October, 1916. The paragraph of their report relating to cinema houses runs as follows—

" Nearly all the witnesses were agreed that constant attendance at cinematograph theatres has an injurious effect upon juvenile mind and character. Not only are children frequently induced to steal in order to obtain admission (it is quite a common excuse in theft or begging cases that the money was wanted for ' the pictures '), but what is perhaps of even greater importance, is that in very many cases the intellectual morale of the child is injured, and its powers of concentration are weakened by a too frequent attendance at such places. It is suggested that, where desirable, the magistrates should introduce, by way of a condition in Probation Orders, restrictions as to the attendance of the probationer at cinema exhibitions. The evidence adduced has also impressed on the committee the urgent necessity for continued strict supervision of the theatres, and illustrative posters, with insistence upon the observance by licensees of the Justices' Rules and Regulations regarding films, and the attendance of children."

There is some educational value in films of such subjects as—

1. Scenes in foreign lands.
2. Historical incidents.
3. Travel and adventure.
4. Nature study.
5. Pictured plays and novels.
6. Industrial and agricultural life.
7. Noteworthy events of the day.

---

[1] There were 1783 children in attendance in the evening. Much fuller statistical evidence with regard to the attendance of children at cinema houses is desirable.

But this educational value can easily be exaggerated, granted the most careful selection of films. The residuum of history left after reading a historical novel is small; still less is that left after witnessing a film. The use of the cinema for definite teaching purposes, particularly with regard to nature study and science, is of far more value in the case of older students who have some conception of abstract ideas of space and time, and whose impressions are not too confused by the bewildering rush of a film across the field of vision. Much more might be done than is done at present to present films which inculcate high qualities, such as courage, self-sacrifice, and generosity. Cinema houses do not realise how popular with children would be films of class 6, giving pictures of the interior of factories, works, agricultural operations, the life of a sailor, and so forth. Boys have a perfect passion for watching men at work.

Defects from the educational point of view are the exciting influence of the cinematograph entertainment. It is one thing to make education interesting, and quite another to make it exciting; and in modern days too much stress has been laid even on the former. Thoroughly objectionable, from the educational and moral point of view, are not only films depicting crimes, immorality and fraud, but also scenes of love-making, vulgar buffoonery, horseplay, practical joking of a mischievous type and successful imposture, which is none the less to be condemned if it is supposed to be comic.

It is in the recreative aspect that there is the strongest justification for the existence of the cinema house. It presents about the cheapest and most comfortable entertainment obtainable. It is brought within easy reach of almost every family, and affords an escape from inclement weather and comfortless homes. The comic film, though generally vulgar, has its recreative value. The cinema house is, in itself, a counter-attraction to the public-house, and if we are not satisfied with the cinema house as the best rival to the public-house, we must make our attack by way of better housing (the problem which lies at the heart of all social reform, from which we can never get away), and the provision of counter-attractions for healthy indoor as well as public outdoor recreation; and here it is a grievous mistake to regard the children as a class wholly separable from their parents. The witness merely mentions the recognised agents for children : Boys' and Girls' Clubs, Cadets, Scouts, Guides, etc., etc. Healthy means for indoor recreation for children and their elders might be found in reformed public-houses, the popularising of music, including brass and string bands, the development of the free library into a club, rooms for the practice of art, the vitalising of museums and galleries by the employment of trained guides, glorified gymnasia, mixed family bathing, possibly also dancing-rooms under direct municipal control. On the outdoor side may be mentioned playing fields and recreation grounds, drill grounds (the most suitable purpose for which the ordinary school playground can be utilised), athletic grounds, and allotments, while in parks and also in smaller open spaces more encouragement might be given to what may perhaps be called formal gardening, *e. g.* old English gardens, rose gardens, etc.

Finally, the effect on the problem of such measures as—

1. Compulsory education schools.
2. National Service.

Both of which have much to recommend them, must not be lost sight of. It is to be hoped that no system of continued education will be introduced which does not secure for the adolescent population at large one of the great privileges at present reserved for the Secondary School boy, viz. the privilege of engaging in home work up till nine o'clock at night. The Continuation School system should provide for one, or if possible two, tutorial evenings a week. So, too, with regard to National Service. A great deal of the physical instruction connected with this will have to be given, and may wholesomely be given, in the evening.

MINUTES OF EVIDENCE

Mr. J. G. Legge. *Examined.*

1. The Chairman. Mr. Legge, you are the Director of Education for the City of Liverpool?—Yes.

2. You have also had a long connection with education in London?—I have; I was in the Home Office for sixteen years, and then I was head of a sub-department of the Home Office, the Reformatory and Industrial Schools Department, for nine years.

3. In Liverpool I see there are forty-nine licensed cinemas, although in 1914 there were only thirty-eight. Therefore, even during the war the number has been growing?—Yes.

4. In Liverpool who decides whether films are suitable for children?—The Justices, and they delegate their duties to a rota of one or two.

5. As a matter of fact, I suppose that this Committee would be very rarely overruled by the Committee as a whole?—Very seldom, but from what I gather from the Head Constable of Liverpool, films do slip through even with the supervision of the Justices, films that are not proper for the children to see.

6. Do you think that would be at all obviated supposing children's films were regulated, say, from a single censor instead of by local censors?—I think that would certainly be very effective if for no other reason than that it would prevent films from being rushed. The difficulty is that a man says : " I have got these films and I am sorry I was not aware that the Justices wished to see them, but I will stop them if after they are started you object to them."

7. And you think if dealt with by a central authority rather than by the various localities, it might be better?—I think it might be very effective in preventing the display of improper films for children.

8. " At exhibitions for children no child shall be allowed to view the exhibition from a distance of less than fifteen feet from the screen on which the pictures are shown." Is that purely because of the eyes; a question of the danger to the eyes ?—I take it it is also to allow full room for dispersal. I think it is a combination of the two.

9. Now have you met in Liverpool the difficulty in the way of regulations for children by attaching the music licence to the cinema licence ?—That is so. The powers under which Liverpool acts in this regard are derived from the Liverpool Corporation Act of 1899.

10. You say : " Children under fourteen, unaccompanied by their parents or guardians, are often smuggled in by strangers to whom they give their penny or twopence."—Yes; the principal of one of our large schools took stock of the children who entered a picture house during one week of last year, and he found that of the children entering after 6.30, 40 per cent. got in without parents or guardians. They handed their money to some one to pass them in in their company. Ten per cent. got in without any guardian or even step-guardian. So that only 50 per cent. of the children entering after 6.30 got in legitimately with their parents or guardians.

11. Has any attempt at supervision been made ?—That is a point I would not care to press the Head Constable very hard upon, but it does seem that it could be very easily checked if an example were made in two or three cases. It might be made a positive offence for a person to smuggle a child in.

12. I notice that you would desire very much more careful statistical evidence with regard to the attendance of children at cinemas ?—Yes, I think it is of enormous importance, particularly from the point of view to see whether it is growing or not. One very interesting point has come out lately over the Summer Time Act of last year. The inspectors under the Education Committee at Liverpool, stated as one of their arguments in favour of the re-enactment of that provision this year, that it had a marked tendency to keep children all through six light months of the year out of the cinema house. When I pressed them as to what they based their opinion upon, they said observation. Well, observation is not enough; one wants actual figures.

13. Your Joint Committee was formed to consider the question of juvenile crime, and they issued this report, which is very condemnatory, of the attendance of children at cinemas ?—I think it is, on the whole.

14. You have handed in a paragraph of their report which is a serious paragraph, is it not ?—Yes; in that connection, my lord, may I mention that a better report than that of the Joint Committee of Liverpool may not be known to you. It is a Manchester report. It is a very much more useful report than the Liverpool one, largely because it was not the work of a committee, but the work of one man, one office, the Education Office at Manchester. The man had also the assistance of the police, and has drawn up

a remarkable report from the statistics. He deals with juvenile crime, and analyses the very question your Committee is dealing with very ably indeed.

15. Now this paragraph : " Not only are children frequently induced to steal in order to obtain admission ; it is quite a common excuse in theft or begging cases that the money was wanted for ' the pictures.' " Now has that not become rather a thing that a child says all over the country ?—I think not, because the authority on which that statement is made by the Committee, is the stipendiary magistrate, and he is perfectly satisfied by questions from the Bench that the statement is well founded.

16. In every case is it usual to take the statement of a prisoner as something which cannot be questioned ?—Oh, no, this is not based on a statement of any one who has accepted the prisoner's statement or the accused's statement. The stipendiary magistrate has examined the child from the Bench, and also I have first-hand information on that point from my school attendance officers making inquiries with regard to industrial school cases ; the parents have complained that the parent's money has sometimes been taken by the child, and that in many cases it is not safe to leave money in the teapot on the mantelpiece because of the incentive which makes them help themselves out of it for the purpose of going to the cinema.

17. That does not necessarily condemn the cinema ?—No.

18. It speaks of the attraction of the cinema, but of nothing wrong that the cinema does. A child is so attracted to it that it has stolen the money ?—I think when the attraction reaches that point one may take it the attraction comes out of a craving for a stimulant, and at that age stimulant of any sort is not altogether wholesome.

19. Then in giving your personal views on the problem you do them under two heads, first the educational and moral aspect, and then the recreative aspect. You therefore accept, don't you, in taking the recreative aspect that the cinema is, after all, not primarily an educational matter ; it is a commercial matter, and the proprietor of a cinema has no more duty to consider the educational side than has the theatre manager.?—That is so.

20. You say cinema houses don't realise how popular all children would think the films giving pictures of industrial factories and works. Could these things be done ?—Yes.

21. " Boys have a perfect passion for seeing men at work." Do you think it would be an incentive towards work for a child to see people at work in a cinema ?—Yes, I have a very strong view on that point. If a child saw in a cinema illustrations of different kinds of factories and workshops, and also pictures showing handymen manipulating their tools and things of that sort, and also the life of a sailor boy, then I think that would be doing a real good thing.

22. And you think it would be a commercial success for the cinema to conduct it ?—For the children, yes.

23. Then we will turn to the recreative side. You will admit

D

that the comic film is recreative although it may be a vulgar film sometimes ?—Yes, I feel forced to make that admission.

24. And you lay stress on the fact that a cinema is a counter-attraction to a public-house ?—Yes, and that is one of the best things that can be said for it. (Hear, hear.)

25. Mr. T. P. O'Connor. Are you a frequenter of cinema theatres ?—No, I go very seldom. I went frequently at one time, but I never go now except to see a particular film, and that is never a comic film.

26. Well, do you ever go to a music hall ?—I have not been to a music hall since war began except, perhaps, to see a film, but I have been to a good many in my time.

27. Have you not found yourself rather saddened by the comic business of music halls ?—Yes.

28. So that that applies to many classes of audience as well as those of the cinema theatres ?—Yes, but there is this difference as I have noticed : I have never seen to my recollection a scene on a music hall stage where the exhibition of comic horseplay was given when the hero was a child. I have constantly seen the hero of a comic film as a child of the Buster Brown type.

29. Well, I do not think your information is quite complete on that point. I would like just to analyse a little the statement you have quoted about children stealing to go to cinemas. I suppose the eager desire of children for enjoyment leads to stealing for other purposes as well, does it not ?—Yes, for cigarettes, if nothing else.

30. Is it not your experience as an educationalist engaged mainly in the welfare of youth, that the confectionery shop is the shop the child goes to with any loose money it has ?—Yes.

31. I put it then, that the stealing is just a part of that general and impulsive desire of enjoyment common to all children ?—No, I cannot quite agree there, because I do not think the child gives up the sweet shop for the cinema. It has become a recognised thing that a child shall have its weekly pence for buying sweets, but this is a need that has come on top of that, and the whole economic idea of the child is certainly disturbed by a demand to find 100 per cent. more money in the week.

32. Before the cinema the child probably found its amusement in the street ?—That is so.

33. Which might have been much more prejudicial than the cinema ?—Yes, but in the summer months I have noticed that the effect of the cinema house has been to keep the children out of the parks, which seems to me to be unfortunate.

34. Could not that be met partially by cinemas in the park ?—Yes, that is a very good suggestion.

35. Now, I will take you a little on the educational side, although I think this, my lord, is not quite so relevant to our inquiry as the other side. You are acquainted with the Berlitz system of teaching English ?—Yes.

36. May I not state that the fundamental principle of that is the combination of the eye with the ear and the memory ?—Yes.

37. Don't you think that system can be applied through the cinema to many other forms of education?—Yes, I think I have practically admitted that the film is quite as good as a picture book to a child, but of course, I need not go so far as to say that the moving picture is better than the picture book.

38. Would it not be better if instead of learning geography in the old way of simply committing to memory rivers and other particulars of nations, that the child should see on the cinema in some form or another a picture of the city and its streets, and its general life, and a picture of the river and the countries it went through?—I would not substitute one for the other. The combination would be of value, but if I had a child educated by the old system and another educated by visits to the cinema house up to the age of sixteen years, I should expect the child educated on the old system to have a very much better working knowledge of geography than the other; in fact, an incomparably better knowledge.

39. I do not think any one suggests you should educate the child in the cinema theatres. The point is that the cinema would be a very useful addition to the study?—Yes.

40. You suggest that probationers should not be allowed to attend at cinema theatres?—Well, that was a suggestion thrown out by the Liverpool Joint Committee on Juvenile Crime.

41. I suppose you are not aware of the fact that some of the probation officers of the large police courts actually take these probationers to the cinemas as a reward for good conduct?—No; I will convey that information to our stipendiary.

42. You object to the fact that there are not enough stories showing courage, self-sacrifice or generosity?—Yes.

43. Do you make that statement on your own personal experience or on information conveyed to you?—On questioning the police. I have gone into that matter in order to form some idea of the variety of films exhibited on occasions when children are expected to be present. I have not gone into what is being displayed in the evening, in the entertainment in the second house.

44. I suppose you would be surprised to hear that stories of this particular kind are to be found in every programme of almost every cinema theatre in the country?—I dare say there are, but I do not know whose word I would take for it. I have seen stories of adventure of the Buster Brown type, but they are not creditable adventures.

45. You know in the melodrama that the hero does deeds of courage and daring; you know what a popular feature that is in all our popular theatres?—Yes, but in many of those I have seen myself the hero is represented as exposed to certain temptations which he triumphs over. Now the temptation on the film takes five-sixths of the time, and the heroic triumph at the end is very short, and the temptation leaves more impression on the child's mind than the triumph at the end.

46. Well, I think you are addressing your mind to one set of

ideas and I am addressing mine to another. I was not talking
of the temptation; I was talking about the story of the melodramatic type where the hero goes through a number of difficult
adventures such as setting about ten Huns at a time, and so on.
Don't you know that is a very popular form of appeal, and that is
to be found in the cinemas?—Yes, I think there is an amount of
good in it, undoubtedly.

47. And my information is that a large number of films have
been produced which give that useful addition and impulse to the
child's education, I mean the war films, and it gives them interest
in the great victories?—Well, there have certainly been some very
popular war films and also films showing munition making.

48. Mr. Newbould. Are you aware that the Courts have held
that when music is subsidiary to the pictures then a music licence
is not necessary?—No, the point has not been raised in Liverpool,
and in any case I think if you look at the report the powers under
the local Act are very extensive and——

49. I notice you are referring to the Justices' rules in Liverpool.
Without a knowledge of your local Act it is impossible for me to
say anything, but in other places are you aware that such rules
have been found to be *ultra vires?*—I know of the Halifax case,
but you mean the bringing in of those drastic rules in connection
with the music licences.

50. My point is that if a music licence is not necessary these
conditions could not be enforced?—That is so, but as a matter of
fact I am told that no licence is ever applied for in Liverpool
without the application for music as well.

51. But if the exhibitor chose to do without music those conditions could not be imposed upon his licence?—That is so, and if
the Committee like I will send them up an extract from the local
Act.

The Chairman. Thank you, will you do so, please.

52. Mr. Newbould. Do you think it either practicable or
sensible that a doorkeeper should inquire into the relationship
between the guardian or the parents and the child going into the
theatre. Would you throw the onus on the cinema proprietors
to ascertain that?—As the law stands I do not think the owner
of the cinema or the proprietor of the cinema can escape the onus
of responsibility.

53. The Chairman. In answer to me you said you would
throw the onus on the police?—I would throw the onus on the police
for checking the proprietor. I would have a system by which
people were followed in and asked, and it would be ascertained
whether the person was the *bona fide* guardian of the child; and
having found out a case, I would prosecute.

54. Mr. Newbould. In the case of a theatre holding, say, a
thousand people, all of whom are admitted in ten minutes, is it
practicable that an attendant should be able to inquire about that
in the time he has, I mean as to the relationship of the child?—
Yes; a certain man can be told off for the work, and only a certain
number need be inquired into, and it can be done by having a set

of turnstiles. If, for instance, you make all the adults going to the cinemas go in alone at one entrance, you would reduce your problem very much.

55. Do you consider a police superintendent a fit and proper person to censor films? I see you say that the synopsis is sent to the police superintendent?—I should think he is pretty good. He is pretty good on the question of what incites to crime.

56. Are you aware that Mr. Justice Darling found that three magistrates could not legally censor films?—No, I was not aware of that.

57. It is unnecessary to ask if a police superintendent should do what three magistrates could not legally do. Do you think that a synopsis could be relied upon as a sufficient indication of what the film portrays?—It is rather a difficult question; it all depends on the synopsis.

58. I see you do not think that there need be much difficulty in enforcing rules and conditions to which you have referred with regard to children. I suppose if they were proved to be illegal you would consider that an obstacle to enforcing them?—Yes, naturally.

59. I see it is stated that 40 per cent. of the pupils of a Liverpool school were smuggled in. I also see that another 10 per cent. got in without being smuggled, and I take it that the other 50 per cent. were properly accompanied by their parents or guardians. Can you tell us how these figures were arrived at and what the actual totals were? Does the 40 per cent. mean forty in one hundred or four in ten?—I have not got the return with me, but you may take it from my recollection that they were about forty per hundred in a week.

60. Do you think that any quantity of statistics proving the popularity of the cinema can provide evidence of its moral effect? —Yes, because it was tremendously interesting to find how many children went three or four times a week.

61. Have you any direct evidence of children stealing money for the purpose of going to cinema theatres?—I have this evidence, that the stipendiary has definitely stated in public that he has had to sentence boys for stealing money to enter picture houses.

62. Supposing that the cinema theatres were not in existence, and ignoring for the moment the question of the war, do you know of any other factors which would be likely to account for the increase of juvenile crime?—Yes.

63. Leaving the war entirely out of the question.—Yes, I do not think the cinema house is by any means the chief agent in creating crime.

64. THE CHAIRMAN. Let me get that quite clear. You mean if the cinema were conducted on the principles you hold you see no reason that it should have any effect on juvenile crime whatever?—It would always depend on the way it was done. If it was done the way I suggest or on my principles, I think it would decrease the crime.

65. MR. NEWBOULD. Does your idea of educating the child

include the total elimination of temptation?—I do not think it is possible to exclude temptation, as a certain amount is inevitable.

66. You advocate more films of an industrial nature and films showing sailors' life and that sort of thing?—Yes.

67. Are you aware that almost every filmable industry has been filmed and shown throughout the country several times?—Several times. It should be shown continually; there should be no show without it.

68. Are you aware they have been shown so frequently that the audiences say: "Take them off, we have seen them"?—You mean adult audiences?

69. Mixed audiences. Do you know that the films showing the sailors' life have been shown so frequently that mothers complain that their boys run away to sea?—No, that is news to me, but if it is true I am pleased.

70. You are rather anxious as to the effect of the excitement of these films. Would you eliminate all exciting games such as the game of football, for instance?—No, I do not think you have got quite clearly what I mean by excitement.

71. THE CHAIRMAN. I think it is very stimulating.—It is one thing to make it educational only, and another thing to make it exciting. I use the word "exciting" there because I think it is a bad mental state for a child to get into.

72. MR. NEWBOULD. You speak of the desirability of popularising music.—Yes.

73. Do you know any factor that has done as much to popularise music as the cinema theatres?—Yes, there is one greater than the cinema theatres—church and chapel music.

74. You say that in view of the fact that over one thousand million people visit the cinemas every year?—Yes, but I am speaking of thousands of years of church and chapel music.

75. Is it a fact that if the Queen's Hall Symphony Orchestra was engaged by a cinema proprietor in Liverpool, the magistrates would not allow it to perform?—I do not know. I do not think so; I should be sorry if they did not.

76. Is it not a fact that in the music licences they prohibit the use of brass instruments?—That I do not know, but I would rather they prohibited brass instruments than string instruments.

77. MR. NEWBOULD. Is it a fact that if a cinema proprietor were to engage Ben Davies to sing a song in a cinema theatre the Liverpool Justices would prohibit that song?—That I cannot say.

78. DR. SALEEBY. You say in your evidence, Mr. Legge, that the powers of concentration of a child are weakened by frequent attendance at cinemas. May I ask whether you have observed what degree of concentration children exhibit at cinemas?—Yes, a child does not show much concentration at any time up to a certain age. I have seen them very attentive at a cinema, but I have never seen a child lost, forgetting the world altogether. I think that comes in the later stage.

79. You have not seen them absorbed in a story or in a sequence of events ?—No, I have never seen a child absorbed in a cinema house, never in the way one sees a child absorbed in a story book. I think the value of the visual presentation of things to a child is very much exaggerated.   I do not think they can see things up to a certain age as after the age of puberty.   I do not think a child can see a picture properly.

80. Well, now, have you made yourself any observation, or can you record any observation of people in cinemas who have noted what they have heard children round about them say, or the questions they ask of their parents or guardians ?—I heard a girl say the other day after the Somme film, when her companion was about to go before the end, " Oh, stay, Jack, there's a comic film coming next."

81. You said your objection was that the shows were so stimulating to the child ?—Yes.

82. And later on you pressed for the exhibition of the Jack Tar's life and so on, saying that you cannot imagine anything more stimulating ?—Yes.

83. Well, we must analyse that word.—Well, I will substitute thrilling for the first and stick to stimulating for the Jack Tar's life.

84. It is the question of degree.—Yes.

85. We were told last time and a point was made that only one-eighth of the time spent in showing films is devoted to education, and the proportion was so deplorably small.   Now, as an educationalist, can you mention many professed amusements which devote more than one-eighth of the time in teaching, say, natural history ?—While I should like the cinema made as harmless an institution as possible, I should think that one-eighth of definite educational effort in it was an ample proportion.

86. You raise some most important questions we have not gone into about the cinema being a counter-attraction to the public-house.   You are, I am sure, with me when I say that the working classes spend more on drink than they do on rent ?—I believe that is true.

87. You say, dealing with the suggestion as to substitutes, " Healthy means for indoor recreation for children and their elders might be found in reformed public-houses."   May I ask you very definitely whether you mean the non-alcoholic house or the continental café ?—No, I distinctly mean the place where you can get alcohol.

88. I should like to know whether Mr. Legge would suggest that the continental café plus alcohol is preferable to the non-alcoholic cinema for the recreation of the family ?—Yes, I do.

89. Preferable to the non-alcoholic cinema ?—Yes, I do.

90. MR. EDGAR JEPSON.   In regard to the question of stimulants; do you want films which stimulate the ordinary effort only ?—I say it is not a wholesome stimulant.

91. No matter how exciting the film is, it stimulates ?—No, there again I think the element of excitement is bad.

92. Well, taking the cinema as it is, would you prefer it to continue and children to go to it, or for them to be prevented going to it and remaining in the streets?—I would rather they were allowed to go to it, under such safeguards as we have in Liverpool.

93. Well, are the authorities in Liverpool, while they are inclined to discourage children going to the cinema, are they taking any steps to provide anything in its place?—They are not discouraging them going to the cinemas except to the second house, the later house.

94. MRS. BURGWIN. What time is that; is it an evening performance of the cinema?—The late house is defined, that is, commencing at 8.30.

95. There are not any afternoon performances?—Yes, in some houses there are, but then the school attendances keep the children clear of them up to 4.30 or 5.

96. Have you found your school attendance affected by the opening of the cinema?—No, because no child can escape. We have got more than eighty school attendance officers, and we can have one at every cinema in the town and make raids.

97. May I ask what age you call a child?—I call it a child up to the age of puberty.

98. You would say from five to fourteen?—Roughly.

99. Have you had any charges of indecency as taking place in the cinemas in Liverpool?—I have only heard of one.

100. That was proved?—I do not know, it was only incidentally mentioned to me.

101. I gather you do not think that the cinema has really any educational value to a child?—Very little indeed.

102. You also think it rather injurious to sit within fifteen feet of the films?—Yes.

103. For the child's eyesight?—Yes.

104. You would think, too, that if there is this afternoon performance, it would be rather difficult to ventilate because of the continuous films, with the result that the atmosphere would be rather injurious to any child?—I have been rather struck not only with the comfort of the cinema houses, but also with their ventilation. They are well ventilated.

105. SIR JOHN KIRK. Have you any boys or girls in your reformatory schools who are there through the influence of the cinema?—Well, I ceased to have any connection with them ten years ago. This has grown since then.

106. THE CHAIRMAN. On that point, is it not a fact that boys were in reformatory schools years ago because of the hooliganism? There was nothing but the streets for them?—Largely.

107. SIR JOHN KIRK. Are you aware there has been an experiment at the Settlement to provide cinemas for the children?—Yes, I was associated with it.

108. It was a failure?—It was not a success; but the war cut it short, and it all depends upon the help we receive from the teachers. If we conduct that experiment again I would associate half a dozen of the head teachers with it.

109. Had you any difficulty in getting any particular film you desired?—Well, I had not the management of it, but I think the head of the Settlement had a good deal of trouble.

110. Is that the only experiment that was tried there?—Yes, the only genuine experiment.

111. MONSIGNOR BROWN. Mr. Legge, would you suggest, or do you suggest that there was any collusion on the part of the exhibitors or the owners with these people who have smuggled the children in; that there were any professional people to do it?—No.

112. Has that been considered specifically?—No.

113. I was dealing with the investigations of this observer, the principal of a Liverpool School. Did he give any information of the people having taken the children in and then going out again immediately?—No.

114. That is an important point?—I think it is.

115. Can you try to get some information about it?—Certainly.

116. Because it seems to me a little difficult that there should always be at hand a sufficient number of benevolent outsiders to take this large body of children in?—But I find it very difficult in the present state of the public mind to try and check it.

117. I should have thought that as people have been the subject of public charges, that the average man would have been very careful in taking children in. As to the stealing which is said now to be very extensive by juveniles. Is there any evidence beyond that of the culprits in their pleading?—There is the evidence of the cases before the police court.

118. But I suppose you have a good deal of experience that adults don't always speak the truth when they charge children for certain purposes. Adults sometimes charge children to get rid of them?—That is so.

119. Now take the stipendiary before whom the boy is brought up and charged. You see the magistrate leaning over the Bench, and he says: "My boy, why did you do that?" and the boy says: "I did it to go to the pictures." Do you attach any importance to that?—No, but I am quite sure in the case of our stipendiary he would turn to the police and ask them if there was any ground for it.

120. But would you attach any very great importance to the excuses a culprit gives which he thinks will mitigate a sentence?—No.

121. Has it not been written about very extensively in the papers?—Yes, it has.

122. It is stated in the daily Press and I think it is given prominence to, that children have been led away by this?—I do not think the Magistrate has the command of the daily Press.

123. One magistrate has made a very strong pronouncement, Mr. d'Eyncourt, upon the worthlessness of such excuses put forward, and he has said that he disbelieves in them. I suppose you agree that there has been more money available since the war in the poorer districts?—Yes.

124. And therefore children have been able to go in many cases with much greater frequency to the cinemas. Will you accept that?—Yes.

125. SIR W. BARRETT. Have you any regulations in Liverpool as regards the non-admission of children to cinemas where the public schools have been closed for infectious diseases?—Yes, we have.

126. They are prevented from admission?—Yes, in the event of any department of a public elementary school within a radius of a quarter of a mile being closed for infectious diseases the pupils are not allowed admission.

127. Do you think a great deal of advantage would accrue if the cinemas were better lighted?—Yes; I think they are unnaturally dark, and I think it would, of course, obviate some of the moral difficulties.

128. You think it would be better?—Personally, I should like to sit in darkness, but I see there are reasons why it should be light.

129. What do you mean by the reformed public-house in your evidence?—Well, I do not mean a public-house where alcoholic drink is not allowed. I mean a place where people can meet and sit down, where you are not practically forced to drink because you have to stand up at the bar of the place, and also where meals can be provided at the same time.

130. Do you think there would be an advantage for children to attend a reformed public-house?—Yes, if it was a place where the family could meet or where two or three families could meet and sit round the table.

131. Where intoxicating liquors are sold?—Yes.

132. MR. GRAVES. With reference to the Justices and their opinion upon the films which should be shown. Are the films presented chosen by the Justices alone, or by the Justices and the members of the Education Committee?—The Justices.

133. And the Education Committee have nothing to say to it?—No.

134. Why should they not? Surely they are the people who would be most likely to advise, on the educational side, at any rate?—As a matter of fact that difficulty does not arise, because I think the members of the Justices' Bench who take the most interest in the matter are also members of the Education Committee.

135. Is the cinematograph used by your teachers either in the form of pathescope or in any other form in any of your schools?—No.

136. But occasionally children have been taken to educational cinematograph shows at certain centres. Do I understand you to say that some cinematograph education shows have been given in the town to which the teachers have taken the children?—Yes, there was one experience of the sort.

137. Was that successful?—It was not.

138. Why was it not? Did you have a successful show or was

it that it was not well shown so that the teachers objected to it? —Well, I do not think it was sufficiently well advertised.

139. Or organised?—Or organised.

140. Do you think it a good thing that the local authorities should have one cinematograph theatre of their own at which educational and other films of a better type might be shown?— Yes, I think it would be a good thing. It would perhaps keep alive the system of municipal lectures and so on. It would work hand in glove with that.

141. I merely suggest that they should have one of their own? —Yes, but I should not feel enthusiastic about it; I should feel that it was a valuable experiment.

142. MR. LAMERT. You quote in your report that the constant attendance is injurious to the children. Now, how would you define constant attendance?—I should say once a week regularly.

143. Once a week is too much. Is once a fortnight too much? —No, not in the winter months.

144. In the winter months you would be inclined to allow a child once a fortnight?—At least.

145. But you said just now that once a week was too much? —Yes, but I mean twice in three weeks.

146. Well, about that amount, twice in three weeks?—Yes.

147. And anything above that you would regard as an excess? —Yes.

148. Now with regard to this question about children stealing to see the pictures. You have quoted one stipendiary and Monsignor Brown has quoted another. Have you in point of fact ever consulted with another stipendiary, except the one you quoted, on this point?—No.

149. We have got here two stipendiaries, one says one thing and the other says another. You have not taken a consensus of opinion?—No; but I am inclined to adopt the opinion of our own stipendiary.

150. Now the question has come up about the children stealing, and that the cinema was fatally attractive, too attractive. Now, I am in a little difficulty; children steal because the cinema is too attractive, but in this evidence you put before us you show us how to make it still more attractive?—Yes.

151. You are not, surely, inciting us to get the children to steal more?—No; but I say that the success of the cinema shows to me the miserable conditions under which millions of our countrymen live. If we have got to accept that, let us do our best to improve things; let us at the same time provide good alternatives which will take away the impulse to go to these cinemas as the one resource.

152. You have used the word " comic." Have you any general objection to the comic films? It seems like King Charles's head; you seem to have a rooted antipathy to anything comic.

THE CHAIRMAN. Mr. Legge when dealing with the recreative side says : " It is useful to have a comic film, even if it is vulgar, because it is recreative."—I think nearly everything I have seen on the music hall stage or on a film which professes to be comic is vulgar. That is to say, it is a bit degrading, it is a poor type of humour.

153. MR. LAMERT. I think one of the films we have showing is the meeting between Betsy Prig and Sarah Gamp?—I would not select that as a typical scene to amuse the child.

154. Do you think it would do a child harm to see that among other things?—Not much, not that particular scene.

155. Have you seen Charlie Chaplin yourself?—In film, yes.

156. Did it strike you as being vulgar and stupid?—Yes; but I confess I enjoyed it very much.

157. Have you seen him a second time?—Yes.

158. Did you enjoy it as much as ever?—Yes; I have only seen him twice.

159. Remarkable! Now you mentioned in reply to a question from Mr. T. P. O'Connor when he was asking you this question about comic films, that some films showed a child as the hero of these knockabout comic incidents?—Yes.

160. Can you give me the name of one of these films?—I am afraid not.

161. Can you give me the name of the company which manufactured it? The name is always found on the screen first.—No; the latest film I have seen with reference to it is where a party of cyclists arrived at an inn.

162. May I interrupt you? We do not want to go into the story. You must bear in mind that some of us here represent the cinematograph industry, and we are only too anxious to eliminate anything which ought not to be there. Now, is it helpful or is it fair to us for you to refer to a film whose name you cannot give, which was manufactured by a company whose name you cannot give, and was exhibited at some place so that we cannot trace it?—I do not see any hardship in it. I do not think this Commission in any case would take action against that firm.

No, this Commission would not; but, as I have said, there are persons here interested in the cinematograph industry, and it would be useful if we could know what the film really was and who the manufacturers were.

THE CHAIRMAN. At any rate you cannot get it, as he has not got it.

163. MR. LAMERT. Can you give us one of these?—I will use my best endeavours. You have never seen a film of the Buster Brown type, then, where there is a famous child actor?

164. THE CHAIRMAN. If Mr. Legge can at any time give us some details about that, it would be all right?—I will.

165. MR. LAMERT. You say there are objectionable films and things like that?—Yes, for children.

166. And things like love-making. Does that cover all love-making?—I do not mean the affection between father and child.

167. No, I do not mean that; but can you imagine literature with the love interest cut out?—No.

168. Can you imagine the cinematograph or the author of cinematograph writing plots with the love interest cut out? —No; but I think it is very bad for children to see an adult love-making on the film.

169. You would not press the point to cut it out and therefore spoil the cinema?—No; but I would have them very closely watched, particularly the scenes of love-making in the kitchen between the policeman and the cook.

170. MR. CROOK. You say you have a Joint Committee in Liverpool?—That is a Joint Committee to go into the question of juvenile crime.

171. Whom does that Joint Committee consist of?—Five magistrates, exclusive of the stipendiary, and five members of the Education Committee.

172. Did you ever contemplate the advantage of having a teacher on this Committee?—There was one, one of the five, who was the teachers' representative on the Committee.

173. You talk about the difficulty of getting statistics. Would it not be possible for you, as the Director of Education of Liverpool, to get the head teachers to get out your statistics?—Yes; but just now the teachers are complaining so much about the strain of the war.

174. Well, would you have any objection to my asking them? —I think my Committee would rather ask them.

175. Well, if I ask your Committee, would they do it?—Well, I am not sure at the moment, because we are endeavouring to confine ourselves to our business as far as possible.

176. Yes, but this is your business. You yourself have talked about the effect of cinemas on children, and it is the duty of the Committee to see that that is nullified as far as possible. Now you could in two days get the figures, say, for a week, from your head teachers if you wanted them; not only that, you could get figures to show how many went to the cinemas and who had taken them?—Well, I am not sure.

177. THE CHAIRMAN. Before you go any further, I should like to allude to one point. I consider it a very important point when you say you would like to eliminate love-making from the cinema. Of course, if you did so, commercially you would interfere very strongly with the cinema?—I have been thinking over the point, and I have thought of a word which I think would cover love-making. The word I would have no objection to is " idyllic." I have only got the children up to fourteen years of age in mind:

178. So that at the Saturday afternoon performances for children you would like to eliminate the love-making scenes and films from that entertainment?—Yes, I think that is all I had in mind.

179. The child does not concentrate upon it, and therefore, is there much harm in the child seeing the love-making scene which may be part of a very interesting film? The last time I was in a cinema there was the love-making scene, and there happened

to be a lady and two children behind me, and the questions they asked showed that they had noticed nothing of the love-making.—I think the danger is largely mitigated if there is no love-making. Of course, that is bound to be understood by the child.

STATEMENT OF MR. CECIL HEPWORTH

PRÉCIS

My Lord Bishop, Ladies and Gentlemen,
The cinematograph is undoubtedly destined to exert a tremendously powerful influence upon thought and understanding in every phase of life. No one doubts the vast influence wielded by literature to-day as exemplified in the modern Press, yet who, in Caxton's time, would have dared to foreshadow its immense and far-reaching power? But in this wonderful new art of Living Photography we have the beginning of something which is certainly shaping as the greatest vehicle of the conveyance of thought and idea that the world has ever known. Greater even than literature if only on the one count that it appeals direct to the intelligence and understanding through the eye without the necessity of any previous education in its interpreting.

In order to illustrate the universality of appeal of the living pictures and their influence as a national asset, I should like to quote a simple instance. Suppose that ten years hence one of our smaller colonies has reached a stage of expansion when it is realised that vast new municipal undertakings in the shape of numerous steel bridges, say, must be faced. Suppose that for those ten years the young men of that colony—the men who have the shaping of her destiny—have been mentally nourished on moving pictures made, say, in America. Their knowledge of their mother country will be confined to hearsay and to such pleasure as their technical training may have left them leisure for. On the other hand they will have a clear and vivid impression of the multifarious industries and activities of America; the very essence of American thought and influence will have been brought right home to them. Now, let us suppose that both England and America tender for the supply of those bridges and that their terms are equal. Can it be in doubt for a single moment to which country those orders will go?

The illustration is merely intended to show how deep and far-reaching an influence the cinematograph must necessarily exert upon all receptive minds, and since the youthful mind is more receptive and more retentive than that of the adult, the influence is necessarily the greatest there. It is intensely important, from a national point of view, that good and worthy pictures of home production should be exhibited in the cinema theatres of the Homeland.

But apart from these broader issues, international trade is

itself a thing of vast importance, becoming vastly more important as time goes on. Among the industries to be fostered, cinematograph picture making will be one. The pictures will find their way into new countries because the new men and the children of the new men will want to see what the old countries are doing, and trade, and after that many other things, will automatically follow them.

The little illustration which has been given to indicate the influence of the living photographs upon growing thought was purposely confined to pictures made with no deliberate intention other than that of entertaining. It is the unintentional influence, absorbed unconsciously in the ordinary course of leisure and pleasure, which has the deep and lasting effect. But there will be an immense field for the cinematograph in the domain of deliberate education as well as in that of intentional advertising. The adaptability of the cinematograph to educational purposes must be obvious to every one. Delicate surgical operations can be repeated indefinitely before a practically unlimited number of students, where only a few could see the real thing once. The dramatic moments of history can be re-enacted by skilled players before recurring multitudes of youthful learners, while the geographical features of foreign lands can be literally brought home to the young with a realism which is second only to that of actual foreign travel. This immense and unexplored field for cinematography in the domain of education is waiting only for a cheaper " base " than celluloid, for expense is practically the only thing which stands in the way of progress now.

Nevertheless, the greatest influence of the pictures will always be that which they exercise unconsciously. The greatest influence of the Press is wielded by its general writers—those who make books and papers for entertainment and informative interest; not those who write textbooks of science and education.

And it is the pictures of general interest which can most easily be hurt by injudicious control now. If this wonderful child-genius, whose babyhood we are watching, is to grow into the great and beneficent leader we believe it is destined to be, it must be wisely led and encouraged, not hampered and thwarted at every turn by an ignorant and cowardly fear of a possible inherent vice. Cranks and faddists from time immemorial have arisen to condemn every art for the sake of the grain of evil of which they can see it to be capable. It is for us to see that this great new art, fraught with wonderful possibilities of happiness and enlightenment for us and our children and our children's children and for our nation as a whole, shall not be emasculated, shall not be rendered harmless and therefore powerless for good as well. By all means let us control or suppress those who would misuse it, but let us beware of hurting the thing itself by injudicious pruning or unwise guiding.

It will be interesting to see what the picture makers of this country are doing. The first and most obvious point, which will strike any intelligent observer, is the fact that, compared with their foreign rivals, they are doing very little indeed, but though few in number, British-made films are among the best in the world. The climatic conditions here are, it is true, not as easy as those which obtain, say, on the west coast of America, yet the fact that the photographic results are equal to those from any part of the world is sufficient proof that what difficulties there are, are certainly not insuperable.

One of the principal causes of the slowness of progress in this country, compared with its foreign competitors, is to be found in the curious objection which English people have to change. The possibilities of art in the cinematograph, even now only recognised by comparatively few, were scoffed at for years by all those who should have helped to bring it forth. The great actors of this country delayed giving their aid, almost until their aid had become superfluous, almost, indeed, until it came to be recognised that acting for the cinematograph is more than a mere variant of stage acting; something new, something different, something requiring new and different characteristics beyond those which stage actors are able to give. Nevertheless, amongst those who have turned their attention to the cinematograph we now find great names.

English picture makers have always been short of capital. For some reason the English investor has regarded this industry as far too precarious to command his serious attention, and opportunity after opportunity has slipped by and fallen to the credit of our rivals. The budding industry has been looked at askance by all those in high places. It is almost an impossibility for an English picture maker to obtain such facilities for his work from railroad and steamship companies as in America are freely and gladly given. The proposal to make pictures of serious historical interest in such a place as Hampton Court Palace, for instance, although it can be clearly proved that no single right or privilege would be thereby usurped, evokes only a scornful wonder from those in authority.

The ambitious nature of the picture drama of the present day as compared with that of its prototype of twenty years ago is reflected in its changed dimensions. The pictures at first were forty to fifty feet in length, and now the average length of a picture is 5000 feet, and much greater lengths are reached in special subjects. The world's weekly output of original pictures is about 500,000 feet, and if the average number of prints to meet the world's demand be put at fifty copies, we have the colossal figure of 25,000,000 feet a week.

But though millions of British capital be involved in the cinematograph industry as a whole, though thousands of pounds are spent by producers upon every single picture they make, though hundreds of thousands of people are kept in clean, healthy, remunerative employment, none of these things count, or should be allowed to count, if the industry in itself were not a good and worthy one, exercising a beneficent and creative influence upon the growth of the nation.

Perhaps we are suffering from the rapidity of our growth, perhaps some of the symptoms which have been diagnosed as malignant disease are really only growing pains. The demand for pictures has increased far more rapidly than the supply could properly keep pace with, and the result is that pictures have been made crudely, unsympathetically, of subjects which—by their very nature—demanded the most careful and delicate treatment, and thoughtless people, seeing these pictures, seeing only the faults and not recognising the possibilities, have condemned the whole industry in consequence.

It has been said that no pictures dealing with any kind of crime should ever be shown to young people, lest the desire for crime might be engendered, but surely that is not a proper view. The works of Charles Dickens deal almost entirely with crime and its results, and those works find a place, unquestioned, on the bookshelves of young people. It is incorrect to state that that which the child may with advantage read about, he may not also see in pictures, provided always that the subject is delicately and sincerely treated. The famous burglary in " Oliver Twist " is no more likely to incite a desire to burgle when its tragic consequences are shown in a picture, than if they are merely described in print, and such incidents as the murder of Nancy can, it has been proved, be far more effectively shown by suggestion than if they were crudely and disgustingly portrayed in the full view of the picture.

Probably it will be realised in the future that there is practically no subject which cannot be effectively and properly dealt with by a producer who is sincere and earnest and has sufficient knowledge and control of his craft. It is not the subject which matters, but the treatment of the subject, and after all, that is equally true of literature, painting, sculpture or any other art under the sun.

MINUTES OF EVIDENCE

Mr. Cecil Hepworth.[1] *Examined.*

1. Principal Garvie. In your evidence you speak of injudicious control. What would you call the injudicious control of the cinema,?—Well, unwise control, control which is limited. I do not know if I can define " injudicious."

2. I should like some concrete instance. Would you consider objections to stories of crime as injudicious ?—Not necessarily, no.

3. I am very anxious that we should know exactly what measure of control those who are specially interested in the trade are prepared to accept. Would you give an instance of what you consider injudicious control ?—The control which eliminates every form of love-making; I should regard that as injudicious control.

4. Then you speak of cranks and faddists. Would you include

[1] See also pp. 74–80.

E

under that those who hold that there is a great need for purification of the cinema?—No, I would not.

5. You admit there is need for purification?—Yes, I think so, certainly.

6. Then you speak of a certain form of control and suppression. Would you make that a little more definite? What form of control would you favour?—A wise censorship.

7. Local or national?—National if not imperial, certainly. Not smaller than national, because a local and consequently a varying control would hamper the industry.

8. There are different districts and naturally there are different ideas. Some cities might feel that they can draw the moral rein a little tighter than other cities, with the support of the public generally. That being so, do you think national and imperial control would be fair? Don't you think that local sentiment should have a say in this matter?—I should hope that local opinion and local sentiment could be sufficiently represented upon the choice of the censor to meet their views.

9. Then you deal with the subject of crime, and refer to a contention that no pictures dealing with any kind of crime should ever be shown to young people. Would you say that in the cinemas as they now exist the pictures are generally and properly presented?—Well, I do not know what suits the word " generally." They certainly are in some cases.

10. Would you say that at the majority of houses when a film is presented dealing with crime, it would meet the demand if it was properly represented?—I have not seen many cases where it has been indelicately and improperly presented.

11. THE CHAIRMAN. You don't see the smaller houses?— Yes, I see many of them. I make it a practice of going to as great a variety as I can.

12. You are Managing Director of the Hepworth Cinematograph Company?—Yes.

13. You are on the Committee of the British Board of Film Censors, a member of the Cinematograph Trade Council, you have been connected very much with the industry from its institution, and your firm is one of the oldest producing firms in this country?—Yes.

14. Now I want to ask you this question. You feel that there is for an ordinary person a very considerable advantage and effect psychologically produced by seeing something than by hearing about it?—Yes; the effect is more direct and is more readily retained in the memory.

15. Therefore it comes to this important point, that something we see should be something we deserve to see?—Yes.

16. Has the educational world and the artistic world left the cinema trade very much to itself. It has had to work out its own salvation?—Yes, with the exception of a few spasmodic efforts, I think it has. The only voices that have been raised have been against us.

17. Do many writers suggest to you original work for films?

Do they write something really good and original?—Well, as a rule they write us stories of crime which we do not care to accept.

18. I take it that the literary men have rather found the technique of the photo play beyond them?—They don't seem to have troubled to interest themselves about it. The stuff they send in is very crude; in fact, they have not studied the technique, which is very difficult.

19. Do you think it possible that the people who produce things for the cinema sometimes rather under-estimate the desire of the public for good things?—Yes, I think perhaps there is a tendency that way.

20. Now, I do not like to go into the question of the performers, but may I take it that it is possible even to be a very good actor on the theatrical stage and to be a very poor film player?—Yes, that is demonstrated constantly.

21. And therefore some of the effects produced by the cinema are less satisfactory because in some cases you have not got a proper cinema player?—Exactly; we do not even now know what a proper cinema player is, for, you see, it is undeveloped.

22. You say here that the American trade is very enormous as compared with ours, with the result that the people get to know a great deal more about what is done in America and get attracted towards America, which attraction might be afterwards used commercially?—Yes.

23. You really think that a person would be inclined to get machinery from America because he had seen on the film that this was a common thing in America?—I put it in a very concrete way. I feel that the influence of the film is very strongly in favour of the country in which the film originated.

24. Then you say: " The adaptability of the cinematograph to educational purposes must be obvious to every one. Delicate surgical operations can be repeated indefinitely before a practically unlimited number of students where only a few could see the real thing once." Now it seems to me that if a medical student saw a surgical operation on the cinema he would not be getting as much out of it as if he saw the actual thing?—Yes; he might see the actual thing once, but then he would have the details driven home to him by a constant repetition of the picture. The camera could be so placed as to gain the most favourable possible view of the operation, and could be sufficiently close, closer perhaps than any one student could get to observe it. With the camera the film could be shown so that the subject could be brought home to all the students with equal clearness.

25. Don't you take rather too black a view of what has been done to your trade by saying: " If this wonderful child-genius whose babyhood we are watching is to grow into the great and beneficent leader we believe it is destined to be, it must be wisely led and encouraged, not hampered and thwarted at every turn by an ignorant and cowardly fear of a possible inherent vice "?—I am speaking there of the future, not of the past.

26. You don't imply that is the attitude?—No, I am only fearing that may be the attitude.

27. Apparently England was leading in supplying the public demand for moving pictures once upon a time?—Yes, I think that was so.

28. How did England lose that?—It is a long story. Am I to go into it?

29. Who is the proper person to go into that?—I think I should.

MR. LAMERT. Mr. Hepworth has been right through with this industry from the start. He is in a position to deal with it better than anybody living.

30. THE CHAIRMAN. Why the English have failed? That is what I want to know. I think that would help our inquiry very much—that is, if the Commission thinks so. (Hear, hear.)

MR. HEPWORTH. Well, it is largely a matter of personal history. The films were being made in this country, and I was making a number of films in this country about eighteen or nineteen years ago.

31. THE CHAIRMAN. You have brought some of them with you?—Yes, I did bring a specimen of the films of those days when they were fifty feet in length. The one I have here is about eighty feet. The films consisted in the old days of pictures of railway trains in cuttings and of omnibuses in Piccadilly—any little thing which tended to movement. There was no attempt to make a consecutive story. Any form of movement satisfied us, because it was a miracle to see moving photographs, and that was what the people were asking for. That idea caused a great many people to believe that this would be a nine days' wonder, and as soon as curiosity was satisfied, it would be all over. They did not foresee that this new thing would be a means of telling stories and recording important events, and that the interest in the actual fact of the movement of the photograph would cease, but the interest would be in the things recorded. Well, while we were satisfying the craving of the people to see movement in a photograph, we were supplying showmen all over the country, such as circus proprietors and travelling booths, and so on. They were the people who consumed our pictures; also lecturers and the successors of the lantern-slide lecturers, who visited the mechanics' institutes throughout the country. The demand for pictures in America was a good deal greater than it was in England. We were in the habit of supplying, forty, fifty, or sixty copies of every one of those innocent pictures which we produced for England.

32. THE CHAIRMAN. Or for other countries?—Yes, and which we produced for other countries. It seemed to take different nations in turn. The Americans later took to the pictures, and then there was a trade storm in America. Then it was discovered that certain patent rights were being infringed wholesale, patent rights held by Edison, and Edison conceived the idea of putting up what he called a trust. He licensed certain cinematograph people and gave them the right, on payment of

a royalty of half a cent a foot on every film they used, to utilise his patents.

33. THE CHAIRMAN. Was he practically the only person then producing in America ?—No, there were several, but he held the master patents. The kinetoscope used a continuous film, and in order to move it, it had a sprocket wheel on the drum with a number of teeth in it which took the perforation in the film. The only thing that people could use was the sprocket wheels for driving their machines, and this sprocket wheel was what Edison had, and upon this he put a tax. Then the Biograph Company found they had an arrangement which was almost as good as Edison's, and they said to the exporters : " Send your films to us and pay us the royalty, and we will fight Edison for you and protect you."

34. MR. LAMERT. Was that Biograph Company an American Company ?—Yes, it was an American Company, but it had an English branch. The Biograph Company had bigger pictures, and their pictures were very expensive, and they could not long hold their own against the smaller and cheaper pictures of the Edison gauge. The Biograph Company, being on its last legs, apparently made this offer to the importers in America, that they would protect them against Edison, oppose the trust, and grant them an entry into the American market. We paid to the Biograph Company—I speak now of the European companies generally—the same rate of royalty that the other firms were paying Edison, until the time came that this Biograph Company joined with Edison and refused to have anything more to do with us. By various means, and I think it is only fair to say by the greater insight of the financial people of America, it gained a large financial leading over the European market, and certainly over the English people. The English people had been hampered by the want of capital from the beginning, but when the Biograph Company joined hands with Edison and formed this big trust, it immediately stopped the import of films from England—in fact, from Europe generally—and that hampered, naturally, the English producers very much indeed.

35. MR. LAMERT. Did we retaliate by refusing to allow the American films to come into this country ?—No ; nobody could retaliate except the Government. There was no trade force strong enough to do so. Just about that time the first picture theatre proper was opened in this country.

36. THE CHAIRMAN. Which was the first ?—I think it was the one in the Strand just by the old Tivoli.

37. THE SECRETARY. The place is there now ?—Yes. They opened picture theatres on the Boulevards in Paris, and there were hundreds in America at that time, and yet there was nothing in this country ; we were still relying on the mechanics' institutes and the circus proprietors. At that time the American people decided to make pictures on their own account instead of importing from Europe. The first picture palaces were opened in this country about the same time, and it followed as the natural

sequence that the picture theatre proprietors were educated in the belief that the only pictures they could obtain were those sent over from America. At this time the Americans were making much better pictures than the Europeans. The Europeans had been having everything their own way beforehand, and they had been supplying the markets practically unhindered, but they made no progress. The Americans had to fight that big competition, and having apparently unlimited capital at their back, they were able to do so, and suddenly startled us by making infinitely better pictures than it was possible for us to make.

38. THE CHAIRMAN. We must remember they had better climatic conditions, or was it by pooling their brains?—Yes, by pooling their brains.

39. THE SECRETARY. And they make better films to-day than we do?—No, we won't admit that, but they make very much more. Then the picture theatres of this country were fed in their sudden demand, by pictures made in America, and they were remarkably good pictures, which to this day have never been beaten.

40. DR. SALEEBY. What is the date of this?

THE CHAIRMAN. I understand 1908.

MR. HEPWORTH. Well, from that point the Americans have realised the possibilities of this cinematograph from the commercial point of view more clearly than the English people have. There has not been that support of the English manufacturers; it has been hard to obtain capital to develop the picture industry in the way it should be developed. The money that was available for the cinematograph progress was put into the theatres for many years, and it cannot be denied that for many years the theatres of this country were infinitely better than the theatres in America.

41. THE CHAIRMAN. That has had a very considerable effect in popularising the cinema here, the excellence of the building?—Undoubtedly.

42. And now you are producing very much better pictures?—Yes, the pendulum is swinging in the opposite direction. We found it was necessary to make better pictures in order to oust the Americans from this country and, if possible, to get a hold on their market, but we have never been able as yet to do it.

43. What is the proportion, roughly, of films made in this country as compared with films made in America?—I should think 5 per cent. would be very optimistic. Eighty-five per cent. American, 5 per cent. English, and 10 per cent. various.

MR. LAMERT. I doubt if there is 10 per cent. outside America.

44. THE SECRETARY. How many manufacturers have you in this country making films?—That is a very liquid thing for the moment, because they are closing down every day for the want of staffs.

45. You have three or four left, I take it?—I doubt it now. Three have closed down during the last few months.

46. THE CHAIRMAN. That is an explanation of the present state of things?—Yes.

Dr. Saleeby. Is it proper to ask whether or not enormous sums of our money are going over to America for this business?

47. The Chairman. I suppose there are a number of English people in the American companies?—Yes.

48. Dr. Saleeby. We are pouring an enormous amount of money into America?—Undoubtedly.

49. The Secretary. I saw a bill the other day which showed that one particular firm paid £36,800 in ten months for Customs duties on films coming to this country. You have many firms doing likewise?—I do not know the actual figures, but it must be a big amount.

Mr. Lamert. Some time ago the British manufacturers attended as a deputation before the Customs to go into this question of taxation. Unfortunately the Treasury saw the Americans first, and I think it would be interesting to ask Mr. Hepworth if he will give some particulars as to what the official attitude was towards the British manufacturers.

50. The Chairman. You attended the meeting with the Customs on the subject of the taxation of American films?—Yes.

51. What was the result?—Well, the actual net result was a small tax placed on the Americans. I think it is one-third of a penny.

52. Mr. Lamert. I think it is one-third of a penny on un-impressed stock, a penny a foot for positives, and fivepence a foot on negatives?—Yes, it is somewhere round that.

53. The Chairman. Might not the effect of that be to rather tempt the manufacturers here to make really bad stuff?—Yes, it might.

54. And that has not been yielded to?—Certainly only in a very minute degree, if at all.

55. Now it is sometimes said that the Americans are no longer producing crook films and what we may call the lower type of moral film. They are no longer producing them either for themselves or for England?—I have not heard that, and they would not be likely to produce them for one country only.

56. The Secretary. Well, the cowboy film?—Yes, that has been to a very large extent overdone, but it is only dead for the time, probably.

57. You say this: " The demand for pictures has increased far more rapidly than the supply could probably keep pace with, and the result is that very many producers have stepped in." Is there no power of control in regard to that matter?—No; anybody can set up as a producer of films and everybody thinks he can do it.

58. Rev. Carey Bonner. I take it that the cinematograph theatres in Great Britain are really running 90 per cent. of American stuff?—Quite 90 per cent. The Americans can import their films to this country upon the payment of a small import duty.

THIRD DAY

Monday, January 22, 1917,

The BISHOP OF BIRMINGHAM in the chair.

STATEMENT OF MR. JOHN D. TIPPETT

PRÉCIS

As an American, born and bred, I have been in intimate touch with the conditions of things in the United States. and have been connected with the cinema trade virtually ever since its earliest days.   I have had ample opportunity in the last three years, while holding the control of the Trans-Atlantic Film Company, which is a British company, to study the ramifications of the British film trade in its relations to American pictures in its most intimate details.

At present, owing to the war and other causes, there appears to be a decrease in the quantity of film subjects turned out in the States, while at the same time, signs are not wanting that both in quality and in excellence all round the film output is vastly improved.   The major proportion of the films shown at present in British picture houses are American, and we can realise from this fact alone that American manufacturers have every reason to raise the level of their productions.   Practically 75 to 80 per cent. of American motion picture negatives are produced in Southern California, an ideal country for motion pictures on account of the brilliance of its sunshine and the permanence of its climate. Here are turned out at least 125 reels a week of 70 different brands.

There have been a great many arguments advanced as to the reason of the universal predominance of the American picture. These include the advantages derived from greater investments of capital, more favourable climatic conditions, a greater field for distribution in the United States with its, say, 20,000 picture houses as against some 5000 in the British Isles, greater sumptuousness in production, better casting and characterisation, more varied scenery and such general attention to minute details which the disposal of very large means would bring about.   All these causes no doubt have their value, and to them must be added the present restrictions on our general European output caused through this world war.

From the point of view of one who has sold American films in great quantities and has at the same time had experience in manufacturing in England, there is one important factor which has not been mentioned, and that is, the large scale on which American pictures are made.   The tremendous output of film in the United States necessitates enormous plants which mean bigness in everything.   I have in mind one company that has a city in itself covering about a thousand acres and surrounded, as you might say, by

a fence. It has several thousand employees, and between thirty
to forty stages or theatres, all busily employed in production work
simultaneously. I know of several other American organisations
working on almost the same scale.

In this country conditions are entirely different. There is
probably not a single producing company in England which has
employed more than three producers (what we call in America,
directors), and usually there is only one. The whole structure
of the motion picture, and indeed very often the entire story (for
the average director does not hesitate to take liberties with the
author's script in case he thinks fit), rests upon the producer, who
re-manipulates the story according to his lights, inexorably ex-
cludes any intervention by the author, and takes the lion's share
of the kudos. Therefore, it is upon the producer that the responsibility of the success or non-success of a picture must rest.
In America, upon one of these large plants that I have referred
to, where there are forty producers working simultaneously, each
one has access to the brains and ideas of his fellow-workers. The
English producer seems still to be working in the spirit where every
craftsman considered his trade a " mystery " and screens himself
in, fearful that a competitor might learn something of the " tricks "
or " stunts." The large-minded attitude of the American producer
has influenced and improved the American productions in many
directions.

When one considers that there are practically four times as many
motion picture theatres in America as there are in Great Britain,
and that the renter receives from the exhibitor far larger prices
than are paid here, it is obvious that the American manufacturer
has far greater scope and opportunity to devote his time and
money to the production of the best of pictures.

In the United States in the building of a picture theatre the
money is to a certain extent spent on the outside of the building.
The interior is cheap-looking and flashy, although the greatest
care is always taken regarding projection, lights, and music. The
programme is changed daily. The prices of admission are as a
rule as from 5 cents ($2\frac{1}{2}d$.) ranging up to 2s. for the average picture
house, the holding capacity of which is, as a general thing, greater
than that of similar establishments in England and ranges as high
as 3200 to 3500 seats. American theatres are almost entirely
owned by individuals.

Every impartial observer will realise that whereas the technique of the film play has improved by leaps and bounds, on
the other hand the stories have not advanced in corresponding
excellence.

It was not till the advent of the exclusive picture that a distinct
improvement took place. At the same time, the powerful acting
and direct simplicity of method employed by such artistes as
Mary Pickford, probably considerably added to the increase of
human interest in the story. To create a human story likely to
be successful is not so easy as it looks. The whole story has to
be told in action, and we have no soliloquies or asides to explain

the state of mind of the actor which forms the essence of a dramatic situation.

The sub-titles were the only means by which you could supply this deficiency, and these, in many cases, being crudely done, have not even to-day received the full prominence and care that they deserve. Hence it has happened that the so-called fount of inspiration of the present-day school of filmwrights has run dry, and it has been recognised by the principal manufacturers that there is an urgent demand for a more modern, more human, and a more up-to-date kind of film story. We all recognise that " the play's the thing."

In pursuance of this idea, I organised, about a year ago, a scenario department on this side, with the intention of bringing the manufacturing end of our big American companies into closer touch with English and European thought. It was generally felt that the film story could not be adequately conveyed by transposing the classics of the drama, and other forms of literature, such as celebrated novels and short magazine stories, upon the screen.

I organised a series of meetings with the Authors' Society and individual writers, in which we tried to convey to them the necessity of their studying the technique of the screen art in order that there might arise a new school of filmwrights who should handle the main problems of life and express them with full knowledge of the limitations of the picture screen. Unfortunately, this scenario department failed in its objects, its non-success being really owing to the producers in America, who still have the final say as to which pictures shall be produced. Producers, in many cases, are never keen to produce works of other men. Some generally have a sheaf of plays up their sleeve, and the scenario editors of such firms, instead of being in the position to decide what shall or shall not be produced, are obliged to work into shape such ideas or stories as the producer thinks fit to use. This condition of things, in part, forms the insuperable bar to the employment for screen stories of the work of the bulk of independent authors, especially European ones who are too far away from the American places of production to establish their claims to being filmed.

The difficulty about making a success with anything that pertains to education either on the screen or off is, because " there is no money in it." Of course, sooner or later the educational authorities, both in America and England, will come to realise that the motion picture is the finest method of education by the eye which exists. In the year 1911, in New York, I was manager of a motion picture company devoted exclusively to educational subjects. Eventually we had to give it up. The authorities were not yet convinced as to the feasibility of introducing motion pictures into the schools. Various objections were put forward. The question of eyestrain to the children was especially investigated. Now, eyestrain was in the main due to causes arising from defects in the earlier machine which have now been remedied. The average modern apparatus projects a perfect and a rock-steady picture. Exhaustive medical investigations in the States have not been able to discover a deterioration of juvenile eyesight owing to the pictures.

The objections raised against the cinema for school purposes, on account of defective ventilation and doubtful hygiene of the picture houses will not hold water. Cinema houses, being of newer build, are far more up-to-date, comfortable, and healthy than most theatres. Throughout America and England a great deal of attention is paid to ventilation. In the bulk of the better-class theatres there is an electric installation for circulating the atmosphere, drawing out the foul air and sucking in the fresh. In many cases the atmosphere is invigorated by impregnations with ozone.

It has been a standing puzzle to many people that hitherto all attempts to organise an efficient service for the schools have proved abortive. There are millions of feet on every subject under the sun lying idle to-day on the shelves of most of the various companies which could be had for such a purpose at a nominal price.

Perhaps the real reason why the cinematograph has not proved adaptable to school education is, that through the very vastness of these ungrouped subjects, the task of re-editing them and putting them together appears such an herculean one, that no organisation or individual has been bold or public-spirited enough to grapple with it.

In the United States the reason of our failure to secure the support of the educational authorities was mainly owing to the machinations of the politicians who play such a large part in every form of American public life. It was the municipal authorities, the fire commissioners, etc., who were against us. It must not be forgotten that the organisation of an educational company, to be efficient, would require an immense amount of money and very complete facilities for distribution.

In New York no children are admitted to the picture houses (or were not three years ago, and I presume the same state of affairs still exists) unless accompanied by an adult. However, this salutary regulation was continually avoided, as the children would stand outside the picture theatres with the money in their hands and entreat grown-up people to take them in. Latterly I am given to understand that a greater stringency in the carrying out of these regulations has eliminated this abuse.

There is, or was, no law in America regarding non-flam film. It was tried over there some years ago, but at that time it seemed impossible to make the non-flam base of a strong wearing quality, and therefore the attempts were abandoned.

Each one of the United States has its own separate laws, and the Sunday opening question is adjusted according to local conditions. Some States allow the cinemas to open and some do not. When they do open, they give the regular performances without being obliged to set apart a certain portion of their proceeds as on this side.

In America the censorship question is all-important. Formerly the American Board of Censors was an organisation organised on the same lines as the present board in England. This was supported by all the manufacturers. However, in time there grew to be a strong agitation throughout the different States on the censorship question, and many laws were passed to regulate it. A number of States have their own censor board, the diversity of their different rulings resulting in much confusion, for the simple reason that as motion pictures are put out to-day, the various States of the Union are supplied with fresh sets of titles to suit the local board of censors' likes and dislikes. With a number of different persons airing their views and opinions upon these subjects, a picture, about which there is the slightest question, is liable to become so mutilated by the time it is finally passed, that its own father would not recognise it. I cannot speak too strongly in favour of film pictures being censored. No manufacturer in his senses would invest his money in a picture which was indecent or immoral. As a matter of fact, such pictures to-day cannot be said to exist. But the real crux of censorship, in my opinion, lies in discriminating as to the effect a picture will have upon all kinds of audiences, old and young, and whether the methods of presentation employed are such as not to offend the canons of good taste, nor to present life from such an angle as to glorify crime or wrong-doing and to make probity ridiculous. Of course we must not be debarred from presenting a powerful story, or facing sex problems of vital import to the future of our race, but it is certain that all this can be done with propriety, decency, and proper dignity.

MINUTES OF EVIDENCE

Mr. John D. Tippett. *Examined.*

1. THE CHAIRMAN. You are the Managing Director of the Trans-Atlantic Film Company, Limited, the representatives and distributing agents in Europe of the Universal Film Manufacturing Company of America, probably the largest film producing company in the world?—Yes.

2. Your company is British, I understand?—Yes.

3. British money?—Yes; well, what do you mean by British money?

4. Well, whether your shareholders are here or the other side? —Our capital is very small indeed; we do not require very much.

5. You say that the conditions of the industry in the United States are more and more assimilating themselves to those of Great Britain. Will you explain that?—Well, the American pictures take over here, the people like them. The different countries have different tastes. On the Continent we have nine offices, and I cannot send more than one picture out of four to every continental office. What may be liked in Russia is not liked in Spain, and what may be liked in France may not be liked in Italy.

6. In America do they like the same as we do here?—Yes, universally so.

7. With the American films their text of explanation is not very careful, not very grammatical?—No, it is not.

8. There has been no very great seeking of literary people in order to do that work?—No; apparently not. In many cases it is very crudely and badly done. At times, the men who make these pictures seem to imagine that the audiences view the subjects through their own glasses, as it were.

9. The choice of the subject for a film. Who, generally speaking, would you say has to do that? Is that the producer?—Yes, to a great extent; as, for instance, in a large company making a great variety of films.

10. Is one of the principal points they work upon to select subjects more suitable for the eye than the ear?—I do not exactly follow that question.

11. I will put it this way: Not long ago there was a film called " Macbeth " produced. And all I could grasp when I saw it was that there had been a hideous and brutal murder committed. And the text was cross-headings to fill the place of the wording of the book. Now is " Macbeth " a suitable thing for a film?—In a commercial sense, it is impossible. I brought it over here, a fair production, but we could not sell it.

12. As a matter of fact these producers take a great liberty with the books and the plays?—Yes.

13. It is a little difficult to take great liberties with Shakespeare, for instance?—They do it.

14. I am rather inclined to contend that you have to be extremely careful as to what you select for a film. It has to be just suited for the eye, and is not dependent on the glory and beauty of the literary side?—Yes, to a great extent.

15. What is exactly meant by the " exclusive " picture? Would you mind explaining?—An exclusive picture is the property of one man who has the sole rights for Great Britain.

16. Generally speaking those would be the most important films, with a considerable amount of money in them?—Yes.

17. And on these films the industry would stake its reputation for a good deal of its beauty and other things?—Yes, on the most important pictures, but there is a commercial reason for a good picture on the open market that should be explained. For instance, take three very popular picture houses in the same vicinity at Hammersmith; a good open market subject is shown; they all book it, showing at the same time. Naturally, none of the houses make money, but if this had been an exclusive picture, it would only have been booked in one of these houses, which would have had a chance to make some money. The very best and longest pictures to-day are sold exclusive. In Great Britain on the open market, forty prints of a very popular subject could be sold and make money for all the buyers, but if any number like sixty, seventy or eighty prints are sold, nobody is going to make any money.

18. MONSIGNOR BROWN. Does that mean that it would be showing simultaneously in forty different places in England?—

It means that forty copies of a picture are sold for England. They are circulated; some houses would have it one week, and others, another week.

19. DR. SALEEBY. The " Battle of the Ancre " was sold in hundreds, I should think?—That is an exception; everybody naturally wanted to see this picture.

20. THE CHAIRMAN. In the United States you have not been successful in getting the educational film going? You put that down to the politicians?—Yes; but it is an expensive idea, and requires an immense amount of capital, for the subjects would have to be changed every week. Edison tried it and spent a great deal of money, but could not make it a success.

21. Why were the educational authorities against the educational films?—Well, say that School Boards in America, as a rule, have politicians on them.

22. You mean they have not any educationalists?—From the experience I had in handling educational pictures in America, I should say they were not all educationalists. In any event, they would not spend money in that direction. Probably the educational pictures were not far enough advanced.

23. The Fire Commissioners were against you. Is that on account of the buildings?—Yes; there is a danger unless the booth is well protected.

24. Then there are the religious pictures. You showed the " Life of Christ " exclusively in churches. Was that well attended? —Yes, and it was quite an interesting picture. It was usually shown under the auspices of a church society, and they sold the tickets. Pictures have been shown a great deal in American churches, not regularly but periodically.

25. And so much is paid by the church authorities for the use of the film?—Some church society took the matter up and sold the tickets, perhaps for charity.

26. THE SECRETARY. And it paid you?—Financially it was a very small proposition.

27. THE CHAIRMAN. Then with regard to the children in New York. No children are admitted into a picture house unless accompanied by an adult. Does that apply to other towns?—I do not know. I remember in New York the law was passed, and if I am not mistaken children were not to be admitted from nine o'clock to four o'clock up to the age of sixteen years, on account of school, and after four o'clock they would have to be accompanied by an adult; but the practice was abused, because the children used to stand outside the picture houses and solicit people to take them in.

28. Can you say whether that is done largely here?—No, I have no experience in England on the exhibition side, but merely in the selling of pictures.

29. And as regards the Sunday opening?—The different States have different laws.

30. And they can open the same as any week-day?—Absolutely.

31. THE SECRETARY. Is there much opposition by the churches to Sunday cinemas?—I do not think so.

32. THE CHAIRMAN. Are the theatres open?—In some places.

33. Does the cinema open in the same way as the theatres do in New York?—The cinemas are open in New York on Sundays, but they are trying to close them.

34. MR. LAMERT. Are the English cinemas largely supported by the films from the United States?—I think they are.

35. THE CHAIRMAN. Is there a duty on American films and stock of an ordinary nature?—Incidentally, I went before the Custom House Board and advocated it when the matter came up.

36. Did it produce much revenue?—We paid them £37,000 in ten months.

37. Does it have much effect in protecting the home industry at present?—The home industry depends on the quality of the pictures.

38. Is the quality of the English picture not equal to the American?—I do not see why it should not be, but there are several reasons. Take, for instance, the weather. I read that there have been only two and a half hours' sunshine in London for some time past, and to a man who takes pictures that is a very serious thing.

39. Is there any check on introducing indiscriminate pictures into this country; I mean every type of film?—England is not picked out for any special picture. The negative is made and the picture is supposed to be sold throughout the world, to Great Britain and Australia, etc.; no special picture is sent to England that cannot be sold in America.

40. Are there certain American films which are not popular in this country and it is no use sending them here?—Not as a class. Of course, we do not expect to sell every picture.

41. Does our film stock compare favourably with American?—Absolutely.

42. MR. LAMERT. Does that not all come from America?—No; I have not used any American stock for a year.

43. THE CHAIRMAN. As far as you can judge, do the undesirable pictures complained of come from America?—A percentage of them.

44. As a business man, do you consider there is any money in the undesirable picture?—I am against this class of pictures, and knowingly would not sell or have anything to do with them.

45. As a commercial man, considering the public opinion and the censorship, and so on, is there money?—I do not see how there can be money. I have never known anybody to consistently make a success on these lines. I take it that a man, I don't care how low he may be, if he has his fifteen-year-old son or daughter with him, cannot enjoy such a picture.

46. THE SECRETARY. May we take it that your pictures are family pictures?—Yes; we have some pictures come over here which we do not think right, and we do not put them out.

47. THE CHAIRMAN. What is the reason of the great preponderance of American pictures?—America has 20,000 picture houses. I do not think there are more than 4500 in Great Britain. The prices are higher there, and likewise they can afford to pay more. I know of some picture theatres in New York and other large cities which pay from £150 to £300 for one week's run of a picture. In this country no such rental could be obtained—in many cases not over £15 per week.

48. Are the prices for admission in America cheaper?—The universal prices are five cents and ten cents, twopence halfpenny and fivepence.

49. Is the attendance very democratic?—It is like this country, yes.

50. Will all the classes mix in the nickel house?—Yes.

51. DR. SALEEBY. Is the nickel house inferior to the two-nickel house?—It is according to the locality. If the two-nickel house is in a good locality, such as in the West End, it is as easy to get two nickels as to get one.

52. The same pictures and the same music?—Yes.

53. THE CHAIRMAN. As regards the eye-strain of children in America. Can you tell us anything about that?—I think since the great improvements have been made in the picture machines it has all been eliminated.

54. What is the distance of the nearest seat you can sit in in America?—Well, I do not think they ought to be nearer than fifteen to twenty feet.

55. That is, comparatively speaking, near?—Yes. I consider that twenty feet is quite enough. I look at our pictures twenty feet away. Of course, some theatres have not sufficient room to have the first row of seats fifteen to twenty feet from the screen.

56. We should like to hear from you with regard to the censorship in America.—I favour censorship first and last. The censorship there arose because there were certain undesirable pictures getting out. The manufacturers got together and had their committee the same as in England, and finally the State took hold of the question, and now it is a perfect jumble, as every State has its own censorship powers.

57. In America are there performances given for children only?—I believe some theatres give performances to children, but they do it chiefly for the purpose of advertising.

58. You say: "We must not be debarred from facing a powerful story or facing sex problems," but that you would not have at a children's performance?—This class of picture should not be shown to children.

59. Then you confine it to adults?—Well, many of these pictures should not be made at all.

60. I should be glad if you would go a little more into the detail. You say that some should not be made at all?—Here is a woman supposed to be a vampire woman. You see her in a luxurious apartment with a lot of men around her. I do not

think a picture like that does any good shown down in the East End to a working girl, although, mind you, I do not say that it would lead her astray.

61. I suppose at the end there is a tag or moral?—Perhaps, but some manufacturers do not make them for this purpose; apparently only sold to make money and appeal to a certain class of men and women. There have been pictures made in Great Britain that were condemned most vigorously by the papers in America. I do not say it was imperfect censorship here. To my mind it was an accident they were passed. I find the censor here, as a rule, has been very careful.

62. Would you consider this a proper thing to present? It is called "—— ———." A girl is sent away from her place in a shop because she gave a pair of stockings that had been bought by a young lady to a young man and a pair of gloves that had been bought by the young man to the young lady, and there was a row and she was discharged. Now interest is taken in her by, I rather fancy, the gentleman who got the stockings by mistake, and he falls in love with her and looks after her. His father is written to and is told that this boy is playing about with a shop-girl. The father objects to this and the son leaves his father. The son's leg is broken later, with the result that his wife—that is, the shop-girl whom he marries—has to go on the stage to try and keep the wolf from the door. Now this boy's father, a lascivious old creature, goes to the theatre, sees her performing there, and eventually asks her to go to supper. For a month, during which time we do not hear what happens, he hangs around her, and at the end of the month there is an interview and the father asks : " May I go home with you? " and she says : " Yes," and takes him home, where her husband, the old man's son, is in bed with his broken leg, and a reconciliation is effected. There is an unsavoury sort of idea about the father going about with the son's wife. Not only that, but we had a good deal of the dressing-rooms and scenes behind the stage, and the important thing seemed to be to show as many people with as little clothing on as possible. Now that seems to me to be absolutely unwholesome?—Yes, if it were my picture I should agree. These kind of pictures do not do any good.

63. In America, we see from the illustrated papers that come over here, pictures of people at the American watering-places spending most of the day in very light attire, young men and young women as far as one can make out. Now, this rather undressed condition is taken less notice of in America than here because it comes into the cinema so much. The motor-car and the light attire seem to be indispensable things in the American films?—This is customary. Some ladies wear very elaborate costumes and do not go into the water. Of course, the weather there is very, very warm.

64. The idea in America in regard to that sort of thing is different from what it is over here. It might be the climatic

F

conditions. Would you agree ?—I do not think moral conditions differ greatly in the two countries.

65. I was not dealing with the question of the morals. I was dealing with this question of the use of costumes. I was rather trying to explain ?—I understand now what you mean, and you are probably right.

66. MONSIGNOR BROWN. Is that general in America, or is it confined to a certain class of watering-places ?—I think to the fashionable watering-places. I know some of the ladies do not intend to go into the water with the costumes they have on.

That is the point we want to bring out.

67. THE SECRETARY. You can show these films in America quite freely ?—Yes; it seems strange to English eyes because they are not accustomed to it over here.

68. MONSIGNOR BROWN. Would there be parts in America where the country audiences would be surprised to look at these things ?—I hardly think so, because they see them in the illustrated papers. You notice that the costumes are not abbreviated costumes, and I do not think there is any idea of indecency.

69. THE CHAIRMAN. But I think the men are in abbreviated costumes ?—Yes.

70. I am not suggesting anything evil at all, but there seems to be a different standard of modesty ?—I think there are more of the continental ideas there than in England.

71. MR. NEWBOULD. Do you submit all your films to the British Board of Film Censors ?—Yes.

72. Are you the proprietor of a film called " Where are my Children " ?—Yes.

73. Did you submit that ?—Have not done so yet.

74. Has it yet been publicly exhibited ?—No.

75. I understand it is going to be exhibited under the auspices of the National Council of Public Morals ?—So I understand.

76. And if the censor had any doubts as to such films you think he would be well advised to consult a body of that sort ?—I should like to have the censor see the picture first.

77. I want to illustrate that there might be difficulties in the censor's mind and he would like to consult an important public body ?—Yes.

78. Do you know whether the American manufacturers submit their films ?—There is an association called the Manufacturers' Association, and they are supposed to submit films to the members of that Association before they are put out.

79. You don't know whether there are some Americans who do not ?—No.

80. THE SECRETARY. You censor your own films before you send them to the censor ?—Yes, our pictures are first viewed by a man who is specially selected for this work, and who has the assistance of two ladies. In the case of American expressions which might be misunderstood, new titles are inserted. They also eliminate any scenes which might seem objectionable.

81. DR. SALEEBY. In your evidence you mention the difficulty of making a success with anything that pertains to education, and you say : " Every publicist knows that to devote oneself purely and simply to educational matters either through the Press or other forms of literature spells ruin."—My remark, in this case, was probably far-fetched.

82. REV. F. C. SPURR. You tell us that educational films in America have been a failure ?—Comparatively speaking, yes.

83. You make the statement : " There are millions of feet on every subject under the sun lying idle to-day on the shelves of most of the various companies, which could be had for such a purpose at a nominal price." Has that been put before the educational authorities ?—Certainly to some extent they must know all about these pictures.

84. Are these pictures shown to the general public ?—Yes, but the probability is that the cinemas will not use much of that class of picture. The audiences like to see something sensational.

85. You really put it down to want of taste on the part of the public ?—I put it down to that, for the exhibitor would not show it unless it was wanted by the public.

86. My experience, in Australia for instance, has been that the pictures that crowded the houses were scenic pictures and what I call educational pictures. These were received with tremendous applause. I want to know the experience in America ? —When I was in the business there they were not received with applause.

87. I have been to a number of picture houses during the last two months with my children, and four or five times in connection with this Commission, and I have been struck by the fact that there has never been an educational picture on the screen ?—What would you term an educational picture?

88. History, travel and interest pictures.—We have plenty of these if you want them.

89. Has there been any attempt made in America to supply what Mr. Ponting has been doing in this country, a lecture with a cinematograph ?—Yes, Burton Holmes is very popular. He takes the pictures himself and lectures on them at a very high price in America. From twenty-five cents to one dollar is the charge for a seat, and he plays at the very best houses.

90. You believe in a censorship, but you prefer it central and not local ?—Absolutely.

91. You do not believe indecent or immoral pictures exist ?— They are made, but the censorship has been so strict in America that they are modified.

92. You say : " As a matter of fact, such pictures to-day cannot be said to exist."—They exist in a sense, but not to a great extent.

93. My final question is this. I see that you are quite against the " presentation of life from such an angle as to glorify crime or wrong-doing."—I do not suggest any picture is made for the purpose of glorifying crime; there is always a moral, is there not ?

94. But would you include in that such pictures, for instance, as show the methods by which poisoners go to work, methods that you scarcely ever read of in real life, even in the annals of the police court or the assize courts, and also show men penetrating rooms on board steamers and burgling jewellery, would you include things of that kind under that heading of glorifying crime?—It seems to me that we could do without these scenes, and that a title would do just as well.

95. Would you exclude from exhibitions to young children all that kind of thing?—I do not know. It is according to how the story ended. The supposition is that the crime should be shown, so that a lesson could be learned by the child. You see crime everywhere; in every story it is brought before the child.

96. You spoke to us about not liking to take a boy or girl of fifteen or sixteen years of age to see certain things. You would make a distinction between exhibitions given to children and exhibitions given to adults? There are certain things an adult might see, and there are certain things, perhaps, it is desirable they should see?—Take the subject " Where are my Children? " That class of story, perhaps, should be told to the child by the father or mother. At that, I have a boy of sixteen, and know it is very difficult for a parent to discuss such themes with his children.

97. THE SECRETARY. In relation to that question about the crime, would you not hold that the methods of the crime should be hidden, and that there should be only an impression?—Yes, in these cases, either an impression or a title.

98. MR. GRAVES. With regard to education in America, I have got before me an interesting article written in June 1910 by J. R. Wallace Waller in the *Pedagogical Seminary.*—I was interested in educational pictures at that time.

99. It was going for the cinemas for educational purposes and suggested that something had already been done, particularly in New York, where there were meetings attended by both the parents and the scholars at which lectures were given with the aid of a cinema with great success. I gather from this that the American Government had done something in the way of popularising the Navy in that way?—Yes.

100. And a good deal has been done to popularise trades and businesses?—Yes, quite a great deal.

101. So that really the Government has taken the thing up from an educational side?—Yes, to a slight extent.

102. Mention has also been made about there being a good deal of danger from inflammable films unless special arrangements are made?—It is necessary to have a special room or booth.

103. It has also been suggested that children should either be taken to a centre for a series of lectures with the aid of a cinema or that a cinema should be fitted up at one of the schools?—Yes.

104. Do you think this failure to work things out in America has been due partly to the effect of the fear of fire and partly because the cinematograph picture got occasionally into wrong hands?—No State to my knowledge has ever elected to put educational films in a school.

105. Has any one approached you to deal with this question of educational films?—No, not in a broad sense. At that time, in America, they were all too busy looking at Charlie Chaplin and sensational class of films.

106. MONSIGNOR BROWN. Making money?—Absolutely.

107. Do film proprietors do anything except make money—I mean, they do not think of these educational films?—The making of money seems to me to be the main object of being in this business.

108. And if there was any money in it, the exhibitors would take it up?—They would.

109. There is no money in it, yet it is cheap compared with other films?—No, the prices are the same, except, of course, for exclusive or costly pictures.

110. Would there be any difficulty in getting properly educated English people to deal with the question of the text?—No difficulty.

111. You state that undesirable films were made. Have there been to your knowledge some very undesirable films taken?—Well, yes, but I have not seen them.

112. Have you heard that such things have been filmed?—I have heard of obscene scenes being filmed.

113. And have you any reason to believe that such films do not exist at the present moment?—I think they do. I was approached a year or so ago by a man who wanted to show me a film of this class in our theatre.

114. Do you suppose that there is any market for them?—I imagine that a market exists in some private clubs.

115. And therefore if people are prepared to pay a high fee it is possible to get a private exhibition of disgraceful films?—I think there are some loathsome things made in motion pictures.

116. MRS. BURGWIN. Would the educational authorities have the power in the United States to pay for the exhibition of films as part of the education grant?—Yes, but I think they would meet with objections.

117. I suggest that a very beautiful educational picture was the cutting of the Panama Canal?—This was filmed by several firms, but I remember distinctly that the picture did not meet with any great success in the cinemas.

118. THE SECRETARY. You spoke just now about these indecent pictures being taken up by clubs. You do not mean political or social clubs?—I mentioned the word clubs, but not in a literal sense. What I meant was a gathering of men who have a dinner, and then perhaps see the picture afterwards.

119. In a house, a private view?—Yes, that is it. I do not mean an organisation, but a gathering of men.

120. In a house of common prostitutes?—No, among a gathering of men.

THE CHAIRMAN. He means that it sometimes happens that individual men come together and see it.

121. DR. SALEEBY. Have they the apparatus there?—They can rent the apparatus.

122. MR. KING. Do you know, if in New York these sort of pictures are shown, whether the police authorities have any power to go into the house?—Yes, they have that power. They have done this where there have been indecent scenes and dances. They do not wait for any search warrant; they go to the house, break the door down and arrest the people. They can walk right in and batter the place down. I remember one place where a number of wealthy men were arrested some years ago.

123. And still, in spite of that, do you know if they are shown?—I know these things are made. I do not know where they are shown.

124. You know the system that exists, I mean the methods that exist in New York for the control of a picture house. You do not know the conditions that exist in other States, in respect particularly to what we call here local control?—No, not fully.

125. For instance, is the cinema licensed by the State?—It is licensed usually by the cities. The cities can govern the cinemas in their own way.

126. Would the State have power to overrule the city with respect to any of them?—Yes, but the Federal Government could not make laws to overrule the various individual States.

127. Do they put any conditions on the licence?—Yes, they put certain conditions on the licence. In New York State, for instance, a cinema could not have more than 299 chairs. Over that, it had to be built with full theatrical arrangements, openings at front and back, and a passage on either side.

128. These conditions would also deal with the ventilation, which you have described as being high-class?—They are very well ventilated.

129. Do they really believe they have got the proper ventilation in New York?—Yes, the supposition is that they have.

130. Do you find that in some parts of the house somebody is freezing and in another part that their head is being blown off?—I do not believe there is perfect ventilation.

131. THE CHAIRMAN. Is smoking allowed in the cinemas over there?—Smoking is not allowed to any extent.

132. DR. SALEEBY. How do you mean, " to any extent "?—It is very rarely allowed.

133. MR. LAMERT. How long ago was that?—I do not know of any American cinemas that allow smoking.

134. THE CHAIRMAN. As a rule in cinema theatres in America smoking is not allowed?—I think I am safe in saying that.

135. Is that a regulation?—It would be a regulation by the manager of the house or it might be a city regulation.

136. MR. KING. Has there been any attempt made in New York to your knowledge to insist on there being special entertainments for children and special entertainments for adults?— I do not think to any extent there has been an attempt in that way.

137. MR. SOOTHILL. Is anything done in the States or townships of America in the way of State ownership of the cinema?— I do not know of any State owning its own cinema. I know of churches that run pictures on Sunday afternoons and evenings.

138. Would you consider that city or township ownership of cinemas would be helpful so far as the trade is concerned and so far as the educational pictures are concerned?—Well, it all depends, in America, upon who is going to have the authority in that city or township cinema.

139. MR. LAMERT. I gather that in one part of your evidence you rather blamed the exhibitor for not showing interest films, and I further gather from you that in your opinion he sometimes mistakes what his audience wanted?—This is a question, perhaps, which goes back to the public. My experience of American cinemas was that the educational films were shelved, for the exhibitors did not seem to be able to make money out of them.

140. In your opinion if the people had an opportunity of seeing these scenic films they might like them?—It seems so to me.

141. You said you did a good deal of exhibiting in America. You were then in a position to try it?—My experience in showing scenic films in America was that they met with very indifferent success, as far as the public were concerned.

142. Were you satisfied?—Personally, yes, and I think, where possible, they should be on programmes.

143. You say there are forty-eight States in America. Does the manufacturer over there have to submit his films to forty-eight different censors?—Yes, the manufacturers have offices in every State, and they have to submit their pictures when there is a State Censorship Board.

144. Does it sometimes happen that a film is turned down in twenty-four cases and it is allowed in twenty-four other cases?— Yes, there are certain States very lenient, and they at times allow a picture which perhaps should not be shown. I read in one of the most prominent American trade papers of a certain manufacturer who would make a salacious or suggestive picture, and send same first to the States where he knew it would be turned down by the State censor. After this was done, he would release the subject in the other Sections, and advertise the fact that it had been turned down in the aforesaid States.

145. On the whole, is this State censorship acting well or is it acting badly? Would it have been better to have a central censorship which would take the view of the whole of the United States or the view of humanity, a broad view, and say that such things shall go and such things shall not go?—Well, to-day they

are trying to put through Congress a National Censorship Board, but the film people are fighting it to a man.

146. THE CHAIRMAN. Have you any theory as to why the manufacturers are against this?—I have read different reasons.

147. MR. LAMERT. Will you give us the real reasons?—Personally, my opinion is that the manufacturers are afraid of a politician.

148. You mean they would have to pay somebody to get their films through?—Yes, in some cases.

149. THE SECRETARY. And the censorship in America would be a political institution either of one party or the other whichever is in power?—Yes.

150. MR. LAMERT. The manufacturers are afraid, in fact, that if they get this sort of censorship they would have to go to the man and say: "Here is 100 dollars or 500 dollars for you to get this picture through"?—There might be a possible danger of such a thing happening.

151. The point is of great importance over here. I think the manufacturers are whole-heartedly in favour of one censorship here?—Yes.

152. About these absolutely vile pictures, the filthy things. There are certain parts of the world where they are shown. Have you ever been in Cuba?—Yes; I have seen pictures in Cuba which were absolutely indecent. I saw these things in a picture show.

153. Now I take it these pictures are made primarily for exhibition in these places?—Yes.

154. And if they are shown here it is only to a certain type of neurotic men?—Yes.

155. The expenses of showing a picture of this kind would be so great that you could not show it for a charge of, say, threepence or sixpence; in fact, you could not show it to less, say, than one hundred people; that is if you are going to charge a small sum?—I do not see how this class picture can be shown at all.

156 If it is shown in this country it would be a very exclusive business?—It would cost a large sum of money. For instance, if a party of men had a dinner, a proportion of the cost of that dinner would be set on one side to pay for the expense of showing the picture. That is what I think.

157. THE SECRETARY. It would be a private show by a private individual?—I assume it would.

158. Then I can go to some place to-night and put down £20 and take that picture to my house?—I suppose you can do that.

159. That is not a public exhibition?—No.

DR. SALEEBY. Is that legal?

THE SECRETARY. I suppose so.

THE CHAIRMAN. But surely it is an offence to buy them?

MR. LAMERT. It is an offence to show them in public.

THE SECRETARY. I think you can write what you like and read it privately to a friend; you can make it and show it to him.

THE CHAIRMAN. I do not think that this matter would have anything to do with our report.

MR. LAMERT. My whole point is that this is a small thing and does not affect the cinemas.

THE CHAIRMAN. No, I do not think it has anything to do with us. It has nothing to do really with what I am called here for.

MR. LAMERT. It is only possible for a few men to get these things, and I suggest that it is done on such a small scale that it would not be important.

THE CHAIRMAN. It is a private matter.

160. DR. KIMMINS. Is the serial story developing very much? —We make a speciality of serials. I have put out ten of these pictures, and they seem to be filled with sensational episodes.

161. How many parts would a serial consist of?—Perhaps twenty weeks. Two thousand feet in each programme.

162. DR. SALEEBY. And lots of people go every week for twenty weeks?—Yes.

163. DR. KIMMINS. Have any statistics been prepared to show how many people go to these things?—There is no question about it. They tell me that the serials in many houses, especially in Lancashire, pay better than the most expensive features.

164. A weekly interval?—Always a week.

165. THE SECRETARY. But these serial stories are no more exciting or worse than those which appear in the magazines?— They are usually an innocent story.

166. DR. MARIE STOPES. I wish to deal with the position of the author. What responsibility has an author for his own film?—That is according to the contract. Most of the films are made from stories which men and women bring in. They are then generally re-edited by the producers.

167. I gather with regard to the final say in the form that a picture takes that that is in the hands of the producers?—Yes.

168. If you have an author of standing who allows you to dramatise any work of his, how do you allow the producer to alter that work without studying the author?—They would have to consider the author.

169. If the producer was more under the control of the author, would they be likely to get a higher class of production?—There is sometimes a difference of opinion between the author and the producer on these matters.

170. REV. CAREY BONNER. We are inquiring into the educational value of the pictures, and I understand that a small percentage of the pictures shown are actually of educational value?—I think there are very few made as a whole.

171. So that practically your evidence comes to this: that there is no education in the cinema in our national life, and the chief pictures are of a sensational character?—There is a great deal of education in motion pictures, but the chief pictures are to a certain extent dramatic or sensational.

172. THE SECRETARY.   Now with reference to these films :
" Ivanhoe," " Annie Laurie " and " Macbeth " are educational ?—
Yes, I think to a certain extent, but I do not think we put out
more than one educational film a week.

173. And the remainder of the 95 per cent. are not educational in any sense of the word ?—They could not be called
educational.

174. You think the inculcation of a moral lesson in a film is
not educational ?—It is educational to show the right and how to
do right. There is supposed to be more or less education in
every picture.

175. THE CHAIRMAN.   Your business is not to be a philan-
thropist, you are carrying on a commercial business ?—Yes.

176. And you are bound to consider that very strongly indeed
and what you want. If you are to produce an educational
film you must first of all have the public educated up to it ?—
Yes.

177. Is it not a fact that at the present time the kind of
amusement that the people are seeking is an amusement with
as little artistic taste as possible, so that they are easily interested ?
—It seems since the war began we have had more comedy.

178. I suppose there must be an agreement between the two
sides. If the cinema has to help education, then the people
should be educated so as to like higher-class cinema ?—Yes.

MR. CECIL HEPWORTH.[1]   *Recalled.*

179. MR. LAMERT.   The first question I wish to ask is with regard to the lighting of the cinemas. Sir William Barrett has referred
to the fact that in giving lectures he had projected, I think he
said, lantern slides on to the screen, and the room was sufficiently
light to enable his students to take notes. He argued that
similar lighting would be possible in cinema halls. Is the analogy
complete ?—No. The gentleman who asked the questions probably alluded to microscopic lantern slides, which, as a rule, are
very largely made on clear glass ; that is to say, they are not
films, and the designs are more or less on a light background. In
the majority of cases these slides measure three inches across,
whereas our films are less than one inch across ; that is to say, they
are nine times as large. Then the slides are projected on a screen
of, say, six, eight, or ten feet across, whereas we project our films
on screens thirty to thirty-five feet across, so that a very much
higher degree of magnification is needed. Then, again, you must
bear in mind that our hall is generally full of smoke, whereas a
lecture hall very seldom is.

180. If you had a screened light ; if you had lights making these
places lighter in an ordinary cinema theatre would it spoil your
picture ?—Not if it is properly done ; not if it is sufficiently
screened.

[1] See also pp. 46–55.

181. You think it is possible to get more light than is at present given in the cinema theatre ?—Well, than in some cinema theatres, perhaps.

182. A point was made some time ago about the tax. There was some suggestion made that the Customs put it in such a way. that there was a slight on the educational varieties, as it was the Customs who had to decide whether the cinema film was educational or not ?—There is no discrimination at all, all the imported films have to be taxed.

183. Now I want to ask one or two questions with regard to this question of local authority over films. You have to think of the whole market, have you not ?—Yes.

184. If certain areas were restricted, would it make any difference to you when you were making films ?—Yes ; I should have very much less market to rely upon.

185. If you had to rely on what one might call the local discretion, would that increase your difficulties in making films ?—Yes, of course, as I should not know what I was up against.

186. And if you had a central authority you would have an idea of what to make ?—Yes.

187. In practice, in making a film you think whether it would be a successful film from a popular point of view and whether it would pass the censor ?—Yes.

188. Now if you had to consider all the views and possibilities of various places, how could you proceed ?—It would be very hard to keep track of them, especially as the local authorities in these places would be changing automatically.

189. And in practice, if you had to make a film to suit all these people you would have to make it so exceedingly carefully that no exception could be taken to it by any of these places ?—Yes, I think so, and by the time it was cut to suit them it might not be interesting.

190. Your view is that a local veto would hamper you as a British manufacturer very much ?—Yes.

191. Now there is another point : If British manufacturers are further limited and further difficulties are put in their way, if their markets are to be further restricted, do you think it is possible for them to go on ?—No, the limitations are already rather heavy. I mean from a commercial point of view. We cannot get our films into America except by an occasional fluke. Consequently we have only to make for this country and the Colonies.

192. If the British manufacturer found it commercially impossible to go on, from what other sources can the exhibitor get his films ?—All the foreign manufacturers.

193. And, I take it, that would mean that he would have to rely on America ?—To a very large extent. There are a few films other than those from America, I mean those which come from France and Italy.

194. Now I want you to say something about the educational films. In the first place, these educational films of travel and historic interest, as they are described, are they more difficult to

take and more expensive than the films of the photo play order? Which would you find the least costly?—The films which are rather unkindly said to be "interest" films. Travel and industrial pictures are, of course, very much easier to take.

195. And if the demand came for these interest films, you could supply any number of them?—Yes; speaking personally, I can always supply a number of these films. You see, I like taking travel pictures, and I do it when I get a chance, and commercially I am willing to sell them cheaper than the usual run of my pictures.

196. But there is no demand for them?—Well, a very small demand.

197. Do you deal direct with the exhibitors?—No; I deal through an intermediary called the hirer, the man who hires the films out.

198. Have you any renters who say: "If you make any interest films I can place them"?—No; they occasionally show an interest film, but very occasionally.

199. Have you ever made films that were to be used for educational purposes, such as a surgical operation?—No, I have not.

200. THE CHAIRMAN. Are they all American?—I have seen one a long time ago; it was made by Dr. Doyen of Paris. He made a series of them.

THE SECRETARY. They were made by Pathé.

201. MR. LAMERT. You think, or you believe, that the film has great possibilities in that way?—Yes.

202. Can you tell us of any direct advantage which a film would have in that way?—Well, I have suggested, in the case of a surgical operation, that it would enable a large number of students to witness the essential details, whereas only a few could otherwise have seen it at sufficiently near quarters.

203. MR. GRAVES. Do you think sufficient light might be secured to prevent immoral practices from being easily indulged in?—Yes, I do. So far as I can see, all the better-class theatres are now sufficiently lighted to deal with that.

204. MONSIGNOR BROWN. In your evidence you say: "The little illustration which has been given to indicate the influence of living photographs upon growing thought was purposely confined to pictures made with no deliberate intention other than that of entertaining. It is the unintentional influence, absorbed unconsciously, which has the deep and lasting effect." Will you admit that a dangerous suggestion in a film accentuates a dangerous suggestion spoken of?—I should have thought so myself, but Mr. Legge, if you remember, had quite a contrary opinion.

205. Well, take for example this advertisement which is an advertisement in the current number of a trade paper. (Witness was handed a copy of that paper showing a coloured advertisement of a man and woman kissing.) Do not you think this is suggestive?—Well, it is suggestive of vulgarity.

206. You don't think anything more?—I think it is distinctly unpleasant.

207. And, therefore, that type of advertising and that type of film would be undesirable for young people ?—I should think so.

208. Not so much because of what it actually portrays as of what may be read in it. The title is " —— —— ——." It suggests to the ordinary person playing with something dangerous ? —Yes.

THE CHAIRMAN. Is that American ?

MONSIGNOR BROWN. It is from ——.

209. THE SECRETARY. That is the advertisement in the paper ? —Yes.

210. MONSIGNOR BROWN. Over which the exhibitor has no control. Has the manufacturer any control ?—No; I should think it was the agent's work.

211. And therefore you would not like films which you manufacture to be put out to the public by appeals of that kind ?—No; I have to be very careful indeed, and I have made a restriction that none of my films should ever be shown in company of any posters I have not myself passed.

212. There is one delicate question I should like to ask. You are speaking for the British manufacturers. Are films of a very undesirable character manufactured and in existence ?—No, I do not think so now.

213. Is it possible, on a high payment, to have provided in certain places a private display, even in London ?—I would not like to say; it has not come under my notice.

214. Then probably for yourself you would say it is impossible ? —I should say it was impossible for British manufacturers as a whole. That I am sure of.

215. SIR JOHN KIRK. I understand that the educational films are not in demand. How do you arrive at that conclusion ?— Well, I do not say merely educational films, but these " films of interest." I have made them more as a matter of experiment than anything else, but to put the matter in figures, the demand never exceeds ten copies at 4d. a foot, whereas my ordinary subjects I sell for 2s. 6d. a foot for fifteen copies.

216. What choice have the audience in the films ?—The exhibitor tries them, and evidently takes notice of the demeanour of the public as to whether they want them or not.

217. DR. SALEEBY. What is the hirer or the renter ?—He is the medium of exchange. The manufacturer sells, if he can, to the renter, and the renter hires the pictures to the exhibitor as he wants them.

218. You complain that you have had a great deal of destructive criticism and practically no constructive criticism ?—Yes, I think that is so.

219. The general rule of the profession is to regard the outsider as the outsider; I mean, take the case of the medical profession, and so on. You don't go to the people who might be expected to help you ?—Well, no, I suppose not.

220. I was thinking of your consulting people with, say, special historical knowledge, and so on ?—Certainly, if I was producing

a historical film I should want costly advice and everything I could get.

221. You do that ?—Undoubtedly.

222. Don't you think that there is some very bad grammar published on some of the films ?—Most of the films that are seen are imported, and perhaps the translations from the French and Italian are made by illiterate people.

223. When you are making educational claims for the films, it seems a pity that a matter like this grammar should spoil them.— It does indeed.

224. You say it is almost impossible to get a film into America ? —Yes.

225. Why is that ?—The American people have a very strong national instinct; they stick to their own films very largely, and they accomplish the exclusion of foreign films by means of rings and combines.

226. It is not a prohibitive tax at the port of entry ?—No, the Government tax is small like our own.

227. Did you film " Far from the Madding Crowd " ?—It was done in my studios.

228. Did it go to America ?—Yes.

229. Did it run in America ?—It was made in my studios by an American and he took it over with him.

230. " Annie Laurie." Did that go to America ?—It is waiting in America now.   It is sealed up, blocked out by the trade rings.

231. When you take a classic from a living master, how do you deal with the author ?—Well, when we have filmed his play he generally makes a few suggestions, which are adopted if possible, and then he sees the finished product as a whole and expresses his approval or the reverse.

232. THE CHAIRMAN.   And if he disapproves ?—That is only in very exceptional cases, I think, but he has a right to stop the film.

233. MR. LAMERT.   I think that all depends on the contract ?— Yes.

234. DR. SALEEBY.   In the case of " Far from the Madding Crowd " did you go to Mr. Hardy first ?—They are generally brought to us by the agents.

235. Where did Mr. Hardy come in ? for, you see, it might have been a mutilation of his work.—I am afraid he has no redress there unless he has protected himself; that is, if he has once seen the scenario.   His protection appears to be to select the best producers; if not, he might get his works mutilated.

236. THE CHAIRMAN.   You cannot produce anything without the author's consent ?—If it is a copyright work.

237. MR. LAMERT.   Have you made a practice of agreeing when the author says he must pass the film ?—No; you see, when it comes to spending three or four thousand pounds on a film dependent on the author passing it, that would be too risky.

238. DR. SALEEBY.   Did Mr. Hardy see " Far from the Madding Crowd " afterwards ?—I think he did.

239. MR. NEWBOULD.   You refer to what you term injudicious

control. May I take it that in the main you mean injudicious censorship?—Yes, that is what I mean.

240. Do you submit all your productions to the Board of British Film Censors?—Yes.

241. Do you know if all the British manufacturers do so?—Yes, I think they do.

242. Do all the American manufacturers do so?—No; I think there are a few exceptions.

243. Have you ever had a film turned down yourself?—No.

244. THE SECRETARY. In how many years?—Since the censorship was instituted.

245. MR. NEWBOULD. You would consider the censorship of films by the police injudicious censorship?—Well, it might be.

246. It all depends on the policeman?—Yes.

247. You would not like to submit your films to policemen?— Preferably not; local control would not be any use unless it reflected local opinion.

248. You would consider anything in the nature of faddist control, either educational or religious, to be injudicious control?—Yes, it might be.

249. THE SECRETARY. By religious you mean the censorship of cranks, you do not mean religious people?—That is so.

250. MR. NEWBOULD. I take it you depend for commercial success on the number of copies of your film which you sell and the price paid for them? Therefore, before producing a film it is essential that you should know that it will not be interfered with by injudicious control or injudicious censorship?—That is my point.

251. THE SECRETARY. Would it not be cheaper and less risky to censor the negative?—It would save 2 or 3 per cent., not more. It is the negative that costs the money.

252. Is it possible to censor the scenario?—It would be possible, but I do not think it would be effective. You have no right to judge a man by anything else than the finished work.

253. COMMISSIONER ADELAIDE COX. You have said something about the royalty. Do you mean that the author gets a royalty merely by the sale of the book or that he gets a royalty every time the film is shown?—The royalty I mean is the royalty he gets on the films.

254. So he has some interest in the takings?—A very large interest. I am alluding to the copyright films for which the author has given his authority to produce.

255. PRINCIPAL GARVIE. The question I am about to put is not put in any hostile spirit, but I should like to give you the chance of making your meaning clear. If local veto would prevent your business being carried on successfully, does that mean that its success depends on the morally doubtful?—I do not think it is quite fair to say that my business would depend on the morally doubtful, because cranks and faddists might be in a position at some place to veto the film.

256. THE CHAIRMAN. You are more likely to get a proper view

from a central than from a local censorship ?—Yes, and the possibility is that it would be a homogeneous view, and it would not differ. When the decision was given we should know it was finished.

257. And you would be more seriously condemned if the central censor condemned than if you were accepted in half the localities and refused in the other half ?—Yes.

258. MR. GRAVES. Is it necessary that the local censorship must be one of faddists ?—No.

259. But it has been said that local censorship would affect your business. Are there so many faddists among these local censors that it would really have that effect ?—I think there might be sufficient faddism to lead to a degree of uncertainty. We should not know in the least where our films might be turned down, and if there is 1 per cent. of danger of that, our customers are not going to risk it.

260. THE SECRETARY. As a matter of fact, you have had films passed in some places which have not been passed in others ?—Not I personally, but there have been.

261. MONSIGNOR BROWN. What would happen to the exhibitors if your films are shut out ? What other films could he buy ?—He would have to buy foreign films.

262. Are they more likely to be passed than yours ?—I do not think so.

263. MR. NEWBOULD. The objection is not so much to the local control as to the fact that the local authorities delegate the censorship to the Police Superintendent, as you will see is done by the Liverpool regulations ?—Yes, that is so.

264. If the local opinion is left to the Police Superintendent, there is an obvious objection ?—It stands to reason it would not be so well done as by one central authority.

265. MR. KING. Have you had any applications from educational bodies for educational films to be made or prepared ?—Yes, I have had applications for lists of what educational films I possess. I have always sent the lists, but the films are not always engaged.

266. You have spoken about the illumination of a hall varying. Would it be possible to have a superior illumination for the hall which would not interfere with the picture ?—It is rather difficult to standardise.

267. It could be standardised ?—It might at a certain distance. Of course, it really matters nothing how much light there is in the hall so long as the screen is in darkness and so long as the people's eyesight is not interfered with by the light.

FOURTH DAY

Monday, January 29, 1917,

The BISHOP OF BIRMINGHAM in the chair.

STATEMENT OF MR. F. R. GOODWIN

PRÉCIS

IN regard to Sunday Evening Cinematograph Entertainments in London I would only venture to offer evidence on the actual method without entering into the merits of these entertainments further than to say that the privilege allowed in this matter in London is held by the pledged undertaking, at the last election, of both parties within the London County Council, and is supported also by the Labour Party of the Council. The exact position is as follows : The London County Council Cinematograph Licence is granted for week-days only, and halls must not open upon Sundays, Christmas Days, nor Good Fridays, but the Council will consider applications to open upon such prohibited days upon the following conditions—

1. The entertainments will be of a healthy character and properly conducted.

2. An amount to be determined by the Council as representing the profit from the entertainment will be paid in respect of each Sunday to a charity to be approved by the Council.

3. No performance shall begin before 6 p.m., or finish later than 11 p.m.

4. No person shall be employed on Sunday who has been employed in connection with cinematograph entertainments for each of the previous six days, and a notice to that effect shall be prominently displayed in a position or positions in which it will be seen by all the staff engaged at the premises.

5. The rules required to be observed on week-days for securing the safety of the public will be complied with.

Upon the application being received by the Council, the person applying is required to furnish details concerning the whole of his expenditure in rent, rates, taxes, wages, films and other items in connection with the business. Figures are required also as to the average takings and the average profit to be expected from the performance is arrived at. The proprietor then agrees to pay the agreed sum weekly to an approved charity, which undertakes with the London County Council that it will keep its accounts in the manner laid down by the Council.

During the past year the Lord Bishop of London, in dealing with Sunday evening entertainments in London, said that attempts by the trade to obtain permission for Sunday shows were always backed up by the plea of charity. To show that this is specious he gave the following figures for a year. The gross receipts from the entertainments opened on Sundays were £182,000; while

G

the amount received by the charities was £33,000, and he said, " If that does not show up what a blind this charity is, I do not know what will."

From the same source as that from which the Bishop of London obtained his figures—the returns of the London County Council in this matter—these further details are given. As the Bishop has done, omitting shillings and pence, the total gross receipts for one year were £182,000; the same returns show the wages at £45,900. The supply of the films came to £45,473; £33,000 was handed to the charities. The total, therefore, for charities, for wages and for the supply of films is £124,373; there is then a balance of £57,627, which went to the owners of the theatres. But what the Bishop did not realise apparently was that this amount was taken in satisfaction of the expenditure on rent, taxes, heating, gas and electric light, and all the odd items of expenditure attending the business were furnished for that sum of money.

The total number of entertainments was practically 15,000; therefore the expenditure per performance in regard to the use of hall with all appliances, electric light, carbons and other essentials was rather less than £4 per performance. It will be noticed that the net profit of the venture, after paying all expenses and wages, is 18 per cent., which I submit is a very satisfactory return indeed, and one which would well satisfy most commercial enterprises.

Regarding the character of the films I beg leave to place the following letter before the Commission from the Cinematograph Exhibitor's Association of Great Britain and Ireland, Ltd. (London Branch) to all exhibitors in London—

February 4, 1916.

RE SUNDAY PROGRAMMES

DEAR SIR,

I am instructed by my Committee to strongly urge London Exhibitors to direct particular attention to the character of their Sunday programmes. Although in the majority of cases *Members* provide a special programme for Sunday, there are instances where the films provided do not differ from the ordinary weekly programme.

My Committee would strongly advise the exclusion of purely comic and wildly sensational pictures, and the substitution of good dramas, travel pictures and films of educational interest. If this is done my Committee feel sure the care exercised in film selection for the Sunday evenings will remove a great deal of the prejudice which exists in some quarters against Sunday amusements.

Your Association are in active negotiation with the renters of films to secure an adequate supply of the proper films for display on Sunday evenings.

Yours faithfully,

ERNEST W. P. PEALL, Hon. Sec.

In regard to the labour question, it has been mentioned that it is a rule of the Council that no one shall work on Sunday evening if he or she has worked each of the previous six days, and in this connection the following clause is operative as between labour and the Association. "Sunday evening, Good Friday evening and Christmas evening shall be deemed equal to a full week-day and paid for accordingly. A worker shall reserve the right to refuse to work on Sunday evening, but if he or she does accept the Sunday evening duty, he or she shall compulsorily take one day off during the week. No worker shall under any circumstances work for seven days continuously."

I therefore and with confidence ask for a ruling of the Commission that without going into the merits and whether or no the houses should be opened on Sunday, that in pursuance of arrangements made by the governing body—the London County Council—the bargain is being loyally carried out by the exhibitors.

In the second place, I desire to refer to the question of indecent conduct, alleged to occur in picture theatres, and to point out to the Commission my earnest conviction that this matter has been very grossly exaggerated. When investigation is made it is usually found that the alleged misconduct is nothing more than the privileged manifestation of affection between the sexes. Most unmarried couples sitting in close proximity at entertainments, or in other places of relaxation or amusement will hold hands, or link arms, or even an occasional arm will be found around a waist, this under the strongest as well as under very much diminished lighting. In this connection I am reminded of a very true and tender remark once made by Mr. Newbould, the chairman of my Association, on this subject, when he said that such a sight so "far from deserving censure should . . . make our hearts glad." I say that in general the cinema is not the abode of indecency, and recall attention to the visits by vigilant workers of the National Union of Women Workers to 248 halls, when as was returned by the Chief Commissioner of Police for the Metropolis to the Home Secretary, no cases of indecency were observed. It is a lamentable fact that certain undesirable characters have lately been found to be endeavouring to make use of the halls in the West End, and in this connection my Association has lately addressed the following letter to the Home Secretary, and is pursuing the matter so far as it sees opportunity.

London District Branch,
Broadmead House, Panton Street,
Panton Street, Haymarket, S.W
January 5, 1917.

Rt. Hon. Sir George Cave, K.C., M.P.,
Home Secretary, Home Office, Whitehall, S.W.

Dear Sir,
On behalf of the above Association we venture to approach you to direct your attention to, and to make some observations upon an extremely urgent matter which affects the well-being of the public in general, and the cinematograph trade in particular.

Certain abnormal conditions unfortunately exist in the West End of London at the present time which tend gravely to endanger the good name of the cinematograph trade, and the comfort and morals of its patrons, and which without the aid of the State cannot be altered.

It has recently been stated that there are at the present time 60,000 prostitutes in the County of London, 40,000 of such being of alien birth. Many are refugees from France and Belgium, and very many are ordinarily resident and have been so for many years in this country. Recent arrangements and adjustments have closed certain quarters in which the women in question have been used to ply their occupation, and the result has been that in addition to using the streets in vastly increased numbers, such women are found to be endeavouring to establish a new market place by invading the tea shops, cafés and cinemas in the West End and vicinity. Having abandoned the glaring garb of the music hall for a more sober raiment, the abnormally darkened conditions of the vestibules of cinemas in the early evenings make it exceedingly difficult to detect the character of women seeking admission.

A campaign for more illuminant within the auditoriums has considerably aided the women in their calling. It has been suggested that indecent and immoral conduct takes place within cinemas. This is entirely without foundation, and the cry for more lighting came from this unfounded charge; the real evil being that the women seek to solicit and are aided rather than otherwise by any attempt to raise the standard of indoor lighting. The difficulty of dealing with this matter is well known. Actions for libel are so easy to manufacture, while the calling of these women is so lucrative that any fine inflicted is paid with ease.

The Association prays for help in this matter, and ventures to place before the Department a series of proposals having for their object the better control of the health and morals of the town.

Under the National Registration Act of 1915, steps might be taken to re-register the woman power of the country, and by this means exact details of the age, occupation, and means of support of every female over the age of fourteen would be obtained. A personal card would be issued to every female giving certain particulars, and this card would be producible on demand by any authorised person.

No opposition should be offered to this course, which only equalises the conditions between the sexes.

Suitable penalties could be inflicted for failure to produce identity cards, and it might be found possible that in future a convicted prostitute would have the identity card marked to that effect.

The result of this registration would be to tabulate clearly the numbers and nationalities of the pests now poisoning our city.

Deportation should follow of the foreign element, and some method of isolation and reclamation for the British nationals adopted forthwith. Woman labour is wanted, we understand, in vast quantities, and it appears to this Association that no better work could be undertaken than the provision of a working settlement in which these women could be placed for stated periods of time, during which organised effort could be made for their better education and reformation.

The Association begs the consideration of His Majesty's Secretary of State for Home Affairs of the information contained in this letter, and hope that some means may be devised to deal with evils alluded to.

We have the honour to remain,

Your obedient servants,

MINUTES OF EVIDENCE

MR. F. R. GOODWIN. *Further examined.*

1. THE CHAIRMAN. I think you produce a poster in consequence of something that was said by Canon Brown on the last occasion ?—Yes. I have a message from the Gaumont Film Company, from whom I got this poster. They say they had no idea that any such meaning could be read into the poster as was pointed out—that the heads of these figures were looking at the girl's legs; it was just a fanciful portrait of the principal girl in the piece, and the faces round were intended to be various actors taking part in the thing. If this Commission thinks it is likely to have any widespread interpretation of the kind referred to, the Gaumont Company are prepared at once to withdraw the poster.

2. Was that prepared in France ?—No, this was done by Waterlow Brothers & Layton.

3. Was that passed by the Billposters' Association ?—I could not say.

4. I think the question might be asked of the Billposters' Association. Now you have come to give us some information on the subject of Sunday entertainments ?—Yes.

5. Do the cinema authorities lay stress upon having Sunday entertainments ? Is it considered an important part of the trade that you should have them ?—Oh, yes; permissions to open are greatly sought after.

6. And there are not a great many places where they are open, are there ?—Very few.

7. Principally London and Brighton ?—Yes, and one or two towns in the North—Blackpool, for instance. There are more places just now, because the military authorities have been asking for Sunday evening entertainments in certain places. Then there are one or two places in Scotland.

8. Are they always open with a kind of condition that a certain amount is to be given in charity ?—I think not. I think that is peculiar to London, and when it has been allowed in Birmingham, I think I am right in saying there has been some charity; but I am not sure of the position in other places.

9. Supposing—it is a question rather of ethics, of course—it were undesirable to have Sunday cinema entertainments; would

that undesirable character cease because any portion of the money were given to a charity ?—No.

10. Would it not be rather intensified ? If the thing is undesirable, and some part of the money received is devoted to charity, does not that rather increase than diminish the impropriety of the matter ?—Yes.

11. What restrictions of hours are there ?—They are not allowed to commence before six o'clock, and they must finish by eleven. That is Rule 3 of the London County Council Regulations.

12. What difference is there between the Sunday programmes and the week-day programmes ?—There is beginning to be more difference. At one time there was no difference at all. My Association have been working for some time on that business. I am happy to say that gradually we are getting exhibitors in London who do open, to see the force of the attempt to do away with some measure of the prejudice that exists.

13. You say that you take care that nobody works more than six days in the week ?—It must not be done. It is a rule—it is an order.

14. I notice you quote the chairman of your Association as making a " true and tender remark " when he said that the sight of people linking arms, or with arms round each other's waists, is a thing rather to rejoice to see in a cinema theatre than to be down upon. You accept that ?—Yes.

15. It would depend upon who are the people who are doing this, would it not ?—Yes.

16. Most of them, I suppose, are presumed to be people engaged to be married ?—Yes, we assume that that is so.

17. I think that assumption shows a very wide charity on your part, but still, what you in effect say is this : Your judgment would be that indecency does not occur in cinema theatres ?—No.

18. Would you say that what goes on is very much the same thing as you may see in any of our parks ?—Yes, and on a bus or tramcar ; it is everywhere the same ; but real indecency, of course, goes very much further than that, and I say that as a fact it does not take place in our theatres.

19. In regard to this matter, it is true, is it not, that you ought to have as much light as possible, compatible with the entertainment going on, in order that there may be correct inspection ?—Yes ; conditional, of course, upon not spoiling the entertainment.

20. Now do you think that has entered into the calculations of the proprietors of halls in regard to entertainments as a rule ?—The question of more light ?

21. Yes ?—No, I should not think so.

22. I suppose the first thing they would say is that the less light there is in the hall the better for the entertainment ?—The proprietor would say that. If I am a proprietor and I am to do the best I can for the picture I am showing, I must show it in the dark.

23. But on the whole you cannot say that this very great darkness is absolutely necessary ?—Well, it is not so necessary now as

it was. The pictures are better, the lenses are better, the halls are better.

24. MR. LAMERT. I think it was this witness who made the suggestion that if there was more light it would be easier for women at the back to attract attention ?—That is the one drawback.

25. THE CHAIRMAN. We ought to get that point. There is, in your judgment, a good deal of that element—of undesirable women coming to the theatre and moving about in order to get into touch with the males ?—We have had cases of that kind before us in the West End.

26. And now you are instituting a kind of watch over that ?—Yes.

27. You have almost a small detective system in a way, and if a person moves more than twice he or she is ejected—it is something like that, is it not ?—It depends ; he or she is placed under observation ; we should always be suspicious of a man or a woman who shifted his seat three or four times.

28. Have you power to eject a person under those circum stances ?—Yes.

29. DR. SALEEBY. On what ground ?—Well, we use the right to refuse admittance to anybody. We simply turn them out. We have never got into trouble over that but once, and then we thought a man had not paid. It turned out that he had, and it cost us £150.

30. But these people have already paid you, and you have admitted them ?—Yes. We have turned them out, and we were probably right, because we did not get into trouble over it.

31. REV. CAREY BONNER. Could you give us any information as to how far there has been an improvement in the Sunday pro-grammes ?—Some of the best of the pictures that were ordinarily only put on on week-days—longer and finer films—we are gradually getting them to show those on Sunday nights instead of the more tawdry two-reel things. There is some really good stuff getting on.

32. You think this has had a practical influence in lifting up the character of Sunday performances ?—Yes.

33. MR. CROOK. Do you get the same clientele on Sundays as during the rest of the week, or do you get a different kind of people ?—Many people come on Sundays who are unable to attend at any other time. They would be the shop-assistant class, and more the real working people. There is only the Saturday even-ing, perhaps, when the man is home, and then he must shop with his wife ; but on Sunday evenings they would have nothing at all to do unless they went to the cinema.

34. And the man has the choice of going to the public-house alone, or going to the cinema with his wife ?—Yes.

35. I remember when I was about twenty-five going to the Pavilion and the Empire, and finding that there were any amount of women of what I may call the accosting class in the upper circle, accosting men right and left. Do you think the same thing would result if you had the same amount of light in the cinemas ?—Where the promenades are big enough for that sort of thing,

certainly; where the promenades are not so big you do not get it so much, but you get spasmodic attempts to have a word with two or three men.

36. But greater lighting would give an increased opportunity? —Yes; that is the opinion I have formed.

37. MR. LAMERT. Are you satisfied with the powers you have at the present time—the legal powers, I do not know what they are exactly—to deal with these undesirable things?—Oh, no; we are always running the risk of making a mistake, but we have never had that happen yet.

38. Any action you have taken has been rather high-handed?—Very much so.

39. You have simply had the luck not to tumble against somebody who has got heavy damages out of you?—Yes.

40. Would it assist you very much if you had powers to deal with them?—Very much.

41. Can you suggest what powers you would like?—Well, I suggest that one power we ought to have as a licensee is a power the same as a constable would have—the right to say, " Where is your registration card? " and not get summoned for asking that question.

42. Of course, by " constable " you mean not a special constable, but an ordinary constable, who has very special powers?—He may demand to know who you are. I say that if a licensed man, a publican or other man holding a licence, who could not carry on his business without a licence—if such a man is entrusted with the conduct and honour of a certain establishment he ought to be armed with sufficient authority to say to anybody on his premises, " Who are you, and where do you live? "

43. You are referring now to the registration card which was instituted in August of 1915?—Yes.

44. Prior to that there was no registration, and that will get out of date pretty soon; that will not help you in five years' time?—It would; the women were registered at the same time.

45. Yes, but in five years you would get another set of women who had grown up in the meantime?—The card would be renewable every year, the same as for your motor-car or driving licence.

46. Do you suggest that we are going to go on with this register? —Yes.

That opens up a very wide question.

47. MONSIGNOR BROWN. May I ask what is on the registration card that would notify you that the woman was of a bad class? She might put herself down as a shop assistant or an actress, or anything?—But it would be an offence to put in anything that was untrue.

48. But how would you get a card telling you what the woman was?—Because it would have her name, her address, her nationality and her business or means of support.

DR. SALEEBY. None of them would put themselves down as prostitutes.

THE CHAIRMAN. I think you have got the witness's answer. I do not think you can carry it any further.

49. MR. LAMERT. Do you suggest that one should have to take one's card in order to get into a cinema?—I see no reason against it; you are supposed to carry your registration card, and you can be called upon for it at any time by a policeman.

50. MR. GRAVES. Do you regard cinemas as a counter-attraction to places of worship?—No. I have only gone so far as to regard them as a counter-attraction to public-houses.

51. But you will grant that they are more or less in opposition to another form of spending the evening in collected numbers—that is, to places of worship—and that undoubtedly there is a considerable number of young people who prefer the counter-attraction of the cinema to places of worship?—Yes, I think some would prefer it.

52. MONSIGNOR BROWN. Would you agree that the very dark state of the London streets at present makes objectionable behaviour possible in the open streets which would not have been possible when there was a stronger light?—Yes.

53. Therefore darkness does, to some extent, make cases of indecency possible, even in assemblages of people?—Yes.

54. And therefore there is a risk of indecent actions following what you might call the affectionate attitude that engaged couples or courting couples might take up innocently in a broad light?—Yes.

55. What would be your procedure, supposing a person in the hall complained to you that near them, within their range of sight, they saw objectionable actions going on; would you require that person to come and face the people that he indicated, or would you take his or her report that certain things had been seen going on?—It would help me very much if the accuser would come forward and assist me.

56. But you recognise that that would be a very painful thing for private people to do?—Yes.

57. Would you require the person who saw it to come up and point them out to you?—I think I should.

58. I was trying to get at that. Therefore, suppose I go into a cinema, pay my shilling and sit down, and within neighbouring seats see that kind of thing going on; if it is to be stopped I must get up in my place and ask to see the manager or some one in authority, and say that that is going on?—It would be better for you to call the attendant.

59. Suppose the attendant, I having called him, says, "That has nothing to do with me"; am I then to press and say, "I insist upon seeing some one higher than you"? I am speaking of what has happened, not of an imaginary case.—That would be very bad indeed, if an attendant did a thing like that.

60. You will recognise that these are very painful things for an ordinary private member of the community to do?—Yes, but it is a question of duty.

61. But you would admit it is a very painful duty for a person to discharge, because such a person might be subjected to molestation afterwards; and therefore there is a certain shrinking on the part of the average member of the public from intervening in such a case?—Yes.

62. Could you say that in most of the halls of exhibitors who are members of your Association there is such a supervision carried on continuously as to make that kind of gross indecency practically impossible?—Yes.

63. You cannot answer for the halls which are not in your Association?—No.

64. One other point. What other methods have you for detecting possible acts of indecency of boys towards girls; especially girls a good deal younger than themselves? Say a boy of fourteen, and children perhaps of ten and nine and so on, especially girls. Parents have told me of very painful things that have happened which the children have told them of afterwards. Is there supervision of a character that makes that a very risky thing for a boy to attempt?—Yes; there is an attendant in charge of these children. The case you put is rather difficult, because the fourteen-year-old boy may be a big boy, and may look older; but if they are children they are all together; they are sitting in seats which are specially reserved for them, and are in the charge of an attendant who is there specially while the children are on the premises. If it was a girl of ten and a boy who was nearly sixteen, or who looked more like sixteen, that is a different thing.

65. I was not putting it so high as that at all; I was putting it more with reference to occasional acts of indecency taking place among children and boys of that age. When you get these rather cheap displays to which children are admitted at reduced rates, when the house is practically full of children, is there any supervision that makes the kind of thing I have described reasonably improbable?—I have never had a question put to me before of indecency to children by children; that is a thing that absolutely I have never heard of. There has never been a complaint made to our Association, as far as I know, of that kind, nor have I had anything said to me by parents on such a subject. Indecency of the adult to the child, yes; but of children to children never; I have never come across that.

66. Professor H. Gollancz. If it was considered necessary or desirable to open the cinemas on Sunday evenings, say, at eight o'clock instead of six, so as to give a chance for those who wished to go to church, so that there would be no excuse for them not going, would it pay?—I think you would still get a fair return for the evening.

67. Mr. King. Can you tell us how it came about that the charity condition was imposed on the cinemas in connection with the Sunday opening? Was it not, as a matter of fact, a condition laid down by the London County Council?—Yes.

68. And is the condition that the entertainments shall not be for profit?—Yes.

69. THE CHAIRMAN. Is that clear? This is very important. Do you mean to say that on Sunday entertainments no profit is made?—No.

70. MR. KING. My question was, is it not a condition precedent to the Sunday opening being granted that, in the terms of the London County Council's regulation, the entertainment shall not be for profit?—Yes. I think I can give you the exact words of that. No, they have been altered. This is the 1916 undertaking. No. 1 : "The entertainment will be of a healthy character and properly conducted "—and now following that it used to be, " and not for profit nor by way of trade."

71. THE CHAIRMAN. That does not exist at all now?—Oh, the principle is the same.

72. Is it an act of philanthropy, then, on a Sunday?—No. In my statement there is shown actually what the proprietor gets. The total number of entertainments was practically 15,000, therefore the expenditure per performance—that is, all he got with regard to the use of the hall with appliances and so on—was rather less than £4 per performance. He has been able to let his theatre which he pays for by the year; he has got this use of the other day, for which he can charge a certain sum of money to somebody else. We cannot disguise the fact that that can be called a profit.

73. MR. KING. Prior to cinemas being granted permission to open, a large number of music halls were already open under the auspices of the National Sunday League?—Yes.

74. What proportion do the staffs employed by cinemas bear to the staffs of music halls or theatres?—Very small. There is a tremendous staff engaged in a music hall behind the scenes that we never see.

75. And if they were open on Sundays those people would be employed?—Oh, yes.

76. MR. EDGAR JEPSON. With regard to children's matinées, are adults admitted to them unless they take children with them? —Yes.

77. DR. SALEEBY. There are still comic pictures to be seen at the very best places on Sunday evenings?—Yes.

78. You nevertheless continue to advocate their exclusion?— Yes; we would like to stop it.

79. You still hold that what is right to show on Saturday is wrong to show on Sunday?—There are the feelings of people to be considered, and I consider the comic film is wrong.

80. MR. NEWBOULD. I take it that since the war the actual condition of the cinema staffs is not so good as before the war. Owing to the difficulty of getting first-class attendants and perhaps having to replace them with older people, supervision has been rendered more difficult?—It is a little more difficult to eject people; we have not so many stalwarts at our back now, but we carry on pretty well. We have had to put perhaps two women where there was one man before.

Mr. W. Percival Westell, F.L.S. *Examined.*

81. The Chairman. Why were your educational cinema lectures started at Letchworth?—Because I was so utterly disappointed with the character of the films being shown at the Letchworth Picture Palace; and because I wished to show the public that they could get a great deal more intelligent interest out of films that mattered. I commenced this series on New Year's Day, 1913. It was a tremendous personal effort to have to fight—although Letchworth is only thirteen years old—a cinema which had been there practically since its infancy, and had got a good hold. There is a big working-class population. I wrote a large number of letters and went round to a large number of educational people and others who I thought would back me, and they readily did so.

82. What kind of films do you exhibit?—I have exhibited films showing industries, travel, physical geography, natural history, historical films, and recently I introduced a sort of light fairy story, " Red Riding Hood," " The Three Bears," and so on.

83. No novels?—No. Dickens's " Christmas Carol."

84. No comedies?—No; with the exception of light fairy stories.

85. The Chairman. Are you an official connected with Letchworth Garden City?—No; my only connection with it is that I hold a plot.

86. Did you have any collection or subscriptions towards the starting of this institution?—Yes. Certain supporters took blocks of tickets and gave them away to school children or deserving people.

87. What prices do you charge?—One penny, threepence and sixpence.

88. Monsignor Brown. What is the accommodation of the hall?—About 800.

89. The Chairman. Does it pay commercially?—Well, that is rather an awkward question, my lord. With regard to one series of six lectures which I gave in November-December, 1914, there was an attendance of 3200 (you can take about three-fourths of these attendances as children), and a profit was made of £15 1s. 8d.; and sandwiched in between those six lectures, I gave a special lecture on behalf of the Belgian Refugees, at which there was an attendance of 660. That is bringing you into the neighbourhood of 4000 for seven lectures, and I handed over the total proceeds of the Belgian Lecture, which amounted to £10 16s. 6d.

90. Is this a work of love on your part?—Well, I get a small fee, but it is not at all commensurate with the enormous amount of work I have had to put in.

91. Are these audited figures, or your own?—These figures were audited, because a Committee was appointed at my request for the purpose of assisting me in these entertainments.

92. What rent do you pay?—When we started it was £2, but it was afterwards increased to £2 5s. My idea was to replace the undesirable Saturday afternoon matinée, which was perfectly dis-

tressing; but, unfortunately, the children revel in it, and so my rent went up from £2 5s. to £3, which I am now paying.

93. Are your attendants paid ?—No.

94. Yours is a work of philanthropy ?—That is practically what it amounts to.

DR. SALEEBY. May we ask about the expression " perfectly distressing " ?

95. THE CHAIRMAN. What particular films do you refer to in this connection ? Can you give us some particular instances ?— There has been produced, on Saturday of last week, a film called "——— _ ——— ———." I call it distressing to have, in a film of that kind which children are permitted to see, both murders and suicides. A week or two previously there was what I call a distressing film, a coiners' den, in which any one who had attended the cinema could have become *au fait* with everything connected with the making of counterfeit coins.

96. Were these for children ?—There was no option; it was either that or stay away.

97. Was this called a children's entertainment like we have heard of at some other cinemas ?—No, it is simply called a Saturday matinée, but is primarily for children.

98. Then it is not what you would call a children's perform- ance ?—The proprietor of the picture palace would tell you it was.

99. MR. CROOK. Do they charge lower prices on Saturday afternoon ?—Oh, yes.

100. Then, really, it is a children's matinée ?—Yes.

101. THE CHAIRMAN.—You want me to ask you something about what appeals to children, and to adults, respectively ?— Yes. As regards the films which I have exhibited, the least appeal is made generally by pond and marine life, insects, snakes, and lizards; and the films which have made the most appeal to children have been the birds, which seem to quite fascinate them, and the light fairy story, which is, of course, absolutely the tit-bit of the afternoon. I am inclined to think that if I showed my light fairy story first, and did not leave it till the last, the show would be more or less empty. The grown- ups, without whom I could not carry on the entertainment, appreciate plants, industries, and birds, and they also do not like the wriggly creatures, especially if it is, say, a water beetle devouring a worm in a tank, which they say is horrible. I point out that it is just what is happening every second, but they say : " Oh, we are grown-up and understand, but we do not want to show these things to the children."

102. Then even your entertainment is regarded sometimes as undesirable ?—Yes. I do not say it is so, but it is criticised as such. I am not in favour of showing these creatures killing one another myself, but the supply of the kind of film which I feel justified in showing is so small, that I have simply got to take what I can get or go without.

103. It is contended that there is an enormous supply of educa- tional films at hand for people, and that they are not being used

at all. You have not, at any rate, been able to get a very wide supply?—Well, I gave thirty lectures and used up the whole of the educational films of Pathé Frères; and I have had to go to another firm now, so I do not know where this great supply is.

104. Mr. Crook. Did you succeed in closing this commercial undertaking?—On Saturday afternoons?

105. The Chairman. At all—at any time?—Yes, I closed it for twelve Saturdays and reclosed it for ten more, twenty-two in all. Now it is simply going on again.

106. Now, as to the scientific and educational value of nature films?—Well, that I feel is very important, because I am a life-long field naturalist, and the result of my having lectured with a large number of natural history films has been that I have myself been educated in many points which I do not think I should ever have seen otherwise. Perhaps I might mention one or two : that the hedgehog is such a good swimmer; that the lizard is so fond of drinking; that the jerboa has a danger signal; that the deer moves with such lightness and fleetness of foot, and springs with such adroitness; that the dormouse successfully tackles a large snake; that the heron carries its legs outstretched as it flies; and the remarkable forms of motion to be seen in jelly-fishes.

107. Mr. Lamert. Did you see these on the films, or did you see them in nature?—The point is that I observed them on the films, and they had escaped my attention in nature, and, I believe, would have continued to do so. I might state that the exhibition of such films seems to me of great importance.

108. Now with regard to the value of standing slides at cinema entertainments?—Well, I have felt it to be very important that the children should not look at moving pictures during the whole of a performance, and the reason I have adopted some other method was because the parents have reported to me that if their children had to look at moving pictures during the whole of the lectures, they complained at night of headache and of their eyes aching.

109. You want to give some facts and figures as to attendances? —I have given some. I should like to give one more. In the twelve lectures which were concluded last Saturday, the attendance has been larger than any since I started some four years ago; it has been 7700.

110. And the people appreciate what you are doing, do they?— Might I quote one or two examples?

111. Yes, if you please.—School managers and staffs, for instance. One of the head masters writes : " During all the twenty-five years of my experience of school work, I can honestly testify that I have never had such assistance in the school as that which has been rendered during the course of the lectures which have just been concluded." The parents certainly appreciate it. I have a letter from our representative upon the County Council. He says : " I was unable to be at the picture palace on New Year's Day, but some of my family were there, and enjoyed your lecture immensely. So much was I impressed

with the educational value of same that I am impelled to send you a cheque, which I should like you to devote to providing as many school children as can be catered for at the lowest price, so as to extend the interest as far as possible." I should like to give just one other instance of a factory, which, I think, may be rather interesting to the Commission. We have a good number of factories at Letchworth, and there is one called the Spirella Corset Company. This is a notice which is put up all over that factory, which employs 700 people : " Cinema Nature Lectures, by Mr. W. P. Westell, F.L.S. Season 1916–17 : Mr. Westell is planning to give twelve of his Nature Lectures at the Letchworth Picture Palace on Saturday afternoons, beginning November 4. In conformity to past customs, and because of our interest in educational work of this kind, the Company have offered to subscribe for a certain number of tickets for free issue to employees."

112. THE CHAIRMAN. Then as to essays written by the children attending ?—Yes, that is rather important. We have invited children attending to write illustrated essays on the lectures. I have a number here. The illustrations are very remarkable when you remember that the whole thing had to be memorised ; the children were in the dark and could not even make any notes. There were just one or two pocket flash-lamps used, I believe.

113. And they have written good essays ?—Excellent essays, with some remarkable illustrations.

114. You want to give a brief resumé of the results obtained, I think ?—Well, I think I have proved, at any rate, to the public of Letchworth, that natural history is not a subject which is only fit for the kindergarten, as most people imagine. I know I have aroused a tremendous amount of interest, and, at any rate, I have replaced the undesirable show some forty-four times, and I am now arranging ten more lectures, which will bring me to over fifty.

115. MR. NEWBOULD. You made some reference to the bad behaviour of the children since the war. Do you attribute that to the influence of the cinema, or to conditions arising out of the war ?—Partly both.

116. What percentage would you attribute to the cinema ?— I should think about 50 per cent.

117. SIR JOHN KIRK. Do I understand you are acting from a philanthropic point of view entirely ?—Oh, yes.

118. Looking at it from the national point of view, and regarding it as on a commercial basis, how would you regard your experiments ? Have you any suggestions to make in a national and commercial sense, arising out of your experiments ?—Yes. I think it would be very difficult to make it a commercial success unless you made quite sure of the support of a large class in your neighbourhood.

119. MR. GRAVES. Do you give your lectures and your cinematograph exhibitions only on Saturdays ?—Only on Saturdays, from October to March. Previously on Wednesdays at 5.45.

120. Is there a general support of your movement from the general body of teachers at Letchworth?—Previous to continuing it on Saturday afternoons, yes; since then, no.

121. To what do you attribute that?—Because it is not fair to expect them to come on Saturday afternoons; they have seen quite enough of the children by Friday night.

122. MR. CROOK. Your last answer rather surprised me. I happen to be a schoolmaster of a large school, and from my knowledge I should say that many schoolmasters would prefer children to go on Saturday afternoons rather than on any evening in the week?—Yes, but the question asked me was whether I had received support. I took it that that meant, did they give their attendance.

123. MR. GRAVES. No, I did not mean their attendance.— The schools have supported me most loyally by selling tickets.

124. MR. CROOK. Has the National Union of Teachers supported you?—Not as a body, only as individual members.

125. You said that the behaviour of the children had been tolerably decent before the war, but that it was now absolutely hopeless?—Yes.

126. You also said that this absolute hopelessness was half due to the cinema and half due to the circumstances of the war?— Yes, the lack of home influence.

127. Who do you think before the war were the people who kept the children in a state of decent behaviour?—I think there was a better home influence, because the father was there, and they rather feared him, and they have got round the mother more.

128. THE CHAIRMAN. But there was a worse cinema then, because you had not started?—Oh, yes, I started two years before the war.

129. MR. CROOK. But besides their homes, they are in school for five and a half hours every day?—Yes.

130. They were before the war under the influence of men teachers—the boys, particularly?—Yes.

131. And now they are not; now they are under the influence of women teachers, who have not the same control over them?— Yes.

132. So there was a loss in regard to the two controls, the home control and the school control?—Yes.

133. Do you still put 50 per cent. on the cinema, having regard to that?—No; you have raised a very interesting point there. I must alter my 50 per cent. I must put, at least, 25 per cent. down to the absence of the men teachers, and to the largeness of the classes, and to women having to deal with them.

134. I want you to see all round the statement you are making. —Yes, I am very glad you raised that point; I had quite over-looked it.

135. And, as a matter of fact, the influence of the cinema was there before the war?—That is so.

136. And, therefore, there is nothing due to the cinema during the war?—No.

137. And so you knock it down to nothing in the cinema?—Oh, no. The way they have been allowed to behave at Saturday afternoon performances is largely due to three or four things, I think : the absence of staff at the picture palace, the war taking away the father, the large classes in the schools, and the women supplementing the men teachers.

138. May I just sum up what I think we have come to? Your statement was that before the war the behaviour of the children at cinemas was tolerably decent?—Yes.

139. Cinemas have not deteriorated since then?—I do not think so.

140. But the influence of the teacher and the parent has gone?—Yes.

141. Therefore, any change in the behaviour of the children cannot be due to the cinema?—No.

142. DR. MARIE STOPES. When you are lecturing on a film, you say it is rather difficult, because the film passes so quickly. Have you never used an apparatus for stopping the film at a certain point, and lecturing on that?—No, because the local people with whom I work would not purchase it. I suggested it, but they would not support me.

143. Should you not think that with regard to educational films in general such an appliance was absolutely necessary?—I should say absolutely essential, to do it properly.

144. MR. T. P. O'CONNOR. May I take it that you regard the cinema as a very valuable aid to the education of the young?—Most certainly; I heartily support such a vade mecum.

145. Would you agree that, as far as possible, the cinema should be attached to every elementary school in the country?—Most certainly.

THE EFFECTS OF CINEMATOGRAPH DISPLAYS UPON THE EYES OF CHILDREN

By N. BISHOP HARMAN,[1] M.A., M.B., F.R.C.S.

Senior Opthalmic Surgeon to the West London Hospital and Ophthalmic Surgeon to the Belgrave Hospital for Children.

IN general it may be said that the effects of these exhibitions on the eyes of children do not differ from those experienced by adults. There are few, if any, adults who do not experience some annoying effects; very many of the more sensitive or impressionable feel considerable strain; and children may be taken to fall into the class of the more impressionable of adults, owing to their lesser power of resistance and readier experience of fatigue.

The unpleasant effects associated with the cinematograph

[1] See also pp. 116–18.

H

exhibition so far as they affect the eyes may be set out as follows—

1. Glare.
2. Flicker.
3. Rapidity of motion.
4. Concentration of attention.
5. Duration of exhibition.

Some of these effects are peculiar to the cinematograph; others are found in the same or some degree in other optical exhibitions. But none of them are natural, and as the more they depart from the effects of natural phenomena, so much the greater is the adverse influence on the eyes increased.

1. *Glare*

The human eye has a wonderful power of adapting itself to varying conditions of illumination. But to one effect it is well-nigh incapable of adapting itself. That is the effect of a single light in a dark place. The light may be but a feeble light, but if the space in which it is exhibited be dark this feeble light will be relatively intense, and therefore irritating to the eyes. These conditions are found exemplified in the highest degree in all optical lantern exhibitions. To enhance the effect of the show the room is made as dark as possible, the light of the lantern as bright as possible, and the transparency as strong as possible. The light from the lantern is projected on to the whitest possible screen, and therefrom it is reflected directly into the eyes of the observer. All these necessary conditions of the show are the worst possible conditions for the eyes; they all tend to produce the maximum of fatigue. The effects of glare are further intensified in the cinematograph show by the programme screen shown between the films. These slides are often far too brilliant in the contrast between the white print and the dark background. Particularly bad are the impromptu slides, made by scratching the writing on a screen of coloured gelatine. These slides should be prepared so that the contrast between the print and the background is the smallest necessary for visibility.

Glare cannot be dissociated from the shows. It can be reduced by providing a sufficient illumination of those parts of the room or hall removed from the immediate region of the screen; by attention to ordinary details connected with the use of fixed slides; and by care in the degree of illumination of the hall during the interval.

2. *Flicker*

Most people will acknowledge that the flicker of the cinematograph is peculiarly irritating. Flicker is of two kinds. First, there is the effect of the rapid change of the moving film. The effect is irritating according to the slowness of the flicker. The more rapid the change of the film, the less is the effect upon the eye. If the film can move at a rate slightly greater than that at which the keen eye is able to perceive variations of light, this sort of flicker will cease to worry. There is already a great improvement in the newer films and machines. The effect is most evident now in the coloured films, where attempts are made to give a natural colour to the scenes by the rapid alternation of different coloured films.

There is another kind of flicker due to bad films. Scratches and patches produce faults in the films which allow of the sudden exposure of the eyes to bright flashes of light; when these flashes follow in rapid and irregular succession, as in a badly damaged or worn film, all the irritable effects of flicker are intensified.

3. *Rapidity of Motion*

This defect in the cinematograph is to some extent connected with the previous defect. With the intent to reduce flicker, films are moved through the machine at a rate greater than the natural rate of progress of event depicted. The eye has a habit of work, just as any other part of the body or the whole organism, and there is a resentment expressed in terms of fatigue when it is required to work at a rate different to the habitual rate. The defect in the film is most evident in those scenes which depict movement near at hand; when the scene is a distant one the variation in speed is little noticeable.

4. *Concentration*

The cinematograph requires a concentration of attention greater than that necessary to follow any other kind of show. For the whole duration of the scene the eye must be fully alert, and constantly varying its condition according to the variation of the light on the screen.

Such a concentration of effort is quite unnatural, and especially for children. Ordinarily the eye wanders freely over objects; the time of concentration on any one object is very short. One can gain some idea of the frequency of variation of movement of the eye by looking at some object in the sky near enough to the sun to cause the sensation of after-images of the sun. Although the eye was apparently engaged in looking fixedly at the object, the number of after-images of the sun will prove that even for that short space of apparent perfect concentration it had moved several times.

5. *Duration of exhibition*

Cinematograph shows commonly last from one and a half to three hours. During that time, save for the short intervals, the eye and the mind are on the stretch. The attention of the child is not naturally capable or willing to concentrate for any but the shortest time. It is common knowledge with teachers that lessons to be effective must be short, and the shorter with the youth of the child. With a lesson longer than half an hour, the attention of the small child flags, and the time is lost and the child tired. Conversely, if the attention can be forced by the thrill of the picture show for a longer period than is natural, the nervous effort is increased out of all proportion. It is well known that to increase the speed of a fast steamship from, say, fifteen to sixteen knots requires almost a doubling of the coal consumption. Similarly, the energy required of the eyes and nervous system of the child to respond to the thrill of the picture increases rapidly and out of all proportion with the length of the show.

These are the main defects associated with cinematograph shows. Some are remediable, others may be mitigated by an alternation of the exhibition with other kinds of entertainment. And all of them may be reduced in intensity by shortening the duration of the show, and preventing small children from attending two shows in direct succession.

It will be asked : What evidence is there that children's eyes suffer from the picture shows ? The evidence is of such a nature that it cannot be presented by figures and percentages. Fortunately the effects are temporary, and unless the indulgence be frequent it is easily recovered from. The effects that have been set out are those which have been ascertained from personal observation, and confirmed by the observation of children of intelligent types who have been attending the shows. Indeed, as was stated at the opening, the effects are experienced by adults ; the child only suffers from this in a higher degree because of its frailer organisation. It may be asked : Is there any evidence of permanent defect arising out of attendance at the show ? It is difficult to answer this question. But there is a recent observation which I am inclined to think has some bearing on the point. The examination of the case papers of a large number of school children who have been referred to eye clinics on account of a failure to pass the standard vision tests at the schools, shows that there is an increasing number of children who on examination at the clinic are found to have nothing the matter with them. At the school they did not pass the test ; at the first examination at the clinic they did not pass the test ; when their eyes were examined nothing amiss was to be found, their eyes objectively were normal, or so nearly normal as to be quite capable of passing the standard test ; at a later subjective examination they did pass the test satisfactorily. There may be several conditions to account for these occurrences, but by far the most likely cause is a condition of fatigue in the children, so that at the time of the test they were incapable of putting out sufficient energy, either ocular or mental, to read the standard types. In some cases I have ascertained that children of this sort were habitually at the picture shows, and it is possible the increasing attendance at these shows may be associated with the increase in the number of children who fail at the vision tests without objective cause. If the normal-eyed children suffer, it is certain that the result will be more serious in those with defective eyes, and possibly lead to permanent aggravation of those defects.

So far as eyes are concerned, the best protection for the child will be secured by the following provisions : 1. The reasonable illumination of all parts of the hall not directly beside the screen. 2. The improvement of the movement of the film so as to reduce flicker; and the withdrawal of films immediately they are damaged. 3. The improvement in taking the picture so as to bring the rate of motion of the objects depicted more nearly to the natural. 4. The increase in the number of intervals to the show, and the interposition of exhibitions other than that of the optical lantern. 5. The limitation of shows for children to one hour, and the prohibition of " repeats." 6. The reservation of the children's seats to the " optimum " position in the hall—as nearly as possible in a line with the centre of the screen, and as far away from the screen as twice its full height.

MINUTES OF EVIDENCE

Mr. N. Bishop Harman, M.A., M.B., F.R.C.S. *Examined.*

1. The Chairman. You have given special attention to the effect of the cinema upon the eyes of children ?—Yes.

2. You are very careful in all you say about glare. You do conclude that the more light that can be given to the auditorium the less danger to the eyes of the children in looking upon the films ?—There is no doubt about that; it is my experience not only with the cinematograph, but also with the optical lanterns which we use largely for medical lectures. We find these are quite satisfactory even if the room is fairly light, provided there is a dark part round the screen; the screen is in a recess, and the rest of the room is quite light enough to take down notes and so forth.

3. Mr. Lamert. Do you have smoking where students are ? —Students are not allowed to smoke at lectures.

4. The Chairman. With regard to the flicker, the more rapid the change of the film, the less the effect, you say, upon the eye ? That is so. The eye is only capable of seeing a change of light within a certain speed; it varies with different people. In the case of the present films the arrangements are very much better than they used to be.

5. There is continuous improvement, is there not ?—Without doubt. The worst flicker I have seen has been in the case of coloured films, where there is an arrangement for mixing; there is a series of colours shown one after the other, and the different colours are, as it were, mixed; they are very irritating indeed.

6. With regard to a damaged or worn film, I understand sometimes it is produced very well in its new condition at the great or important halls, but it goes off to a cheap place when the plate has become rather damaged ?—Well, if that be so, it is particularly bad, because the cheap places are mostly used by children. I find that they have a halfpenny Saturday afternoon performance for children.

7. Then you would recommend as one remedy a happy despatch and a more rapid despatch of the film ?—Certainly.

8. Then there is the effort required to refrain from blinking. Now does one get rather to stare without blinking before a film? —While the film is being exposed the tendency is to stare; then afterwards the blinking is excessive, because, as we get fatigued, the tendency is to blink so as to wash the eye more and more, and to remove the sensation of " crumbiness " which comes to every one when the eye is fatigued.

9. You are strongly in favour of a short entertainment for children?—Oh, yes; I think an hour ample for any children.

10. You are also in favour of the subjects being many for children instead of only one or two?—Well, I would not like to dogmatise on the subject. It is quite possible there might be a whole play, for instance, but the ideal is, it should be broken up by frequent intervals, and, if possible, there should be two sections or more. It is a good thing if a recitation or a song came on to break the pictures. That would be a great help for children, particularly.

11. In your opinion, should children be farther away from the screen than adults?—I suggest that the distance should be, at least, twice the height of the screen.

12. It would be better still farther back, would it not?—Farther back you would have a great effort to see.

13. Your remedies would make, in your judgment, for very great improvement for the children seeing at a cinema?—Yes. I am sure they are quite simple matters and within the range of possibility.

14. DR. SALEEBY. Will you define " glare "? I am not quite certain as to what you mean by " glare "?—Glare is produced by a point of light in a dark place. We do not suffer from glare in daylight, because the light is so diffused, although daylight is immensely more powerful than any artificial light. Exposure of the eyes to a naked, unbalanced, artificial light produces immediate effects, the sensation is as though you are partially blinded; you cannot see the things at which you are looking. That is an example of glare.

15. Then you think glare cannot be dissociated from picture palaces? You have not recently been to picture palaces where you found no glare at all?—Quite recently I went to the Scala, which I believe, is supposed to be about the best, and the glare was manifest. I am very sensitive to glare myself, and I have never yet found any of these exhibitions free from it.

16. You are yourself more sensitive than most people to glare, are you?—I would not say than most people. I took a number of children purposely to check these impressions, and they gave me very interesting accounts of what they felt.

17. You speak of the optimum position. The more expensive seats are further back, as a rule, than the optimum position, are they not?—Well, at the Scala the most expensive seats were, as far as I could judge with the eye, perhaps two and a half to three screens back.

18. Take the Pavilion at the Marble Arch; the expensive seats there must be, I should say, six times the height of the screen?—Is there a tremendously powerful lantern there?

19. Oh, yes. Mind you, I like your optimum position; I never go to the farther back seats myself, and I gather that what you say is that at many of these cinema theatres the higher priced seats are too far back?—Yes.

20. The distortion of which you have spoken tells very strongly, does it not, in those converted theatres where you have people at the side and at all sorts of vile angles to the screen?—Yes. I was once in a box when a cinema performance was given, and it was atrocious.

21. Then you would prescribe an optimum form from your point of view as an oculist?—Yes.

22. There is a definite point there which you lay down for the proper shape of the building of these places?—Yes, I should say that, but I rather incline not to lay any stress upon this so far as adults are concerned, because as soon as they find they have had enough they go; but it is not so with the children; the children will hang on to the very end; they miss nothing. So that I should not lay much stress upon special buildings, provided you secure the best seats for the children.

23. That also applies as much to being above the screen as at the side, does it not?—Yes.

24. Say with the gallery position at theatres like Terry's in the Strand?—I should think that would be very unpleasant.

25. THE CHAIRMAN. It is better to look down than up?—Oh, much easier.

26. DR. SALEEBY. Could you give us some definition as to what constitutes too frequent indulgence in this form of entertainment?—I should say once a week is quite enough for any child.

27. Now as regards your evidence, it is very non-statistical, of course?—Yes. You could work out statistics in plenty on flicker.

28. And you could work up attendances of people whose eyes are susceptible of injury?—Yes, but you cannot check those who are individually susceptible; it cannot be done. There have been a great many tests, but when these tests are made it is found that they are never quite satisfactory.

29. The injury is never organic, but purely functional?—Quite functional.

30. Of course, as a clinician you see the cases that are injured, and the hosts that are not do not trouble?—That is true; I believe some of the hosts we do not see are injured, but not so seriously as to bring them to us.

31. It might very well be that the overwhelming majority have no occasion to come to you?—The overwhelming majority reckon that there must be a small penalty upon all their pleasurable indulgences.

32. You lay stress in this paragraph, which seems to me so

extremely weighty, upon intervals. You want the picture part of the show shut down for a time?—Yes.

33. You want musical interludes, and so forth?—Yes, that is the kind of thing.

FIFTH DAY

Monday, February 5, 1917,

Principal A. E. GARVIE, D.D., in the chair.

STATEMENT BY ONE OF THE EXAMINERS
From the British Board of Film Censors

PRÉCIS

WHEN Mr. Redford commenced the Censorship the only two rules he laid down were that the living figure of Christ should not be permitted and that nudity should be in no circumstances passed.

The examiners, therefore, have been guided by the broad principle that nothing should be passed which in their opinion was calculated to demoralise an audience or any section of it; that could be held to extenuate crime or to teach the methods of criminals; that could undermine the teachings of morality; that tended to bring the institution of marriage into contempt; that lowered the sacredness of family ties. They have refused their sanction to incidents which brought into contempt public characters acting in their capacity as such; *i. e.* officers wearing H.M. uniform, ministers of religion, ministers of the Crown, ambassadors and representatives of foreign nations, judges, etc. They have objected to subjects calculated to wound the susceptibilities of foreign peoples, of members of any religion. And, especially recently, they have rejected films calculated and possibly intended to foment social unrest and discontent.

Their experience has made it very clear to the examiners that every film must be judged on its own merits, and that, while it was very essential to be consistent, it was impossible to aim at strictly logical decisions. They have had to consider the impression likely to be made on an average audience which includes a not inconsiderable proportion of people of immature judgment. A harmless story may become unacceptable through the actions of the characters, and a film which depicts no indecent or even suggestive action may be prohibited from the nature of the story. The examiners have also been compelled to take objection to what I may term the cumulative effects caused by the repetition of, and insistence on, incidents which in themselves might be passed, the impression in such cases being that certain lapses from virtue or honesty were usual, and even unavoidable, in the given circumstances; young and unthinking people might thus be accustomed to the idea that such lapses were excusable and even deserving of sympathy.

In stories turning on the relations of the sexes the examiners have had many difficult problems. They have frequently to decide where embraces overstep the limits of affection or even passion, and become lascivious, the efforts of the actors, and still more the actresses, to obtain a dramatic effect leading them sometimes to proceed to lengths which are quite prohibitive.

Naturally when such a vast number of stories is presented the variations on the " triangle " theme are numerous and often complicated. Some of them, while involving departure from virtue, do not necessarily suggest actual depravity; and there is a distinction between errors caused by love, even if guilty love, and the pursuit of lust, and the examiners have always endeavoured to eliminate manifestations of the latter character. In the same way they have always objected to scenes in which the intention of rape is so clearly shown as to be unmistakable.

The examiners are glad to say that they have succeeded in stopping entirely the introduction into this country of " first nights " subjects which at the beginning were fairly numerous.

At one time there were numerous stories in which attempt was made to obtain dramatic interest by representing the characters as bearing abnormal relations to each other; for instance, a father making love to his unknown daughter, or a brother and sister unknown to each other as such, etc. These situations have appeared to the examiners as repugnant, and they have insisted upon such alterations in the sub-titles as would remove the unwholesome complications.

The question of seduction is very difficult. In these cases much depends upon the treatment, and, when the story is depicted with restraint, it seems impossible to exclude the subject as the theme of a story. But the examiners have objected to the treatment of this subject in such a way as to suggest that a poor girl is morally justified in succumbing to temptation in order to escape from sordid surroundings and uncongenial work.

It is impossible to refer to all of the many different developments of the sexual play; but the examiners have steadily borne in mind, when dealing with them, the general principle that, while it is impossible to exact that poetic justice should always overtake the evildoer, it is at least essential that no halo should be placed round the heads of the delinquents.

There have been stories which portrayed the progress and surroundings of women leading immoral lives. The examiners have held that these cannot be wholesome, as the exhibition of gaiety, luxury and admiration might prove more of a lure to young girls of weak principles than the debacle at the end might be of a deterrent. For much the same reason they have objected to scenes in which a woman is shown dressing up and rouging and painting preparatory to going out into the streets for an immoral purpose. They have, in fact, steadily discouraged all scenes showing vice in an attractive form, even though retribution may follow, and the story claims to afford a warning and point a moral.

In dealing with " crime " subjects the examiners have had to discriminate between such stories as are calculated, in their judgment, to familiarise young people with theft, robberies and crimes of violence, and so to leave them to conclude that such are normal incidents and not very greatly to be reprobated, and those stories which deal with " costume " crime—*i.e.* cowboy shootings, " feather and rapier " stabbings, bandits' and Mexicans' robberies, etc. It seems to them that the latter are regarded by the young as simply dramatic and thrilling adventures, with no connection with their own lives or probable experiences. When the same crimes are committed by people in ordinary dress and home surroundings, the examiners aim at eliminating details which make them too realistic, and entirely forbid any scenes which depict the actual method of committing theft. In this case, also, they draw a distinction between subjects in which theft, burglary or murder is simply the dramatic motive round which the story with other interests turns, and those in which the crime is the sole and entire interest.

In dealing with indecorum of dress, the examiners are met with the objection that on the stage a licence has been permitted which makes it very difficult for them to enforce so strict a standard as seems to them desirable, but they insist upon deletion when the dress appears to be meant to be indecent or suggestive. No absolute rule can be applied. In the case of bathing dresses, if girls are shown swimming and bathing there is little harm, but if they pose before the camera with the evident intention of displaying their shape, it is regarded as prohibitive.

When the Censorship was instituted it was decided that two forms of certificate should be issued; one (U) for such films as were considered suitable for universal exhibition, and one (A) for films for exhibition before adults only. The Censorship, however, had no means of enforcing that children should not be admitted to performances where films with the A certificate were shown.

MINUTES OF EVIDENCE

One of THE EXAMINERS. *Examined.*

1. THE CHAIRMAN. How long have you been an examiner of films?—Four years.

2. We should like to know whether the Censor, Mr. Redford, saw every film or whether he acted on the advice of an examiner? —He did not see every film. The practice was that there were four examiners who examined the films. If there were no objections or if there was nothing questionable about the films, they were simply passed and a certificate granted. If we questioned anything, we referred the films to Mr. Redford and he saw the films himself and decided. We used to report to him, and then he decided whether to grant or withhold the certificate, and whether he should ask the producer to make such alterations as in his opinion would make the films acceptable.

3. Would a film be objected to on the report of one examiner ? —No. We were four examiners, and two examined each film.

4. You say : " They have rejected films calculated and possibly intended to foment social unrest and discontent." Would those be the films which represented life in the slums or the conditions of labour of men and women ?—No ; we considered scenes depicting conditions under which the people live, or the hard life in the slums to be perfectly legitimate. What we had especially in our minds were the films which came forward at one time in which the actual conflict between Capital and Labour was depicted in rather crude colours. There were strike breakers, armed forces, killing, the throwing of bombs, and mines laid to blow up the strikers. The impression was that these were of such a nature that they could not be passed.

5. Would you consider that some kind of standard should be applied to the films to deal with the place in which they are shown ? Do you feel that some audiences like different films ?— Well, our feeling is that as a general fact people going to see a play do not go without making some inquiry. From what we hear it seems more likely that people would drop into a cinema show more at haphazard than they would into a theatre. Consequently, we think that greater discretion ought to be exercised in the class of films, because you are dealing with a different kind of audience and a more comprehensive audience.

6. I should like to know whether statistics have been kept of the number of films submitted and passed and the number refused ? —Our secretary, Mr. Brook Wilkinson, has all these particulars. I know generally, but I could not give you the exact figures.

7. MR. NEWBOULD. At a meeting of the British Board held last week a resolution was passed to the effect that the whole of the books and papers should be placed at the disposal of the Commission ?—I have here the annual report. I do not think the last one has been brought up-to-date, but, roughly speaking, I think the year before the number of subjects submitted was 4767.

8. THE CHAIRMAN. It would be interesting to know what proportion of that number was passed and what was rejected.— What you mean by rejected is those films to which objection is taken. Of course, the number finally rejected is not so very large, because a great deal can be done by the modification of what the trade calls the subject title, that is the letterpress, and scenes can be modified. You cannot alter the picture, but you can cut bits out and make a scene perfectly different. To illustrate that, you can understand in the case of a very fervent embrace, that if the man is represented as a husband of a wife, and the woman represented as a wife of a husband, it is inexpedient; but if they are husband and wife it is legitimate, and possibly, laudable. And so a great deal can be done by the alteration of the subject titles.

9. We have been told that in some parts of the States the rejection of a film in one State was used as a means of advertising it as something specially attractive in another. I understand that films not passed by the Censor may be exhibited in this country ?—That is

so, and of course, in our position as censors we regard that as a regrettable fact.

10. You do not know any instance where actually the refusal of the licence for the film has been used as an advertisement of the film ?—I have no idea of such a case.

11. Have you any information as to what proportion of American as contrasted with British films are either approved or not passed ?—I do not know, but I do not think that is a point on which we keep statistics. As far as possible we judge a film absolutely on its merits, without regard to who sends it in or the country of origin or anything connected with it.

12. Have the reasons for objection been in any way classified ?—Yes. I have brought here a copy of the report for the year 1915, and we have got a considerable list of reasons for the rejections; and when I say rejections, I mean objections. We have got forty-three reasons.

13. The members of the Commission might have copies of that report, I take it ?—With pleasure.

14. When one of these films you have passed is accepted is it intimated to the audience that the film about to be put on has been passed by the Censor ?—It should be, and we hope it is. I find that the majority of films have the certificate on them. That is the idea of the gentlemen who send us the films to go through.

15. REV. CAREY BONNER. There is one point I should like to ask information on. THE EXAMINER states here that the living figure of Christ is never permitted in the films ? — Not the materialised figure.

16. Is it not a fact that recently there has been a film with the figure of our Lord represented by the actor who took the part in the Ober-Ammergau play ?—The only one we have ever passed was a film called " Quo Vadis." In that there was a figure of Christ, and the figure moved, and therefore it was a materialised figure of Christ. It was represented in a kind of filmy way, and presented an appearance of an apparition and not a corporal body. That is the only case in which we have ever passed a materialised figure of Christ.

17. It is quite clear if there has been such a film it has not been before your Board ?—That is so.

18. It is clear that there are a number of cinema theatres exhibiting pictures that are never brought to your Board ?—I have no idea how many there are, but the majority make a stipulation that all the films to be exhibited are furnished with our certificate. I should not like to say that there was any theatre that made a practice of showing films that were uncensored.

19. Supposing an exhibitor, having got the film passed by you, cut it and inserted certain pictures that are undesirable, could you prohibit that, have you any power at all ?—Being a voluntary Board, we have no power of control except in extreme cases. I think I might say that if we found any one doing that we should never look at a film of his again. It would be known that his films would not be examined by us. That is all the control we have.

20. So that if a man did such a thing you could do nothing to him?—We could do nothing. We have never had an instance of that sort. There may have been cases where an accident has arisen. When we have asked for certain deletions or modifications of scenes, sometimes several films are printed, and it is possible that one might have been shown without the alterations having been made. I do not say it is so, but it is possible that that might have been an error and not a deliberate act.

21. THE SECRETARY. If you put your certificate on a film and the film afterwards is altered, have you any power to withdraw your certificate which is being exhibited in a film which you did not pass?—Absolutely.

22. Have you ever done that?—No.

23. You have never had occasion to do it?—No.

24. You have no knowledge of any film which you have censored being altered in such a way that you withdrew your certificate? —I have no recollections of such a thing. I do not think it has happened.

25. MR. GRAVES. Is there any distribution of the duties of the four examiners, or do they all do the same work?—We all do the same kind of work. As things began to develop we thought possibly it would be inexpedient that the same two examiners should always work together, because it might be noticed that the same two initials were always on together, and, therefore, we made a practice of changing the examiners week by week. Again it is possible that we do not all see the same thing from the same point of view, and we think it useful that one opinion should be supplemented by another in different weeks.

26. Supposing two of you thought there was something objectionable, would you consult the other two, or would you act on your own considerations and go to the Censor and lay the doubtful point before him?—If one examiner felt strongly that there was something objectionable, we have considered that the matter should be referred.

27. If there was a minor objection in the film, would you have power to cut it out without going to the Chief Censor, or has everything to be done by the Censor himself?—When Mr. Redford was there, every objection, however slight, was referred to him. Mr. Redford interviewed the producer, explained the situation to him, the deletion was made and the certificate granted by Mr. Redford.

28. Perhaps you can give us a rough idea of the number of films put before the Chief Censor in a week?—When Mr. Redford was alive I should say perhaps ten a week, but I do not know for certain.

29. So that the main part of the work would be done by the examiners?—Every film was examined by the examiners.

30. Did you have anything to do with that film " From the Manger to the Cross ",from which the figure of our Lord appeared? Was that passed by you?—I think that was about four years ago. I cannot say I remember it.

31. You know a good deal of fuss was made about it, and it was to a certain extent censored and produced in another way; it was

not considered so objectionable, but it was not exhibited in some parts of the country at all ?—I am afraid I should find it very difficult to give any valuable information about any one particular film.

MR. NEWBOULD. May I say that within my knowledge that film was rejected by the British Board.

32. MR. GRAVES. When you say you object to the nude female figure that does not apply to statuary ?—No ; but we have objected to statuary when we have seen it shown in certain positions which seem to us to be indecorous, and we have asked for it to be cut out.

33. At the same time, you would confess that a half-nude figure or a scarcely concealed woman's form might be more suggestive than a piece of statuary ?—Personally I see nothing indecent in a nude figure ; if it is properly shown it is not indecent. It would make it very difficult to draw distinctions, and therefore the rule was laid down that the nude should be excluded from the film.

34. DR. SALEEBY. You mean the living nude ?—Yes.

35. MR. GRAVES. Bathing, for example ?—In bathing, of course they are clothed, but certainly we should object to bathing if they were in the nude.

36. MR. LAMERT. Has your experience led you to the general conclusion that it is possible to reduce to writing rules for governing the Censor ?—No.

37. You would say that no set of rules can be formed as everything has to be judged on the merits of the film ?—You must consider that in one year we had something approaching five thousand subjects, and therefore I think we should have to have some one with quite exceptional powers to lay down rules. We were guided by the principle. If we were to lay down rigid rules we should have to pass things which we are now able to exclude.

38. Did you personally see a film called " —— —— —— ——— " ? Do you remember it ?—I am afraid I should not like to trust my memory to speak about any one film.

39. It is a type of religious film ; in fact, it is semi-religious. It is based on the idea of a man who loses his soul, and the object is rather to show what degradation a man comes to under certain circumstances. You have seen that sort of film ?—That sort of thing, yes, or, at least, something of that nature. Of course the Americans were rather fond of problems of that kind.

40. Now you can realise that that film has possibly affected different people in different ways ?—Yes.

41. I am alluding to this particular film because subsequently you gave it a U certificate ?—Yes.

42. And subsequently a number of opinions were received. Did you ever directly get opinions from people to say you should never have passed this film ?—We had a letter the other day from a gentleman who told us it was very depraving, but we never get any valuable criticisms.

43. I am going to read a letter from the Rev. Father Vaughan, who writes : " I can't write you anything about the '—— —— - ——.' After reading your synopsis of the story I prefer to leave

it severely alone. To me it seems a vulgar production, and runs quite counter to what I know of the genesis of good and evil. It is a false hothouse growth, and would not stand the storm of real tests. I speak plainly because life is too short and sacred to be veneered with." That is a pretty strong condemnation?—Yes, but I should gather that the gentleman did not see the film.

44. The synopsis finished him?—Well, a great deal depends upon seeing the film.

45. And of the same film the Rev. F. B. Meyer, after seeing it, writes : " This is a film which every one should see. Its exhibition can do nothing but good." You would not be prepared to say that the Rev. F. B. Meyer's standard of morals is different?—I should say that he saw the film and the other gentleman did not.

THE CHAIRMAN. What is the idea of bringing forward these two gentlemen?

46. MR. LAMERT. I want to bring forward the point that one gentleman did not see the film and the other did. I have not the authority to mention the name, but an Anglican bishop denounced it very strongly, and I had two clergymen of the Church of England who thought very strongly of it. The whole point is that some people may approve of a film and others may strongly disapprove? —I should say that that was unquestionably the case, but I think myself that some of these films are treated in rather a crude manner.

47. You see here one says that every one should see it and that it is excellent, while another says that it is not. That makes the censorship extremely difficult?—I have found it extremely difficult.

48. If you find it extremely difficult at one centre, do you think it would improve by spreading it over a large number of centres? Do you think it would meet the difficulty if you had different censors in various parts of the country?—It would add very materially to the embarrassments and difficulties of the trade.

49. It is quite clear that the temperaments of people are different. Do you think that a central body could do it sufficiently well?—I should say certainly. The sense of morality and decency is not different in different parts of the British Isles.

50. MONSIGNOR BROWN. Do you know of instances where films passed by your Board have been refused exhibition by local authorities or town councils?—I heard of one the other day, but it was refused in one town and passed on to another.

51. Do you think it is possible to override the local wishes or the local prejudices, or whatever you may choose to call them, which may lead to a different standard in different towns from the standard of the Central Board?—I should say that any local body would accept a Central Censorship.

52. In fact some local authorities have vetoed films passed by your Board?—I know of one case.

53. Liverpool did refuse?—Yes, but I rather think the objectors in that case had not seen the film. I think the name of the film was unfortunate.

54. THE SECRETARY. It was "—— ——"?—There were two films passed of which some people did not approve, and I think they took it for granted that the stories of the films were the same as the books, whereas we had taken particular care that every sort of indiscretion in the story should be changed so as to remove that objection.

55. MONSIGNOR BROWN. I think it was mentioned that this "—— ——" and "—— ——" had been turned down by the Board. I think that some one said that it had been refused approbation by the Censor?—I feel some delicacy in referring to any particular film because they come before us in a confidential capacity. The main objection was based on the name of the film.

56. Have you called attention to the American form of spelling in the script on the film?—I am glad we have not been given the task of being literary censors. The sub-titles of the American films I consider a serious evil. The grammar and the spelling and the language are deplorable, but the task of correcting them was not imposed upon us, and we do not take it upon ourselves to deal with it.

57. Have you had any complaint as to the moral conveyed by a story? If you received these complaints would you simply note them?—I hope we pay attention to every communication made to us.

58. What would happen suppose some one wrote up and said that " the story of a discarded mistress tends to excite sympathy and compassion with a woman who was leading a certain life." Would that come before your Censor or not?—I do not think one can assume that the attitude of the *bona fide* criticism of the public does not concern us, if it gives us an idea of the public feeling and standard in such matters; but, of course, one could not always assume that one letter from an individual conveyed the whole of the popular feeling on the matter. But we always pay attention to a serious complaint, and in such cases we have several times had a film back and examined it to see if the criticism is well founded.

59. I have had my attention called to a film called "—— —— ——." The gentleman who saw it took a number of boys there, and the film seemed to turn upon a married woman who, not being certain whether her first husband was dead, became attached to another man. On the script there was a final scene, a bedroom scene, with the words, " Don't be too affectionate to-night," and the gentleman said that the boys asked him what that meant?—I could not say whether I have seen that film, but it is in the nature of the Enoch Arden theme. I know one, but it may not be the same. The man turns up after ten years, in a more or less ragged state, and finds that his wife has married another man. There is a child, and the struggle in her mind is shown, whether she should revert to her first husband or stick to the man; and she says " I shall stick to the father of my child." Whether that is an immoral story or not it is extremely difficult to say.

60. Mr. Edgar Jepson. Were the bulk of the films you rejected, rejected on the ground that they stimulated sexual impulses? —I could not say whether the bulk of them did, but there were some, of course. We have had a variety of films, some of which touch upon what we consider improper lessons, and some showing pictures exciting unnecessary horror. These latter are what we call the " close up " pictures of, say, a man with a wound bleeding in his head. Then we have had some which we have objected to very much, and they are the usual poor girl film who is turned out of her lodging and cannot find work. She applies at an office, and there is the benevolent old gentleman at the desk. She asks for a post as stenographer, gets the post perhaps offered her, and the benevolent employer immediately proposes to take her out to supper. The same girl goes to another benevolent old gentleman, and he makes the same sort of offer to her. Now that might pass, but when it comes to the third or fourth employer all making the same suggestion, we say " no." You see, this is wrong, as it might cause trouble amongst girls who go out to get posts as typists, if they are led to believe that improper proposals will be made to them. It is a wrong lesson for the girl, gives her a wrong view, and tends to throw her off the idea of work. You cannot call that sexual immorality; it is improper conduct.

61. Monsignor Brown. But were the four employers Americans; it was an American film?—It looked like it.

62. Mr. Edgar Jepson. Do you reject the films which present crime as a profitable career for industrious young men?—I do not know that we have had one that holds out crime as a definite career; for the time being they have profited by it, but in a very large majority of cases they have suffered punishment in some form or other, although some of them who have paid the penalty have improved in life.

63. Dr. Marie Stopes. The film manufacturers at your suggestion take out a certain portion of a film?—Yes.

64. Have they ever sent in a plea for mercy on the ground of the expense entailed in altering the film?—During the last year it was my lot to interview these gentlemen on this kind of thing, and I have often had it pointed out that enormous sums of money have been spent on these films, and that the alteration would also cost money. We could not take that into consideration.

65. I imagine that some alterations might be inexpensive while others might be expensive?—Of course the actual cost only consists of the loss of footage. The films are sold at so much per foot, and if you cut out so many feet that means the loss to the proprietor of so many feet in hiring it out. The actual expense of cutting the film is nothing.

66. But it may have to be filled in again?—They cannot do that, because that would be a very great expense. I only know of one case where that has been done, and on that occasion the film went back to America and was redone. In that case there was an indication of the nude to which we had to object.

67. It is within my knowledge that firms refuse to allow the

I

author to have any control of his own story, on the ground that it is too costly for an author to have a scene changed. It would be a matter of interest to know how far they would go to alter a film at your suggestion ?—I should say that to really recast a film would be a very expensive thing if they had to pose before the camera. The suggestions we make mean the deletions of a scene, or the shortening of a scene, or to cut out the insertion of explanatory sub-titles so as to remove some of the objectionable features.

68. Is it within your knowledge that they have never entirely recast the play and brought the story in a different form before you as a result of your objections ?—I do not know how far I can go on that, but we have had stories recast so as to remove what appeared to be objectionable situations, but I do not think it has all been redone in the studio.

69. DR. KIMMINS. I suppose occasionally you have to condemn a film entirely as hopeless ?—Yes.

70. When you have made suggestions and those suggestions have been remedied, do you see the film in its final form ?—Not invariably; only when alterations are important, but we always have the deleted pieces sent to us.

71. COMMISSIONER ADELAIDE COX. Would you refuse to give a certificate for a burglary scene that was to be shown to children ?—We do not generally allow a very realistic scene showing the actual methods. We cannot cut out the burglary entirely, but all burglary scenes we describe as " A."

72. I have had a letter from a magistrate who points out the great harm that is done to children by cinemas that show the whole process of the burglary with the burglar's tools and so on. Can you say that you would put a stop to that ?—I cannot say that we could put a stop to it, but we use every discouragement we possibly can, and we invariably ask for the deletion of that part which shows the actual method of the burglary.

73. And of course you have no real power to prevent people showing these things if they wish to do so, despite what you say about them ?—We have no statutory power.

74. What power do these film censors really have over the four thousand theatres ?—Our relationship is that the producers came to us, and we exist in consequence of their feeling that a censorship was necessary or desirable for the good of the trade. They willingly subjected themselves to the censorship. The large majority of them, a very large proportion of the producers, sent their films to us, and we are entitled to believe that they will adhere to the terms of the contract to submit them.

75. MR. NEWBOULD. I think you were with Mr. Redford from the start, when the trade first imposed this censorship upon itself ?—Yes.

76. Did the trade endeavour to lay down the guiding principles he was to work to ?—They left it entirely with Mr. Redford.

77. And abided by the decisions ?—Yes.

78. And sometimes he might pass a film which you yourself **or your** fellow-examiners would have preferred not to pass ?—

Well, occasionally. Very occasionally it happened that Mr. Redford took what I would call a broader view of the matter than we did.

79. Since Mr. Redford's death there was an interval before another Censor was appointed, when you were responsible?— Practically for the past twelve months he was in the background.

80. You have had a new president now for some weeks. Have you observed any increased tightening up or stricter censorship? —Our present president has shown a disposition to make the meshes a little smaller.

81. DR. SALEEBY. The question has been asked about the discarded mistress causing compassion; I suppose in such a case you recollect a film or a certain precedent of such a compassion, and so pass the film?—Well, I think that could be done; but I do not think that subject should be prohibited so long as it does not exalt the unfortunate woman into a position of a martyr, but that there should simply be forgiveness or the compassion for wrongdoing.

82. PROFESSOR H. GOLLANCZ. I notice that you say that no rigid rule could be laid down. You deal with the poor girl in your evidence; what would you say if the rich girl was in that position? —I do not remember a film where the victim was a rich girl who was the subject of seduction. Of this class of film we get many, and in almost every case it is the poor girl who is the subject of the temptation.

83. MR. T. P. O'CONNOR. How many hours a day do the examiners work?—We go at ten o'clock and we work until six o'clock, and, if necessary, if the boats are late from America we stay until the work is done.

84. DR. SALEEBY. Five days a week?—Yes.

85. Seeing the pictures all the time?—Yes. When I joined this Censorship Board I read a letter from an eminent authority, an oculist, warning the public not to allow their children to attend cinema shows, as any child there for one and a half hours would be running the risk of having its eyesight impaired for life. I have been there four years, and my eyesight was not stronger than it was in childhood. I am bound to say that my eyesight is not affected. That, I think, is one point for the cinema trade.

86. MR. T. P. O'CONNOR. Is that the experience of your colleagues?—Well, they have made no complaints, but one of them adopted the precaution of wearing green-tinted glasses.

87. May I take it that the censorship of the film has to be on more rigid lines than the censorship of the drama?—Yes. You see, we have to take objection to any questionable gestures and things of that sort.

88. You have not allowed any reproduction of prize fighting on the cinema?—No. We have passed boxing on a film, but we have never allowed a prize fight.

89. You do not allow anything to appear which appears to you to be purely morbid?—We try to turn that down.

90. With regard to " —— ——," did not Mr. Redford lay

it down that books with a rather lurid reputation should be very closely examined if not rejected ?—I think that was his idea.

MR. N. B. HARMAN.[1] *Recalled.*

91. DR. SALEEBY. What conclusion have you drawn as to the distance one should be away from the screen ?—Well, I have made several experiments, and I found that taking the height twice over brought me into a position where the flickering was the smallest. The farther away I got the flickering was less noticeable.

92. Can you give any definite measurements for a cinema hall ? —It is difficult to give such measurements, as the question of the building space has a lot to do with this.

93. Children get over-excited in going to a show ?—Yes, but if they go too often this excitement wears off.

94. We were told that in Liverpool there were instructions given against music between the films, and especially against certain types of music ?—Yes, the music has a very brightening effect on you.

95. MR. KING. What is your opinion about the glare ?—I think the glare is most serious. I think the glare is everywhere where there is artificial light, and that is one thing we have been trying to eliminate in the artificial lights in school.

96. I take it that the eyesight might be defective and a child might suffer in a class, and that would be very serious to the child in its school work ?—Yes.

97. If that child were then taken to the cinema, the painful result would not necessarily be the result of the cinema ?—The cinema would aggravate the school result.

98. Probably the initial conditions might exist in the school itself and in the school work, and the cinema only be a contributory cause ?—Yes.

99. DR. KIMMINS. I suppose it would be possible to improve a building very much indeed by paying more attention to the lighting arrangements ?—Yes; and if they got a sufficient illumination of the walls at the side and back, I think that would be all right.

100. Have any experiments been performed to discover the amount of visual and mental fatigue ?—Some experiments were carried out, but it seems that when the children were examined they whipped up such reserves at the moment the tests were made that we could not pay much attention to these experiments. There was no doubt they were fatigued, but they appreciated that an experiment was being done and brought up their reserve forces to deal with it.

101. MONSIGNOR BROWN. We have had a good deal of evidence with regard to the use of the film for educational purposes. Do you think it is possible without severe strain upon the children to give them a cinematograph lesson which could be memorised

[1] See also pp. 97–104.

as a result of seeing the film ?—Yes, I am quite sure the cinemato-graph can be used without any damage to the children's eyes and with great value from an educational point of view. I have seen myself medical demonstrations which were excellent.

102. Would you say that the cinematograph demonstration would have to be restricted as to the time ?—Well, I see no harm at all in giving the children, say, one hour.

103. A continuous show ?—For the older children, yes.

104. You would not think it very educative for the children lower down in the school ?—Not for the little children. They might be shown birds and flowers and simple objects like that, as that would interest them. For any other pictures the apprecia-tion of the small child is too slow for them to understand the pictures.

105. Children under twelve ?—No, I should say under eight, the children in the infant school or the first standard.

106. MR. LAMERT. With regard to the shape of a theatre. When I was in New York I was talking to a Mr. Rotherville who is a great cinema builder, and his idea of the perfect theatre is that it should be more or less of a triangle, coming down to a point with a stage at the end ?—I made a note of that matter, and I believe the best building I know of in London for this and any sort of public demonstration or performance where the audience look at things is Dr. Horton's church at Hampstead. I went in there the other day and noticed the shape of it. It is something like a fan with the point cut off, and the sides slope rapidly, and there were galleries. The rostrum is at the point. I went round to various parts of the building, and everywhere I went you could see perfectly well. I thought for an auditorium, for a visual display, this place was ideal.

107. How many people, roughly, would it hold ?—One thousand to 1500.

108. And at the maximum point how far would it be from the rostrum or the screen ?—That is a little hard to say; four or five times the height of a good cinematograph screen.

109. That would give you 150 feet at 30 feet ?—It must have been more than that.

THE SECRETARY. I think it is about 180 to 200 feet to the back of the gallery.

110. MR. LAMERT. Do you know that a cinematograph picture was shown at the Albert Hall ?—I was not aware of that.

111. " The Miracle "—and it was seen from all parts ?—Then they must have arranged for an extra-sized screen.

MR. KING. It was thirty-four by forty-five feet.

WITNESS. That would make a great deal of difference, but they would have to have a powerful lamp.

112. MR. LAMERT. Speaking broadly, in the American theatres you have longer distances than that, and it is a curious fact that a higher price is usually paid for the gallery which is over the back ?—Well, the gallery is a better place to sit in. If you look down at a picture it is better than looking up.

113. Have you considered a frontal projection from the back? —I have seen a lantern shown from the back, but not a cinematograph.

114. It can be done?—It would have to have a fine screen.

115. You have never considered it?—I should think it would be quite impossible, as you would have to have a long building.

116. I mean the projection from behind altogether?—There you lose a certain amount of light. The denser you make your screen the less light would come through it.

117. REV. CAREY BONNER. Has there been any investigation made as to the effect of the cinema on the children's eyes?—I am afraid not, it will always be a matter of opinion.

118. I suppose your judgments are based on the children's eyes you have examined?—Exactly.

SIXTH DAY

Monday, February 12, 1917,

The BISHOP OF BIRMINGHAM in the chair.

STATEMENT OF MR. JOHN KAY, B.A. (LOND.),

Head Master, " Major Lester " County School, Liverpool, Pres. Lancs. County Assoc. of Teachers (N.U.T.), Former Pres. Nat. Assoc. of Head Teachers

PRÉCIS

I HAVE been for fifteen years head master of schools mainly attended by children of a low social class. I have made inquiries in my own school into the relations between the school and the cinema, and have gathered the views of teachers in neighbouring schools in the city of Liverpool. I am also in possession of the general opinion of the teaching body on the subject.

A committee of the Lancs. Teachers' Association has for some months been gathering information from a large number of representative schools in the county. A full report is now in course of preparation. Some of the results are adverted to in this statement.

While appreciating the cinema as a popular and legitimate form of public amusement, teachers are gravely concerned about the results of many injurious films that are exhibited from time to time. That such films are very frequent is clear from a scrutiny of a large number of synopses of entertainments, as well as from personal observation.

At an inquiry in Liverpool held by justices and the education authority into the subject of juvenile crime, all three teacher witnesses were of opinion that the cinema is a factor in the problem.

In an inquiry recently conducted by the Lancs. Teachers' Association into the same subject, our correspondents in large industrial areas almost invariably suggested the cinema as a contributory cause.

Returns from ninety-five Lancashire schools, embracing 31,990 children, show that during a single week in December 12,251 children attended once or more, a percentage of 38·3 of the school population. It becomes quite clear that the children must be absolutely protected from any deleterious influences in the exhibitions.

From twenty-three schools came reports of misdemeanours, mostly petty thefts, which were attributed to the influence of the cinema. Children frequently state that they have stolen " to get money for the pictures." Teachers recognise that it is most difficult to establish cause and effect, and that in many cases the thefts would probably have occurred in any case. The picture shows only afford a ready means of disposing of part of the booty. But two facts clearly emerge. In the first place, children of criminal tendency in a school are found among the most regular frequenters of the shows. Secondly, the " street trading " class in large centres, already beset by many handicaps, are frequent attenders at the " second house " when their papers or other wares are sold.

In a few cases the attendance and punctuality of children are thought to have been adversely affected by attendance at shows, but the great majority of teachers have observed no change in this respect.

Frequent complaints have been made of physical evils resulting from habitual attendance. Although our inquiries have revealed a few cases of eye trouble, and nervous or other affections declared by medical men to be the result of such attendance, it must be stated that the cases bear a very small proportion to the number using the pictures, and it is seldom quite clear that the trouble is the result of the cause assigned.

Inquiries were made with a view to ascertaining what educational effects can be ascribed to the cinema. The replies were almost entirely negative. The great majority of teachers consulted have observed no perceptible increase in general knowledge, or vocabulary, or other reflection of cinema subject or incident, except in direct composition on the subject of the cinema, where it becomes evident that some little addition has been made to the children's stock of general knowledge and to their vocabulary, notably by American slang phrases. It seems probable also that there is a development of the imaginative faculty. The addition to the child's stock of mental pictures provided by the better films must be of value, especially to the children who live in the cramped and barren slum environment.

There does not appear to be a large place for the cinema in primary school work. In the essentials of instruction it can be of no service. As an interesting and attractive aid, purely illustrative, to the teaching of a small group of subjects, industrial geography, travel, contemporary history, natural history, and the like, there is a small field for it. Used in conjunction with lecture and letterpress it can give much colour to fact and terminology, but the cost would have to be small to justify its employment.

In conclusion, I venture to suggest that every film might be licensed either (*a*) for adults only, or (*b*) for general use; and that children should not be admitted when any of the former are on exhibition. For the rest, I can only urge insistence upon a high standard of cleanliness and sanitation in all cinema houses, and the protection of the plastic eyes of children by properly regulating their distance from the screen.

MINUTES OF EVIDENCE

Mr. John Kay, B.A. (Lond.). *Examined.*

1. The Chairman. You say teachers appreciate the cinema as a popular and legitimate form of public amusement, but that certain films which were produced were considered to be dangerous and injurious to the children ?—Quite.

2. Can you give us one or two special instances you came across ?—I do not know that I could recollect the titles, but I can certainly quote some of the films. I have seen as late as last week a film shown which I consider quite unsuitable for children. The film was with regard to the sex problem.

3. You would say, then, that the general films dealing with the sex problem are undesirable for the children altogether ?— Most inevitably.

4. Now with regard to the question of inciting to crime, by what we may call films dealing with criminal incidents. Have you any opinion with regard to that, I mean the effect upon children ?—Yes, I have a very strong opinion. I do not think it is generally understood to what extent these pictures can be an incentive to children. It is a matter of common knowledge amongst teachers, particularly amongst teachers in the infants' schools, that the very suggestion even of warning against anything means to the child an incentive to do the offence. That is not generally understood by people; if it were they would understand that pictures of a certain character might be a real incentive to the children.

5. Films are largely attended by your children ?—Yes.

6. And cinemas are far and away the most popular class of entertainment ?—Far and away.

7. Have you known cases where money has been taken by the children so that they can attend the cinemas ?—Well, many have taken money and used it to attend, but it is a very difficult matter to say how far the pictures were an incentive or an afterthought.

8. Have you anything to say with regard to eye trouble produced by going to cinemas? Well, we have had a number of replies, but there again we have difficulty. You cannot establish cases of defect.

9. What educational value would you put upon the cinema?—I am afraid slight. I have not been able to observe any effects.

10. There would be, would there not, a widening of knowledge of certain subjects?—Yes, but that is only small, because, after all, the purely educational films are very rare.

11. Now, with regard to the films that purport to be educational and helpful, such as the way in which flowers come out, showing them from their earliest infancy to their fullest completeness. We have had it put before us that it is rather harmful showing the film that way because of the rapidity with which the matter is shown. This would give the impression to the child that it is all done in about three minutes?—I do not think that argument is a very weighty one. I think the child, if not of very tender years, would be quite able to adjust the balance in its own mind.

12. Would you see some advantage in films of that sort?—Undoubtedly.

13. And films that are strictly educational you would approve of?—Of course.

14. You would not expect the whole film entertainment to be educational all through?—No, that would be extravagant.

15. You say there does not seem to be a large place for the cinema in primary school work? We are dealing here with a matter which is still more or less in its infancy. Don't you think there are possibilities with regard to the future of the cinema?—It is these possibilities I have tried to estimate. As regards the humanities, that is, writing, and reading, and also arithmetic, it is of no value, and those are the subjects on which the great bulk of our time has to be centred.

16. You lay great stress upon the high standard of cleanliness and sanitation in the cinema. Do you find in Lancashire that there are some defects of this kind in the cinema houses?—I should not say generally, but we have had indications that advances might be made in the direction of cleanliness, and my own observation has shown to me on many visits that the sanitation with regard to the air is not all what it might be.

17. Have you any information as to immoral conduct of any kind between children and adults in the cinema house?—None; I have neither met a case nor had one quoted.

18. PRINCIPAL GARVIE. A suggestion was made that films might specially be marked as suitable for children. Do you approve of such a suggestion?—Yes.

19. MR. T. P. O'CONNOR. Are you aware that already in the present form of censorship there is a distinction made in films for adults and films for children?—No, I was not aware of that.

20. There are two kinds of films, one marked " U," which means Universal, for adults and children, and another marked " A," which means it can only be exhibited to adults?—That is new to me.

21. You think that is a good arrangement?—I quite approve of such an arrangement, but I still say that I do not think the

classification which exists now has been satisfactory in its application. I have seen frequently films which must have been passed for general consumption which I consider totally unfit for children. The idea of a separate classification for children and general use I consider to be a good one.

22. Of course, children is a general term; the child of eight and the child of fourteen, fifteen or sixteen have quite different opinions?—Quite.

23. I take it that as there is a difference in the class of children, so there is a difference in the impression they have with regard to certain films?—Yes.

24. I understand that the film that makes a profound impression on children is the story of adventure rather than the stories of love; that is, up to a certain age?—Yes, I think that is so.

25. So that a story of love which would produce no impression, and, indeed, might be profoundly uninteresting, to a child up to twelve or fourteen years of age, might make a different impression upon a child beyond that age?—Yes.

26. I take it that a boy of fourteen or fifteen or sixteen is what I might call a melodramatist in the sense that adventure appeals to him more than any other form of film?—That is so.

27. And therefore your opinion is that what I might call the crook drama has to be very carefully scrutinised?—Yes, I quite agree.

28. Mr. Newbould. In regard to these inquiries which have been made as to the influence of the cinema upon children, can you explain how they are carried out? Were questions put to the children or merely answered by the observations of the teachers?—The question as regards the numbers of attendances would be put to the children, and the other question, as to the educational effect and as to the criminal effect, so to speak, obviously could only be answered by an expression of opinion from the teachers.

29. Dr. Saleeby. About these sexual films. Have you heard of cases where injury has been done to a child by seeing this type of play?—No, I can hardly conceive the possibility of a danger.

30. In point of fact you have no experimental evidence of such an injury. I suppose you assume there is an injury, but you will agree that a great deal which is very significant to an adult would be like water rolling off a duck's back to a child?—Yes; but my opinion would vary with the age of the child.

31. I suggest the cinema would be of great aid in teaching, say, natural history to a town child. How would you teach a child natural history except by such a means?—Natural history is not a subject for the curriculum of the ordinary school.

32. Mr. Crook. It has been suggested that the film would be extremely useful in teaching geography in schools. Would you show only one film in a school, or would you not require separate films for each class?—Each class has its separate curriculum in geography.

33. And therefore you would want seven films shown each week for geography alone ?—That is so.

34. Would you not prefer to have a picture of a set scene which can be shown every time, rather than films to illustrate geography ?—Yes, since the one is capable of much more liberal treatment. You can get a far larger number to illustrate in the matter of pictures than you could with films.

35. With regard to natural history, I think with a great variety of birds the child would be confused ?—I should think so.

36. MR. KING. You say : "Teachers are gravely concerned about the results of many injurious films that are exhibited from time to time, films of a vulgar, suggestive, or openly indecent character." Will you give us an instance of a vulgar picture ?— I can remember seeing a film in which the hero was called " Fatty," and in one of the scenes there was the loss of his nether garments, and he goes into a dancing-room with a blanket wrapped round his lower extremities.

37. Have you ever seen an openly indecent picture, or do you know anybody that has ?—I know of many people who have told me they have seen indecent pictures. I do not remember one that I can describe, but I have certainly seen programmes depicting openly indecent pictures.

38. In Liverpool ?—No, I cannot say exactly where they came from. I had a large number of programmes collected, and I selected a number of them which were of the class mentioned there.

39. Do you know of the rules issued by the Justices of Liverpool and also copied by a large number of other towns, amongst them Burnley, Blackburn and St. Helens ? (Mr. King read extracts from these rules.) Did you know these rules were in existence ?—Yes, I know they have been in existence for two years past.

40. And yet you say there are indecent films shown—Yes.

41. That is not very kind to the magistrates ?—I am sorry. I do not say Liverpool, but I see no reason to qualify what I have said.

42. I see you say there was an inquiry by the justices and the educational authorities into the question of juvenile crime, and that the teachers said the cinema was the factor of the problem. What kind of evidence was given ; evidence of fact or evidence of opinion ?—Facts as far as we could secure them, but largely opinion, of course.

43. You say something about the cinema proprietor or cinema company receiving the booty. Do you suggest that the cinema proprietors were the receivers ? Will you qualify that ?—I do not wish to give any impression of that kind. It has been alleged that children steal with the direct intention of getting money to see the films. I say it is not possible to say that the children have stolen for that purpose. It is probably an afterthought, and in that way the cinemas afford a child the opportunity of getting rid of his booty.

44. Any more than a sweetstuff shop?—No more, except that they are more prolific in Liverpool.

45. Then you refer to the street trading class, and you object to them getting into the theatre after nine o'clock. Do you think the picture palaces are worse places than their homes?—Their homes are bad enough. We are speaking of children under fourteen years of age.

46. Commissioner Adelaide Cox. You say: "Children of criminal tendency in a school are found amongst the most regular frequenters of the shows." Do you mean they go to the cinemas and increase their wrong tendencies?—I do not know. I only say it is a well-known fact among the teachers that they are the class that visit the theatres largely.

47. The Chairman. What do you mean by criminal tendencies?—I was thinking of children who had been known to be guilty of theft sometimes.

48. Dr. Kimmins. Do you find that the boys or the girls are more attracted to the cinema?—I have drawn very little difference. Of the 30,000 children that our inquiries included, 16,000 were boys and 14,000 girls.

49. Have you discovered at what age the cinema gives the greatest attraction to the children?—I should say about twelve.

50. It falls off at thirteen and fourteen?—Yes, I think my largest numbers were about Standard V. I would not say it falls off; it is rather that our class diminishes towards that age.

51. I suppose your view of the educational possibilities of the film is that the action is too rapid on the screen for the children to derive much instruction?—Yes, very largely.

52. Dr. Marie Stopes. You mean that the cinema as it is at present has not the educational value. You are not contemplating the ideal advance?—I scarcely know what the ideal is. I think it will be admitted that you cannot teach mathematics by the cinema, and a large proportion of our curriculum comes into the same category.

53. There are a lot of things, though, which can very well be shown on the screen, and these would have especial interest to children, such as pictures of the Niagara Falls, which are a source of electricity?—Yes, but you see our considerations must be relative to the whole of our work.

54. Do you agree that a series of films collected by teachers and circulated around the various schools would be of use?—Quite. I think that must be the way in which the cinema will probably make its appearance amongst us.

55. Mr. Edgar Jepson. I take it that you would have no objection to using the film for educational purposes, but you would be against the heavy cost at present entailed. Supposing they were cheap, would they be of great service?—Yes, within the narrow limits as regards the subjects in the curriculum. I would be delighted to welcome the cinema as an aid to teaching if it came within our needs financially.

56. The Chairman. What you mean is that there is a certain

amount of work to do in primary education. For that work the cinema is, comparatively speaking, of little value, but from the educational point of view generally you consider the cinema may be of considerable value?—Quite.

57. MONSIGNOR BROWN. Do you think you would be able to satisfy either the local authority or His Majesty's inspector on the knowledge required and the lessons given on the films for geography.—No.

58. (Monsignor Brown read an essay written by a girl of thirteen on a picture she saw at a local cinema.) Do you think that girl has followed the plot of that little drama without grasping anything more than the girl going out with the boy and the father?—It would appear that she had grasped it.

58. Would you think the impression made on the child's mind was that the film was undesirable?—It does not certainly appear from her writing.

60. Would you think that type of film was quite harmless exhibited promiscuously to children, say, under fourteen years of age?—No, I would not.

61. Would you consider that there was a danger that the child might define what was going on?—I am sure of it. I am sure in the bulk of cases it would be defined. I think the children would generally see more than is imagined, especially the children that come from the homes I have largely in mind, because these problems are not new to them.

62. SIR JOHN KIRK. Are children at all distracted at school after they have been to the cinema the previous night?—I have not observed any ill results.

63. Does the same thing apply to the conduct in the playgrounds?—I think it is generally agreed that the children's conduct in the playground is becoming much rougher of late years.

64. Is that because of the cinema?—It is generally thought so. We have watched the games and we have seen reflected there the cinema.

65. Does that deal with their retiring-places and the scribbling on the walls?—I have not seen that.

66. THE CHAIRMAN. Did your scholars attend the music halls before the cinemas came in?—Not to any extent.

67. Are you in a position to say that the class of entertainment of the picture palace is inferior or superior to the music halls?—It is difficult to answer.

68. Do you think the cinema might be used to advantage in the night schools?—Yes, I think so.

69. DR. SALEEBY. Have you had any opportunities of comparing the roughness of these children with the roughness of, say, the upper-class children. Do you think they are rougher?—I have not had much opportunity of comparison.

70. Do you think it possible that the children during the last few years have been better fed, and are much more likely to have animal spirits?—Yes, no doubt that has an effect on the type

of games that are played. We have noticed that the cinema is with them all the time. They reproduce the story they have seen, a cowboy story, for instance.

71. MR. CROOK. In saying that the children are rougher now than they were, have you allowed for the fact that many of the parents are away at the war or on munition work?—Yes, it has been particularly noticed lately, but even before that it was noticed that the playground games were much rougher. I won't say rougher, though, but they were of another type altogether.

72. And you know that not only has the influence of the parents gone, but the influence of the male teacher in the boy school has gone?—Yes, since the war that has been particularly noticed.

73. And therefore it would be difficult to indicate how much of the increased roughness is due to the cinema?—It would be.

STATEMENT OF MR. J. W. BUNN,

*Head Master " The Cloudesley " L.C.C. School, Islington, N.,
Member of the Executive, National Union of Teachers, National
Cinematograph Association, Social Welfare Association.*

PRÉCIS

I AM head master of a school for mentally defective boys. The boys are drawn from the poorest quarters of Hoxton, and are between the ages of twelve and sixteen. I am also a member of the Executive Committee of the National Cinematograph Association, and a member of the Executive Committee of the Social Welfare Association. I have had opportunity of obtaining direct evidence on the question of the cinematograph from the children themselves, and also of hearing the opinions of many other social workers interested in the same subject.

A considerable number of people look upon the attendance of children at cinematograph entertainments with dislike if not with horror, and are apparently inclined to accuse the picture shows of being the main cause of juvenile misdemeanours. I do not agree with this view, and am firmly convinced that there is great exaggeration committed by this class. In my opinion these people are always to be found on the side of opposition to popular and cheap amusements for the working classes. The picture show is undoubtedly very popular with the women and children of the working class, but then it is still new enough to be a novelty, and it must be remembered that no other form of entertainment has ever offered to the poor the same value in variety and comfort for a very small outlay.

I have paid many visits to the shows which cater for the class amongst whom I work. I have made it a rule to go always into the cheapest seats and have carefully observed both the programme and the audience. The entertainment is not, of course, on a high intellectual level, but an entertainment on such a level would not be an entertainment at all for the lower classes. Many films of the "farce" variety are absurdly stupid, and sometimes rather vulgar. I have seen many sensational films, presenting incidents in some cases not fit for public presentation, but I have never seen a film that I should call obscene, and the most vulgar and stupid items I have witnessed are not nearly so objectionable as some " turns " I have seen on the music-hall stage.

In the summer of 1914 I took the opportunity at school of obtaining indirect evidence of the popularity of the picture show among the children. I arranged for a series of " free " drawing lessons throughout the school, that is to say lessons where, having served out materials, the teacher tells the class to draw anything they like which they have seen lately. Ninety per cent. of the drawings were of incidents seen on the films. There was no attempt to reproduce the comic or stupid items, all the drawings were on the heroic side with a sensational bias. As examples of the most common, I may mention " Rescue of Prisoners from Indians by Cowboys," " Rescue of Women and Children from Fire," " Rescue of Passengers from a Sinking Ship."

After the drawings were finished, I held long conversations with the classes in which the artists were asked to explain their own drawings. This enabled me to inquire into the conduct of the entertainments and the number of visits paid. I found that in the great majority of cases once a week was the most, a few had been twice in a week, and three boys had been three times. These last, however, I found, went to a house where children could gain admission for a halfpenny and were only in the show for about half an hour.

In the autumn of 1916 I tried the same experiment over again, and found a great change. Nearly all the pictures drawn were of war subjects—soldiers, guns, etc.; the most popular of all being Zeppelin pictures, which were wonderfully good and showed both imagination and observation. Inquiry as to the number of visits to picture shows proved that a great reduction had taken place, chiefly, I think, because the novelty has worn off.

I do not think that there is in the films any educational value worth mentioning at present. Some houses, in deference to the clamour for " improving the mind," put in films showing manufacturing processes and natural phenomena, but I believe these only bore the audience and are tolerated till the real entertainment commences again. I think that in poor neighbourhoods where the children need more change and variety in school work than among the well-to-do, it would not be a bad plan to have a cinematograph lesson once a week. It could be done by arranging for children from three or four schools to go for an hour to a suitable cinema, and the Education Authority could pay proprietors a penny per head, exactly as they do now for visits to the baths. I should arrange for the programme to be selected by the teachers, and for one of the teachers to explain the films in a few suitable words as the lesson proceeded. The film proprietors have hundreds of suitable subjects, and there would be no difficulty in getting the managers of local halls to admit school children during school hours at a penny each.

MINUTES OF EVIDENCE

Mr. J. W. Bunn.   *Examined.*

1. THE CHAIRMAN.   You are a member of the Executive of the National Cinematograph Association ?—Yes.

2. What is that association ?—It was started about a year before the war. It was a voluntary organisation, and had for its object the idea of getting some control over the cinematograph in relation to the child, especially with regard to the development of the cinematograph for educational purposes, as well as exercising some control over the popular entertainment to which children went. Of course the outbreak of the war upset the arrangements. The secretary enlisted and went abroad, and since the first two or three meetings the association has been in a comatose condition. The association was composed of representatives of educational and public bodies. At the inaugural meeting Sir Albert Rollitt occupied the chair and moved the resolution that the association should be established. There were a number of well-known public people there, including Dr. Lyttelton, Dr. Kimmins, Mr. Bernard Shaw, and representatives of other associations.

3. Do your defective children go to the cinema ?—Yes, about the same as the elementary school children.

4. And their view is pretty much the same as the view of the child not defective; they take the same interest ?—Yes, they go because it is somewhere to go in the evening.

5. You say " the picture show is undoubtedly very popular with the women and children of the working class." Do you mean to exclude the man ?—I do not think the working man goes as much as the women and children.

6. The working man likes going to another public institution ?—Yes; I suppose you mean he prefers going into the public-house ?

7. And on the whole even those people who object to the cinema might prefer that the working man should go to the cinema and not the public-house ?—Quite so.

8. You lay stress upon the cheapness of the cinema as one of the attractions ?—Yes, and upon the variety of the entertainment and the general comfort. They have a comfortable seat in a warm, well-ventilated hall.

9. You have gone as a rule in the cheap seats ?—Yes, I always go into the threepenny seats.

10. That means the seats nearest to the film ?—Yes.

11. Have you found any effect on your own eyes through being so near the film ?—No, not a bit, but I must say that I have not enjoyed the entertainment.

12. " The entertainment is not, of course, on a high intellectual level." Now I sometimes go to an entertainment because I do not want something very highly intellectual; I want to be amused.

You agree that amusements and the brightening of life are helpful to some people?—I think so.

13. You say, " Many films of the farce variety are absurdly stupid and sometimes rather vulgar." Farce need not always be vulgar?—Quite so.

14. It does happen that what to one person seems vulgar would not be thought so by another?—That is true.

15. Can you give us instances of sensational films which present incidents not fit for public presentation?—The sensational films I object to are those that depict in detail horrible scenes of torture, such as where the robbers get hold of a police officer or something of that sort, and proceed to torture him, with the inevitable motor-car dashing up at the correct moment. I saw a case the other night. It was really wonderful as regards the ingenuity of the film, because the robbers got the police officer, a detective, tied his ankles together, and then strung him up by his feet on to a hook on the ceiling and cleared out. Well, he hung there a considerable time, and commenced to swing backwards and forwards, increasing the swing each time until he was able to grasp the telephone box on the wall. He then got hold of the telephone, and was able to telephone to headquarters. It was really very depressing to watch the man's expression; in fact, I do not think it was a fit thing to see.

16. You realise there are certain theatrical pieces to which the same criticism would apply?—Yes, and I say that a lot of the attack on the cinema is quite unfair because people are not taking any notice of other things which are just as objectionable.

17. You arranged a number of " free " drawing lessons. Was that in your defective school?—Yes.

18. Does the result lead you to the impression that the more permanent effect in the cinema entertainments is produced by the things that are not comic; that they forget the comic things sooner than they do the others?—They forget the comic, but they remember the sensational and romantic part.

19. You say that some of the children have been three times in a week, to halls where children can obtain admission for one halfpenny. Are there many halls you know of where the halfpenny admission is still in existence?—No, I do not know of many. It appears that the children with the half-pennies are stood on one side, and the attendant takes them in and puts them in one seat. After they have seen three pictures out they go.

20. Now you have noticed since the war that the pictures they draw are mainly war pictures, and whatever for the moment is the leading thing?—I do not mean that they draw cinema pictures. I did not mean that. On the first occasion they drew cinema pictures, but latterly they drew war pictures.

21. You say that the novelty of the cinema has worn off, and there is a reduction in the attendance. Does that lead you to the idea that in a year or two of cinema shows the children care less for them?—Personally I think so.

K

22. With regard to the educational value ?—The cinema might be used in education.

23. By the State ?—Quite so.

24. You would not consider it the duty of the management of a cinematograph entertainment to be sufficiently philanthropic to educate the children who ought to be educated by the State ?—I do not think it ought to be left in their hands, because they are not the people to know what education is.

25. But you would like special entertainments to be arranged for children in order to help the educational question forward ?— Yes, I think there is room for that. I say that the way to do it is to combine sufficient schools to take a hall and then let the teachers take the children there.

26. Mr. Lamert. You gave us one or two reasons for the popularity of the cinema. One is its low price. You do not mention one particular point, and that is the question of time. To a cinema show a person can go at any time ?—That is another reason for its popularity, no doubt.

27. In the modern stress of work don't you think it is a good thing for grown-up people that there should be a cheap show to give them a little entertainment after their work ?—I agree.

28. Do you think it is equally good for children that after the work of the school they should have some relaxation of this sort ? —Yes, I think so.

29. At present is there any alternative to the cinema ?—Nothing, except the appalling entertainments provided by the Churches in the way of bands of hope and mission rooms, and so on. They are absolutely dreadful.

30. Monsignor Brown. You have seen some of the statements made by Mr. Cecil Chapman, the magistrate ?—Yes.

31. Do you think there is any possible means even for a metropolitan magistrate to form a valuable opinion upon the excuses given by offenders ?—That is purely a personal opinion ; I should say no.

32. It is said that the cinema depicting offences against the law has been a great incentive to young people to imitate such doings. Do you take that seriously ?—No, I think that is all nonsense.

33. Then as to the increase in petty thefts which it is alleged has been produced by the desire to go to the cinema, do you attach much importance to a boy, when asked by the magistrate, " Why did you do that ? " answering, " Because I wanted to go to the pictures ? "—I think it is absurd.

34. Dr. Marie Stopes. Do you agree that the film should be in the hands of scientific people, or teachers, or somebody who has expert knowledge of what is wanted ?—Yes, but practically all the big manufacturers have an official whom they call their educational adviser.

35. Are you satisfied with the films that are provided and labelled as educational films ?—I am satisfied there are a good many educational films, but I do not think that field has been properly explored yet. I know that Pathé Frères have lots of

splendid films from which schoolmasters can pick out, say, half a dozen films for an afternoon.

36. But they are not made in connection with any course to be given ?—No.

37. And you agree that it is not suitable to leave the matter in the hands of the manufacturers ?—That is so.

38. Do you agree with me that those who direct destructive criticism towards the cinema would be better employed in constructive work in getting cheap theatres of good quality scattered about the country ?—Yes.

39. DR. KIMMINS. Do you find that the mentally defective boys are as interested in the cinema as the normal child is ?—I think so.

40. And they like particular kinds of films ?—I think they like sensational films which they can follow better. Very dull people are very difficult to amuse.

41. Do you think there are possibilities with regard to the cinema in teaching mentally defective children ?—I should think it would want a lot of careful thinking out.

42. Could you not awaken a more vivid interest with the cinema than with the ordinary appliances ?—I think the great thing to be borne in mind for the mentally defective is to keep them physically occupied as much as possible, and I don't think there is great value for improving their intellectual outlook by looking at pictures.

43. Have you noticed whether the mentally defective boy tires of the cinema performance more rapidly than the normal child ? —I could not answer that, because I have never been in the theatre right through the whole performance. I do not think they tire while there is value left for money.

44. COMMISSIONER ADELAIDE COX. When you compare the cinema shows with the mission halls and bands of hope, are you speaking of the atmosphere of the place or the entertainment provided ?—I think both are unspeakably dreadful. There is also an absolute want of control in keeping the children quiet and interested.

45. MR. CROOK. Supposing you had liberty to use the cinema at the ordinary primary school, how many hours a week would you use it for one class ?—One or two lessons, perhaps forty-five minutes each time, but I think I should prefer only one.

46. So that its educative value is only one-thirtieth of the curriculum as regards time ?—Yes, it works out like that.

47. Would you use the same pictures for the whole school, or would you want different films for each class ?—I should have different films for each class.

48. THE CHAIRMAN. Would you regard it as useful to have in connection with your school work a cinema exhibition once a week for forty-five minutes on something not absolutely in the curriculum but yet in the education ?—That was in my mind.

49. PROFESSOR H. GOLLANCZ. Have you had any opportunity of judging whether the eyestrain affects the defective children the same as any intelligent boy or girl ?—I have not found any

eye difficulty or any eyestrain, and I have had no complaint as to sight being affected by the cinema.

50. DR. SALEEBY. Do you think your children get more excited? —No, the mentally defective are, as a rule, no more excitable than the other children. In fact, the great difficulty is that they are not easily excitable; they are lethargic—the great thing is to arouse them.

SEVENTH DAY

February 19, 1917,

The BISHOP OF BIRMINGHAM in the chair.

MINUTES OF EVIDENCE

MISS MARGERY FOX. *Examined.*

1. THE CHAIRMAN. You represent the Head Mistresses' Conference?—Yes.

2. Does that include all types of schools?—No, only the head mistresses of public secondary schools.

3. Do I take it, therefore, that you are dealing mainly with children of the High School type, or what type of school?— Mainly with the High School type, but I think I touch on all the other classes of children.

4. And have certain people attended some of the cinemas on behalf of the Association in order to prepare a kind of report to bring up?—No, this is on my own observation.

5. You realise that the educational side, if it comes in at all with regard to the cinema, comes in accidentally and not primarily? —I do not think the cinemas are educational.

6. It is not the first purpose of the cinema to be educational?— No, certainly not.

7. It is something to amuse, an entertainment to amuse, that is one of its purposes. You would consider it an entertainment that excites sometimes?—Yes, certainly.

8. You bear in mind that it is something carried on for profit by people who are risking their own means?—Yes.

9. And you agree that to be successful it has to appeal to various tastes?—Yes.

10. You say there is no educational value?—Yes; and there I go a great deal further than many on the Conference I represent.

11. Do you go to the cinema a good deal yourself?—Yes, a very great deal.

12. Have you seen the picture of the Tanks?—No; I only go to the bad cinemas, those I think are going to be bad.

13. You would realise that a great many people had not the

slightest idea of what a Tank was until they saw them on the cinema?—That is so.

14. Is there any educational value in that?—I think the films of the Tanks could be made educational if they were given by a lecturer, and if they followed some of the children's lessons which had been given during the week. I cannot call anything educational that is divorced from the child's usual education.

15. Supposing in the schools nothing is taught about the Tanks, how is the child to get to know what a Tank is?—I cannot conceive a child at the present day who has not been taught something about the Tanks.

16. You consider it better that a child should have an explanation of the Tanks than that it should see a representation upon the film with some letterpress in front saying what the Tank is doing?—I doubt whether the child can follow what is meant by the letterpress, as this moves so quickly.

17. Is not concentration one of the greatest difficulties to deal with in regard to a child?—I think the cinema panders to that lack of concentration, and that is why I think it is bad educationally.

18. You do not like a constant change of subject; you think it is a bad mental strain?—I think it is very bad.

19. We have had witnesses who advocate constant change of the subject for the child?—I think psychologically it is extraordinarily tiring for the child, as its mind would have to turn so rapidly from one type of subject to another. I think what one wants is variety with some logical line of continuity running through it, and these you don't get in the cinema.

20. With regard to the physical strain, I mean the strain on the eyes, I should like your opinion?—The cheapest seats are in front, and the nearer you are to the front the greater the strain on the eyesight. I consider there ought to be seats for children behind.

21. Have you any ideas of the kind of films you would like to have for children?—Assuming that the cinema industry must go on, I think the films should be connected with the child's own school as far as possible. Different schools, if they guaranteed a certain number of attendances—although I think the attendances should be limited from a physical point of view—could induce the proprietors to put on films in connection with their work. I think that is the only way they should be tolerated.

22. Are you a believer in a child getting pure amusement without instructional education?—Yes, certainly, but I would far rather it take its amusement in the open air than in the cinema.

23. What would you have a child go to for amusement indoors?—I should say simply dancing or acting. I think dancing has been brought down to the level of the poorest child.

24. We have heard that the child is so active that it perpetrates the crimes afterwards?—I do not think so, because of the unreality of the films; I have seen crimes so absurdly represented.

25. You have said a good deal about the unhygienic condition

of the palaces. I understand that the trade is entirely in favour of building as hygienically as possible?—I have been in both theatres and picture palaces constantly, and I have never once been in a theatre which is anything like as bad as six picture palaces I have been in during this last week.

26. With regard to the darkness, or as you would say, the halls that are illegally dark?—I had an impression that some of the halls were illegally dark. I say it is quite easy to see in comparative lightness. In Gravesend we have advertising films thrown on the screen when the lights are turned up, and you can see these films quite easily.

27. You speak about particular plays. I should like some instances of any plays you have seen?—There is far too much stress laid on the sexual passion, so that it would seem there is no other passion worth reckoning. In most of the plays I have seen there are instances of attempted rape carried on to the last minute, and the rescue takes place in that last minute, so that the whole house is in an unhealthy excitement. I was in one of the palaces last week, and there was a row of children in front from elementary schools who were talking about it in a way showing that they quite understood what was going on. I think the child soon learns to understand from a cinema.

28. Don't you think that a child, with the unsatisfactory housing conditions and environment, has an opportunity of learning these things early?—I think very often the children have learned these things from the cinemas. I have heard of this from the mothers. Now I should like to give you some of the plays I have seen. In —— there was a girl who was lodged in a house of ill-fame without her knowledge, and the house was raided in order to provide wives for the colonies. I might say that the staging of the play was of about the eighteenth century. Then there followed a ship filled with these girls all going out to the colonies, and it was boarded and captured by pirates, and there followed disgusting scenes of the women being on show while the pirates came round and inspected them. This went on four or five times, and I think the vividness of the scene and the expressions on the men's faces were almost disgusting. This was followed by a struggle between a man and a woman, who did not want the man who had chosen her. I have noticed that in nearly all these plays there has been a struggle of a very revolting kind between a man and a woman, and, speaking perhaps not from the point of view of a young child, but from the point of view of the adolescent, I do not think there is anything more suggestive or more dangerous for the adolescent to see than that struggle. This was followed by a travesty of the marriage service. The parson in this case was forced to marry the girl. This travesty of the marriage service also occurs in the ——. In this play a girl wants to marry a man, and they try to kidnap the parson to marry them, but by mistake they kidnap the father instead. There is the same story of travesty in ——, and there the bridegroom has a fight with a man who has

ill-treated his bride before the marriage. Then again, in this
—— there is one scene where a woman in delirium has a
struggle with a man, and her clothes are torn. Then you
have the posters, and in many cases they are even worse than
the real thing. To illustrate what I mean, I heard one boy
say to another : " Don't go to this theatre, go to another
where there is a murder on." —— is a very bad play. The
scene is laid in South Africa. A man breaks into the woman's
room, and you see on the stage alternately the man's eyes and
the woman's eyes. It is a horrid sight. Then in —— there
are two men and a woman, and one of the men offers £100
to the other one if he will spread a slander about the woman,
because he is weary of her as his wife, and he offers this large sum
of money as a bribe for the other man to induce her to be un-
faithful to him. Then, again, you get the plays where the girl is
just rescued from the clutches of the villain, which is worse, I
think, because one's sympathies go out to the defeated. I think
there is far too much of this kind of crime shown on the cinemas.
You see safe-breaking, robbery and burglary, and I think it is
a pity that such things are allowed to be shown.

29. But in theatrical performances do they not touch upon
the same points as the films do, although, of course, they treat
them in a different way ?—I have seen things on the films you
would never see on the legitimate stage, in Paris or London.

30. The subjects are very much about the same sexual passions.
In fact, we have been complaining there is too much of that in
the theatres; and we have been having " crook " plays in the
theatres ?—Yes.

31. At the present moment there is on the stage a scene where
the selling of girls takes place for the purpose of immorality?
—Yes.

32. It is rather in the treatment, I mean in the way in which a
thing is treated, than the style of subject ?—Yes, that is so. The
thing is treated on a legitimate stage in a different manner from
the way it is treated on the cinema, and certainly some things
are shown on the cinema that no manager would allow on the stage
of a theatre.

33. You mean that you cannot, strictly speaking, in your
own judgment, deal modestly or honestly with such questions as
sexual passion on the film, as you would if they were spoken on
the stage ?—That is so.

34. Have you any other plays you can call to mind ?—There
is one play called ——. I think it is worse, because it
gives an example of every sort of thing. It begins by a man
perjuring himself by swearing that another man is a forger.
There is a horrid scene in the court where the prisoner
grapples with another person. There are scenes of convict life
in France, and you see the men dragging along with cannon
balls on chains behind them, possibly to prevent their going too
fast. Then you see two of the convicts escape, and one of the
men rushes into a field where there are women. They all scatter

and go to a shed, which he sets on fire, and afterwards you see him carrying her away. The other convict meanwhile has been hidden by a fisherman, and the woman there brings him food, and this leads to several scenes of love-making. You see the girl go down to the beach, and she is pursued by the other convict, a madman, and there follows a violent struggle between the man and the woman. The hidden convict sees this from the window, rushes to the rescue, and there is another struggle, the girl joining in the fracas. Later on you see the son trying to rob his mother's safe, and there are furious death-struggles because he did not know that the burglar trap was set in the safe which shot him. The —— has some of the same sort of elements. I say many of these scenes when you see them on the film are far more intolerable than when you read of them in the books.

35. PRINCIPAL GARVIE. When you say that children should be active in their amusement, would you apply that all round? Would you approve of a child being taken to a circus or to a magic-lantern entertainment?—I do not approve of circuses because of the cruelty to animals. I do not object to magic-lantern entertainments, although a magic-lantern is trying to the sight, because it is very dull. On the other hand, a cinema is not dull.

36. Why do you object to the faces that are thrown upon the screen?—I object to them because they are magnified so much, in fact, some of the faces are so large that you can see the pores of the skin.

37. It is the very impressiveness of the cinema that aggravates the danger of it to the child?—Certainly; the better it is the worse it is.

38. MR. NEWBOULD. You say that the sense of sight is used to the neglect of the other senses. Would you make the same remark with regard to the sense of hearing in music?—Well, I suppose it is, but of course as a matter of fact a child does not hear a great deal of music unless it joins in. The instinct of the child is always to join in the music.

39. At the cinemas you have been to is there any music?— If you can call it music, there is a certain amount, but I do not think you pay any attention to the music.

40. But you have only been to those you expected to find bad?—I have been to some of the halls with the best reputations, and I very often find that they have the worst films.

41. You have spoken about the increase of sensational films. Has it occurred to you that the causes arise out of the war, that the public desires something more sensational?—I should not like to say that. I should think that they found sensationalism paid better, therefore it was put on.

42. Have you noticed the changes which have taken place in the class of films shown?—They are certainly far more sensational than they were when the war broke out.

43. Do you think we are getting rid of the bad cinema?— I know of no place of my own observation where cinemas have

been closed. I know of two towns where cinemas have been increased.

44. Dr. Saleeby. Would you object to taking a child to a concert?—Not if the child was of an age to understand music, but I would not take it to a concert night after night. A child going too frequently to a cinema must suffer.

45. Rev. W. E. Soothill. What is the effect of the cinema on the child next day?—Those children who go to the cinemas overnight are very discontented and tired next day.

46. Mr. Graves. You say you do not think that there is any educational value in the cinematograph in its present form. Are you aware of any experiments in the way of teaching by the cinematograph that have been made in the primary or secondary schools?—I have only heard of those in Letchworth.

47. A lesson might be given illustrating a certain process, and this lesson might wind up with a cinematograph summary of the process, which, say, might be lumbering?—I should always want it safeguarded so that the child did not go too often.

48. You don't see any objection then to, say, the magic-lantern lessons being reinforced by the cinematograph once a week?—No.

49. Dr. Kimmins. Have you ever been to a cinema where there are children's attendants?—I dare say there are some in London. I have always looked, but I have never seen any.

50. Have you noticed any improvements in the lighting of the cinema theatre?—No; and when I have sent in my card to the management the lighting has been improved.

51. And when they were lightened they did not interfere with the picture?—No.

52. You could see quite as well?—To me it was much more comfortable; there was less strain.

53. Mr. Edgar Jepson. Are they the poorer children or the upper middle classes that attend the cinema chiefly?—The poorer children chiefly. The children who go to my own school do not go to the cinemas.

54. Do you think that the cinema is more impressive than the drama or less? Does the scene on the film impress you more strongly than the scene on the stage?—It frightens me more because I have never seen such frightening things on the stage.

55. That is to say the subject is stronger?—Yes, and the treatment.

56. You said that it would be a good thing for a child to spend its evening in dancing and acting. That would be all very well with regard to your pupils, but what about the poor children?—There are some centres and clubs for poor children.

57. It is only a small proportion of the children that can get this dancing or acting at night?—Yes, at present.

58. Mr. Lamert. You refer to the extraordinarily vivid impression a cinema has on a child, and you have given an illustration of a child remembering something you did not wish it to remember. Is there any reason why the cinema should not give

an extraordinarily vivid impression of something you would like the child to remember?—It certainly would.

59. If a film projected on to a screen can give an extraordinarily vivid impression for evil, it can also give a vivid impression for good?—Yes.

60. So you would want the right type of film?—Yes, if you could get away from the physical and mental strain of cinemas.

61. REV. CAREY BONNER. Have you ever seen films suitable for children?—Yes.

62. You think these might be of educational value to the children?—If you are going to have any educational value you must repeat, repeat, and repeat, and if you are going to allow the child to go too often to the cinema it will be bad for it.

63. THE CHAIRMAN. With regard to the elementary school child. If the child lives in a rather wretched house, and has a bad environment, and goes to school most of the day, and has nothing whatever afterwards to do, is it to be wondered at that it flies to the cinema?—No, I do not think so, because the cinemas are much cheaper than anything else and they are very warm and comfortable.

HON. AND REV. DR. E. LYTTELTON.   *Examined.*

64. THE CHAIRMAN. Are you going to deal with the educational side of the film entirely?—I have very little to say outside the educational aspect of the matter, and I should be disposed to confine my remarks almost to that.

65. Still at the same time do you realise shortly that the primary objects of the cinema is not to educate?—Yes.

66. It is a commercial undertaking carried on for profit with the intention of amusing people to some extent, of exciting, no doubt?—Yes; so much so that I should be prepared to say that any practical suggestions as to improving the influence of cinemas would have to take that into account. I believe a great deal ought to be done and can be done to restrict the number of children who attend these shows, and also the time they can give to them. Other restrictions, too, are most advisable in the case of children, but, realising the hold they have got on the life of the country and how vast are the vested interests as regards adults, I have no particular suggestions to make. I think the influence of cinemas on adults is not good, but on children it is positively bad.

67. But the public which licenses these entertainments has the right to demand that no moral, mental or physical hurt should come to any one?—Yes, certainly.

68. And you would say at once that the child has to be specially cared for as distinct from the adult?—Yes.

69. Now your contention is that there is no such thing as sound knowledge acquired without effort? Would you mind developing that for a moment?—Of course, as I have put it down very briefly, that might be a point for dispute. I think I should

prefer to begin with No. 1, because there we touch upon the principle in education that as soon as you advance to the unknown from the unknown it becomes what we call in the profession cramming. If you try to do that in education you get knowledge which is not assimilated, but merely held in the mind a short time and then forgotten. Then we come to ask about the opposite principles. Suppose the knowledge is gained by the advance from the known to the unknown. Is it accompanied by effort? I for one may say that normally it is the process of effort and the process of joy at the same time. Now, that is all ignored by people who believe that a heterogeneous mass of children can be taken into a cinema show and look week after week at pictures which have not been assorted to their minds, and believe that that can be called learning. Of course, there is no guarantee whatever that there is nothing from the known to the unknown. Nobody knows what those children know. I do not profess to have much personal experience of cinemas, but I have heard enough of them and seen enough of them to know that what goes on is a presentation of pictures to attract the largest number of people, whether adults or children; and, further, that there are things to be said in favour of them, such as giving adults who have got no literary or intellectual interests of a certain kind—of giving them a pastime which can be said to be harmless. I am assuming that amongst the pictures shown are possibly some which are meant to be educational, but in order to make the display attractive to the mass of the people there must be others which are not educational, and which in the case of children become positively harmful; but that is a further point. Those that are supposed to be educational cannot be so, because of the difficulties which attend on that class of teaching. That difficulty has enormously increased, especially when you have children brought in of different ages and different interests and no time to make them a homogeneous class.

70. Do you think it fair to ask of a business which is run for a commercial profit and intended to amuse and interest people generally that they should be an educational influence upon the country?—No. I think we should ask that there should be some restrictions enforced upon the frequency of these pictures to children, as they only become harmful.

71. Can you suggest any type of film that would become absolutely educational and could be used for both adults and children? Would you take, for instance, such a thing as the showing of the Tanks, or lumbering in Canada, or the growth of flowers, and so on? Would you think these things could be made reasonably useful educationally without being absolutely educational in intention?—I think that all depends upon whether a good, clear and intelligible explanation of them is given at the time. That certainly should be a condition.

72. I think you have very strong feeling that sight and hearing should go together?—Yes, certainly.

73. You don't believe, generally speaking, in teaching entirely by sight?—That is so. I do not.

74. Do you think there is any advantage, or any different effect produced by the cinema shown to a boy from Eton and a boy from the elementary school?—Well, supposing they are two youngsters of the same age and attend the same pictures and the same number of pictures. The Eton boy would start with this advantage: he would probably know more to begin with. More pictures would appeal to his mind and give him useful information. Suppose we take the case of timbering or lumbering. He might have read a novel on the subject, and if he has, the pictures would be instructive to him and not the least harmful. In the case of the elementary school child, assuming that the picture comes before him, long before he has time to know anything about it it passes and another one comes. I am anxious to emphasise this, that the effect upon that child is very bad, even though the pictures are perfectly good. It is bad in more ways than one. I hold that the English boy, as compared with the American and the French boy, requires to be slowly taught. That is to say, the mind works slowly and he is not so advanced at the age of sixteen as the American boy is. Well, what happens? The child either gives up the effort to keep up with the pictures, in which case he merely becomes befogged or confused, or if he has an active brain and an inquiring mind he does his utmost to keep up with them when he has not the knowledge to do so. And there I am convinced in the case of young children that you run a very serious danger, because there is not the intellectual effort that an adult can make. If the child's mind is over-active the effort is really greater than it ought to be called upon to make, especially if you have had one picture rapidly succeeded by another one. Amongst the children going to cinema shows you have a good many with active brains, but they are largely ignorant of the matters shown them. You have therefore a growing mischief to deal with, the over-exciting of excitable brains. A large number of people come out of the cinema shows in a state of coma.

75. I gather that you are dealing with the educational value of the cinema as at present put before you; that really education has nothing to do at present, or only accidentally, with the cinema?—I am afraid I can go further and say from the nature of the case it is bound to be bad education.

76. I presume the cinema authorities would be prepared to say, " If you think our efforts at giving you education are bad we will either omit the educational side altogether, or ask the State how education may best be produced from the cinema." That would be reasonable?—Yes, and then there would be a distinct answer given, namely, that all children, indeed all young people under eighteen years of age, should be barred from cinematograph shows, and that the cinema should be used only in schools.

77. What would you do with the elementary child at present

who has no amusement in the evening?—There are efforts to be made to deal with this question after the war. I do not say that the cinema should be entirely banished, but it should be controlled by people who understand children.

78. MR. LAMERT. In the London Press of last December you were reported to have said this : " The cinema only made an appeal to silly people." Do you remember that?—I do not remember having said that. I would dispute it as it stands without the context.

79. You say that in the case of boys and girls class-teaching depends upon the class being fairly homogeneous in brain power. In the case of the ordinary national school how many classes do you get that are homogeneous?—Undoubtedly very few indeed, but there are degrees in this matter. A good teacher before long finds out what subject he can take which will interest the children.

80. Is it not conceivable that something like the cinema would make a ready and quick appeal to the mind and might assist the child?—Yes, when properly managed.

81. You have said about the impressions given in the cinema, " The deepest impressions are given by experience in early youth. Those given by the cinema where they are not definitely corrupting tend to be hedonistic in tone or at least in effect." I take it that the film which is hedonistic conveys the impression, " Eat, drink, and be merry, for to-morrow we die " ?—I take it that those who have invested money in films have to make them attractive to bring the people there.

82. You might have a film with a murder, you could not call that hedonistic?—That depends entirely on the context and the light in which the murder is done. I hear that a large amount of small crimes, with the outwitting of the police, and petty larceny and dodging are shown on the films, and that there is also a great deal of forgery and other evils and bloodshed. So, you see, the subject is put before the children in an exciting light. The child when he sees the picture of somebody like himself outwitting the police or the public in the street, is he not certain to say, " That is a thing I might do " ? And he tries to do it, only his idea is that he shall not be found out.

83. Can you name a film, or have you ever seen a film where one of the characters steals or commits a murder and does not pay the penalty for it?—I have not seen any of them.

84. In a number of countries no crime film of any sort will pass the censor unless that point is made clear?—That, no doubt, will diminish the evil which I am apprehending.

85. Is it your belief that children always believe what they are told?—If you were to provide some one who is an educator, then I think the pictures would be instructive; but do not dabble in those difficult moral problems, and don't have anything in the least approaching the presentation of sexual questions in any shape or form. Then, again, I think there should be a long interval in between each picture which ought to be employed in stimulating the curiosity of the children as far as

possible in what is coming next. Children should not go more than once a week, and the performances should not be more than one hour long. We have discovered that no man can keep children under the age of thirteen interested in a lesson more than fifty minutes, but I have heard of cases in the cinema where children will sit for over three hours. Dealing with the question of the length of the performances, I should say there should be seven to ten pictures in fifty minutes. That would be quite enough if a proper explanation were given before each picture.

86. MONSIGNOR BROWN. Do I understand that you want all young children up to the age of eighteen to be excluded from the cinema as now conducted ?—I think so.

87. Do you think that is a reasonable requirement to make of the community ?—I think it is very reasonable, but perhaps it is not very practicable.

88. You say there should be a performance restricted in character for the protection of the children ?—Yes.

89. Can you organise a performance which would hold the interest of children whose ages range from six to eighteen ?—I should have thought so ; at any rate I think I could give something better suited to them than the performances which are given now.

90. Bear in mind that this is the recreation of the very poor who are living under very squalid conditions. Is it quite fair to say that they should never have such recreation ?—I should put it this way : that however squalid their conditions may be, we have no right to give them baneful recreation, intellectual y baneful.

91. That, of course, would carry us to prohibiting children from going to the music halls, or, say, one of your boys from going to the Coliseum to see George Robey ?—I know much less about music halls than I do about cinemas. I think that the public seem to be awaking to the fact that there are dangers in connection with music halls, but they do not seem to be aware that there are dangers in connection with the cinemas.

92. THE CHAIRMAN. I was wondering whether you have not placed the age of the children rather too high. You say you would not allow children under eighteen years of age to go to a cinema. Now eighteen seems high, because by that time the bulk of the young people have started out in life, so that they can hardly be hurt with the cinema. If you had said sixteen I should have understood it better ?—I may have been influenced by the fact that if you want to get sixteen you had better ask for eighteen.

EIGHTH DAY

Monday, February 26, 1917,

The BISHOP OF BIRMINGHAM in the chair.

PRÉCIS OF REPORT REFERRED TO IN EVIDENCE

THE Cinema Investigation Report presented to a gathering representative of all the religious bodies of Worcester City, January 1917, reads : Your committee has carried out inquiries along three lines : by personal visits to the four cinema halls in the city; by an inquiry through teachers of elementary schools; and by correspondence to ascertain steps taken in other towns.

Fifteen independent visits to cinemas were made by members of the committee since your last meeting.

The films presented were, with few exceptions, not objectionable on grounds of indecency, but often highly sensational and melodramatic. And there is evidence that some at least of the exhibits—for instance, in " society dramas " and the like—are helping to lower the standard of reverence for woman, and familiarising the minds of young people with loose ideas of the relation of the sexes. Further, such features as murders, drugging, and various forms of brutality, with the usual incentives thereto of money-greed or unlawful passion, when repeatedly witnessed, must tend to make such actions seem possible to imitate, and perhaps attractively easy; and the films are not free from revolting scenes, as where, in a Red Indian film, corpses are seen piled, and people walking over them. One report refers to a small boy's only sign of interest, his chuckles at seeing the heroine of the film being kicked about like a football. One report says : " In my visits I saw very little of indecency, but I consider many of the features immoral in consequence of the way in which robbery, treachery, murder, deceit, and other vices are depicted."

It seems evident that many of the melodramatic play-films are unhealthily exciting for young children, especially when the rapid action, intensified gesture and concentrated episode inevitable in the dumb-show are considered. Some teachers remark that younger children dream about the pictures.

Head teachers were very obliging in carrying out the inquiries we asked of them. It appears that of 1843 boys questioned, 718 called themselves *regular* cinema goers, and of 1868 girls, 477, *i. e.* 39 per cent. boys and 25 per cent. girls. About 23 per cent. of all had attended once during the previous week, and just over 1000 visits had been paid in that week by some 800 children.

Boys attend in larger numbers than girls and more often, and analysis bears out the general inference that scholars from the poorest districts, who have fewer inducements to stay at home, and generally less home control, attend in a much higher ratio

than those from better homes, though these figures are complicated by the fact that schools at a distance from the cinema
areas show lower cinema attendances.

An effort was made to find out what types of film were most
popular, and what, if any, were disliked. *Cowboy* films got 16
out of 23 possible votes, being put first in six schools. *Comics*
of all sorts got 15 votes, being put first in seven schools. *Army*
and *War* pictures got 14 votes, put first in four schools. *Detective*
and *Burglary* films got 11 votes. Other classes, such as weekly
budget, travel, dramatised novels, romance, illustrated industries, etc., got a few votes each.

As to pictures of which children expressed dislike, films with
murders stand first, then burglaries (this apparently apart from
the detective interest often involved in this class), then tragedies
generally—disasters, fires, etc.—then love-making, generally
described by boys as "silly." Broadly, it would seem that
children of school age, unlike their elders, do not like pictures
that harrow their feelings.

The teachers' personal comments are full of interest, but
difficult to summarise. Three boys' teachers and six girls'
teachers note ill effects on school work of habitual cinema-going,
by loss of sleep, lateness at school, listlessness, or inferior work.
On the other hand, a good many teachers agree that the pictures
widen general knowledge, stimulate the imagination, and perhaps
quicken observation and the critical faculties. Most of them
have found the better type of picture a help and incentive in
the essay writing of their scholars.

On the effect on health and eyesight the opinion of teachers is
most emphatic. Several interrogated their scholars ; nine schools
find scholars complaining of eyestrain after the pictures ; two
mention that the cheap seats nearest the screen produce most
eyestrain ; six or seven schools mention the ill effects of close
and stuffy air, and one boys' teacher considers the cinema habit
has helped to spread the cigarette habit.

No direct question was asked as to moral influence, but some
of the teachers say more or less directly that the general effect
of habitual cinema visits is detrimental to character, and two
teachers of large boys' schools note that the most regular attenders
are poor and backward scholars.

The general inference is that the teachers of the schools most
affected by the cinema would welcome some restraint upon too
frequent and indiscriminate visits to the cinema by school children,
and some effective means of regulating shows which children
might attend alone, and of selecting the films which they
might see.

The third section of the report gives information obtained from
correspondents as to action elsewhere—London, Birmingham,
Liverpool, York and Middlesbrough—and concludes—

The correspondence has shown us that where the public is
awake to the evils and the dangers of the present cinema system,
they can successfully press their local authorities—

1. To make special cinema by-laws;

2. To appoint special inspectors, or a special committee of people who care about this question, to see that the by-laws are observed. Birmingham has shown how possible this suggestion is, and how well it has been found to work.

RECOMMENDATIONS

I. The most desirable course would be the immediate formation of a strong permanent Vigilance Association to which all further action on this subject would be entrusted, and which might affiliate itself with the National Council of Public Morals.

II. That a deputation be sent to the bench of magistrates for the city, presenting the substance of this report, and asking them to consider the appointment of women inspectors of places of public amusement, with powers, in respect of cinemas, to visit the halls, and to report to the police any films unsuitable for children, and any infringement of licensing conditions, or failure to carry out any regulation that might be agreed upon.

III. A deputation should also be sent to the City Council or its Watch Committee, calling their attention to the powers given to local authorities under the Cinema Acts 1909, 1910, and to the model conditions for future licences when issued by the Home Office in connection with the proposals for an official censorship. The City Council might be asked to give official recognition to the Vigilance Association, if formed.

IV. If it is decided that a deputation should interview the managers of local cinema halls, your sub-committee suggest that the following results of our investigations be emphasised—·

(1) That under the existing film censorship the programmes are so uneven in quality that those who go can never be certain that they may not witness something objectionable or revolting.

(2) That many children confess to eyestrain, headache, etc., from the conditions under which the films are shown, and that head teachers of the schools most affected find the effects of habitual cinema-going detrimental to punctuality, attention, and work at school.

(3) That the attendance at all of children in the later hours of evening is undesirable on many grounds.

(4) That pictures portraying crime and evil should be excluded from performances to which children are admitted unaccompanied by adults, and that the effect of sad and harrowing pictures, and even of much ordinary melodrama, on the imagination of very young children, and on nervous and excitable natures, is disturbing and bad.

The managers might be invited to discuss these three points—

1. Whether children under fourteen, who are not with adults, can be refused admission to the second evening houses, or in the case of continuous performances, after a certain hour, say 7.30 p.m.

L

2. Whether their programmes can be so arranged that the matinees and early houses shall not show any film unsuitable for children, or in the case of continuous performances, that such films should not be shown before a certain hour, say 9.30 p.m.

3. Whether they can arrange that no children shall be seated nearer the screen than fifteen feet.

MINUTES OF EVIDENCE

The Dean of Worcester. *Examined.*

1. The Chairman. In the course of your social and moral interest in the city of Worcester you have been able to make a thorough study of this question?—Yes, but I do not know whether I have much to add to my report. This report did not originate with me, but with the clergy and churchwardens of St. Martin's Church, Worcester, arising out of the action of a study circle which led them to think something ought to be done in relation to cinemas and their influence, and so they drew up a circular which was sent to every church, place of worship and religious organisation in Worcester, asking them to join in protest against demoralising pictures at the cinemas, against certain revues, and against the posters advertising these performances. The circular suggested that such protests from the different religious bodies, when drawn up, should be sent as a memorial to the City Council and express disapproval of the present lax state of affairs, and urge that (1) there should be a stricter local censorship of public performances; that (2) there should' be performances suitable for children, from which pictures of crime and evil should be rigorously excluded; and that children should no longer be admitted to the ordinary performances, except possibly with their parents. The circular continued : " We know that a Government Film Censor Board is under consideration, and suggest that it would strengthen the hands of those who are pressing for this needful reform if a corporate protest from the religious bodies of Worcester were sent to them as well as to our own Council. We feel it will be important to make it clear that, as Christian people, we recognise that the cinemas, if rightly censored, might and should be a great power for good, and also a legitimate and healthy recreation, and that what we are urging is, not their abolition, but their cleansing. Whether such a protest as we suggest has a practical effect or not, it seems to us of the gravest importance that all right-minded people should manifest their disapproval of this moral evil."

2. How many cinemas have you in Worcester ?—Four.

3. Are they varying in size ?—Yes. In the matter I have referred to we acted with the full knowledge of the leading person in Worcester who has to do with the cinemas, who is also the proprietor of the theatre, Alderman Carlton, who is also Mayor of Worcester at the present moment. When we had our report

made and epitomised, we sent a copy to the representatives of all the cinemas and asked them to meet us, but one of them, which had its headquarters in London, declined to do so. We told them we thought we could act locally without interfering with anything that might be done here or with any regulations the Government might bring into force, as we wanted to act together in a friendly way and make things as good as possible locally. The position we took up was not one of hostility, but of friendly co-operation with a view to getting things made better than they are, and first of all we wanted to ascertain how far things were undesirable. The original report was a little longer, but there were things which we thought better should not be inserted, such as the special names of cinemas, and there were one or two names of pieces which people objected to.

4. We have no objection to these names being stated. We are rather glad to know what particular films were objected to.— At the smallest theatre, where the average is lowest in character, there was a serial film named ——, which was very un-favourably commented on, and later on, at the same one, there was another film called ——, a very broad farce in bedrooms, arising out of a page altering the numbers on the bedroom doors of the hotel.

5. Might I ask whether the films you mainly objected to were at one particular house or whether they were at all houses?— There were degrees; in some there were more objectionable ones than in others. The two I have mentioned were in one particular house.

6. Can you give us the accommodation of the house?—It is a very small one, holding not much more than 150 people.

7. Can you tell us whether the quality of the films varies in regard to the kind of public before whom they are shown, whether the worse things are amongst the very poor, or whether there are worse things in other parts of the city?—The worst things are in the poorest part of the city.

8. I gather indecency was not very prominent in the films you took objection to?—Except that one, ——. I do not say there was none in the others.

9. Would you say they were more sensational and melodramatic than some of the pieces presented at a theatre?—Some much more so.

10. I see you think that the standard of reverence for women is a good deal hurt by the character of films presented?—Yes.

11. You mean that woman is dealt with in an undignified way? —And also very often in a suggestive way, which is a degradation to the relations of the sexes.

12. I notice that your houses run two houses nightly; that means they are not open in the afternoon?—They are open on Saturday afternoons and Thursday afternoons. The Saturday afternoons are very largely for the children.

13. Are adults in Worcester admitted at all to the children's entertainments?—Yes; I am not aware of their being excluded.

I have heard that for the children's entertainments, if you have children only, a certain tax is not payable.

MR. NEWBOULD. If you apply for the exemption of the tax you are not allowed to admit adults. That is the case where the admission must not be more than one penny.

14. THE CHAIRMAN. In regard to the attendance at the cinemas, have your people who have visited them come across any case where they consider that adults were present with children for the purposes of immorality?—None whatever. I was very careful to inquire as to whether there were any grounds for complaints of want of light, because I saw that in some places complaints were made that the cinemas were so darkened as to give opportunity for indecent action. I questioned every one of the members of our Committee about that, and they all said it was dark, but they did not consider it was unduly dark, and that there was nothing in the darkness that was likely to cover anything of that kind.

15. You say: "As to pictures to which children express dislike, films with murders stand first." Now, does that mean that you think the children realise to any extent what was being presented before them?—We have summarised the evidence that we had from the head masters and mistresses who made the inquiries for us. Of course, it is open for people to say that boys and girls, when asked questions by head masters and head mistresses, say what they think will please them rather than what they really think; but knowing the teachers and knowing their attitude in relation to these things—for they were not attempting to make a case—I think the summary in that report is as correct as we can give it.

16. I see the cowboy films are put down as the most popular? —Yes, and I should like to say that when we discussed this matter with our Mayor he said that the public taste differed, and what is popular to-day was not popular a year ago, and may not be popular six months hence.

17. Have you had war films?—Yes.

18. And are they popular?—Yes; you see, there is the interest in the thing itself.

19. With regard to the eyestrain and the class of buildings. Are your cinemas modern buildings that have been put up for the purpose of showing these films?—Two out of the four are.

20. And there is not much complaint about the stuffiness of the air there?—No, we have not much complaint about that with regard to any of them; but, of course, where there is a continuous performance you must expect the air to get stuffy.

21. Supposing you had to choose between a censor appointed by the city, with assistants under him, or a censor appointed by the State, which would you think the better?—Well, there are town councils and town councils; I would trust some of them, but I would not trust the others.

22. Would you trust the State?—I would trust the State to be honest, but probably wooden in its methods.

23. More wooden than the local authorities?—Oh, yes, but wooden in their methods.

24. Then it is rather difficult for you to say which you would prefer?—I think for the country as a whole I would certainly prefer the State, because I think the pressure that the financial interests might bring to bear upon local governing bodies, urban and district councils, and some town councils, would be very undesirable. Perhaps I might read you something which would interest you in my report : " That under the existing film censorship the programmes are so uneven in quality that those who go can never be certain that they may not witness something objectionable or revolting." We had a long talk with the cinema proprietors about that, and I told them : " It seems to me you are losing a great deal of custom because decent people go, and there is flashed on the screen some objectionable thing, and all the rest of the performance is quite satisfactory; and they say they cannot go again and take their friends because they do not know that something objectionable may not appear." I also said to the Mayor : " Cannot you give a guarantee to the public that nothing in your place shall be shown that anybody will object to?" and he pointed out the difficulties. One of these difficulties is connected with the present time, with regard to the railways and so forth. He explained that sometimes the cinema proprietors are disappointed in the film, and at the last moment they have to telegraph to Birmingham to send them down something. They cannot guarantee what it is, and sometimes it is undesirable and they have not had time to inspect it beforehand. Then I would like to read you what the Mayor said on other matters : " It was pointed out that the existing Board of Film Censors, appointed by the trade, were not able to prevent a film which they had not passed from being advertised in the weekly lists from which selections were made for the cinema halls, and those lists did not indicate which films were passed by the Board. A Government censorship would, therefore, be a real boon both to the trade and to the public, and would be much more certain and satisfactory than any local attempt at censorship, because it would check any evil at the root. Alderman Carlton thought he might speak for all the local cinema managers in saying that they would welcome an efficient and wise Government censorship; and, personally, he regretted the announcement of Sir George Cave that the proposal of the late Home Secretary for the creation by Order in Council of an official Censor of Films had been abandoned."

25. You say in the interests of the trade it is all-important that what they produce before the public should be void of offence?—Most emphatically.

26. In the interests of the cinema trade I might say that the people attracted by what is unworthy are the people they would most desire to keep outside their places?—Yes, and I do think some of the films they use have a demoralising effect upon the children. For instance, to illustrate what I mean, speaking of

Satan we had this report : " It was greeted with roars of delight, and it was only too plain that it was its wickedness that called forth this excitement, as there was nothing amusing in the picture."

27. MR. GRAVES. Have you seen any change since these pictures have been in existence, showing there has been a deterioration in the morale of the neighbourhood ?—Well, I should be very slow to say that the cinema did this or did that unless you have some real standard of comparison.

28. How young do children go to the cinemas ; do the children attending the infants' school go ?—Quite little tots go if they can get a penny.

29. Do you suggest that the children have really been frightened ? Are children of an imaginative mind ?—The evidence of the teachers is that there are certain children who are affected in that way.

30. How often do they attend the cinema ?—Two or three times a week, while some children go every day.

31. REV. CAREY BONNER. Have you any knowledge of your local cinema proprietors adapting the entertainment for children alone, or do they put on the same films as shown to the adults ?— There are special entertainments or programmes where there have been invitations to children, but there is not much variation.

32. In Worcester are the children always in the front seats, where there is the most strain to the eyes ?—Yes, and the cinema proprietors have agreed in three of the cases that they will respect that fourteen feet from the screen to the utmost of their ability.

33. MR. LAMERT. In Worcester are you well off for what they call play centres ?—We have done a good deal in the way of children's playgrounds, but not children's evenings in school.

34. Then in the winter there is no provision at all for the children ?—No, but we have not said that we think the cinemas in themselves are undesirable. It is.in the poorest parts and by the poorest children that they are most used, and I think the children are much better there than in the streets.

35. You approve of some sort of entertainment ?—Yes, but I want it kept clear of anything that tends to lower morality or anything of extreme sensationalism.

36. MONSIGNOR BROWN. Can you tell us how this information was acquired by the teachers ; was it by questioning the class orally or had they to write down the questions and answers ?— The masters and mistresses talked to the children in a friendly way and got them to make statements.

37. SIR EDWARD BRABROOK. Having regard to the great educational value of the moving pictures, do you look forward to the time when it will be possible to produce them so economically that they will be used in ordinary school entertainments like the magic lantern ?—I have no means of knowing what possible economies there may be in that direction, but I remember when the cinemas began, and I know what strides have been made, and I see, therefore, no reason to doubt that the time will come

when they can be dealt with in such a way that they will be used for certain subjects.

SIR ROBERT WALLACE, K.C. *Examined.*

38. THE CHAIRMAN.   You wish to deal solely with the question of the cinema from the point of view of the police court and the incidents arising there from the suggestive nature of the films on young minds, and as to the indecencies of the pictures themselves, or the opportunity which darkness affords?—I think it would be much better to confine myself strictly to that which comes within my own experience.   I would like to say, in the first place, in regard to the topic that has often been raised as to the indecency of pictures themselves, that I have quite satisfied myself from the general information I have received—and I have been trying in every direction to find out—that indecency does not exist in any general sense in the pictures themselves.   The pictures may be vulgar, they may not conform, perhaps, to the standard of taste that some would desire, but they are not indecent, and I do not think that charge can be made against those who are responsible for the pictures.   That is the result of the inquiries I have made in regard to the matter.   In regard to indecency arising out of the circumstances under which the pictures have to be given, there is perhaps more to be said.   As you know, cases of indecent assault, if they are contested, are not dealt with by the police magistrates summarily; they are sent for trial to the Sessions, and in that way they come before me, and a considerable number of cases of that kind have had to be tried in the last year or two.   I was very much afraid from the nature of the evidence given in connection with these cases that there were a great number of cases which never came for trial because the girls or women who are the object of the assault do not care for the publicity which attends the trial.   They shrink from having their names connected in any way with a thing of that kind.   Every one knows that to be mixed up in a police court at all, even if you are a complainant, is a disagreeable thing, and the conclusion which I arrive at after hearing several of these cases is that there are many more of them than the number of cases which are actually tried.   In regard to that, I suppose pictures are best shown in total darkness, but in Birmingham, I understand, they have half-lights or something of that kind.   If it is possible to show the pictures in such a way as to give interest to those who see them, and at the same time to have sufficient light, that would largely prevent what has been going on in London.   The first suggestion I make would be that it would be desirable to adopt some such system as has been adopted in Birmingham.   The other point in connection with this question is this : I think the whole system of having a promenade is most undesirable, allowing the standing together promiscuously of people at the back of the hall.   I have had a great number of letters since it was known that I had expressed

myself on this subject, from fathers of girls, telling me things which really are rather horrible, with regard to the result which followed on the standing room at the back and the opportunities which are presented for indecency.

39. Is it within your knowledge that there are large promenades at the back of the halls?—In some theatres there are standing places. I do not know whether they are intended for promenades, or whether this is an easy method of providing for a large number of people. My suggestion is that every one should have a seat, and there should not be much moving about from seat to seat or from seat to promenade. I will now come to the other question which occupied a good deal of my attention, and that is the effect of the pictures themselves upon those who see them. I am looking at it simply from the point of view of crime. Now you have to consider first, of course, the character of the audience, for you are not dealing with a theatre audience; you are not dealing with the grown-up; I am dealing more especially with young people who go in their thousands to these places. Now as to the audiences in the cinemas. You start with the fact that you have the young and impressionable minds, and you consider the conditions under which they have met. There is the mystery which darkness in itself produces, and then the condition of mind to which they are reduced by the atmosphere and by the effect of constantly going there to see the pictures, for, you see, I am dealing simply with pictures suggestive of crime.

40. Do you distinguish between any of the kinds of crime, such as the " crook " crime, the murders; while there are some adventurous crimes?—It is the adventurous crime that has come chiefly before me. The other type of crime is repulsive. I will deal with what I call the bold crime. Now if an adventurous, bold boy with an active mind and body sees a man climbing up a rope to get into a window, and then balancing himself on the window-sill and using a knife—well, what is the effect? There is the natural desire to reproduce largely, if it is a bold thing and of that type of crime I am referring to. Even if the crime is that of the "artful dodger "—you know what I mean : the sleight-of-hand movement, quickness—they like to try that. Now, I will mention to you two cases. I tried a boy of about seventeen years of age, who was sent for trial to the Sessions. He had committed six burglaries, he had stolen watches and small jewellery, not very valuable, but all amounting in the aggregate to some £80 or £90. Well, he had no defence, because he was at last caught red-handed. Now, I am not putting before you his account of the cause, because it may be that a boy, a quick boy, knows the best way of giving an excuse, but I am dealing with the evidence of the police. As you know, in our courts, before sentencing any one, we insist on the fullest investigation by the police as to the antecedents of the boy and the history of the crime as far as possible. Now this boy in the first place had the highest character. He occupied a good position in business, and his employer said he was one of the most trustworthy boys,

had had money entrusted to him and had never lost a penny, and here he had committed six burglaries. The police then said that the remarkable thing about it was this : that of this £80 to £90 worth of burglary he had never realised one pennyworth. When he was taken at the end of the sixth attempt he told the police where they would find the things, and every article from the first burglary to the last was carefully stored up there together, and they were all recovered. It was simply adventure. Then I asked the police the history of the boy, and they told me they had investigated the matter. He had got into this habit—it seems to be a habit—of going almost daily to these picture palaces. He had been going day by day, steadily and regularly, and seeing how things of this kind were done, and he had an adventurous desire to try to realise himself that which he had seen on the stage. That is one illustration, and you can draw your own conclusions from it. The other case to which I referred was a case of two young men seventeen or eighteen years of age. They went into a shop in the south of London; they were armed with a stage pistol, a sort of weapon which is said to be very dangerous if employed at close quarters. They went into this shop; the shopkeeper was there by himself, and they both presented their pistols at his head, and called upon him there and then either to hand over what money he had or take the consequences. Well, the timid man—I suppose we are all, perhaps, more or less timid in things or circumstances like this—proceeded to hand over his money, but they were captured almost immediately. Now these two boys had been members of the Boys' Brigade. The particular branch of the Brigade was watched over very carefully by two young Admiralty clerks, who were very careful and keenly interested in the boys. And what was the character they gave of these two ? They were the two best boys they had ever known; not a thing against them in any shape or form. In their employment and in their daily life they gave them the highest character, and all that could be gathered from the evidence was that they had seen something on the stage—" Your money or your life "—and they thought it a good opportunity. Well, the authorities looked into this matter, and they could not send the boys to Borstal, because the Prison Commissioners would not have them because of their previous good characters. The alternative was to send them to Dartmoor, which was then a convict prison, because there was a sort of modified Borstal system carried on there. Now, I was in communication with the Home Office on the matter, and I said I would do nothing of the kind. I said I was quite satisfied from the inquiries the police made that they were not bad characters, and that it was the spirit of adventure which alone actuated them, and that they were acting on that which they had seen, so I bound them over for judgment, and those boys are following their occupations to-day properly. Well, now, that is what I want to bring home to you, so that it may be realised what I am driving at. I have spoken very strongly from the judicial bench on this subject and in connection with this subject, a greater number of cases can be given, but I will leave it at that, as the point I want to make is the temptation that is there for these young people. Then the next point is the other temptation that is offered to them to steal in order to go. The police have told me of cases where it is not a weekly visit or a bi-weekly visit, but practically a daily visit that these boys make to these places. Of course, I recognise what has been so often stated, and that is the peculiar times we are living in. They are under no control, their fathers are all fighting for their country abroad, their mothers are all working to keep them at home; there is no one to look after them. The boy goes there day by day, and the result is that he exhausts his own money first, and then arises that which has been so frequently the case : he takes his employer s money to go, and so begins his criminal career. Now I have put very shortly and simply what I wanted to say.

41. Can you suggest any remedies ? Here is a great industry which is practically for the whole of the people of these islands. In itself it may be an absolutely desirable thing and may give a great deal of reasonable recreation, but it has certain objections which you have stated to-day. Will you suggest to me how you think a remedy might be applied for the evils ?—We have already dealt with one or two. I will not deal with the question of the light. Of course, you may say that what I propose is a very drastic remedy. I do not believe it is a very good thing for the very young people to go to the cinema at all. I say that frankly.

42. What age ?—I was going to try and put it without actually naming an age, because age is not a measure of intelligence, I am afraid, in these days. It is difficult to get at. In going around London I see long strings of little ones standing outside these places waiting for them to open. You will see perhaps two or three hundred children waiting for half an hour. Some of them can hardly toddle, being three or four years of age, and it may be they are brought there because their guardians, who perhaps are eight years of age, are taking charge of them. I should doubt whether the average age would be more than eleven years. In fact, it may be a year or two less. Now, it may be a strange thing to say, but I doubt very much whether anybody under twelve years of age should be admitted to cinema entertainments, except, of course, when it is a special entertainment for children. Then, again, you are up against the decision with regard to the censorship, whether every picture ought to be censored or not, and I think that is a very difficult thing to do.

43. If you had to choose between the central censorship by the State or the local censorship by local authorities, which would you be inclined to have ?—I would prefer myself that every locality should look after itself—that is, on the whole. I am not at this moment offering a strong opinion upon that, because from that point of view I do not pretend that I have considered it, but I think myself it would be better that every locality

should take charge of itself, and I think in London the censorship should be the County Council.

44. When you get smaller local authorities, do you not think it would be well for them to be advised from the censor?—Certainly, as I do not think they can have the means of providing the machinery. You require a larger and wealthier body to deal with that.

45. PRINCIPAL GARVIE. Would you think a censorship exercised by the trade, which must be voluntary, would be adequate? —I do not believe in it at all; I do not think they could do it.

46. Then about the " promenade "; is it used by women of bad character for immoral purposes, or is it used accidentally?—I do not think it is used as largely as many of the old music-hall promenades were used. The cinemas are used by the poorer people, and the indecency is perhaps the more sorrowful because it is the indecency of those who are not naturally bad.

47. MR. NEWBOULD. I want to ask you about the accuracy of a report that you have said that the cinemas are the curse of London?—No, I never said anything of the kind. I said the cinemas under certain conditions and used in a certain way would be the curse of London. I never suggested the other for one moment; quite the contrary, as you may gather from the observations I have made to-day.

48. MR. KING. Might I ask you to refer to the increase in the number of cases during the last year or two? What is the comparison? What are you comparing with?—Well, the only comparison that I have is in regard to the increase in the number of cases coming to the courts.

49. How many years are you covering?—I have been chairman of the London Sessions for ten years, and that, I think, covers the whole active history of the cinemas.

50. It is within the last two or three years you have seen this increase?—I think so.

51. You speak of the promenades; you have not actually seen the promenades?—I have heard of them a great deal. If you mean, have I studied any one myself, I say no, but I have heard from the police, and I have also heard the statements of the witnesses.

52. You suggest that the boys steal to go to the cinemas?—Yes; I have tried a good many of these boys brought up for embezzlement, and some are at Borstal, while others are bound over and are at home.

53. You know the price they can get in for is a penny or twopence?—That's the very point. You can get in for twopence, and twopence is the easiest thing to remove from the drawer of your master; and if you start at twopence you get on to fourpence.

54. With regard to the censorship, is a policeman any good?— I have not offered any opinion, but I do not believe in the police censorship; I believe in something more.

55. SIR EDWARD BRABROOK. Would you suggest that those

under twelve should be accompanied or unaccompanied?—They should be accompanied. I doubt very much whether you can separate a mother and a child. As long as they were under proper guardianship I would not say anything.

56. SIR W. BARRETT. You agree that the amount of lighting is a vital question both from a moral and hygienic point of view. Would you not recommend that there should be a regulation issued as to the amount of light?—I think so.

57. MR. GRAVES. Have you heard of any other form of crime committed by boys apart from those crimes of boldness, such as incendiarism?—None have come before me. I have heard of one or two cases in the country, but they have not come before me.

58. DR. KIMMINS. Have statistics been kept of the cases where the cinema has been the cause of the downfall?—No, but I suppose the Clerk of the Peace would be able to give you some of the figures.

59. MONSIGNOR BROWN. Before the cinema came in the newspapers were constantly telling us that the boys committed crimes because of what they read in penny dreadfuls?—Yes, I do not deny it.

60. Would you suggest that children under twelve years of age should not be admitted at all?—Yes, except in the case where the child is accompanied or under guardianship.

61. THE CHAIRMAN. You don't want to drive the children on to the streets?—That is so.

62. You only want to secure that everything shall be as suitable as possible?—That is all I desire.

63. MR. LAMERT. Have you anything to suggest as an alternative to the cinema?—I have not; I regret the children do not have more outdoor opportunities, but it is very difficult in London.

64. In our climate the child will only have a few months of the year for outdoor enjoyment?—Yes.

65. THE CHAIRMAN. I should like to hear what you have to say about the slackness of parental influence and responsibility in recent years?—You are asking me a question on which I have a strong view. I think there is a lack of training to-day which is largely responsible for what is going on. I do not know what it is that is lacking, but I seem to realise that the children are not trained as a child ought to be trained; they have not gripped the moral responsibilities that rest upon them, and I think that it is the loss of belief which has led to this condition of things.

NINTH DAY

Monday, March 5, 1917,

The BISHOP OF BIRMINGHAM in the chair.

STATEMENT OF MR. SPURLEY HEY
Director of Education, Manchester

PRÉCIS

I. THE present population of Manchester is estimated at about 750,000. The city boundaries enclose an area of about thirty-three square miles. The population is so disposed that the " Central " area, which is roughly about a quarter the size of the " Outside " or remaining area, and one-fifth the whole area, houses half the population.

The number of licensed picture houses in each area is practically the same—forty-nine in the " Central " area, fifty in the " Outside " area.

These facts are important in considering the statistics submitted in this abstract of evidence.

II. The evidence submitted takes the following form—

A. An extract from " Juvenile Crime "—a paper which I read at a Conference on Special Schools Work, held in Manchester in October last.

B. Statistics relative to an inquiry covering 360 Manchester Elementary School Departments.

C. Particulars relative to an inquiry addressed to the Managers of Cinema Houses in Manchester.

D. Conditions on which Licences are granted to show films in Manchester and which are particularly applicable to Children.

E. Some Suggestions.

A. AN EXTRACT FROM MY PAPER ON " JUVENILE CRIME "

The Influence of Boys' Literature and Picture House Films.

Many adverse criticisms have been passed from time to time on the type of cheap literature which boys read, and, more recently, on the type of film which they witness at the picture houses. It has been thought desirable to include in this report the results of certain inquiries into the degree and type of influence of these two very similar factors, and these inquiries included many visits to picture houses and the reading of many " penny dreadfuls."

Reasons for the Demand for Amusement.

Reference has been made previously to the industrial, social, and economic conditions which, in their cumulative effect, both create the desire for amusement—that is, change—and provide the means to satisfy it.

The sequence may be developed briefly as follows—

1. (a) Children are under less restraint from their elders;
   (b) School hours are shorter; therefore
   (c) (Some) children have been thrown more into the streets; but
   (d) Throughout the winter the streets have been darkened, and the weather is often inclement; and
   (e) (Many) children's homes are uninviting.
2. (a) There is no lack of employment; therefore
   (b) More money in the home; and
   (c) More pocket-money for the children.
3. (a) There is a shortage of provision for child-entertainment; but
   (b) There is a large number of picture houses; and
   (c) These are popular with parents as being near home and as providing interesting, comparatively short, and cheap entertainment.

The parents' demand created the supply of picture houses; the supply has created the demand in children. The craving for the " pictures " evinced by children is very marked, and many cases are known to teachers of children begging and stealing in order to obtain money to spend in this way. A number of boys banded themselves together as a begging society. Evening after evening they hid away their boots and stockings, and begged in the streets for money for the " pictures." The society came to a sudden end when one of its members stole the hidden boots and stockings of his companions and pawned them.

Prevalence of the Picture House Habit among Children.

There are ninety-nine halls in Manchester which are licensed to show films, and some indication of the extent to which children attend these picture houses is indicated in Table XII.

The table shows that only 22 (or 11·4 per cent.) out of 193 boys did not attend the picture house during a certain week, and that more than half of these were children (Example 3) in whose case the three days for which the statistics are given are Monday, Tuesday, and Wednesday.

Types of Films.

The type of films shown may be classified briefly as under :—

Miscellaneous—

    1. Travel.
    2. Natural History.
    3. Passing Events.

Narrative—

    4. Stories of Everyday Life.
    5. Stories of Adventure.
    6. Stories of Crime.
    7. Comic.

Effects of Different Types on Children.

The effect of picture-shows on the child's ethical outlook cannot be treated exhaustively in this report, but their positive or negative influence on juvenile crime may very properly be considered.

The main arguments for and against picture-shows as constituted at present would appear to be as set out in Chart XIII.

Suggestion and Imitation in Children.

From the brief summary in Chart XIII it is clear that a categoric condemnation of the picture house, even as organised at present, is impossible; further, it would appear that the use of films might be made an educative instrument of a high order. The limits and character of subconscious suggestion cannot be measured or defined; and whereas certain imitative criminal acts committed by boys have undoubtedly been traced to a suggestive film, it is more difficult to trace the impress on other boys who have witnessed the same film and who have been influenced more by the abstract courage or endurance portrayed by a character than by the concrete acts he performed; yet suggestion and the imitative faculty should be considered as operative in their case also.

But it is possible to produce films for boys which would be at once stirring in action and manly in tone, and from which, therefore, no criminal imitative action could accrue.

B. Statistics re Attendance of Children at Picture Houses

The inquiry covers the week ending February 3, 1917.

Number of school departments giving information—360.

Number of children present in these departments during the week—93,010.

Number of children who went to the cinema house at least once during the week—46,116 (approximately 50 per cent.).

Approximate average number of attendances for children who went at all—1·3.

Detailed statistics are given in Tables I and II.

Note—In considering these tables, the following points should be kept in mind—

(1) The table is prepared on figures supplied by the head teachers.

(2) Table I gives the number of children under ten years of age, the number of these children who attended once or more, and the number who did not attend at all.

(3) Table II gives the number of children above ten years of age, the total number of attendances they made, and additional details as to the number of attendances made by those who went once, twice, three times, four times, five times, six times.

(4) In each age-group, the children are divided into those resident in the " Central " and in the " Outside " area.

(5) The figures are in respect of both boys and girls.

CHART XIII.

Giving Outline of (a) Intellectual and Moral Effects of Various Types of Film on Children; and (b) Physical Effect of Picture-House Attendance.

TYPE OF FILM.	INTELLECTUAL AND MORAL		PHYSICAL	
	Good	Bad	Good	Bad
Travel, Natural History, Passing Events.	*Informative.* *Recreative.* Children less apt to form wrong ideas from moving pictures than from the verbal or written description. Arouse intelligent interest in everyday affairs.		Conservation of child energy, which expends itself too rapidly. Street-playing children are afforded a cheap shelter from inclement weather.	Ill effects of bad ventilation. Some picture houses are disseminators of vermin and disease. Eyestrain: children are often placed at the front where the pictures are most out of focus and the flickering of the lantern is accentuated.
Stories of Everyday Life, Adventure, Crime.	*Recreative.* Create admiration for courage, endurance, skill. Quicken the intelligence. Develop knowledge of human nature. Good triumphs over evil. Train the imagination.	Entirely pantomimic, therefore exaggerated in action and in reflecting the workings of the mind. Unrestraint is presented as normal. (Some) Films too sentimental in tone presenting details which tend to make children precocious. Crime Films bad because suggestive and awaken imitative faculty in children. Unreal and untrue to life.		Too exciting for children. Cause mental unrest, loss of sleep, and bad dreams.
Comic.	*Recreative.* Develop sense of humour.	Increase buffoonery and practical joking.		

TABLE XII

Giving Statistics, collected from Three Classes in Three different Schools, relative to Attendance at Picture Houses.

Example	Type of School	Type of District	Standard selected	Period selected	No. of Boys	No. of Boys who attended Picture Houses					Total Attendance per week	Average No. of times per week per boy
						Not at all	Once	Twice	Three times	Four times		
1.	Mun.	Poor	VI & VII	1 week	85	10	22	47	4	2	136	1·6
2.	Mun.	Poor	IV	1 week	70	0	47	20	3	—	96	1·3
3.	N.P.	Very Poor	VI & VII	½ week (3 days)	38	12	14	11	1	—	78 (39 × 2)	2
				Totals	193	22 (11·4%)	83 (43%)	78 (40·4%)	8 (4%)	2 (1%)	310	1·6

M

(6) On the whole, there is little difference between the aggregate number of attendances made by girls and that made by boys.

(7) Younger girls in the " Central " area attended the cinema houses in greater numbers than the younger girls in the " Outside " area.

(8) Older girls in the more industrial areas are useful in the home, since there are more working mothers in such areas; and this is a phase which has been accentuated during the war. Probably this accounts for the fact that the older boys in the " Central " area appear to attend rather more frequently than the girls.

(9) The older girls in the " Outside " area probably have their actions more carefully supervised by their parents, and attend, therefore, not quite so frequently as the boys of the same class.

(10) Comparing children with attendances, the figures are very similar for each of the three age-groups; about 50 per cent. of the children in each age-group went to the " pictures " at least once during the week under survey, and an average number of attendances of approximately 1·3 for each child was recorded.

TABLE I

Ages	Areas	Total No. of Children	No. of Children who did *not* go at all	No. of Children who went *at least once*
Under 10	C	28,530	13,892	14,638
	O	24,489	13,384	11,105
	Whole of Manchester	53,019	27,276	25,743

TABLE II

Ages	Areas	Total No. of Children	No. of Children who did *not* go at all	Attendances						Total No. of Attendances
				1	2	3	4	5	6	
10–12	C	12,156	5,921	4,876	2,192	660	132	30	24	7,914
	O	11,232	5,660	4,436	1,880	474	100	60	6	6,956
Over 12	C	8,670	3,948	3,560	1,810	621	152	35	30	6,208
	O	7,933	4,089	2,879	1,570	417	88	60	42	5,056
Totals	C	20,826	9,869	8,436	4,002	1,281	284	65	54	14,122
	O	19,165	9,749	7,315	3,450	891	188	120	48	12,012
	Whole of Manchester	39,991	19,618	15,751	7,452	2,172	472	185	102	26,134

C denotes Central crowded area.
O denotes areas Outside the Central area.

C. PARTICULARS SUPPLIED BY MANAGERS OF CINEMA HOUSES.

1. Number of houses to which an inquiry was addressed—99.
2. Eighteen of these are either
    (*a*) Ordinary theatres, or
    (*b*) Rooms belonging to social organisations.
3. Number of replies received—44.
4. The number of houses giving special shows for children was twenty, and these special shows were usually held on Saturday afternoons.
5. At fifteen of these houses, adults were admitted to children's shows, so that in reality there were only five houses which gave performances exclusively for children.
6. Only five houses state that they provide special programmes for children's shows.
7. The charge for admission to children varies from 1*d*. to 4*d*.
8. The number of children visiting a single cinema house during the week varies according to the managers' returns, from 100 to 1200.
9. Only six houses exclude children from " second houses " unless accompanied by an adult.
10. Only two managers state that children unaccompanied by adults are excluded from certain parts of the hall.
11. As a whole managers take no steps to exclude children suffering from ringworm or other infectious disease. The managers generally state that this is the parents' duty; one states that the Education Committee should deal with the matter; some few state that the children are watched as they enter; and some that they have excluded children so suffering. Some managers state that they have their halls flushed regularly with disinfectant fluid.
NOTE.—It is clearly most difficult for the managers of cinema houses to take any *effective* steps to exclude children suffering from infectious diseases.

D. THE TERMS AND CONDITIONS ON, AND RESTRICTIONS UNDER, WHICH LICENCES IN MANCHESTER TO SHOW FILMS ARE GRANTED AND WHICH ARE PARTICULARLY APPLICABLE TO CHILDREN ARE—

1. No indecent or objectionable incidents must be shown.
2. No incidents which are likely to encourage or incite to crime must be shown.
3. No poster shall be shown which is likely to be injurious to morality or to encourage or incite to crime.
4. Good order and decent behaviour must be maintained.
5. There shall be sufficient subdued light in the auditorium to enable any person present to see clearly to all parts.
6. The giving away of sweets, etc., by way of inducement to children is strictly forbidden.
7. Performances must not continue later than eleven o'clock.

(No restriction is placed upon the attendance of children at " second houses," either accompanied or unaccompanied by parents).

8. The means of ventilation shall be efficiently maintained and used.

9. All floors, carpets, etc., shall be thoroughly cleansed at frequent intervals.

10. No rubbish shall be deposited or allowed to accumulate in the auditorium.

E. SOME SUGGESTIONS

The cinema house as a recreative factor is firmly established, and will undoubtedly extend its influence upon both adults and children. It is necessary that immediate steps should be taken to counteract any evil effects from picture-house attendance which may arise from present conditions. It is unfair to make a sweeping condemnation of cinema houses, even as carried on at present, but undoubtedly many improvements might be made. Children learn much by seeing actions performed, and the natural corollary to seeing is doing. With children the imitative act often follows the suggestion : and herein lies the danger, as well as the educative value, of the films.

I have taken a deep interest in this aspect of children's welfare and education, and have endeavoured to preserve an open mind in considering the effects of the films on children. When in New-castle-on-Tyne I inaugurated a trial scheme whereby children in the elementary schools were taken in drafts to a certain school hall at which films were shown which had been chosen by a committee of educational experts. In Manchester I have frequently encouraged head teachers to send drafts of children during school hours to cinema houses showing approved films.

(1) The interest of children in the films is such that education committees must either
    (*a*) Co-operate with the managements of the cinema halls, or
    (*b*) Establish halls of their own.

(2) The conditions on which licences are granted and which are particularly applicable to children, should be more effectually carried out.

(3) Certain additional conditions should be attached to the issue of licences.

(4) The attendance of children after a stated time in the evening should be prohibited.

(5) There should be more effective control over the admission of children suffering from infectious disease or coming from houses in which there is infectious disease.

(6) Children should not be placed in such seats as, in their relative position to the screen, might cause eyestrain.

(7) There should be longer intervals between the showing of successive films.

(8) Explanatory addresses might be given by people with an expert knowledge of children.

(9) Crowding children in cinema houses is bad, and there should be much closer supervision than appears to obtain at present during the performances.

(10) A higher degree of diffused light should obtain in the halls.

(11) Sufficient lavatory accommodation should be provided for both boys and girls.

(12) A censorship of films for children is an urgent necessity, and should embrace also the survey of the posters exhibited advertising the films.

(13) A Board of Censors should include both men and women having intimate knowledge of child life and of the educational requirements and capacity of young children.

(14) Education committees should have the right of supervision of all cinema houses so far as the children's interests are concerned.

MINUTES OF EVIDENCE

Mr. Spurley Hey. *Examined.*

1. The Chairman. You come from Manchester, where you have a population of 750,000 people. In your statement you first of all deal with juvenile crime. Now you say, do you not, that children must have some kind of amusement ?—I agree.

2. And that for certain seasons in the year they cannot possibly even have these amusements ?—Yes.

3. And the cheapest and easiest form of amusement provided for them under cover is the cinema ?—I think that is so.

4. I notice that at Manchester some boys banded themselves together as a begging society. They took off their shoes and stockings and asked people for money for the purpose of providing boots and stockings, and this money they used to go to the pictures ?—That is so.

5. You have ninety-nine halls in Manchester. That is a very large proportion as compared with other cities ?—I think it is larger than other cities when compared in size.

6. Some are large and some are small, some are new and well founded and sanitarily perfect and satisfactory, and then they come down to the unsatisfactory ?—Yes, some are quite unsatisfactory, whereas others are well ventilated and well fitted up.

7. With reference to juvenile crime, I want to take up some of the bad effects you have put down. " Some picture houses are disseminators of vermin and disease." Are there many houses in Manchester of that kind ?—I think there are picture houses in which the sanitary conditions are not at all satisfactory, and in which children living in the crowded areas might and actually do attend, such children in certain cases having been excluded from school on the ground of ringworm or some other equally infectious complaint.

8. Now, can you suggest to me any way in which at any place

of entertainment—not merely the cinema, but any other places of entertainment to which the child goes—the proprietors can tell whether the child has ringworm ?—No, I do not think I can, and I do not suggest that by any arrangement you will be able to exclude all children, but I think it is possible to arrive at some arrangement for the exclusion of the worst cases of suffering children.

9. Can you tell us in what direction that might be done ?—I think it would be very difficult for those who manage the picture houses to do this kind of thing themselves, but that is one of the points upon which there might be co-operation with the Education Committee.

10. You do not suggest anything like a ticket office examination ? —I do not.

11. Do you say from your educational experience that children are placed too near the front where their eyes are strained ?—I am positively certain they are placed too near the front, and I am afraid that that position has a bad effect on the eyesight of the children.   I have evidence from our own medical staff and teachers on that point.

12. Has Manchester with its Corporation or its Council ever taken into consideration how best to provide cheap entertainment and amusement for children out of school hours ?—Not to any considerable extent.   They have considered the question of throwing open the school playgrounds in the evening, but that, of course, is not during the winter.   They have also considered the question of taking the children into the parks, and a certain number of playgrounds and special parts of the park have been thrown open to them; but that, of course, is only touching the fringe of the question.   But where the greatest need arises there are no parks.

13. Now these stories of everyday living with the excitement the children get, did you get your evidence from the schools ?— Yes.

14. Now I notice you say something about the bad effects of these stories, and in looking through your bad effects which you say have been produced, it occurs to me that some theatrical entertainments would produce the same effects where there is not only seeing but hearing.   For instance, you have a detective or a comic story and such things like that ?—I think it is a matter of degree.   I do not think the effect would be quite so bad at one place as it would at another, for, you see, in the theatre you have the " balance " of the conversation to set off the action.

15. Well, you have the story book of an unsatisfactory kind— I mean the story of crime.   Would you tell me what the difference between a bad story book and an unsatisfactory crime film is ?— Without saying how unsatisfactory it is, I think in the same sense it is unsatisfactory watching the wrong kind of thing at the film and seeing the wrong kind of thing on the stage.

16. And you are satisfied that these crime films do suggest and do awaken the imitative faculty in the child ?—I think that is

perfectly true, but that is only half the story. It does mean that some children may commit crimes because of what they have seen. On the other hand, it is difficult to say how many children are saved from committing crimes by being in picture houses. I am quite sure that certain crimes have been committed to some extent as the result of visits to picture houses, but I am not very sure in my own mind at the present time as to how far there is a greater aggregate of crime than there would have been without the pictures.

17. In London we used to have hooliganism in the streets. You would imply that supposing some of these boys had been in some place of entertainment they would have been less likely to develop that hooliganism?—That is so; and it is especially true of the conditions during the last two and a half years when the streets have been darkened and there has been this abnormal excitement. I am inclined to think that the picture house is a safer place than the streets in many instances.

18. I notice that you say " that the poorest district seems to be the one in which the children go to the cinema."—The word " poorer " is used to a large extent from the point of view of the children being badly clothed, badly nourished. I do not know that there is less money altogether there than in certain other areas. There may be more extravagance and more waste.

19. In your evidence I am struck with the large number of children who do not go at all. This information has been carefully prepared by your teachers?—Very carefully; and I had another week taken which I have not put in, and that verifies this result.

20. That 50 per cent. of the children do not attend at all?—Practically 50 per cent. did not go during those weeks.

21. That strikes me as being high. Now, you addressed your inquiries to ninety-nine cinema houses and only forty-four replied? Have you any reason in your mind as to why the other houses did not reply?—There were quite reasonable grounds for no reply. It was probably somewhat unusual for them to be asked these questions, and although I impressed upon the managers that it was perfectly friendly from my point of view and entirely with the object of co-operating, I think there was some ground for wondering what the information was required for.

22. Would you say that this new industry was a little suspicious of inquiries being made by public authorities?—No, I would not say that. You see, they have not dealt with the Education Committee in the past, and I suppose any one who deals with this kind of thing is rather suspicious of any department, or even a central authority, approaching them.

23. I notice there are only five houses that give performances exclusively for children. I want your opinion as to children's entertainments; for instance, if the entertainment is for children absolutely, whether adults should be admitted?—I should not say that children and adults should not mix at the same entertainment or in the same building. I think it is reasonable to arrange under certain conditions for special entertainments for children and for

special entertainments for adults, most of all for special entertainments for children.

24. You would never have an entertainment for children from which you exclude the adults ?—I think that any entertainment exclusively for children might be considered satisfactory for adults and adults might be admitted, but I do not think the opposite is true.

25. And the restrictions you have at Manchester with regard to the exhibitions, there is nothing very out of the way about them ? —So long as the regulations are carried out.

26. It is stated there that the performances must not continue later than eleven o'clock. Does that mean that the children are allowed to go there up till eleven o'clock at night ?—That is so, and I think I said in my evidence that only six houses exclude children from the second house unless accompanied by an adult. I certainly think children should not be allowed to stay until eleven o'clock at night.

27. Would you be inclined to say that the second house should be closed to children ?—I should certainly say that, and I would prefer to see children—that is, those under fourteen years of age —excluded after eight o'clock.

28. These children are to come out at eight o'clock, and you must bear in mind their parents do not see that they go to bed at eight o'clock ?—I am thinking mostly when I say eight o'clock of the fact that you will not make a child go to bed at any particular time, whilst you can make them leave the picture house.

29. Would you like an adult attendant to be provided to keep order in regard to the children's entertainments ?—I think that is a very important point. One of my real complaints is that great harm may be done, and I believe is done, by the lack of proper supervision. In regard to this matter, when the houses were built and the films prepared and the general arrangements made, children were forgotten, and had to fit in under the conditions provided for adults. Now not only at the entrance is there a great deal of supervision required; but the lack of proper supervision when the children are in their seats is, in my opinion, detrimental to them. I will take one point, the question of seating. Children are made to sit in a way detrimental both to their health and their morals. I can give a case, for instance, where something like this occurred that, say 300 children, have had to sit upon seats prepared for 200 adults. The seats are tip-up seats with no arms, so that the children can be pushed together, and that is bad and ought not to be allowed. Then again, the children are allowed to mix together, and there is no arrangement in some of the halls where children at the back can see over the children in front. All these things are bad for the children, and I feel in this matter that the physical side is of great importance.

30. Supposing you had the cinema supervised, would you have that done by people appointed by the trade or the local authorities ?—I have not thought of that, but on the spur of the moment

I would say I would like the trade to make their own arrangements, but I should like supervision by the educational authority. By supervision I mean such things as the right of inspection.

31. I think you would find then that the better part of the trade would be aware that the wisest thing would be to fall into line with the local authorities as far as possible?—I have found that to be the case.

32. In your evidence you say there should be longer intervals between the showing of successive films. Will you tell us why? —If there were longer intervals I think the eyestrain would be considerably relieved. The actual concentration on the pictures would be reduced throughout the performance. I would like to see an interval of that kind utilised, say, by explanations from a capable man. If that could not be done, I would like to have music between, something to relieve the concentration and make the show educational.

33. Supposing you were absolutely free to decide, would you like a central Board of Censors who shall be supreme, or would you like a censorship in each locality?—Speaking from the point of view of Manchester, I would rather have the censorship in Manchester than in London.

34. Supposing the censorship was of this kind, that it included people from, say, Manchester, and people from London who met at a centre and dealt with the matter from a central point of view, that would not please you so much as the local censorship?— Personally, it would not, but I think the great point is that the right people should be on the Board of Censors. It requires people who know something of children, their capabilities and their outlook. So long as the right men and women—and if there should be a difference in the number I say more women than men—are on the Board, I am not concerned so much where the censorship Board meets.

35. Do you think anything can be done in the school with regard to teaching education by means of the cinematograph?—When I was in Newcastle I tried an experiment of that sort by setting up a screen and an apparatus generally in a school, and that experiment was carried on for a little over six months. All I can say about it is that it justified a further experiment. That was at a time when really good films for children were few. I believe there is an opening for a large authority to deal with this question from an educational point of view.

36. With regard to the entertainment or amusement of children, do you think that any kind of amusement is definitely satisfactory to a child if that amusement to some extent is regulated and ordered by the authority the child is under for the rest of the day? —I will answer that by the action I have taken myself with regard to the recreative play centres we are about to set up in Manchester. We may do that through organisations already in existence so long as the Education Committee approves, or we may do it ourselves in co-operation with them. I say it will not be done adequately or satisfactorily unless the local authorities take it in

hand, but I do not suggest that the local authority should do it exclusively itself.

37. What you would really like would be that the Education Committee and the cinema trade should, for the benefit of the children from an amusement and educative point of view, co-operate generally for the children ?—Yes.

38. PROFESSOR H. GOLLANCZ.   You agree that a subdued light does not in any way interfere with the performance ?—I have seen very dark halls and really light ones, and I would prefer the light ones from every point of view.   I believe that while relieving eye-strain, apart from other matters, from my point of view the value of the pictures did not suffer because of the more highly diffused light.

39. LIEUT.-GEN. SIR R. BADEN-POWELL'S REPRESENTATIVE. Are there promenades or standing room in the halls ?—I have not been in the ninety-nine halls, as you will understand, but I have been in some of the best houses and in some of the worst.   I have never seen any promenading down the sides or down the middle of the hall beyond going to the seats.   I have never seen a real promenade at the back, but I have seen people standing at the back; in fact, I have stood at the back many times myself.   I have been in no house in Manchester where people are allowed to stand at the back to such a depth that the passage is interfered with.

40. Have you ever known of improper behaviour in the standing room ?—I have never seen it nor heard of it.

41. Which type of film attracts the children the most ?—I am sorry to say the comic.

42. MR. NEWBOULD.   In your evidence you say : " The Education Committee should have the right of supervision of all cinema houses so far as the children's interests are concerned."   Should they not first of all have the supervision of the children's homes and home life ?—To some extent I suppose some other local authority is supposed to carry that out.   The whole root of the matter is the question of housing and the bad conditions of the streets.   I mean the mean, narrow streets where there are no playgrounds, and then I should say there is not the slightest doubt that the picture houses are more comfortable than the home.

43. DR. SALEEBY.   Can you give us any idea why in Manchester singers are not allowed between the films ?—This is the by-law : "Singing shall not be permitted and no variety entertainment shall be allowed in any premises licensed under the Act which does not have a theatre licence."

44. MR. KING.   Would you require a child which has been accompanied by its parents to be sent away at eight o'clock and the parents remain ?—I think the parents must make up their minds as to what to do.   I think that children under fourteen years of age should generally be in their own houses at nine o'clock.

45. MR. GRAVES.   How often do you think a child ought to attend ?—I think one attendance a week is sufficient for any child who is still in attendance at school.

46. MR. EDGAR JEPSON.   If the choice were open, would you

prefer a child to go once a week to a music hall or to a cinema?
—To a cinema. I might tell you that I have had evidence from
teachers that children who go to cinemas habitually suffer from
lassitude.

47. Are those who go once a week more intelligent than those
who do not go at all?—I was only speaking from the physical side.
I think in some respects the children who go to cinemas gain
intellectually, but in some respects they suffer. It is difficult to
compare these things. You must remember this, that this habit
of going to cinemas is so deep in the lives of the children, that those
who go once now will probably soon be going oftener, and this is
likely to spread.

STATEMENT OF EDWARD NICHOLLS

PRÉCIS

In addition to the theatres under my control I have repeatedly
visited many others in important towns, and I am able to say
that the music does not fall short of the standard observed at the
theatres under my control; but on the other hand a healthy competition tends continually to raise this standard to a higher and
higher level.

The permanent musical staff under my control number 250,
all first-class musicians, an average of twelve per theatre, but this
number is occasionally augmented for special performances.

The combination of the orchestras varies from trios, quin-
tets, septets, and so. on, two separate orchestras (with one or
two exceptions) being employed at each theatre to ensure continuous orchestral music throughout the day's performance.

In addition, we have a permanent Symphony Orchestra of forty-
five most highly skilled musicians. The object of this orchestra
is to tour the Company's theatres from time to time for a season.

The cost of the Company's orchestras is approximately £33,000
to £34,000 a year.

The standard of music played varies from the old classics,
modern classics, suites, overtures, entr'actes, etc., down to the
modern up-to-date musical comedy, rag-time, etc.

Instructions have always been to make high-class music a
feature at these theatres, but unfortunately owing to the many
idiosyncrasies of the existing music licences in some of our provincial towns it has not always been an easy task to carry this
out.

For instance, some months ago, I wished to install the Symphony
Orchestra for a season at our theatre in Oxford Street, Manchester,
but the magistrates most strongly opposed the scheme, and it
was only allowed after a strenuous effort on our part on condition
*that the Symphony Orchestra only accompanied the pictures and
did not play any special selections!*

Recently on another occasion we applied for a licence for the
Symphony Orchestra to play at our theatre in Wolverhampton.

Again I was informed by the Magistrates' Clerk that they had no power to grant us the favour as the music licence clearly stipulated *that no brass instrument could be allowed in any picture theatre orchestra in that town!* I pleaded that the Directors were most desirous of giving to their patrons a season of entertainment of the highest educational order, but the only satisfaction I received was a humorously absurd suggestion: " Why not send the Symphony Orchestra without the brass instruments ! " Similar absurd conditions prevail in other towns on the circuit.

At the commencement of war my Directors, wishing to stimulate patriotism with a view to recruiting, requested me to engage one or two well-known singers to tour their theatres and *sing only patriotic songs*. Having engaged these artistes at very heavy fees, we were confronted with the same opposition. In some towns they were not permitted to appear. In Manchester after very great trouble one singer was allowed on condition that the sum of £50 was given to the local branch of the Prince of Wales's fund.

In many of our theatres we have solo instrumentalists of very considerable merit, and a practice was instituted to give a short musical selection or solo between the pictures. This innovation met with considerable success, but unfortunately in several places we were informed that it was contrary to the provisions of our music licence.

During my experience for the last five years I have come to the conclusion that music plays and will play a still more important part in this class of amusement.

MINUTES OF EVIDENCE

EDWARD NICHOLLS. *Examined.*

1. THE CHAIRMAN. You are a composer? You have been through France, Germany, Holland, Belgium and Italy in a musical capacity? You are now a director of music of a company controlling twenty-one cinema theatres, all in the provinces?—Yes.

2. As far as you can judge, do you find that music attracts to the cinemas? The better the music the more likely the people are to come?—I think so; I think music has played a very important part, much more so in the last five years. It is gradually growing and playing a still more important part.

3. And is there a great deal of pains taken now as regards the music appropriate to a particular drama or whatever may be on?—That has been our greatest difficulty. We have certainly battled with it as far as possible. It could only be dealt with by some sort of automatic arrangement which would be impossible. So far as the synchronisation goes, we do that as far as possible, but to try and synchronise to the very moment is almost impossible; and therefore we deal with it by creating an atmosphere in keeping with the picture.

4. Now is there a direct opposition to the cinema having singing

and also excellent music on the part of the other entertainments such as the music hall?—Of course, there are occasions when there is certain opposition, but I have known of none in my experience in that way. The opposition has simply been the pig-headedness of the magistrates.

5. Has there been an opposition engineered by the music halls?—No, and I can prove that in Wolverhampton the music halls wanted us to get the necessary licence.

6. I am a little puzzled as to what the objection can be.—It has also been a great puzzle to me. Now in Manchester on one occasion we wished to install a symphony orchestra there, and no one could object to that orchestra, but permission was refused. It seemed rather absurd to think that the restriction was simply placed there by some licensing law that ought to be obsolete. On this occasion the police passed it, the Watch Committee acquiesced in it, and the magistrate said : " What is this ? Why, your music licence says so-and-so. Is it going to play to the pictures ? " I said : " Yes "; but still they refused it. This orchestra was going to play special selections, and I wanted to know what difference it made to have a special selection.

7. But they allow special individuals to play?—Yes.

8. You had a Russian violinist playing in Birmingham?—Yes.

9. But supposing he wanted to sing a song, that would not be allowed?—No.

10. Do you have to get a separate licence in those cities where you are allowed to have music and singing?—I think there are only one or two theatres where there is a singing and music licence.

11. Some of the objections taken to the cinemas as they now are will be immensely lessened if you have music in between, and therefore, it seems to me they would be helping the authorities to make the cinemas more what they ought to be like, that is, of course, if they allow the music and singing. Do you think the authorities understand this point?—Yes, I do, but it seems that they are such a long time in conceiving the benefit that would arise.

12. Do you get requests for special pieces of music?—Yes.

13. Do you think there is now considerable evidence of musical progress?—Yes. For instance, it was a great surprise to me only quite recently in Manchester and in Glasgow to see our first and second row of seats in the stalls filled with musical students, as I have myself sat several times, simply to watch the symphony orchestra and to follow them with the scores.

14. Why are singers or brass instruments barred?—We do not know.

15. Are musical entr'actes popular?—Very.

16. Do other theatres than yours announce their music on the programmes?—I think so; most theatres do.

17. May I take it that there are two important senses engaged at your cinemas, the eye and the ear?—Yes, not only seeing but hearing the music, but I have heard a man say that a first-class orchestra put him off the picture.

18. A complaint against the cinema is that you are only exercising the eye. If you are having beautiful music at the same time, you are doing something for the ear as well. I am rather defending the cinemas from that point of view, if you see what I mean?—Yes, and I quite agree.

19. Monsignor Brown. Are the selections played in full, or are they only parts?—In full, but of course, they might be cut on certain occasions.

20. Have you any considerable knowledge of the music which is given in halls where they have a small orchestra or only a piano?—I have only seen such things when I have been into an opposition house. You must bear in mind that the cheaper halls cannot afford grand orchestras, whereas there is a very healthy competition in the better-class houses for these orchestras.

21. Dr. Kimmins. When you have a new film, how do you manage to get the proper music for it?—If it is a very special film for our own company, I endeavour to see it myself some weeks beforehand, and then I arrange the special music for it and send on my suggestions to all my conductors. They see it on the morning of the day it arrives, and fit their pieces in. Those are only special films, as it would be impossible for me to arrange music for every film.

22. Rev. F. C. Spurr. Would it not be an educational help if people knew what kind of music they were listening to?—Yes, and the houses should have programmes as we do, with the names of the pieces printed on them. I know of no better system.

23. Principal Garvie. Would the theatre be kept in darkness while the special selections are played?—No, we put the lights up, certainly.

24. So the objections could not be on the ground that the darkness gave any chance for misconduct?—No.

25. Supposing each cinema had an orchestra, would a considerable space be required in front of the film, and would that do away with the objection of having the front seats too near?—It would be a decided advantage to the audience.

26. Did you ever feel that the music was too good for the film it accompanied?—I know this, that music has lifted a bad film up into a good one; it has helped it.

TENTH DAY

Monday, March 12, 1917,

The BISHOP OF BIRMINGHAM in the chair.

STATEMENT OF MR. RODERICK ROSS, M.V.O.
Chief Constable of Edinburgh.

PRÉCIS

IN the social life of the people during recent years there has been nothing more outstanding and remarkable than the growth and development of the cinema as a means of public entertainment and amusement.

Not only in large towns but in country districts the cinema has met with phenomenal success, and received the support and patronage of all classes of society.

Edinburgh has been no exception to this rule. Every principal thoroughfare has its picture house, and the large queues which form every evening—more especially on Saturdays—outside these places waiting for admission testify to the popularity of this form of entertainment, and to the fact that the public are satisfied with the enjoyment the picture houses provide, and that the cinema has become part and parcel of the people's amusement and of the social life of the community.

There were many who predicted that the popularity of the cinema would gradually wane, and that it was only the novelty of the exhibition that had caught the popular fancy and attracted so many, and that, after the novelty had worn off, the power of the cinema as a means of public entertainment would gradually decrease. The years have proved the fallacy of such predictions. The cinemas — at least those in Edinburgh — are as popular as ever, and this notwithstanding the fact that we are passing through a period when amusement, it is thought, would be least indulged in by the people.

What, it may be asked, is the reason of the cinema's popularity?

In my opinion this is brought about by the fact that the entertainment provided meets with the approbation and approval of the public in respect that an educative, morally wholesome, and bright entertainment is given at a price within the reach of all.

In this undoubtedly lies the secret of the popularity of the cinema, and from this fact it has, without doubt, come to stay, and is destined to continue as a permanent form of amusement in our midst.

The cinema, in consequence of its popularity, must, therefore, of necessity exercise a certain influence either for good or evil in the social life of the community.

In my opinion, the popularity of the cinema among all classes and conditions of men and women is a guarantee of its power for good in the community. Were the lessons it taught to exercise an influence for evil in the people, that evil would ere now have made itself manifest in some form or other; but such has not been the case.

It is scarcely possible that thousands upon thousands of our citizens could nightly come under an influence detrimental to their moral character without some manifestation, however slight, of the evil inculcated making itself apparent in their conduct and mode of living.

It is my opinion that the cinema, as a rule, has proved to those who patronise it an educative, morally healthy, and pleasure-giving entertainment.

It has also, without doubt, been the means of attracting many who otherwise would have resorted to the public-house, and in this connection my divisional officers, who have opportunities of judging, emphatically state that the picture houses have been instrumental in reducing intemperance in the city.

The cinema, however, is not without its opponents and critics, although I must say I have had surprisingly few complaints made to me with regard thereto so far as Edinburgh is concerned.

The complaints made were generally as to the films exhibited being of an indecent character or suggestive of immorality. On investigation by the police, all complaints made were found to be such that no action could be taken, as the police were of opinion that the films complained of were not indecent representations, and accordingly did not come within the scope of the criminal law.

One of the complaints made, I remember, had reference to a film entitled " —— ——," where the innuendo was that immorality had taken place.

Such films which contain suggestions of this kind ought, in my opinion, to be eliminated from the cinema. It must be remembered that of the great number of people patronising the picture houses many are girls and youths of impressionable age, and while such exhibitions may, on the majority of persons, have no impression, there is always the fear that in some instances these exhibitions suggesting immoral conduct may have a deleterious effect.

It is true that in the reading of novels as much evil, if not more so, may be gleaned by the young, but that is no reason why the cinema in this respect should not keep clear of this pernicious phase of the question.

There is another matter on which the cinema has been criticised. In some quarters it has been alleged that the exhibition of films which showed burglars and other criminals at work have been the means of inciting boys to emulate the example given by committing crime.

No such case has come to my knowledge or to the knowledge of my detective officers. I, however, consider that there is grave danger in such representations. Boys are generally of an adventurous disposition, and ever ready to emulate anything in the way of an example which would afford them vent for the inherent love of adventure which is in their natures. For this reason I am decidedly opposed to representations of such a character being shown to the young.

It has also been frequently alleged that juvenile crime was in measure due to the love of the cinema on the part of boys who took to stealing for the purpose of procuring money with which to pay for admission to the picture house, and thus gratifying their insatiable desires in this direction

I am unable to find a single case where any juvenile set out to steal for this one purpose.

I admit that the proceeds of several thefts have been spent on the cinema, but this fact cannot be brought as a fault against the picture houses.

In most instances I have found that the proceeds of theft by juveniles have gone to satisfy their fondness or craze for gambling, which is more in keeping with their vicious tendencies than witnessing an exhibition of living pictures.

Independent of the cinema, boys will continue to steal and to devote the proceeds of their dishonesty to whatever purpose may take their fancy.

I am satisfied that, so far as Edinburgh is concerned, the cinema, in this respect and as a means of inciting the commission of crime on the part of juveniles, has had little or no effect on the crime committed by children and young persons.

I have shown the foregoing statement of evidence to the chief constables of Dundee and Aberdeen, and they concur therein.

MINUTES OF EVIDENCE

MR. RODERICK ROSS, M.V.O. *Examined.*

1. THE CHAIRMAN. You have no figures, I suppose, as to the numbers that go to the cinema in Edinburgh?—We have twenty-four houses in the city, and I understand that their seating capacity is about 17,000. There are special performances on Saturday afternoons for children.

2. Are children only admitted to these performances?—Well, adults go too.

3. Are there any suggestions as to the numbers that attend each week?—No, I have not got that. Most of these houses are pretty well filled at all times.

4. What is the population of Edinburgh?—Between 320,000 and 330,000.

5. You claim, of course, in Edinburgh that the population is, from the point of view of intellect, rather above the average?—It is supposed to be a fairly intellectual city.

6. And you find that all classes of society go to the cinema entertainments?—Yes.

7. Now you say that it is approved of because it gives an educative and morally wholesome and a bright entertainment?—That is my opinion.

N

8. Are there any houses in Edinburgh of which you could reasonably complain as to the want of wholesome entertainment? —The only complaint I remember was a complaint in regard to the film "——— ———." I went down to see the film, and sat in the house while it was on, and from a police point of view I could see nothing objectionable.

9. What would be the police point of view?—There was nothing that brought the management within the meaning of the criminal law; there was nothing indecent about it.

10. MR. T. P. O'CONNOR. Speaking outside the criminal law would you find anything indecent?—Well, it was not exactly a film I would like to send my daughter to, but from a police point of view there was nothing objectionable.

11. THE CHAIRMAN. You mean a young girl or woman under eighteen years of age?—That is so.

12. Would you mind telling me in what you consider the cinema educative?—You see films depicting the customs of countries which common people would not know about unless they saw them on the films.

13. You do not mean technically educative, but that it widens the mind and gives people knowledge which otherwise they would not be likely to obtain?—That is what I mean to convey.

14. Have you had any complaints in regard to any houses as to the possibility of immorality taking place within the building? —I do not think it is possible for immorality to take place within the building. I have had one or two complaints of indecent assaults having been committed, and I have spoken to other chief constables who have had similar complaints, and I have no doubt that is due largely to the fact that the cinema is carried on in a state of darkness more or less. If you will allow me I will read what the Chief Constable of Aberdeen says.

15. You bring a good deal of accumulative information from other chief constables?— Your secretary asked me to submit evidence, and I have two letters here, one from the Chief Constable of Aberdeen and one from the Chief Constable of Dundee. They write me—

" I duly received your letter of the 28th ult. with copy of your statement of evidence. I have carefully considered the same and I concur therein. Personally, I seldom visit the picture houses, but I know that they are patronised by large numbers of citizens and are visited by members of the force, and I am satisfied that if anything far wrong occurred my attention would soon be directed to the matter. In variety theatres I have seen acting of a more objectionable nature in my opinion than anything I have seen at a cinema show. At the same time, it appears to me a censor of films would be a step in the right direction.

" (Signed) W. ANDERSON,
" Chief Constable of Aberdeen."

" I am in receipt of your favour of yesterday enclosing copy of your statement of evidence regarding cinematograph exhibitions,

in all of which I concur.   There is one point which you may have
an opportunity of touching on, *i. e.* lighting of the premises.   I
have heard it suggested that in the darker parts of some houses,
the behaviour of some of the patrons, if not altogether indecent,
sexually, has been at least suspicious.   Were due attention paid
to the construction of the premises—boxes, lounges, and promenades—and the highest degree of light consistent with the proper
working of the lantern insisted on, cause for complaint in this
respect would be removed.

" (Signed) J. CARMICHAEL,
" Chief Constable of Dundee."

16. THE CHAIRMAN.   Do you think that the possibility of any
indecency of that sort is much more due to the comparative
darkness than to the fact that the cinema is an extremely cheap
entertainment and, therefore, it is easier for people of a low moral
standpoint to get in; people who would not be sorry for the opportunity of some kind of indecency ?—I should think that there is a
good deal in what you suggest.   The low standard of morality of
the individual and the darkness combined, I have no doubt leads
to this kind of thing.   Probably both phases of the matter should
be taken into consideration.

17. I notice both from Dundee and Aberdeen there is only
this one point of objection raised at all.   That, I suppose, might
imply there is nothing else to which they might object ?—The
chief constables of Dundee and Aberdeen have nothing to say
against the picture houses.   I have come to the conclusion that
they have done a great deal more good than harm.   I mean in
this way.   Many people prior to the picture house coming into
existence adjourned to a public-house and there got more or less
drunk.   The view I take is that it is much better for them to come
to a picture house than a public-house.

18. MR. T. P. O'CONNOR.   That applies also to keeping children
a little more off the streets ?—It does.

19. THE CHAIRMAN.   Now with regard to juvenile crime,
which is supposed to be due to the cinema influence, have you
come across that in your police courts ?—Well, we have from time
to time complaints that juveniles steal for this purpose, but I
have not been able to get one case or one conviction.   I made
some notes on this matter, if you will allow me to read them.

" The first picture house in Edinburgh was opened on 18th July,
1910.   Special performances for juveniles are held on Saturday
afternoons in twelve houses, the charges being a penny and three-
halfpence.   One of the conditions of the cinema licence is that a
child under twelve years of age shall not be allowed to remain in
said premises after nine o'clock unless accompanied by a parent
or guardian.   It is the custom in picture houses in the poorer
quarters of the city for a considerable number of women with
children in arms to attend these places late at night.   In one
picture house in one evening after 8 p.m. no less than forty-two
women with children in arms were seen to leave the premises.

This is a matter to be deplored, but it is no doubt due to the fact that most of the husbands of these women are at present on active service with His Majesty's Forces, and no doubt the women are glad to have a little relaxation from the weary round which is theirs; and being unable, of course, to leave the children behind have perforce to take them with them. As a proof of the fact that the cinema, which came into active being in Edinburgh in 1910, is not responsible for juvenile crime, I give the numbers of persons under sixteen years of age convicted of crime during the five years from 1912 to 1916.

1912	.	.	.	.	.	.	335 persons
1913	.	.	.	.	.	.	309 ,,
1914	.	.	.	.	.	.	352 ,,
1915	.	.	.	.	.	.	423 ,,
1916	.	.	.	.	:	.	553 ,,

" In several recent cases of juveniles coming before the court it has been pleaded on their behalf by agents appearing for them that the cause of their downfall was due to the excitement brought about by attending the cinema. I caused inquiries to be made into the truth of a plea of this nature put forth in the case of a number of boys who were before the court for housebreaking last week, and find that there was no truth whatever in the allegation that the picture house had been responsible for their delinquency. The boys themselves admitted that they committed the crime through pure mischief, and that they had not been influenced in any way by what they had seen in any picture house. As will be seen from the figures of juvenile crime a great increase has taken place since 1914. The cinema was established in 1910, and from then until 1913 juvenile crime was normal. It is, in my opinion, very significant that the increase of crime amongst juveniles should synchronise with the outbreak of war. This undoubtedly points to the fact that with so many fathers and guardians absent on military service, the lack of the necessary parental control has been the principal cause of increased crime amongst juveniles."

20. REV. CAREY BONNER. Are the theatres well lit in Edinburgh? —Yes, quite well lit, but the light is subdued when the films are exposed.

21. Are they in total darkness ?—No.

22. Can you give us any information as to opening on Sundays? —They do not open on Sundays, but they may open for a charitable purpose where the proceeds are given to a charity.

23. Did you notice whether the film " ——— ——— " had been passed by the censor?—Yes, it was passed by the British Board of Censors. I had complaints about it prior to it coming to the city, and it was alleged that it was stopped at Preston and Dublin, or Belfast, and I wrote to both those cities and I found that my information was not correct. The film was passed by a British Board of Censors, and I was not going to interfere with it.

24. SIR JOHN KIRK. Do the school teachers take parties of children to the cinema?—I do not remember any such case. I would get a notice of anything of that sort, because of arranging for the safety of the children in crossing the streets.

25. MR. LAMERT. Have you had any complaints whatever that the children have been molested at these theatres in Edinburgh?—No, I have not. The only case in which I remember a child having been interfered with was in one of the ordinary theatres.

26. You say that under the magistrate's orders the children are not allowed to go unaccompanied after nine oclock. The suggestion has been made that children possibly accost people outside cinemas and hand them their money with a view to seeing whether they would palm them off as their own son or daughter and so get in?—I do not think it occurs to any extent, but there may be an isolated case.

27. MONSIGNOR BROWN. As to the increase of crime, would you agree that that may be due not only to the fact that the father is away, but that there are many cases in which the mother is employed and away from home much more, and that this leads to the children being out of control and on the streets?—There is little doubt about that.

28. As to " —— ——," have you heard of any action being taken in Manchester as regards that or " —— —— "?—No.

29. You say you would not allow your own daughter or anybody else's daughter to see that film; therefore, you would not regard it as a film suited for general display?—No, were I a censor I should certainly ban it for young people under eighteen or twenty years of age.

30. Have you noticed any display bills that are objectionable?—I have never been struck by some of these things being indecent.

31. You have never heard the police speak of them?—No.

32. DR. MARIE STOPES. With regard to the question of nudity, is that always objectionable even if it is presented from a moral or gymnastic point of view? Would you always object to nude figures?—Well, that is a somewhat difficult question to answer. It depends entirely on how the figure is presented.

33. I believe the censor looks upon the nude figure as always objectionable?—We might consider it objectionable, but it is another matter as to whether we should interfere or not.

34. THE CHAIRMAN. The nude figure is not necessarily under the police ban?—No.

35. DR. KIMMINS. Have you any association in Edinburgh which looks after the cinema, or is it left entirely to the police?—There is certainly no association that looks after them.

36. And films are not subjected in any way to criticism unless some objection is raised?—I have never seen any criticism upon any film which has been presented. These complaints that I had with regard to " —— —— " were from private individuals or private letters to me. There was no criticism in the Press or anything of that sort.

37. You do not in any way look through the programmes regularly?—No, but I may say the places are visited daily by the police.

38. REV. F. C. SPURR. Would you tell us if you advocate special performances for children?—I think it would be quite a good thing that special films should be exhibited to children only.

39. Have the Edinburgh police the power, as I believe they have in most cases, to seize objectionable prints and photographs? —Yes, any objectionable or indecent.

40. But you have not the power to seize objectionable films? —If the films were indecent we should not seize them, but we should proceed against the management.

41. With regard to the cheaper houses, where I think you mention the price is one penny admission, will you tell us whether you consider the ventilation is what it should be, and whether the front seats are as far from the screen as they should be?— I am afraid the structure of the premises does not come within my purview. I have never had any complaints brought to my notice that these places are ill-ventilated. I think if other departments of the Corporation had had these complaints I should have heard about them.

42. SIR W. BARRETT. You say that the lighting of the cinemas is quite adequate. During the showing of the films is the light adequate to allow the audience to read their programmes?—I do not think they could read the programme unless it was pretty large print. I should imagine that it is not necessary for the audience to be in darkness.

43. What degree of lighting is there in the theatre when the films are being shown?—A fair amount.

44. MR. G. KING. You have had an opportunity of comparing the cinemas in Edinburgh with the lighting in the theatre and the music halls. In the case of the theatre did you find you were able to read a newspaper during the period when the lights are lowered?—I think the lighting in the cinema is quite as good as in the theatre.

45. MR. T. P. O'CONNOR. Did you ever read the book ——— ———?—I did after I saw the film, with a view to seeing whether it was dramatised fully.

46. Did you find some difference between the book and the film?—Yes.

47. Rather in favour of the cinema as against the book?—Yes.

48. Are you aware that in connection with that particular film the censorship laid down the rule that even though the cinema might be unobjectionable it was undesirable it should reproduce novels which had an undesirable reputation?—I believe that is so.

49. THE CHAIRMAN. What is your control over books?—I have no control over books unless they are of an indecent nature.

50. And ——— ——— would not come under that category? —No. Would you allow me to say one word with regard to drunkenness?

" With regard to my statement as to the picture houses being instrumental in reducing intemperance, I came to this conclusion as far back as the year 1911, and in my annual report of that year I find the following occurs with regard to drunkenness—

" ' The reduction recorded in the number charged may be due to the large increase in places of amusement opened during recent years which cater for the adult as well as for the youth, and divert their inclinations from the public-house.'

" The following year a further reduction in the number of persons charged with drunkenness took place, and in my annual report for that year I make the following statement—

" ' I am more than convinced that people are behaving themselves better than formerly, and I am of opinion . . . that the gradual decrease in drunkenness has been brought about by the opening up to the people of more means of rational amusement such as the picture house, of which the city contains a considerable number. These places of amusement, which always seem to be well patronised by the public, have without doubt brought about a wonderful improvement in the sobriety of the city.' "

STATEMENT OF THE REV. T. HORNE,

Rector of Syresham, Northants, and Senior Chaplain to the Showmen's Guild of Great Britain and Ireland.

PRÉCIS

WITH the experience of half a century as a social worker, directly concerned with the working classes, and with special inside knowledge of the cinema industry, I claim to know the subject before the Commission.

I have been inside the cinema movement from its invention and application to entertainment purposes. Long before the cinema appeared as an item on music-hall programmes and picture halls were established, my showmen with large portable theatres were using the cinema for show purposes.

In many ways I was the one and only censor of films in those early days, and I am proud of the fact that my suggestions were invariably carried out, and that my travelling showmen sought opportunities of submitting films to me prior to exhibition.

I was, in those early days, to a very large extent able to prevent the growth of a class of film manufacture largely French and in my judgment unsuited to a British audience.

When the cinema began to develop rapidly in permanent buildings a considerable number of my showmen were concerned in the settled movement, and have prospered in it. My association with the cinema in its settled form was owing to the fact that

I had been with the showmen in its itinerant days. As the industry began to organise itself, immediately after the passing of the Cinematograph Act in 1909, I was asked by the cinema exhibitors to help them in their trade defence movement.

I have been welcomed and my advice much appreciated at all great meetings of the leaders in the industry.

At these great gatherings of all the branches of trade and enterprise in the cinema world I have never failed to find an immediate response to the appeals I felt impelled to make from time to time that they should work their business in accordance with the highest ideals of moral and civic good.

Coming to what I consider to be the main objects of your inquiry and in answer to the serious allegations brought against the cinema by its opponents, I have to state that I entirely agree with Mr. Herbert Samuel's opinion that the increase in juvenile delinquency is more attributable to the lack of parental control and to the unfortunate absence of many of the good agencies that the war has closed down in our great centres of population than to the cinema or other forms of amusement.

With regard to the influence of the cinema and of amusements generally on the young life of the nation I wish to make this point —that the splendid heroism, the dauntless courage, the magnificent comradeship and self-sacrifice of the lads and young men who passed from the cinema and its influence to the fighting line, give a direct contradiction to the aspersions cast upon the popular and cheap amusements of the people.

I am in full agreement with the constructive policy for dealing with the possible evils of the industry by combination within it as outlined by the Exhibitors' Association, the Cinema Trade Council and the Board of Film Censors under the presidency of Mr. T. P. O'Connor.

I have been intimately concerned with the development of this constructive policy, and I hold that it would be wise for the Home Office to co-operate with this policy and to give it compulsory powers for its necessary work.

MINUTES OF EVIDENCE

REV. T. HORNE. *Examined.*

1. THE CHAIRMAN. In regard to what women who go to these entertainments feel and their reasons, have you any inside knowledge ?—My knowledge is of tired-out mothers working hard during the greater part of the day. They are only too glad to know that their children are able to go to an interesting entertainment such as the cinema, and that they are enjoying themselves and out of the dangers and risks of the streets. I should think the mothers send their children purposely, not to get rid of them, but for love of them, to give them a pleasant hour or two hours; and then they are more amenable to home discipline.

2. Do you think the mother ever asks herself the question : " What are they showing? " or simply sends the child because

she knows it will have a bright time?—Entirely from the point of view that it is a bright entertainment.

3. You are a pioneer of the cinema?—Yes, I was concerned with it in its earliest days when it was shown by the shows which went from town to town. I remember the awful days of the uncensored funny pictures that came from France. Any one connected with the first stage must feel that the improvement has been so great and continuous that there is no serious cause for any censure or serious alarm at the present aspect of affairs.

4. With regard to juvenile crime and the cinema?—I think it is a very negligible and doubtful charge that the cinema has had any influence on juvenile crime.

5. Mr. NEWBOULD. Would you say that at any time the trade was unreasonable in its attitude towards the Home Office proposals for a trade censorship?—The trade takes a most diplomatic line in its dealings with the Home Office, and I was keenly disappointed at the result.

6. With your knowledge of the trade organisation and what it is doing and what it is aiming at, do you think it will in reasonable time deal with anything that is undesirable?—I do. I have found on every occasion perfect unanimity in the desire to eliminate anything objectionable.

7. Mr. GRAVES. Are you in favour of introducing the cinema into religious teaching?—I am to a large extent. I might point out that some years ago I wanted to get the picture of the Life of Christ, but the price put upon it was prohibitive.

8. Dr. KIMMINS. You have noticed a very marked improvement in the nature of the films during your long association with the cinema?—A very marked improvement indeed.

9. In the early days there was something wrong with the films? —Well, they were very French films. In the early days of the travelling cinema there was a great deal of effort by English firms to give local pictures, and it was very successfully done. You could be on the fair ground at ten o'clock in the morning and you could see yourself on the screen at five o'clock. It was these pictures which completely banished the objectionable pictures.

10. Dr. MARIE STOPES. Are you satisfied that the Home Office is alive to the great danger of the trade being swamped by the American films?—The American film has really been a tremendous good to the cinema industry. Without the American supply we should not have been able to develop so rapidly for exhibition purposes as we have done.

11. THE CHAIRMAN. In regard to the censorship, supposing you had to construct a censorship yourself, would you have a central censorship or local censorship?—I would construct a Board of Censors on the identical lines that we have already set up. I am now speaking for the trade. I would have a central office and have its powers compulsory so that no film should be shown unless it be passed by that Board. I would have one censor for the whole of the country and not a local censor.

ELEVENTH DAY

Monday, March 19, 1917.

The BISHOP OF BIRMINGHAM in the chair.

STATEMENT OF MR. CECIL LEESON,
Secretary of the Howard Association.

PRÉCIS

IT is certain that, in the public mind, the effects of the cinema on juvenile conduct are greatly out of perspective. It does not appear to have struck those who attribute juvenile delinquency exclusively to the low-grade cinema that among the children who form the bulk of cinema patrons are included precisely the children from whom adult guidance had been suddenly withdrawn by the war taking parents away from the home.

The outcry comes from two kinds of people. There are the well-intentioned and ignorant and, secondly, there are saner critics who object on moral and partly on hygienic grounds.

The first kind of critic, unfortunately, cannot be ignored, for he it is to whose public utterances much of the present misunderstanding of the problem is due.

Objection to cinemas by the second class of critics demands more serious attention. It is fourfold. First, that the cinema is too sensational; second, that by showing to the child how wrongful acts are committed it induces him to imitate them; third, that it proves so overwhelmingly attractive to children that they will do anything to procure the coppers for admission, and, fourth, that it is harmful to children on hygienic grounds.

On the score of hygiene, the absence of sunlight produces a physical condition favourable to the propagation of colds and other infections.

Moreover, children often suffer because they do not get sufficient sleep, and the cinema, by inducing them to keep late hours, aggravates this, with the result that the boy, whether at school or at work, comes next day to his task in a jaded, lifeless condition, both of mind and body.

On the mental effect of the cinema it is urged that whereas the act of reading—even the reading of penny " bloods "—demands some mental effort, the witnessing of moving pictures does not, and that the impression made by the pictures is much stronger than that made by the book, no mere printed word appealing nearly so forcibly as does an actual representation. Further, the printed story proceeds at a much slower pace than the picture story; also, whereas in the book the villain becomes as bad a villain as the child is capable of imagining, in the picture his villainy is as great as the villain is capable of imagining—so that to permit children to witness any and every kind of picture is much worse than to permit them to read any and every kind of book. Again, while one does not go to read half a dozen different books at one sitting, one does go to see half a dozen different kinds of picture at one sitting. Thus the combined effect of the pictures, the absence of mental effort, the intensity and the multiplication of impressions, are held to exert an undesirable effect on the child. Moreover, by over-elaborating the sensational, they evoke in the young mind emotions too strong for it to withstand, night terrors and other nervous disorders resulting.

Nearer to the charge of inducing criminal conduct in children is the criticism—and it appears well founded—that the pictures give to children quite wrong ideas of life and conduct. The villain is often " lionised," he does wrong things in a humorous way, he does " smart " things—things the youngsters wish they had thought of doing. At the same time, the reception of pictures such as these convinces me that the attractive thing to the child is not the wrongness of the act, but the humour or the cleverness of it. The cinema villain who is villain and nothing else invariably gains a satisfactory measure of execration from the audience ! Clearly it is not good to present to a young child wickedness in the guise of humour, but my chief objection to the films is that they make children, whose thoughts should be happy and wholesome, familiar with ideas of death by exhibiting shootings, stabbings, and the like. Nor are these death scenes merely brief incidents in the stories, for where a character is represented to be mortally wounded the story pauses while the children are shown an enlarged view of the victim's features during the death agony. Owing to this deliberate emphasis of the repulsiveness of such situations, it is difficult to see how the child's nerves can maintain their tone; we should look for a want of balance in children subjected repeatedly to these ordeals, and thence delinquency would not be unlikely. At any rate, such exhibitions are highly objectionable for children, whether they lead to delinquency or not.

On the charge that the cinema leads children to steal by showing them how to steal, I confess I should welcome more, and better authenticated, information. The argument by those who hold this view seems to be that, since all thoughts, no matter how arising, have their influence on conduct, the pictorial representations of theft or violence cause the children who witness them to commit similar acts through the principles of suggestion and imitation; that the picture suggests the wrongful thought and shows how it may be acted upon. The place of suggestion and imitation on conduct is admitted, and the absence of the restraining influence of adults indicated above may cause these factors to have been more greatly operative in children during the past two years than before; further, if it should prove that a case here and there of juvenile theft is directly attributable to these films I should not be surprised. But even so, the case against the films would, on this head, still remain to be proved; for though these isolated offences may aggregate to a considerable number, I would point out that in the past two years there are some twenty-five thousand children whose misconduct requires to be explained, and that nothing more reliable than general impressions have at the moment been advanced to show the part the cinema has played in producing this great number of offences. I do not acquit such films of responsibility for juvenile theft, of course; all I urge is that at present sufficient evidence exists neither to acquit nor condemn them, and that judgment on this aspect of the cinema problem must be suspended until more information is forthcoming on one side or the other.

There remains the overwhelming attractiveness of picture shows and the fact, clearly enough established, that the visits of children to them are often preceded by theft. Let it be admitted at once that much of the attraction children see in the films is obtained by illegitimate means. But the cinema can forgo vulgarity and sensationalism and still remain attractive, for the fact that a picture is a picture is enough for children, especially if it is funny.

The fascination of the cinema is an indictment of the child's dull home conditions. He leaves school at four, often earlier. If he goes home neither father nor mother are there. An elder sister prepares his tea, or maybe a neighbour gives him some, but no one really wants him. He requires to be interested, and positively the only interesting things still remaining in his little world are the picture palace and the street it stands in. Left thus to themselves, the wonder is that children should stick at anything to get away from their dullness. Bundles of energy, suppressed during the few hours' confinement at school, now in reaction, spoiling for something to vent themselves upon, and with no one to say them nay—this is the condition of these lads. Some of them steal. The wonder is so few of them do. For there is risk in stealing, and excitement, which is what healthy-minded lads need, and which, if it avoid the ultra-sensational, is good for them. When the charge that lads are taught to steal by the films comes properly to be investigated, it will possibly be found, not that they deliberately steal as a means to an end, to procure coppers for admission to the pictures, but that the great majority of them steal because they are dull. That the proceeds of their thefts are spent on the pictures is what would be expected. The pictures are the one bright spot in their drab lives, their only remaining interest.

MINUTES OF EVIDENCE

Mr. Cecil Leeson. *Examined.*

1. THE CHAIRMAN. The Howard Association has taken special interest in the question of children and what are called child offences, and with regard to the establishment of children's courts?—That is so.

2. You have thoroughly looked into this matter, and in con-

nection with that you have been brought up against the cinema question. You say that without the cinema the child's life would be even very dull?—Yes, that is so. The thing I complain of is that the children have very few alternatives to the cinema.

3. That applies more particularly to the long winter days?—Yes.

4. A great deal of this country's time is taken up with unsatisfactory weather and short days when the children cannot be in the parks?—Yes.

5. And you find they fly to the cinema?—In my position as probation officer in Birmingham I found that the cinema entered the lives of the probationers very considerably, and therefore it was my work to be cognisant with what the cinemas were doing.

6. Would you know whether children's crime was due to the cinema?—I have heard it said so, but one often gets that kind of excuse. The child and the parents of the child are in a difficulty, and the first thing they want to do is to get out of the difficulty, very often irrespective of the truth. This applies also to the cases of adults in police courts, where perhaps they say that their action was due to horse-racing, particularly if the magistrate suggests it first.

7. And once the suggestion is made, it is taken up by other children?—Yes, I think the excuses are passed round. With regard to children's offences, I have made very careful inquiries, and I have tried to get a case proved. To do this I think it should be proved on the lines of a case where circumstantial evidence comes into consideration. If a child went to the pictures and saw a burglary, say, like two men climbing up an outside spout and entering a house through the bedroom window, and then becoming acrobats and starting all sorts of foolery on the bed, possibly adjourning to the bathroom, the first dominant in the child's mind would be one of fun, but at the back of the child's mind there would be this other matter, the question of the burglary. If, having left the picture house, the child goes along the street and sees a house which reminds him of the house he saw burgled, the child might imitate the film.

8. Would that not be more the spirit of adventure than of crime?—Yes.

9. Do you think impressions produced by entertainments are very lasting?—I think it does produce that effect, and I find it is nothing for a child to go every night. In fact, I know of one little girl who went three times on a Saturday. Very often they are encouraged to go, as their mothers think they are out of harm's way. I am afraid that the cinema is used much in the same way as the Sunday school is.

10. Do you think a more lasting effect is produced by what is seen at the cinema than by what is seen at the theatre?—I do not think so, except, of course, that the cinema is more accessible.

11. What is your opinion about entertainments for children

only?—Well, frankly, I cannot give an opinion. I cannot see any solution unless you are to treat your adults as children. It is a question of how far you have the right to prescribe for the adult.

12. I suppose you would consider it a reasonable thing that everybody connected with the cinema should seize every opportunity of seeing what the public opinion is with regard to it?— Yes. My trouble is that they diagnose quite correctly what attracts the child most, and the question is whether it is quite desirable to pander to what the child wants.

13. Your feeling is that for a child to go frequently is not very good for body or mind?—No.

14. You lay stress on the insanitary condition of the halls?— I have got that opinion from the structure of the picture palaces. You see, the palaces are constructed so as to exclude light and to give the proper conditions for showing the pictures. I do not think they ought to stop at that. I think they are built wrongly. I have found hundreds of picture houses with no side windows. There are often roof lights, but through them the sun's rays do not come properly. I think it is wrong to exclude the sun's rays from the structures. Many medical officers of health have informed me that the absence of the sun's rays is a thing they complain of.

15. Do you like the idea of children going to late performances?—No; our difficulty at the courts was that the children do not get enough sleep. Of course, when considering the cinema you cannot interfere with the parents' domestic arrangements about putting the child to bed at a certain hour, but I think you could answer this question indirectly by not encouraging the cinema to take children in after a certain hour.

16. But are there not some houses which are quite as unhealthy to live in as a cinema?—Yes.

17. PRINCIPAL GARVIE. You are strongly in favour of special entertainments for children?—Yes, at special hours.

18. And that films should be marked if they are specially suitable for children?—Yes, I should like to see some common sense exercised in the selection, but I do not want to see picture houses as namby-pamby houses.

19. Would you say that the influence of the picture houses on the child was worse than that of its home surroundings, or that it is a better influence?—I am afraid I cannot answer that question. I was dealing with the children whose home surroundings are less favourable, and if some one took the view that the picture house was better than the home I would not dissent.

20. MR. NEWBOULD. Supposing special entertainments for children were not a commercial proposition, have you any suggestion to make so that it would be?—Simply by censorship.

21. The children's performance to which adults are not admitted is not a commercial proposition, and therefore special films would have to be provided so that the entertainments for children must be assisted or subsidised?—Is that so? Has it not been tried?

I cannot for the life of me see why we cannot have a children's programme on the same lines as we have children's literature.

22. MR. KING. To what extent is your opinion respecting unhygienic conditions of the cinema based on your experience?— I am afraid I cannot give you any statistics. I am alluding to the foul atmosphere in these places and to the absence of sunlight. There have been some houses I have been in where I have been glad to get out. I remember visiting twenty-seven houses in one week in Birmingham.

23. How many of them were unhygienic?—All, so far as the absence of sunlight was concerned.

24. You were talking of the foul air?—Well, pretty well all of them, I should think.

25. You think so, but do you know it is so?—There is no standard on which to work.

26. You had some comparison, such as a church or school?— A church is difficult to ventilate, but a school is different. I should say that the atmosphere was far and away better in a church than in a cinema.

27. MR. CROOK. Your experience is with abnormal children?— No, the delinquent children.

28. Is it your experience that hooliganism has increased on the streets?—You would not call a child of ten a hooligan.

29. And the cinema is not to blame for that?—No.

30. And the effect of the cinema would be rather to decrease hooliganism than increase it?—It would take the children off the streets.

31. Don't you think that five and a half hours a day under a teacher is sufficient for a child?—Yes, I should think so.

32. MR. GRAVES. Have you had any complaints from the teachers as to the immoral influence of the cinema on the children? —No, I am afraid the views obtained have been rather the other way. I am not at all blind to the advantages of the cinema. I might add that the boys' organisations in several towns have got together, and in one town, that of Newcastle, I think it is, they have got their own private cinema and a club-room as well.

STATEMENT OF MR. W. ARTHUR NORTHAM,

Member of the Council of the Kinematograph Manufacturers Association, Member of the Renters Association.

PRÉCIS

I HAVE been connected with the cinematograph trade for nearly five years, during which time I have held positions of trust in all sections, *i. e.* exhibiting, renting and manufacturing.

I have managed one of the largest picture houses in this country, have controlled the advertising for a large circuit of theatres, have occupied the position of sales manager for the London Film Company, Limited, am the general manager of a renting house, and spend most of my time negotiating for the hire of films and assisting in the arrangement of the programmes for more than twenty important picture houses.

During my connection with the cinematograph trade I have made business trips to America on two occasions, France, Germany, Austria and Belgium each on one occasion.

GENERAL STATEMENT

The evidence given herewith deals with—

- A. Definitions of " Open Market " and " Exclusive."
- B. Methods of Selection of Films by Renters and Exhibitors.
- C. The Machinery for Recording Reviewers' Criticisms.
- D. Method of Distribution of Films to Theatres.

To obtain a full knowledge of the arrangement of a programme, which is made up of both Open Market films and Exclusive films, it is necessary to make clear the difference between these two classes of films, at the same time, by so doing, the difference between Open Market Renters and Exclusive Renters will be demonstrated.

A.   DEFINITION OF " OPEN MARKET " AND " EXCLUSIVE "

(1) *Open Market Films*

This class of film, which is the shorter film, is sold by the manufacturer to any Renter wishing to purchase copies. The Renter hires out such films to his regular customers, who each half-week take from him the short films shown in the programmes. The Exhibitor requests his Renter to obtain the subjects he selects, knowing that his immediate opposition—in fact, all the houses near him using the same run of film as himself—may be showing these same subjects. Such subjects are, therefore, as the description makes clear, Open Market films.

(2) *Exclusive Films*

Each separate subject of this class of film is sold to one Renter, who purchases the exclusive right to rent that subject, and who in due course contracts with Exhibitors in any town to give to them the exclusive right to show it for first run, second run, and so on. This means that only one Exhibitor in a town or district of a large town at a time can show such a subject. It may be that the film will return to the town in a few weeks, but only one theatre can show it on any given three days.

By these explanations you will see that the Open Market Renter has a regular list of customers who half-week by half-week rent the short films, whereas the Exclusive Renter appeals to every Exhibitor in the country for custom. From the Open Market Renter the Exhibitor may obtain the productions of any maker of Open Market films, whilst the Exhibitor must go to Fox for Fox Exclusives, to J. D. Walker for Famous Players

Exclusives, to Jury for London Films, to Triangle for Triangle Exclusives.

B. METHODS OF SELECTION OF BOTH OPEN MARKET AND EXCLUSIVE FILMS BY RENTERS AND EXHIBITORS

(1) *Open Market*

In the instance of the purchase by the Renter of Open Market films this purchase is governed in the main by the selection of the viewers for first-run houses. The first-run house pays a high price for the advantage of playing first run, and is therefore allowed to select the films required. Such selection is supplemented by the purchases made by the Renter, who employs viewers to report and select. (You will therefore note that the films which appear on all theatres, from first run in towns to the last run in villages, are selected by the largest houses and by the Renters.) To allow Exhibitors the opportunity of viewing these films all manufacturers of Open Market films have private projecting-rooms in which the films are screened for reviewing purposes. They are shown to reviewers, roughly, six weeks before release date, to allow of time to order the necessary copies and for those copies to be printed. The ordered copies are, in due course, delivered to the Renters the day previous to release date, which ensures all copies appearing in theatres on the date announced as the release date. Therefore first run of an Open Market film is its release date.

(2) *Exclusive*

The viewing and selection of this class of film differs in many ways from that of the Open Market. The films are viewed by the Exhibitor, but not at the manufacturer's projecting-room, with the object of ordering through a Renter as in the instance of Open Market films. The Exhibitor attends trade shows of these larger subjects, or the projecting-room of the Renter who has purchased the subject, and, having viewed and approved a film, enters into a contract with the Renter for the exclusive rights of the showing of that subject for a given period.

The completed programme, containing both Open Market and Exclusive Films, is then, in its due time, sent to the theatre.

C. MACHINERY FOR RECORDING REVIEWERS' CRITICISMS

(1) *The Specially Employed Viewer*

This naturally varies, but it can be taken for granted that every Exhibitor adopts a method of collating information from which selection is made. In many instances Exhibitors engage the services of individuals or a staff whose sole work is that of viewing and passing judgment on films. Attached is a card used by a firm controlling over twenty important houses. This firm employs four viewers (three men and one woman), all of whom write reports on that card, which is marked " B." By

o

these means a thorough and reliable report is obtained and filed
of all films placed before the Exhibitor.

(2) *The Free Lance Viewer*

There are a number of viewers, both male and female, who
spend their time in viewing films for many theatre proprietors,
and whose reports can be purchased by any Exhibitor who wishes
to subscribe to such service.   These reports contain a suggestion
as to the type of story, whilst the actual value of the film is
indicated by marks.

(3) *The Trade Papers*

Each of the trade journals (three in number) print reports of
all important films and most of the others, but even of the unreported films (unreported because of lack of space) there is a
synopsis.

D.   METHOD OF DISTRIBUTION OF FILMS TO THEATRES

This is carried out principally by rail and in specially made
boxes.   The railway companies refuse to carry films unless
packed in boxes made according to their specification, which is,
roughly: galvanised iron, wood lined, with special hinges and
strengtheners.   The boxes are very expensive at ordinary times,
whilst at present they are practically unobtainable.   They are
the cause of much worry and labour, for elaborate systems have
to be maintained to keep track of them.   When it is remembered
that there are at least 4000 theatres, each needing three boxes
to carry the programme (one each for Open Market, Exclusive,
and Topical), it will be seen that there are 24,000 boxes per week
wandering about the country.   To take an imaginary case:
" A " purchases an exclusive film which he shows to the trade
by means of trade shows held at the principal centres.   He
obtains as many bookings as possible on, say, sixteen copies.
These bookings are consecutive bookings, for it is the essence
of the Renting business that no copies shall remain on the Renters'
shelves.   He must get his returns quickly, for films, like fashions,
become old very rapidly.   Therefore, having made all his arrangements, he, on the day before release, sends his sixteen copies to
the first sixteen customers with instructions to forward, immediately after the last performance, to the next theatre (which is
always made as short a journey as possible).   The films from that
moment commence to travel from theatre to theatre, with as
frequent return to the Renter's office as possible for overhauling
and renovation.   As they come in, new beginnings and ends are
added, as required, for it is those sections which suffer most.
This travelling from theatre to theatre is known as the " cross-
over," and is fraught with worry and anxiety, especially during
the mid-week.   Closing time is generally 10.30 p.m., and opening
time any time from 11 a.m. to 3 p.m.   Therefore each half-week
20,000 films are hurrying from theatre to theatre, whilst during

the mid-week change it has all to be accomplished within twelve hours. This, in these days of reduced train service and depleted railway staffs, frequently means the non-arrival of films in time for the opening performances. In such an instance the " stand-by " programme is called into use. This programme is comprised of films which have, in the main, run their course, but may be used for such a purpose, and which were selected originally in the manner described heretofore.

This statement has resolved itself into a description of the links which bind Manufacturer, Renter and Exhibitor, and has perhaps more particularly demonstrated the position in the industry held by the Renter.

MINUTES OF EVIDENCE

Mr. W. Arthur Northam. *Examined.*

1. THE CHAIRMAN. You are going to explain to us the method by which the trade is organised ? Now, will you explain to us the three classes, the manufacturer, the renter and the exhibitor, where the province of the one ends and the other begins ?—The manufacturer, as you will see from his title, is the man who manufactures films. Until about two years ago he was purely a manufacturer of films, and he sold to the middleman, who is known as the renter, and he is the distributor of the films to the exhibitor. Since those days the manufacturer has entered the renting field, and is now manufacturer and renter, with the result that the middleman's usefulness has in a measure declined.

2. The manufacturer, is he almost entirely American ?—Yes.

3. And what he manufactures is primarily of American taste ? —His object is obviously to make films attractive to the public, and as he is an American, he has in the first instance to attract his own public, which is the greatest public, with the result that the films are more American than anything else. Further, an American producer, given a British story to produce, produces that story with American surroundings and American ideas, for very often he has never been in England, and this is undesirable.

4. Is there any reason why the British manufacturer should not be able to dispose of his goods in America in the same way as the American disposes of his goods in England ?—No; with that question you touch upon fundamental differences between the two countries. An English manufacturer might produce a film and wish to show it to the entire trade in Great Britain. He could show it in the main towns of the country in seven days. For an American manufacturer, wishing to show it to the whole trade in America, it would take, roughly, seven days from New York to San Francisco without stopping, and the consequence is that the American builds up an enormous organisation throughout the United States to carry on his work. Now, the American can come over here with the object of selling films, and if he cannot find a buyer he can set up an organisation here, whereas the Englishman cannot do that over in America, on account of

the enormous organisations up against him. If an Englishman wanted to sell a film in America he would perhaps approach these people, who would refuse to take the film, and they might inform him that if they required more pictures they would prefer to make them.

5. Why should not the British manufacturer have the complete hold over the British Isles?—The American has enormous sales in his own country, and he has the sales in his hands, and possibly the sales in this country. You must take into consideration that there are 30,000 cinemas in the United States, as compared with 4000, approximately, here. The result is that the American can spend much more money in excess of the Englishman, with the result that the American production is generally more magnificent.

6. Taking things as they are, if the cinema is to go on in this country it would for a considerable period have to rely upon the American manufacturer?—Yes, to a great extent.

7. Would you be able to say that there is more effort made in America to produce films for the British market?—I should be disposed to think they are taking more care of the British market than they did. I should say that British-producing has been stationary for two years.

8. And, of course, there is not so much manufactured in the British Isles since the war began?—It has fallen quite 50 per cent.

9. And there is no decrease in America?—No.

10. Now as to the renter?—The renter has two branches of his business, the open market and the exclusive renting. The renter goes to the viewing-rooms, and is the selector of the open market subjects. We will say there are fifty open market renters. Well, these fifty renters will have viewers viewing films in London, and in addition to this the trade papers and exhibitors will have a man to view. These men, having viewed the films, will hand in their reports, and in due course orders are sent in for the films. I might say that at the present moment orders are being placed for April 23rd. Many renters are purchasing copies of the open market subjects. The other type of renter is the exclusive renter, who goes to the producer of exclusive films and, having selected something likely to appeal to the exhibitor, he goes to the owner and purchases it entirely, and therefore he is the only man who owns that subject and has the right to it. Each exhibitor then goes to him to negotiate for the hire of that subject. Usually the manufacturer holds rights for the whole world, and he disposes of those rights to people in the different countries.

11. Viewers are of two classes?—There is only one type of viewer, but, of course, he is viewing the two types of films. His duty in each instance is to view the film and make a report as to the desirability of the subject. If we wanted the opinion of another viewer, we would supplement that opinion by that of an impartial viewer or a free-lance viewer.

12. What is a free-lance viewer?—An individual who sets out

as being an expert film viewer or critic. He sees all the films shown and writes a report, which any exhibitor might subscribe for. He sells these reports at a comparatively nominal sum, and these reports come up to us each week.

13. How is the free-lance viewer paid?—From his subscriptions. He depends purely on the number of people who want to have his notes. He says : " I view films, and I will sell you my notes for so much."

14. Does he take all sides, the moral side, the paying side and the language side?—Yes, he will tell you whether it is sensational, whether it is bordering on the immoral, and so on. The viewers in the trade are looked upon as censors.

15. How many copies of films, generally speaking, are there?— One or two extraordinary films have sold 100 copies on the open market. This was the case with " Ivanhoe." In the main the open market subject will sell for an average of seventeen to twenty, and sometimes as many as thirty copies. To arrange for a small number of copies to be used, the renter works his districts very closely and during a sequence of weeks, with the result that when a picture is finished with in one town it can be sent on to the next town with smallest loss of time. With regard to exclusive films, in pre-war days bookings would be made on these films even two years after they were released, but, of course, they would be new copies. The average contract is two years, but certain subjects, religious and spectacular subjects used at Christmas and Good Friday, go on for ever.

16. SIR R. BADEN-POWELL. Has the English industry any chance of getting up to the American output?—I do not suppose it will come up to the American output.

17. Is there any truth in the statement that American firms are trying to oust the British manufacturers by supplying films to exhibitors at a lower price than that for which they can obtain British films?—No.

18. MR. NEWBOULD. Have you any knowledge of the fact that when the British manufacturer acquires, say, the sole rights of a well-known play, he also frequently acquires a series of lawsuits in other countries to establish his rights?—Yes, and particularly so in regard to America. That is one of the weaknesses of the copyright law.

19. PRINCIPAL GARVIE. I gather that there are films in this country that have never been censored?—Censorship at the present moment is a kind of voluntary censorship supported by the trade, and here and there there has been a certain amount of disloyalty.

20. Do you think it is possible the trade will organise themselves so that uncensored films cannot be shown?—That is the view of our organisation, and we have the matter in hand.

21. THE SECRETARY. What sort of productions were those which were not censored?—Such as " —— ——," " —— ——," and " —— ——."

[Three South London schoolgirls were examined together].

22. THE CHAIRMAN. How often do you go to the cinema?—I don't go very often, as it is very injurious to my eyes when I go.

23. Do you sit right in the front?—Well, if they put you there you have to go there.

24. What do you pay generally?—Fourpence.

25. Do you go only for entertainments which are for children?—Not always.

26. Are you a great cinema-goer?—Yes.

27. How often do you go?—Once a week. Sometimes I go once a week for six months and then have a rest, and then start all over again.

28. What seats do you go in; what do you pay?—Sevenpence.

29. You sit right in the front?—No, it is all according to how much you pay. If you pay a low price you go into the front.

30. With your sevenpence, is that not a first-rate seat?—Just about in the middle of the cinema, and I can see all right there.

31. And you don't find your eyes hurt?—When I go out it generally gives me a headache.

32. How long do you sit in the cinema?—Two and a half or three hours.

33. Do you go very much?—About once every three weeks.

34. What do you like best? Comic things?—I like pretty pictures about dancing and horses.

35. Do you like seeing people breaking into rooms and taking things?—Not very much.

36. It never gives any of you an idea that what you see you want to go and do yourself?—No.

37. How about your eyes? Do you get a headache?—No.

38. Where do you sit?—I pay fourpence and sit about two or three seats away from the front.

39. What part of London do you come from?—We are all from the middle of South London.

40. Have you any particular picture palace which appeals to you?—I used to go to the Oval Cinema, but now I go to the Queen's Hall, Newington Butts.

41. Where do you go?—To the Palladium, Brixton, and the Arcadia, Brixton.

42. What kind of things do you have at the Arcadia?—They generally have very good pictures, and I went once and saw "_____ _____ — —." It is not a very good picture to go to.

43. Why, what was the matter?—Because I do not like the way they used the crucifix. They used the crucifix to hit one another with, and it might make children think less of religion.

44. That was the principal thing, and you did not notice anything else?—No.

45. Where do you go?—I go to the Queen's Hall, Newington Butts.

46. Did you see " —— —— — — " ?—No.

47. Do the girls sit amongst the boys?—Yes, all mixed up, and the attendant comes round, and if the boys start whistling about and do that again he turns them out.

48. I suppose girls never do that sort of thing?—That all depends.

49. Do you go to the late entertainment?—No, mother won't let me.

50. Do you go late?—I get out about 9 or 9.30. Very often it is 9.30. If I go to Brixton by myself and my sisters are that way they meet me, otherwise I come home by myself.

51. Do you feel the influence next day?—I do not feel any bad effects.

52. SIR JOHN KIRK. Is the place very dark?—Yes, very dark. You can see over it while the performance goes on.

53. What would happen if the boys started fighting?—They would not start fighting, because they are always too anxious to see the pictures.

54. MR. LAMERT. Have you any other amusement to go to beside the cinema?—Sometimes a theatre.

55. Do you pay to go to the theatre?—Sometimes mother lets us go into the pit, as she doesn't like us to go up the stairs to the gallery. The price is one shilling and twopence tax.

56. When you go to the theatre what do you see?—Pantomimes, and if there is a revue mother thinks we will understand she will take us to it.

57. At the picture palaces do you take any steps to find out what is on?—No, we take our chance.

58. MONSIGNOR BROWN. What sort of picture do the children like best?—When the cowboys and Indians come on they clap very loudly.

59. Do you like flowers?—No, not very much.

60. Birds' nests?—No, they don't like those.

61. Charlie Chaplin?—They like those.

62. Do you get tired when they begin to show views and landscapes?—Sometimes some of them do.

63. Are they short films?—Yes, and sometimes they are the topical budget, and then a lot of them go out.

64. Do they like a long drama?—Yes.

65. How many minutes do the dramas last?—Sometimes one and a half hours.

66. Do they like dramas with a lot of love mixed up?—We don't care for them very much; some like them and some don't.

67. Would many like them?—I should not think many of them would like them. I think they would prefer other pictures

68. How many different picture houses have you been to?— Sixteen.

69. How many have you been to?—Eight.

70. How many you?—Six in London and Manchester.

71. DR. MARIE STOPES. Have you seen any picture which you thought at the time was bad to see?—No, but I saw a picture

once which I thought was vulgar. It was called "——
————."

72. Supposing you went into a picture house and you met a fairy at the door who told you you could see any picture you liked, what kind would you like to see?—I should like to see a picture about a circus.

73. What sort of picture would you like best?—I should like a good drama, but not a love drama. A drama like " Little Miss Nobody," which I thought was very nice.

74. Why don't you like love dramas?—There is too much fooling about in them, and there is always a hatred between two men and two women.

75. You don't like to see two men hating each other?—Well, it is a lot of silliness. I do not think it would happen in real life.

76. You never got any disease at the cinema?—No, but once I got scarlet fever, but not in a cinema.

77. Did you ever get anything?—No, I did not catch my disease there.

78. Dr. Kimmins. What is the nicest picture you have seen in the cinema?—I think it was " Cleopatra."

79. And you?—" Little Miss Nobody."

80. And you?—" The Prisoner of Zenda " and " Rupert of Hentzau."

Mr. Newbould. These three were of British manufacture.

81. Do you like serials?—I have seen " The Broken Coin," but I did not like that, although I liked the acting.

82. Commissioner Adelaide Cox. Did you see anything that frightened you?—I saw one picture where a man was in the cell, and he was supposed to have an apparition, which breaks through the wall, and the wall falls over. It was in " Monte Cristo."

83. And when you went to bed, did you think about these things?—No, I went to sleep.

84. What do you like the least?—I do not like the topical budget.

85. And you?—Love stories.

86. And you?—I think the same—love stories.

87. Mr. Graves. Have you seen any pictures which help you at school?—I have seen the picture about Nero.

88. Would you like some singing in between?—I should like to have some singing.

89. Mr. Newbould. Are you quite sure it was a crucifix you saw in " —— —— — — " ?—Yes.

90. Have you any idea why she hit the man with the crucifix?—She was a servant in his father's house, and he wanted to be in love with her, and he started cuddling and kissing her, and she gets up the crucifix quite unconsciously and hits him with it.

91. Have you ever seen films you do not understand?—Yes, I can never understand pictures on general plays.

92. Mr. Crook. Have you ever had a man who wanted to pay for you at night?—No.

93. PRINCIPAL GARVIE. Have the boys ever been rude to you in the cinema?—No, but they have pulled our hair and taken our hats off.

94. THE CHAIRMAN. Do they only do that in the cinema?— No, and if the attendant is about he puts them outside.

TWELFTH DAY

Monday, March 26, 1917,

The BISHOP OF BIRMINGHAM in the chair.

MINUTES OF EVIDENCE

TWO SCHOOLBOYS. *Examined.*

1. THE CHAIRMAN. What are your names, where do you come from, what are your ages, and what standards are you in?— —— and ——, ————, ——; ages thirteen and eleven, and in Standards VI and VII.

2. How often do you go to the cinema shows?—About once a week.

3. And what price seats do you go in?—Fourpence or twopence.

4. And you?—I always go into the fourpenny.

5. And your parents give you the money to go with?—Yes.

6. And they like you to go?—Yes.

7. About what time in the day do you go to the performances? —On Saturday afternoon.

8. And you?—On Friday after school.

9. And what time does that performance begin?—Five o'clock.

10. And your performance on Saturday?—About a quarter to three.

11. And it lasts about two hours?—Yes.

12. What is the picture theatre you principally go to?—The Grand Hall.

13. And you?—I go to the Tower Cinema.

14. Have you any particular fancy for any particular kind of picture?—Well, I like war pictures and I like geography pictures.

15. When you say geography, will you explain exactly what you mean?—Like the different kind of things that come into England, and the exports.

16. You like to see things unshipped?—Yes.

17. And do you like the comic films?—Yes, sometimes, if they are not too silly.

18. Do you consider Charlie Chaplin too silly?—Sometimes.

19. What about the love stories?—I do not think much of those.

20. Do you like the films where the people are stealing things? —Yes.

21. And where the clever detectives discovers them?—Yes.

22. Have you ever thought it would be a fine idea to copy these people and steal these things?—No.

23. Has it ever made you think what a fine sort of life it is to go round and break into people's houses?—No.

24. And what are your favourite films?—(Second boy) I rather like tragedy.

25. What do you mean by that?—A play where sorts of deaths come in.

26. Where somebody kills somebody else?—Yes.

27. Seeing a bad man trying to kill a good fellow, you never want to go and kill the best boy in the school?—No.

28. Now, why do you specially like that film? Is it because it is adventure?—Well, it is; it rather makes you—like, jumpy.

29. It excites you?—Yes.

30. Does that excitement last with you after you leave the theatre; do you feel nervous?—I feel rather nervous when I get home and when I go up and down stairs in the dark.

31. Do you feel nervous next morning when you go to school? —No, I have never felt any effects in the daytime, but I do in the night.

32. But you still like it?—Yes.

33. What else do you like besides?—Robberies are all right.

34. And you like to see how a fellow cleverly cuts things with a glass and gets into a window and over walls?—Yes, but a man has to be pretty good and have a good bit of sense to do all these things.

35. And you really think there is something rather clever about it?—Yes.

36. Have you ever met any boys who are?—There are one or two ruffians who sometimes go for other peoples' things when they ought not to go.

37. And have they sometimes told you that the pictures made them anxious to go?—I do not believe the pictures do, but they read some of these penny books.

38. Now do you like the comic things?—No, I do not like them.

39. Do you like the love stories?—Well, they are a bit trying sometimes.

40. Do you know those pictures which show you birds growing up and flowers coming out?—Yes, I like them all right.

41. Would you like the whole entertainment of two hours to be composed of that kind of film?—Well, they are not so bad, but sometimes they are a bit trying.

42. If an entertainment lasted two hours, would you object to half an hour of that?—No.

43. Do you find that seeing these things teaches you something?—Yes.

44. MR. T. P. O'CONNOR. Do you find that films assist you with your geography?—Yes.

45. If you saw a picture of Russia, say, would that make you study up your geography more about that country?—Yes.

46. PROFESSOR H. GOLLANCZ. Have you ever had any head-aches on the same evening?—No.

47. Have you?—My eyes seem to be affected.

48. Did you notice any flickering?—Yes, during the performance.

49. Have you noticed any rough behaviour to some of the girls?—No.

50. MR. NEWBOULD. Is there a special attendant to look after the children when you go in?—Yes.

51. MR. KING. Have you ever felt sleepy?—Yes.

52. When do you feel that?—When there is a dry picture and you don't care about looking at it.

53. MR. GRAVES. Would you like cinema lessons to be given in your schools the same as the magic lantern?—Yes, that would not be bad.

54. MONSIGNOR BROWN. Supposing a geography film lasted for half an hour, how do you think the children would take it?—They would not like it.

55. Are the children crowded in at the cinemas?—Not in all the places, but there was one place I went to where they were crowded together and there were no divisions or arms to the seats.

56. REV. CAREY BONNER. Have you seen any rough play going on?—There has always been decent behaviour, unless some ruffians get in.

57. THE CHAIRMAN. Do you see these films better if the hall is lighted better?—No, the darker the place the better you can see the pictures.

STATEMENT OF MR. F. W. BARNETT

PRÉCIS

I AM Probation Officer and Court Missioner at the Westminster Police Court, and have been engaged in this kind of work for the last twenty-five years.

The Westminster Court covers the areas of Westminster, Chelsea, a portion of Lambeth, and deals with all juvenile cases under sixteen from the West London Police Court district as well.

The district comprises the well-to-do, middle class and extremely poor. There is a high proportion of slum property. In fact, in the Notting Dale district probably the worst slums in London are to be found. Among the poor the children are wage-earners at an early age. Among these poor the home conditions are indifferent, as is shown by the large proportion of prosecutions for neglect, keeping children from school, and wilful neglect and cruelty.

In the Westminster and West London police divisions there is a population exceeding three quarters of a million. The picture houses are in most cases of a fairly satisfactory type as regards ventilation and cleanliness, but a few are considerably below the others in this respect. I should say that the buildings compare more than favourably with other buildings designed for the general use of the community.

The war conditions have largely affected the type of audience in the immediate vicinity of Victoria and Westminster. This district is the centre for the Colonial troops. Immorality is frightfully prevalent, and the picture house audiences have suffered in consequence so far as prestige goes. As soon as the war conditions are removed these conditions will improve.

I am a frequent attendant at the picture theatres, and have always found the audience orderly and well-behaved, and have never seen the remotest suggestion of any sort of disturbance.

A very large proportion of the audiences are children, especially at the afternoon and early evening performances. In a very large number of cases the children are accompanied by their parents.

The intense appreciation of these children has always formed one of the big attractions of the picture theatres so far as I was concerned. I have been pleased to note the moral sensibility the children display in denouncing trickery and fraud, and applauding the instances of benevolence, charity and honourable behaviour, and so forth.

It has seemed to me that the restrictions on the children so far as demonstration was concerned have been, if anything, too strict. In their desire to secure orderly audiences sometimes I think the attendants erred on the side of repression. In my judgment the type of the audiences has been, to a large extent, a guarantee of general decency both as regards the nature of the entertainment, and the behaviour of the audience. Many religious people with a Puritan strain in their blood, who hold music halls and theatres in abhorrence, are regular patrons of the picture houses all over London.

I should say that, in general, the cinemas compare favourably with other means of recreation in the district, and are much safer for the children than suburban music-halls, or the " Funland " type of exhibition, where the spirit of gambling is often stimulated.

There has been a great increase in " juvenile crime " in our police division in recent years. This is not remarkable when one considers the circumstances. We now have boys of from fourteen to sixteen doing the work of men and getting men's wages. These boys have very little leisure. They are often employed for fourteen or fifteen hours a day as carmen, lift-boys or on the railway. Fathers are away at the Front; the mothers, though better off financially than ever before, have acquired drinking habits, and often leave the homes neglected and the children at liberty to do what they please. In a large number of cases there is really no parental control or discipline at all.

There has been a tendency in recent years to increase the *variety* of offences with which children may be charged. For instance, children are now charged with wandering, with being without proper guardianship, with being " beyond control."

Our streets are now more rigidly supervised than ever before. There is a large and increasing army of officials whose duty it is to watch over child life. In many cases it has seemed to me that the zeal of these officers was not always adequately tempered by humanity and expediency. The practical result of their activities has been a systematic increase in the number of charges brought against children.

Although I have been specially interested in the question of juvenile crime for many years I do not, at the moment, recollect a single case where a juvenile crime was attributable to the children's attendance at the cinemas. I remember one case in which that was the excuse offered, but after the child in question had been remanded I made inquiries and found that the home life and environment of the child directly conduced to criminal degeneracy, and it was not necessary to look further for an explanation.

A great many cases have come under my notice of children who have stolen money. As soon as these thefts have been effected, the confectioner's shop is the first place visited. Then sometimes the picture show, or, if the money stolen was sufficient, the first houses of the music halls are commonly patronised.

So far as films depicting burglaries, robberies and other infringements of the law are concerned, I have this to say—where a good home influence is wanting I think quite possibly such films may have a pernicious effect on the young. It must be borne in mind that children who are looking at these pictures are at the impressionable period. Their home life does not provide for the inculcation of the cardinal virtues, and in a large number of cases they are children of unhealthy body and mind. In such cases films of this type may give a wrong impetus to the imagination of the child. Even in these films the moral lesson is always satisfactory. It is always demonstrated that vice brings its own penalty in suffering both for body and mind. Undoubtedly this spectacle of inevitable retribution must tend to offset the fictitious glamour of wrong-doing.

In my opinion the closing of the picture houses, or their prohibition to children, would have most unbeneficial results. In many cases the cinemas are the only form of healthy recreation available, and this is particularly the case during the long winter months. The children in question have neither the taste nor the facilities for indulging in any sport, and if the cinemas were closed to them, so far from the condition of the streets being improved, I am convinced there would be an immediate and immense increase in hooliganism, shop-lifting and similar street misdemeanours. Fifteen years ago street hooligan gangs were a real menace and problem. Now such gangs are quite unknown in my district.

There is another side to this question. We must not forget that the stress of present conditions affects child life very directly. The father is absent, and the irritability of the mother left at home is a very serious factor. She is affected by the monotony and drudgery of her daily life and by the constant anxiety as to the safety of those dear to her in the war. The atmosphere of the picture theatre with its unobtrusive entertainments is a very positive relief to her, and tends to lessen for a time at least her nervous tension. I am of opinion that there is no entertainment to be compared with the pictures for dispelling the little cares of the children, and the bigger difficulties of their elders.

It has often seemed to me that when films illustrating the virtues of life were shown, the inculcation of right principles has been more effective and impressive on the silent screen than the spoken word would have been. I do not think, for instance, that the pulpit can exercise its influence quite so vividly or so directly in illustrating such virtues as generosity, charity, chivalry, honesty, and so forth. The pictures drive these lessons home with a directness of appeal which the spoken word, save in exceptional instances, cannot equal.

I think it is obvious that the cinemas are a strong counter-attraction to the public-houses, and, in my experience, the attitude of the average parent to these shows has been very friendly indeed. If there is any serious antagonism on the part of religious people to the picture shows, I should say it arises from the violent objection of such people to the Sunday opening of places of amusement and recreation. So far as the official opposition of the churches is concerned, I should say this is due to an entire misapprehension of the position. In many cases there is an entire lack of understanding as to the practical conditions in which the poor live. Owing to this there has been a relative failure on the part of the churches to attract the poorer classes, and as a result the churches tend to quarrel with any well-ordered recreation that *does* attract the poor.

The point has often been made that attendance at the cinemas makes it increasingly difficult to secure the attendance of the child at Sunday schools, night schools, guilds and similar organisations for the welfare of the young. I do not think that the attendance at these places would be materially increased by restricting the cinema. Night schools do not attract the boy of fourteen who is physically tired by a heavy day's work. So far as social guilds are concerned, these, in my opinion, are not generally very attractive concerns, and the various clubs for children do not retain the interest of boys and girls for long.

I might add that I very frequently take my probationers to picture shows with beneficial results, and the general phases of life there shown are, in the main, what I should wish them to be for such a purpose—that is to say, they give a faithful representation of city life in which both the failings and virtues of humanity are thrown up in bold relief. From my point of view I should not wish to give my probationers a view of life which was too widely different from the actual conditions they would themselves later have to encounter.

MINUTES OF EVIDENCE

Mr. Barnett. *Examined.*

1. The Chairman. Do you find a variety in the quality of the theatres, such as in the sanitary arrangements and buildings?— Yes, there is a variety.

2. Some are very fine houses ?—Yes, some are ; but it largely depends upon the street and locality. There is a picture show just off the Horseferry Road, and that house, although of recent construction, is not to be compared with the houses, say, in the Strand or some of the main streets.

3. Would you say that the quality of the house varies with the quality of the class living near that house ?—Most certainly.

4. The better the private houses in the locality, the better the cinema houses ?—I do not mean that. If a house stands in a main street, where you have a big stream of people, then you have a better house than you would have in a mean street.

5. You think on the whole the cinema palaces compare favourably with some of the music halls ?—I do most certainly ; from the point of view of sanitation and general building.

6. You say the war conditions have largely affected the type of audience in particular parts of Victoria and Westminster where there are so many Colonial troops. Do you mean by that that a great many more undesirable women have come to these houses in consequence ?—Certainly, yes ; and we are getting women who are strangers. At Westminster Police Court this morning we had quite a number of cases of prostitution with girls whose ages ranged from fourteen and a half to nineteen years of age. They have come up from the country without any protection, without any money and without friends, and they go to the picture shows in the districts, and that is where they sometimes meet our Colonials.

7. These young girls come out with the intention of leading an immoral life ?—In many instances they do, because they have been corrupted in the towns where they have resided owing to the fact that the military have been training there.

8. They lose their virtue there, and they say : " Now London is the place for me " ?—Yes.

9. Have you seen enough of these young girls to be able to answer this question ? Do you think the relaxation of parental authority in those country towns that they come from might lead to their first folly and then their absolute abandonment ?—In part I would admit that, but I say that many of these girls have come from good and religious homes. They have been the victims of mock modesty ; their training has been imperfect, and they have become the ready prey of men ready to seduce them.

10. But you don't say their first fall is due to the picture houses ? —No.

11. Have you seen any rough play or indecent behaviour on the part of boys towards girls at the cinemas ?—Never, apart from perhaps a little pushing outside at the ticket office.

12. I see you say : " It has seemed to me that the restrictions on the children so far as demonstration was concerned, have been, if anything, too strict ? "—Yes, at the picture shows, the behaviour there is a great deal better than amongst worshippers in churches or the chapels.

13. There has been an increase in juvenile crime, you say ?— Yes, and I say the main cause is the absence of the father,

and I want to say that history is only repeating itself.   During the South African War for two years I had boys under my control whose fathers, being Reservists, had been called up for service.

14. And the same experience you are getting now?—Absolutely.

15. And there were no cinemas then, during the South African War? Well, I do not remember any. In a number of cases I also find that the mothers go out to work, and I have known cases where families of nine and ten children have been left entirely to the care of a girl of twelve or thirteen years of age, and even, in some cases, those children are left all night.   I should like to add that I consider the cinema to be the most harmless form of recreation we have ever had.

16. Have you ever had a case where the boy had stolen in order to go to the cinema?—I did hear a boy say that on one occasion, but inquiries did not bear that out.   Before the cinemas were started the boys stole money and said they did it because they wanted to go to sea.

17. Supposing you closed all the cinemas?—I wonder what would happen to child and adult life of London if you did that. Why, look what good it does! It does more good than the music halls.   May I tell you an instance of a couple which will interest you? They had applied for separation orders, and I took up their cases. I took them to a picture show and made them squeeze close together, as close as they could, and with the pictures and the appreciation of them a new understanding came into their lives.

18. Do you see any advantage in the cinema in keeping the people away from the public-houses?—I do.   I have kept watch in one district and I have seen 200 couples come out of a show and only one couple went into a public-house. This was before the days of the restrictions.

19. REV. CAREY BONNER. Would you indicate the improvements you would like made to the cinema?—Well, for one thing, they are not heated properly; they are very cold, and that is pretty general.   Then again, I should like to see adopted in all shows the spraying of the house with disinfectants.   Then there is another improvement which will come in after the war.   I have noticed there has been a great deterioration in the films since the war began, and think it was because we are so largely dependent on America.   Before the war we had films from Italy and France, but now they have something more to do.   Then, again, I have noticed that the posters are very bad.   If I had my way I would have a special film censorship for the children, and it would not be done by justices of the peace, but by men exclusively from the scholastic profession.

20. PRINCIPAL GARVIE. May I take it you would be satisfied if the censorship had a special Advisory Committee to advise them on children's matters?—That is so.   I should like to add that in Westminster I have only known one case of indecency within the precincts of the cinema halls coming up at the court.

21. MR. LAMERT. Have you ever seen any films which were indecent in themselves or suggested indecency ?—Not to my mind.

22. MONSIGNOR BROWN. Have you ever seen films that dealt with the problems of seduction ?—I believe I saw one in Liverpool, but never in London.

FOUR SCHOOLBOYS. *Examined.*

Two of these boys were aged eleven years and two thirteen years. They lived in the Bethnal Green neighbourhood, and two of them attended cinemas on Saturday night and two on Saturday afternoon, only going once a week.

23. THE CHAIRMAN. What do you like best at the cinema ?— All about thieves.

24. The next best ?—Charlie Chaplin.

25. And you?—Mysteries; and then Charlie Chaplin.

26. And you?—Mysteries, and Charlie Chaplin.

27. What do you mean by mysteries ?—Where stolen goods are hidden away in vaults so that the police can't get them.

28. And you ?—Cowboys; and then Charlie Chaplin second.

29. When you have seen these pieces showing thieving and people catching the thief, has it ever made you wish to go and do the same thing ?—Yes.

30. Do you think the fellow who steals, then, a fine man ?—No.

31. But you would like to do it yourself ?—Yes.

32. Do you like the adventure or what ?—I like the adventure.

33. You have no desire, then, to steal in order to get things for yourself, but you like the dashing about and getting up drain-pipes and that sort of thing? Yes.

34. And you ?—No, I don't like that, I should not like to do that.

35. Do you like pictures where you see flowers growing?—No.

36. Do you like ships coming in and bringing things from distant lands ?—(One boy replied " No," and the other three " Yes.")

37. You like to have a consistent programme of detective stories and Charlie Chaplin, and you don't want any more ?—Yes.

38. Do you sit amongst the girls ?—Sometimes.

39. What do you pay ?—1½d. and 2d.

40. Do you ever have to sit on the ground ?—No, we always have a seat.

41. Have you ever seen the boys behave roughly to the girls ?— Yes.

42. What do they do ?—Aim orange peel at them.

43. Do they pull the girls about ?—Yes, their hair.

44. And do the girls pull back again ?—No; they seem to enjoy it.

45. Do your sisters go ?—I take baby every night; it is four and a half years old.

46. Does baby like it and laugh ?—Yes.

47. She likes Charlie Chaplin best ?—Yes.

48. Is your father at the war ?—(One boy here stated his father

P

was on the Midland Railway; another one on war work; the third, a sailor; and the fourth, working at Woolwich Arsenal.)

49. Then your fathers are away a great deal, and you don't see much of them ?—No.

50. And mother ?—Mother looks after us at home.

51. I suppose mother is very busy on Saturday night, and she gives you the baby to take to the pictures ?—Yes.

52. Do you pay for the baby ?—Yes, a penny.

53. Do you go to Sunday School ?—(One boy stated he went to Sunday School, but the other three said they did not.)

54. Are you able to sleep long on Sunday morning after going to the pictures ?—I do not feel tired.

55. PRINCIPAL GARVIE. Can you tell me the film you like best ? —(One boy liked " The Broken Coin," and three boys preferred " Red Circle.")

56. Can you tell us the story of the " Red Circle " ?—A man has a red circle on his hand and it forces him to do crime.

57. MR. KING. If there were no picture palaces what would you do ?—Stop at home; but sometimes we go out and play football.

58. Why do you like the cowboy films ?—Because they are exciting.

59. DR. KIMMINS. What other films do you like besides the " Red Circle " and " The Broken Coin " ?—Tragedy.

60. What is the nicest one you have ever seen ?—A picture about the death of a boy's mother and he revenges her.

61. Do you care about love stories at all ?—No.

62. MONSIGNOR BROWN. If there were two picture houses together, and one was showing flowers and geography films, and the other one Charlie Chaplin films, which would you go to ?—The one showing Charlie Chaplin.

63. Supposing they put on some of the films you do not like, what would the boys do ?—They would grumble and shout " Chuck it off."

64. MR. LAMERT. Did you ever on a film see a man do anything with any apparatus or things which you could get hold of ?—No.

65. Would you know how to get any of these things ?—No.

Thirteenth Day

Monday, April 2, 1917,

The Bishop of Birmingham in the chair.

MINUTES OF EVIDENCE

Mrs. Garnett. *Examined.*

1. Monsignor Brown. You are familiar with the working women in your locality?—Yes; it is one of the poorest and one of the most thickly populated districts in Woolwich and Greenwich. I come in contact a good deal with the children through the Invalid Children's Aid Society, the National Society for the Prevention of Cruelty to Children, and on a group of three schools for Children's Care Committees.

2. Have you much knowledge as to the extent to which the women and children go to the cinemas?—Yes; I am afraid they go a great deal, especially in the very poor districts. Some of them go practically every night. We used to have children's performances on Saturday mornings, but these have now been stopped, and the children have to go in the evenings. I do not think their parents take them, but leave them on their own. I have spoken to the parents as to their impressions of the cinema, but they do not seem to think there is any harm. They seem to think the children are sharper by going to the cinemas, as they are taught a good deal by going to these places. I have not had any complaints about the overcrowding, but the Care Committee have complained very much of the crowding of the children, the seating accommodation not being adequate. We think there ought to be some one who should go with the children, in addition to the attendant at the cinema.

3. Can you tell us anything as to the state of the atmosphere?—We have had complaints of the atmosphere of the places, and we think they pick up a good deal of infection through the overcrowding.

4. Have you any complaints to make against the ventilation of the halls?—I do not think there are any complaints.

5. Have you been to many of the halls in these areas?—I have been to two or three of them in the poorer parts just to find out what they are like. They are not very large buildings, and they get a number of children in the audience.

6. Have you any remark to make upon the character of the films shown?—No, except in one when we had a performance given to the children. The first films were very nice, a sort of fairy story, which the children enjoyed, and the latter part was very good, but the middle section really spoilt the whole thing. It was not indecent, but it was Charlie Chaplin pilfering.

7. Have you received any complaints as to the character of the films?—We thought it a pity that Charlie Chaplin should use his abilities to show the children how to pilfer. The Care Committees, of course, complain a good deal about the class of the films. For instance, the children are left to guess a good deal about the films. The films I have in my mind are mostly love stories and questions dealing with seduction.

8. REV. CAREY BONNER. You say they did not like the middle lot of films?—Well, they cheered Charlie Chaplin. I might say that the mothers complain that the children will do anything to get money to go to the cinemas, even to the extent of pilfering. I have distinct evidence of that.

9. SIR JOHN KIRK. Do the teachers complain of the conduct of the children next day?—Yes, they complain very much. They say it takes their minds off their work.

10. MR. LAMERT. You will admit that children have to have a certain amount of recreation. Now do you take exception to this form of recreation, or do you think they have too much?— I think they have too much. You see, there is a great deal of recreation for children nowadays.

11. Do you think that is a correct statement. In your district do you think there are enough play centres for the children to attend?—No, I do not think so.

12. Take the case of Greenwich, where there are no play centres?—Then they are tempted to go to the cinemas. There is no alternative, I am afraid, and I cannot suggest any.

13. Supposing the cinemas were regulated so that the children do not get an excessive amount, do you think there would then be any harm in the cinemas?—It is a question of degree.

14. DR. MARIE STOPES. Take the case of perhaps ten people in one or two rooms, can the children see anything at the cinemas which they are not already acquainted with at their own homes?—No, perhaps not, but it might impress them more at the cinemas.

15. Do you think in homes like that the children are given the money for cinemas which ought to go in boots and food?— No, I think not. But down there now they are practically wealthy.

16. You think the attitude of the mother is to give the children as much enjoyment as possible in spite of what the effect might be on the child's life?—Yes; and the poor mother is very pleased to have the cinema to send the children to.

17. DR. KIMMINS. And the Care Committees would be sorry to see the cinema go?—Yes; but we think there should be more care in the selection of the pictures.

18. THE CHAIRMAN. In regard to the Play Centres there is a certain amount of discipline there?—Yes.

19. Is it not rather natural for the child and perhaps for the grown-up to get away to something where there is not quite so much discipline?—Yes; probably they do enjoy it where there is no discipline.

20. Do you think that if the cinema was properly conducted it would be hurtful to the child's life ?—Well, we say in the medical inspections that it is hurtful to the eyes. We also think they do see a great deal they ought not to see.

21. Supposing there was a control of these places, could not the cinema be more helpful for the child ?—It could be.

STATEMENT OF MR. J. BROOKE WILKINSON

Secretary to the British Board of Film Censors

PRÉCIS

I HAVE been associated with the cinematograph industry, in one way or another, for over twenty years. Having regard to a certain class of film which was being introduced from Germany, the trade early in 1910 considered the question of censorship.

On November 1, 1912, Mr. Redford was appointed as President of the Board of Censors, which Board commenced active duties on January 1, 1913, Mr. Redford having nominated four examiners, who were in no way, directly or indirectly, connected with the trade.

As the Board has no statutory powers, it was decided, in order to assist to make its work effective, to issue a certificate to those exhibitors who only showed censored films. A parchment certificate was prepared (Exhibit A) which could be displayed in the theatres, but the scheme proved ineffective. The licensing authorities were then approached, and of them, so far as can be ascertained, between forty and fifty have shown their confidence in the censorship by making a rule that only such films as have been passed by the Board are to be exhibited in the halls under their jurisdiction.

At the commencement of the censorship, what are known as " topical " films were not included in the scheme; but in August 1914 a report became current to the effect that the exhibition of any film subject dealing with the war would be prohibited. After careful consideration, it became apparent that such a course would be unwise and against the general interest. Consequently, it was decided to take every possible step to deal with the situation that had arisen, and after consultation with the Home Office, it was considered that the Board would best serve the interests of the community generally by amending its policy so far as topical films were concerned. With the approval of the Home Office and the Press Bureau, it was ultimately arranged that topical films relating to the war should be censored. The manufacturers of such films realised the necessity for censorship, and the question of films dealing in any way with the European crisis has been dealt with to the apparent satisfaction of the authorities.

The following table gives a summary of the amount of film dealt with by the Board from its inception to December 31, 1916.

Year	Amount of Film Examined (Feet)	No. of Subjects	Passed Universal Exhibition	Passed with "A" Certificate	Rejected
1913	7,628,931	7,488	6,861	627	22
1914	6,881,614	6,282	5,866	416	13
1915	6,273,924	4,767	4,395	372	22
1916	7,061,681	5,334	4,430	904	25

During 1913 exception was taken to 166 films, in 1914 to 148, in 1915 to 214, and in 1916 to 502, on various grounds.[1]

In 1915 the Board was asked to assist the War Office in the matter of the censorship of films intended for export, and in this connection it was felt that the Board would be acting not only in the interests of the trade, but also in the interests of the State in undertaking the work required. One of the conditions of every licence issued by the Privy Council is that each film must be submitted and sealed by the Board prior to exportation. This seal, attached to the tins, serves to show the Customs authorities or the postal censors, as the case may be, that the films have been submitted to and sanctioned for exportation by the Board. The following table shows the amount and value of the films dealt with from April 1 to December 31, 1916.

	Amount in feet.	Value. £	s.	d.
Africa	2,759,470	24,382	11	6
America	5,414,206	86,063	10	4
Asia	6,301,879	40,389	14	5
Australasia	3,934,299	56,110	11	0
Europe	11,445,044	204,165	6	8

Early in its career the Board was instrumental in eliminating from the screen pictures of an objectionable nature, but there has been a growing tendency, on the introduction of the longer films, to develop stories turning on sexual relations, some of which have been very daring in their conception, and a very definite line of action had to be taken. In this connection, the publication of films based on books of a doubtful nature led to misconception on the part of the public, as the films, as finally passed by the Board, bore no relation in character to the books in question. The Board has also suffered in the eyes of the public on many occasions on account of the character of the posters and literature advertising the films, giving altogether a distorted impression of the actual treatment of the subject. In consequence of this, it was decided last year that the Board should undertake the censorship of cinematograph posters, but owing to the proposal

[1] Far too numerous in range for individual characterisation.

of an official censorship by the Home Office, the matter has not
been carried into effect.

The Board has been encouraged and fortified in its work by the
expressions of approval from the Home Office, and the recognitions
from the Home Secretary of the usefulness of the work accomplished.
Similar recognition has also been made, amongst others, by the
War Office, the Admiralty, and many licensing authorities.

The work of the Board must not only be judged by the films
which have actually been passed, but also by what has been
eliminated and rejected, together with the influence which has
been brought to bear on the producers and importers to discourage the many subjects which were considered altogether
unsuitable for exhibition in this country.

In certain quarters there appears to be a feeling that the Board
simply examines films from the standpoint of immorality and
indecency. It cannot too emphatically be denied that this is not
so, as may be seen from the list of exceptions taken to films during
the past four years.

In several cases, the Board has anticipated the action which
authorities eventually deemed necessary; for instance, by subjects
tending to familiarise the public with the " drug " habit; dealing
with inflammatory treatment of the relations between Capital and
Labour; subjects calculated to hurt the feelings of our fellow-
citizens in the East, and other subjects associated with the war.

Mr. Redford, after a long and serious illness, passed away at
the beginning of November last year, and the trade secured the
services of Mr. T. P. O'Connor, M.P., as President of the Board,
who began his duties on 1st January, 1917.

MINUTES OF EVIDENCE

Mr. J. Brooke Wilkinson. *Examined.*

1. The Chairman. Will you describe to me the British Board
of Film Censors ?—The question of the censorship has been considered by the trade since early in 1910. The matter was first
introduced owing to the fact of certain German films coming into
this country which were considered to be daring. That was in
1908 or 1909. This matter was considered by the manufacturers
of films, and it was felt that something should be done to keep
control of the type of film which was then being introduced from the
Continent, and on November 1, 1911, the matter really took more
or less tangible form. Censorship was formally introduced to the
trade and a long discussion took place. Early in 1912 a resolution
was passed in favour of an independent Board of Censorship, as
it was felt by the trade that it was time to have an independent
Board established which should be absolutely impartial and independent. The matter was considered for some considerable
time, and in October 1912 a report was submitted and received to
carry the proposal into effect. On November 1 Mr. Redford was
appointed as Censor of Films by the trade. I can assure you

the censorship has been carried on since its inception with absolute impartiality and has been absolutely independent. If it had not been so Mr. Redford would not have remained in office. Mr. Redford and myself have on several occasions gone before licensing authorities when the question of censorship was under discussion. The trade have co-operated with Mr. Redford in every possible way, and no request has been made for the decision of the Censor to be altered.

2. MONSIGNOR BROWN. What were the terms of the appointment of the censor?—Mr. Redford was appointed for a year, but if a Government censorship was established it was understood that the appointment should lapse. Just about the time the trade was considering this question of censorship Mr. McKenna, the Home Secretary, asked for a deputation from the trade in order to consider this very matter, and he was then told that the trade was considering the censorship, and that they were about to appoint an independent censor. Mr. McKenna said that he would smile on the proposal, and there is no denying the fact that the Home Office assisted us materially in the early days.

3. What distinction do you make between a dependent and an independent censorship?—To my mind the word independent implies this : whatever decision the censor may give, the trade honourably abides by that decision.

4. DR. KIMMINS. Then Mr. Redford's appointment, when did that come up for renewal?—As a matter of fact, after the first year he went on. He was not reappointed.

5. THE CHAIRMAN. He was liable to go?—Yes. Very possibly if Mr. Redford had undertaken censorship duties in a manner which was absolutely silly, the trade would not have put up with it.

6. THE SECRETARY. Is it a clean and open censorship; as clean as a Court of Justice?—Absolutely.

7. Had Mr. Redford any financial interest in the trade?—Not the slightest.

8. Can you tell us how he came to be appointed?—The question of the appointment of a censor was naturally a very difficult matter for the trade. Two or three names were suggested, but Mr. Redford had been, up to a few months previously, Examiner of Plays under the Lord Chamberlain, and it was felt that he was just the person to examine films if his services could be obtained. He was approached by a person who had never met him before. We made it a rule that none of the examiners must have any interest in the trade.

9. And they have none?—Absolutely none. The Home Office was satisfied with the proposal, and said that if things were done on the lines suggested, they would no doubt allay the present criticism.

10. THE CHAIRMAN. But there are parts of the trade who do not have their films censored?—That is not a very considerable proportion. The amount of film censored is about 97 per cent. of the output.

11. Will you tell me why the percentage of films to which exception was taken in 1916 is more than double the percentage of the films of the previous year?—Well, there is no doubt that the type of film now is very different to what it was in the old days. There is a difference in the class of subject produced.

12. Would any objection be taken to having the films marked " Suitable for children " ?—I think there would be some objection, as the audience would think it was a children's performance. I will say that there are no films passed for universal exhibition, to my mind, that I dare not show in a Sunday school. You will see that in 1916 the number of films which were reconsidered is higher than in any previous years.

13. Do you think the films which are not passed by the Board become popular in some districts for that reason?—That was so in a case four years ago. There was a film advertised, " This film has *not* been passed by the British Board of Film Censors," but I have not heard of anything for a considerable time. It seems to me they found it did not pay. No film which has been rejected by us has been put on the screen, although attempts have been made to do so. In certain cases we have had the good-will of the Home Office and the co-operation of the licensing authorities throughout the country, which has diminished any prospect of a profit if the film were shown without a certificate.

14. How many manufacturers at the present moment do not send their films to the censor?—At the present moment there is only one, but he has now promised to send in his films.

15. MONSIGNOR BROWN. Was " —— —— " passed by the censor?—Yes; we had to consider whether we should be influenced by something which was not on the screen, whether we should, in fact, become censors of literature or whether we should keep entirely to films. After certain eliminations, there was nothing objectionable in that film. You see, this film, like " —— ——," had behind it a certain reputation in the form of a book. I know of no instance of a film which has had a lot of money spent on it having different measure meted out because of that fact. All films are treated on their merits. I might say we have had representatives of the American censors over here to study our methods, and they have adopted some of our ideas.

STATEMENT OF MR. JOHN MASSEY

PRÉCIS

I AM the Court Missionary and Probation Officer of the Old Street Police Court, having occupied these posts for the last twenty-seven years.

The adult court comprises Shoreditch, Hoxton, St. Luke's, Bethnal Green, Spitalfields, Old Ford and parts of Whitechapel and Bow.

The juvenile court embraces the Thames Police Court, the North London Court and the Old Street Court.

The population of these districts might be classified as follows—

(a) A few middle-class.
(b) Poor.
(c) Very poor.
(d) Criminal.
(e) Hebrew.

There is a large population of children in the district, and nearly all the boys and girls go out to work at the age of fourteen.

The average home conditions are bad, and, in some parts, very bad. In a very large number of cases entire families live in one and two rooms.

There are a good many picture palaces in the district, though some have closed since the war began. These houses seem generally clean, well-kept and ventilated during the day. They are very well attended, and the level of behaviour maintained is good. It is rare to hear of disorder except at some of the picture houses. The audiences comprise many mothers with their children—not so many fathers since the war—but many soldiers on leave and others who have been wounded attend them. These audiences are representative of those who live in the neighbourhood. The factory lads and lasses attend in great numbers.

I consider the entertainments are a great improvement on the old penny gaff, the old music hall and club entertainments, particularly in view of the fact that there is no drinking permitted.

As regards juvenile crime, I should say there has been a large increase in the number of children charged, but I do not agree that there has been a large increase of crime. Many children have been picked up in the streets by school officers and charged with being found wandering; also more mothers have charged their children with being beyond control, and with petty thefts from home—a practice which should be deprecated. It is absurd that children of eight or ten years of age should be beyond control. I admit that the absence of the fathers at the war has had much to do with this, and, in some cases, the want of tact on the part of the street school officers. The lists of juvenile offences have been greatly swelled by this kind of charge.

So far as the influence of the cinema on juvenile crime is concerned, there have been very few cases where it has been strictly proved that the offence was the result of the influence of the picture houses; but to my knowledge I have never heard it said in this court that the defendants had been led to do it by " seeing it on the cinema." It is frequently stated by school officers that the children have been to the picture palace. It has been a statement merely, and these statements are not taken too seriously. Sometimes these statements have been suggested by others, but it is evidence on oath that decides the case. These other statements are made not on oath, but when the officer is asked for particulars of the home and school life of the boys and girls in question after the *evidence* has been taken. That is how we hear so much of the picture palaces when thefts have taken place. Sweets, cigarettes, tram rides, music halls, as well as picture palaces are the reasons frequently given for stealing.

The films chiefly complained of, crime and " crook " films, have, in my opinion, little if anything to do with the increase in juvenile crime. Let any keen observer attend a cinema when a " crook " film and detective story is shown and listen to the children's cheers when the " crook " has been run to earth and punished. To my mind the effect is neutral, if anything, and almost forgotten in the pictures that follow. The children of this district could learn little, if anything, about crime from such films. They see and learn very much more in their miserable so-called homes, and sometimes in the places of detention. They recount to one another their exploits.

In my judgment it would be a great blow to my neighbourhood if the cinemas were suppressed, or closed against the children. Just imagine what the cinemas mean to tens of thousands of poor children herded together in one room—to families living in one house, six or eight families under the same roof. For a few hours at the picture house at the corner they can find breathing space, warmth, music (the more music the better), and the pictures, where they can have a real laugh, a cheer and sometimes a shout. Who can measure the effect on their spirits and body ?

To be able to make the poor pinched-faced, half-clad, and half-nourished boys and girls in the crowded slums in cities forget their pain and misery and their sad lot is a great thing, and the pictures do it.

You could not get these children to anything else except in the case of a few to whom a club or a school would appeal. To my mind the picture palace is, and can be made increasingly so, a wonderful counter-attraction to the public-house. It is much better that the parents should be with their children at the picture palace instead of at the public-house.

What is there to hinder the cinema from becoming the best night school or social club ? Why should not the school teacher be used for this purpose and give appropriate lessons from the films on certain nights ? Why should not the influence of the London County Council be brought to bear on them and introduce singers, glee parties and lecturers into the cinemas ? Why should the parson and the district visitor hold aloof ? Those who have the least knowledge of the habits, the difficulties and the squalid lives of these one and two-roomed tenants talk the most foolish things against the cinema. Why should not district visitors who hold Mothers' Meetings take them once a week to the pictures ? Why should not the parson meet the street crowds in his district (those who never darken the door of his church or chapel), at the pictures one night a week and say a word on the subject of the films—preferably on a Sunday night ? What is needed to-day is real, first-hand knowledge of the conditions in which the poor live. Lack of this is the explanation of so much silly talk about pictures being harmful.

MINUTES OF EVIDENCE

MR. JOHN MASSEY. *Examined.*

1. THE CHAIRMAN. You seem in absolute agreement with Mr. Barnett over this cinema question ?—Yes.

2. Now with regard to juvenile crime, will you tell me what you think about that matter ?—I think the cinema has very little effect on juvenile crime. This is caused by the receivers of stolen property, and quite young people go to them.

3. Do you hear the excuse when children are brought up that they " saw it in a cinema " ?—No, never once. I have never heard it, and I have attended every children's court.

4. And you think from the point of view of health that the cinema is a better place to be in than some of these children's homes ?—In many cases, much better, and I would be very sorry to see the cinema closed. I have been trying to imagine the district of Hoxton or Whitechapel during this war, with the dark nights, what it would have been like without the picture palaces to brighten up the children's lives. The public-house proprietors have made a complaint that the picture palaces have interfered with the takings, and one man told me that he lost from £15 to £20 a week.

5. Do you think the cinema can be made educational in up-lifting the general life of the child ?—I think so ; I think if the day school teachers were to take their classes once a week to the cinema and get the children next day to write an essay on what they saw of the film, and offer them a prize, I think that would be excellent. I have not seen anything to object to on the film, and I do not think that undesirable women go to the cinema in my district for the purpose of soliciting or getting into touch with other people.

6. You have not come across any case in your children's court when a boy has been brought up charged with molesting or doing anything indecent to a girl ?—During four years we have had one charge of indecent assault at a cinema. It was about 1911, and I think it was only an attempt to put his hands up a little child's clothes. ' I might point out we have had more charges of indecency taking place in open spaces than in the cinemas. I should like to see travelling cinemas which could visit every village once a week, so that the children of those villages could be allowed to write essays for which prizes would be given. I think this can be done commercially, or by the public school authorities.

FOURTEENTH DAY

Monday, April 16, 1917,

The BISHOP OF BIRMINGHAM in the chair.

STATEMENT OF MR. CHARLES PASCALL

Chairman and Managing Director of Pascalls Ltd. and other Companies, Billposting Contractors; Past President of the London Billposters' Protection Association and of the United Billposters' Association, and ex-Mayor of the Borough of Hammersmith.

PRÉCIS

In 1891, when the present London Billposters' Association was formed, provision was made for the formation of a Censorship Committee.

Subsequently, the Censorship Committee became a Joint Committee of the London and United Billposters' Associations, having also upon it representatives of the Poster Printers' Association, the Theatrical Managers' Association and Touring Managers' Association. The decisions of this Censorship Commitee are acted upon by billposters throughout the United Kingdom and practically by the theatrical interests.

The broad principles on which the Committee have acted are that nothing should be exhibited upon the hoardings depicting murder, acts of violence, or which, in the opinion of the Committee, was calculated to demoralise, or could be held to excuse or extenuate crime or incite to its commission, or which depicted obscenity or nudity.

Certain religious subjects which might give offence, subjects calculated to wound the susceptibilities of foreign peoples, or members of religious bodies,.or calculated to ferment social unrest, are also objected to.

The result of the Committee's work soon became manifest, inasmuch as the class of poster printed became less and less open to objection. Printers and advertisers had become aware of the general lines upon which the billposting trade had dealt with objectionable posters, and besides largely avoiding objectionable features, rapidly improved the general tone and artistic design in poster production. Consequently the posters which the Censorship Committee had to deal with gradually became less and less.

With the advent of the cinema, the number of sensational and objectionable posters again increased, most of them coming from abroad, and as a result the work of the Committee for a time considerably increased.

Strong exception was in some instances taken by proprietors of cinema posters to what they termed the interference of the billposting trade. However, for some time past the proprietors of films and cinema halls, and also printers of film posters, have seen the force of our objections.

Much of the adverse criticism to which the billposting trade has been subjected has been occasioned by the general, but erroneous, impression that the billposter was responsible for the cinema posters. At first, the cinema halls did not use the hoardings to any considerable extent, and even now some halls do not do so, and posters that have been censored by the Billposters' Censorship Committee and have been refused by the billposters have frequently been displayed on cinema premises.

At the present time, however, objectionable cinema posters have practically disappeared from billposters' hoardings throughout the country, but not, unfortunately, from the private boards and premises of some cinema proprietors. The continued exhibition of these posters upon cinema premises caused complaint from local authorities, societies and individuals.

Having regard to the latter fact, representations were made to the cinema people who were invited to a conference with the billposting trade, and who, when meeting, expressed their appreciation of the work of the Censorship Committee, and intimated that they were in accord with the lines upon which the Committee worked and the reasons by which they were actuated. They were then invited to appoint representatives upon the Censorship Committee, but possibly the appointment of this Commission has delayed this.

One feels that there is generally a sincere desire on the part of the cinema people not to use posters to which any reasonable objection can be taken.

I understand that information is desired as to " whether objectionable posters have been sent for display." As to this there can be no question. It is not necessary to go through the whole of the posters that have been considered objectionable. I will, therefore, only quote a few appearing between 1912 and 1916. (A dozen examples given.)

The trade claims that the work of the Censorship Committee of the past quarter of a century has not only had most excellent and satisfactory results, but has done all that any officially appointed censorship could have done—if not more.

The trade has established a precedent which might well be followed by other trades. The success which has attended their efforts has met with the approval of numerous councils, societies and others. Mr. Herbert Samuel (late Home Secretary), recently stated—

" It was greatly to the credit of the trade that they should have taken up the attitude which they have for many years past and endeavour to exercise an effective control over the posters put on walls. Posters have a very great influence on the public life and character. The public ought to be grateful to the deputation for having done their best to see that nothing really offensive to public taste was accepted.

It was mainly owing to them that it had not been found necessary for the Government to take any measures with regard to the general control of hoardings throughout the country. Some of the posters advertising cinema plays have given a deal of offence here and there, and many of them were of an ultra-sensational character and had a bad effect on young people. There are also the posters(over which the Billposting Trade had no control) which are on the premises of the cinema theatres themselves."

Under these circumstances and in view of the practical experience I have had in the past, I am convinced that there is no need or necessity for any official censorship of cinema posters, and that it is only a matter of time, and a very short time, when the posters advertising the cinema will be brought into line with those of the theatre, and that there will be very little in the near future for the present Censorship Committee or indeed any other Censorship Committee to do in the matter of censoring posters.

Even if the cinema proprietors or the cinema exhibitors formed a Censorship Committee of their own, or some other method of censoring cinema posters were established, the billposter, who is in a somewhat similar position to the proprietor and publisher of a newspaper, must have the last word as to what could or should not be exhibited on his hoardings, both in his own interest as well as that of the public—and because some other committee or body had passed a poster, it would not follow that our Censorship Committee would refrain from censoring it.

MINUTES OF EVIDENCE

MR. CHARLES PASCALL. *Examined.*

1. THE CHAIRMAN. Might I ask you to tell us the exact powers of the Billposters' Protection Association and the limitations of those powers?—The London Billposters' Protection Association deals with the membership of London and, roughly, twelve miles round, and practically embraces every billposting firm of any standing. It is a limited company trading under a special permit of the Board of Trade, without profit, and it is not in any sense a trade union. It has no absolute legal control over its members, but practically it has a control to which members agree to submit; it is purely voluntary.

2. What disadvantage would there be to any one who says he will have nothing to do with the Association?—I am not aware that there are any particular disadvantages, but the advantages of belonging to a protection society are almost self-evident.

3. Have you a legal fund?—No; levies are made from time to time.

4. With regard to the censoring of posters. Over a building which is used for purposes of public display of any kind, you have a control?—Actually no control in this sense. We could not say

to the people, " You must not put that bill up " ; but the fact
of our having a control over our posters to a very large extent
gives the control over all others.   This Censorship Committee of
ours has grown and has been recognised by many bodies.   Years
ago when the Censorship Committee began its work with the theatrical posters that had its effect, because owing to the justices calling
attention to the exhibition of posters, the theatrical people saw
it was no use putting up certain bills.   Then, in addition to that,
the printers themselves are more particular with regard to the
printing of posters, because there is a practical standard set up
which it is to their interest to follow, and the same thing is coming
about now with regard to the cinemas.   If we live long enough
the cinema people will see that they must not issue things which
have been banned.

5. There is the temptation that when they find the Billposters'
Association Censorship Committee saying " We won't put these
things up," they might say, " We can get them put up over our
own premises " ?—It is extremely limited, and I doubt whether
it would be done very much.   I have brought here copies of some
of the posters which have been condemned by us.

6. Your Censorship Committee is composed of members of your
Association only ?—No, it represents the theatrical interests and
the printers, but the billposter's interest is the paramount interest.

7. Are you sufficiently in touch with this Censorship Committee
yourself to be able to say whether these pictures you exhibit were
condemned because of their lurid unpleasantness or anything
indecent in them ?—I do not think that any of these pictures
are banned on the grounds of indecency, but suggestiveness
undoubtedly.

8. With regard to the cinema trade generally, you are getting
into close touch with them ?—We are, and we desire to get even
closer.   We wrote to two of the organisations not long ago on this
matter, and the result was we had a very representative meeting
of cinema proprietors and renters, and they all testified to the
immense amount of good we had done.   They are in hopes that
we can come into line, and the proposal was made that they should
consider the advisability of appointing so many people to go on
the Censorship Committee.

9. PRINCIPAL GARVIE. Would not the poster occasionally be
very much more lurid than the film itself ?—Undoubtedly.

10. Have the cinema proprietors got hoardings of their own
apart from the buildings or the hoardings which are under your
control ?—To a very limited extent there are some, but not in the
sense you can call hoardings.

11. So that objectionable posters would be confined to the
cinema ?—That is so.

12. Supposing this Commission were to advise the appointment
of an Advisory Council to act with the Censor of Films, would
your Censorship Committee be prepared to co-operate in any way
with any such Advisory Committee that might be dealing with the
films ?—That was foreshadowed very strongly by Mr. Samuel.

Personally, I do not think there is any necessity for it. I think that with proper safeguards we might be disposed to agree, but there must always be this factor : that even if they had agreed not to condemn a poster, we must, as an association, exercise our rights of refusing the poster.

13. Such a Committee might be helpful to you in doubtful cases ?—I think the people can keep their own house in order, if they please, very much better than anybody else.

14. Do the police exercise any sort of control over the posters exhibited ?—In London, no, but in some parts of the country they do.

15. Have you had any complaints from the police authorities about posters which have passed your censorship ?—No, but we have had commendation from the authorities.

16. MONSIGNOR BROWN. What would be your action if the printers issued to the cinema proprietors for posting on their hoardings posters which you would refuse on your own hoardings ?—That has been done, but the licensing authorities now have power to deal with that matter.

17. Say ten posters are issued, nine of which you have no objection to, but the tenth you refuse, and it is posted by the cinema proprietor on his own display board in front of his hall: would you take any notice of that ?—We have no power to take action, but we would very probably write to him and call his attention to it.

18. THE CHAIRMAN. What is meant is, that a man deliberately flouts your powers. Cannot you take drastic action in regard to that ?—My answer is, that we have had no instance of that kind.

19. DR. SALEEBY. On what grounds are some of these pictures objected to ?—On the grounds that they would be repulsive. We have also refused to exhibit posters in two forms : one is Christ on the Cross, and the other is the Salvation Army figure of Christ used as a poster for their appeal in Self-Denial Week. We feel that these subjects are not subjects which should be on a hoarding.

MR. JOHN HILL. *Examined.*

20. THE CHAIRMAN. You are the Managing Director of Sheffields, Ltd., Birmingham, and its subsidiary companies, and a Past President of the United Billposters' Association. Does that cover the whole of London ?—The whole of the provinces, but not London.

21. What you would like in dealing with posters is, that a sample of each objectionable poster should be sent to your Committee ?— Our Censorship Committee are competent to deal with any poster, and their decisions have been adhered to by the general billposting trade throughout the country.

22. Then you suggest that the cinematograph exhibitors should accept the suggestions of your censorship ?—That is a matter purely between ourselves and the trade.

Q

23. Altogether you are strongly opposed to any additional censorship beyond that which at present is exercised?—We feel we have been doing this work for a large number of years, and our experience is, that we are better able to do it than any public official that might be appointed. Our general knowledge and intercourse with the public is such that it would be very difficult to get another committee together such as we have, and with such experience. There is not one trade represented upon the Committee, but four. We have the billposters, the printers, and the theatrical people so far, and we are getting the cinema people. There are a variety of interests, you see, and the four should be able to arrive at something better than any public official.

24. A poster is put where every one must see it. People have to go in to see the film?—We recognise that the hoardings must be safeguarded, and we have done what we can to safeguard them. We are quite satisfied that the work we are doing is efficiently done, and we have already satisfied the Home Secretary on that point. If we can see a way of dealing with this question of censorship, we are quite open to consider any point which may arise. As far as the posters go, our Censorship Committee take the greatest care that no bill shall go out which will offend either child or man.

25. MR. NEWBOULD. Do you consider a voluntary trade censorship is far more severe than an official censorship?—I won't say severer; it is more intelligent.

MR. OLIVER H. McCOWEN, B.A. *Examined.*

26. THE CHAIRMAN. You are practically the head of the Y.M.C.A. in France, and only arrived from France this morning? —Yes.

27. Will you tell us something about the cinema over there amongst our troops?—We have sixteen or seventeen cinemas in France. We have large wooden halls that hold about 1000 men, and they run the cinema performances six nights a week, but not on Sundays. All the takings from these cinemas, after paying expenses, we devote to a farm colony in Dorset for disabled soldiers. The men pay for admission twenty-five centimes, the non-commissioned officers fifty centimes, and the officers one franc.

28. Will you tell us the kind of things you have on the film?— Pretty much the ordinary kind of film.

29. Charlie Chaplin?—Oh yes, he is the most popular man in France. Then we have noticed that the cinema in France makes a very remarkable contribution to the behaviour and *morale* of the troops. I have repeatedly had testimony from Town Majors and men in charge of the discipline of the various places, that the opening of one of these cinemas in a town has meant an immediate diminution, amounting in some cases to fifty per cent. in drunkenness and crime. In one town at the northern end of our line we

opened a cinema. The drunks there had been 100 a night, and the Town Major told me that the night we opened this went down to sixteen, and they have not gone up to twenty-five. In another town, not twenty miles from that, the Town Major said it meant an immediate diminution of crime to the extent of 50 per cent. In our large reinforcement camps where the men are sometimes for three weeks or a month with nothing to do, it is the greatest boon in the world for them to get in and have a real good laugh and spend a pleasant hour without the drink. Then in every programme we have a film of an instructive or scientific character. The performances last about one and a half hours.

30. Do the soldiers take to the instructive film?—They do not like it very much, but we insist on it, as you see we are in the happy position out there that they have nowhere else to go. We have a number of religious films, but they are not popular because they have not been properly produced.

31. Is there any improvement you would like to see in the cinema?—Yes, with regard to the films I think the tone of them might be higher. A lot of them are very silly, and the plots in the dramas of the Wild West are very obvious from the beginning. Then, again, we have music in some of the places where there are small orchestras played by the men. The films are selected by a man who used to be with us. In the first place we purchased £400 or £500 worth, but they got out of shape and got ruined, so we find it is better to hire them.

32. Have you tried applying to the great cinema industry itself to make you a grant of the films?—Quite recently I wrote round to practically all the big companies in London; and the reply was, that there was a difficulty in getting the films back from France, with the result that they found it was not practicable to send the films over.

33. Is your audience very critical?—No; they are very appreciative. We also have travelling cinemas which perform in barns and big buildings like that.

34. Have you seen anything produced in the cinema under your direction which you think could lead anybody to think that crime was a desirable occupation?—No, I am bound to say I have not. All our films are censored by the Secretary in the particular districts in which they are to be produced.

35. REV. F. SPURR. Is the magic lantern with the lectures very popular?—Yes, it is very popular, and I think the reason is, that the lantern lecturer insists upon an effort of memory, and he explains the pictures as they appear.

36. THE CHAIRMAN. Do you get as large an audience for the magic lantern as for the cinematograph?—Every bit; but that is, of course, because they have nowhere else to go.

37. And there is real gratitude for the cinema out there at the Front?—Yes, and the authorities help us all they can.

STATEMENT OF THE REV. W. E. SOOTHILL, M.A.,
Religious Work Secretary, Y.M.C.A.

I have obtained the views of some of those members of the Y.M.C.A. who have had personal experience of the running of cinemas, and the evidence I have selected is that of three members of our staff who are able to speak from three different standpoints. One of them, whom I will style " C," has had a great deal to do with the cinema in a large central building, both before and since the outbreak of war.   Another, whom I will style " O," has considerable knowledge of educational films along a special line.   The third, whom I am styling " M," has gained his experience in a large camp, where he has established and run a most successful cinema for the soldiers.   I have taken the evidence of these three as typical of that which the Y.M.C.A. is able to supply.

Eight questions were issued, and those questions with the answers received from the three sources already indicated, are given below.

Question 1.   Have you found educational features specially appeal to audiences ?

" C " says—Yes ! so long as they have been interspersed with films of an entirely different character.

" O " says—Yes ! especially where lecturers were in attendance giving more detailed descriptions than could be given in the printed sections of the films.   The public want more of this.

" M " says—In an audience composed entirely of soldiers we have found that films dealing with naval or military matters have been decidedly appreciated.

Films showing men in action at the Front or actual fighting are not liked ; but films dealing with transport of troops, distribution of letters at the Front, military supplies, ceremonies, parades, military engineering works, the making of munitions, etc., are liked.

Films dealing with travel, animal life, insect life, take a second place in the men's interest ; but there is a distinct liking for films which show horses, monkeys, dogs—and in fact any animals who have been cleverly trained and can do clever tricks.

We have found that films which show life under the sea are also liked.   There is an intense appreciation for films dealing with submarines ; or films which show life in coalmines, fire stations, quarries, diamond-mines, naval dockyards, boys' naval training-ships.   Films showing rough seas, storms, effective sunrise or sunset scenes are also liked.

Films having anything to do with aeroplanes, airships, or interesting machinery are also appreciated.

Question 2.   Is there a demand for vulgar films ?

" C."   No.   They are just tolerated.

" O."   Yes, as there is a certain demand for vulgar books and many other things.

" M."   A certain section of a military audience will laugh and apparently enjoy a vulgar film, but if vulgar films are not shown the fact is certainly never commented on, nor does one ever receive a request to show any questionable film one of the men might know of.

It is advisable for the person in charge where possible to see the programme through himself before it is shown publicly to the men. Occasionally one finds that a certain scene in a film, whilst it was never intended to be vulgar, will call forth some unnecessary, rude remark from a noisy member of the audience; and experience teaches that it is advisable, where possible, for the manager of the picture show simply to have the offending portion of the film temporarily cut out and then put back again when he despatches the films to the agents.

No opportunity should be given which would tend to create a dirty impression on a man's mind; and occasionally, although it might never have been intended by the film producer, some scenes do produce an undesirable effect on a man's mind.

There is such an abundance of absolutely clean and intensely interesting or comical film productions that it makes it at any time absolutely unnecessary to show anything which is in the very slightest way questionable. The whole tendency now-a-days, I firmly believe, is for film productions to be cleaner, more interesting, and at the same time instructive; yet we find these very films are not lacking in intensely exciting plots and features.

There is a distinct demand for dramatic films, but no call for long-drawn-out deaths or suicides.

Question 3. How far can the cinema at present be used for definitely religious purposes?

" C." The so-called religious film is a very doubtful quantity. It leaves room for tremendous improvement and seems to be received generally as a caricature. On the other hand, films of national events from which lessons may be drawn are of undoubted value, and I think that some of the booked films also lend themselves to a good story teller as a very great aid indeed in matters religious.

" O." To an unlimited extent many an empty church might be filled if it were equipped with a cinema or other means of ocular demonstration for the purpose of illustrating the speaker's remarks, and in my opinion every church should have one.

" M." The cinema hall, as a hall, is always a quite suitable place for holding religious meetings either on week-days or more particularly on Sundays. This does not mean that cinematograph pictures need necessarily be included, but it has been found from experience that the inclusion of same results in crowded houses. And it is perhaps a matter of personal opinion whether we ought to consider that offering the men a free cinematograph show on Sunday evening along with a short definite religious service is a legitimate and recommendable policy.

It is important, however, to let the men know definitely what they are to expect, *i. e.* a religious service at the end of the cinema picture. From experience it has been found that the men do not go out after the picture is finished, but that they stay, with very few exceptions, to the religious meeting. On the other hand, suitable films can be procured which lend themselves as a suitable subject for a lecture or a distinctly religious address actually given whilst the film is being shown. Existing films treating Biblical subjects are not recommended; but films adapted from the works of well-known authors of fiction are procurable. These pictures are always popular, and result in a large demand by the men for books from the Y.M.C.A. library of the same title as the film. Such films as " The Sign of the Cross," " The Eternal City," " The Rosary," " Quo Vadis?" " Jane Shore," " In the Ranks," and films of a similar nature have been tried with conspicuous success for Sunday evening cinema shows.

The moral of the pictures is good, and I believe leaves a good impression on the men.

We have tried the following arrangement, and it has met with great success on Sunday evenings : A small military orchestra has been in attendance, and has rendered first-class and quite suitable Sunday music. A suitable film picture has been shown whilst the orchestra has played. This film might last one hour; then the distinctly religious address has been given, and the " house " has closed with a hymn and prayer.

This arrangement has been gone through twice in the one evening. In a case of this sort, of course, no admission charge is made. When an admission charge has been made, the following arrangement we consider has been a suitable one, and has certainly been greatly appreciated by the audience. Special attention has been paid to ensure that really high-class music has been provided at the same time as the pictures have been showing.

The programme would consist of, first, a short film of, say, 1000 feet, consisting of either topical news budget or a travel subject, then a long suitable film (preferably one of J. D. Walker's productions, which can always be relied on for Sunday shows) of about 6000 feet in length. The Sunday show is then finished off with a suitable sacred song by a lady or gentleman singer. This would happen twice in the same evening.

Cinema shows meet a great need in camps where a great mass of men are congregated. They make provision for the section of men who will not under any circumstances attend church. If these men did not attend the cinema show they would in the majority of cases spend their time in their own huts or hanging about the camp and public roads, thereby meeting temptation which we are out to keep them from coming into contact with.

If every church or place of worship, every recreation hut or room in and around the camp within a walking radius were packed to overflowing with men attending service on any Sunday night, there would still be a considerable number of men in the camp for whom room could not possibly be found in these churches.

Cinemas on Sunday certainly do not encourage men to attend church, but they certainly make provision for the man who does not want to go to church, or who would never go to church, and also for the man who for lack of accommodation could not get into a church.

I suggest that cinemas on Sunday could be made a means of enabling men to spend their time, if not definitely profitably, at least harmlessly. Moreover, Sunday cinemas can be made instructive as well as interesting. They can be used as a means to an end.

Whilst the foregoing remarks may not apply to Sunday cinemas in ordinary towns, I feel they are certainly applicable to Sunday cinemas in military camps where vast numbers of men are gathered together under unusual environment and conditions.

Question 4. Is the present Censorship of films satisfactory, or is it necessary to apply a double censorship, that is, an additional one of our own before films issued under the censorship can be safely used?

" C." I do not consider the present censorship of films any censorship at all. It only cuts out the absolute lewd and stamps things as being correct which are to say the least, extremely vulgar—as instance Charlie Chaplin films. There is no doubt in my mind that it is absolutely necessary that a strict censorship should be given by any Y.M.C.A. officer to all films proposed to be screened. This is an exceptionally difficult matter. The method we have adopted is to go to the firm of highest repute, tell them exactly what we stand for, and ask them when supplying films to always bear this in mind. The result has been that Gaumont's, who have supplied us here, have made not more than two errors, and these probably ninety per cent. of people would take no objection to.

" O." No. A double censorship is strongly advisable.

" M " considers that he has replied in some measure in his previous answer.

Question 5. Have you any suggestions to make in regard to a more vigorous censorship?

" C " is of opinion that a more vigorous censorship would ensure better public results, and he considers that the Censor should have the support of a Committee consisting of men representing education, science and literature. He omits altogether a representation of religion, which is probably not intentional.

" O " considers that a more vigorous censorship is necessary, that the Censor should be appointed by the Government, and that a fee should be charged for films submitted for approval.

" M " considers that he has answered this question in some measure in his previous remarks.

Question 6. Can you speak of the general level of the public cinema shows in your district or area? Are they satisfactory?

" C," who has been much occupied with his own work, says: On the whole, I think this area is well served; the films in the majority of cases being of the highest possible order.

" O," who lives in the same area, says: Have not visited public cinema shows since outbreak of war. Previously, the cinemas in this area were not satisfactory.

" M " says: Experience suggests that the programmes provided in the local cinemas are about the average as far as general level is concerned. They are certainly no worse than the usual picture show in the town.

Programmes shown might be of a much better type, but as far as I know nothing has been shown in these picture houses which one might take public objection to.

Question 7. What has been the result of Sunday cinema? Has it prejudicially affected church attendance? Is the tone of the entertainment better than the week-day cinema. Has it been a good or bad thing? Has it reduced the amount of Sunday drinking, and the spending of time in places of less helpful results?

Personally, I strongly deprecate the Sunday cinema, as I do the so-called Sunday sacred concert, but this is entirely a matter of opinion. I am certain of one thing, namely, that it does prejudicially affect church attendance, especially on the part of young men. As far as I am aware, the films featured on a Sunday are the same as on other days—no difference is made. I do not think that its influence has been to reduce the amount of Sunday drinking, inasmuch as the performances are continuous and give ample time for any attender to make up for lost time.

" O." Fairly good. I do not believe church attendance has been affected. Tone on Sunday same as week-day. More a good thing than a bad thing. I believe it has reduced Sunday drinking and attracted people from less desirable places.

" M " has been answered to some extent in my answer to question No. 3, but I add the following—

In my experience Sunday cinemas have not prejudicially affected church attendance as far as we are concerned at this camp. The Sunday cinema has helped the attendance of our Sunday evening services tremendously. When the men leave the first house of the cinema most of them come straight into our large recreation hall adjoining the cinema hall, and the regular Sunday evening service (7.30), conducted by a chaplain, then commences. The same thing again happens with the men coming out of the next house of the cinema at nine o'clock. Thus the great crowds which are attracted by the cinema also afterwards attend the Sunday evening service. Certainly the entertainment provided in the cinema on Sunday is distinctly different in tone from the week-day programme. Sunday cinema has been a distinctly good thing for us and for the men. It has certainly reduced the amount of Sunday gambling and Sunday drinking to a tremendous extent.

Question 8. What has been the effect of the cinema on boys and younger people? Is there anything in the police court reports relative to the suggestion of crime in the young mind?

I do not think that the effect of the cinema on boys has been more prejudicial than the fiction recommended for boys' reading. It all depends upon the boy; if he has a well-developed imagination, both cinema and fiction will lead him into doing things over which he can get into trouble.

" O." I do not think it has had a bad effect on boys. Cases that have appeared in the police courts do not suggest to me that serious crimes have been committed as a result of young persons frequenting cinemas.

"M." We do not admit boys under sixteen to the cinema at any time, but to my mind, cinemas which cater for adults cannot cater for the youthful mind. There should be a distinctly different programme provided for young people, and generally speaking I do not think it advisable for young people to be allowed to attend and to see cinema programmes which are produced primarily with the idea of appealing to the adult mind. The quantity of films now obtainable which are specially suitable to be shown to children is very big; suitable story films, instruction films, travel films and news budgets only should, I think, be shown to children.

Some dramatic and detective films have, I think, a bad effect on the youthful mind, whilst when shown to an adult the effect produced is only one of interest and not of ill effect. Naturally, there are exceptions even as to the result of showing certain films to an adult; but I do not think many adult people are greatly affected by what they see on the screen. I have known children to be worked up to a most unhealthy state of excitement in viewing films which to an adult produces little or no excitement. Therefore, I say let us by all means have a special programme for children and a special programme for adults. Notwithstanding all this, many of the programmes shown to adults are quite suitable to be shown to children, but this does not apply by any means to all programmes which are shown.

I believe that an unsuitable picture shown to a boy or girl may produce very wrong and unhappy results on a childish mind; and I cannot help but think that many of the crimes committed by very young people could, if carefully looked into, be traced to the result of seeing an unsuitable picture screened.

Concluding Remarks.—The observations made above, whilst they may apply to cinemas in military camps, may not all necessarily apply to cinemas in town.

To my mind it is important and a great asset to provide high-class orchestral music in the cinema.

It is important that the films should be clearly and steadily shown on the screen.

A good light should be used, but not too brilliant a one.

Films which are old or scratched should not be tolerated for one moment.

Films which are newly released from the producers should be secured where possible. If this is done, although the cost is more, the result will be (providing you have a good operator through which to show your film) a creditable show.

If we are to run cinemas at all, I believe we should aim at using the best mechanical equipment possible.

The initial cost is, of course, greater, but it pays in the long run. A second-rate cinema projector, a second-rate light producing engine or dynamo, whilst it might enable you to show a picture on the screen, only results in your picture being dazzling, alternately brilliant and dull, unsteady, and a source of disappointment to your audience and discredit to the Y.M.C.A. Let us have the best mechanical equipment, a good operator, and a good and suitable programme of fairly new films, and a hall well managed.

Rev. W. E. Soothill, M.A. *Examined.*

The Chairman. I see in your evidence you have got hold of the views of three people ?—Yes, three people in this country, all of whom have been running cinemas, and they are men of some standing. (Witness gave the names.) I have here a few notes from Mr. Yapp, which he wishes me to put before this Commission. " Influence depends entirely on the films. We carefully censor our films and allow no uncensored films to appear. Success can only be assured by a varied and up-to-date programme which must include films : (1) Thrilling, but not sensational or morbid ; (2) Funny, but not vulgar ; (3) Educational, but not dry ; (4) Clean, with nothing suggestive of the unclean. If properly run a good cinema is helpful in town or city, as it occupies time and attention that might be spent in worse ways. Its influence may be positive and altogether helpful. In large out-of-the-way camps—particularly in Flanders, France, Egypt and Mesopotamia—we have found our cinemas a perfect godsend. In an advanced position in Flanders I found about 1000 men in the Y.M.C.A. cinema, and the Town Major said since its advent crime had decreased seventy per cent. Our pathescopes are in great demand, and the services of our men are constantly requisitioned to give shows to isolated detachments of men in their huts or tents, billeted in barns, cellars or ruined houses—and frequently even near the trenches. We have many Y.M.C.A. cinemas in France and Flanders, most of them in big buildings specially constructed, but others in ruined houses, tents and barns ; also two or three travelling cinemas."

Fifteenth Day

Monday, April 23, 1917,

The Bishop of Birmingham in the chair.

STATEMENT OF MR. J. GRANT RAMSAY, F.R.E.S.

Principal of the Institute of Hygiene.

Précis

I am convinced that the cinema can be utilised to great advantage, not alone in education, by facilitating the spread of knowledge, but also as an influence for good by raising the moral standard of the people.

The first cinema in England, for purely educational work, was installed at the Institute of Hygiene about eight years ago. The London County Council considered, later, the feasibility of installing 200 cinemas in London schools, but, owing to the expense and other obstacles, no action was taken.

The cinema has proved of great service at the Institute in illustrating lectures, and at demonstrations of first aid, sick nursing, and cooking, and also at special exhibitions—such as the Domestic Economy and Child Life Exhibitions. It is also utilised for showing medical films of germ life (greatly magnified), the working of the heart and stomach, and even operations, but these are exhibited only to medical audiences. Films are also shown illustrating hygiene and sanitation to men of the Royal Army Medical Corps. Children, representing a school at a time, are brought regularly, and annually, to see the pictures at the Institute, and on these occasions interest and instruction are blended judiciously together.

The development of the cinema on educational lines can hardly be said to have come up to anticipations, but this is not altogether surprising. Messrs. Pathé Frères and other makers have devoted much time and money to the production of scientific and educational films, but at a great loss. The reason is simple. School books would not be popular on bookstalls, and before educational films can be in any demand there must be facilities for showing them. Further development rests largely with the educational authorities.

I have visited a number of cinema theatres in London and the provinces, and while most of them are good buildings, are well fitted, and conform to the local regulations, I have not yet found one that could possibly be classed as healthy or hygienic. Darkness, a humid atmosphere, and the heat developed from a congregation of people, all participate to make the most suitable culture for germs, and the consequent spread of infection and disease. This is a serious danger, and should receive attention and be remedied, if at all possible, in the public interest.

The films generally shown, too, leave much to be desired. Long dramas, of the " shilling shocker " character, have lately been largely chosen to attract the public, but I am not at all sure that this sort of film is what the public mostly wants. Some of the films, also, are very suggestive and can only have a harmful influence.

The hygiene of the mind is deserving of much more consideration than it has received. We have an elaborate and very complete organisation for preventing adulteration and poisoning of the body, but we have no system whatever for preventing the poisoning of the mind. Body poisons may be thrown off, but mental poisons take root and are lasting in their influence for evil.

I have no practical evidence that the effect on the nerves and brain, through looking at pictures, is seriously detrimental to the adult. It is exhausting, especially if the films are long, and more rapidly exhausting if the films flicker and are old and bad, but the result largely depends on the condition of the person, and recovery from any strain generally follows from a little rest.

Children deserve, and require, very special consideration in regard to cinema pictures. They are more readily influenced than adults, and their nerves are more delicate and more easily exhausted. I do not think they should ever be taken to a cinema at night, as it affects their sleep and development. I am altogether in favour, however, of cinema pictures for children—under proper conditions. They might with advantage have special theatres and pictures devoted to them. I have received many proofs that children prefer interesting and instructive pictures, such as those shown at the Institute, to the weary dramas and other pictures usually shown at the popular theatres.

As regards the possible improvements and future possibilities of the cinema, I think that better ventilation and greater air space should be required in the theatres, so as to ensure a more hygienic atmosphere. It would also be of great advantage to show the pictures in the light, and the obstacle to this may soon be overcome, as it has already been almost achieved. The shorter films—say, under a thousand feet—are to be preferred, and when the films run into thousands of feet there should be more frequent and longer intervals. The question of intervals is most important in regard to children. Other methods of entertaining the audiences can be introduced to fill up these intervals, but they should not be of movement, such as dancing, if it can be avoided. Singing is very preferable.

Cinema proprietors should recognise their obligation to the public more fully than they do, and if they aimed at elevating the people, they would also elevate their calling. I do not think, either, that they would lose in any way by showing pictures slightly above, rather than below, the public taste, and it would not be too much to require of them that a certain percentage of instructive or educational films should be shown at each performance.

I believe the cinema has a great future if directed on right lines, and if installed in schools, Sunday schools, and even churches, it could be made a most attractive and influential factor for improving the education and raising the moral standard of the people.

MINUTES OF EVIDENCE

Mr. J. Grant Ramsay. *Examined.*

1. The Chairman. I notice you say you visited Paris some years ago, and the idea occurred to you that the cinema could be made very popular for illustrating lectures?—Yes, but at that time the cinema was very crude. It was more a novelty than anything else, but the possibilities appealed to me, and long ago I suggested to my council the possibilities of the cinema. We went later into the cost, as we thought it would be an advantage to introduce it into our lecture-room, and the council took up the idea.

2. The cinema trade took very kindly to you?—Yes, very kindly indeed.

3. Can you say what service the cinema has been at the Institute to illustrate your lectures?—It has been a very marked feature of our work. We either give educational pictures before the lecture starts, and so gather the people, or we give them afterwards, using the cinema also to illustrate the lectures. We found, however, that it was better to give the cinema show first, as it brought the audience there early and they stayed for the lecture. One of the first pictures we had was to illustrate the fly pest.

4. You state that some firms have produced scientific films at a great loss?—Yes, so much so that one well-known firm has shut up its educational department. Many of the films, more especially the medical films, were produced in collaboration with the Pasteur Institute in Paris.

5. Your feeling is that if we are to get the cinema used in an educational way, it must be done by the educational authorities first of all to find out its value, and then they will have to educate the British public to spend its money?—I think so. For instance, Pathé's are a very wealthy firm, and they have been very generous over this matter. When I visited them in Paris three years ago they said they were quite ready to spend a great deal of money if it would enable them to promote education in any way.

6. I notice you are not quite satisfied with the buildings?— Not with the atmosphere, at all events.

7. Can you suggest any improvements?—Yes, ventilation and more air space. I look upon proper ventilation as more important than air space : that is, if you can get sufficient fresh air into a building. I might say that a French doctor has brought out an invention of a new lantern, which throws such a strong picture on the screen that the picture can be well seen in daylight.

8. The films themselves leave much to be desired, you say. Are you still looking at this from an educational point of view? —No, I am looking at it from the point of view of mental hygiene.

9. You mention the long drama of the " shilling shocker " character, and that brings us back to the fact that there have been " shilling shocker " books. Which would you say was the more dangerous, the " shilling shocker " film or the book?—I think the picture is the worst, because it gets more impressed upon the mind. The " shilling shocker " book depends upon the memory of the reader, whereas the impression conveyed from a picture is fairly lasting. I think that sort of film is not wanted.

10. Are you prepared to say what the juvenile public requires? —I think the juveniles like interesting and instructive pictures even more than comic pictures; that is my experience.

11. Of what social class are you thinking?—We have had the lower middle, the middle and the upper classes at our pictures, but not the very poor. I have tried to find out what is the natural bent more indirectly than directly, so as to get a true impression. Their ages are about seven or eight to about fourteen.

Some schools come to us and see the pictures, and when the children return to school they are required to write an essay on what they have seen, and it is most interesting to find the impression conveyed to them by certain pictures.

12. Supposing next door to you there was a film theatre where the entertainments were of a different type to yours, such as Mr. Charlie Chaplin, and the children were left absolutely free, into which place would they go?—If you take the average picture palace and the pictures we show, if they had the opportunity they would come to our pictures. I have asked children after having seen the Charlie Chaplin pictures whether they prefer the Charlie Chaplin pictures or the pictures at the Institute, and they replied that they preferred the pictures at Institute; and the reason they gave was that they could not always see the jokes in Charlie Chaplin. We give them pictures of things in common use, such as the supply and distribution of milk, and there is always a lesson in our pictures.

13. Have those pictures been prepared for you specially?— No, we have mostly picked them up from different sources. Whenever we heard of an educational film we tried to get it.

14. Are they British or American films?—Nearly all the medical films are French. The French predominate in scientific films.

15. You are strongly of opinion that the sleep of the child is affected by going to the cinema at night?—I think so, and this is the opinion of medical men who have strong views on that subject.

16. You are satisfied that if the cinema were used and directed in the right lines, it could be helpful in educational, moral, and even religious matters?—I think so. For instance, if the educational authorities installed a few cinemas in schools around London, the popular cinemas would be only too pleased to follow up and take advantage of the development.

17. PRINCIPAL GARVIE. Do you disapprove of a series of pictures running on without a break?—I do not think it is advisable to have a continuous run of films.

18. You are in favour of music?—Yes, including singing.

19. MR. CROOK. Do you think the cinema, accompanying the lectures, is a great advantage, greater than a magic lantern?— Yes, as one appeals to them as being alive and the other as dead.

20. MONSIGNOR BROWN. About what interval do you suggest as a pause between the pictures?—That would depend largely on the length of the film. A thousand feet takes twenty minutes, and I should say five minutes would be quite enough. After a film of fifty minutes to an hour, there should be a pause of about ten minutes. During those intervals I suggest music or singing.

21. Do you think that seriously practicable in the poor houses? —Yes.

22. MR. LAMERT. You recognise that if vocal music were introduced it would very largely add to the cost?—Not necessarily, but you would want more than one singer.

23. If there is a disposition shown here in England for a better-class film, they would be made?—Yes.

24. THE CHAIRMAN. Do you say it is quite as easy to find a good film as a good play for production?—I think so.

25. MR. LAMERT. But do you realise that you would have to find fifty-two or one hundred and four of these good films, as they do not run continuously at the cinemas?—I have not fully considered that.

26. MR. T. P. O'CONNOR. Would you object to the idea that there should be a cinema attached to every school in the country? —I think it is coming to that.

27. And you don't agree with the theory that the cinema rather interferes with the method of education?—No, I think it is the best way of illustrating subjects.

MRS. BASIL L. Q. HENRIQUES. *Examined.*

28. THE CHAIRMAN. I want to get from you how you are interested in this question?—In peace time my husband runs a boys' club in the East end, at St. George's in the East, and I run a girls' club round the corner. We live over the boys' club, and now he is away I see after the boys' club as well. I was not directly interested in the Cinema Commission, but I always had felt very strongly on the subject, and I had a letter from Mr. Marchant saying that the Chief Rabbi had given my name as living there, and that perhaps I would be able to tell something. Before that I had not been in a cinema at St. George's because they bear bad reputations. As an example to the children I would not go, but I have taken children to cinemas in the north of London to see certain films. I speak about the local conditions because the trade of the people down there has a great deal to do with the large numbers who visit the cinemas. Most of the children are tailors or cigarette-makers, and the work is not a great strain on them mentally, so they have plenty of time to think and talk of things, and in the evening when they have finished their work they feel they must have some excitement. Now the housing question settles the matter, because down there nine or ten people are living in one house, and the luxury of only four people in one bedroom is something to be envied. You will thus see it is impossible for the children to stop indoors in most cases. Their homes are usually rather dirty, and in many cases there is a consumptive father and the smaller children are screaming. Anyway, there is every inducement for the children to go into the streets. Round about St. George's there are quite a lot of undesirable houses and loose women, and the amount of evil which surrounds the children is appalling. It is either a question of stopping in the streets and seeing what is going on, or going to the pictures; and there are a number of cases where the parents like them to go to the pictures because of these things. The next point is that it is a dark place, and if you have a young lady it is very convenient to go there. It is also a convenient rendezvous for family parties, but the elder children do not go with their parents; they go with their " bird." The expression down there is that you take your " bird " to the

pictures. They have, roughly, two types of entertainments, and where you get the children in hundreds there are sensational pictures of the blood-and-thunder type, and Charlie Chaplin is quite the most refined thing about the pictures.

29. Can you remember any of the names of the plays?—I cannot remember the titles, but there is a picture, say, of the trousers coming off in front of the audience, and the things that happen until the new trousers come. I notice that the couples go for the love stories. The children are always in the cheapest seats, which are under the exit lights, whereas the couples go where it is darker.

30. Have you seen some of the love stories that are objectionable?—I have seen some very objectionable ones. I saw the " ———— — ————," and these are my remarks on it : I visited the Old King's Hall, Commercial Road. The hall was well ventilated and the audience composed mostly of adults or boys and girls over sixteen. The behaviour on the whole was more seemly. There were, of course, the usual couples absorbed in one another. The film shown was one in which a woman causes a man such temptation as to make him lose control of himself—shows him carrying her off—and was so very suggestive that the man next to me groaned repeatedly and could not keep still in his seat— he left after the climax. I am certain that the film could not do otherwise than have a very dangerous effect on any one at all given to sensuous thoughts, and could not fail to cause impure thoughts to any of the couples watching it. I thought it was something really rather more than suggestive. The sensational pictures are what the children flock to, and I saw the children in one cinema so excited that I am certain that had any panic happened it would have been absolutely impossible to control them. With reference to the condition of some of the cinemas, the bigger ones are good, but the smaller ones are badly ventilated, and some of them are dirty and appalling. Then, again, with reference to the attendants at these cinemas, some of them are a very low type of men. The lights in many do not go up, and I feel that if they were to go up fairly frequently it would put a stop to a lot of the behaviour.

31. Have your boys or girls come to you with complaints about anything being done to them by members of the opposite sex?— Not at cinemas. I saw at one cinema a man trying to behave objectionably to a girl of about eleven years of age, and she moved away. The effects on the children are rather peculiar. I found that a girl of fourteen and a half years of age who was in trouble and had fallen, told the story that she was in a room and fell asleep, and when she woke up there was a bottle by her side. She gave that as the excuse for her falling. In some cinemas I have seen the boys behave in a very nasty manner towards the girls. I have spoken to head teachers of schools, and they have said that pictures, as they are shown at present, are very bad, and that they are so distinctly uneducational that they never show anything to raise the children. With reference to the

desirability of proper supervision at performances, I am certain this would do a lot of good. They should give a little more travel and topical films.

32. Have you anything to say with regard to the effect of the cinema on drink?—There is very little drink amongst the Jews. If the child is in the cinema seeing horrors, that child will not be in the streets stealing things off a barrow.

33. Do you think it has had some effect upon decreasing hooliganism in the streets?—Yes, certainly.

34. MONSIGNOR BROWN. Have you noticed acts of impropriety yourself?—Yes.

35. In a way that people passing up and down the gangway would see it?—Well, I looked closely for it.

36. That is the first time we have had a specific mention of an act of indecency. Have you observed that more than once?—Twice or three times.

37. Separate couples?—I have several times seen couples in regard to whom one would have no doubt as to what is going to happen.

38. In the interests of every one, I want to know whether this was a covert act of immorality which might easily have escaped the attendants, or whether it was a thing which no one paid attention to, and which could be seen?—I used to pay for the dear seats, so that I could move about into the different seats.

39. How far away were you then?—I was walking up the gangway and they were almost at the edge of the seat. I was scrutinising.

40. Supposing the attendant was passing up and down, do you think it would have been observed by him?—Not easily.

41. DR. KIMMINS. I take it the people sitting next to this couple must have noticed?—Well, perhaps they were interested in themselves. I think if a couple are sitting with their arms around one another they can fairly easily manage anything they want to.

42. MR. KING. Did you see any indecent pictures?—I saw something a little suspicious about a great many of the pictures.

R

SIXTEENTH DAY

Monday, April 30, 1917,

The BISHOP OF BIRMINGHAM in the chair.

STATEMENT OF BISHOP WELLDON,
Dean of Manchester

PRÉCIS

I AM quite sure the cinematograph show may be one of the most valuable of educational agencies. Teaching through the eye is the most effective kind of teaching in the education of the young. If I may take the films which display the proceedings at the great Durbar in Delhi, it is not too much to say that any person who saw those films saw more of the Durbar than he would have seen if he had been at Delhi himself. Therefore, I cannot imagine that teachers will be so foolish as to make a general attack on cinematograph shows. I hope the shows will be more and more used in education, and I believe they are capable of giving teaching which it is impossible to give with equal effect by any other means. In my judgment, whatever faults may attach to the shows, the shows are far better than the public-houses, and now, in the community from which I have come, I am told that, owing to the monotony of industry, the people will not go to a play which is prolonged, as they are not able to endure the strain, and that the cinematograph show answers their need very well. I hope, just as magic-lantern lessons have been found beneficial in churches and chapels, so the cinematograph shows will be equally used there. Therefore, I cannot at all associate myself with the general condemnation of the cinemas.

MINUTES OF EVIDENCE

THE RIGHT REV. BISHOP WELLDON, DEAN OF MANCHESTER.
Examined.

1. THE CHAIRMAN. Would you consider it desirable to attach the cinema to actual details of education in the school?—I can well conceive that in the elementary classes it would be useful.

2. As regards the teaching of a particular subject, do you think it would be helpful?—Certainly. I have never been able to learn any geography at all except by going to places, and the nearest thing to going to the places is to see the places at the cinematograph show. I was going to say that as far as I am able to form an opinion, there has been of late years, and particularly during the war, a serious increase in juvenile crime, but I do not think it is so much due to the cinematograph show as to the absence of parental control. I do not dispute that certain films have done, and are doing, harm to children, and I think it is the duty of the

State or the municipality to control the exhibition of these films. I think there should be a serious and strenuous censorship. I do not sympathise with the plea put forward in Manchester that these films cannot be inspected before they are exhibited because they never arrive until the morning on which they are to be exhibited. I think the municipal authorities should claim that there should be an interval of two days between the arrival and the exhibition of the films. I think the presence of children over and over again at exhibitions of cinematograph shows during late hours is undesirable. I do not see any reason why children should be allowed to go more than once a week. They might go with a certificate from their teachers, or again, they might go accompanied by their parents. I think the cinematograph show is a potent agent for imparting information, and its managers should welcome discipline which should prevent it from doing evil.

3. REV. CAREY BONNER. Where would you have the pictures shown? Do you mean that the children would have to go to the cinema theatres?—I think the cinemas may be useful in the schools and in the churches.

4. SIR JOHN KIRK. How would you use it for religious purposes?—I should look upon it as suitable for occasional services.

5. DR. SALEEBY. Do you object to the cinemas being open on Sunday?—I attach very great value to the observance of Sunday, and I think that if once this boon were lost it would be difficult to recover. I would not forbid the exhibitions, but they should not take place during the recognised hours of divine service, and the proceeds should be handed over to some charitable purpose.

TWO GIRLS AND TWO BOYS. *Examined.*

Two girls, aged respectively eleven and thirteen, and two boys, aged fourteen and eleven, were then called. One went to a cinema once a week for some time, two others were continuous attendants, whilst the fourth, a boy of fourteen, attended the Cable Street cinema every night for the purpose of selling chocolates.

One of the girls stated that her father and mother did not like her going to the cinema, and if she wanted to go she had to save up her own money for that purpose. The films she liked best were of the tragedy variety, the name of one of which was " Too Late."

The second girl, in reply to Principal Garvie, said she did not like all of Charlie Chaplin's films. It all depended upon what parts he took in them.

The boy who sold sweets at Cable Street said he had never noticed misconduct amongst any of the boys and girls, but there was plenty of roughness going on.

The boy of eleven, in reply to the question, " When you see a hero, do you feel that you would like to be that hero? " replied, " Not always."

The girl of fourteen said that Cable Street was a very noisy cinema, and very often the children were turned out.   The grown-up boys also made a considerable noise and were very rowdy, and on a Saturday night the porter was stabbed with a knife. Very often they turned the children out on a Saturday night to make room for the grown-ups.

All the witnesses were unanimous that more ventilation was needed in the cinemas, which they described as very stuffy.

STATEMENT OF MR. T. P. O'CONNOR, M.P.,

President of the Board of Film Censors.

PRECIS

I WAS approached about November of last year—on the death of Mr. Redford—to accept the position of President of the Board of Film Censors, and, as I understand, by the unanimous vote of all branches of the trade.

I hesitated about accepting, for the reason that I did not know the exact situation between the trade and the Home Office and that I deprecated the idea of myself coming into collision with the Home Office and still more to the trade doing so.   It was represented to me, however, that there was a necessity for immediate action because films had to be submitted for censorship every week and therefore films could not be sent out unless in the name of Mr. Redford, who is dead.

There was about the same time some confusion owing to the fact that by a ministerial crisis the Home Office was in process of being transferred from Mr. Samuel to Sir George Cave.

I accepted, but always gave it to be understood that I thought it was necessary to keep, not only in touch with, but on the friendliest relations with the Home Office, and that I think I have succeeded in doing.   Ultimately I was officially appointed and began my duties in the month of January.

I approached my duties with the knowledge that certain criticisms in the newspapers and from the magisterial bench had represented the films as bad and in many cases bad in their effects, and therefore I had anticipated finding either a careless or ineffective method of censorship.   I was surprised and pleased to find that, on the contrary, the censorship had been conducted with remarkable assiduity, usually with great success.

I found that Mr. Redford had under him a body of four examiners, one of whom, however, before my appointment had been compelled to go into military service.   Since my appointment I have filled this vacancy by replacing this gentleman with another gentleman whom I have known for thirty years and who is a man of the finest character.   The three remaining gentlemen I found to be men of education, of long experience and of high character.

They sit in a small room and two films are exposed simultaneously; each of these films is examined by two of the examiners, and when any question of difficulty arises all four give their opinion, and, as a rule, no film is passed which has not received the unanimous approval of the four.

I found also that a code of censorship had been established and rigidly adhered to. The chief points in this code have been already given to the committee by the chief examiner and I need not recapitulate them here.

I call especial attention to one decision of my predecessor as showing the scrupulous care with which he exercised his functions.

When complaint was made to him of films founded on certain books he made the decision that though the films in these cases might in themselves be quite innocuous, yet, owing to the lurid repute of the books, audiences might be tempted to go and see them on false grounds, and therefore that in future it was inexpedient to allow the production of the innocent film of a book with a lurid reputation.

The chief difficulty of the censorship arises from the number of what may be called " crook " films, which come mainly from America and which have been brought partly into existence by the popularity of the detective story. On these films I found the examiners had already laid down some severe restrictions—as, for instance, that none of the methods by which thieves can carry out their purposes should be exhibited.

I have somewhat extended these restrictions, and I have sent out a circular urging the trade to give as few films of this character as possible, and I think there is already a steady diminution in that form of film.

I have endeavoured to think out a whole code of film censorship, but the question is not so simple as it appears and I think can only be done by a comparison between our methods and those of other countries where the censorship is established.

In a codification I hope to have the assistance of an advisory committee when this Commission has finished its work.

I would like to say, as showing the difficulties of such codification, that the analogy between the methods of censoring the drama and the film is false in many particulars. Many things which may be permissible on the stage when living beings are acting the parts, are quite inadmissible on a film where action has to take the place of words and where, therefore, things which can be suggested by the voice or by a gesture or by a look even of the actor or actress have to be put in what I may call the crude concrete of the film. I would therefore say that censorship of the film must be, if not severer, certainly different from that of the drama.

The position of President of the Censor Board is conferred by the trade and my term is for one year. It was indicated to me that the intention of the trade was to continue my office as long as I pleased, but that is a matter which must be left for future consideration by them and, of course, by myself.

Except in the fact that I am appointed by the trade, my position is perfectly independent—I am perfectly free to accept or reject any film without appeal and, indeed, often without complaint. In most cases and up to the present I have not only been encouraged to take up an attitude of absolute independence, but have been backed without any hesitation by the trade and in the most loyal way.

If the owner of a film feels that any modification of the film could make it acceptable he asks and receives an interview with me. It happens very often that a film may be for the most part quite unexceptionable, but there may be some scenes which are not permissible. In these cases the examiners and myself go through the film carefully, eliminate the objectionable scenes, and then see the film again after these alterations have been made. If the alterations be not sufficient or have not been carried out according to our suggestions, further modifications are made. In some cases this requires repeated examinations of the film. In the case of one film which was seen at my invitation by the members of the Commission I have myself seen the film four or five times, and in other cases I see the films two or three times.

I think myself that the present position is not quite satisfactory, and that to make it satisfactory a closer co-operation should exist between the Home Office and the Board of Censors, and that the Home Office should have the right of veto of the appointment of the president, and on the other hand that the president, if accepted by the Home Office, should have the co-operation of the Home Office in having his decisions supported. This is the more necessary as there are no fewer than some 300 licensing authorities in the United Kingdom, and of course it would produce an undesirable state of things if each of these authorities were to insist on a separate and perhaps different decision.

I am bound to add that a letter of mine to the licensing authorities has received very favourable reception, and most of them promise me their co-operation. I may add as a mark of the confidence the Government put in our censorship that every film which leaves the country is sent to our Board for examination lest anything prejudicial to our interests should be upon them, and nothing is sent out of the country without our approval.

Hard-and-fast rules are open to two dangers : on the one hand, they might, if narrowly interpreted, prevent the production of films not objectionable on the whole—say, for instance, " Oliver Twist " or " Hamlet "—and, on the other hand, might lead to skilful adhesion to the letter though not to the spirit of the rules.

MINUTES OF EVIDENCE

Mr. T. P. O'Connor, M.P. *Examined.*

1. The Chairman. When you were appointed you did not yourself know the exact position of the trade and the Home Office. Are you satisfied as to that position now ?—No, I am very dissatisfied. I quite sympathise with the trade in their disinclination to be under what is called bureaucratic control,

because in a public department you generally find that the decision is that of a single gentleman, and he might be the worst kind of man to deal with the complex question of the censorship of films.

2. It is quite a new industry?—Yes, and it deals with people and with subjects of a complex kind.

3. And the prominent official is not a person whom the public knows anything about and who is the head of the department?— Yes, and more or less he has to stand by his officials.

4. Because the official knows more about the subject than he does?—Yes.

5. And so far as you can judge at the present time the position is that the Home Office has not yet made up its mind as to the attitude which it shall adopt?—The position, I understand, is this. There were some negotiations between Mr. Herbert Samuel, who was the Home Secretary, and the representatives of the trade, and while these negotiations were being considered there was a change in the Ministry and Sir George Cave came in. I was appointed in the interval between these negotiations and the succession of one minister by another.

6. You came in really at the interregnum?—Yes, and that is the reason why I consented to become Censor without first obtaining the approval of the Home Office. It was represented to me that it was a case of urgency, because the cinema goes on from week to week and from day to day, and unless some one was appointed they would have to refuse to send out any films, or send them out with the name of the gentleman who is dead on them. At first I was unwilling to give my decision, because I said I did not want to be in conflict with the great Government department. I am strongly of opinion that the Home Office should not appoint one of their own officials, nor should they appoint the Film Censor, but they should have a veto on the appointment, so that the Film Censor might be a man not selected from the Civil Service, but that at the same time the Home Office should have some say in the matter.

7. You were surprised and pleased to find that the censorship before you came into office was careful?—I came into the office at the moment when there was rather a bitter blast blowing against the trade. There were several remarks which the daily papers reported from the Bench and there were remarks from other people which would give the impression that stealing and impurity and other evils were the unavoidable result of the cinema theatre; and, not having investigated the case, I was rather afraid that I would find that the films had been more or less allowed to run loose. When I came in I found there was, on the contrary, a highly formed censorship already. I knew there was Mr. Redford, but I did not know of the expanse of the organisation behind the censorship.

8. You have complete control, have you not, as to the appointment of the examiners? I do not mean those already in existence?—There were four already in existence. They sit in rather a small and not very comfortable room, and there are two films

exhibited simultaneously. One film is examined by two examiners on the right, and another film examined by two examiners on the left.

9. Could all four see both?—Yes, easily. Well, then, if there is any doubt by the two on the left as to their film, or if there is any doubt by the two on the right as to their film, they enter into consultation, so that practically no film is passed except with the universal assent of the four examiners. It does not come to me unless there is a doubt. I am a kind of court of appeal. Of the four examiners one of them has been called up for some sort of military service, and I appointed another examiner. There was no Irishman or Catholic among the three and I thought from a religious point of view I should appoint an Irish Catholic.

10. I find that these gentlemen work daily from ten to five practically without any interval in a small room?—Yes.

11. I should like to know whether this affects their health?— I do not think it affects their health, but I cannot say whether they are altogether free from boredom and fatigue. They do not suffer in their health nor their eyesight.

12. You have practically all agreed that a film produced based upon a book that is objectionable, even though that film be itself quite without abuse or wrong, had better not be shown?— Yes, and I had mentioned two of these books in my evidence, but I was warned by one of my advisers that I might let myself in for an action for libel, and consequently I have had to knock it out. I should like to say a word about the examiners. You have all seen the Chief Examiner, —— ——. I think he is a university man, and he is a gentleman both in manner and in mind; and then we have a gentleman who is an ex-bank official, a fairly experienced man of the world. The third man I do not know anything about except that he is a sort of Joan of Arc, that is, vigorous of criticism of anything which approaches indecorum. And there is the fourth man, a good Catholic and a high-minded man. You have four very good men there.

13. I understand you have taken a strong line about the " crook " film?—Yes.

14. I should like to know why, because the " crook " film up to a certain point rather appeals to me, and I have taken a fearful interest in anything to do with detective stories. Will you tell me about these films?—Of course, the " crook " film to a certain extent is in some cases the questionable result of an extremely good thing, namely, the detective story, because you cannot have a detective without having the " crook."

15. But you can sometimes have the " crook " without the detective?—That is so. In these detective stories you have the romance and melodrama of crime, and it is undeniable that that appeals to the young minds who love adventure, and that led, of course, largely to the creation of the " crook " fims. There was another reason. I must, of course, be careful what I say about the American enterprise, because it forms so large a part of the cinema industry, and a very great proportion of our films are

manufactured in America and exhibited in England. Of course, they have a different state of society from ours. You see over there they have the mining camp, they have the world of Bret Harte, and over here since Hounslow Heath has been abolished the highwayman has been done away with. Well, the result is that there is a large amount of the detective spirit and adventure which comes from the civilisation where there is still the fight with Nature. Now, I will deal with another point. I think the point in the armour of the trade which is most vulnerable is the charge that was made of the film leading to juvenile crime.

16. Are you still of that opinion after the evidence you have heard?—I am not of that opinion. I think in the interests of the trade and the morality of the nation it was desirable to devote more attention to that point first. Well, I found that there I had been anticipated by my predecessor, who had laid down as one of the rules that methods of crime which might suggest crime to the youth should not be exhibited. For instance, we should not allow a man to do a burglary according to the fine art of burglary. We do not allow a man to pick a pocket according to the fine art of pocket-picking. I should like at this point to refer to a film which came before us. It was called " —— ———.'' It began with a scene outside a gaol where there was a young man, evidently in poor health, just released from prison. It was an American film. He was met by a young woman, and was given a very pleasant shake of the hand by the warder, who begged him not to come back again. This girl was a thief also, and apparently not his wife. She was known as " Diamond Daisy.'' A little while afterwards there was a scene in the Jewellers' Club at Philadelphia, and the Head of the Police was there. It was a brilliant, club-like scene. In came a gentleman who was somewhat vain, and a discussion started as to the methods of a burglary, and each jeweller claimed that he had taken effective remedies against burglary. The vain, self-conceited old gentleman said that he had organised his shop with such absolute perfection that no burglary was possible. The Chief of the Police and some of the other jewellers made a bet of 5000 dollars that a burglary could be committed at this gentleman's shop. The Chief of the Police hears of the release of this man, and of this girl who is known as " Diamond Daisy,'' and he takes it into his head that through the well-known success and skill of these two people a burglary might be committed. The burglary is committed as a matter of fact. When they get into the jeweller's shop you see the girl, " Diamond Daisy,'' there. Like all other American girls, she is chewing gum. She takes up a diamond ring, attaches it to the chewing gum and fixes it under a tray. She is, of course, suspected of taking the diamond ring and is searched, but nothing is found. A confederate comes in and puts his hand under the case and so goes off with the ring. Well, the story ends quite pleasantly, because these people in the club get their 5000 dollars, and you see the burglar and the girl end up their life in the country. It all ends very well. Now I said this was a film that I could not

permit. Well, I am bound by the rules of the organisation, if I reject a film, to see it and discuss it in a friendly spirit with the proprietor. That is for two reasons. In the first place he may convince me; but the second reason, which much more frequently occurs, is that he will have pointed out to him certain alterations which no doubt he will consent to make. Well, I saw the proprietor and he said that it had never occurred to him that this film could be objected to, as he thought it was all a joke, and it taught the lesson that dishonesty did not pay. I pointed out to him that undoubtedly the people did reform, but not in the right way, and I said that if he made it clear that it was a joke and only a joke, if he could clean up the " crook " and the criminal girl and make her a devoted wife with a view of trying to redeem her unfortunate husband from his crimes; and if he would undertake to point out the joke by making the Jewellers' Club, where the wager is made, the main scene, then I would reconsider the thing. Well, he carried out all my wishes, and I think the film is now a perfectly decent film.

17. Monsignor Brown. Did you succeed in eliminating the actual manipulation of the theft?—Yes, that went out at once.

18. The Chairman. Now I saw something on a film about a theft being committed, and nobody knew how it was done, and eventually a lady is seen to undo the heel of her shoe, and there is a hole inside which she has the diamond necklace. Now that is a method which I should have thought undesirable to show to the British public?—I should have thought so; but it may not have been passed by us. The greatest film being shown in London to-day has not been passed by us. It has never been submitted to us at all; I have never seen it.

19. Now that leads us to ask this question: Do you think it would be desirable that any film which has not been passed by the Censor should not be exhibited?—I should think so, and there I have the support of the Home Office. I am glad this film was not submitted to me, as there are questions of church history arising out of its scenes. Of course, at the same time I think it would be desirable, if you have a censorship at all, that it should be universal.

20. You would advocate a censorship which was approved by the Home Office so that all films should be censored?—All films which are intended mainly for the cinema theatre and mainly for the purposes of amusement should be submitted for censorship, but I would have nothing to do with the propaganda film, such as " The Ghosts " of Ibsen, and " Damaged Goods." I would rather not be asked to adjudicate on a question like that.

21. Monsignor Brown. Can you say how it is people are in a position to show such great films in Drury Lane so as not to come under the censorship. Are they films owned by people who submit other films?—As a rule we act on the principle that anybody who is associated with this organisation shall, as a matter of fact, be under an obligation, upon honour, to submit all films. I should rather think that the gentleman who is the proprietor

of this film is outside this organisation. You see, we have no
legal power.

22. THE CHAIRMAN. As a matter of fact, you do not know
whether he belongs to any of the usual firms ?—The members of
the trade would know.

MR. KING. He is a producer who produces films for the purposes of the trade.

23. MONSIGNOR BROWN. Who are the exhibitors ?—I rather
fancy that as Drury Lane is a theatre it is therefore under the
control of the Lord Chamberlain, and that it would be the Lord
Chamberlain who would have to deal with the matter.

24. THE CHAIRMAN. Supposing I liked to produce a film at a
theatre which is licensed by the Lord Chamberlain. Has that
anything to do with you ?

MR. KING. Yes, it has, if the theatre has a cinema licence.
If he puts in a projector he must have a licence.

25. THE CHAIRMAN. You have looked through the methods
of other countries as regards the censorship ?—Very slightly, but
might I refer to a circular I sent out to the trade upon certain
subjects ?—" Dear Sirs,—I have to inform you for your guidance
that the following rules will be observed by my Board in censoring
films. (1) No serial dealing with crime will be examined in
future except as a whole." The origin of that rule was that they
had a number of serials running into three, four, five and six
numbers. The first may be fairly innocent ; the second pretty
bad ; the third, fourth, and fifth good, the sixth bad, and so
on.   Of course, if we passed the first without having seen the
rest, which we may reject, we give them the right to say that
we have spoilt their film. Now I will go on : " (2) No serial in
which crime is the dominant feature and not merely an episode
in the story will be passed by the Censor." We had some very
shocking films in which there were extremely brutal things and
which were really " crook " films. To show you the difficulty of
laying down a general rule, I will read you a letter which I got in
regard to this particular rule. But I will first of all finish reading
the circular : " (3) No film will be passed in which the methods of
crime are set forth and form the chief theme. This rule will have
to be applied even in cases where at the end of the film retribution
is supposed to have fallen on the criminal ; and equally when the
detective element is subordinate to the criminal interest, or when
actual crime is treated from the comic point of view. (4) The
Board proposes to issue monthly to the licensing authorities a
list of the films which have been passed by them." As regards
No. 4, I believe legally we have gone as far as we can. If we went
any further we might lay ourselves open to litigation, especially
if we sent out a " black list," so we send out a " white list "
showing which films we have passed. Now as regards No. 3,
we got this letter : " I am in receipt of your circular letter setting
forth for my guidance certain rules which will be observed by
the Board in censoring films, and, while I cordially appreciate
your effort to save producers unnecessary expense by outlining

beforehand subjects which will not be allowed to pass, I wish most respectfully to protest against the making of broad generalisations which may easily prove harmful to an important and growing art which is as yet in such early stages that no man can foresee its possible development. As an instance, allow me to call attention to paragraph 3 in the above-mentioned circular: 'No film will be passed in which the methods of crime are set forth and form the chief theme.' Permit me to trouble you with a single instance. Here is in brief the synopsis of a film: ' Small boys rebel more or less successfully against constituted authority— the hero is apprenticed to a tradesman from whom he deserts— a school for crime in which young boys are taught the methods of street robbery—the result of the lessons; picking pockets in the streets—a burglary shown in full detail with methods employed; the illicit relationship of a brutal man with a young woman who, but for his influence, would be capable of better things—she drugs him in order to escape temporarily from his power—her foul and brutal murder by the man—his flight from justice and eventual downfall.' This is a fair synopsis of the story of " Oliver Twist," which has twice successfully and harmlessly been made into a cinematograph film. One of the films, at least, has been shown all over this country and largely in America, and has earned praise and gratitude everywhere. It has never brought disrepute or hostile criticism upon any show which has exhibited it, and it is, moreover, a film version of an English classic. It is clear that this picture could not have been produced under the embargo placed upon films by paragraph 3 of your circular. I submit, with all respect, that a film can only be judged upon its merits after it has been produced, for the methods and manner of production are all important—the matter practically negligible. (*Signed*) Cecil M. Hepworth." Well now, in answer to that, I should say that methods of crime do not form the chief theme of the film, and again, although we do not generalise, our rules cannot be regarded as like the language of Statute Law, which judges are compelled to interpret quite literally.

26. MONSIGNOR BROWN. How about cutting out the actual manipulation of the crime?—I admit there may be a certain contradiction on this matter, but pocket-picking is so well-known an art that I do not know that anything new can be thought of it. I might say that the result of this circular is already showing itself, and we do not get so many of these " crook " films as we used to.

27. THE CHAIRMAN. Your appointment is a yearly one?— Yes.

28. Does that mean that you get three months or six months' notice?—I really don't know; I think it is a year certain.

29. Have you any idea as to why an appointment of that kind should be a yearly one?—Well, in the first place I was an unknown man in the world of films; I was quite ignorant; I might have turned out no good, and I think they were entitled to a preliminary canter with me. Then in the next place I might get ill,

and they could not well be expected to give an appointment for long.

30. Do you think that the Home Office would favour the idea of their putting a veto on a censor who is being sent away at the end of a year?—They may do, and for this reason, that when the next man came along they would say : " You have made a bad choice." Everything depends upon the attitude of the trade. My view of the attitude of the trade is that they regard a censor as a necessary protection to them against, on the one hand, undue interference and, on the other, any attempt by less scrupulous members of the trade to expose the whole trade to prejudice. It seems to me it is a compromise. I am bound also to say that some of the members of the trade have rather found fault with me for being rather too considerate and not dictatorial enough. Their idea is that I should use my ukase and allow nobody to approach me with any modification of the film, but I do not think that is fair. I think I am much more likely to get the trade to work cordially with me if I consider their feelings in the matter, but I may say that really I have been left absolutely free.

31. That film which was seen by members of the Commission, might I ask if it has been passed?—Yes, subject to great modifications, and I am sorry to say that some of the cinema Press have got hold of the statement that I made in a lighthearted way that I thought the Commission was rather more indulgent, perhaps, than I could have been. I do not blame them for their indulgence, but, of course, I have to judge not merely by the film itself, but by the principles lying behind it, and by those things that precede it and the things that follow. Now, what one has to consider in that film is how far you can allow the nude to appear, and on that question there is practically an unbroken rule of my predecessors and my present colleagues. That rule is not to allow the nude almost under any circumstances. Well, of course, as you remember, that film to a large extent was centred around ⸺ ⸺ ⸺, who was in the act of swimming. I would not expect her to take a dive of 200 feet in a walking dress, and so far as that was concerned, especially as the action was a rapid one, I was not entitled to hold to the strict rule that it should not be permitted. If it was a mere pose showing the woman in repose I was entitled to condemn it. I have now cut out all exhibitions of ⸺ ⸺ ⸺ in very close-fitting garments, where she was in repose.

32. Then, as I understand it, the censorship we are speaking of is the censorship purely of films, and has nothing to do with the building?—No, nor the conduct in the building.

33. Would you be inclined to leave that subject to the various local authorities where the film was presented?—Yes, I think it would be impossible for me to take it up.

34. Or for anybody?—Or for anybody.

35. This would be a local matter?—Yes.

36. Dr. Saleeby. And the posters?—The posters do not come under my jurisdiction.

37. THE CHAIRMAN. You have views, have you not, with regard to 'the educational value of the film ?—Very strong views. Take the question of geography. Imagine showing the school or even the class a cinema picture of Russia, where you see Petrograd with the life of Petrograd, the people going through the streets. That would be an appeal to the eye and to the imagination of the child, and would be much better than learning from a book. I think geography, history, physiology, and any number of subjects can be learned much more rapidly and pleasantly with the aid of the cinema than otherwise. I do not think our elementary schools will at all approach modern and proper methods of education until there is a cinema attached to every school. Now, would you allow me to put in the rules which are laid down by the Board of Censors? There are forty-three rules, and I think they cover pretty well all the grounds that you can think of.

(1) Indecorous, ambiguous and irreverent titles and sub-titles.
(2) Cruelty to animals.
(3) The irreverent treatment of sacred subjects.
(4) Drunken scenes carried to excess.
(5) Vulgar accessories in the staging.
(6) The *modus operandi* of criminals.
(7) Cruelty to young infants and excessive cruelty and torture to adults, especially women.
(8) Unnecessary exhibition of feminine underclothing.
(9) The exhibition of profuse bleeding.
(10) Nude figures.
(11) Offensive vulgarity, and impropriety in conduct and dress.
(12) Indecorous dancing.
(13) Excessively passionate love scenes.
(14) Bathing scenes passing the limits of propriety.
(15) References to controversial politics.
(16) Relations of Capital and Labour.
(17) Scenes tending to disparage public characters and institutions.
(18) Realistic horrors of warfare.
(19) Scenes and incidents calculated to afford information to the enemy.
(20) Incidents having a tendency to disparage our Allies.
(21) Scenes holding up the King's uniform to contempt or ridicule.
(22) Subjects dealing with India, in which British officers are seen in an odious light, and otherwise attempting to suggest the disloyalty of Native States or bringing into disrepute British prestige in the Empire.
(23) The exploitation of tragic incidents of the war.
(24) Gruesome murders and strangulation scenes.
(25) Executions.
(26) The effects of vitriol throwing.
(27) The drug habit, *e. g.* opium, morphia, cocaine, etc.

(28) Subjects dealing with White Slave traffic.
(29) Subjects dealing with the premeditated seduction of girls.
(30) " First night " scenes.
(31) Scenes suggestive of immorality.
(32) Indelicate sexual situations.
(33) Situations accentuating delicate marital relations.
(34) Men and women in bed together.
(35) Illicit sexual relationships.
(36) Prostitution and procuration.
(37) Incidents indicating the actual perpetration of criminal assaults on women.
(38) Scenes depicting the effect of venereal diseases, inherited or acquired.
(39) Incidents suggestive of incestuous relations.
(40) Themes and references relative to " race suicide."
(41) Confinements.
(42) Scenes laid in disorderly houses.
(43) Materialisation of the conventional figure of Christ.

38. PRINCIPAL GARVIE. I notice you say in your evidence that in a codification you hope to have the assistance of an advisory committee. I should like to ask you how that advisory committee should be constituted. Would it be by yourself or by representatives of public interests?—I think we should have those who represent public interests.

39. You think the advisory committee should include the educationalists who might strengthen your hands in any point of difficulty?—Certainly; I want all the assistance I can get from everybody.

40. Have you any idea as to how you would like such a committee appointed?—I would not like to express a personal opinion, as I have not consulted the trade, and I must bring them along with me. Until I have gone into the matter properly I cannot bring it up. Of course, I want the best men I can get, and the most representative body of men.

41. You are aware that in America there are these advisory committees, and they have gone thoroughly into the matter?—So I understand.

42. DR. SALEEBY. A good many films are still shown that you have never seen?—I have only seen the films that are referred to me.

43. Which your Board has never seen?—I do not know.

44. For instance, at one of the best places in London I saw a ——— ——— comedy called " —— —— — ——." It was an odious composition, extremely vulgar, and I do not believe you would have allowed that film to pass you. When I arrived at the cinema it was half-way through, and I waited until it came on again and found that no one had passed it. How does that get there?—You see, we are a voluntary association, and a member of the trade may or may not join; that is left to his own judgment.

As a matter of fact, I understand very strong pressure is being exercised to bring practically everybody connected with the trade in our power. For instance, Mr. Seddon, who is now practically the organiser of the trade, is going the round of the cinema people and trying to get them to join.

45. If a person belongs to your body does he submit everything to you?—He is supposed to.

46. ——— ——— people's films are everywhere. Do they submit their things to you?—I do not recollect that, because I really do not look at the name of the producer, but if they do not they ought to.

47. A great many places have a ——— comedy every week?—I know the name very well, but I cannot recollect whether I have seen that particular film.

48. Will it be possible for you to get at the people about that?—I believe they are got at by the members of the trade.

49. And the exhibitor also is under the obligation? It is the ———, ——— ———?—Yes, and I should say every member of the trade who joins the organisation is under the obligation not to submit any film which has not been passed by the British Board of Film Censors.

50. THE SECRETARY intimated that he would obtain this film for exhibition before the members of the Commission.

51. DR. SALEEBY. Your view is that you should have the control over every film that is shown in this country?—Yes; and in that I am backed by the Home Office.

52. You made an exception to propaganda films?—I would not call " Ghosts " a propaganda film.

53. Well, " Damaged Goods? "—That is a play. I have in my mind a certain film about which I am not a little troubled. It is " Where are my children? " which is a propaganda film against what is called race suicide. You see after all, my business is with the cinematograph manufacture and the cinematograph proprietor who produces films for the purposes of profit, and I am a bit unwilling to enlarge my sphere.

54. Some one else can deal with this?—The Home Office and the police authorities and the Lord Chamberlain can deal with that as well as the licensing authorities. I may say I make it a rule to welcome all objections, and I make inquiries into those objections; that is to say, I get letters objecting to certain pictures, and I have inquiries made immediately, and the letters are answered giving the result of the inquiries.

55. Objection has been taken now to scenes depicting the effect of venereal diseases?—Well, remember that opinion on this question has changed considerably. The attitude of the newspapers and the theatres has changed.

56. MR. KING. His lordship asked you whether you thought that other matters should be dealt with by local authorities, and I think you expressed the opinion that that would be desirable?—I think it would be well for broad general rules to be laid down. You can lay down general rules from the Central Office

in London and find that they are disobeyed or evaded, and therefore you require certain powers of vigilance on the part of the local authorities.

57. You know there are certain regulations issued by the Home Office which are incumbent upon all?—I assume so.

58. MR. CROOK. Talking of these educational films, do you think that if any boys in a class were studying, say, Russia, with Petrograd and Moscow and other things for a fortnight, they would have as clear vision at the end of the fortnight if they studied with the aid of a cinema instead of with fixed pictures?—Well, of course, it would depend on the boy a good deal, and it would also depend on the film a good deal and the rapidity with which the films succeeded one another. Mind you, I do not exclude the necessity of going to books before or after seeing the film.

59. Don't you think that pictures which lay permanently before them would be more effective in impressing views of a particular place upon the boy?—I do not know; but you see you cannot give the same sense of reality as with the cinema. Take the pictures of geography, for instance. You would be showing the buildings or the rivers or anything like that, whereas in the cinema you would have moving views, and in that way you would bring the pictures more like reality.

60. It depends on the moving picture; they would have to be chosen with remarkable care?—Of course.

61. If the other subjects you mentioned were taught, and you gave two hours a week to each of the subjects, that would mean that the children would be looking at the cinema for ten or twelve hours a week?—Well, these things must be done with discretion and with regard to the health of the child mentally and physically.

62. There are about 30,000 schools in England and about 5000 of them contain less than eighty children. It is rather a big proposition to put a cinema into all these schools?—Not at all.

63. SIR WILLIAM BARRETT. Are these four assistants of yours all male assistants?—All male.

64. Don't you think it would be desirable to have lady assistants as well as male assistants? This seems to me to be a very important point?—I am bound to consider that in the first place this is purely a voluntary organisation, kept in existence by voluntary subscriptions, and although the expenses are pretty heavy, I have no power to force them to do these things, and again, if we had a lady I should insist that we should have different premises in which to perform our duties.

65. Don't you think at the present time instructional and educational films can be shown in connection with the preparation of cooking and saving of food? I have seen demonstrations at different Board schools which can be easily produced and would be useful.—I am sure they would be.

66. You say that the Government send films to your Board to be censored?—Yes, that is so, and I think it only fair to the trade to point to the fact that already there are enormous possibilities in times like these for appealing to the patriotism of the

people.   Various war films and economy films have been produced,
and these have been submitted to our Board to be censored.
Then again, they have given us practically all the censorship of
films for export.   In this respect you can see how valuable it is,
as I have heard of cinema films being used for the purpose of
espionage, and I believe these parties have been detected by
Mr. Brooke Wilkinson, our secretary.   You see, there are films
which can be sent abroad which would give important information
about this country.

67. DR. MARIE STOPES.   Do I understand you to suggest that
you would like a separate authority to deal with propaganda
films?—Well, propaganda is a somewhat general term.   There
are certain types of propaganda films which have to be carefully
dealt with.   We would not allow the films showing a dispute
between Capital and Labour or serious things like that.   You
see, a department like ours, if we took these things on, would
have a very large and a very delicate issue to decide, and we are
not anxious to add to our responsibilities.   We exist mainly,
almost exclusively, for the cinema theatre alone, for the amusement of the public and for the profit of the proprietor or the owner
of the film.   I would not bring educational films under our Board,
as I think they are entirely outside our skill.   They are for the
educational authorities to decide and not for us.

68. What is to prevent an ordinary exhibitor saying he wished
to have an educational film in his exhibition and taking something
of a propagandist nature which you disapprove of very much?—
He cannot do that if he is an exhibitor belonging to our organisation.   If he exhibits an educational film, then we have the right
of censorship over that.   But, of course, when you come to the
general educational film you have to consider many different
questions.

69. The propaganda film, " Where are my children? " was, I
understand, to be shown in all the ordinary houses?—No, I do
not think so; I understand it was only for special halls and special
audiences, and was only to be shown to adults.

70. MONSIGNOR BROWN.   Assuming that the present censorship
works satisfactorily, what hope is there of bringing every concern
under it?—You mean without further legislation?

71. Yes, first voluntarily, is there reasonable hope?—If you
ask my personal opinion I think there is a very strong hope.   I
do not know the exact number of members, but I think it is
something like 95 per cent. who belong to our organisation.

72. We are in a position of being attacked, and to some extent
being discredited by attack over many matters, and I should like
to know, if this censorship continues, whether all the other exhibitors will come in?—I can only speak of the information that
is in my possession, and that is that every member of the organisation has loyally and faithfully carried out his pledge.   I should
be surprised to find that any one has broken out outside that
5 or 10 per cent. who are still outside the organisation.   We are
endeavouring so far as we can to put the cinema industry on trade

unionist lines, and the trade unionist has plenty of methods of dealing with the recalcitrant members. For instance, the manufacturers will be perfectly entitled to say that they will not sell to any hall any film that does not come under the censorship. By that I mean that if a hall shows a film which has not been dealt with by the Censor, then the manufacturers will refuse to supply it with any other film.

73. THE SECRETARY. As a matter of fact, they are doing that now?—I believe they are.

74. SIR JOHN KIRK. In the event of a direct censorship being instituted, should it supersede the present censorship?—I think it ought to, because otherwise it would put the trade in an intolerable position if they had to work under various standards.

75. You are in favour of a local censorship?—No, except as regards the conduct of the halls.

76. THE SECRETARY. Will you tell us whether there is any possibility of your reviewing films which Mr. Redford has passed? I ask this because " —— —— " and " —— —— " are still being exhibited, and I have had a complaint from a chief constable that one has been exhibited quite recently. He went down to see the film and strongly objected to it?—I must inquire into that.

SEVENTEENTH DAY

Monday, May 7, 1917,

The BISHOP OF BIRMINGHAM in the chair.

STATEMENT OF MISS VICKERS

PRÉCIS

MY personal experience of cinemas is limited to Central London, and the schools with which I am in closest touch are in the borough of Holborn. It is difficult to estimate how often the children go to cinemas, but from the returns from two schools in Holborn and one in South St. Pancras I should say generally not more than once a week or once a fortnight. In a Holborn school, boys' department: two classes, II and IV, were questioned, and the number who had visited cinemas in the preceding week was 33 per cent. The head master in this school has done much to deter boys from going. In another school the percentage of boys and girls attending cinemas during April was 16 per cent. In February the percentage of boys had been 33 per cent., which shows that the cinemas relieve a felt want of somewhere to go to in the dark and cold of the winter, away from their overcrowded homes. When the children can play in the street the cinema is not so much frequented. I have been supplied with information concerning the real tastes of the children of one school.

The questions set were answered by the boys of the classes IV, V, VI, VII, and by the girls of classes V, VI, VII. The boys vote first for detective and burglary stories, and the girls for love stories. War pictures take the second place with both, and comics the third. Nearly half the children confess to dreaming about the pictures, noticeably the elder boys, who dislike murder being represented on the film. "The Light that Failed," "King Arthur and His Knights," "The Merchant of Venice," "The Battles of the Ancre and the Somme," "Sons of the Empire," are all favourite films. Practically every child mentioned Charlie Chaplin; he is a universal favourite. When asked what part they would like to take, the great majority vote for the detective hero. Some would like to be comedians, not many want to be cowboys; *only one boy at this school wished to take the part of a burglar or murderer.* They are evidently on the side of justice with a strong bias towards the *Heroic Ideal.* The girls also want to be the heroines. I think the pictures are better now than they were a short time ago, but I do not think they are nearly as good as they were in their early days. French pictures are undoubtedly the best, both from the artistic point of view and because they can be funny without being vulgar. The type of pictures generally shown is most unsuitable for children, for without being absolutely immoral or indecent, it turns the most beautiful things in life into ridicule and degrades them by making them ugly and absurd. The exaggerated gestures and actions which appear to be necessary to explain the plot are themselves an evil, as self-control of mind and body is the first lesson we try to teach children. I do not think that the detective stories which have always enthralled boys since reading became universal do so much harm as the sickly sentiment, coarse love-making, and infidelities of men and women, seen in the "dramas." The comic films are often very vulgar, but they are so far removed from everyday life that their effect on the child mind is not so evil. I wish there could be healthy, wholesome cinemas to which parents could send their children, confident that they would see nothing to soil their minds. Educational films such as those dealing with plant life are useless unless explained by a teacher or some competent person and taken as part of the school curriculum. But good stories from standard novels such as *Ivanhoe* and *The Last Days of Pompeii* are both instructive and really thrilling. Fairy tales might be more used, and pictures of foreign countries, their people and their history.

Would it be too much to ask that certain cinemas might be selected where the management undertook to provide suitable programmes for children on Saturday afternoons, and then a list of those cinemas hung up in the schools and the children encouraged to patronise them? At present the cinema is too exciting, it should be more normal and not so exaggerated, and should deal with the beautiful things in life rather than the sordid aspect of human nature. The children often live among such sordid surroundings that it is surely a mistake to accentuate them.

MINUTES OF EVIDENCE

Miss Vickers. *Examined.*

Miss Vickers explained that she was a voluntary worker in Hatton Garden, and had been for some years Secretary of Tower Street, Seven Dials, a school which was now closed.

1. Principal Garvie. You say there should be an "hour limit." Do you refer to a period of time or to time generally?—Oh, a time limit generally.

2. As to how long they should stop?—I mean the hour at which they are allowed to be present.

3. Not merely the length of time, but the hour of the day they should be there?—Some of these children were there for three or four hours at a stretch. Cinemas are beginning to turn them out at a specified time. The ——— ———, ——————— ———, was very rowdy the whole time. A man was walking about trying to keep the children quiet, and there was great commotion at the beginning of the second performance owing to those outside fighting to get in.

4. Was there no adequate provision for keeping order?— They were shouting—it was like Babel.

5. You did not notice any rude conduct by boys towards girls? Were the children all crowded together? Were they sitting too close to each other?—The seats were divided, at least where I was. There was no separation of the sexes.

6. Was the lighting adequate?—I could see dimly. But to give an idea, a man came in and sat down on top of me because he could not see the seat I was in. Lighting ought to be better than that.

7. Mr. Newbould. You wish for wholesome cinemas to which parents can send their children. Do you mean to assert there are no such places?—We do not know them. They are probably the better-class cinemas. I would suggest a list.

8. Dr. Kimmins. Don't you think children better in the cinema than in the streets?—Well, it's a difficult question. I really cannot say. I have not made up my mind on the subject.

9. What alternative is there to the cinema?—It might point to this, that we ought to have cinemas where children can be catered for, and have amusement suitable for them. I am not against the cinema in the least, provided the children don't sit there too long. In this district of London it does not seem to have become a passion with them as in other districts.

10. Mr. Lamert. You have referred to cinemas where children can be catered for. Are you referring to commercial cinemas, or state-aided or rate-aided institutions?—I don't mind either. It is a question whether the ordinary cinema would find it worth while.

11. Do you think it advisable that public funds should be used for the purpose?—If public funds could be used in connection with the schools.

12. I think you will find as a commercial proposition nobody is likely to do so. Do you think it of sufficient importance to be done in the other way? Otherwise it is merely a pious hope.— I think the cinema trade would make just as great profits.

13. If this is a commercial thing and could be made commercially possible, it would be done. If it is not done, will you agree with me there is no profit in it?—Take a building like Victoria Hall. They have a splendid performance of opera, Shakespeare and so on.

14. And the prices?—2*d.*, 4*d.*, 5*d.*, 6*d.*, and I believe 1*s.*

15. The audience is drawn from all over London?—Probably South London provides most.

16. Somewhat different from the cinema, which is local?—If you give people good stuff they will appreciate it. The cinema managers should co-operate in the right way. It is quite possible the Education Committee will put restrictions upon children going to cinemas. After the war there is sure to be stronger control.

17. MRS. BURGWIN. Is not the great attraction of the cinema not so much the subjects as the price at which the child may get in?—In the case of the worker, yes. It is somewhere for a mother to get her smaller children out of the way on a Saturday afternoon. People must have amusement.

STATEMENT OF MR. A. E. NEWBOULD,

Chairman of the Cinematograph Exhibitors' Association of Great Britain and Ireland, Limited; Chairman of the Cinematograph Trade Council; Director and Manager of Provincial Cinematograph Theatres, Limited; Director and Manager of Associated Provincial Picture Houses, Limited; Director of London Film Company, Limited; Director of Fenning's Film Service, Limited.

PRÉCIS

THE first witness to appear before the Cinema Commission prefaced his evidence with some remarks in regard to the abnormality of the times. I wish to associate myself with, and even to emphasise those remarks, because I am now firmly of opinion that but for the war the charges against the cinema would never have taken the serious line which they have done. Of all the charges brought against the cinematograph industry, the most damaging is the charge that the cinema is largely responsible for the increase in juvenile crime. The trade, quite apart from the work of this Commission, has made an effort to find out what the actual truth in this connection is. It has been at some pains to collect and examine the available evidence, and the results have been embodied in a pamphlet just published by the Cinematograph Trade Council. I submit that this pamphlet is a fair and comprehensive statement of the case, and that the conclusions arrived at must commend themselves to any unbiassed student. The other serious charge is that indecent conduct takes place in the cinema audiences. My experience teaches me that this question of indecent conduct is simply one of supervision, and not of lighting, as is generally supposed. Supervision since the war has necessarily been increasingly difficult and inefficient at a time when it possibly should have been more thorough than ever. But for this fact the question of lighting would never have assumed so serious an aspect if it had arisen at all. I am frankly unable to sympathise with the mental attitude of those who would prohibit darkness everywhere on the ground that it necessarily conduces to evil. I could as readily sympathise with a proposal that all walls and roofs should be of glass, and all doors abolished on the ground that privacy and seclusion are incentives to immorality.

Prior to the war there was little criticism in regard to the censorship. The films were improving automatically week by week. But for the war there would have been a considerable increase in the number of British productions, and trade organisations tending to general improvement would have reached a higher stage of efficiency. These things would in themselves have dealt adequately with any attempt to place undesirable films on the market. The films of this type could not under any circumstances be commercially profitable in an industry which expected to last for more than six months, and that fact has from the first been fully recognised by the responsible trade leaders.

Prior to the commencement of the war new and up-to-date cinema theatres were rapidly ousting the older and less satisfactory places. Unfortunately, the suspension of all building operations and the crippling of all efforts towards architectural improvement has given a new lease of life to many places which, under normal conditions, would have been put out of business by simple competition.

Finally, there is the question of the social evil, which has assumed an acute aspect as the inevitable result of war conditions. It has been very difficult to keep cinema theatres, as well as all other places of entertainment, entirely free from an undesirable element which was controlled with comparative ease prior to the war.

In regard to the increased illumination of theatres there are several aspects to be considered. The moral aspect I have already referred to, and, in my judgment, the amount of lighting in cinema theatres should be sufficient to allow of proper supervision.

On the physical side there is the question of eyestrain. A certain amount of strain undoubtedly exists, particularly in the case of young children, but it appears to be entirely temporary, and is not worse than other contrasts which are of daily occurrence, such as drawing the bedroom blinds suddenly on a bright, sunny morning, or entering a brilliantly lit room from a dark street, and so forth. In this connection I would suggest that anything that tends to destroy the definition and brilliancy of the picture, such as excessive and distracting lighting in the auditorium, must involve a greater strain on the eyes in the endeavour to distinguish imperfect detail.

I hesitate to mention the financial side of this question, but in view of the present difficulties of the trade it must be mentioned. The increase in lighting means a very serious increase in expense on account of the very much greater power required to project the picture through a lighted auditorium on to the screen. Recent instructions issued by the Board of Trade make it imperative on all theatre proprietors to reduce and not to increase the amount of electricity consumed during the continuation of the war.

On the question of special children's performances I wish to say that a specially selected programme is not at present a commercial proposition. It will be found that where the price of admission is sixpence and upwards children's matinées are seldom if ever given, and the proportion of children attending these places is negligible at any time. Those who do attend are nearly always accompanied by their parents, and are seldom seen in the theatres after 8 p.m. The number of children attending cinemas increases as the prices of admission decrease. In other words, the problem of the child and the cinema belongs chiefly to the poor-class districts. Until housing and home life conditions are improved, and until something is done to provide other equally attractive forms of wholesome entertainment for children, it does not seem to me to be wise unduly to restrict attendance at the cinemas. The probable result would be that children would simply roam the streets, with their attendant evils and temptations.

An experiment has been started in Birmingham, where the cinema proprietors and the authorities are working together to improve the conditions of children's attendance. The experiment is in its infancy, but is worthy of sympathetic encouragement, for it is probably in this direction that a practical solution will be found.

Censorship

The full report of the negotiations between the Home Office and the trade on the subject of censorship is a somewhat lengthy document, and I propose, therefore, briefly to recapitulate the Home Office proposals and the attitude of the trade towards them. Briefly, the proposals were—

1. A voluntary censorship under the control of the Home Office for which the trade was to pay a sum of not less than £6000 a year. As the Home Office had no legal powers either to enforce such a censorship as final throughout the kingdom, or to compel renters and manufacturers to submit their films for censorship, or to prohibit exhibitors showing films which had not passed the censorship, these proposals offered no improvement on existing conditions.
2. The Chief Censor and Examiners were to be selected and appointed by the Home Office.
3. There was to be " a strong Advisory Committee appointed by the Secretary of State, including representatives of local authorities (including educational authorities) well-known members of the general public, authors of standing

not connected with cinemas, with a representative of the manufacturers and a representative of the exhibitors. One member at least should be a woman."

The Trade was asked to make observations on these proposals, and the objections the trade raised were as follows—

1. That a Government Censorship must be compulsory, universal in its application, and final in its decisions.
2. That the Chief Censor should either be selected or appointed by the Advisory Board or the Home Office in agreement with the trade, and that one Examiner should be appointed by the trade.
3. The trade asked for a better representation on the Advisory Board.

After very considerable delay, the Home Office had to admit—

1. That it was unable without legislation (which was out of the question) to make the censorship compulsory, universal or final.
2. The Home Secretary adhered to his decision that all the appointments should be made by him, although all the salaries would be paid by the trade.
3. The Home Secretary intimated his willingness to concede three representatives on the Advisory Committee instead of two.

I wish émphatically to deny the statement which has been made that the trade was inconsistent in its attitude, and that it refused to go on with the negotiations. I personally conducted those negotiations on behalf of the trade from start to finish. I entered them with a sincere desire to assist the Home Office to bring about a settlement, and that I was unable to do so was in no way my fault or the fault of the trade.

I am convinced that a voluntary trade censorship as at present conducted will be found the most satisfactory form of censorship to all concerned. I 'personally think it desirable that to the present organisation should be added an Advisory and Appeal Committee, which should be appointed by some such body as the National Council of Public Morals in consultation with the Home Office.

MODEL REGULATIONS

The Cinematograph Act is an Act to provide for the safety of the public, and regulations to that effect are included in the Act, but the local authorities are given certain powers to vary or add to these regulations, with the result that between 200 and 300 different sets of regulations are in force, according to the views of the various licensing authorities.

Many of these regulations have nothing whatever to do with the question of safety, and even those that have that aim are, in some instances, highly absurd.

I suggest that a committee should be set up consisting of representatives of (1) the trade, (2) the local authorities and the Home Office, and (3) this Commission, with a chairman appointed by the Home Office to consider these regulations and draw up a model set, which should then be issued by the Home Office for use throughout the entire kingdom.

THE BRITISH MANUFACTURER

A good deal of comment has been caused by the fact that something like 90 per cent. of the films shown in this country come from America, or other foreign countries. There is a big public demand for British films, but it is not articulate, and British manufacturers are working under serious commercial difficulties as against the American manufacturer inasmuch as they have great difficulty in selling their productions in America.

A joint advertising campaign urging the public to insist on seeing British productions, together with the setting up of an efficient sales organisation for the handling of British-made films in America, would, in my opinion, quickly result in at least 50 per cent. of the films shown in this country being of British origin, while the development of the American sales of such films would enable the British manufacturer to expend more money on his productions.

THE NATURE AND EXTENT OF THE CHARGES AGAINST THE INDUSTRY

It was my intention to go very thoroughly into this matter, but I believe this to be unnecessary as the Commission has already been able to throw a good deal of light on this question from the evidence which it has examined. I am further of opinion that the unfair and unjust attacks which have been made upon the Commission itself are sufficient to indicate the prejudice which existed in some quarters, and I am willing to leave this aspect without comment.

MINUTES OF EVIDENCE

MR. A. E. NEWBOULD. *Examined.*

1. THE CHAIRMAN. I want you to explain to me a little more fully why you think but for the war there would not have been the charges against the cinema. Supposing I put it this way. If there had been no war, we should have had more leisure for minor things and the cinema would have more attention thrown on it ?—Natural development was arrested when war broke out. The general nervous condition of the people, their unbalanced mental attitude, have tended to throw these things out of proper proportion and perspective.

2. In the matter of juvenile crime. The trade has gone into that very carefully ?—The Trades Council, which is a body composed of all branches—manufacturers, renters and exhibitors—

to deal with all matters of general policy concerning the trade, thought that this thing had assumed a very serious aspect and was likely to damage the trade considerably. We have a very able secretary, Mr. Frank Fowell, who is rather used to this sort of work, and we instructed him to collect, as far as possible, all available evidence, interviewing as many people and writing to as many as possible, and to draw up a report for the Council.

3. Why do you consider the question of indecent conduct is not in any sense a question of lighting?—Well, I should be loath to think, my lord, just because it was dark, that this gave rise to indecent conduct. There are many dark places other than the cinema. I do not walk about in these dark places suspecting indecency.

4. You don't require supervision in these cases?—Supervision is possible. It is reasonable there should be proper supervision.

5. Tell me as closely as you can, what is the objection of the trade to better lighting than prevails usually?—The more light the worse the picture. Till you can eliminate that view you cannot expect them to welcome additional light at the expense of the picture on the screen. A secondary consideration is that more light means more cost. To project light through light is difficult, and doubling the amount of light in the auditorium would probably require much more than double the amount of current for projection to get an equally clear picture. We shall insist that every cinema shall be sufficiently well lighted to permit of proper supervision. A man walking down the aisle should be able to see to the end of the seats fed by that aisle. It is the attendants' duty to walk down behind the seats and see what is going on, and any inspectors, police, etc., ought to be able to do the same. It is unreasonable to expect that inspectors standing at the back of the gallery should see at once to the extreme end of the building and see what is happening to people in the front.

6. Do you have many complaints brought to you of any particular theatres where there is carelessness of supervision and indecent conduct?—The Exhibitors' Association heard some months ago that complaints in regard to conduct were made to the L.C.C. and Scotland Yard, and we as an association took the matter up and sent a circular to the theatres complained of, and informed them that if any more complaints were received the Association would oppose the renewal of the licences.

7. There were supervisors in these places?—They were not so well conducted as before the war. We had trained supervision then, now it is only casual. Twenty-one of my theatres before the war had highly trained men. It is a very, very delicate thing to handle. You instantly find yourselves in a lawsuit if you say a few words.

8. Yes. But increased lighting means less temptation?—I suppose it is so.

9. In regard to British productions, you say there would have been a great many but for the war?—The British producer was gradually coming into his own. I speak from personal experience.

The London Film Company was turning out prior to the war about thirty big films a year, of about 5000 feet each. It is entirely closed down at the moment; every single producer and operator was taken for the Army, and nobody was left to continue it.

10. What is the average life of a film?—One copy does not last more than twelve weeks of continuous showing, *i. e.*, say, four times a day.

11. Could it then still be shown in inferior theatres?—Not that copy. Of course the junk merchant might buy it and sell it to some outlying village. A new copy takes its place, and so it goes travelling on.

12. Are many copies of the same film made?—That's a question of finance. Some films run ten or twelve copies.

13. That depends upon the popularity of the film?—Naturally. A film of topical interest would be exhausted in a shorter time and would require more copies with which to cover the ground.

14. Classic films like " Macbeth " and " The Merchant of Venice," is their life short?—These films are very apt to crop up from time to time. A Shakespearian revival would cause reissue to be made.

15. There are certain things that go on practically for ever. Charlie Chaplin, for instance?—No, two or three years.

16. Detective stories?—There are so many new ones coming out.

17. Is it a fact that very few of the high-class novels have been a failure—comparatively speaking?—Comparatively speaking, good literature has not been.

18. Commercially doubtful?—It depends. Romantic literature is constantly in demand; it is in particular favour at the present time.

19. You say the war is interfering with the building of better-class theatres. Is there a process going on something like the absorption of the smaller theatres? Would you be building palaces capable of holding more people?—The original theatres were made too small, and the expenses of new construction are enormous compared with what they were.

20. Would it be incorrect to ask whether you were projecting anything of that sort?—We had thirty odd sites and options on similar lines when war broke out.

21. That would have meant the absorption of smaller places?—Closed them down by healthy competition.

22. In regard to the social evil, have you much difficulty?—Not much in the provinces. In one or two towns more difficulty than others. There was not much trouble in London prior to the war, but since the war it has been very considerable. There has been a certain laxity of behaviour in perfectly respectable girls owing to the presence of soldiers. It is probably quite harmless, but frivolous and stupid.

23. THE SECRETARY. Emotional disturbance!

MR. NEWBOULD. It is very difficult to speak to them.

24. THE CHAIRMAN. Is there any advantage in having private boxes in cinemas?—As a rule, no. There are snobs who think

the cinema is a place where they have to mix with undesirable people. We have not a single box in any cinema I am connected with—twenty-one theatres; average accommodation, 700 people.

25. With regard to eyestrain, I am not going to take you as an authority on that.—I am not. I may say my Company have a most elaborate method of selecting their pictures. They have six people—two ladies and four men who sit each day from 9.30 to 6 at night. They have never complained of eyestrain and headache. The pictures are rushed through at top speed.

26. Now the censorship?—I represented the Association officially on some occasions, and sometimes alone, and saw Mr. Herbert Samuel and others informally.

27. You are still more or less in touch with them?—The Home Office proposals are for a voluntary censorship under the control of the Home Office. It was rather a contradiction, censorship by consent, and we were to consent to whatever the Home Office liked to do!

28. You were required to pay? That was not to be voluntary?—That is so.

29. Was the idea that without an Act of Parliament it could not get an enforced censorship?—There are criminal penal laws dealing with immoral and indecent publications. They have no powers outside that.

30. There is nothing to compel you to send your films in?—No.

31. THE SECRETARY. You could say: "We won't send our films"?—The whole of the manufacturers 'of films signed an undertaking not to do so so long as the Home Office censorship assumed.that form.

32. Would you go so far as to say that at the present time supposing this Commission were to recommend compulsory censorship it could not be carried out except by Act of Parliament?—The Home Secretary said it was contentious, and they were under pledge not to introduce it during the war.

33. THE CHAIRMAN. The second proposal was that the Chief Censor and Examiners were to be selected, and a larger number.—Six. We have four. Government officials don't like to work as long as other people. We were to pay for the six.

34. At the present time the films produced only require four examiners.—They sit in couples.

35. Supposing it were not war time, do you think four would be sufficient?—No, the footage is larger than can be inspected. The inferior stuff doesn't get on the market at any price—there is so much good stuff.

36. You have objected as a trade. Supposing what you objected to had been eliminated?—We still think something of the sort will ultimately come.

37. And considering how reasonably fair our great public authorities are, the trade would not find itself entirely antagonistic?—There would have to be very great safeguards. Nobody

claims that the Lord Chamberlain's censorship of plays is very satisfactory.

38. Is it not possible that we may learn a lesson from the failure of the Lord Chamberlain's department? You cannot imagine a Government censorship of films now appointing a man far removed from any knowledge?—Governments come and go—Home Secretaries come and go. They bring their own views.

39. THE SECRETARY. Can you indicate the kind of man who was suggested for the censorship? I think the public should know the kind of names.—The men suggested were in each case very well-known literary men and writers of romantic and imaginative novels.

40. In the case of the Lord Chamberlain, there was no thought of a type of person fitted for censoring plays?—The Lord Chamberlain appointed a type to carry out the work, as in the case of Mr. Redford.

41. REV. S. SOOTHILL. Has the Lord Chamberlain no power over cinema representations?—No power.

42. For instance, there is a cinema at Drury Lane. Has he no control?— No control over it.

43. THE CHAIRMAN. The Advisory Board, what of that?— I quickly came to the conclusion that the Advisory Board was, to use a slang expression, merely "eyewash." It was never intended to be active or have any views in the matter. It was a sort of sop to the public. They were only intended to pass pious resolutions.

44. Have you any idea how many they were to be?—About twenty.

45. One was to be a woman?—" At least " one !

46. Was it feasible to suggest that one examiner should be appointed by the Advisory Board?—I think so.

47. Was only one for you?—None.

48. Would it have given the public greater confidence if one examiner was appointed by the Advisory Board?—I think so.

49. Was it not rather curious that you went into all these negotiations with the Home Office and then the Home Office found they were not able to appoint some one in that capacity? —They thought the trade was not organised and could put up no sort of defence, and were vastly disappointed when they found this was not so.

50. Were the meetings with the Home Secretary or with officials?—We had three with the Home Secretary, and there were others with permanent officials, but there was a lot of correspondence.

51. Have you much experience of permanent officials?—More than I sought for.

52. Do they realise they are fallible?—I'm sure they don't ! I shall always be theoretically in favour of a voluntary trade censorship, but in their form it would not be satisfactory. The trade would not be averse to a Government censorship if it would

silence this everlasting talk. We want peace and quietness, and not to be fighting all the time. We propose to perfect the trade organisation so as to deal with blacklegs; we have started to apply Trade Union principles fairly and properly, to entirely suppress blacklegs.

53. With regard to other things besides the character of the film—the lighting of the buildings, etc.—you are prepared to leave these to the local authority?—My experience of getting anything passed by local authorities is such an ordeal that I am astounded to hear of some places ever getting licensed. It seems to me it is entirely up to the local authorities to see that these insanitary places are not allowed. I am surprised to hear they are.

The Chairman mentioned a certain house in the Strand which was insanitary and dangerous.

54. THE CHAIRMAN. You would like some model regulations in regard to these matters?—Very much. All over the country.

55. Knowing how jealous the local authorities are in respect of their powers, don't you think it would be extremely difficult to get them to accept any model regulations?—They seem fairly willing to adopt regulations issued by the Home Office, provided they are of a very stringent nature.

56. You think the local authorities would be prepared to accept an agreed set of model regulations?—They would be glad of the solution.

57. Supposing you had anything like a censorship partly trade and partly Home Office, what kind of proportion would you like the trade to have?—The trade don't insist on any representative upon a censorship which can be trusted. It wants to be sure it has a democratic censorship. It wants to be safeguarded against bureaucrats, cranks and extremists. What we want is to place ourselves in the hands of sane, rational, reasonable people.

58. You say the public wish for British films but are not " articulate." What do you mean?—If you mix amongst the people going in and out you hear them say: " What a pity we are always looking at American films—Yankee policemen, etc.—we want British films ! " You only get that sort of thing if you ask for it. They don't go to the manager and ask for them. British films are so few and far between that they would wear their boots out trying to find them.

59. Would the advertising scheme you mention be a combine?—No one firm could afford to carry it out—we should have to co-operate to get British films everywhere.

60. Very well. Then to use a Yankee phrase, " It is up to the trade." My last question is this—do you feel that the complaints which have been made against the cinema generally are very numerous or of very great importance?—If you were to see my collection of press cuttings you wouldn't ask that ! All grossly unfair; and also such pamphlets as that of Prebendary Carlile. You see reports in the Press with headings " Crime and the Cinema " or " Suicide and the Cinema "—it is nauseating, because

when you read the reports you can discover no reasonable connection with the cinema at all.   I agree that the criticisms refer to other things than cinemas.

61. Has there been much talk?—There has been very unfair talk..

EIGHTEENTH DAY

Monday, May 14, 1917,

The REV. PRINCIPAL A. E. GARVIE, D.D., in the chair.

STATEMENT OF DR. C. W. KIMMINS.

PRÉCIS

An Investigation of Children's Interest in the Cinema.

IN order to see what type of film proves most attractive to boys and girls of different ages, the children in six elementary schools in very poor districts, and six in well-to-do districts, were asked to write an account of the moving picture they liked the most of all those they had seen at the cinema, and they were told that they would only be allowed to write for fifteen minutes.   There was no notice given and no preparation nor preliminary discussion, and the children wrote the essays at practically the same time.   The boys' and girls' departments in the same schools were used for the experiment.   A similar test was given to a girls' central school in which the ages are from eleven to fifteen.

The numbers of children in the different schools are given in the analysis.   The totals are as follows—

In the 6 boys' schools in poor districts there were 1413 children
„ „ 6 girls'   „   „   „   „   „   1334   „
„ „ 6 boys'   „   well-do-do   „   „   1861   „
„ „ 6 girls'   „   „   „   „   1909   „
„ „ girls' central school   „   „   184   „

6701 children

It was found by a sample test that children from eight to ten years of age wrote accounts of films they had seen quite recently, so that they simply represent selections from one or two programmes.   In the upper classes, however, the selection was made from a larger area.   In the analysis A and A etc., represent boys and girls at the same schools—

ANALYSIS OF RESULTS.

Schools in Poor Districts	War Films (1)	Comics (2)	Cowboys and Adventure (3)	Domestic and Fairy Stories (4)	Crook Films (no other interest) (5)	Serials (6)	Love Films (7)	Educational (8)	Cannot describe (9)	Never been (10)	Total (11)
(a) Boys—											
A	16	48	53	43	10	107	—	2	36	5	320
B	28	60	107	30	39	49	2	—	45	7	367
C	31	55	53	37	34	—	—	1	—	5	216
D	17	23	57	48	36	38	—	—	—	7	188
E	3	38	22	47	12	17	—	—	9	4	173
F	24	19	33	30	9	17	—	1	12	4	149
	119	243	325	235	140	211	2	4	102	32	1413
(b) Girls—											
A'	15	21	25	94	6	54	34	12	71	16	348
B'	42	60	36	88	—	17	2	3	101	7	356
C'	11	30	13	57	18	—	—	2	—	19	150
D'	6	26	19	136	14	—	—	1	—	2	204
E'	11	22	1	85	4	18	—	—	—	2	143
F'	8	22	6	80	1	4	—	—	8	4	133
	93	181	100	540	43	93	36	18	180	50	1334

T

ANALYSIS OF RESULTS.

Schools in Good Districts	War Films (1)	Comics (2)	Cowboys and Adventure (3)	Domestic and Fairy Stories (4)	Crook Films (no other interest) (5y)	Serials (6)	Love Films (7)	Educational (8)	Cannot describe (9)	Never been (10)	Total (11)
(a) Boys—											
A	20	29	66	12	6	23	2	7	1	22	188
B	107	43	36	26	12	4	2	18	26	7	281
C	56	46	95	49	24	42	7	5	64	36	424
D	43	107	76	44	23	17	3	4	11	40	368
E	14	103	59	54	13	7	2	1	—	9	262
F	55	89	53	49	20	30	3	5	1	33	338
	295	417	385	234	98	123	19	40	103	147	1861
(b) Girls—											
A'	12	21	31	76	10	18	12	—	17	13	210
B'	96	10	24	65	—	1	25	16	—	32	269
C'	29	63	35	107	4	11	21	7	52	62	391
D'	51	30	34	139	7	13	22	17	8	70	391
E'	10	64	27	128	5	12	33	3	9	13	304
F'	34	36	18	136	—	—	37	20	—	63	344
	232	224	169	651	26	55	150	63	86	253	1909
Central Girls' School	13	14	37	66	2	5	16	5	3	23	184

Notes on Analysis.

1. The great point of difference between the boys' and girls' favourite films is, that the girls are much more interested in domestic and fairy stories than the boys, and are far less interested in cowboy stories and adventures.

2. Comics are much more popular with the boys than with the girls. In the upper standards of most of the schools there is evidence that the film of exclusively comic interest is less popular than in the lower standards.

3. The boys in both classes of schools are much keener on serial films than girls.

4. The interest in war films varies from school to school. The boys are rather more interested in this type of film than the girls. In the schools in well-to-do districts they are far more popular than in those in poor districts.

5. The boys are much more keenly interested in the purely Crook films than the girls. This may account for the greater interest of the boys in serials, in many of which, *e.g.*, " The Laughing Mask," " The Clutching Hand," " The Red Circle " and " The Broken Coin," the Crook is the predominant interest. In " Liberty," which is the favourite with the girls, there is a strong love interest. Serials are not so popular in schools in well-to-do districts.

6. Exclusively love films are far more popular with the girls than with the boys.

7. Of the children who have never been to a cinema, there are fewer boys than girls. The numbers in the schools in well-to-do districts are much greater than in those in the poor districts.

8. Comparatively few children name films but are unable to give any description of them, and these are in the lower standards.

9. Purely educational films are not popular, but are more so in the schools in the well-to-do than in those in the poor districts.

10. In the girls' central school the only points worthy of mention are the fall of interest in comics and the comparatively large number of girls who like stories of cowboys and adventure. In other girls' schools an increased interest at twelve and thirteen years of age in this type of film is to be noticed.

11. The interest in purely love stories starts in most girls schools at about eleven years of age.

12. The children who have never been to cinemas very often state as the reason that " Mother says it is bad for the eyes."

The most striking result that emerges from the investigation is, that the older children have a remarkable power of giving good accounts of films they have only seen once. This not merely a passing interest. In one of the schools about thirty girls had promised their teacher in 1914 not to go to the cinemas during the war. In spite of this, girls who had kept the promise were able, with one exception, to give good accounts of films they had seen more than two years before. This would seem to open up possibilities of great educational developments if films could be produced

which, in addition to being of value from the educational point of view were of sufficient general interest to command the concentrated attention which is evidently given to popular cinema films.
April 21, 1917.

MINUTES OF EVIDENCE

DR. KIMMINS. *Examined.*

DR. KIMMINS : I think the simplest way would be for me to elaborate the evidence, and give you a few extracts from essays showing you the mind of the child with regard to the cinema. I would urge you not to attach much importance to the results from the girls' central school, because I only had 184 papers sent in, which is not a sufficient number from which to draw a very definite conclusion. In many of the children's essays they simply refer to the last performance or the one before that. I have thoroughly analysed the papers and there are several points which come out very clearly. I have noticed that the girls take a greater interest in domestic drama and fairy stories. Quite a large number of fairy stories have been filmed, and they have been described in great detail. As regards the comics they are very much more popular with the boys than the girls, and when one analyses every age one finds that in the upper standards the boys are less attracted by the comics than the boys in the lower standards. The boys are much keener on serial films than the girls, but this may be explained by the fact that the boys have more opportunities of attending the cinema than the girls. The interest in war films is very great and varies from school to school. Then, again, the boys take a keener interest in the crook films than the girls, while love films are more popular with the girls than the boys; and it is very noticeable that in the schools in very well-to-do districts the purely love film is more popular than in the poorer districts. To carry on this investigation I selected six schools from poor districts and six schools from good districts, in order to get a great difference in the home surroundings. One point comes out in the analyses of the papers of the girls' central school; and that is, that there is an increased interest at twelve and thirteen years of age in films about cowboys and adventure. I will quote some extracts from essays as to why some of the children do not go to cinemas.

The first is rather pathetic, it is from a child of nine : " I have never been in a cinema. It was my dada's wish that I was not to go in a cinema. Mother likes to keep his wish because he was killed " (in France).

Then another child of nine says : " My reasons for not going to cinemas are that the heat gives me a headache. I also found that germs like the dark and so cinemas are unhealthy, so father and mother decided I better not go. I like books very much and having many at home I do not want to go."

Then a child of ten : " I have never been to cinemas. Last year my two sisters went, and in two or three days, one had scarlet fever and the other measles, and so mother would not let me go because she thought I might get it."

Then a girl of thirteen says—and I must say here that a girl of thirteen is much more critical than a boy of thirteen : " I do not go to the pictures because of these reasons : (1) I save money by stopping at home; (2) it don't do your eyes any good; (3) it's not healthy to be stuck inside a hot place taking other people's breath."

Now I will read some extracts from essays on films. Here is a rather remarkable one from a boy of ten : " A girl had an extremely heroic mother whose husband was locked up in a den of tigers. The woman, who was determined to save her man, boldly went to the circus train where she begged pitifully and melancholily to give her the keys of the den. After a long argument they answered in the affirmative. When she got to the place they said ' You can have the keys on one condition only,' and that was, when she got to the door and unlocked it they must give back the keys. At first she answered in the negative, afterwards she agreed. The second she got into the gloomy cavern she heard her husband's voice. ' Is that you, John ? ' ' Who is that ? ' came a dreamy and fatigued voice. ' It is me your wife, Charlotte.' Then the tears flowed."

Here is an extraordinary account of the impression a girl of thirteen obtained from seeing a film dealing with the death of Nurse Cavell : " They took her to a prison in a German neighbourhood and ordered her to tell the British plans. When she thought of her God and country she said : ' I will not be a traitor to my own country.' The German Emperor, who is called the Kaiser, said : ' You will suffer for it if you do not tell us.' Nurse Cavell knelt by her stony bed and said her evening prayer. When Von Bissing saw her he spoke some German language to her, and she did not understand it. The following day the Kaiser ordered his soldiers to fetch her to the place where she was going to be shot. When she was led through the market the people laughed and teased her. When she arrived at her destination the Kaiser said : ' Fancy you trying to fight against me.' He then ordered Von Bissing to level his revolver and shoot her. He did so, and then he was given an Iron Cross and some money for killing her."

One small child after describing a country scene says : " The picture I like best is like a meadow. It had flowers and little hills. Why I like it is, because it makes you think that you are in the country yourself. It also learns you your Nature study."

Then a child of eleven says : " I always look forward to pictures about people who do daring things. I like to see people climb mountains under great difficulties, or people running away and being pursued. There is one picture that I think is very good. It is called Liberty. It is a very daring play and the people go through very dangerous things."

The girls, by the way, take very much more interest in scenery than the boys, and here is what one of the girls says : " The picture that I enjoyed most was one delivered in six parts and dealing with the wild life of Alaska and the Yukon District. I cannot exactly recollect the details, but I have a rather hazy, it is true, remembrance of them. It is about a man who, in disguise, tracks to the snowy regions of Alaska and there kills the man who ran away with his wife. The music that was played at the time, I think, has a great deal to do with my decision."

Here is another : " It was a beautiful picture and beautiful scenery too; as we sat looking at it, it seemed to dazzle our eyes. The lady of the house was dressed in green velvet, while her son had a green suit; her son's sweetheart also had a green dress, but it was trimmed with black fur. As they sat under the trees, on a seat made of oak, in the moonlight, it was picturesque. The green made it look more beautiful than ever. We held our breaths as we watched it, for it was so beautiful."

At the age of thirteen, the girls like to describe the appearance of the people who are acting. That comes out very strikingly in one or two essays I have here : " Joan was a young and beautiful girl of about seventeen years of age, who worked in the mines. Her friend was Lizzie, a pretty girl of about the same age, but fragile and obstinate. Their ' boss ' as they called the manager, was a young man, handsome and kind. Many a time had he saved Joan from blows from the foreman, and she had grown to love him. Joan's father was a bully and the terror of the mine."

Here is another short description : " It was a dull day, and a heavy storm was raging overhead ; and a man, evidently a newcomer, entered the inn. He was tall and respectable, with large bright eyes, which seemed to influence everybody. Having had his fill, and the storm having abated, he left the inn and proceeded homewards. On arriving there he sat down and seemed lost in meditation."

Here is a good description : " The picture that I liked most was not a funny story nor a drama, but just views of water waving and curling, and also some falls. It gave some most beautiful falls and fountains splashing and sparkling in sunny France. The water first turned a beautiful blue, and then on the fountains it sprinkled with a silver tint. Then came the fall, with its beautiful waters jumping and bubbling over sharp stones and rocks, making many pools of white foam. Another picture was the river, and sometimes it did not sparkle but was dark and sullen."

This is a remarkable production for a young child.

Then another child says : " I like mysteries and detective pictures, from them you can learn many things : first, you can learn to copy detectives' ways ; secondly, you can be careful of whom you make acquaintance, whether a nice girl or a nasty mean girl."

Here is something for the Censor : " Some pictures are degrading, and they do not do one any good; but they would help to make the people who see them less pure and have less moral support. These pictures are only shown in cheap and degraded picture palaces, and are only supported by the people of inferior education. Some pictures are degrading, and these never ought to be passed by the Censor."

The age of that girl is only thirteen and she goes to an ordinary elementary school.

Then you have : " Pictures of foreign scenes, exploration and aviation give one ideas that are not to be found in books and do a great deal to improve our ideas. My opinion is, that pictures could be utilised for the education of children along with the form of education that is taught in our schools. Pictures about foreign countries are highly valued for their aid to education, and in the improvement of children's minds."

Another girl says : " Love pictures are sometimes ridiculous and are only meant for grown-ups. Pictures such as ' Quo Vadis?' ' John Halifax, Gentleman ' and ' The Three Musketeers ' are really a help to education and give one a good idea of the habits of the people at the time."

Then here is a delightful child who gives this description : " I have an æsthetic taste for scenery, and one of the best pictures I have seen is ' Doran's Travels in China.' This young lady travelled on the tranquil winding river. The mountains glistened in the sun and the traveller stood amazed at the wondrous spectacle. The people in the massive building were similar to the ancient people of years ago. The beautiful scenery helps to uplift one to purer thoughts. It helps to give one a better idea of the beauty of the world and gives one ideas of different countries."

In one essay a girl traces the extraordinary influence of one person upon another : " Bob believed in crime, and reared Daisy, as the little girl was called, to believe in the same principles. One day Daisy was hungry, and being now a girl of seventeen and very pretty, she decided to pick some one's pocket, but also was detected and carried to the police station, where a middle-aged man took pity on her and took her to his own home, which was situated in Park Lane. Daisy had never seen such a lovely house, and even after she was dressed in lovely clothes, the impulse to steal would come to her, and at last, while the haughty footman was asleep, she cut off the gorgeous gold braid from his shoulder, and tied it round her own waist."

Then here is the essay of a boy of eight years of age : " There was a girl about fourteen years of age. She had a very nice young man. There was another lady who was very jealous, because she wanted the young man. So she made up her mind to murder this young lady. She got two young men to capture her. One day they saw her out. They blindfolded her and took her away. They put her in a house and left her there. While she was looking out of the window she saw her sweetheart. She opened the window and called out to him and told him all about it, so he knocked the door down and got her."

Here is a boy of nine : " The best film I have ever seen is ' The Man Who Stayed at Home.' I like it best, because it ended up nicely, and some pictures end up so funny. But ' The Man Who Stayed at Home ' ended up where the Man Who Stayed at Home saves one of our biggest liners, and sunk one of the German submarines, and killed a lot of German soldiers. So you can see that it did end up very nicely."

The boys' descriptions of war films are extremely well done, as you will see by this one : " Name—Battle of the Ancre. Crash ! Boom ! The Tower Cinema Band is imitating the battle of the Ancre. You see the Tanks in action, also men slushing about in mud. Now you see a transport wagon being guided round a shell hole by an officer; the officer takes an unlucky step and has a bath in mud. Now the eighteen-pounders in action, making frightful havoc over in the German trenches. Now the whistle shrills, and they leap over the parapet, rat, tap, tap, tap, go the German machine guns, but nothing daunts our soldiers. Crack ! and their gallant captain falls. This enrages the men to fury. At last they reach the German lines. Most of the Germans flee for their lives shouting ' Kamerad ! Kamerad ! ' etc. Now the British and German wounded are brought in, some seriously, others slightly. Soon after follow the German prisoners, some vicious-looking scoundrels that I should not like to meet on a dark night, others young boys, about sixteen years of age."

Here is the essay of a boy of eleven : " Moving pictures are nice, and although I have seen and enjoyed many, that which I liked most was a film entitled ' His Mistake.' In the first picture one saw three evil-looking men in an old shepherd's hut, plotting to kill Lord Harston of Myrtle Manor. The next shows these men slinking home in the dark to a dilapidated cottage. Third, one saw Lord Harston riding out with his faithful dog ' Rufe.' As Harston came down a leafy lane a masked man with a revolver calls upon him to stop. Harston speaks to his dog, which, unnoticed, creeps behind the masked man and then, with a low crouch, darts forward upon Harston's would-be kidnapper. He, startled by the attack, falls and is immediately attacked by the dog. Part II shows Lord Harston's Manor, which he is using as a convalescent home for wounded soldiers. Part III films a second attempt on Harston's life, in which he receives a mysterious threat in a note brought by a shaggy dog. Last part : Lord Harston's baby is kidnapped and threatened with death unless Harston turns up at a certain spot. Lord Harston takes ten constables, captures the robbers or plotters and imprisons them."

I have had some fine descriptions of Tom Brown's Schooldays. It is a very favourable film with the girls and many of them write upon that. Then just one description of the way in which the boys describe Charlie Chaplin—

" Charlie by the Sea. In this two-reel farce we see the inimitable Charlie Chaplin garbed in the clothes of a seaside lounger, bowler hat and baggy trousers complete, strolling along the front at Mud-splosh-on-Sea, winking merrily at the oysters and twiddling the toothbrush on his upper lip. A fair form hoves in sight, which gradually changes itself into a fair maiden, escorted by a fierce old gentleman with a moustache which nearly hid his uncomely face from view. She soon left him asleep, at which Charlie gaily tripped along, his golden locks waving gently to and fro in the breezes. On being asked, the fair damsel agreed to go for a stroll along the sands with our hero. After a game with another of the young maiden's admirers in which a lifeboat came prominently into action, Charlie left his young lady to meet his friend Jerry Swiller, whom he treated to some ices. At the end of the picture we see all the irate maidens he had jilted chasing our hero.''

This is, I think, one of the best of the Battle pictures: "The best picture I have seen was the Battle of the Ancre and the Advance of the Tanks. It shows us in Old England the privations Tommy has to undergo in blood-sodden France and Belgium. The Tommies went to the trenches stumbling and slipping, but always wore the smile which the Kaiser's legions, try hard as they might, could not brush off. Lords, tinkers, earls, chimney sweeps, side by side, were shown in this splendid film. It showed and proved that although England was small and Germany large, the British Lion was a match for the German Eagle any day. The film also showed that monster terror and fear of the Germans, the Tank. Snorting, creaking, waddling, the huge bogey started for the German first-line trenches. The film showed the huge British guns. Day and night, night and day the huge monsters of destruction roared never ceasing."

That I think is a remarkable essay for a small boy from an elementary school. I will conclude with one or two extracts from the girls' essays.

A child of eight says : " When I went to the picture palace I saw a picture of a fire. It was a large house which was on fire. The fire was caused by a little girl dropping a lighted lamp. When the house was burning a boy came walking along. He saw the house on fire and three little girls looking out of the window. He threw up to them a large rope. They took hold of it and climbed down in turns. The mother came down after her children and the father came down last. The mother and father were very pleased with the boy for saving their children's lives and their own."

Then a girl of ten says : " The pictures I like best are dramas not too sad. I like about when people get bankrupt. A lady has to marry a person she does not like to get her father's business back. She loves another gentleman and she tells him her trouble. Then just as they are going to church a telegram boy comes to say that her uncle has died and she is an heiress. Then she marries her real young man. Her father is then able to keep his business on."

Here is the extraordinary story of the reformation of a beer-drinker : " Once when I went to the cinema I saw a picture about a little girl named Mary, whose mother was very ill and whose father was a drunkard. One night her father came home very drunk and he aimed a jug at his wife and killed her, and when Mary saw it she ran away. Presently she came to a motor and got under a covering and went to sleep. Later, a gentleman got in who was very rich, and whose *fiancée* had broken off her engagement with him because he drank beer. When he got in the motor he put his feet on the blanket and he woke Mary up. He sat her on his lap and she said : ' I don't like you; your breath smells like my daddy's.' He took her home with him determined not to touch beer again."

This next one is very typical and shows the child's extreme love of detail : " ' The House of Fear ' was the moving picture I enjoyed most.   It was a drama in four acts, but it was not as long as some dramas.   It was about a very old lady, named Mrs. White, who was bedridden.   She had only one child, a girl named Margaret, who was married to a certain Mr. Fairley, who had no relatives.   Margaret had one child named Elsie, who was thirteen months old.   Soon after Elsie's second birthday her father was accidently shot through the head and died immediately.   Her mother, hearing of her husband's sudden death, is taken very ill and dies soon afterwards. She then lived with her grandmother until she had turned five, knowing but little of her parents' deaths.   In her ninety-ninth year Mrs. White dies, leaving the child in the care of an uncle who is her godfather, but the uncle was a miser and did not wish to keep her.   After the funeral of her grandmother Elsie is brought before a meeting in her house and the uncle is asked to keep his promise.   He does not wish to, but in the end, wishing not to appear ungrateful, he consents.   In the end Elsie is married to her uncle's nephew, and here we leave her with a good husband, a comfortable home and two children."

STATEMENT OF MR. PERCIVAL SHARP, B.Sc.,
Director of Education for Newcastle-upon-Tyne.

Précis

1.—*The Function of the Cinema.*

THE cinema show is a place of legitimate entertainment.   The proprietor claims for it that it is nothing less; nothing more. Against the cinema show no criticism can fairly be directed therefore, because it may fail to fulfil in any wide sense the functions of an instrument of education.   The function of the cinema is primarily to make a profit, and this it can most easily do by making the show a place of interest and amusement.   In so far as it may do this with detriment to, without detriment to, or with benefit to public taste, morals or general *bona mores*, the cimena must be held blameworthy, blameless, or worthy of praise and support.

2.—*Juvenile Crime and its Association with the Cinema.*

It is most difficult to estimate the effect of the cinema on the good taste or general manners of the child, inasmuch as the standard of reference must vary so largely with the identity of the observer.   My own observations lead me to say that I have seen exhibits in distinctly bad taste, which could but have a bad effect on the development of child mind towards a love of the beautiful; but I am bound to say that I have seen many more of which the effect must be entirely for good.   I am speaking now of the development of good or bad taste and good or bad manners, as distinct from the development of criminal tendencies.

Vulgar pictures are shown on occasion, and such exhibition is to be deplored, but I think the general movement is in the direction of what is beautiful and of what is legitimately interesting.

With regard to the origin or development by the cinema of criminal tendencies in the young, I desire to say at once that in my opinion no good ground exists for attack upon the cinema in this connection. It is fortunate that in this, the most serious aspect of the influence of the cinema, the matter can be put to some extent to a quantitative test—for crime, unlike taste or manners, is not a matter of opinion or local convention. The extent—in a thickly populated area closely served by picture shows —to which juvenile crime can justly be attributed to the influence of the cinema, is a question capable of some definite investigation.

I set out below some facts with regard to Newcastle-on-Tyne, which may be regarded as pointing to a well-considered conclusion on this particular point.

Newcastle is a city with a population of 278,000 (approximately). The acreage is 8452 acres, which includes 1294 acres of town moor, parks and recreation grounds. In many parts of the city the population is closely gathered, owing to the existence of tenements and to the system of housing in flats. There are in the city twenty-four picture houses. On the rolls of the public elementary schools of the city are over 49,000 children. All the elements of the problem are therefore brought into association.

The number of children committed to industrial schools from the city area and under maintenance at the present moment is 262.

These committals fall under one of the following heads—

Section 58 (1) (*a*): " Found begging."
    ,,   ,, (1) (*b*): " Found wandering, no proper guardianship."
    ,,   ,, (2) and (3): " Shopbreaking and Larceny."
    ,,   ,, (6): " Non-compliance with Attendance Order."

SECTION 58

Year	Sub-Sections 1-3	Sub-Section 6	Total
1914	44	27	71
1915	41	22	63
1916	29	23	52
Totals	114	72	186

By far the greater number of these committals are at the instance of the police.

As the Local Education Authority is responsible for the maintenance of all children committed to industrial schools, whether at the instance of the police or otherwise, it is laid down in Section 74 (6) of the Children Act that no child may be committed to an industrial school to be maintained by a local education authority until the local education authority has had an opportunity of being heard with reference to the case.

The Local Education Authority have laid upon the Director of Education for the city of Newcastle the duty of examining the facts and circumstances of all proposed committals to industrial schools and determining whether opposition shall be offered in any particular case to such commitment.

In this capacity I have dealt with a large number of cases in Newcastle during the last three years, and my scrutiny has brought under survey in each case—

(*a*) The report of the police on the facts of the case including in most cases some comment on the tendencies of the boy or of his guardians.

(*b*) The report of a school attendance officer whose duty it is to inquire and report closely upon the previous record of the boy, his habits, his companions and his home environment.

(*c*) The report of the head-teacher upon the habits and conduct of the boy in school and upon his school record.

Upon these three records I form a judgment as to whether opposition shall be offered to a committal.

I have dwelt upon this procedure in some detail in order that the Commission may form a clear idea as to the kind of case and the nature of the information I am called upon to examine and pronounce upon in the ordinary routine of my work.

I have not during the last three years of investigation (covering 186 cases of committal) *had a single case brought to my notice, in respect of which it has been alleged or even suggested by police, school attendance officer or head-teacher that the genesis of the wrong-doing was to be found in the cinema show,* EITHER IMMEDIATELY OR REMOTELY.

I have mentioned the period of three years because that covers the period of my work in Newcastle up to date.

I may add, however, that I do not recall a single such instance in the preceding ten years during which I acted in a similar capacity in a Lancashire county borough of 100,000 population.

I have gone further, and examined the records of my predecessors, which have been preserved in this office, of seventy-six other cases from this city area now being maintained in industrial schools, and I cannot find any trace of a single child whose wrong-doing has been attributed, either directly or by inference, to the influence of the cinema show.

Having regard to the fact that when I leave the region of conjecture, and seek over so wide an area of wrong-doing, for concrete instances of crime, directly traceable to the influence of the cinema, and finding none; and having regard to the further fact that in no single instance has it been alleged or suggested by those instituting proceedings or by those whose duty it was to report upon the facts that such connection between crime and the cinema existed;

I am driven to the conclusion that, so far as this city is concerned, no case can lie against the cinema show as the genesis of juvenile crime, or as being responsible for the marked increase of the crimes of juveniles during the last three years.

But although in my opinion the grave accusations against the cinema, to which the foregoing notes refer, must be dismissed as resting largely on a confusion between *propter hoc* and *post hoc*, it is none the less desirable that so far as is possible, all exhibitions calculated to deprave public taste, whether of adult or child, should be discountenanced. This is an obvious truism, and can be held to be no more applicable to picture shows than to any other form of entertainment.

CENSORSHIP.

This naturally leads to the question of censorship.

I am of opinion censorship is desirable in relation to picture exhibits as it is in relation to stage exhibits.

I suggest that any censorship in the public interest should be entirely maintained at the public expense, and be free from responsibility to any authority other than that of the State.

The standard of censorship should be constant, and censorship should be exercised before films are allowed to be exhibited publicly.

I am, therefore, in favour of a State Established Censorship, consisting of a staff of people efficient in quality and sufficient in number to deal with this matter at its source.

I view with distaste proposals for differentiating between exhibitions " for adults only " and those for children. The child mind is intensely inquisitive, and when such distinctions are established, the juvenile boy is very anxious indeed to see what his big brother may see from which he himself is excluded.

It predisposes the mind of the child to look forward with a nasty expectancy to those exhibitions to which he is for the time denied.

It is, I think, unfortunate to recognise as an expedient thing, forms of entertainment for adults not fit for the sight of children.

THE CINEMA AS AN INSTRUMENT OF EDUCATION.

I do not regard the cinema as a serious instrument of education.

The subjects of instruction in the elementary schools are broadly : Reading, writing, English composition, arithmetic, some history and geography, handicraft and some Nature study.

In the secondary schools we have also : Mathematics, languages other than English, physical science.

The subjects in respect of which claims have been made for the educational value of the cinema are : History, geography, Nature study.

One recognises the value of good pictures—whether cinetic or static—as an aid to the formation of mental pictures of scenes, geographical or historical, but to claim more than that would be —in my judgment—confession of a very inadequate concept of the true meaning of the study of either subject. A much more insidious claim can be made for the cinema as an educational aid to Nature study. No doubt many very interesting processes can be brought to the intellectual door, but I feel strongly that the effective study of science must be based on personal observations, comparisons, measurements and deductions. Observation by proxy is vicious. Indeed, there is a real danger of making study too easy—even without the cinema. Peptonised mental pabulum of any kind atrophies the intellectual digestion. Education by cinema would ruin it.

GENERAL CONCLUSION.

My general conclusion is, that the cinema show can only be regarded as a legitimate form of entertainment suffering from the present day defects which characterise other forms of entertainment.

The remarkable and immediate popularity of this form of entertainment has directed to it criticisms which in its minor forms may be justified, but which, in its more serious forms has, in my opinion, very often been founded on prejudice or even ignorance.

The cinema show will pass through a process of evolution— as other forms of entertainment have done, improving with the public taste and probably itself improving the public taste.

It is remarkable that the type of entertainment is generally so high, having regard to the short period of its development and to its possibilities for evil, if those possibilities were exploited—an event which, in my opinion, has not happened.

MINUTES OF EVIDENCE

PERCIVAL SHARP, B.Sc. *Examined.*

1. THE CHAIRMAN. You are the Director of Education for Newcastle-on-Tyne, and have taken a great interest in the cinema and its influence upon young life ?—Yes.

2. On the whole you say that the influence of the cinema is for good rather than for evil ?—That is so; but it depends very much upon the child's home, and it also depends upon its power of observation.

3. Then I see you have a very decided opinion that a great deal said about the criminal influence caused by the cinema is unwarranted ?—Well, I am strongly of that opinion, but my opinion, of course, is formed entirely from my own experience. I have thoroughly investigated all these cases, and that is the opinion I have formed. You will find that many of these children are born with criminal tendencies. There are such things as naturally warped children, but I think they are relatively few. The other cases are mainly due to parental neglect. If you take the children that attend cinema shows late in the evening by themselves, you will find that the greater proportion of these children are neglected children from homes in which there is no good parental influence.

4. Have you noticed that there has been an increase in juvenile crime since the beginning of the war ?—There has been an increase of crime amongst juveniles, certainly.

5. Would you attribute that to the absence of the father from home?—I should have done had I not been careful not to jump at conclusions without a very careful examination of facts. I examined all the circumstances of these commitments since the war broke out, and it was remarkable that of the 150 cases which had been committed in only seven of them were the fathers at the Front. Of course, the industrial conditions of Newcastle would probably account for the larger proportion of the fathers being at home than in other districts.

6. Coming to the censorship, you would distinctly favour a State censorship as contrasted to a censorship exercised by the trade?—Yes, certainly, as it would set up a better standard, as a censor must be above suspicion.

7. And you think, if connected with the trade, it may be regarded as not impartial?—I think that is the kind of uncharitable thing which might be said.

8. You think that on the whole a distinction between exhibitions for children and separate exhibitions for adults would tend to hinder the progress of the cinema?—Yes, I think it would. If you had a special performance for the adults the natural curiosity of the child would be to see that performance.

9. MONSIGNOR BROWN. Will you develop that remark of yours as to the better standard?—I think that films should be censored from the source, and this would be far better than if you left it to 230 or 240 localities to censor it. If you left it to them you would be having different standards.

10. THE CHAIRMAN. Coming to the cinema as an instrument of education, as an educationalist you do not regard the cinema as really a very serious educational agent?—No, I do not. There are very few subjects which lend themselves to teaching with the aid of the cinema.

11. Would you consider that explanations, spoken along with educational films, might increase the usefulness of these films?—Undoubtedly.

12. You would not accept it as a substitute for instruction?—Certainly not, but as a supplement merely for the purposes of interest and stimulant. I do not think it is worth the great expense that would have to be incurred in fitting up rooms for it; in fact, I do not think the school is the place for the cinema.

13. SIR JOHN KIRK. Has there been any complaints of the pictures themselves at Newcastle-on-Tyne?—No.

14. MONSIGNOR BROWN. What do you say about the censorship? What should constitute the censorship?—There should be a number of sufficiently qualified people to carry out the work.

15. DR. KIMMINS. You would not exclude the children from going to the cinema?—No, I should not.

16. MR. KING. Failing a State censorship, I take it that you would approve of a voluntary censorship in preference to the individual censorship of the local licensing authority?—Undoubtedly.

The Bishop of Birmingham in the chair.

STATEMENT OF MR. J. A. SEDDON.

Précis

The Cinematograph Exhibitors' National Union is intended to succeed to the Cinematograph Exhibitors' Association. For some years the parent body has been actively engaged in creating a national organisation to advance a common policy for the government and control of the business from the exhibitors' standpoint. The legal disabilities of a limited liability company compelled the members to substitute a new basis of organisation so that the executive authority could enforce the rules and also apply the agreed policy of the Union for self-preservation and resistance to any unfair attacks that may be made. The process of transition from the Exhibitors' Association to the National Union is progressing rapidly, and should be completed within a very few months.

In accepting the appointment of Organising Secretary to the Union, two considerations governed my decision. Speaking as one who has been closely connected with the working class and trade union movement for upwards of twenty-five years, I am profoundly convinced that the cinema exhibitions have given to the workers a form of entertainment which in the main constitutes a real pleasure and respite from the drab surroundings of many. No one conversant with the actual working class conditions can fail to be struck with the monotony of most of our modern industries. Specialisation, the mechanical habit produced by consistent attention to one operation or one part of a complex production, has created a new problem amongst most of our workers engaged upon machine productions. These are denied the mental activity and the personal pleasure of a former generation of mechanics and artisans who were the creators of a complete article. For those who are the victims of this change the cinema provides a mental stimulus which in hours of bodily rest gives knowledge and pleasure without fatigue. For this reason, speaking for my class, who are overwhelmingly the greatest proportion of patrons, I am convinced that the question of control cannot be left to those, however high and lofty their motives may be, who condemn upon hearsay, or make incidents into general charges. Nor is it in the interest of national betterment that a source of harmless amusement should be threatened with destruction, thereby reducing tens of thousands to a choice of the street or the public-houses.

My second reason for accepting the position was partly based upon the labour aspect of the industry, and partly upon the finance involved; but chiefly the possibility that through effective organisation and disciplinary power it would be possible to prevent the attempts of any individual for personal gain to bring discredit upon the whole trade. The labour question is of some considerable importance, the employment of nearly 100,000 directly engaged, and the vast sums spent on subsidiary employment, printing, building and its allied trades, commands the attention of every one who is interested in the question of employment; and the possibility of their unemployment, unless for very real and grave reasons, is a vital national question, especially in view of the great problems that will confront us at the end of the war. The chief question, however, that I wish to deal with is the scope and possibilities of organisation to regulate and control the exhibitions. The rules of the Union contain the following objects—

(*a*) To promote goodwill and a good understanding between all proprietors of cinemas and other places of entertainment, and between them and such men as work for them, and between them and the manufacturers and renters of films.

(*b*) To provide a fund for the protection of the interests of the members of the Union, to relieve them when in distress and to protect them from oppression.

(*c*) To secure unity of action among proprietors of cinemas and other places of entertainment.

(*d*) To promote by all lawful means the adoption of fair working rules and customs of the trade.

(*e*) To organise and, when necessary, supply means whereby a free and unrestricted circulation of films and other trade requisites may be secured for members of the Union.

(*f*) To resist by all lawful means the imposition by public authorities or other persons of terms and conditions upon the trade which are unreasonable or unnecessary.

(*g*) To secure legislation for the protection of the interests of members, and to promote or oppose and join in promoting or opposing Bills in Parliament.

(*h*) To adopt such means of making known the operations of the Union as may seem to the council expedient.

(*i*) To adopt any means which in the opinion of the council may be incidental or conducive to the above objects.

The government of the Union is vested in a general council elected annually by vote of the members, district councils and local branches. The maximum fine for breach of rules is £100. It should be said here that the change from the Association to a Union was carried almost unanimously at the last annual meeting. During the last few months I have addressed meetings in the following towns : Leicester, Nottingham, Derby, Hanley and district, Birmingham, Cardiff, Liverpool, Manchester, Sheffield, London, Bradford, Leeds, Newcastle, Edinburgh and Glasgow. These meetings were not confined to members, but were open to all exhibitors in each district. It is not possible to say the exact percentage represented at the meetings, but it is a simple statement of fact to say that the great majority of exhibitors, either in person or by proxy attended. The aggregate vote was equal to ninety-nine to one for stringent organisation and the use of combination to secure effective means for dealing with members guilty of acts detrimental to the whole, which demonstrates that the vast majority of exhibitors welcomed any means whereby the charges that were constantly being made could be met and dealt with.

U

It is felt generally throughout the trade that except in rare and isolated cases the charges made against the cinema are based upon innuendo, hypothesis, or prejudice; and even the exceptions have been used for general condemnation without a shadow of justification. The Union welcomes any agency that will examine in a broad and comprehensive manner the charges brought against the cinema. There is absolute fearlessness that inquiry, judicial in character, can result in general condemnation. The vast bulk of the members feel acutely many of the unfair attacks by irresponsible people and the uncertainty arising from some administrative decision by local authorities. They are fully conscious of the vast influence placed in their hands, and entirely endorse the statement made by Mr. Newbould, chairman of the Cinematograph Exhibitors Association: " We are honourable and responsible citizens, we realise our great responsibility to its fullest extent, and it is our policy to so organise, conduct and control this vast business as to eliminate all undesirable element and utilise wholly for good the enormous influence at our disposal."

The question as to what power the Union possesses to deal with defaulting or non-members is the crux of the policy of the Union. It is recognised that an industry of such gigantic proportions, involving millions of capital and universally bound up with the amusement of millions of the population, cannot be left to the old doctrine of *laissez faire*. To those who are members fines can be applied, and, failing this, disciplinary method, expulsion. In the case of non-members who for selfish motives remain outside and whose conduct of their business is inimical to the general good of the whole trade, the use of a white list will be a protection for all who are united for clean business as well as self-preservation. The white list will be a guarantee to the public that the subscribers thereto are bound by common obligation to collective action against the unscrupulous. The local authorities for licensing buildings will have a guide in their decision and good cause to question any applicant who is not prepared to co-operate with his fellow exhibitors for regulation and control within.

Another weapon equally powerful with a strong combination is the influence with renters. The relationship of the exhibitor with the manufacturer and the renter has well been compared to that of the circulating library with the publisher and the author. The success of the business is equally shared by the three interests involved. In securing a circuit, the renters desire to be in the good graces of the greatest number of exhibitors. Any small minority who resisted the collective efforts of exhibitors would soon find its supply so limited that competition with rivals would be hopeless, and self-interest would soon compel a change of attitude.

The powers of the Union are not selfish but self-defensive. No national undertaking with such great moral, social and financial responsibilities can permit anarchy in its ranks. The vast majority of the trade are pledged to control. As business men they claim that such control should be national in character and based upon the legitimate use of the cinemas as places of amusement As citizens they desire that the educational side shall be an aid to the school and an opportunity to visualise the beauties of Nature and the charms of other lands denied by actual travel to so many. As men whose standard of morals is not low, they are anxious that an industry that gives pleasure to millions shall be an auxiliary to all that elevates and helps to higher citizenship.

MINUTES OF EVIDENCE

MR. J. A. SEDDON. *Examined.*

1. THE CHAIRMAN. You are the Organising Secretary of the Cinematograph Exhibitors' National Union?—Yes.

2. And does that National Union practically cover all the exhibitors?—Well, we are hoping that by the machinery we are setting up, by peaceful persuasion and other methods known as trades union activity, we shall be able to being them into line at no distant date.

3. As a matter of fact, you would not find many who would be opposed to it as joining the Union would be to their interest?—Yes.

4. If they do not belong to the Union, it would be extremely difficult for them to get hold of the things they want to show?—That is one of the weapons of organisation, one of our levers.

5. Of course, that all depends upon the kind of help you get from the people who produce the films?—Well, that all depends on the strength of the organisation. If 90 per cent. are in the organisation, then the manufacturers would want the custom of that 90 per cent. rather than the custom of the 10 per cent.

6. Supposing they said : We can practically sell all we want to sell in America and we are not going to be hampered in this way by being told : You must not sell to so-and-so. Supposing they said : We can depend on our American trade?—That would depend on the law of competition. I cannot conceive any business firm deliberately taking 10 per cent. from pure cussedness and trying to fight 90 per cent.

7. I see the rules of the Union are to promote goodwill and a good understanding between all proprietors of cinemas and other places of entertainment. I suppose there has not been much friction between the cinema and other places of entertainment? —Not to my knowledge. There is the usual trade rivalry, of course.

8. We were told that music and singing were prevented as far as they could be by certain local authorities on the petition almost of every other kind of entertainment?—Well, that is merely the spirit of competition and rivalry, and in that way using the power of the local authority.

9. I see there are about 100,000 people directly engaged in the cinema industry?—Yes.

10. Have they formed themselves into anything like a trade

union yet ?—Well, that 100,000 refers to the whole of the trade in its three branches and the number directly employed in the exhibitions. The latter would probably be about half that number, or a little more, say 60,000. The musicians are effectively organised, and harmonious relationships have been established between the musicians and the new exhibitors' union. With reference to the others, they are not organised to any great extent, but they are trying to be, and whether they will succeed or not, time will tell. I see the Union has to provide a fund for the protection of the interests of the members of the Union, to relieve them when in distress, and to protect them from oppression. There has been very little of that ?—It has not had time to find out yet, but I think there has been considerable distress owing to the many factors arising out of the war. You see, over 700 houses have already been closed.

11. Then, again, I see you are formed to organise and, when necessary, supply means whereby a free and unrestricted circulation of films and other trade requisites may be secured for members of the Union. What difficulty has there been in regard to that ?— There have been attempts on the part of some firms to place irksome conditions on the trade. For instance, the ——— Company were having a great draw, and they wished to impose these burdens. Now our object is to organise against such things as that.

12. Should you say that up and down the country there has been very much attack upon the cinema trade ?—The attacks that have been made are more or less hearsay without any specific charges being made.

13. You are depending upon your White List ?—Not altogether; but the White List would be an additional weapon to the obstreperous member.

14. How long has the Union been started ?—It has been registered for over a year, but is only now actually at work.

15. Would you like powers given for the local authorities to deal with the private person who floods the small town with the wrong sort of film ?—I would prefer that the power be given the Union.

16. PRINCIPAL GARVIE. How would you work the white list ? Would you send the white list to the magistrates ?—Yes.

17. Would each house belonging to your Union bear any particular badge or sign ?—We are hoping so. We already have a very artistic card of membership, and we are going to insist upon members displaying it.

18. You think you will be powerful enough to so influence the renters that it will be difficult for those who remain outside the Union to be supplied with the films ?—Yes.

19. MONSIGNOR BROWN.—How do you propose to deal with a case like, say, Drury Lane, where they are showing " Intolerance," which has not been submitted to the British Board of Film Censors and which attracts, apparently, enormous public support ? —Well, that is an isolated case, and when the trade is sufficiently organised, they will be able to deal with a situation like that by

taking that film and trying to get that film for general production all over the country.

20. What is to stop Drury Lane from going on as they are ?—Well, the final step to deal with them would be through Parliament. You see, the Association would go to the local bench and would say that this picture is contrary to the Union, and is against the interests of the community.

21. I am afraid with the public sanction that it has already got, I do not think you would get the public authority to stop " Intolerance."—Then it cannot be immoral. You see, we would appeal to the local authority and if the local authority refused to act, then we would have a case for legislation.

22. Seeing that the vast majority of the films that come into this country are American, how are they to be made to conform to the standards that we should like here ?—Well, I should say the best means would be to cultivate home productions.

23. We are told that the home manufacturer is struggling against the American and that he does not see his way to crush it ?—The proposition is, that we as an Association are out to make the business reputable and respectable, and we are anxious for censorship where the public and the trade will have confidence in the man who has been appointed as Censor because of his experience.

24. MR. NEWBOULD. I should like to explain, first of all, that Drury Lane is not a cinema theatre, and the next time Drury Lane applies for a licence to show a film, the Association will appear at the application to oppose it on the grounds that they have shown a film which is detrimental.

25. REV. CAREY BONNER. Every exhibitor who comes in has to bind himself only to use films that have passed the Board of Censors ?—That is one of the objects of the Association. The Association could not allow any film or the conduct of any member to go unnoticed that was going to bring any disgrace or injury on the whole.

26. Is there a black list ?—The law will not permit you to issue a black list, but you publish a white list and every one who is not on the white list is on the black list.

27. THE SECRETARY. " Intolerance " has been brought into this country. If you govern all the cinema halls you can say that this picture shall not come into our halls because we will not allow it to pass our censor, as you have paid a good deal of money for your buildings, etc., whereas Drury Lane has not ?—It is because they are not in the Association that they are blacklegs to the organisation, and as such we should not permit them to show.

28. MR. NEWBOULD. Mr. Marchant's question contains a statement which is entirely wrong. He says that the trade can say 'We won't let our Censor pass it.' The trade says nothing of the sort, and it has not been seen by Mr. O'Connor. The trade have no power to say to Mr. O'Connor that he is not to pass a film. The film has not been before the Board of Censors, and nobody knows what the action will be.

29. THE SECRETARY.   The effect of the Union, you say, is not to give undue power over the censorship?—That is so.

30. MONSIGNOR BROWN.   When you have the whole concern under your control, what is there to prevent you saying that now we have got the trade in our hands we will deal with the Censor, and the Censor will have to agree to our terms?

MR. NEWBOULD.   I think the Government can control that. If the censorship is unsatisfactory, sooner or later there must be a Government censorship.

WITNESS.   With reference to the censorship I think it is in the interests of the public as a whole.   I object to a State censorship, after many years' association with the civil servants of this country.

NINETEENTH DAY
Monday, May 21, 1917,
The BISHOP OF BIRMINGHAM in the chair.

MINUTES OF EVIDENCE

MR. R. H. FASTNEDGE, of the L.C.C. Licensing Committee. *Examined.*

1. THE CHAIRMAN.   You are the official in connection with the London County Council to whom have been deputed more particularly duties in regard to details of the cinema?—That is so.

2. What are the powers of the L.C.C. in regard to the cinema? —Well, the powers of control are very wide.   The Council has absolute discretion to grant or refuse licences, and it can attach conditions.

3. Any conditions regarding particular things, such as building?—Well, the building would be seen to before the Council granted a licence.

4. With regard to the condition of the auditorium of a theatre, have you any powers with regard to darkness or the lighting of the building?—One of the most important of the conditions which the Council attaches to its licences is with regard to lighting, but prior to that the building would be dealt with *qua* building.

5. You cannot build below the street level, for instance?— That would follow, but in the case of a building above street level the Council has given instructions regarding the provision of windows which, of course, are not used when the performance is on.   There are two systems of lighting.   In the hall itself both systems must be maintained to such an extent that in the event of the failure of one system, the other would enable people to see their way out.

6. Of course, under this system of lighting it would still necessitate attendants going about with small lamps?—No.   Take the

case of Deptford, where four little children were unfortunately killed, the lighting there was quite good. Even in the best lighted theatres it is quite possible that on entering it would strike one as dark, and the Council inspectors never arrive at a decision until they have been in the building at least fifteen minutes. Of course, there is a lot of reflected light from the screen.

7. Have any new regulations been laid down?—There is a new one, of which you have probably not heard, to stop cinema proprietors putting two children in one seat at children's matinées. I believe that was a common practice in the East End and the poorer districts.

8. Have you had any difficulty with the cinematographic proprietors? Have they objected very strongly to any condition?—I think not, except with regard to Sunday opening.

9. With regard to Sunday, what are the conditions?—There is a condition on the licence that the premises be not opened on Sunday, but, subject to certain regulations, applications are granted and the proprietors given to understand that the condition on the licence will not be insisted upon. When the Cinema Act came into force there were about 200 cinemas open every Sunday.

10. You mean to say 200 were open in London without control, seven days a week, before the Act came into force? What happened when the Act came into force?—The cinemas were closed for one Sunday, then they came open under the Council's regulations. The profits were to be allotted to some charitable society.

11. I see. They are supposed to be entertainers six days a week and philanthropists on the seventh?—Nobody is under that impression.

12. Can you make a logical proposition of the Sunday opening? —They presumably would not open unless there was reasonable profit.

13. MONSIGNOR BROWN. Why does any one open at all if there is no profit?—Some income accrues from the performance. One-seventh of the rates and taxes and rent.

14. They must have to employ extra persons?—Oh, that goes into the expenses. Wages are all expenses.

15. THE CHAIRMAN. It has been very much said up and down the country that it was easy to chuck your money away in charities so long as you were putting money in your own pocket? — The Cinematograph Exhibitors' Association could possibly tell you more than I about the motives which actuate their members. I cannot see where the hardship would come in if every place was closed. Obviously the Council was thinking of the hundreds of thousands of people in poorer parts who had nowhere else to go.

16. They might be doing a great deal worse than going to cinemas?—That must have been a consideration in the Council's mind.

17. It would be absurd to say that what London does should

be followed by provincial towns, say Newcastle?—That is a matter for the locality.

18. You would say that London does stand by itself in these matters?—Yes, with regard to amusement the argument would be quite sound.

19. Answering MONSIGNOR BROWN, the witness said that the Council's instructions were that every part was to be illuminated. The Council had had reports from the London Council for the promotion of Public Morality of halls which were too dark, and they had sent a further letter.

20. Have there been complaints as to boxes, etc.?—There have been a few?

21. What was the action?—In some cases the lighting has been improved.

22. The lighting which you have prescribed in that way has always been maintained?—Nobody would say that. The basic principle of the Council's system of inspection is that the visits are surprise visits, made on an average once every ten days. Any breach of regulations would mean a warning, and sometimes a summons. Almost certainly a warning the first time, and instructions to the Council's solicitor the second time to take proceedings.

23. Does the Council exercise control of cafés and refreshment places in connection with the hall?—If on the premises, yes. All suggestions of impropriety would be investigated.

24. Have the officers going round ever observed any misconduct on the part of the audience?—They have not reported any.

25. Answering further questions, the witness said the Council relied upon the public to write to them and report any objectionable feature in the performance. He agreed that notices might be put up in the buildings to this effect. All communications, signed or otherwise, would be treated as confidential. The question of a systematic patrol had been considered by the Council, and they did not consider it desirable to alter their system. In explaining the system on which the profits on Sunday performances were based, he said it was on past profits. All societies did not come under the War Charities Act. A considerable number of applications for Sunday opening had been refused, usually on the grounds of the hall being in proximity to a place of worship or a hospital. There were some proprietors who did not wish to open on Sundays, but he attributed that to covenants in the lease.

26. THE CHAIRMAN. There are not many theatres that have boxes?—Very few.

27. You have had no difficulty with the box question?—Very little. I don't think we have had any complaint.

STATEMENT OF MR. LEON GASTER,

Honorary Secretary of the Illuminating Engineering Society,
Editor of " The Illuminating Engineer."

Précis

SOME aspects of the lighting of cinema theatres were discussed at a meeting of the Illuminating Engineering Society,[1] at which representatives of the Commission were present. It was then suggested that a small committee of the Society should be formed to co-operate with the cinematograph industry in regard to lighting problems.

I am of opinion that this step is desirable in order to obtain fuller evidence of existing practice, and to ensure that any recommendations made will not impose undue hardship. In the inquiry carried out by the Home Office Departmental Committee on Lighting in Factories and Workshops, of which I am a member, a large number of observations and measurements were made in typical factories, and were found most valuable in showing that recommendations made on theoretical grounds were justifiable in practice. A similar series of tests would be necessary as a preliminary to standards of lighting in cinema theatres. Such standards should be clear and free from ambiguity, and if carefully framed would be in the interests alike of the industry and the public. Uniformity of procedure would be desirable in view of the technical nature of the problem. I understand that at present the requirements of licensing authorities in different parts of the country vary considerably. It would be a great advantage, as regards lighting, if common procedure throughout the country could be adopted.

I wish to offer some tentative suggestions regarding the chief principles to be observed in cinema lighting. While requirements as regards wiring and installation work from the safety standpoint are covered by the London County Council regulations, there do not appear to be any detailed requirements in regard to lighting from the standpoint of its effect on the eye; official requirements appear to be framed in general terms, and are based mainly on moral aspects.

The questions brought before my notice relate, first, to the illumination of the screen, and, secondly, to lighting of the theatre, passages, entrance hall, etc. While in the better-class theatres the conditions are frequently all that can be desired, it is suggested that in the cheaper places of entertainment inferior lighting of screen, incorrect angle of observation, use of poor films, and unsteadiness of the source of light are productive of eyestrain; and that the arrangements for lighting the theatre and adjacent stairs, passages, etc., are sometimes inadequate. Fuller statistics on these points are needed.

The following matters appear to deserve special consideration—

[1] *Illuminating Engineer*, February 1917, pp. 47–62.

1. In the darkened condition of cinema theatres the eye is very sensitive to glare from bright sources. It is therefore suggested that no source brighter than the screen should fall within the angle of vision of the audience when looking towards the picture. Also that any lamps used to indicate exits or for general lighting in the theatre should be properly shaded.

2. An excessive contrast between the bright screen and the dark surroundings is trying to the eyes. The walls and ceilings of the theatre might, therefore, preferably be fairly light in tint; this would also assist the effect of any permanent artificial lighting.

3. With a view to the proper display of pictures the lantern should be capable of giving an illumination on the screen of not less than one foot-candle,[1] before the film is interposed. The operator could then adjust his light according to the nature of the film.

4. In order to meet the views of authorities as regards propriety, and to diminish the objectionable contrast between the brightness of screen and surroundings, and also as a measure of safety, a small amount of permanent general artificial illumination, maintained while the display is in progress, appears desirable. A minimum of value of one-tenth foot-candle is suggested. The running cost of providing such an illumination would be small, probably within 5 to 10 per cent. of the cost of the electricity provided for the lantern and other illumination in the theatre building.

By careful direction of light it should be possible to provide such an illumination without prejudice to the image on the screen. Stairs, both within and without the theatre, should be lighted to the minimum value specified above, and the edges should preferably be white, so as to be easily seen.

The full lighting should be provided between performances, but the lights should be gradually raised or lowered by "dimmers" (resistances gradually inserted in the lighting circuit), so as to avoid the shock to the eye of sudden transition from darkness to brightness, or *vice versa*. In order to prepare the eye for the conditions within the theatre the illumination in vestibules, corridors, etc., should have a value intermediate between that prevailing in the theatre and outside, and all lights should be effectually screened.

5. It is common knowledge that observation of the screen at close quarters is productive of eyestrain. The distance should be such that the angle subtended by the screen at the eye does not exceed forty-five degrees, and the angle of obliquity at which the screen is viewed should not exceed thirty degrees. Children should not occupy seats which do not comply with these requirements. In view of the irregularities produced by screens giving a certain amount of polished reflection (*e. g.* powdered aluminium), a screen of dead-white material is to be preferred.

[1] A "foot-candle" is the illumination produced by a source of light equivalent to one candle, at a distance of one foot.

6. Due regard should be paid to the vision of lantern operators. A window provided with glass of suitable opacity and of a nature to absorb ultra-violet rays should be provided for observation of the arc, and the eyes of the operator should be screened from direct light as far as possible.

I desire also to refer to lighting conditions in rooms where film preparation goes on. The industry should take steps to secure that the conditions are hygienic, on the lines adopted in dealing with lighting of the theatrical stage.

MINUTES OF EVIDENCE

Mr. Leon Gaster. *Examined.*

1. THE CHAIRMAN. It has been suggested that in regard to the lighting of cinema theatres, a committee of your society should co-operate with the cinema commission. Would it be a good thing if you were to meet us and advise the Commission?— It would be a good idea. It has not been sufficiently studied in the past. There must be no undue hardship to the exhibitor.

2. It is important that we should have something in the shape of uniformity. Local authorities vary; unless we have some sort of central method, the whole thing would be chaotic?—So I understand.

3. SIR W. BARRETT. What is the proposed method of measuring the "foot-candle"?—In reply the witness demonstrated the method of ascertaining the power necessary to light the screen and auditorium, and, in answer to Dr. Kimmins, he agreed that excessive contrast between the bright screen and the dark surroundings is very trying to the eyes. It induced headaches and other effects. He suggested that the shortest distance at which children should be seated should preferably be about thirty feet away from the screen. Concluding his evidence, the witness suggested that reduced lighting outside cinemas should be made a special feature of the Commission's report. Under present circumstances, in view of the urgency of economy in fuel, it was sheer waste of coal to use electricity for lavish display of brilliant lights.

Mr. W. Gavazzi King. *Examined.*

The witness put in the following letter, which he was called upon to explain—

THE CINEMATOGRAPH EXHIBITORS' ASSOCIATION OF GREAT BRITAIN AND IRELAND, Limited

Broadmead House, Panton Street, Haymarket

DEAR SIR,

It is hardly possible to exaggerate the serious peril which is now threatening to bring ruin upon the business of the exhibitor. The trade is in immediate danger from a most drastic Government censorship which will have the effect of depriving you of 75 per cent. of the films which are most popular with your patrons. Why this particular form of entertainment should have a more drastic censorship imposed upon it than is imposed upon any other form of amusement or publication we fail to understand, but this, nevertheless, is what the Home Secretary proposes to do. The establishment of such a censorship, unless the association is successful in preventing it, will drive your patrons from the cinema. Your executive, which has been in the closest touch with this matter for six months past, and in frequent consultation with the Home Office, and therefore has first-hand knowledge, views the situation with the gravest apprehension. Your very existence as an exhibitor is at stake. The immediate inauguration of a powerful campaign on the screen, in the public Press and the law courts, is the only effective method of preventing this catastrophe, and it is therefore evident that there is an urgent and imperious call for the sinews of war.

Ever since the association was established, its operations have been greatly hampered by lack of funds. The annual subscription is proved to be much too small for an organisation which represents so large an industry, and one in which so much capital is involved. It is, moreover, not generally remembered that one-half of the annual subscription is absorbed by the district branches.

Manufacturers and renters will be asked to participate in raising funds for the protection of the industry, but every exhibitor must take a generous share in the financial responsibility.

We therefore appeal to every exhibitor, large and small, to send us as much as he can possibly afford. It is suggested that those who have benefited from the appeal in the Excess Profits case should, in addition to such sum, add the equivalent of at least 10 per cent. of the amount saved.

This appeal is *serious and urgent*, and should be responded to by one and all. *Do it now!*

On behalf of the Executive Committee,

A. E. NEWBOULD, Chairman,
W. GAVAZZI KING, Secretary.

₊ Cheques should be made payable to the association.

1. THE CHAIRMAN. Can you tell me on what date this letter was written?—I think October 1, 1916.

2. What led to it?—A series of negotiations which were conducted with the Home Office, not the Home Secretary. At that time there was a distinct disposition on the part of the permanent officials to exclude children from cinemas altogether. I am not in a position to give the actual evidence. But it was due to a statement made by certain persons. What followed was that action was taken by the Home Office, who suggested to various local authorities that they should insert in their conditions a clause excluding children under fourteen from cinemas. Liverpool put it into force, and at Halifax they went a little further. There at nine o'clock children were turned out whether accom-

panied by parents or not. My association took action, and the High Court decided that the condition was *ultra vires*. My association took the view that the proposed censorship would only allow pictures to be shown which would be suitable for children, and they came, to the conclusion, after investigation, that these represent only about 25 per cent. and that, therefore, 75 per cent. of the pictures would have to be entirely cut out of the programmes. In view of this position we had to take strong action and communicate with members of the association, asking them to interest M.P.s and prevent this censorship being imposed.

3. You were aware at that time that the Home Office had not the power to appoint a permanent censor. Your letter suggests that they could have?—Of course, a censor could have been appointed, but he could not have acted without the agreement of the trade.

4. You had no idea of any Commission when this letter was written?—Absolutely none.

5. This letter was written in a private way?—It was confidential.

6. How did it get scattered broadcast?—We have a very large membership. I have no doubt our members asked M.P.s to take action. They may have sent copies to a number of them.

7. In consequence of a certain amount of talk about this letter you have not issued any explanation of the letter?—It would be necessary to give an amount of explanation which I am afraid would involve the association in practical difficulties. We should have to explain matters which could not be fully explained to the public except at great length.

8. If you had known that the Commission was to be appointed, would this letter have been issued?—I think not.

9. You had been in communication with the Home Office before it was drafted?—We say: " Six months past."

10. From this letter it would seem you had gathered something which caused you grave apprehension?—Yes; a conversation I had with one of the chief officials led me to the conclusion that he would exclude every film of a dramatic or sensational nature, every film which had the slightest allusion to sex, every film dealing with crime even when incidental to the subject, and, I think, all rush and knockabout films.

11. Is your association with the Home Office a little more friendly now?—We have always been friendly, although we have had differences.

I know those differences. I cannot help feeling that in view of the way in which this letter was used, it might have been advantageous to send out something a little explanatory of the circumstances under which it was issued. The impression got abroad that this Commission was the reply of the Cinematograph Exhibitors' Association to a thrust which had been administered to them by the Home Office. It was almost a pity there could not have been something in general terms.

12. Did the official say that he had inquired into the influence of the cinema, and that the cinema itself was evil?—Yes, and he would like it stamped out.

13. THE SECRETARY. Was that the same permanent official who was devising the proposed censorship?—I believe so.

14. Can the Home Office, at present, as the law of this country stands, establish a compulsory censorship?—No.

15. And that fact was known to the Home Office and yourselves all the time these negotiations were proceeding?—Yes.

16. COMMISSIONER ADELAIDE COX. Do you mean that there were only certain films which it was desired children should see, educational pictures—scenic, travel—developments of industry, and fairy stories?—Yes. The official objected to dramas, comedies, love interests. The official particularly objected to the latter.

17. DR. KIMMINS. I have received copies of this letter from six different sources. The impression it would produce was that 75 per cent. of the films were considered undesirable.

[In answer to Dr. Kimmins, the witness said he could not say if there would be a reply to the letter. If the Commission thought it desirable, it might be dealt with.]

18. THE CHAIRMAN. You will forgive me for saying that your denial of this was not made very clear?—The letter was not intended for the public.

19. THE SECRETARY. Did you mean that in your judgment the action of such a censorship as you believed the Home Office would propose would have destroyed 75 per cent. of the films in existence?—Yes.

20. THE CHAIRMAN. Was this letter marked *Private and confidential?*—I believe so.

21. If it was marked *Private and confidential*, then those into whose hands it fell and who published it violated that confidence?—Yes.

There has been some great misunderstanding. I hardly think any man of the present day, even of my age, could take the line that the cinema is in itself an evil.

STATEMENT OF MR. ALFRED PERCEVAL GRAVES, M.A., F.R.S.L.

Formerly H. M. Inspector of Schools ; Chairman of the Representative Managers of the L.C.C. Elementary Schools, and Originator of the Educational Councils within the Metropolis.

PRÉCIS

As a Government Inspector of Schools from 1875 till 1910, I have given special attention to methods of instruction. After my retirement from the Government service I found time for educational work in directions where I had been moving during my Inspectorate.

When in the year 1912 I began to feel that a new and vital educational force had arisen in the cinematograph, capable of effecting perhaps as much for the improvement of the mind and spirit as the aeroplane is effecting for material locomotion, I made inquiries as to what steps were being taken in Germany, America and elsewhere, and then wrote on picture teaching for the Educational Supplement of the *Times*. I followed this article with lectures on the same subject to teachers in training and as a consequence was asked in 1913 to organise an Educational Conference at Olympia at the International Exhibition there held by the Cinematograph Exhibition Association. This led to conversations and discussions with such men as Sir Albert Rollit, the Hon. and Rev. Dr. Lyttelton and others, and brought within my experience much valuable data and opinions.

At the second educational conference of the Cinematograph Exhibition Association, held in Glasgow in February 1914, a resolution was adopted : " That this conference, representing members of educational institutions throughout Glasgow and district, strongly supports the adoption of cinematography in schools and colleges as an aid to education."

I now come to my more personal views as to (I) how, (II) when, and (III) where the cinematograph may be best used in education.

I. 1. And first, as regards the elementary school. The question of apparatus and installation arises first. In my opinion the teaching by cinematograph should be both by the larger instrument and the pathescope used side by side with the magic lantern, perhaps in an apparatus combining static and dynamic teaching.

2. The lantern slides should be used as the first illustrations in lessons of from twenty minutes to three-quarters of an hour according to the ages of the children. They should be followed by a cinematograph film which would summarise the illustrations given by magic lantern.

3. The films used might be inflammable or non-inflammable. The inflammable films cannot be presented upon the screen for more than a couple minutes, if that, but their pictures are much more telling, and if by screening or some other device they can be maintained upon the screen for a little longer they would be the most suitable for teaching purposes, the more so as danger from fire has been guarded against in a manner which makes them now safe for schools. The non-inflammable films do not last as long and do not project as good an image, but the image can be kept longer on the screen, and if their material can be improved they might furnish the best means of teaching. They are specially adapted at present to daylight screens, which have the advantage of enabling students or scholars to take notes with the illustrations before them.

II. 1. The instruction should as a rule take place not more than once a week, and generally on a Friday morning or afternoon as a summing up of the week's instruction in some particular subject or sets of subjects.

2. On special occasions such as Empire Day, St. George's Day,

St. Andrew's, St. David's and St. Patrick's Days, and on special occasions of national interest.

III. 1. The class lessons should be given in the school lantern-room. which should be in full use during the week for the various classes.

2. In the school halls, where longer films relating to the occasions suggested under II. 2 should be used.

3. In halls outside the school belonging to polytechnics or other educational institutions, or in picture halls lent for the purpose.

As regards the subjects to be taught, I need not specify. They would from time to time be determined by the school authorities, and if the Board of Education follows the example of the French Government Education authorities, instructions will doubtless be issued to Government Inspectors advising them how to deal with applications from local educational authorities as to what is to be taught and how and when instruction is to be given.

In the matter of the censorship as far as it applies to education, I should hope that if the Government takes it over there will be a combination of the Board of Education and the Home Office to see that the public in general, as well as children and young people, may be able to see pictures which are both recreative and educative, at the same time that the sight and general health of the community are guarded by the best lighting and ventilation procurable. Such a joint censorship should be supported by a committee of trade and education experts, who would advise upon the practical as well as the moral and educational side of cinematography.

MINUTES OF EVIDENCE

Mr. A. P. GRAVES. *Examined.*

1. THE CHAIRMAN. Will you give me, briefly, what assistance you can as to the value of the cinema in connection with education?—I think the cinema is, from the point of view of teaching, of great value in geography, especially in nature study, in science and contemporary history. As far as geography is concerned you can use it, as Professor Gregory points out, in the depicting of geysers and volcanic action, and so on, things it would be quite impossible for the ordinary child to see.

2. THE CHAIRMAN. These are things which would come under ordinary public entertainment?—They might.

3. Do you think it would be of advantage in the school?—I do. Ordinary object lessons given in the schools could be dealt with in the same way. I should use a magic lantern in the first instance and the cinema at the end with a cinematograph and static lantern. Every London school of importance has a magic lantern, and elementary teachers have done a great deal to prepare slides. They have made 35,000 slides, and 30,000 are in constant use.

4. There has been a good deal said to the effect that children don't care for the film which is more or less educational?—Both

the adult and the child you are trying to educate do not care to have a story or a " crook " film followed by an educational film or a romantic story. I think one of the reasons that these films have not been successful is that they have not been properly placed.

The witness handed in documents relating to the manufacture and production of films by the boys at Oundle School.

5. THE CHAIRMAN. How would you place the film? Would you begin the entertainment by giving the educational film first and working up?—It depends upon the nature of the entertainment. In the case of a mixed entertainment you ought to have the solids first. It is a very good rule to begin with these and have the sweets after.

6. In answer to Mr. Crook, the witness, although admitting that the ages of the boys at Oundle were higher than those of an elementary school, considered that in application the effects of self-made educational films would be identical. He would like to say that in his experience of the last ten to fifteen years there was very little to choose between the natural capacity of the elementary scholar with small educational advantages and the scholar of better social position.

7. THE CHAIRMAN. My experience goes further than that. I should say that up to the age of thirteen the elementary scholar is above the other.

8. Replying to Sir Wm. Barrett, the witness said he thought that the proper authority to deal with these educational films would be the Board of Education. Only on the crime side had the Home Office a status at all.

STATEMENT OF THE REV. CAREY BONNER,

General Secretary of The Sunday School Union ; (Hon.) Secretary United Board of Sunday School Organisations ; (Hon.) Joint Secretary World's Sunday School Association.

PRÉCIS

THE Sunday School Union introduced into Great Britain the better educational Sunday-school methods known as " Graded," resulting in the provision of residential colleges for training Sunday-school leaders; the issue of new educational textbooks and other literature; and in the generally broadened scope of the teacher's work for the scholar.

In carrying out these methods it has strongly emphasised the need for leaders to be interested in the week-day life of the scholar; and in its " Presidential Campaign " for the present year is organising conferences aiming to strengthen the co-operation of Sunday-school teachers with after care, child welfare, organised play committees and similar organisations.

Pursuing this policy, I, as general secretary, sent a " Questionnaire " to the secretaries of 290 affiliated metropolitan auxiliaries and provincial unions, asking for information concerning the cinema in relation to children and young people.

x

The results of the inquiry are now summarised and presented to the commission for consideration.

METHOD AND SCOPE OF INVESTIGATION

The Questionnaire was accompanied by the following suggestions designed to aid the thoroughness and fairness of the investigation—

I. General statements and resolutions are useless as evidence. Specific information as to films and picture palaces only is of value.

II. In order to get specific evidence, appoint two people, if possible to pay personal visits to the cinemas.

III. SUGGESTIONS FOR VISITORS.

1. If you have never been to a cinema before, do not go as a biased critic whose knowledge is based wholly on hearsay or newspaper reports. Go with an open mind, remembering that your sole interest is the welfare of the children and young people.

2. Do not imagine that by your criticism you can do away with the cinema. It has come to stay.

3. Do not criticise the performance wholly from the educational point of view, for no claim is made that the moving picture is an educational asset. Even expert educationists are divided in their views on this point. But the cinema *is* intended to be a place of amusement, and if it amuses and at the same time adds to the general knowledge of the people who visit it, and is free from objectionable elements, no one will wish to have it removed.

4. Do not go alone when paying a critical visit to a cinema. A companion will enable your facts to be verified, and your judgment to be confirmed by one who has had exactly the same experience as yourself.

5. If an objectionable film is shown, it would be well to lodge a complaint with the proprietor of the theatre with as little delay as possible.

6. If possible, on the occasion of each visit, secure a programme of the films shown. In any case note the exact title of the picture and the name of the producer of the film. In all but the most objectionable films this information is given on the screen.

Two hundred and forty-four unions have sent replies, including—

(a) *Large cities*, such as London (various districts), Liverpool, Manchester, Newcastle-on-Tyne, Leeds, Sheffield, Bristol, and Cardiff.

(b) *Towns in manufacturing centres*, such as Oldham, Rochdale, Bolton, Dewsbury, Stoke, Kettering.

(c) *County towns*, e. g. Maidstone, Oxford, Ipswich, Carlisle.

(d) *Seaside or health resorts*, e. g. Brighton, Tunbridge Wells, Southport, Blackpool, Whitley Bay, Bexhill.

(e) *Suburban districts*, such as Barnet, Ilford, Eltham, Bowdon.

(f) *Village and country districts*, e. g. North Wiltshire, Sawston, Saffron Walden, East Herts.

Note.—The large majority of the replies were of peculiar value, as they gave the results of personal visits, the visitors having attended from one to twenty theatres, according to the size of the town.

CLASSIFIED SUMMARY OF REPLIES

1. *Sunday Opening.*—The first query concerned Sunday opening of picture palaces. The replies show that Sunday exhibitions are quite exceptional, as only the following places reported them—

> London West: Bermondsey, Islington, West Hampstead. Ilford (one only out of five, from 6 to 9 p.m.). Hackney (5 to 10 p.m.). Battersea (6 to 11 p.m.). Wandsworth, West Ham.
> Kettering (one only).
> Hartlepool (after church service).
> Brighton (2 to 10 p.m.). Middleton (occasionally for charities).
> Southport (but children under sixteen not allowed to attend).

In these places generally more adults attended than children.

In Rochester a cinema was for a time opened at 8.15 p.m. for the soldiers. A census taken on five Sunday evenings showed that the military only attended in the proportion of one to five civilians, and the shows were therefore stopped.

2. *Lighting and Ventilation.*—In connection with cinemas during the week, the next question dealt with (*a*) sufficient lighting, and (*b*) good ventilation : both points of special importance to child life.

> On Lighting—70 per cent. reported this as good.
> 20 per cent. as insufficient or bad.
> 10 per cent, as only fair.
> On Ventilation—72 per cent. good.
> 17 per cent. bad.
> 11 per cent. fair.

In the instance of large towns, typical figures are : eighteen theatres visited—

> 10 lighting and ventilation good.
> 6 insufficient.
> 2 fair.

In one town the licence of the local justice requires dull lights, so that every part of the auditorium is visible to every person throughout the performance.

3. *Position and Attendance of Children.*—As to the position of the boys and girls in relation to the pictures—

> 55 per cent. found them too near—approximately from 12 to 15 ft. from the screen.
> 44 per cent. report them as being in good position further back than 15 ft. also scattered in various parts of the building, in many cases the children being seated with parents or friends.
> 1 per cent. simply thought position " fairly good."

In practically every instance the visits were paid to evening performances for mixed audiences, and all visitors found boys and girls present. The numbers varied according to the size of the theatre and were reported in figures varying from 10 to 250, or in percentage from 10 per cent. to 40 per cent.

Other Points.—One theatre proprietor in Southend supplied the information that the daily attendance of children in a large theatre was from 100 to 300, and in a small one 25 to 30.

In Bradford, Yorks, out of 42,257 children under the education authorities, 16,865 attended the cinemas in one week.

Character of Films.—The next question dealt with the character of the films seen. If anything injurious to the child mind was observed, the visitor was asked to give the title, etc.

The reports are characterised by impartiality, and even where some objection is taken to certain films, due admiration for the good ones is expressed. In dealing with " crook " films the observers noted the enthusiasm of the youngsters when the wrong-doer was brought to book. Many testify to the greater care now exercised by proprietors in showing better-class films.

Seventy-five per cent. replied that in the pictures seen there was nothing they deemed injurious to children. Another $7\frac{1}{2}$ per cent. replied similarly, but with a slight modification, such as " for the most part "; or " many were silly " or " inane," but not harmful; or " out of twenty-eight films viewed, only two were objectionable." The remaining $17\frac{1}{2}$ per cent. considered that the pictures they saw were (for the most part, at any rate) objectionable, or were, in their judgment, likely to be harmful to young people. In the more general answers under this heading, several visitors strongly objected to details of crime being shown, such as they had witnessed, *e. g.* house-breaking, card-sharping, cheque-forging; others objected to ultra-sensationalism or the exhibition of impossible and dangerous feats of daring; and others to the " innuendo and suggestiveness " of several of the situations in sex-problem films.

Effects of Cinema upon Children

Again, specific information was requested upon any other features personally observed at the show, likely to be physically, nervously, or morally injurious to children.

The averages work out almost as in the previous question : 75 per cent. replied they had observed nothing injurious; 10 per cent. answered similarly for the most part, but making slight exceptions chiefly on physical grounds; 15 per cent. mentioned definite objections.

Omitting certain sweeping statements as of no value, I note the following as typical results of visitors' observations of ill effects from attendance at the cinema shows—

" Over excitement and loss of sleep "; " undue nervous strain "; " eye-strain and headache " (one union secretary—a doctor of science and professor at university—names this as from personal observation and suggests wider expert inquiry); " disinclination for steady work after frequent visits " (a schoolmaster); " young children harmed by late hours," in some cases infants in mothers' arms taken to evening shows (several note this).

Local Censorship.—To the last question, as to local censorship, many forms were returned blank; but of those where the answer was given, 40 per cent. reported " No local censorship "; 25 per cent. none " as far as the correspondent was aware," while 35 per cent. gave affirmative replies. By far the greater proportion of these stated that the police or chief constables act as censors; others, that censorship is exercised by licensing committees, town councils, education authorities and watch committees. The L.C.C. regulations, of course, obtain in metropolitan areas, while several districts are under the model rules issued by the Secretary of State.

THE CINEMA AND JUVENILE DELINQUENCY

I realise the exceeding difficulty of getting material to enable the Commission to form a sound judgment upon this vitally important matter.

In order to obtain something more satisfactory than the wild general statements so frequently made, I addressed a letter to the chief religious weeklies, asking for specific instances of juvenile wrongdoing that could be supported by substantial proof.

In response, material of differing value has been sent, including certain facts and statements that at any rate merit further investigation.

Authorities upon the psychology of child life and adolescence generally are agreed as to the principle of the imitativeness of youth, especially where actions are concerned. This principle has been recognised by the cinema trade in the issue of a picture of a little " cinema hero " who had rescued a small child from drowning, because he had witnessed a rescue scene upon the films. Manifestly, the faculty which led this child to perform a noble deed might in other instances lead children to perform ignoble actions.

It seems to me clear that the truth will be found, not in extreme statements on either side, but only after investigation of a sufficiently thorough nature to cover the area of facts. We have received evidence on the one side from three or four witnesses with expert knowledge, and I respectfully suggest that, in order to enable us to form a true judgment, further inquiries should be made (perhaps by two or three appointed members of the Commission) into facts to be supplied. If evidence is widely sought from probation officers and from those connected with juvenile courts and children's welfare committees, it should prove a firm basis for a final judgment.

Various Points of Interest.—The following points may be worth noting—

1. In Rochdale no child under eight years is allowed to attend the cinema theatre.

2. In one small town where there is no censorship, the pro-

prietors of two or three theatres expressed their willingness to consider any suggestion made by the local union committee.

3. Many instances were reported of cinema proprietors or officials who were connected with the Sunday school or the Church; in two or three cases the proprietors being Sunday-school superintendents. It was stated that in these instances no objectionable pictures were shown.

4. In some cases the replies were supplied by local magistrates.

5. In Bedford the County Band of Hope Union has a first-class cinematograph apparatus, and has given hundreds of shows in schools, churches, colleges, and out-of-doors. The union possesses 40,000 ft. of films, mainly of natural history, travel, science and industry, child-life and humour. The union has occasionally loaned the films to picture theatre proprietors for children's shows.

I also know of an instance where a London minister in a poor district has for some years had a cinema apparatus installed in his school, so that he might give the best type of pictures to the children of the district.

6. Salford Sunday School Union appointed twelve ministers and laymen to visit the cinema theatres of the district. The work was very thoroughly done, with the result that, on the whole, a decidedly favourable report was given, both on films and theatres.

As one who fully recognises the place of recreation, especially in the lives of young people, and who has had a fairly wide experience of theatres and films, I have come to the conviction that, in the best sense of the word (and even in a commercial sense) the better class of films " pay." The success of the Ponting and Besley experiments are cases in point. My faith in the soundness of British hearts and minds leads me to decline to believe it necessary to stir up moral cesspools in order to find something interesting to the people.

I have seen audiences spellbound and enthusiastic over picture stories far removed from sex problems and crimes, stories featuring purity, high ideals, and yet of intense human interest.

If British producers will follow such high standards and free us from the nauseating stuff, much of which is imported from America, they will help to make the cinema a worthy asset in national life.

MINUTES OF EVIDENCE

REV. CAREY BONNER. *Examined.*

1. THE CHAIRMAN. You determined to try and investigate matters relating to cinemas in this country, and had great opportunities of getting information because of the number of varied societies connected with you. Was the question taken up by yourself alone ?—With the editor of our paper.

2. On the whole, bearing in mind that from your point of view you are apt to think upon the moral side, you found the lighting conditions to have been good ?—Yes.

3. Regarding the position of children at the pictures, you

found 55 per cent. placed too near, within twelve or fifteen feet. This I take it, was due to motives of cheapness. Regarding the character of the films, these were remarkably satisfactory, when you bear in mind what subjects have been focussed upon, to elicit the statement that 75 per cent. were not injurious to children.— It was a surprise to me.

4. What class of person was it who made these visits?—In some cases Sunday-school teachers, magistrates and business men, officials of the union.

5. People who carried a high moral tone, and would have readily discovered anything injurious to a child's mind?—Yes.

6. With regard to the films which were objectionable, have you yourself seen any of these?—I have seen over 250 in the last twelve months. I wish particularly to emphasise the sixth paragraph on page 310. All the probation officers should be asked to give their opinion. I had two before me recently who give quite a different opinion.

7. THE CHAIRMAN. You have come to the conclusion that the better-class films pay, and you instance those of Ponting and Besley. Don't you find an entirely different audience present at these films from that in the poorer theatres. Prices are higher than those in the other theatres. Can you expect the same kind of conditions?—At the Pavilion, Marble Arch, yes. The 75 per cent. of films seen represented visits by 200 people, say 20 in a big town, 18 in Sheffield and 20 in Liverpool.

THE CHAIRMAN remarked that indecency would probably grow less with better lighting.

APPENDIX I

CINEMATOGRAPH CENSORSHIP REGULATIONS IN OTHER COUNTRIES [1]

RÉPUBLIQUE FRANÇAISE

Le Ministre de L'Intérieur

Arrêté

Article 1.—Il est institué au Ministère de l'Intérieur une Commission qui est chargée de l'examen et du contrôle des films cinématographiques dont la représentation est projetée en France, et qui arrêtera la liste de ceux de ces films qui lui auront paru susceptibles d'être représentés.

Article 2.—Il sera délivré, pour chaque film admis, une carte spéciale qui devra être produits aux autorités compétentes avant toute représentation.

Article 3.—Sont nommés Membres de cette Commission—

M. Lemarquant, Chef de Bureau au Ministère de l'Intérieur ;

M. Labussiere, Chef de Bureau au Ministère de l'Intérieur ;

M. Esteve, Sous-Chef de Bureau au Ministère de l'Intérieur ;

M. Guichard (Xavier), Commissaire Divisionnaire à la Préfecture de Police ;

M. Isnard, Sous-Chef de Bureau à la Préfecture de Police.

Fait à Paris, le 16 juin 1916.
Le Ministre de l'Intérieur.
(*Signé*) Malvy.

Pour amplication :
Le Directeur de la Sureté Générale.
(*Signé*) Richard.

Pour copie conforme,
Le Directeur du Cabinet,

(*Signé*) Maunoury.

RÉPUBLIQUE FRANÇAISE

Paris, le 24 juin 1916.

Le Ministre de L'Intérieur

a MM. les Préfets

Par une circulaire en date du 19 avril 1913, l'un de mes prédécesseurs vous a recommandé de faire usage des pouvoirs que vous confèrent les articles 97 et 99 de la loi du 5 avril 1884 pour interdire, dans toute l'étendue de votre département, les représentations, par les cinématographes, des crimes, exécutions capitales et d'une façon générale de toutes scènes à caractère immoral et scandaleux.

---

[1] Owing to the numerous delays occasioned by the war, it has not been possible to include the returns from other countries.

313

Le Conseil d'État, saisi de plusieurs pourvois formés contre les arrêtés municipaux qui avaient règlementé les représentations cinématographiques ou interdit certaines catégories de films dangereux pour l'ordre public, a décide, le 3 avril 1914, que les cinématographes rentrent dans la catégorie des spectacles de curiosités et autres établissements de même genre régis par l'article 4, du titre XI, de la loi des 16–24 août 1790, l'article 3 du décret de la convention du 1ᵉʳ septembre 1793 et l'article 6 du décret du 6 janvier 1864; que par suite, ces spectacles sont soumis à l'autorisation des Maires, dont les pouvoirs, en cette matière ont été confirmés par les articles 91 et 97 de la loi du 5 avril 1884. En conséquence le Conseil d'État a déclaré que les Maires ont le droit de soumettre les représentations cinématographiques à la réglementation qu'ils jugent utile d'édicter en vue du maintien de l'ordre public, de décider qu'aucun film ne pourrait être reproduit publiquement sans être, au préalable, soumis à la censure de l'autorité municipale, et d'interdire les scènes qu'ils jugeraient susceptibles de provoquer le désordre ou dangereuses pour la moralité publique.

La Préfecture de Police a adopté comme règle de ne permettre la représentation publique d'un film qu'autant qu'il a obtenu son visa, consigné sur une fiche mentionnant le titre du film. Estimant qu'il convient d'étendre ce régime à toute la France, et, considérant qu'il est matériellement impossible aux autorités locales d'exercer le contrôle préventif, j'ai constituer une Commission chargée d'examiner les films dont la représentation est projetée. Pour tout film admis, il sera remis une carte signée par l'un des Membres de la Commission. Au point de vue strictement légal, cette carte ne peut constituer, par elle-même, une autorisation. Ce droit n'est réservé qu'aux autorités municipales en vertu des articles 91 et 97 de la loi du 5 avril 1884 ou a l'autorité préfectorale en vertu de l'article 99 de la dite loi. Mais elle est destinée à donner à ces diverses autorités une indication précise leur facilitant l'exercice de leurs droits.

En conséquences, je vous prie de prendre les dispositions nécessaires pour interdire, dans votre département, la représentation des films qui n'auront pas obtenu le visa de mon Administration, ou qui ne seront pas munis des cartes délivrées, jusqu'à ce jour par la Préfecture de Police.

Je vous recommande de porter ces dispositions à la connaissances des Maires, en leur signalant l'intérêt qui s'attache à ce qu'ils ne permettent que les films admis, à l'exclusion de tous autres. En outre, il y aura lieu de prévenir les exploitants de cinématographes que, dans le cas où ils représenteraient des films non visés ou substitueraient à un film admis un film non visé, l'autorisation qui leur a été accordée leur serait immédiatement retirée. Il vous appartient, en vertu de l'article 99, de vous substituer aux autorité municipales, si vous estimer que cette façon de procéder constitue une garantie nécessaire.

J'ajoute que les autorités préfectorales et municipales ont le droit d'interdire les films admis dans le cas où elles jugeraient, pour des considérations d'ordre local, que leur reproduction peut présenter des inconvénients.

Le Ministre de l'Intérieur,

Malvy.

RUSSIA

Instructions issued to Cinematograph Inspectors in Russia

1. *Court Chronicle.*—Films representing the sacred person of the Emperor or any of the imperial family are only permitted by special order from the Court Censorship.

2. *War Chronicle.*—Films showing military life and containing soldiers of any rank are only to be shown with the permission of the Military Censorship.

3. *Religion.*—(a) Any representation of Our Lord Jesus Christ, of the Holy Virgin or of the holy angels and apostles are forbidden. (b) The

image or sign of the holy Cross are forbidden. (c) The exteriors of churches of any sects and also statues of saints may be shown. (d) The interior of any church other than Orthodox may be shown. (e) Churchyards and cemeteries may be shown provided that there be no scene represented unfitting for such surroundings and that no actual dead body be shown; separate graves may be shown with the above reservation and also provided that they be closed; graves opened for burial or for judicial investigation may not be shown; graves on the field of battle may not be shown (by order of the Military Censorship). (f) The Holy Gospel, sacred banners and other church furniture may not be shown; icons, cross or crucifix in the corner of a room or on the wall may be shown provided that the surroundings be inoffensive to such sacred objects. (g) Religious processions other than Orthodox may be represented. (h) No form of Christian Church service may be shown, with the exception of marriage ceremonies other than Orthodox. *Note.*—Orthodox religious processions may be shown with the consent of the Religious Censorship if taken from *life*.

4. *Politics.*—It is forbidden to represent political gatherings or processions except such as depict scenes from the distant past of purely historical interest. Strikes and anything relating thereto may not be shown. Political murders or attempts at murder may not be shown except, again, when having merely a distant historical interest.

5. *Profanation.* — (a) All scenes depicting dead bodies are forbidden. (b) All scenes including coffins are forbidden. (c) Scenes of cremation as practised in ancient times as a rite and even at present in certain countries are forbidden. (d) Representation of persons mentally afflicted is forbidden save in the case of well-known characters from literature such as Ophelia, King Lear, etc.

6. *Science, medicine and medical jurisprudence.*—(a) No sort of operation may be shown without special authorisation; such permission can only be given for special demonstrations with a scientific object, the audience being limited to persons professionally interested. (b) Anatomical demonstrations showing the human body may be shown to professors and students only, a special permit being obtained on each occasion. (c) Autopsy or post-mortem examinations may be shown under the same conditions.

7. *Miscellaneous.*—(a) Murders may be shown. (b) Suicides may be shown except by hanging. (c) Tortures may not be shown. (d) Scenes of execution whether by hanging, shooting or by any other method are forbidden.

8. *Private life.*—(a) Scenes from the private life of persons now living may only be shown with their consent. (b) Scenes from the life of persons already dead may only be shown with the consent of their near relatives. (c) Scenes from the life of public men already dead—statesmen, writers, artists, etc.—may be shown provided that they are concerned only with their actual work.

9. *Pornography.*—(a) Scenes of love-making may be shown provided that there be no sign of licentiousness therein. (b) Scenes representing attempts at rape or seduction or anything of this nature are forbidden.

ITALY

(Kindly translated for the Commission by the Very Rev. Wm. Canon Barry, D.D.)

INSPECTION AND CENSORSHIP OF KINEMATIC FILMS

Ministry of the Interior (Home Office).

1 (a). Law of June 25, 1913, No. 785; (b) Law of May 31, 1914, No. 162.
2. Regulations of May 31, 1914, No. 352.

(The whole extract is from Official Bulletin of the Ministry of the Interior, July 21, 1914, No. 21.)

1 (*a*). The Law : Victor Emanuel III, King of Italy, etc.
Decrees as follows—

The Royal Government is hereby authorised to inspect and censor (*escritare la vigilanza*) the production in public of kinematic films, whether home-made or imported, and to lay on them a tax of ten centesimi for every metre of film.

The Minister of Finance is charged with the details of execution as regards the Home Office in this matter.

We ordain that the present decree should be sealed with the Great Seal, and published in the Official Record of Italian Laws, etc.

Given at San Rossore, June 25, 1913.

VICTOR EMANUEL,
GIOLITTI,
FACTA,
TEDESCO.

Seen by the Keeper of the Seals—
Finocchiaro,—Aprile.

1 (*b*). Victor Emanuel III, etc.—

Whereas the Law of June 25, 1913, No. 785, authorises, etc., as above; Now, therefore, we ordain and approve of the Regulation in question (set forth below), after it has been seen and approved by our Minister of the Interior, etc.

Rome, May 31, 1914.

VICTOR EMANUEL,
SALANDRA.

The Keeper of the Seals—
Dari.

The Regulation follows in twenty articles—

1. The purpose of inspection and censorship of these films is to hinder the exhibition in public—

    (*a*) Of pictures offending against morals, good manners, public decency, and private persons.

    (*b*) Of spectacles injurious to the national fame and self-respect, or against the public order, or likely to trouble our good relations with foreign Powers.

    (*c*) Of such as would lessen the name and fame of public institutions and authorities, or of the officers and agents of the law (*forza pubblica*).

    (*d*) Of scenes of violence, horror, and cruelty, even where animals are concerned, or of crimes and suicides realistically given; and, in general, of scenes representing perverse actions or facts which would be lessons or incentives of crime, or be calculated to unsettle the mind and provoke to evil.

2. No film shall be shown in public except with permit (*nulla osta*) or licence from the Minister of the Interior, after previous inspection of the whole picture to be produced.

In case of several copies, one only need be inspected; but the rest must have nothing different in them from that submitted.

3. Request of licence must be made to Minister of Interior (Kinematograph Department), accompanied by the film, in two copies, one with stamp of lire 1.20, on form set out in Appendix (here omitted).

The stamp shall be cancelled, etc. (mere formalities).

Request to be in name and on behalf of the makers or importers by their lawful representative.

Foreign firms (companies) must have a domicile in Italy or a responsible agent.

The two copies of request must be in identical terms, giving—

(a) Name and address of company, likewise of its legal representative.
(b) Title, trade-mark, length in metres of film.
(c) Particular description of subject, divided into pictures, with title, sub-title, and reading matter, in order of exhibition without the least alteration.

Titles, sub-titles, reading matter on the film, and on the requests for licence, must be written correctly in Italian.

Or if in a foreign language must be accompanied by good Italian version.

4. Regulations touching payment of tax, and receipt for same.

5. Inspection and censorship shall be in order of priority of requests, unless where the subject is of urgent present importance. If of great urgency, the minister may delegate his powers to the prefects of provinces, who can extend the licence to the whole kingdom.

Fiscal rules to be observed.

The prefect shall acquaint the minister with what has been done, sending at the same time the unstamped copy of request.

6. Inspection is entrusted to the first-grade officers of Pubblica Sicurezza (Police Department) or to commissaries of the same.

Where the prefect is delegated as above, the theatrical censor may act as censor of films.

The persons interested are not allowed to be present at the official inspection.

7. The censor shall state in writing, on the unstamped petition, whether licence may be given, or any portions of the film are to be prohibited, or any titles, sub-titles, or reading matter.

The minister will grant the licence conformably to the censor's report.

In case of refusal, complete or in part, the decision with its grounds, shall be exhibited to the party interested, who by way of acknowledgment shall subscribe his name and the date on the unstamped petition.

Duplicates of the licence may be obtained on a scale set forth.

8. The party interested, in case of refusal, may appeal within thirty days from the date of information received as above, and demand a fresh inspection.

Except when such party renounces his right of appeal in writing, the film will not be given back to him until the appeal has been decided, or the thirty days are over.

Regulation concerning the tax paid.

9. In case of appeal, the new inspectors shall comprise the vice-director of the Pubblica Sicurezza, and two heads of division belonging to the same.

Should the vice-director be unable to attend, the senior head of division shall take his place. Details of State payment to officials (omitted).

The inspector of first instance shall not take part in the second examination and decision.

The parties interested shall not be present during the inspection.

10. Should the minister have solid reasons for holding that the censor's judgment contravenes any portion of Article 1, he may require the person who has charge of the film to submit it to a Commission formed as in Article 9; and on their report he will decide accordingly.

11. Before a manufactory of films can be set up, notice must be given to the prefect of the province, who will report to the Minister of the Interior.

The same rule applies to importers of films which in whole or part are intended for public exhibition.

The prefect shall return acknowledgment of notice given to the parties giving it.

All makers and importers of films must keep a dated register of the respective films, and note the licences granted in it.

The police may at all times inspect these registers.

12. The company which proposes to exhibit films in localities open to the public must give written notice to the local authorities.

13. The films thus exhibited must be exactly such as have been licensed, and in the conditions required.

The licence must be open to inspection at request of the local authorities and the police.

Before giving leave for advertisement of such exhibitions (Article 65 of Law on Public Security) the local authorities should be satisfied that these bills and notices do not contravene Article 1 of the present Regulation.

14. Under exceptional circumstances, the local prefect may delay the exhibition of films, reporting his action to the Home Office.

15. The possessor of the film must be careful not in any way to change the title, sub-titles, reading matter, nor to change the scenes and pictures, to add nothing, and to leave the sequence unchanged, except by leave of the Home Office.

These points are to be noted down in the licence.

If such directions be violated in any way whatever, the licence shall be considered null and void, and the Penal Code may be invoked according to circumstances.

16. When a non-licensed film has been produced, or another substituted for the one allowed, or unpermitted changes have been made as in preceding Article, or Article 13 has not been observed, the police have power to suspend or revoke the licence.   See Articles 37 or 39 of the Police Laws.

17. The tax on kinematic representations.

18. Regulations concerning purchase of machinery for such.

19, 20. Provisional arrangements until this Regulation.comes into force.

The Minister of the Interior,

SALANDRA.

SPAIN

Madrid, March 9, 1917.

NOTE VERBALE

In reply to the Note of H.B.M. Embassy, dated February 7, 1917, the Ministry of State has the honour to give hereunder a copy of the provisions existing in Spain with regard to the Censorship of Cinematographs, which particulars may interest the " National Council of Public Morals."

" The extraordinary development experienced by the display of cinematograph films in the public halls over all the world has caused educational scientists and hygienists to inquire into the considerable influence which these pictures may have on the public and especially the young public, which is so impressionable and predisposed to imitate the criminal and immoral acts which the greed of gain prompts certain film manufacturers to reproduce by means of photography, thus contributing, no doubt, unwittingly to the rise of grave social and private dangers.

" In different European countries these motives have been invoked for the adoption of a vigilant censorship and stern measures of repression, since it was in many cases established that criminal acts had been committed by children and youths under the suggestion of police scenes and terroristic displays which invariably produce psychic disturbances; it was considered also indispensable to repress all immoral or pernicious tendency due to pictures that generally enjoy preference in display, as well as to foment the educative and instructive influence which the cinematograph is able to exert on the crowd.   The private display of pornographic films has always been the subject of prosecution before the court.

" In Spain, various scientific bodies, such as the " Sociedad española de Higiene," and recently the " Sociodad Pediatrica española," have pointed out the above-mentioned dangers, and the latter association has formulated a strong protest based on facts established clinically, the newspaper press, having co-operated in these campaigns with a rare unanimity and dropping all difference of opinion, has united to demand the immediate intervention of the public authorities so as to avoid such grave evils.

" The Supreme Council for the Protection of Childhood and the Repression of Mendicity, which is always ready to comply with the definite injunctions of the provisions in force, placing the physical and moral welfare of children in its safe keeping and in that of the Protection Committees all over Spain, keeping careful watch so as to protect them from disease, cruelty, perversion and demoralisation, view the present case in the light of a great mission to be fulfilled for which it is urgently necessary to adopt measures of an administrative nature and also to stimulate the zeal of the authorities, of theatrical undertakings, parents, guardians and all who are charged with the care of children, and to apply the laws issued for the protection of childhood rigorously, paying special attention, as said above, to whatever may favour and advance the physical and moral welfare of minors under ten years of age.

" In these moments when congresses and scientific meetings are being held for the purpose of organising the combating of all avoidable disease, thus demonstrating in practice the need of spreading hygiene and its manifold redeeming influence in all directions, the opportunity would seem a favourable one for all of us to try and co-operate in this good work, and prevent children from frequenting alone displays like the cinematograph, where a numerous public is gathered in the dark, breathing vitiated air and, what is more lamentable, having daily reflected before them the image of lust, passion or crime, a spectacle that may exert lifelong deplorable consequences of a moral and pathological nature on the delicate organism of the child.

" These displays should be, as they were in their beginning, an element of culture and honest recreation, showing the real scenes of natural life, the marvels of geography, great scientific or industrial undertakings, pictures of normal and sane life, views of charitable and educational institutions, and whatever scenes of an historical and moralising nature may stimulate to good actions, and which exalt the love of country and of home and extol the heroism of sacrifice for the welfare of humanity, instead of giving the appearance of reality to fantastic, tragic, comic, terrifying or disturbing scenes.

" In virtue of the above, I call on Your Excellency as *ex-officio* President of the Provincial Society for the Protection of Childhood and Repression of Mendicity, to exert strict vigilance over all public displays which may contribute to the growth of the above-mentioned evils, and to repress same with the greatest energy.

" In view of the Law of August 12, 1904, and Articles 4 and 39 of the Royal Decree of January 24, 1908—

" His Majesty the King—whom God save—has seen fit to order—

" 1. That the titles and subject-matter of all films offered to the public by any theatrical undertaking should be submitted to the Civil Government offices and municipal secretaries in due time before they are to be shown for verification as to whether they are free of all pernicious tendencies. If it is thought advisable, the assistance of a special commission may be made use of, which is to be appointed by the Committee for the Protection of Childhood, for the purpose of making a suitable selection. If it should become known that pornographic films have been shown privately, they shall hand over the offenders to the Courts of Justice.

" 2. Any infringement of what is laid down in the preceding article shall be punished by the competent authorities with a fine ranging from fifty to two hundred and fifty pesetas, besides any further liabilities that may arise in this connection.

" 3. It shall be absolutely forbidden for children under ten years of age who are unaccompanied to enter any closed hall where cinematograph or so-called variety shows are given, during the night performances, and the responsibility for this shall lie with the parents, guardians, or others entrusted with or legally under the obligation of watching over the children.

" 4. Cinematograph displays, but only these, may, however, be given specially for children in the daytime, at which films of an instructive or educational character, such as scenes of travel, or from history, shall be shown.

" 5. The subordinate officers under Your Excellency and unpaid assistants of the Supreme Council for the Protection of Childhood and Repression of Mendicity who will be nominated for this purpose, will watch over the due observance of the preceding provisions, notifying any case of non-fulfilment of same to the Civil Government offices and municipalities of the locality where this class of shows are held, the unpaid assistants belonging to Madrid having the faculty of officially informing the Secretariate of the Supreme Council.

" 6. Within a term of fifteen days, which shall in no case be exceeded, Your Excellency shall communicate to the theatrical companies of this capital and to the mayors of the province, the contents of this royal order, with the object of ensuring the due fulfilment of what is laid down herein.

" The Civil Governors shall order the text of this royal order to be published in the official bulletins, for the better compliance with the instructions issued herein.

" By Royal Order, etc.

" Madrid, November 12, 1912.

" (*Gazette of Madrid* of the 28th November, 1912)."

NEW ZEALAND

1916, No. 10

An Act to provide for the Censoring of Cinematograph films.

August 7, 1916.

Be it Enacted by the General Assembly of New Zealand in Parliament assembled, and by the authority of the same, as follows—

1. This Act may be cited as the Cinematograph Film Censorship Act, 1916.

2. On and after the first day of October, nineteen hundred and sixteen, it shall not be lawful to exhibit any cinematograph film unless it has been approved in the manner hereinafter provided.

3. (1) There shall be appointed from time to time by the Governor such fit persons as the Governor deems necessary as censors of cinematograph films, who shall hold office during the Governor's pleasure.

(2) The provisions of the Public Service Act, 1912, shall not apply to the persons so appointed.

4. (1) It shall be the duty of every person so appointed to examine every cinematograph film submitted to him for approval.

(2) Such approval shall be signified by a certificate in the prescribed form.

(3) Such approval shall not be given in the case of any film which, in the opinion of the censor, depicts any matter that is against public order and decency, or the exhibition of which for any other reason is, in the opinion of the censor, undesirable in the public interest.

(4) Such approval may be given generally, or may be given subject to a condition that the film shall be exhibited only to any specified class or classes of persons.

(5) There shall be a right of appeal from every decision of a censor under

this Act to such person or persons, and in such manner and subject to such conditions, as may be prescribed by regulations under this Act.

5. A film to which any matter has been added after it has been approved by a censor shall be again submitted for approval, and until it has been again approved shall be deemed not to have been approved.

6. There shall be payable for every film submitted for approval under this Act such fees as are prescribed.

7. (1) Every person who exhibits any film in contravention of this Act is liable to a fine not exceeding fifty pounds, and the film may be ordered by the convicting Court to be forfeited to the Crown.

(2) Any film so forfeited shall be dealt with in such manner as the Minister of Internal Affairs directs.

8. The Governor may from time to time, by Order in Council, make such regulations as he deems necessary for giving effect to this Act.

Regulations under the Cinematograph Film Censorship Act, 1916.

LIVERPOOL, GOVERNOR

ORDER IN COUNCIL

At the Government House at Wellington, this eleventh day of September, 1916.

Present :

HIS EXCELLENCY THE GOVERNOR IN COUNCIL

In pursuance and exercise of the powers conferred on him by the Cinematograph Film Censorship Act, 1916 (hereinafter referred to as "the said Act"), His Excellency the Governor of the Dominion of New Zealand, acting by and with the advice and consent of the Executive Council of the said Dominion, doth hereby make the following regulations for the purposes of the said Act.

REGULATIONS

INTERPRETATION

1. In these regulations—

"Censor" means the Censor of Cinematograph Films appointed pursuant to the said Act.

"Film" means a cinematograph film intended for exhibition.

SUBMISSION OF FILMS TO CENSOR

2. (1) All films shall be submitted for approval to the Censor at his office at Wellington.

(2) Films so submitted may be delivered at the said office, or may be posted by registered letter addressed to the Censor at that office.

3. (1) Application for the approval by the Censor of any film shall be in the form No. 1 in the first schedule hereto, and shall be accompanied by the prescribed examination fee.

(2) If the applicant requires the film to be examined by the Censor and returned within forty-eight hours of the time when the film is submitted to the Censor for examination, there shall be charged, in addition to the ordinary examination fee, a special fee equal to the examination fee—

Provided that the Censor may, in his absolute discretion, and notwithstanding that the applicant may have paid the additional fee required by this regulation, decline to examine any film before the expiration of a period of at least forty-eight hours after the same has been submitted to him for approval, but in any such case the amount of any such additional fee shall be refunded to the applicant.

Y

(3) Where films submitted for approval are required to be returned to the applicant by post the amount of postage (including the registration fee) must be prepaid by the applicant.

EXAMINATION OF FILMS BY CENSOR

4. (1) As soon as practicable after submission to the Censor of any film, and the payment of the prescribed fee, the Censor shall examine the same, and shall either—

(a) Approve the film and issue his certificate of approval in respect thereof; or

(b) Approve the film subject to a condition that it may be exhibited only to a specified class or to specified classes of persons; or

(c) Refuse his approval of the film either absolutely or until such alterations as he directs have been made therein. On being satisfied that the required alterations have been made in any film, the Censor shall issue his certificate of approval in respect thereof.

(2) When the Censor has refused to approve any film until certain alterations directed by him have been made therein, and such film is again submitted for his approval, the examination fee payable on the resubmission of the film shall be charged, at the rate prescribed in the second schedule hereto, only in respect of so much of the film as the Censor requires to examine to satisfy himself that his directions as to the alteration of the film have been carried out.

5. (1) The approval by the Censor of any film shall be signified by a certificate in the form No. 2 in the first schedule hereto.

(2) The refusal of the Censor to approve any film submitted for his approval shall be forthwith communicated to the applicant or his agent, in the form No. 3 in the first schedule hereto.

APPEALS FROM DECISIONS OF CENSOR

6. (1) If any applicant for the approval of a film is dissatisfied with the decision of the Censor with respect thereto, he may, within fourteen days from the notification to him of the decision of the Censor, appeal therefrom to a Board of Appeal consisting of three persons to be from time to time appointed by the Minister of Internal Affairs, one of whom shall be appointed by the said minister as chairman.

(2) Every such appeal shall be instituted by delivering or posting to the Under-Secretary of the Department of Internal Affairs, at his office at the Government Buildings, Wellington, a notice of appeal in the form No. 4 in the first schedule hereto.

(3) Every such notice of appeal shall be accompanied by the prescribed fee, and the film in respect of which the appeal is lodged shall be delivered either to the Under-Secretary aforesaid or to the Censor.

(4) Forthwith on the receipt by him of a notice of appeal under this regulation, the Under-Secretary of the Department of Internal Affairs shall cause the same to be transmitted to the Chairman of the Board of Appeal, and the Board of Appeal shall, as soon as practicable thereafter, determine the appeal.

(5) Notice of the appeal shall be forthwith given to the Censor by the Under-Secretary aforesaid.

7. The decision of not less than two members of the Board of Appeal shall constitute the decision of the Board, and the decision of the Board on any matters submitted to it under these regulations shall be final. In any case where the refusal of the Censor to approve a film is not upheld by the Board, the Censor shall forthwith give his certificate in accordance with the decision of the Board.

8. If the decision of the Censor is reversed with respect to any film, or is substantially modified by the Board, the fee payable by the applicant on appeal shall be refunded to the applicant.

9. The fees specified in the second schedule hereto shall be charged in respect of the matters therein mentioned, and shall be forthwith paid by the persons receiving the same into the public account.

10. (1) Every person who, on the 14th day of September, 1916, is the owner or has control of any films intended for exhibition (whether on circuit or not) shall, within seven days from the said date, forward to the Censor a list of all such films, setting forth with respect to each film—

(a) The title of the film;
(b) The name of the manufacturer; and
(c) The length of the film (in feet).

(2) Every person who, after the said 14th day of September, 1916, imports into New Zealand any films intended for exhibition shall, within twenty-four hours after receiving the same, forward to the Censor a list of all such films, setting forth with respect to each film—

(a) The title of the film;
(b) The name of the manufacturer;
(c) The length of the film (in feet); and
(d) The date of importation.

(3) Every person who, after the 14th day of September aforesaid, makes in New Zealand any film intended for exhibition shall forthwith give notice thereof to the Censor.

11. The Censor, having regard to the time required for the examination of films and to the accommodation available for the storage of films awaiting examination, may from day to day determine the quantity of film to be received by him for examination, and may decline to receive more than such quantity in any day.

12. After the 1st day of October, 1916, a copy of the certificate of the Censor given in respect of any film shall be attached to the film so as to form part thereof, and shall be screened therewith.

13. Where, on the request of the owner of any film, a photographic reproduction of the certificate of the Censor is supplied for attachment to that film, the fee prescribed in the second schedule hereto for such reproduction shall be paid by the owner of the film.

NEW YORK

THE NATIONAL BOARD OF REVIEW: ITS ORGANISATION AND SERVICE

The National Board of Review of Motion Pictures is an organisation of 225 volunteer workers with main offices at 70 Fifth Avenue, New York. Originally local, it began in April 1909 to review the national product of the film manufacturers. Since October 1909 it has reviewed virtually all the motion pictures issued in this country. The Board operates through agreements with the manufacturers under which all pictures are submitted before they are placed on the market, and any change that is suggested in a given picture is carried out not only in New York city, but for the whole United States.

The General Committee, which is the governing body of the National Board, is composed of persons of culture, judgment, and discretion, most of whom are connected in important positions with civic associations, child welfare organisations, and other movements. The General Committee selects members for the Review Committee. These also are men and women whose training and standing fits them for the difficult task which they voluntarily undertake.

No member of the general or the review committees is connected financially or in any other respect with the motion picture industry.

The large Review Committee is divided into thirty sections, each of which has one meeting a week. These sections see each film as many times as may be necessary. Their judgment is based on the published standards of the Board. It is recognised, however, that the standards are progressive and not fixed. Change and progress occur, as the Board from experience ascertains through its national correspondence what public opinion is on various types of pictures.

Not only are standards established with reference to films which are so often publicly censured, such as the social evil drama, but many other important aspects of plays are scrutinised carefully. Vulgarity (immorality or impropriety of conduct), prolonged and passionate love scenes, insufficient clothing, unnecessary and detailed showing of opium joints or dance halls, improper dancing, unnecessary brutality to man and beast, and detailed exposition of crime are all carefully eliminated. The Board, for example, insists on the punishment of the criminal when his crime might be considered by the young and impressionable spectator as an excusable act. The standards, which amount to a detailed code of film ethics, are well understood by committee members who subordinate their own views to them. Thus undue individualism is avoided.

Upon conclusion of the review the members of the committee informally discuss the picture and then cast individual ballots which disclose their opinions. Should there be any uncertainty with reference to the picture, it is referred to another review committee or to the general committee, which acts as a Court of Appeals.

The committees are concerned principally with eliminations or cuts in the films. After the review of pictures the Board notifies the manufacturers of the changes which are to be made. During the year 1915, 9670 reels were viewed. Changes in scenes to the number of 1116 were made, 59 entire pictures were condemned or returned for revision, 58,740 feet of film were eliminated from sample copies and the total cost of manufacturing of negatives, sample copies and sales copies kept off the American market was $258,368.30.

A record of the transactions of the Board is made in a weekly bulletin which gives the names of all pictures passed, together with notation of eliminations and names of pictures rejected. This bulletin goes to a mailing list of over three hundred city officials, such as mayors, license departments, Boards of Public Welfare, as well as many social agencies scattered throughout the United States. City officials, guided by the bulletin, enforce the decisions of the Board in their communities.

So effective is the work of the Board that any manufacturer who might be so inclined would find it impossible to profitably market or exhibit films condemned by the Board.

In addition to the important review duties of the Board, it carries on progressive and constructive educational work. The Board offers suggestions to manufacturers and uses its influence with them in an effort to make the film output of real social value. From time to time it issues special bulletins to the manufacturers, discussing various items which should be borne in mind in directing pictures, and noting situations to be avoided. It carries on active work to develop a demand for special programmes for children; to increase the manufacture of films for children; and to further the now rapid growth of special performances for them. Extensive lists of the best children's books have been furnished to film manufacturers, as suggestions for scenarios. The co-operation of civic societies, women's clubs and public-spirited individuals is sought in this most important department of the Board's work. High principles have been established to govern the selection of children's pictures. The Board has lists of these films for public distribution. Similarly, a list suitable for family groups is compiled monthly, and mailed to all interested in the " Better Films Movement."

Unofficial volunteer review of films, bringing to bear upon manufacturers through well-organised and authoritative channels the force of representative public opinion is the best possible public protection. It carries with it none of the dangers to freedom of speech—dangers of political domination—dangers of class oppression which are inherent and have been for all time a prominent feature of legalised censorship. In its form of organisation, in the character of its membership, in the democracy of its method, the National Board is representative of American ideals and actually represents American public opinion in its judgments. *Public* opinion may be, and usually is, diametrically opposed to the judgment of many individuals—often of considerable groups of individuals. A desire to mould public opinion—to dictate standards of public morals—usually actuates the relatively small groups who would place the yoke of censorship upon the State and the Press. Pre-publicity, legalised censorship, is oppressive, confiscatory and fundamentally un-American.

The Christian Science *Monitor* for July 7, 1915, said : " It was most fortunate that in the first days of photoplay and motion-picture development in the United States a form of censorship on a national scale was worked out. While private and non-governmental in form, nevertheless it has continued to be effective because of the good sense of the persons who make up the Board, and the equal wisdom and public spirit of the leading promoters of the business, now so vast in its proportion. Precedent and rule was early defined, while conditions were still malleable; and the moral gain for the people has been incalculable, nor should it be overlooked or forgotten that because of this understanding between producers of films and defenders of social standards there has been much less recourse to restrictive State law and municipal ordinance than otherwise would have been necessary."

The Board invites correspondence concerning its work, gladly sends its literature, and is in a position to act as a clearing-house of information concerning motion pictures, or to help by advice in any local difficulty.

NATIONAL BOARD OF REVIEW,
70 Fifth Avenue, New York.

THE NATIONAL COMMITTEE ON FILMS FOR YOUNG PEOPLE
By-Laws

NAME

The name shall be The National Committee on Films for Young People.

POLICY

First.—To further the discovery, production, selection, distribution and use of selected motion pictures and programmes for young people, adding as occasion demands the furthering of the use of better films for the family group in the theatres of the country.

Second.—To discover and formulate the principles governing such selection of motion pictures for use by the National Board of Review and other agencies.

Third.—To act as a clearing-house of facts, information and methods to and from the centres of the country, including the producers, exchanges, exhibitors, committees and individuals.

Fourth.—To develop and to further co-operation with existing and future groups dealing with various phases, both of the production and the use of selected motion pictures for young people.

ORGANISATION

There shall be an executive committee of eleven persons drawn from the vicinity of New York from among those volunteers who have intimate knowledge of and interest in both the welfare of society and motion pictures. Six of these shall be members of the general committee of the National Board of Review. The chairman of the National Board of Review shall be *ex-officio* a member of the National Committee.

Special committees may be formed as necessary to deal with distinct phases of the work.

A secretary shall be assigned by the National Board of Review to work with and for the National Committee on Films for Young People in carrying out approved policies and methods.

The office shall be in the office of the National Board of Review.

RELATION TO THE NATIONAL BOARD OF REVIEW

The National Committee shall be closely associated with the National Board of Review by sympathy, by membership on the National Committee, by endorsement of policies and methods, and by the use of the films selected by the appropriate committees of the National Board. After such endorsement of policy by the National Board the National Committee shall maintain independence in the conduct of the work.

METHODS

First.—The acceptance of the judgments of the members of the review committees of the National Board of Review in the selection of films from all those reviewed for general circulation.

Second.—The discussion of inter-relating problems and new ones which may arise with the appropriate committees of the National Board.

Third.—Regular formulation and circulation of selected lists of pictures for use in the communities of the country.

Fourth.—The circulation of publicity to present ideas and methods to those interested and able to advance the work. This will include correspondence, printed matter, articles in newspapers and periodicals, conferences, addresses, etc.

Fifth.—The encouragement of the assumption of local responsibility in working out experiments in local situations.

Sixth.—The development of knowledge and the interchange of information through affiliated organisations, committees and individuals.

Seventh.—This committee shall encourage others to give performances and offer every possible assistance for successful motion-picture entertainments in the cities of the United States.

Adopted June 21, 1916.

NORWAY

Enclosure in Sir M. Findlay's, No. 50, dated May 4, 1917

TRANSLATION OF NOTE FROM THE NORWEGIAN MINISTRY OF FOREIGN AFFAIRS TO H.M. LEGATION, OF APRIL 24, 1917

With reference to H.B.M. Legation's Note Verbale of February 8, 1917, on the subject of the control of cinematographic films in Norway, the Department for Foreign Affairs has the honour to transmit herewith—

(1) A copy of the *Law Gazette*, Part II, for 1913, containing—p. 292— Law No. 4 of the 25th July, 1913, relating to the public exhibition of cinematograph pictures and—p. 347—the Royal Resolution of 12th September, 1913, in which, among other things, the rules for the control of cinema films are laid down.

(2) A copy of Bill in the Lower House of Parliament, No. 26, for 1913, forming the basis of the aforesaid law.

(3) A copy of circular letter from Ministry of Justice of 30th December, 1913.

The Ministry of Foreign Affairs would call attention to the fact that, during the debate on the Bill in the Storting, powers to grant licence for the running of cinematograph exhibitions were transferred from the police to the municipal authorities. In this way an opportunity is afforded to municipalities to take over themselves the running of such exhibitions, and it would appear likely in view of recent developments that this opportunity would be taken advantage of to a considerable extent. It will be obvious that this circumstance will also exercise an influence on the choice of films.

Translation.

SWEDEN

Royal Decree of June 22, 1911, relating to Cinematograph Exhibitions

We, Gustaf, etc., make known that, after having consulted the opinion of the Riksdag with regard to a proposal brought forward by Us for a decree relating to cinematograph exhibitions, We have found good to decree as follows—

Article 1

Any person who wishes to exhibit in public moving photographic pictures, or so-called cinematograph pictures, shall make application to that effect, in towns to the proper Police Authorities, and in rural districts to the district bailiff (*kronofogde*), or where the Provincial Governor has so prescribed, to the *lansman* (sheriff's officer); and it shall be incumbent on the applicant, at the demand of the Police Authorities, to show evidence that the stated premises have been let by the owner, or holder, for the purpose, and also to furnish the Police Authorities with the information they demand as to the exact nature of the exhibition, in order that they may issue the necessary regulations.

Where there is no objection to the grant of the licence applied for, the Police Authorities shall issue the licence. Before such licence has been obtained, admission tickets must not be issued, nor admission fees be demanded or received.

Article 2

If it appears that an exhibition as above referred to, is intended to convey, or involves, anything contrary to morality or law, or conduces to serious disturbance of the public peace, or that the regulations issued by the police with regard to the exhibition are not obeyed, the Police Authorities shall prohibit its renewal. In the cases just mentioned, as well as when the exhibition takes place without proper licence, or contrary to the terms of a licence issued, or if among the audience a disturbance of a serious nature arises, which cannot be suppressed by the removal of the persons who have taken part in it, the performance may be suspended or stopped by the Police Authorities; and all those who have assembled on the premises shall be obliged, at the order of the said Authorities, to leave the premises, on penalty of a fine of not less than five kronor and not exceeding one hundred kronor for each person who does not comply with such order.

Article 3

Children under the age of fifteen may not be given admission to a cinematograph exhibition, where display takes place of other pictures than those which, in the manner hereinafter stated, have been approved for exhibition also to children, nor, where the child is not accompanied by a parent or guardian, to such exhibition which terminates later than 8 p.m.

It shall be signified by clearly displayed notices whether children have admittance to a cinematograph exhibition or not.

Article 4

In exhibitions referred to in Article 1, pictures may not be displayed unless they have previously been examined and approved in the manner hereinafter stated.

This does not apply with regard to pictures which faithfully depict events which have recently occurred and are exhibited during a period of not more than ten days after the events depicted have taken place; nevertheless such pictures also must not be exhibited before they have been approved by the Police Authorities.

Article 5

The examination of cinematograph pictures referred to in the first paragraph of Article 4 shall be conducted for the whole of Sweden at a place determined by the Crown, by one or more censors appointed by the Crown.

The applicant shall pay a fee in accordance with a special tariff. This tariff will be determined by the Crown, which will also issue detailed regulations in other respects with regard to the duties of the censors.

(The text of Articles 5 and 7 is as amended by a Royal Decree of May 9, 1913.)

Article 6

A censor may not approve cinematograph pictures the exhibition of which would be contrary to law or morality, or might otherwise have a demoralising or excitative effect, or be subversive of morality. Pictures representing scenes of terror, suicide, or crimes in such a manner, or in such a context, that such effect may be produced, may thus not be approved.

Nor, with regard to displays to which children under the age of fifteen have admission, may pictures be approved which are calculated to rouse the imagination of children in an injurious manner, or otherwise have a detrimental effect on their mental development or health.

A censor may not refuse to approve pictures of another nature than that above stated.

If a censor finds that a film cannot be approved, unless a certain, minor, portion thereof is excluded, the remainder of the film may be approved, if the applicant so demands.

(The last paragraph of Article 6 was added by the amending Decree.)

Article 7

A film which has been approved on examination shall, in evidence thereof, have impressed on it a stamp, provided with a registration number, besides which the Censor shall issue a certificate of approval containing—

(1) The name of the firm from which the film has proceeded (the manufacturers).

(2) Short description of the pictures with heading and sub-headings, if such are appended to the film, and, if a certain portion of the film has been excluded, a separate description of the excluded portion.

(3) Length of the film, and if some portion of the film has been excluded by the Censor, the length of the film after the exclusion, and—

(4) The registration number on the stamp.

In the stamp and the certificate it shall likewise be stated whether the series of pictures has been approved, or not, for display at an exhibition to which children under the age of fifteen have admittance.

The said certificate shall be shown to the Police Authorities on demand.

If a portion of the film has been excluded, the said portion shall be retained by the Censor, and may only be delivered against the return of the certificate and the above-mentioned stamp. Nevertheless such delivery may not be demanded after two years have elapsed from the issue of the certificate.

(The last paragraph of Article 7 was added by the amending Decree.)

Article 8

Any person who gives an exhibition as referred to in Article 1, without a licence, or contrary to the regulations contained in the licence, or who does not comply with the regulations issued by the Police Authorities, with regard to the exhibition, or who lets premises for an exhibition which is given without licence, shall be liable to a fine of not less than ten kronor and not exceeding five hundred kronor.

Any person who infringes the provisions of Articles 3 and 4 shall be liable to the same penalties.

Article 9

A person who during the time when he is being prosecuted for an offence referred to in Article 8 renews the same offence, shall be liable to penalties under the said Article, each time a summons has been issued and served.

Article 10

Offences referred to in Article 8 shall be prosecuted by the Public Prosecutor, in towns before a police court, if such exists, but otherwise before a police officer, and where such does not exist, at a court of justice, and in rural districts, at a court of justice; with regard to appeal from the decision of a court or police office, in these causes, the general regulations with regard to appeal in criminal cases shall apply.

Article 11

Fines sentenced under this Decree shall go half to the Crown and half to the prosecutor. If there is a special informant, he shall receive half the prosecutor's share.

If a fine cannot be paid in full, it shall be commuted in accordance with the provisions of the Penal Code.

Article 12

Appeal from the decision of the Censor may be made to the Crown in the proper Government office, in accordance with the general regulations with regard to causes affecting " economic " questions.

Article 13

The provisions of this Decree do not apply to exhibitions of cinematograph pictures in connection with lectures held at an educational establishment, nor to other cases where the Crown, on application, grants exemption from the application of the Decree.

This Decree enters into force on December 1, 1911.

This, etc.

The Palace, Stockholm, June 22, 1911.

GUSTAF.

HUGO HAMILTON, Ministry of the Interior.

ROYAL REGULATIONS OF JUNE 22, 1911, RELATING TO THE CENSORSHIP OF CINEMATOGRAPH FILMS

Article 1

The censorship of cinematograph pictures referred to in the Decree relating to Cinematograph Exhibitions shall be conducted in Stockholm.

Three persons shall be appointed by the Crown as Censors, namely, two Censors in ordinary and one Assistant Censor.

The appointment is subject to recall at any time.

Article 2

Any person who applies for the examination of cinematograph pictures shall make a written application to that effect to the Office of the Censor (Statens Biografoyran), containing, as regards each separate film—

(1) The name of the firm of manufacturers, together with the manufacturer's number, where such exists.

(2) The title of the film in Swedish, together with a short description of the pictures with heading and sub-headings, if such are appended to the film.

(3) The length of the film.

Article 3

The examination shall take place in the order which the Censor may determine; nevertheless, where this may suitably be done, it should be seen to that pictures which faithfully depict events which have recently occurred shall be given priority, that several copies of the same series of pictures shall be examined consecutively, and that otherwise the order in which the applications have been received shall be followed in the examination.

Article 4

The examination shall be conducted as a general rule by one of the Censors in Ordinary. If the latter considers this necessary, he shall be entitled to summon the Assistant Censor; and if these two are not in agreement, the third Censor shall be summoned. Decision shall afterwards be taken by vote. In other respects the Censors shall be entitled to distribute the work of Censorship among themselves as they think fit.

No other persons shall be present at the examination than those whom the officiating Censor may determine.

Article 5

After the examination has been terminated, the Censor, if the film has been entirely or partially approved, shall furnish it with a stamp, as enacted in the Stamp Ordinance, and issue such a certificate as is referred to in the Decree relating to Cinematograph Exhibitions, and if the film has been rejected in its entirety, make a written communication to the applicant to that effect.

Article 6

Whether the film is passed or not, fees shall be paid for the examination in accordance with the following Tariff—

(a) For each copy of an examined series of pictures, with the exceptions stated below, one krona plus fifty öre for each fifty metres by which the length of the films exceeds 100 metres;

(b) for series of pictures which are manifestly not taken from life, as well as for series of pictures which require more than one examination before a decision is taken, double the amount of the fees stated in point (a).

In the examination of several copies of the same series of pictures, the Censor's fee shall be reduced to half the amount stated in points (a) and (b), for each copy, if the examination can take place consecutively, and if this is not possible, for each copy except that first examined. Nevertheless, as regards a series of pictures which faithfully depicts events which have recently occurred, the fee shall be paid only for the first five copies.

Article 7

The Censor shall be entitled to demand that a person who applies for the examination of a film shall pay in advance a fee to the amount which the Censor may determine with the guidance of the statements in the application. Otherwise the fee shall be paid after examination.

These regulations enter into force on December 1, 1911; nevertheless, applications for examination may take place from September 1, 1911. As regards old films which the Censor finds to be considerably reduced in value owing to wear and tear, and which are submitted for examination before December 1, 1911, the Censor shall be entitled to reduce the fee to half of the amount stated in points (*a*) and (*b*).

This, etc.

The Palace, Stockholm, June 22, 1911.

GUSTAF.

HUGO HAMILTON, Ministry of the Interior.

NEW SOUTH WALES

Prohibition of Objectionable Cinematograph Pictures

No objectionable cinematograph pictures shall be exhibited in any licensed theatre, public hall, or temporary structure, including any pictures representing—

(i) Scenes suggestive of immorality or indecency.

(ii) Executions, murders, or other revolting scenes.

(iii) Scenes of debauchery, low habits of life, or other scenes such as would have a demoralising effect on young persons.

(iv) Successful crime, such as bushranging, robberies, or other acts of lawlessness which might reasonably be considered as having an injurious influence on youthful minds.

Any licensee, lessee, or other person conducting picture show entertainments shall submit to the police for inspection, at the nearest police station, at least six hours before exhibition, a copy of the proposed programme for the week, or portion of the week, together with the dates of exhibition; and such programme shall be dealt with by the police within a reasonable time, and the persons concerned, notified of the approval, or withholding of approval, of such programme, or any part thereof, nor shall any submitted and approved programme be altered or varied, save by omission or re-arrangement of the sequence of the items, and shall not be added to by the inclusion of other pictures, unless permission shall have been first obtained for such alteration or addition.

All programmes on submission to the police shall be accompanied by a synopsis, or short description, of the nature of each film for the information and guidance of the officer inspecting the programme.

If required any film shall be screened for the information of police. Provided that any film which has passed the censorship of any authority notified by the Minister in the *Government Gazette* need not be so screened. The owner, lessee, or person in charge of any such film shall, on demand, give any member of the police force a written statement that the film in question has been so passed. Any person giving any such statement which is untrue in any material particular shall be liable to a penalty not exceeding twenty pounds.

Any person appointed by the Minister, or officers of police, and such non-commissioned officers as they may select to assist them, may require that the public exhibition of any cinematograph film shall be deferred, pending the decision of the Minister thereon as to whether it shall be, or shall not be, exhibited.

Any person who after due notice shall have been given in that behalf persists in exhibiting a prohibited cinematograph picture shall be liable to a penalty not exceeding twenty pounds.—*Government Gazette*, No. 177, Part V.

APPENDIX II

JUVENILE DELINQUENCY

REPORT TO THE EXECUTIVE SECRETARY OF THE NATIONAL BOARD OF
REVIEW, NEW YORK, U.S.A., BASED ON INVESTIGATION MADE BY
MR. EDWARD M. BARROWS OF THE PEOPLE'S INSTITUTE

["MR. E. M. BARROWS," writes Mr. W. D. McGuire, Executive Secretary of
The National Board of Review of Motion Pictures, "who is considered an
authority in New York on the subject of street life, has made several important
investigations and was for some time connected with the Extension Department of the University of Wisconsin."]

"A short time ago I made a general investigation in New York of the
extent and manner in which certain environmental influences in child life
here affected juvenile crime. During this study I had occasion to look into
the part the movie theatres played in the annals of juvenile crime. I found
scores of cases in which the movies were held responsible by policemen,
judges and reformers for the commission of crime. I found only a very few
cases in which this charge could be sustained by any actual facts. Occasionally the manner of a burglary, or street hold-up, related so closely to the
action of the motion picture screen which the youngster admitted having
seen immediately before that it pointed conclusively to the direct influence
of the motion picture. There were a number of cases in which the children
said themselves in court that they got their ideas from the movies. Many
judges will agree with me, however, when I say that such statements should
be pretty strongly discounted. Generally the children who say this are
only repeating ideas which the arresting officers or adult acquaintances have
put into their heads. Few of them are keen enough analysts to know whether
or not they really were so influenced.

"Specific instances aside, the general influence of the motion picture
towards encouraging lawless instincts among boys is, I am afraid, open to
more serious indictment. Without going into the evidence on the subject
I reached the general conclusion that it was possible for the melodramatic,
garish motion picture dramas dealing with crime, burglary and other situations heroic to youth to have the same general effect that the Diamond Dick
and Nick Carter dime novels of our own youth had on weak-minded and
impressionable boys, if you consider also that the motion picture is a thousand
times more vivid and has an infinitely wider circulation than the dime novel
ever could hope to have. This does not necessarily hold the motion picture
as a bad influence. If the movies were abolished to-day, the same erratic
children that are led to crime through the movies would be influenced by
the next most sensational thing which existed. In other words, an evil
motion picture will influence for the worse weak minds and minds with way-
ward tendencies, just as surely as good motion pictures will influence for the
better weak minds and minds with better tendencies.

"All of which has only reinforced the conviction upon which I base my
present work : that there is no force in American life to-day which through
its direct and vivid appeal so profoundly brings out whatever dormant tendencies, whether for better or for worse, lie in the minds of our impressionable
youth. So you cannot make a case against bad movies without thereby
making a case of equal strength for the good movie.

"E. M. BARROWS.

"*March 22, 1917.*"

332

APPENDIX III

A HUNDRED AND EIGHTEEN REPLIES TO MEMORANDA OF INQUIRY ADDRESSED TO THE CHIEF CONSTABLES OF THE UNITED KINGDOM CONCERNING THE EVIDENCE OF CHIEF CONSTABLE ROSS OF EDINBURGH

THE Précis[1] of Chief Constable Ross of Edinburgh was sent to the following Chief Constables of the United Kingdom with the request that they would state "to what extent they agreed or differed from his statements." The Chief Constables of the following thirty-seven towns and cities "agreed" with the views set forth in the Précis and made no further comment—

Airdrie.	Luton.
Arbroath.	Merthyr Tydfil.
Banbury.	Newark-on-Trent.
Barrow-in-Furness.	Newport (Mon.).
Barnstaple.	Oldham.
Bedford.	Paisley.
Birkenhead.	Penrith.
Boston.	Peterborough.
Bradford.	Rochester.
Bridgwater.	Sheerness.
Colchester.	St. Helens.
Derby.	Stalybridge.
Doncaster.	Sunderland.
Dover.	Taunton.
Folkestone.	Wallasey.
Gravesend.	Warrington.
Hereford.	Weymouth.
High Wycombe.	Worcester.
Leeds.	

Eighty-one replied as follows, and they have consented to the publication and have corrected the proofs of their statements.

BOROUGH OF ACCRINGTON

20th March, 1917.

With a good deal of Mr. Ross's evidence I am in agreement. He truly states the cinema forms one of the most popular forms of amusement we have in the country, but so far as my experience and judgment goes, the film producers do not appear to grasp their opportunities for educating the public and combine education with pleasure. The pictures are mostly, with the exception of the news pictures, which, of course, embraces the war pictures, plays or faked stories of an exciting and sensational character and of no

---

[1] pp. 175–7. See also communications from Chief Constables of Aberdeen and Dundee, pp. 178–9.

educational value whatever. The picture Mr. Ross named in his evidence was a low production, and several others I could name were equally as bad. In one case here a young woman had been to see the pictures, and saw a scene of a person committing suicide by putting a gas-tube in her mouth, and she went straight home and committed suicide in a similar manner. A number of youths here formed themselves into a robber gang on lines similar to what they had seen depicted on the cinema, and only last week I had to refuse to allow a picture to be shown here where an artist's model was taking her part in an almost nude condition.

The cinema has a great future before it if it will use for good its opportunities, but it can have an equally bad influence if pictures of a sensational and low character are displayed. Within a radius of six miles of this Town Hall there is a population of half a million, and their wants for this class of entertainment are liberally catered for, but I regret to say that my experience has not been so happy as that of Mr. Ross, for the reasons stated as well as in other respects.

GEO. SINCLAIR,
Chief Constable.

ASHTON-UNDER-LYNE

21st April, 1917.

I beg to inform you that my sentiments regarding this matter are quite in accord with those expressed by Mr. Ross. There is, however, one suggestion I would like to put forward which I feel sure would have beneficial results in many respects; that is, that some method be adopted whereby a subdued form of lighting could be in operation during the whole of the performance, *i. e.* a number of subdued red or other coloured lights.

HENRY A. TOLSON,
Chief Constable.

BACUP

13th March, 1917.

In general I agree with Mr. Ross. However, I have found that in several districts films which deal with questions of sexual morality, and which, in my opinion, may properly be exhibited to an adult audience, are screened before young children at matinées. Probably the children do not quite understand the moral which the film is intended to point, but I am convinced that they are prematurely set thinking about the subject of the films.

JAS. N. CAMPBELL,
Chief Constable.

BATH

13th March, 1917.

I beg to inform you that I have read your enclosure with great care, and on the whole I quite concur with Mr. Ross.

In one case only can I trace of a boy who stole money from another for the express purpose of going to the pictures, but I am not prepared to say that the offence would not have been committed had there been no such places in existence. This action I consider more spontaneous than contemplative, an irrepressible desire than a person with a criminal motive. The only film to which an exception was taken to in this city was a film entitled ————, which was suggestive of immorality. This film was stopped, and I am given to understand that other authorities since have taken the same course.

J. VAUGHAN PHILIPPS,
Chief Constable.

BERWICK-UPON-TWEED

19th April, 1917.

We have only one picture hall in this borough. A most careful watch is kept as to the class of pictures shown at it. I must honestly say that I can trace no crime amongst young persons to the picture hall. As a matter of fact we have had very little crime amongst juveniles for some years past.

WM. NICHOLSON,
Chief Constable.

BEVERLEY

23rd April, 1917.

I beg to acknowledge receipt of your letter of the 20th instant, also copy of evidence given before the Commission of Enquiry by the Chief Constable of Edinburgh, and I fully endorse all he says. The cinemas are the only means of public entertainment provided in Beverley, and the fact that they are full almost every night in the week testify to the popularity of this form of amusement. During the present war many thousands of troops have been billeted in the town, and it is a surprising fact that only about one per 1000 of them have been proceeded against for drunkenness, which in my opinion is due to the fascinating performances provided for them at the cinemas, of which they take full advantage, instead of resorting to public-houses. From my own experience I am satisfied that the cinemas in Beverley have been the means of reducing drunkenness to a very low standard.

JAMES E. CARPENTER,
Actg. Chief Constable.

BLACKPOOL

24th March, 1917.

I was Superintendent of Police of the Borough of Wallsend-upon-Tyne when the first cinema there was opened in, I think, the year 1907. It was an instantaneous success. Other cinema halls were hastily erected and opened. All were well patronised. I was most favourably impressed. I watched closely the growth and development of the cinema in Wallsend up to my departure in 1912. I saw with pleasure the happiness which cinemas brought into the lives of the thousands of the hard-working folks of Wallsend, living a very drab life indeed. The films then exhibited were varied. There were travel pictures at all shows. During the early years there were, I believe, more pictures depicting other lands and people, natural history and such films as were bound to increase the general knowledge of those attending.

I found at Blackpool, on my transfer here, cinema places capable of accommodating about 20,000 persons, and that these, with other places of entertainment, were and are required for the recreation and enjoyment of the residents and visitors. In my report to the Watch Committee for the year 1913 I made the following statements—

"A great deal has been said and written about the demoralising influence of cinematograph exhibitions on children of tender years who attend them. As picture halls are visited nightly by millions of people of all ages in every corner of the globe, the question is one of considerable moment. We are told that some children steal money for admission; go every evening of the week; deriving a thirst for pleasure, amusement, and ostentatious display, and become disinclined for steady work and effort. Whilst offering no comment on the latter statement, I venture to suggest that were any statistics available on the subject, cinematograph exhibitions would only be accountable for a very small percentage of juvenile depravity and crime.

"If you think of excluding children from the cheap and entertaining pastime of watching, you must consider what they will do instead. When you are satisfied that their homes and the street corners they frequent are healthier, morally and physically, and more comfortable than picture halls, exclude them by all means. I am, however, inclined to regard the suggested cure as worse than the malady. So long as the programmes at picture halls are decent and the halls themselves are clean, well ventilated and satisfactorily lighted and conducted, and children of tender years are allowed to resort there under proper guardianship, during reasonable hours, neither their minds nor their bodies are likely to suffer very seriously in consequence. The British Board of Film Censors appear to be doing excellent work in securing clean programmes for cinema halls. Their report for 1913 gives some interesting figures bearing on this work."

And in my report for 1914 I stated—

". . . During the year no complaints respecting any film exhibited here has been received by me, and so far as the police are aware no crime or offence was committed by a child or young person with a view to obtaining money for the express purpose of obtaining admission to a cinema hall. The British Board of Film Censors appear to be doing excellent work in securing clean programmes for cinema halls. All the pictures, however, are not submitted to or passed by the Board, and at the last annual meeting of the Chief Constables' Association it was resolved that—

"'All films for public exhibition should, before being sent out for exhibition, be censored by a Government official specially appointed for the purpose, as local censorship was quite impracticable. . . .'"

In 1915 I reported to the same effect as I did in 1914.

Since 1908 I have carefully examined all documents relating to detected offences committed by juveniles and young persons. I have not found one case traceable to, or even alleged to be the result of, witnessing films depicting crime and (or) criminals, nor have I found that offences had been specially committed by such persons to obtain money to enable them to go to cinema places. I have on occasions found that the persons charged have attended the cinema with the proceeds or part proceeds. On the 19th April, 1916, I reported to my Watch Committee as follows—

"I beg to suggest that the Watch Committee recommend the Council to attach to all licences granted under the Cinematograph Act, 1909, a condition that no films be displayed which are likely to be subversive of public morality, and that all licensees should be informed of this resolution. Also that licensees should be informed that the exhibition of certain types of films which are said to have a demoralising and injurious influence on children will, in the future, be considered a ground for the refusal of the renewal of a licence. Also that they be informed that posters should, before being exhibited, be seen by the licensees."

Recently a special constable—a solicitor practising in our courts—examined, at my request, the papers relating to all crime committed here in 1916, with a view to ascertaining what evidence there is of indictable crime having connection with attendance at cinematograph exhibitions, and he reports under date 12th February, 1917, as follows—

" Return of Juvenile Offenders

1912.	1913.	1914.	1915.	1916.
43	54	77	75	81

" I have read through the papers, including the reports relating to this class of crime, and find that there is no evidence of a direct or even indirect nature to form an opinion that this class of crime has been suggested or caused by the witnessing of these entertainments.

" The type of crime most largely committed by juveniles is that of larceny, and although I have read carefully through the reports and papers relating to juvenile larceny I am unable to find any evidence or suggestion that this type of crime has arisen through the witnessing of these entertainments.

" It will be noticed from the return that the years of war, 1914, 1915 and 1916 show an increase of juvenile crime, and the reason, therefore, may well be as follows—

" 1. The Military Service Act, 1916 (Session 2), calling up for military service married men between the ages of eighteen and forty-one, has, of course, resulted in many fathers leaving their homes for duty; and—

" 2. Many mothers and guardians, having been engaged on war work, has had the consequent result of parental control being reduced to a minimum.

" I have been unable to find evidence from the papers that the larcenies were committed with a view to raising moneys for the purpose of witnessing cinematograph entertainments.

" In none of the reports do I find any reference either directly or indirectly to cinematograph pictures.

" Having regard to the fact that there is a total lack of evidence of a corroborative nature, and that there is also no evidence of even an indirect nature to presuppose a connection between juvenile crime and the witnessing of these performances, it would, I think, be unwise and unfair to assume that the criminal tendencies of juveniles had their origin in the witnessing of these exhibitions."

In conclusion I have no hesitancy in agreeing generally with the comments and deductions of the Chief Constable of Edinburgh so far as they appear in his statement of evidence, but in addition thereto I would suggest that inasmuch as—

1. The cinemas provide a cheap and suitable form of entertainment for the recreation of the masses;

2. It is a most successful counter-attraction to the public-house, and a deterrent to drinking, and

3. Because of its tendency to cultivate a taste for music amongst the people;

I am of the opinion that the production and showing of more films of an educational character is a matter of great importance to the public generally, and a feature to strive for in cinematograph production. The type of educational film should be produced with the object of inculcating a general knowledge of various subjects of topical and geographical interest.

W. PRINGLE,
Chief Constable of Blackpool.

BLACKBURN

26th March, 1917.

The Licensing Authority in this County Borough are the Magistrates, the Town Council having delegated to them their powers under the Cinematograph Act. The Licensing Authority acknowledge that the cinema is a popular form of entertainment and amusement, and, if properly regulated, will become also an excellent educational asset, and in their opinion I fully concur. The policy in Blackburn has been to limit the number of licences, and to insist upon the cinema halls being specially built and adapted for the purpose; the building being substantial and a credit to the town. It is felt that an excess of licences would have an injurious effect by creating such competition as to compel many to resort to methods not conducive to the best interests of the shows. Cheap prices do not allow of good films, and if the number of licences are in excess of the legitimate requirements of the public, the majority are not able to maintain a high standard of pictures. With a population of nearly 140,000 it is felt that seven licences are, for the present, serving the requirements of the cinema patrons, and it is admitted by the licensees that no town gives a better class of pictures than those presented to the Blackburn public.

The Licensing Authority unanimously passed a resolution in favour of an official censor of films, but as the Home Office have not seen their way to carry out this most desirable proposal into effect, they have added to already stringent rules and conditions those recently suggested by the Home Office. Under those rules, programmes and a synopsis of the films to be produced have to be sent to me for approval before being shown, and a special committee is appointed by the justices to inspect any film if necessary. By special arrangements with the licensees any film which I or the committee consider should not be shown is withdrawn without raising any question of dispute or argument. The authority and the licensees have always worked together in the greatest harmony, and no friction of any kind has so far existed. The requirements with regard to lighting, heating, ventilation, seating, public order, etc., have always been observed without the least question.

With regard to children, very strict rules are in force as to their attendance, and the nature of the films produced is even more essential in their interest than that of adults. A large number attend the cinema, and the craving for moving pictures, if anything, is increasing. I have had several instances of boys stealing money, and even forcibly taking money from small children, in order to provide the price of attending the shows. It is not unusual for boys of from ten to fourteen years of age to visit these places at least twice and often as many as four times a week. This unhappy means of satisfying the craving for entertainment, however, is not confined to picture halls alone, as there have been instances of theft by boys for the purpose of attending other places of amusement.

There are many films offered to licensees which, though not indecent representations or liable to be banned, are yet unsuitable for public exhibition. Any film which contains objectionable suggestions should be excluded. As an instance, films have been disallowed here which depict the objectionable moral liberties of the foreign rich nobleman, or the luring triumphs of the fascinating actress. Anything depicting the doings of the clever burglars or thieves, or kindred subjects, and also all representations of prize fights, are forbidden. The best films are often reproductions of first-class plays, which many people prefer to the actual theatre, as they obtain at a small cost the work of the greatest actors. There is no objection to the comic films so long as they are kept within reasonable bounds.

What the authority think is most important is to bring licensees to recognise that good, elevating and instructive matter is more appreciated by the public, and ultimately more profitable to themselves, than the senseless and foolish extravagancies of questionable pictures. The vast majority do not want the latter kind, and resent it when presented.

C. Hodson,
Chief Constable.

BOLTON

13th March, 1917.

I entirely concur with the statement of Mr. Ross, and I wish to emphasise the paragraphs in which he refers to films being exhibited of an indecent character, or suggestive of immorality. I think it is a pity that such films as ———— and other such pictures should pass the Censor. It is far easier for these films to be eliminated from the cinema by the Censor than after they have been exhibited in parts of the country before complaints reach the police, for the Chief Constable is always up against the cry that " they have been shown at So-and-so and So-and-so without any complaint."

When ———— was shown in this county borough it is true that they had cut certain portions out, but in my opinion the film was worse then than it was at the commencement, leaving vacant portions to the imagination, and I find that the imaginations of some people visiting picturedromes are in some cases most extraordinary. At the same time I strongly agree that all pictures showing the least suggestion of immorality should not be allowed to be shown in any part of the country. Although juvenile crime unfortunately has increased I do not for one single moment put this down to pictures, but more so to lack of parental control. Juvenile crime always has existed, and reformatories, industrial schools and training ships were instituted long before picturedromes were thought of; but at the same time there has been a tendency for children to use the proceeds of the money, etc., they have stolen for visiting picturedromes.

Although no regulation is in force in this borough with regard to the admission of children to cinemas, there is, however, an arrangement between all proprietors in Bolton and myself that children should not be admitted after 8 p.m. unless accompanied by parent or guardian, and I feel that I would like to go one further and make this apply to the whole performance.

F. W. Mullineux,
Chief Constable.

BOOTLE

23rd April, 1917.

I have carefully perused the Précis of Mr. Ross's evidence, and agree with him that the cinema has helped to reduce drunkenness, but I cannot agree when he says the cinema has had little effect on the number of crimes committed by children. I have had a number of cases of stealing by children for the sole purpose of gaining admission to picture houses, and I have also had cases where the culprits have admitted to my officer that the methods adopted by them in committing the crime were suggested to them by the pictures exhibited. Much more could be said on the subject, but I think these two matters are, in this connection, the most important.

John Stewart,
Chief Constable.

BOROUGH OF BRIGHTON POLICE

20th March, 1917.

I have read Mr. Ross's evidence with great interest, and in the main agree with him. On page 7 Mr. Ross states he is unable to find " a single case where any juvenile set out to steal for this one purpose." I regret to say my experience is not so satisfactory in that direction. With this exception, as I have said, I agree with his observations.

(SIR) WILLIAM GENTLE,
Chief Constable.

BRECHIN

23rd April, 1917.

I have read Mr. Ross's statement carefully over, and I am very pleased to have an opportunity of making some observations on the matter.

To begin with, I am afraid there is much in the statement that I could not honestly agree with. Until very recently there have been for a considerable time two picture houses in Brechin, one of which has theatrical performances as well. Of these, one was closed a few weeks ago, owing mainly to the lessee performer being called up for military duty. Speaking from my own experience of about thirty-five years' police service among the criminal, wastrel and other classes, I claim to have seen a few " ups and downs " in the world during these years; and among the many other things that have been got up with a view to giving amusement and pleasure to the people, I consider the cinema is one of the poorest and meanest productions which have yet been produced to waste the time of those who attend them and to get their money. I have never seen any good results from those attending such places. They are credited with being a stage in advance of the public-house in respect that they have been the cause of reduced drinking, which may to some extent be true. But the fact of so many of the working class, male and female, as well as the upper class, attending the cinema several nights weekly, is, according to my light on the matter, nothing short of precious time wasted.

It might be difficult to prove that some of the pictures shown are of an indecent nature, yet some of them are suggestive of that, and cannot, therefore, fail to have a demoralising effect on the young minds. We may be quite sure that the cinema proprietors are not out to give the people a moral education, but to make money out of whatever will take on best. Just the same thing as most of the theatres are out for—profit-making; in some of which women immodestly and indecently appeal to the purely animal passions of men.

There is no doubt at all but the picture house is a great source of temptation to the young. In various instances it has produced pilfering in order to get admission money, which was perfectly evident to the police here at the outset of these places in Brechin.

What I can see in the cinema picture house is, just that it is a pronounced mark of the trend in which public morals has been drifting for the past quarter of a century, viz. more concerned about pleasure and material things than about spiritual and lasting things; and the cinema is, like many other would-be sources of pleasure which have come and gone during the above period; and there is also a great probability that it too, as a novelty, will exhaust itself in the course of the next two or three years. For there is really nothing that I can see good about it, in particular, as an educative institution. On the contrary, the great majority of those that frequent the picture houses are more or less ignorant of the history of most of the pictures shown, and therefore derive no benefit of any kind; but just because it is one of the crazes of the age in which we are living, it is thus sought after. However, in concluding, I may painfully add that while the Churches have failed to find audiences, the cinemas in the former's deserted buildings, where the Gospel used to be preached, have generally succeeded in bringing out large numbers to see their pictures and other performances; and I am sorry to say this applies doubly strong to the rural district; for although the farm-workers as a rule here attend no place of worship, yet they come in in pretty large numbers two or three times a week to the picture houses. Surely there is something morally and spiritually wrong at the foundation.

D. SMART,
Chief Constable.

BRISTOL

19th March, 1917.

The popularity of the cinema and the influence it exercises upon the social life of the community is now well known, and I am confident that the influence for good considerably outweighs the bad. My opinion, however, is, that there is room for improvement in the character of some of the films, which cannot but have an unwholesome effect upon the minds of those of an impressionable age. Pictures depicting infidelity, a veiled but suggestive immorality, licentious leer, and amorous expressions and actions of some of the actors and actresses in the pictures are unseemly and repulsive to a healthy sense of propriety, although I would not be prepared to say they are really indecent, in the general sense of the term.

In actual practice I find that the opinions of police officers as well as cinema critics are very divergent, and this fact often militates against or nullifies a real basis of common censorship in any particular instance. An alert mind, well-balanced judgment, close reasoning, and sound common sense are required to enable any one to censor some films. It has happened, and may do so again, that a film will be shown, say, in five towns, when it gets to the sixth a portion will be objected to by the police and cut out. At the seventh it may again be shown in full, whilst at the eighth it is objected to in its entirety.

To ban a film after it has been shown in various towns requires considerable courage, the risk of an action for damages being great, as witness the notorious film ————.

I am thoroughly in accord with the Chief Constable of Edinburgh in saying that intemperance has been considerably reduced through the attendance at cinemas. It undoubtedly has been the means of keeping a large number of people out of the public-houses. I am confident the moving pictures have, in this city, been the means of giving thousands a healthy, educative, and pleasant entertainment, an entertainment which, I believe, is ever increasingly popular, and with the necessary machinery to eliminate its undesirable features, cannot do other than a large amount of good.

J. H. WATSON,
Chief Constable.

COUNTY BOROUGH OF BURNLEY

21st April, 1917.

Owing to delay in receiving it, I have perused the Précis rather hurriedly, and, generally, I endorse the conclusions of Mr. Ross, but I am unable to endorse page 6, lines 17–18, as in several instances evidence has been given in the Juvenile Police Court here by boys that they have been induced to commit offences by what they had seen at picture shows. Films showing burglars and other criminals at work are, I am glad to say, not now being shown as often as formerly.

W. H. SMITH,
Chief Constable.

BOROUGH OF CAMBRIDGE

28th April, 1917.

I have read with interest the Précis of evidence given by the Chief Constable of Edinburgh before your Commission, and fully endorse what he states in so far as it affects a place like Cambridge. Our picture houses are well

managed, and I have only received one " ungrounded " complaint during
the past year. Their advent has brought brightness into the lives of lots
of poor people, and as long as they are properly managed I see no reason
why they should be handicapped by further regulations.

CHAS. EDW. HOLLAND,
Chief Constable.

CARLISLE

Chief Constable's Office,
12*th March*, 1917.

I fully agree with everything said by Mr. Ross, and my own personal
experience bears out fully that portion of his evidence given on pages 7 and 8
with regard to juvenile crime. I am of opinion that some films, particularly
those used in the smaller halls, are of an unhealthy nature, as, for example,
" The Suicide Club," which was recently given at a Saturday afternoon
children's performance in this city and gave rise to considerable comment,
and would suggest that as far as possible educational and topical pictures
should be used on these occasions.

E. H. DE SCHMID,
Chief Constable.

CHATHAM

Police Office,
12*th March*, 1917.

I have carefully read that statement, and I beg to say that had I been the
person called upon to make it, I should have based it on exactly similar lines.
Referring to the last paragraph on page 6 and continued on page 7, I have
for some time past felt that there must be a danger among boys of an adventurous disposition who witness films of an exciting character, more especially
those showing criminals at work, and on this subject I am also with Mr. Ross,
and although I have not much proof, I feel that this kind of picture would
not, among such boys, have a tendency for good.

I, personally, do not think that the great increase of juvenile crime is due
to cinema exhibitions, but chiefly from abnormal circumstances in which we
are placed at the present time.

ALBT. E. RHODES,
Superintendent.

P.S.—The above also applies to the Boro' of Gillingham, also in my
division.

CHELTENHAM

18*th May*, 1917.

Referring to your letter of the 13th March enclosing a statement of evidence
on cinema shows by the Chief Constable of Edinburgh, I sent that statement
round to the superintendents in this county.

With the exception of one, who objects to cinema shows altogether, their
views seem fairly to coincide with those of Mr. Ross, and I agree with them.

I think perhaps he is somewhat optimistic as to the darker side of the
shows, as I think that quite a large proportion of juvenile crime may originate
in something connected with them, but if this is so it would chiefly indicate
that rigorous control should be kept over the films.

So much that is really good, from both moral and educational points of
view, can be conveyed through the medium of these shows, that there is no
excuse whatever for prostituting their use to any baser service.

M. W. COLCHESTER-WEMYSS,
Chairman Glos. County Council,
Hon. Acting Chief Constable.

CHESTER

24th April, 1917.

I am satisfied that the cinema, properly used, is beneficial to the general public. The greatest possible care *must* be taken that all subjects filmed and shown are of such a character that *all* classes of the community might see the same and not be ashamed of their action. I think that Education Authorities might assist to further the use of scientific films, and that all films suggestive of crime or immorality should not be allowed in any cinema in the country.

JNO. H. LAYBOURNE,
Chief Constable.

CHESTERFIELD

25th April, 1917.

Since the development of these shows, as a police officer, I have looked to them as a counter-attraction to the public-house, and have not been disappointed. There are phases which could be improved, one of which is the admission of children after 9 p.m., without parent or guardian; this, I consider, should not be. There are other little details which I might mention, but on the whole I have not a word to say against the influence exercised by these exhibitions on the morals of the town. Of course, great care should be exercised in the elimination of questionable films.

R. KILPATRICK,
Chief Constable.

COATBRIDGE

20th April, 1917.

I have read the evidence of Mr. Ross carefully, and entirely agree with the whole of it. I think the picture house very much preferable to the low-class music hall, and as to the encouragement to juvenile pilfering, I find that the gambling machines in ice-cream and other small shops legalised by a decision in the High Court of Justiciary has been the cause of most of the thefts which have occurred in this burgh where the proceeds were squandered by young persons. I agree with Mr. Ross that great care should be exercised in the selection of the pictures, and that those showing any suggestion of immorality, and showing burglars and other criminals at work, should be deleted. I am clearly of opinion that this form of entertainment has lessened intemperance in this burgh to a very considerable extent. I herewith return the copy of the evidence which you were good enough to send me.

WM. M'DONALD,
Chief Constable.

CORK (SOUTH)

16th May, 1917.

I may say that I agree generally with the views expressed by him. As regards pictures of an immoral character or suggestive of immorality, I have not observed any of that type exhibited in this city, nor have I received any complaints from any of the citizens in reference to such. I believe, however, that the cinema has led to some increase of juvenile crime in the city, and it has contributed to that increase in two ways: (1) through a desire to see pictures (for which undoubtedly children have a great fondness) children occasionally steal money; (2) through seeing pictures, showing how thefts and burglaries are committed, they are sometimes led to imitate the actions displayed on the pictures. The pictures are, however, a very cheap and, generally speaking, a very harmless form of amusement for the working classes and others who have not the money or the opportunity to go to theatres; and I consider the benefit they confer outweighs any harm they may do in other ways.

C. A. WALSH,

D.I., R.I.C.

COVENTRY

15th March, 1917.

I have to inform you that I accept much of what Mr. Ross says as true and applying to the cinemas of the city of Coventry. I, too, believe that cinemas are here to stay; that they have contributed towards the promotion of temperance and good order in this city; that they have a future before them; and that they are educative, morally healthy, and pleasure-giving entertainments *if suitably controlled by a reasonable censorship.* This qualification is, I think, necessary.

There are sixteen picture theatres in this city, financed by men who have a direct stake here. Complaints of improper pictures since the first theatre was established many years ago have been very few, and the proprietors have always been amenable to a reasonable request from the Licensing Authority, but incidents have occurred which tend to show that unless direct supervision is maintained the pictures would deteriorate. The object of theatre proprietors is undoubtedly to make money. If they can accomplish this object by exhibiting programmes that satisfy both the authorities and their patrons, all is well; if not, it occasionally happens that some proprietor is willing to exhibit something risky. In subjects approaching the marginal line dividing decency from indecency there is money, and the spirit of emulation is strong. If one house can show a daring picture without official interference, why not another? is a reasoning often heard. Some time last year I stopped the exhibition of a film entitled ————. This film was more than suggestive. Only one manager in the city could be found to accept it, and on the nights it was shown, prior to my action, crowds of people were turned away who could not obtain admission. Similar action had been taken in Lancashire, with the result that an action claiming heavy damages was entered against the Chief Constable of the town concerned. These proceedings, I am glad to say, failed.

Many people condemn cinemas without visiting them. This attitude, often adopted by men of standing, renders the official position difficult, because it is not understood. Chief officers have to judge such exhibitions judicially and within the limits of the Acts or Orders controlling them. It is assumed very often that a threat of opposition to licence is sufficient to compel a licensee to accede to any official request, whether such request is empowered by law or not. This is a fallacy. I agree that pictures depicting fast life, the *amours* of faithless husbands and wives, suggestive actions, films showing robberies by violence, gagging, chloroforming, safe-breaking, brutal murders, etc., should be discarded altogether.

There have been cases where boys have undoubtedly been inspired to commit offences by a visit to the pictures, and in Coventry offences by juveniles are on the increase. Perhaps I am unduly optimistic, but I see no cause for alarm in this fact. The times are abnormal, and children are left much to their own resources, and may possess an inventive genius in so far as mischief is concerned. It is true they commit what the law calls indictable offences which, if committed by adults for gain or as a livelihood, are most serious and denote the criminal mind; but the bulk of offences committed by children display, in my judgment, no criminal tendency whatever. There is a risk in their undertaking. Excitement is exhilarating, and children steal articles that they afterwards throw away as useless, not being cognisant of their value. The cinema should not be blamed for this.

The Watch Committee here, subject to the approval of the Council, on Tuesday adopted the new conditions of licences recommended by the Secretary of State. Doubtless you are familiar with them. Wisely and tactfully administered, these rules should create a local censorship that will prevent abuses. Their action, I venture to believe, will tend to check the tendency of film producers to exploit for gain risky films, although I have no doubt many pictures still will be exhibited in questionable taste from the standpoint of art and culture; but the gain to the general public from the prohibition of shows that are morally bad would be unquestionably great, and I trust that the conditions referred to will be generally adopted.

C. C. CHARSLEY,
Chief Constable.

DEWSBURY COUNTY BOROUGH POLICE

26th March, 1917.

From my experience in this borough, I should say the cinema has had very little effect on the crime committed by juveniles, and the Précis almost entirely bears out my views in regard to the matter.

S. BURNACLOUGH,
Chief Constable.

DUDLEY

Chief Superintendent's Office,
16th March, 1917.

I quite endorse the statement of the Chief Constable of Edinburgh relating to picture houses, and to say that I have had very few complaints as to the films exhibited here; but some time ago several lads were arrested for shopbreaking, which was so well done that I felt anxious to know how it was conceived by lads not more than fourteen years of age, when one of them told me they had seen it enacted at a picture house in the town. I have also had to complain of the hideous and indecent posters which are now somewhat suppressed. My own opinion is, that if less tragedy and crime were depicted in these houses the better it would be for the youth of both sexes.

R. SPEKE,
Chief Superintendent.

DUMFRIES

24th April, 1917.

In my opinion the cinema, as it ought to be, should prove an important factor in the education and entertainment of both young and old. The cinema, as it very often is at present, cannot fail to produce a bad effect upon its patrons, particularly the young. While it is true that police proceedings, on the ground that certain films shown are indecent representations, would not succeed, the harm such productions are capable of working to the young of both sexes is very great, although it may not have immediate effect. The subject of many films is a mere string of compromising situations and suggestions of immorality, which, if they have no worse effect upon the spectators, tend to coarsen them and familiarise them with a side of human life which should not be held up to public gaze. These films, unfortunately, seem to be the most popular—leaving out of account war pictures such as the " Battle of the Somme," etc. Recently a film entitled ———— was shown in one of the picture houses here, and the previous week the management issued handbills intimating its intended production, and adding that no children under sixteen would be admitted to view the film. The result was, that the house was packed on the first night, and hundreds were turned away. I witnessed the performance, and while there were no grounds for criminal proceedings, the opinion I formed was that the entertainment was the reverse of elevating.

No cases have come under my notice of juveniles being incited to commit crime by the cinema. It is most unusual to discover a case where juveniles commit crime for any one purpose. Boys commit theft, or theft by house-breaking, almost always in order to have a " good time " with the proceeds. Having a good time invariably includes purchasing confectionery, ice-cream and cigarettes, gambling with the machines usually found in ice-cream saloons, and frequenting picture houses. While the cinema may play a small part in creating the juvenile delinquent, absence of parental control, un-inviting homes, and the absence of a proper system of continuation classes of education in citizenship for youths on leaving the elementary schools are, in my view, the principal causes. I am strongly of opinion that there is great need for the establishing of some authority with power to prevent the public exhibition of unwholesome films which may fall far short of " indecent exhibitions," but nevertheless have a baneful influence upon the minds of the young, and which at present seem to be numerous.

W. BLACK,
Chief Constable of the Burgh of Dumfries.

DUNFERMLINE

Chief Constable's Office,
23rd April, 1917.

I beg to say that I entirely endorse what has been said by Mr. Ross, and would only just like to add that the desirability of eliminating from the cinema films which are in the least suggestive of immorality cannot be too strongly emphasised.

GEORGE BRUCE,
Chief Constable.

DURHAM

6th April, 1917.

I agree with Mr. Ross's views. I supplement my observations on one or two points mentioned. Page 5, paragraph 3 : With reference to a picture entitled ———— being immorally suggestive, I have, in this county, had complaints about two films, entitled ———— (from two of my police divisions) and ————. The first named was at each place banned by the justices, and in the ———— case I instituted proceedings : a conviction, however, was not obtained; but I am satisfied the prosecution resulted in cleaner, healthier and more suitable pictures being exhibited.

Page 7, paragraph 2 : Stealing to procure admission. Cases have occurred in this county where boys have said they stole the money for the purpose of gaining admission to the picture hall. I, however, do not believe that that was the boy's actual motive at the time he committed the offence. An opportunity presented itself, he availed himself of it, and in every instance took more than would pay for admission, and in some instances took other articles in addition. It then became a question of what to do with the money—how to spend it. The cinema hall being so popular, suggests itself at once. Some have been known to spend money at ice-cream shops, etc.

My impression is, that the cinema is not responsible for juvenile crime. In every case my experience is, that although the wrong-doer or the bad man of the play flourishes and successfully carries on his wrong-doing for a while, he invariably lands into the hands of the law and receives his just reward; so that the moral is good, and that should have equally as much effect on the young mind as the first part leading up to it. I am firmly of opinion juvenile crime, if not altogether to a very great extent, is due to lack of parental control, want of interest by parents in their children, neglect of children, and bad home surroundings, examples and teaching.

Granted a good, healthy, moral film, and I am of the opinion its influence has a tendency for good. It is educative and interesting. If humorous, it serves a good, useful purpose, as it creates mirth; and persons worried with the toil of the day may forget their troubles for a time.

W. G. MORANT,
Chief Constable of the County of Durham.

OBSERVATIONS BY THE CHIEF CONSTABLE OF THE CITY OF EXETER

17th March, 1917.

SUMMARY OF MR. ROSS'S EVIDENCE.

OBSERVATION OF CHIEF CONSTABLE OF EXETER.

1. Cinema entertainments are immensely popular with the public.

1. I agree.

2. They are approved by the public because they provide (a) " an educative, (b) morally wholesome, (c) and bright entertainment " at a price within reach of all."

2. (a) In my opinion it is regrettable that only a small part of the average cinema entertainment can be described as educative.

(b) Many of the films might be described as wholesome, but there are others to which that term does not apply. and from which some adults, but more particularly juveniles, are likely to form entirely wrong ideas about life. I feel sure that some of the crime pictures are most harmful to children, and may even suggest methods of crime to certain adults.

(c) Many of the " comic " pictures are inane and vulgar, as, indeed, are some of the stories from every-day life. Obviously film producers are not so much concerned with making the cinema an educative instrument as in making money. If the popular demand is for sensational or inane stuff, they will manufacture it, without regard to its effect, unless they are controlled.

3. Cinemas exercise a certain influence either for good or evil in the social life of the community.

3. I think it may exercise both.

4. The popularity of the cinema among all classes and conditions of men and women is a guarantee of its power for good in the community.

4. I agree; and therefore every effort should be made to prevent its " power for good " from being nullified by the objectionable pictures.

5. That were the lessons it taught to exercise the evil influence in the people, that evil would ere now have made itself manifest in some form or other, but such has not been the case.

5. The influence of the cinema, unconscious as it may be, is of an extremely pervasive character. It is as difficult to produce evidence of the evil influence of pernicious films as it would be to produce evidence of the effect on the minds of readers of an obscene story, but I think in either case evil results may be safely assumed.

I am of opinion, from my personal

6. (*a*) The cinema has been the means of attracting many who otherwise would have resorted to the public-house. (*b*) Picture houses have been instrumental in reducing intemperance.

7. All complaints made to the police as to films exhibited being of an indecent character, or suggestive of immorality, " were found to be such that no action could be taken," as they were not indecent.

8. Films which contain suggestions of immorality ought to be eliminated from the cinema.

9. In the reading of novels, as much evil, if not more, may be gleaned by the young; but there is no reason why the cinema in this respect should not keep clear of this pernicious phase of the question.

10. In some quarters it has been alleged that the exhibitions of films which showed burglars and other criminals at work have been the means of inciting boys to emulate the example of committing crime. No such case has come to Mr. Ross's knowledge, but he thinks there is grave danger in such representations.

11. It has been alleged that juvenile crimes were in a measure due to the love of the cinema on the part of boys, who took to stealing for the purpose of procuring money with which to pay for admission to the picture house, and thus gratifying

experience, that methods of committing crime have been suggested to children by crime pictures.

6. (*a*) I agree. (*b*) I think it is very likely.

7. To enable action to be taken by the police under the criminal law, the films would require to be very bad indeed—more than suggestive; and I have never seen a film which would justify such action.

8. I agree; Mr. Ross suggests that there are such films, and that " on girls and youths of impressionable age there is a fear that they may have a deleterious effect."

I would submit that if films suggestive of immorality may have such an effect on girls and youths of impressionable age, pictures displayed before children making them familiar with death, crime, methods of committing crime, killing, fighting, scenes of anguish, and all kinds of unhealthy excitement, are also likely to have their deleterious effects.

9. With the first part I do not agree. The young who read novels I do not think are numerous, certainly not so numerous as those who attend picture halls; but nothing read in print has the same vivid effect as pictures submitted to the eye. I, of course, agree with the latter part of this section.

10. I think it is most probable that pictures have been the means of suggesting methods of crime to boys. It is naturally almost impossible to find definite evidence that crimes by children have been suggested by pictures, but there are good reasons for believing such to be the case, and I take it that when Mr. Ross says " there is grave danger in such representations " he has in mind danger of that particular kind.

11. I know of numerous cases of juveniles who have spent money they have stolen on picture halls. They have stated, and their parents have also stated, that their object in stealing was to procure money for admission to picture halls.

their insatiable desires in this direction. He is unable to find a single case where any juvenile set out to steal for this purpose.

12. Juveniles stealing to obtain money for admission to picture halls cannot be brought as a fault against the picture houses.

13. In most instances Mr. Ross has found that the proceeds of theft by juveniles have gone to satisfy their fondness or craze for gambling, which is more in keeping with their " vicious tendencies " than witnessing an exhibition of living pictures.

Such confessions have not always related to picture halls, but sometimes to other places of amusement.

12. I agree.

13. This has not been my experience, but I do know of several cases in which money was stolen for the purpose of playing on the automatic gaming machines which were very prevalent in this city in 1915. These have now been removed. The number of juveniles proceeded against last year for indictable offences represented 46 per cent. of the total number of persons proceeded against in this city for such offences, and gambling was not the cause of crime in a single instance.

I do not consider that more than a small number of the children who have passed through this Court could be described as of " vicious tendencies." I know the circumstances in each case, because with regard to each child I have had a very careful inquiry made, which is recorded in the form of a " history sheet."

14. Independent of the cinemas, boys will continue to steal and to devote the proceeds to whatever purpose may take their fancy.

15. So far as Edinburgh is concerned, the cinemas in this respect, and as a means of inciting the commission of crime on the part of juveniles, has had little or no effect on the crime committed by children or young persons.

14. I agree.

15. I think that the responsibility of the cinema for juvenile crime generally has been exaggerated, but I believe pernicious films to be responsible for some of it. There is no doubt, however, that there are deeper causes, and I believe bad environment and weak parental control to be the primary causes.

A. F. NICHOLSON,
Chief Constable.

GALASHIELS

19th May, 1917.

I beg to inform you that, so far as my experience is concerned, I endorse Mr. Ross's views generally. Copy of statement herewith returned.

A. NOBLE,
Chief Constable.

GATESHEAD

16th March, 1917.

I agree with the major portion of what Mr. Ross has said. I am of the opinion that the cinema is playing, and likely to continue to do so, an important part in the habits of the people. I would very much like to see many needed improvements made regarding film production. I also think that in some measure picture houses have been the means of reducing intemperance. I am also of the opinion that a certain amount of juvenile crime has taken place with a view to money being obtained to gratify the desire to see the pictures. In my opinion the pictures to which I see objection are more likely to produce ill-effect upon both sexes between the ages of fifteen to about twenty years.

R. Ogle,
Chief Constable.

GLASGOW

9th March, 1917.

I have to say that I agree generally with the views expressed by Mr. Ross.

The cinema houses became popular at once, and their popularity is rather increasing than waning. There are 102 houses licensed in Glasgow, distributed over all parts of the city, and at all of them waiting *queues* are to be seen almost every evening. The prices of admission range from twopence to half a crown, which enables the poorest to obtain admission.

All licences in Glasgow under the Cinematograph Act, 1909, are granted subject to the following conditions—

1. That no child under fourteen years of age shall, unless accompanied by a parent or guardian, be permitted to be in premises licensed under the Cinematograph Act after 9.30 p.m.

2. That provision shall be made in such premises for separate seating accommodation for children under fourteen years of age who are not accompanied by their parents or guardians.

3. That provision shall be made to the satisfaction of the Engineer of the Electricity Department for the efficient lighting of such premises; and—

4. That the fire appliances in said premises shall be regularly inspected by a member of the Fire Brigade.

Occasional complaints have been made of the character of the films shown, but no case was found where the picture could be considered indecent. Pictures are sometimes shown which are vulgar and unpleasant, as, for instance, ————; sometimes what is called a "strong" play is shown, containing suggestions which are not healthy for young people. The crime pictures show the operations of criminals in burglary, theft, etc., and while no case of crime can be definitely traced to the effect of the pictures, the familiarity with the methods of criminals cannot be good for children, and may lead adventurous boys to imitate the methods shown. While all these objectionable items may be found in books, moving pictures present them in a much more realistic and impressive way. As the pictures appeal so strongly to young people, there should be a rigid censorship, so that everything objectionable should be eliminated.

Cases of petty thefts by boys have come to the notice of the police, where the boys admitted that the theft had been committed to obtain money to pay for admission to the picture houses, but the same boys would, of course, steal similarly to obtain means to gratify any other strong desire. There are many instances of boys stealing to obtain money to play with gaming machines in refreshment shops.

J. V. Stevenson,
Chief Constable.

GRANTHAM

25th April, 1917.

I have read what Mr. Ross says, and am in full agreement with it.

Although we have had an increase here in juvenile offenders, we cannot trace any connection between that increase and any desire on the behalf of such offenders to obtain the means for attending cinemas, nor can we say that they have been influenced in committing the crimes by anything they have seen at the cinemas. I quite agree, also, that the cinemas are a means of taking many persons from the public-houses and so decreasing drunkenness. I am of opinion that the good done by cinemas in the way of education, and in providing a cheap means of entertainment for people who would otherwise be in public-houses or lounging about the streets, far more than outweighs any evil which may be traced to them (a doubtful tracing at the best) in the shape of inciting juveniles to commit crime. My only complaint is that I think such places of entertainment might be better lighted.

I wish to thank you for giving me the opportunity of reading what I consider is a very straightforward and fair statement on this subject.

J. R. Casburn,
Chief Constable.

GREENOCK

8th May, 1917.

I had heard Mr. Ross read his statement at a meeting of the Chief Constables' Club shortly before he sent it in, and at the time it struck me that he was giving rather an exceptional testimonial to the cinema. I have now read over his statement carefully, and, while still of the opinion that the character he gives these places of entertainment is very flattering, my own views are not so pronounced as to warrant me in dissenting from his generally.

I cannot quite follow his reasoning where, on the one hand, he tacitly admits that films of a suggestive character, although not just of such a nature as to bring them within the scope of the criminal law, are sometimes shown, and, on the other, says that were the lessons taught to exercise an influence for evil in the people, the evil would have manifested itself ere now, but that such has not been the case. How does he know? What means has he had of informing himself what are the number of cases of immorality that have been caused through the influence of such films? I do not say it is, but may it not be that many cases of misconduct on the part of the sexes have resulted from the influence of such pictures which are unknown except to the persons who committed them? I agree with Mr. Ross that the cinema has become a popular institution, and that all classes of the community frequent it, and I think that it can with safety be said that its influence for good outweighs its evils.

It has taken many people off the streets who would otherwise have gone into the public-house, and thereby tended to lessen drunkenness. The pictures which are shown are, I am informed, mostly of an amusing kind, and that those of much educational value are the exception to the rule, the reason being that the funny ones are the most popular. There are also, I am told, films shown which are suggestive, and others which depict burglars at work, and I think it cannot be over-emphasised that those are dangerous. There are persons who are very impressionable, and it is difficult to say what the influence of such pictures have on them. Such pictures are of no value to any one, and interest only the few who are in most need of having them kept from them.

JAMES CHRISTIE,
Chief Constable.

GUILDFORD

Chief Constable's Office,
20th May, 1917.

With the opinion of Mr. Roderick Ross, Chief Constable, City of Edinburgh, I practically agree—there are certain exceptions. I also venture a few personal observations not referred to in his evidence.

I am not an opponent of the cinema, but am strongly opposed to the absence of hygienic conditions in regard to the same. Generally speaking, the atmosphere is obnoxious and vitiated, the heat developed by the audience sickly, and the darkness most objectionable.—These defects are very deplorable, and should receive stricter attention from the local authorities in the public interest. Owing to the insufficient ventilation and heat there is undoubtedly a creation and free distribution of bacteria—a fact proved by the proprietors themselves in causing the deodorisation of halls by means of syringes at intervals during the performances. Infantile disease is also spread in a great number of halls, especially where shops have been converted into picture houses, to an alarming degree—a point brought to my notice by several of the medical profession. The properly constructed theatre or variety house does not require deodorisation; therefore the majority of picture palaces are condemned by the precautions and actions of their proprietors. With reference to the darkness (difficult to overcome), it is the cause of many abuses, and one in particular where young men and young women attend together, not for the purpose of following the pictures, but, owing to the darkness, to become spoony, and to work up passions which may be described as " initiative immorality." Cases have been reported to me of young women who have fallen through having been overcome in the way related. This kind of vice, to my mind, could be kept more in subjection if proprietors would administer strict supervision and effective action.

In regard to children going to cinemas at night, I am very much against it, as, from my own experience, I am certain it affects their sleep and natural development. Would advocate special halls and pictures for them.

The cinema has, no doubt, attracted many who would otherwise have resorted to the public-house, and especially the men—the women who frequent public-houses are not, from my observations, patronisers of the picture palace.

I submit that films of an indecent character, as mentioned by the Chief Constable of Edinburgh, are very few and rare. It does not pay the producer of cinema films to produce an immoral picture, because the trade censorship is always antagonistic to showing it. I agree that the public patronising the picture houses consists mainly of girls and youths of impressionable age, and that anything suggesting immoral conduct might have a deleterious effect. Yet, as far as I have acquaintance with the cinema, there is but little innuendo, but, unfortunately, a tangible suggestion of criminality. The Chief Constable of Edinburgh has declared that no case has come to his knowledge of boys attempting to emulate the criminal example as shown to them on the films. This is entirely opposed to my own experience, where boys actually committed robberies, not for profit, but in order to copy the exploits shown upon the screen. In consequence I am entirely against films dealing with thefts or criminal acts.

In my opinion, the cinema to-day is not used sufficiently for educational purposes. Unfortunately, it mainly consists of frivolous comedy or bald melodrama mostly with impossible situations, and combined with a romance which is very often an insult to one's intelligence. If the producers of cinema films could only be induced to keep in view the education of the public mind to a higher level, with popular science and wholesome fiction, then the justifiable criticism of the Chief Constable of Edinburgh would be unnecessary.

His opinion regarding the juvenile craze for gambling is probably local, for while in Scotland, I admit, there is much juvenile gambling, yet in most of the provincial towns in the south of England this offence is practically unknown.

The last paragraph of the statement of evidence in question is of considerable interest. The Chief Constable states that, so far as Edinburgh is concerned, the exhibition of criminal pictures has had little or no effect on the crime committed by young persons. It is surely without question that the example seen of profitable crime, whether in real life or upon the screen, must exercise a detrimental effect upon the impressionable mind of the young person. Hence it is that, in my opinion, cinema films dealing with crime should be eliminated entirely by the censor.

Just a word about posters. During the past year there has been a marked improvement in the character of posters exhibited on the boards and hoardings in and outside the picture palaces in this borough. This has been brought about by the proprietors of cinemas displaying a keener desire to work in concert with the police, and a willingness at all times to comply with reasonable suggestions. The result obtained is an absolute cessation of public complaints.

I am pleased to have the opportunity of submitting these few observations, and trust they may be of some material value.

WILLIAM V. NICHOLAS,
Chief Constable.

HAMILTON (SCOTLAND)

22nd April, 1917.

In comparison with a burgh of this size, the experience of Chief Constable Ross of Edinburgh, concurred in by Chief Constables Anderson of Aberdeen and Carmichael of Dundee, with regard to " picture houses " must, of course, be very much greater than ours. We have five such places in this burgh, but I am unable to offer any personal opinion on the subject, and I have had no complaints—either from members of the public or from my subordinates. We have had a good deal of petty thieving by children, but the almost invariable object has been to obtain money to spend at gambling machines in ice-cream shops, and with reference to that complaints have been very numerous indeed. Speaking from memory, I cannot recall more than one or two instances where children, when brought before the Court, admitted they had spent the money got by the theft to get in to see " the pictures."

JOHN MILLAR,
Chief Constable.

HARTLEPOOL

25th April, 1917.

I have to inform you that we have only two picture halls in this borough, and up to the present time I have had no complaint as to the management or character of the films exhibited. I agree in the main with the views of the Chief Constable of Edinburgh. Juvenile crime in this borough has slightly decreased during last year, and I know of no case which I can ascribe to the cinema.

A. WINTERBOTTOM,
Chief Constable.

A A

HASTINGS

14*th March*, 1917.

I have carefully perused the Précis of Mr. Ross and generally agree with the opinions expressed therein. I enclose, for your information, an extract from my " Annual Report " on the matter, which, of course, was only alluded to briefly.

F. Y. AMES,
Chief Constable.

EXTRACT FROM THE CHIEF CONSTABLE'S ANNUAL REPORT FOR 1916 RE CINEMAS

" Much has been said and written respecting the large increase in juvenile crime almost everywhere in the country, but happily this has not been the experience at Hastings, as, although there has been a slight increase in indictable crimes committed by juveniles here, the total number dealt with for all offences during the past year was 60, as compared with 59 for 1915; 90 for 1914; and 67 for 1913.

" In some cases the boys admitted that the money stolen had been spent in buying sweets and other edibles and in attending cinemas, but it does not necessarily follow that if there were no picture houses they would not have committed the offences with which they were charged. Undoubtedly in some cases the desire to attend such places is an inducement to steal so as to obtain the money for admission, but I am pleased to say that the picture houses in the town are capably managed and well conducted, complaints being extremely rare.

" These places are frequently visited by police in uniform and plain clothes, and the regulations governing the licences are well observed."

HAWICK

24*th April*, 1917.

Although I can endorse what Mr. Ross says as to the effect of the cinema on the reduction of drunkenness, I am sorry to say that my experience with regard to juvenile crime is quite the opposite, and I have had several cases—two in particular—lately where boys deliberately planned the crimes to get money to attend the picture houses, and were found there by the police after the offences were committed.

I do not blame the class of picture shown for creating the desire in the minds of the youths to commit the offences, although I must say that the class of pictures usually shown here is neither educative nor morally healthy, although it may to the patrons of these places be of a pleasure-giving nature. What to my mind has been the cause of picture houses inciting children to commit crime for the purpose of obtaining money to attend them is that every Saturday and during holidays special matinées are run for children during the afternoons. This I have no objection to so long as the pictures are suitable; but, as every one is aware, no child cares to be left out in the cold, and while the better-off classes can afford the money, the poorer classes cannot, and consequently the children cannot attend, and I am sorry to say it is principally among the poorer classes of children that this spate of juvenile crime has broken out here. Of course, one can also blame the want of parental control for a certain amount of this, but I cannot say that parental control is any more lax than in former years.

The craze for gambling which is rampant in many towns practically does not exist here. In my opinion, what is wanted—and I speak for my own town only and from experience—is legislation to prevent children of, say, under fourteen years of age attending picture houses during the evening unless accompanied by their parents, which would ensure that the children could not be there unknown to their parents.

I would also advocate the setting up of a local censure appointed from the Town Council to deal with all pictures intended to be shown at special matinées for children. If this were done it would ensure us that no attempt would be made to show pictures which were not of an educative nature and morally healthy. I do not think I can add anything further, recognising as I do that strong arguments can be made from both sides; and while welcoming the cinema as a cheap and popular means of entertaining the masses, I think, as I have already said, much can yet be done to ensure that nothing will be done to tempt children to commit crime for the purpose of attending the picture house.

DAVID THOM,
Chief Constable.

HOVE

2nd May, 1917.

There are only three cinematograph picture palaces licensed in this borough for regular daily entertainments, Sundays excepted, for a population of over 44,000. They are at times fairly well-attended, but I have never yet seen such large *queues* formed up outside waiting for admission as exists at a place like Edinburgh, the class of resident being of a totally different character. I agree entirely with the statement of the Chief Constable of Edinburgh as regards the popularity, its being instrumental in reducing intemperance in certain towns and also with his suggestions that the exhibition of the films showing burglars and other criminals and those with any suggestion of immorality should be prevented from being shown to the young. I may, however, state that I can speak as to two cases of theft which were committed by the juvenile class entirely by seeing such films exhibited.

W. COCKS,
Chief Constable.

HUDDERSFIELD

16th March, 1917.

In response to your invitation for my views on Mr. Ross' Précis, I beg to state—

1. In this town several instances have been brought to light in which boys admitted stealing for the purpose of getting money to visit picture houses.

2. I think pictures of murders, burglaries and violent crimes are calculated to have a decidedly deleterious influence particularly upon juvenile minds. To give one illustration—a series of pictures representing the operations of a gang of thieves called the " Clutching Hand Gang " were shown in one of the picture houses here. Immediately afterwards numerous complaints of shop-lifting and petty thefts were reported to the police. Ultimately some boys were caught in the act of shop-lifting and the thefts were proved to be the work of a regularly organised band with a recognised leader, styling themselves the " Clutching Hand Gang." Needless to say, the gang was broken up, but this entailed the sending of several of the children to industrial schools and others were birched or placed on probation.

3. Pictures which are objectionable, indecent, or suggestive of immorality should be firmly suppressed. Of course, no cinema proprietor would dream of presenting a picture absolutely indecent. The conditions attached to the licences we issue here include the prohibition I have named and only once have I met with a refusal to withdraw a picture to which I objected. It was undoubtedly very beautifully staged, but the immoral tendency was quite apparent. In spite of my embargo the

picture was shown for a week, with the result that I objected to the renewal of the licence, my objection prevailed and the house was closed. This object lesson to others has been most salutary. In Edinburgh the proprietors of the different shows may be particularly careful in the selection of the films exhibited, but in some of our houses particularly those frequented by the poorer classes, there is a tendency, I presume for the sake of attracting large audiences, to sail very close to the wind, and strict supervision is necessary.

4. Otherwise I am in general agreement with Mr. Ross and do not think the possibilities of the picture properly applied both as an educational and entertaining agency have been fully appreciated, but if improperly applied much mischief may quite conceivably follow.

JOHN MORTON,
Chief Constable.

HULL

19th March, 1917.

With the opening remarks of the Chief Constable of Edinburgh I agree. The cinema is undoubtedly very popular and has come to stay. I also agree that there is in the cinema a considerable power for good, and that an educative, morally wholesome and bright entertainment is very often provided. But the usual programme of the cinema show in a place like Hull contains a good deal that is neither educative nor morally wholesome, and is even calculated to have a bad effect on the mental capacity of young people.

I agree that it is desirable to keep the cinema clear of indecent or suggestive representations, but there are other parts of the programme which, though they cannot be called indecent, are likely to have a bad influence on the development of young people; and I think that while all cinema shows should be rigidly censored for indecency, those to which persons under a certain age are admitted should also be censored from other points of view. A few cases have occurred here where the exhibition of films showing crime has been the means of inciting boys to commit crime, but these cases are not very frequent. There are numerous cases where boys have taken to stealing for the purpose of procuring money with which to pay for admission to the picture house, and I do not agree with the Chief Constable of Edinburgh that these cases are rare; but I do agree with him that it cannot be brought as a fault against the picture houses. Boys must be taught in other ways to resist this temptation in the same way as other temptations which they are bound to meet with.

The chief objection to picture houses, which cannot be cured by censorship, is that they feed and increase the desire for pleasure until it is pursued to the detriment of other necessary things—in fact, it becomes a craze; and it has resulted in Hull in undue neglect by mothers of their household responsibilities. At the same time I cannot suggest any remedy for this, except a better education of the people. It cannot, of course, be used as an argument for the suppression of picture houses.

I agree with the Chief Constable of Edinburgh that the picture houses have been the means of attracting some—but I should say not very many—who otherwise would have resorted to the public-house.

I have a very strong objection to insufficiently lighted picture houses, but it is quite possible now to show good pictures in a properly lighted room, and most towns, I believe, now have a rule requiring the picture houses to be so illuminated that any part of the house can be seen from any other part.

GEORGE MORLEY,
Chief Constable.

BOROUGH OF HYDE

25th April, 1917.

Generally I agree with Mr. Ross, but I am quite unable to endorse his statement as to juveniles. I have found many cases directly traceable to these pictures; and, like Mr. Ross, I cannot too strongly condemn pictures which show any kind of criminal at work.

J. W. DANBY,
Chief Constable.

IPSWICH COUNTY BOROUGH POLICE

17th March, 1917.

I entirely concur. I am, however, of opinion that the increase of indictable offences recently noticeable amongst juvenile offenders is in some measure due to ideas imbibed from melodramatic films dealing with crime. The managers of various cinematograph theatres in Ipswich have recently conferred with the Watch Committee and have given an undertaking not to show any films to which reasonable objection may be taken on the grounds of their being of an immoral, undesirable, or objectionable nature.

ARTHUR T. SCHREIBER (Captain),
Chief Constable.

KETTERING

Northamptonshire Constabulary,
11th March, 1917.

I endorse Mr. Ross's views, with the exception of " Juvenile Crime."

In my opinion juvenile crime on the part of boys is due in a great measure to the love of cinemas, and in my experience, it is inducive to them stealing for the purpose of visiting them. I have had several cases where boys have set out to steal for this purpose, and in my opinion, juveniles under the age of fourteen years should not be admitted at any time, unless accompanied by their parents.

W. G. HOOPER,
Superintendent.

KIDDERMINSTER

13th March, 1917.

I consider it an excellent report, it deals with all sides of the question, there seems to be nothing of importance to add. However, my own experience teaches me, that too much credence should not be given to the excuses of children when before the magistrates; they are very often questioned, and the question often suggests the answer; the youth of the present day is 'cute and soon sees an opening for an excuse. There may be reasons why pictures which show how burglars and other criminals work should be eliminated from the films; some boys no doubt look upon these criminals as heroes, and straightway emulate them. It would be well to prohibit such pictures altogether, with those of immoral suggestiveness; it would be almost useless to limit the ages of boys, it would be unworkable.

I suppose these inquiries have been brought about mainly in consequence of the great increase of juvenile crime. The root of the mischief is want of discipline in the homes, and at school. Masters have very little power over these youngsters; the law is, or appears to be, dead against corporal punishment; years ago constables and schoolmasters used to cane freely with very good results, but that is a thing of the past.

Speaking of cinemas generally, landlords of public-houses dislike them because people cannot be at two places at the same time ; that is some evidence that they are doing good instead of harm, and it is a kind of entertainment that admirably suits the tastes of the rising generation, because there is no mental or physical effort required to understand them ; the pictures speak for themselves.

E. BENNETT,
Chief Constable.

KILMARNOCK

27th April, 1917.

I have carefully gone over the Précis of the evidence of Mr. Ross. There are four picture houses in this burgh, and no case has come under my notice in which the commission of the offence was influenced by the cinema. It is only recently that the picture-going habit has been taken up in this burgh, and consequently I have not had the same opportunity of studying its effects as Mr. Ross. So far, however, as my experience goes I agree with the gist of his evidence.

A. CAMERON,
Chief Constable.

KIRKCALDY

21st April, 1917.

I agree in general with Mr. Ross's views. Since the inauguration of the cinema houses in this burgh, a number of years ago, I have only received two complaints regarding the conducting of these entertainments. The first complaint applied to the film that was being shown, but on visiting the place personally, the occupier most willingly showed me the pictures on the screen, and I saw no cause for complaint. The other was an attempted indecent assault, owing to the darkness of the place, but on my making a representation to the occupiers of these houses, a considerable improvement was made in the lighting, and since then no complaint has reached me. I have, however, had a number of cases of juveniles before the police court, charged with thefts of a paltry nature, whereon the boys being asked why they committed the theft, replied that it was to get to the picture houses. While that was so, I agree with Mr. Ross, that boys will continue to steal although the picture houses were a thing of the past. Since the outbreak of war I have considered these places a necessity, especially where a body of troops are stationed, as these men, after their day's drill is over, have no-where to go, and in many instances would otherwise spend their time in public-houses, which would not be beneficial either to themselves or the country.

D. GATHERUM,
Chief Constable.

BOROUGH OF LANCASTER

20th March, 1917.

I cannot endorse Mr. Ross's views altogether. That the picture houses are popular goes without saying, but that the entertainments provided are educative is true only in a limited sense, indeed, the pictures which are most popular are not educative at all. Whilst there are pictures that come under this category, my experience is that they are very few. If there were more educative pictures, say of natural history studies, foreign travel, and pictures that would give an idea of the extent of the British Empire, and its resources and responsibilities, instead of pictures based upon novels, which exploit the sex problems, wild and impossible adventures, and so-called comic pictures, it would be far better. I agree that the cinema attracts many who would otherwise resort to public-houses, but do not think it has had the slightest influence on the habitual drinker.

There is a wide difference between a picture which could be called indecent, and one which is merely suggestive of immorality; no one would be allowed to exhibit the former, many of the latter we are unable to interfere with. So far as juvenile crime is concerned, it is true juvenile criminality existed before the days of picture houses, but the craze amongst children for attending these houses has added another incentive to those formerly in existence, and in Lancaster we have had several cases where the commission of juvenile crimes have been solely attributable to this cause. In conclusion, I should like to say, that so far as the picture houses prove a counter-attraction to the public-house I consider it to be all to the good, and if the pictures were more educative and less of the silly element introduced, I consider they may be of great service.

CHAS. E. HARRISS,
Chief Constable.

LEAMINGTON

25th April, 1917.

I have read the Précis very carefully, and agree with Mr. Ross's remarks in general. Cinemas are well patronised in this town by all classes and are visited nightly by the police. Nothing has appeared in any of the films to call for police interference and the houses are well conducted.

T. T. EARNSHAW,
Chief Constable.

LEITH

23rd April, 1917.

The cinema as a means of public entertainment and amusement is certainly very popular, more especially amongst the young, and to a large extent do good. During recent years cinema exhibitions have been conducted on a higher moral scale, but I think there is room for improvement still. To people of ripe years and high moral standing there can be no danger from the cinema as presently conducted, but pictures suggestive of immorality, depicting burglaries, and drama full of vulgarities are bound to have an evil influence on youths of both sexes who are weak in morals and require to be protected against their own passions. I have no doubt the cinema has contributed towards the increase in crime among boys under sixteen years of age.

JNO. MACLEOD,
Chief Constable.

LIVERPOOL

See the evidence of Mr. J. G. Legge, Director of Education for Liverpool, pp. 28–46.

LONDONDERRY

20th May, 1917.

I have carefully read over the evidence of Mr. Ross, and I fully endorse everything he has said regarding the cinema. No case of crime has come under my notice which would be attributed to the influence of cinema exhibitions. I, however, think there should be very strict censorship to cut out everything of an immoral tendency.

J. F. RYAN, D.I., R.I.C.,
Chief Constable.

MAIDSTONE

Kent County Constabulary,
27th March, 1917.

I now have the honour to inform you that I have called for reports on the subject of your letter from the superintendents of the thirteen police divisions in this county, with the following result.

The general opinion is that the influence of the cinema upon the public is good, and that it has the undoubted effect of attracting many who would otherwise resort to the public-house for their recreation, and thus has been instrumental in reducing drunkenness throughout the entire county. There is no evidence that immoral displays have been given, nor have any complaints been received by the police on that score. In one or two districts it is held that juvenile crime has been increased by the exhibition of films showing burglars and criminals at work, and it has also been found that the proceeds of thefts have been spent upon the cinema. It is natural that the influence of the cinema should depend upon the films displayed, and there seems little doubt that if there were sufficient control to eliminate such pictures as may be instrumental in inciting juveniles to emulate the burglars, etc., shown on the films, and also such films as may be suggestive of immorality, the influence of the cinema would be absolutely to the good, and that it would form a simple, cheerful and inexpensive recreation for many hard-working men and women and their families. The area covered by the reports received by me contains crowded seaport towns, pleasure resorts, country towns and rural areas, and as such may be considered representative in many ways.

H. M. A. WARDE,
Chief Constable of Kent.

MANCHESTER

See the evidence of Mr. Spurley Hey, Director of Education, Manchester, pp. 157–171.

MARGATE

28th April, 1917.

I agree with Mr. Ross on every point referred to, except that I have come across several instances where boys have committed thefts primarily for the purpose of gratifying their fascination and desire to see the cinema. I am of opinion that there are other classes of films beside those referred to in Mr. Ross's evidence which are harmful to the well-being of juveniles. I refer to the comedy films, more particularly to some of —— and —— films, which, to say the least, are undoubtedly vulgar. I think pictures which show a man expectorating on another, and similar behaviour, as being outside the pale of decency and should be eliminated from public exhibitions. Again, the lighting of the cinema auditorium is a matter which, in my opinion, demands immediate attention, inasmuch as the darkness of these places permits acts of misbehaviour to be indulged in which are offensive to other people who unfortunately happen to be seated near the offenders—indeed, such conduct would never be practised in a public audience in a properly lighted room.

A. APPLEYARD,
Chief Constable.

NEWCASTLE-UPON-TYNE

[See also the evidence of Mr. Percival Sharp, B.Sc., Director of Education for Newcastle-on-Tyne, pp. 282–287.]

17th March, 1917.

I have to inform you that I am of opinion that the cinema should be an educative as well as a pleasure-giving entertainment, and that, on the whole, it is the desire of those who produce films to make it so. On the other hand, there is no doubt that many of the films represent sensational and criminal features which are likely to exercise a baneful influence upon young people, and there has been a tendency shown in some cases to border on what is suggestive of immorality without being actually suggestive. The titles, too, are sometimes more suggestive than the representations themselves. With regard to the inducement to crime, such as thefts in order to obtain means for admission to picture houses, there have been some cases here, and in particular two cases in which the method of the theft was practically that represented in the pictures, the delinquents stating that they had laid their plans on the lines seen by them at a cinematograph entertainment. This matter has for some time engaged the attention of the Chief Constables' Association of Cities and Boroughs, of which I have the honour this year to be President, and at the Annual Meeting held in this city in May last the following resolution was adopted, viz. "That this Conference is of opinion that the establishment of a central Government censor of cinematograph films is essential, and will conduce to the reduction of juvenile crime in the country."

J. B. WRIGHT,
Chief Constable.

NEWCASTLE (STAFFORDSHIRE)

26th April, 1917.

I agree with Mr. Ross, but my experiences respecting the last paragraph on p. 176 and the last but one on p. 177 have been otherwise, as in several instances in this borough it has been found that juvenile thieves have spent nearly the whole of the proceeds on cinemas, and in other cases, although exhibitions of criminal films may not have been altogether the cause, they have, I have found, been a contributing cause.

WILLIAM FORSTER,
Chief Constable.

PENZANCE

7th May, 1917.

I have carefully read the report and agree with most of what Mr. Ross has said, but I do not think the cinemas in West Cornwall give such an educative programme as Mr. Ross says are given in Edinburgh. In county boroughs the licences are granted by the town councils or magistrates, but in non-county boroughs the licences are granted by the Standing Joint Committee of the county in which the town is situate. Take Penzance, for instance; the cinematograph licences are granted by the Cornwall Standing Joint Committee which sits at Bodmin—fifty-six miles from here. If the local justices had the granting of these licences they would have a better opportunity of imposing conditions that were suitable to the town when granting the licences. Then there is the question of children attending the evening performances. My opinion is, that not any child who attends school should be allowed to attend a performance that did not finish by 8 p.m. It would also be much better if suitable films could be shown at children's performances, but the cry of the managers is, that it would not pay to get special films.

H. KENYON,
Head Constable.

PLYMOUTH

12*th March*, 1917.

I have to inform you that I am fully in agreement with practically all that Mr. Ross has said. There is, however, one part in which I do not entirely agree, and that is where it is stated on page 8 that his experience has been that the proceeds of thefts by juveniles have gone to satisfy their fondness or craze for gambling. Such has not been my experience here. In practically all the cases where juveniles have been charged here with theft the proceeds have been spent either in cinemas or sweets. Juvenile gambling here is not very extensive.

J. D. SOWERBY,
Chief Constable.

PORTSMOUTH

14*th March*, 1917.

I entirely agree with the remarks of the Chief Constable of Edinburgh, as stated by him in his report on cinema exhibitions and their influence. I must, however, say that in this county borough, instances have come to light in which boys have left the cinema and immediately tried to emulate films showing burglaries being committed, and in consequence were brought before the justices.

T. DAVIES,
Chief Constable.

READING

20*th March*, 1917.

I have to say that I entirely agree with the Précis. If there is the same supervision over the films produced as there is in ordinary stage plays, there can be no more possible harm in the former than there is in the latter. If this is done the cinematograph is a cheap, healthy entertainment, and can have no more bad effect on the audience, young or old, than a stage play.

J. S. HENDERSON (Captain),
Chief Constable.

ROCHDALE

29*th March*, 1917.

I may say, I am generally in agreement with the statement made by Mr. Ross, but with regard to pages 175-6, I have several cases where boys set out to steal in order to go to the serial class of picture.

LEONARD BARRY,
Chief Constable.

ROTHERHAM

15*th March*, 1917.

I have to state that I do not altogether agree with Mr. Ross, as I am strongly of the opinion that some of the pictures shown in cinema houses have a detrimental effect on children's minds. In support of my opinion, I have to submit that as recently as the 21st of February of this year, nine juveniles (ages ranging from ten to thirteen years) who described themselves as the "Clutching Hand Gang," were brought before the Rotherham Borough Justices upon charges of larceny. Some time before this trial took place, a film named the —— was exhibited in various cinema houses in this borough, and I understand that in one portion of this picture certain persons operate as thieves. It is, therefore, safe to assume that in the case of these juveniles, the idea of styling themselves the "Clutching Hand Gang" originated either in the cinema houses when the film was being shown, or in consequence of the film being advertised by means of posters on the hoardings. Also, if the idea of styling themselves the "Clutching Hand Gang" was obtained by these youthful thieves through the above medium, most probably the idea of actual thieving was derived from the same source. I also submit that at the present time, proceedings are pending against three lads (one aged twelve, and two aged thirteen years), in respect of a charge of stealing eleven shillings in money, a quantity of Woodbine cigarettes, sugar, Quaker Oats and condensed milk.

Inquiries have been instituted with a view to determining the character of these boys, and by the admission of two of them it has been ascertained that, since last September, they, together with the third boy, have been systematically entering lock-up or other premises, and stealing goods. In all, about fifteen offences have been admitted by them. Their methods of entering the premises in question appear to have varied with the difficulties they had to overcome. At one place they got through a skylight, at another they got through the cellar, two more entrances were effected through windows, whilst to show their absence of fear they crossed the Midland Main Line, near to Holmes Lane, at pitch dark. Two of these boys state that they obtained their ideas of breaking and entering premises, etc., from seeing similar incidents depicted at the picture houses, and they specifically mention certain films from which they got ideas.

Probably to evade arrest, they had arranged to board a railway wagon to get away from Rotherham. This, again, was an idea that they had obtained from certain films. However, their courage seems to have failed them in putting their last idea into effect, and in due course they were arrested. It has also been ascertained that these boys have always appeared to be well-clothed and fed, but it seems that there has not been proper supervision by their fathers, etc.

Several other cases have been brought to my notice where boys of tender years have been so obsessed with a desire to attend these places of entertainment (either because they have been before, or because other boys have spoken to them of certain things which they had seen there, or on account of startling posters), that they have stolen money from their homes in order that they might gain admission. In these cases, however, no legal proceedings ensued, but sometimes the thefts were followed by others of a more serious nature, and ultimately the boys have been subjected to police court proceedings.

There is no doubt that some films bring before the view of children and young persons certain acts, which, if emulated, would bring them within the scope of criminal law, and I have a strong conviction that certain films shown in cinema houses together with lack of parental control are partly the cause of the increase of juvenile crime in this borough. To remedy this situation, I would respectfully suggest that those portions of films, which are likely to deprave youthful minds, be cut out by the censor. As regards the effect of cinema entertainments on the sale of intoxicating liquor, I beg to state that the decrease in drunkenness in this borough is no doubt largely due to the counter-attraction provided by cinema houses and music halls.

E. WEATHERHOGG,
Chief Constable.

SALFORD

26th April, 1917.

I have to inform you that I agree with most of the conclusions come to by him. I am, however, in disagreement with him when he says that he thinks there is danger in the representation of burglars and other criminals at work. I rather take another view, and think perhaps a boy who has a *penchant* for pilfering and petty crime, could possibly be reformed by seeing the futility of the crimes appearing in the pictures. There is always a horrible end to the criminal, he is either hung, sentenced to a long term of penal servitude, or in some other way brought to see the error of his ways, and if the boy who is watching the pictures is going to take notice of the way in which the criminal works, surely he is going to take notice of what happens to him in the end. I, therefore, think that pictures generally point out the moral, that honesty is, after all, the best policy.

C. V GODFREY (Major),
Chief Constable.

SCARBOROUGH

16th March, 1917.

I quite agree with the remarks on pages 1 and 2 of the statement which was enclosed with your letter.

I cannot, however, endorse the assertions on page 3 that the popularity of the cinema is " brought about by the fact that the entertainment is educative, morally wholesome, and bright," or that " the popularity is a guarantee of its power for good in the community." Betting, gaming and drinking intoxicating liquor are popular, but that is no " guarantee of their power for good." Again it is stated that " the cinema, as a rule, has proved to those who patronise it an educative, morally healthy, and pleasure-giving entertainment." I regret to say that I have frequently seen films which have disgusted me and to which neither of the above terms can be applied. I agree with the statement that some of the films cannot be classed as " indecent representations," and accordingly do not come within the scope of the criminal law, but I admit that many of them contain representations calculated to pervert and contaminate the minds of those who witness them and are decidedly objectionable for exhibition to young persons.

A film known as —— is referred to. I haven't seen that particular film, but I have seen ——, and surely it is notorious that this film was passed by the " British Board of Film Censors," although it has since then been stopped from exhibition in many towns, and actions have in consequence been brought against the police !

The statements generally on pages 5 and 6 seem to admit that there are films being shown which are " suggestive of immorality," and which are " pernicious " and " which show burglars and criminals at work."

On page 7 the " insatiable desire " of boys to visit cinemas is referred to, and whilst they may be attracted by reason of an entertainment being " bright," I am afraid that the " educative and morally wholesome " pictures do not offer the strongest incentive.

In my opinion the cinema entertainment has become such a great attraction to the public that it is necessary in the interest of the public that exhibitions of pictures should be controlled by some person or persons outside of and independent of the producers and exhibitors of films and that local censorship by the justices or police is quite inadequate and must end in failure.

When questioning small boys as to where they got their ideas from with regard to certain offences with which they were charged, I have been told by them that they saw it " at the pictures," but I have had no legal power to stop the exhibition of films depicting the commission of crime and wrongdoing, and I submit that it is unfair to the proprietors and exhibitors of films as well as to the police that the approval or otherwise of films should be left to the local authority of each town in which the exhibition takes place.

To sum my views up in a very few words I think that the cinema is such a popular institution and there is so much good to be derived by the public from the entertainment provided that it is of national importance that the evil influences which are present in some representations should be eliminated.

HY. WINDSOR,
Chief Constable.

SHEFFIELD

STATEMENT OF MAJOR HALL-DALWOOD

Chief Constable of the City of Sheffield, on Cinematograph Shows
and their relation to child-life.

I entirely agree with the general statements made by the Chief Constable of Edinburgh that cinematograph performances have become a permanent form of amusement of the people, and if systematically controlled are of a highly educative and instructional form of relaxation. Much more could be accomplished by the Education Authorities in producing to the notice of children films of historical and geographical interest as well as travel and other interesting subjects. Facts are more easily impressed upon a child's memory by object lessons, such as pictures would supply, than the older and effete form of lectures, maps, etc., which up to a certain age make little or no impression. In consequence these subjects being uninteresting in the form presented to children, render the knowledge of them imperfect in adult life. Geometry, mensuration and other subjects, as zoology, geology, physiology, bacteriology, and even languages, could be similarly treated. I am of opinion that many of the films exhibited in this and other cities, although of such a nature that no action could be taken in the courts, are undesirable either from the point of suggestiveness or as being contrary to good taste so far as children are concerned. By suggestiveness I mean that they are calculated to engender in the youthful mind the idea of lawlessness, inducement to commit crime and other dangerous activities.

In Sheffield some cases of crime committed by youths have certainly been traceable to the lessons taught in picture houses. One, for example, quite recently where three small boys were convicted of tampering with the mail vans from which many letters had been extracted (the majority were fortunately recovered), the *modus operandi* was conceived from the halls and by the reading of adventurous novels. Undoubtedly picture palaces form an attractive outlet for money either stolen direct or realised by children on articles which they have stolen, and many such cases are disclosed in the prosecution of children for offences of felony, but it is only on very rare occasions that it can be positively said that the felony was committed with the express intention of providing means for admission to cinema houses.

As to the moral effect upon the juvenile mind, the precocious youngster with criminal tendencies will naturally have stirred within him a desire to emulate the exploits of expert burglars, and the depredations of criminals of which faked and exaggerated representation sometimes appear on the screen, and cases have occurred where crude attempts of that description have been made, but I do not think it could be definitely established that such representation has been the cause of leading boys into a consistent and habitual life of crime. Pictures of this class produce no appreciable effect upon the normal adult mind, and consequently judgment cannot properly be formed from that direction as to whether the community is ill-affected. And, in the case of children and adolescents the noticeable effects, except in few cases, are not immediate. It does seem inadvisable that at an impressionable age, pictures of a morbidly exciting character should be constantly viewed by children, and particularly when it is borne in mind that the children, where parental control is lacking and in some cases non-existent, form a large proportion of those regularly frequenting the halls.

The problem is not one easy of solution. A Saturday afternoon children's matinee at each hall would provide a sufficient weekly entertainment of that character for the average child (up to fourteen years of age). The programme in that case would be of an educative, instructive, and healthily exciting character. To secure this arrangement, the co-operation of the cinema proprietors would be necessary. Differentiation between adolescents and adults seems quite impracticable. It would, therefore, appear that what is required is Government censorship.

The objection to the pictures suggestive of indecency or immorality ought not to require any official demonstration to support it, but such films should be their own condemnation, for whatever may be the effect on the individual mind and whatever definite act of immorality the exhibition of such pictures may lead to, there can only be one opinion amongst right thinking people as to the general result upon the moral susceptibilities of the community. Unconsciously almost, the moral tone is reduced and the finer feelings become dulled and stifled. At present authorities in various cities and towns take a different view as to the exhibition of certain films, but so far as Sheffield is concerned the proprietors of the cinema houses have always acquiesced immediately to the wishes of the police, and many objections raised by the authorities have been met with the utmost cordiality.

To place the exhibition of films on a systematic basis I would make the following suggestions—

1. The appointment of a Government censor who would be responsible for the inspection of every film from whatever source, English or otherwise.

2. That it should be an offence for an alteration to be made in a film after it has been inspected by the Censor Department. This would prevent the addition or deletion of any portion of a film.

3. The proprietor of a cinema house where a film was to be exhibited to produce certificate from censor department. This to be countersigned by the chief of police. Disregard of this regulation would be an offence.

4. Censorship of films by private companies should be discontinued.

5. Films produced by firms of foreign countries should be specially subjected to censorship and all present films now exhibited should be re-sanctioned.

J. HALL-DALWOOD (Major),
Chief Constable.

SOUTHAMPTON

21st March, 1917.

In general, I agree with all the remarks of Mr. Ross, although there have been one or two cases here of children charged with larceny, and it has been stated that money was stolen in order that tickets might be purchased for cinemas.

W. E. JONES,
Chief Constable.

SOUTHPORT

1st May, 1917.

In the absence of the chief constable, who is at present serving with H.M. Forces, I have to state that from my observations in this borough I agree with Mr. Ross's statements, particularly with regard to pictures suggestive of immorality, and, when children are present, to those depicting burglars and other criminals at work. Perhaps I may also state that in my opinion films to be shown to children should be chosen largely for their educational value, such as scenes in foreign countries, historical incidents, adventure, shipping, the army and navy, the various industries of our own and other countries, and subjects morally wholesome in the strict sense, not necessarily omitting humorous subjects. The matter of supervision in cinema theatres, particularly where there are so-called private boxes, should in my opinion be considered. Emergency exits, distance of the front seats from the screen, and ventilation, are also matters for consideration.

J. WAREING,
Deputy Chief Constable.

SOUTH SHIELDS

14th March, 1917.

In the main I agree with Mr. Ross, but in regard to his assertion in the last paragraph on page 6 of the report, that no case has come to his knowledge or that of his detective officers of juveniles committing crime in emulation of what they had seen at the cinema, I am not in that happy position. Here we have had such experiences, and I certainly think that films which show means of larceny from the person, acts of burglary, and other methods of committing crime, where the persons are masked and armed, should be prohibited; as well as films which contain amours, the lasciviousness being only too palpable. It is not what is shown, but the horrible suggestiveness which is harmful. If the cinema is kept clean, I consider it a means of educative amusement, and it no doubt affords a cheap form of recreation for those who would spend their time, possibly, in less desirable environment.

WILLIAM SCOTT,
Chief Constable.

STOCKPORT

16th March, 1917.

I quite agree with Mr. Ross's evidence in the main. I certainly think, and can prove, that they have formed a counter-attraction to public-houses, inasmuch as many former visitors to public-houses may now be seen frequently attending the various picture houses. I have also had it reported to me of one man having stated that he was much better in health and in pocket by attending the picture houses on Saturday afternoons and evenings instead of spending his time drinking pints of beer in public-houses, as hitherto. As regards their influence for evil upon the people, I must say that pictures showing how crimes are committed are to my mind calculated to have a serious influence upon children shorn of parental control, and those of criminal tendencies; or even upon grown-up people of weak minds and criminal tendencies. Such pictures, that frequently end in the culprit escaping, following a demonstration of the criminal's cleverness in carrying out the crime so as to baulk the police, must assuredly influence persons of the type before-mentioned to try to emulate the hero of the play. I am also of opinion that pictures suggestive of immorality should not be permitted. Those are the pictures that find favour with youths and girls of immoral tendencies, and there can be no gainsaying the fact that they later form subjects of comment between such youths and girls, either in the workshop or in the street, that must inevitably lead to acts of immorality in many cases — possibly unknown to the police. We have to remember that littles lead to far greater evils, and that evils resulting from immoral influences are usually practised in secrecy; therefore, the police cannot very well be in a position to say that such pictures have or have not had some evil influence upon certain individuals in the audience. As regards children stealing to go to picture houses, such cases have been well established in this town; still, I quite agree such children would steal for the purpose of going to any place to which they had formed a desire to go. To that I attach little importance; still, when we come to remember that there is a possibility of such children seeing pictures of supposed expert thieves at work, hoodwinking the police, it may well be imagined that such a visit to the cinema would not fill them with remorse for their previous wrongdoings.

Personally, I think picture houses have done much good in the furtherance of temperance, and I also think they have a tendency to broaden the minds of people who frequent them. They somewhat take them out of their own little spheres—especially where places of interest are shown. I think there is much good work that could still be done by picture houses of an educational nature if more use were made of them in that direction. Feats of skilful engineering could be shown in the various stages, as also could the manufacture of various goods; also historical pictures, etc., all of which would be interesting and instructive. These, of course, could well be followed by numerous pictures of a mirthful nature without the necessity of resorting to those of the criminal, vulgar, or suggestive type.

FREDERICK BRINDLEY,
Chief Constable.

STAFFORD

12th March, 1917.

The allegations made against picture houses are, I believe, in brief, as follows—

1. That they are rendezvous and meeting places for immoral purposes, and that the conditions of darkness inseparable from the display of films are conducive to this result.
2. That the films displayed are in some cases an advertisement of and encouragement to immoral courses and lead to results of that nature.
3. That the films, in some other cases, surround criminal adventures with a fictitious halo which has an unfavourable influence on young and impressionable minds.

As regards (1) there is probably a small element of truth in it; but the general paying public would cease to patronise the picture theatres if the evil were of a really serious character.

As regards (2) it is quite clear that film representations do not go so far towards indecency and immoral suggestions as may be done with impunity on the stage. The question is merely one of detail and, of course, censorship is necessary.

As regards (3) it is probably the most serious of the difficulties. There is no doubt whatever as to the imitative character of crime among young persons, and pictures of thrilling crimes are more than likely to have a de-moralising effect on young persons of twelve or thirteen years of age up to, say, sixteen or seventeen years of age. Censorship in the case of these films is far more difficult than in the case of films likely to be an inducement to immorality. The difficulty can only be met by censorship; but I do not see how a mere representation (for instance) of a burglary can be banned altogether; and it is not easy to suggest any satisfactory method of dealing with the question. In addition to the above-mentioned objections raised against picture houses, I understand that it is alleged that boys commit thefts for the purpose of obtaining funds to spend on this form of pleasure. The same objection might be made against lollypops. In favour of picture palaces it may be said that they provide a cheap and to a great extent in-structive form of popular entertainment; also that they are to a considerable extent a counter-attraction to public-houses, although in this connection the closing at present of public-houses in the afternoon must be borne in mind in estimating the extent to which this is the case.

G. A. ANSON (Lieut.-Colonel),
Chief Constable of Staffordshire.

STIRLING

25th April, 1917.

I agree generally with the views Mr. Ross so well and ably expresses.

The necessity for the most strict censorship, however, seems to me to be of paramount importance and cannot be too strongly urged, to eliminate entirely from the cinema entertainment such films as are in the slightest degree sug-gestive of indecency or immorality, and also those films which tend to be more harmful than instructive or educative, such as might impress and incite the minds of the young to any act of wrongdoing.

GEO. NICOL,
Chief Constable.

STOKE-ON-TRENT, HANLEY

12th March, 1917.

I have read the statement of evidence submitted by Mr. Ross, and in the main I agree with him. With regard to his reference to the film ——, I may say that the Chairman of the Watch Committee here and myself viewed a private exhibition of the film before it was shown here and we saw nothing indecent; any one having read the book before viewing the film might take an exaggerated view of some portions of the film. I cannot subscribe to the definite statement made in the penultimate paragraph of his précis.

R. J. CARTER,
Chief Constable.

TUNBRIDGE WELLS BOROUGH POLICE

13th March, 1917.

I entirely concur, as everything mentioned by Mr. Ross applies to Tunbridge Wells in a lesser degree, having regard to the difference in the population of the two places. The absence of disorder in the streets has been very noticeable since a hippodrome and cinema theatres have been established in this town.

CHARLES PRIOR,
Chief Constable.

COUNTY BOROUGH OF WALSALL

25th April, 1917.

I agree with many of Mr. Ross's observations. With regard to juvenile crime, however, I have known of several cases where thefts were committed to obtain money for admission. The other week a boy, aged ten years, was caught in the Co-operative Stores with two quarter-pound packets of tea and a tin of condensed milk in his possession. In reply to a question put by the bench as to why he stole the articles, he said, " My mother wouldn't give me any money to see the pictures. I took the tea intending to sell it to get the money."

A. THOMSON,
Chief Constable.

WIGAN

15th March, 1917.

1. *Page* 175. *The cinema as a power for good, etc.*
    It has certainly manifested itself as an influence for evil, as it has been proved beyond doubt that it is partly responsible for the great increase in crime committed by juveniles.
2. *Page* 175. *The cinema as an influence, etc.*
    Many of the pictures are of a character not calculated to edify, therefore must act as an adverse influence.
3. *Page* 175. *As being educational, etc.*
    Why the qualification " as a rule " ? This could only obtain when the films are good.
4. *Page* 175. *As a means of preventing people visiting public-houses and getting drunk.*—AGREED.

B B

5. *Page* 175. *Character of films exhibited.*

    The question of films being indecent or otherwise (*suggestions of immorality*).

    A suggestive picture, as a suggestive book, is most dangerous because of its subtle character. It has a fascinating influence on young life and is very harmful.

6. *Page* 175, *film* ———

    Do not need any consideration. They stand condemned (unqualified).

7. *Page* 177. *Burglars, etc.*

    This is not my experience.

8. *Page* 177. *Cinemas as conducive to theft.*

    I have had cases where boys committed thefts, their object being to obtain money to enable them to go to the cinema.

9. *Page* 177. *Proceeds of theft for gambling,* etc.

    This is not my experience.

10. *Page* 177. *Boys will continue to steal.*

    Yes, but the cinema is responsible for the increase in juvenile crime, which is nearly 50 per cent. of the whole of the crimes committed.

General Baden Powell, on a recent visit to Wigan, lecturing the Boy Scouts, said : " Good pictures are a means of education, but a bad picture has a pernicious influence on young life."

JOHN S. PERCIVAL,
Chief Constable.

WINCHESTER

26th April, 1917.

Generally speaking, I endorse Mr. Ross's views.

I am certainly of opinion that all films ought to be censored before they are exhibited to the public. The question of admitting children to cinematograph performances appears to be one well worthy of consideration by the authorities.

JOHN SIM,
Head Constable of Winchester.

WINDSOR

4th May, 1917.

I inform you that the cinemas in this borough are both successful and popular with all classes and so far have been conducted to my satisfaction. Taken generally, my opinion does not differ much from that of the Chief Constable of Edinburgh. My experience has certainly been that the takings of licensed houses in the vicinity of the cinemas have been reduced.

J. T. CARTER,
Chief Constable.

WOLVERHAMPTON

16th March, 1917.

I consider it an excellent report, although I differ somewhat with regard to child entertainments. Matinees should be set apart for children, and only healthy or instructive films permitted. Children should not be allowed at any other cinema performance unless they are accompanied by either a parent or guardian. Films portraying Wild West or criminal pictures should under no circumstances be shown at such matinees, as they undoubtedly excite the minds of children, and in some cases brought to my notice have been copied and carried into execution in committing crimes. In my opinion there is nothing instructive for children in such films, hence my suggestion for their abolishment. The very few complaints received from the adult population respecting films shown prove conclusively that they are generally healthy and clean, but, of course, there have been and always will be, persons ready and anxious to find fault; they are generally those who only attend such entertainments when what is termed a "doubtful picture" is being shown. They attend more or less with the object of directing criticism at this particular film.

It is difficult to get uniformity of opinion; what might be considered objectionable or suggestive by some may be thought by others to be instructive, healthy, and presenting a good moral.

I think it is far better that there should be one committee of censors, representing the clergy, education, law, police, theatrical profession, novelists, etc., and their decision should be final. The composition of such a committee would save the local authorities much anxiety and secure uniformity of opinion throughout the country.

D. WEBSTER,
Chief Constable.

YORK

17th March, 1917.

I have carefully read the précis of evidence of the Chief Constable of Edinburgh. I think every one agrees that the growth of the cinema has been very considerable, and that the entertainments provided are witnessed by a very large number of men, women and children each week, and that being so it is of the highest importance that such entertainments should be carefully selected in order to ensure healthy recreation and amusement and to maintain a sound moral tone. I think the educational value of the cinema may be over-estimated, the amount of information thrown on to the screen in so short a time makes it very difficult to remember much of it, and in order to be of real use the picture would have to be repeated and a lecture given with it.

All films that have been shown cannot be said to have been morally wholesome. I have on several occasions had complaints, and I consider some thoughtful supervision is necessary to prevent such being shown. An exhibition can be bright and entertaining without bordering on the improper, as some have done. The popularity of the cinema, which must be admitted, may prove its power for good, but only so long as the entertainment given is of the right kind; if not, it may prove its power for evil, and that in some cases it has proved the reverse of good, I think cannot be doubted, particularly in the cases of young persons and children, some of whom, when they have got into trouble, have stated that the idea to commit the offence came from the pictures. I have heard it repeatedly stated by juveniles before the magistrates that they had committed thefts to get money to go to pictures; I agree, however, that that was no fault against the cinema. The cinema may have been, but I consider only to a very limited extent, a means of keeping people from the public-house. If the drink has not been obtained before going, it has been obtained afterwards.

I have had complaints about theatres and music-halls, and a careful supervision is required over all houses of public entertainment. With some exceptions, the cinema has provided interesting and pleasurable entertainments for large numbers of people who cannot afford to pay high rates of charges.

As stated by Mr. Ross, pictures showing burglars and other criminals at work should not be shown, nor should, of course, pictures bordering on the indecent or suggestive of immoral conduct.

JAS. BURROW,
Chief Constable

The following reached us too late to place in their right order—

DUBLIN

Dublin Castle,
29th May, 1917.

I am directed by the Chief Commissioner of Police to acknowledge the receipt of your letter of 8th instant, together with enclosure, and to inform you that he is in entire agreement with the views of Mr. Ross, which he has read with much interest.

No films of an indecent nature have been exhibited in this city, although in one or two instances private persons have taken exception to films which might perhaps be regarded as suggestive, but which did not justify police action.

There is no doubt that films depicting the perpetration of crime are objectionable in view of the effect which they may produce on young people, whose imitative propensities may be thereby excited. On the other hand, films generally illustrate the punishment falling on such evildoers, and this must, no doubt, have a deterrent effect. There have been some cases of theft by juveniles in which the offenders have alleged that their object was to procure the means of admission to picture houses. Children, however, who steal for this purpose would equally steal to gratify any other keen desire, and it can scarcely be said that the cinema can be held responsible for such crimes.

On the whole, the Chief Commissioner considers, having regard to the working of the Dublin picture houses, that the cinema is a source of much innocent amusement, and will, no doubt, as the taste of the public which patronises these theatres becomes more just, become a highly useful educative influence.

W. A. MAGILL,
Secretary.

GRIMSBY

16th June, 1917.

I have carefully perused the Précis of evidence given before the Commission by Chief Constable Ross, of Edinburgh, and endorse all he says. I have always contended that the much-maligned cinemas have very little to do with Juvenile Crime.

My opinion is that if more advantage were taken of Section 99, Sub-Section 1, of the Children's Act 1908, under which parents can be ordered to pay fines for offences committed by the children, this would have a very salutary effect, and we should hear of a substantial decrease in Juvenile Crime before very long.

JOHN STIRLING,
Chief Constable.

NATIONAL COUNCIL OF PUBLIC MORALS

FOR GREAT AND GREATER BRITAIN

Object: The Regeneration of the Race—Spiritual · Moral · Physical

President of National Council: THE LORD BISHOP OF BIRMINGHAM.

President of Ladies' Advisory Council: MRS. MARY SCHARLIEB, M.D., M.S.

Vice-Presidents:

The Viscount Clifden
The Lord Bishop of London
The Lord Bishop of Southwark
The Lord Bishop of Rochester
The Lord Bishop of Hereford
The Lord Bishop of Liverpool
The Lord Bishop of Ripon
The Lord Bishop of Bristol
The Lord Bishop of Peter-borough
The Lord Bishop of Chelmsford
The Lord Bishop of Llandaff
Francis, Bishop of Menevia
The Lord Kinnaird
The Lord Peckover
The Rt. Rev. The Bishop of Barking
The Rt. Rev. Bishop Welldon, D.D., Dean of Manchester
Very Rev. Henry Wace, D.D., Dean of Canterbury
Very Rev. H. Hensley Henson, D.D., Dean of Durham
Very Rev. W. Moore Ede, D.D., Dean of Worcester
Very Rev. P. M'Adam Muir, D.D.
Very Rev. Canon Barry, D.D.
Rev. the Hon. E. Lyttelton, M.A.
Rev. H. Montagu Butler, D.D.
Rev. A. R. Buckland, M.A.

The Very Rev. J. H. Hertz, Ph.D., Chief Rabbi
Rev. Prebendary Carlile, D.D.
Rev. W. Temple, M.A.
Rev. Principal Alexander Whyte, D.D.
Rev. Principal P. T. Forsyth, M.A., D.D.
Rev. Principal A. E. Garvie, M.A., D.D.
Rev. Principal W. B. Selbie, M.A.
Rev. Principal C. Chapman, LL.D.
General Bramwell Booth
Rev. Rabbi Prof. Hermann Gollancz, M.A., D.Lit.
Rev. J. Clifford, M.A., D.D.
Rev. R. F. Horton, M.A., D.D.
Rev. J. Monro Gibson, M.A., LL.D.
Principal T. F. Roberts, LL.D.
Rev. D. Brook, M.A., D.C.L.
Rev. J. D. Jones, M.A., B.D.
Rev. Sidney Berry, M.A.
Rev. Prof. J. H. Moulton, D.Lit.
Rev. Prof. H. Bisseker, M.A.
Rev. R. C. Gillie, M.A.
Rev. R. J. Campbell, M.A.
The Rt. Hon. Sir T. Clouston
W. Joynson-Hicks, Esq., M.P.
Prof. Sir T. Clifford Allbutt, K.C.B., D.Sc., F.R.S.
Lady Henry Somerset
Lady Battersea

Past Presidents:

THE RT. REV. BISHOP BOYD CARPENTER, K.C.V.O., D.D., D.C.L., D.LIT.
THE LORD BISHOP OF DURHAM.

Chairman of Committee:
PRINCIPAL A. E. GARVIE, M.A., D.D.

Vice-Chairman:
DR. C. W. SALEEBY, F.R.S., ED.

Hon. Treasurers:
PROF. H. GOLLANCZ, M.A., D.LIT.
REV. F. B. MEYER, B.A., D.D.

Director & Secretary:
REV. JAMES MARCHANT, F.R.S., ED., F.R.A.S., F.L.S.

Solicitors:
WONTNER & SONS.

Accountants and Auditors:
CARTER, CLAY & LINTOTT.

Bankers:
BARCLAY & CO.,
54 Lombard Street, E.C.

Vice-Presidents:

Lady Rhondda
Lady Aberconway
Lady Rucker
Mrs. Price Hughes
Sir Dyce Duckworth, Bart., M.D., LL.D.
Sir T. Fowell Buxton, Bart., G.C.M.G., D.L.
Prof. Sir J. Macdonell, K.C.B., LL.D.
Sir A. Pearce Gould, K.C.V.O.
Sir Thomas Glen-Coats, D.L.
Sir Thos. Barclay, LL.D., Ph.D.
Sir John Kirk, J.P.
Rev. Prof. T. Witton Davies, D.D.
Prof. G. Sims Woodhead, LL.D.
Prof. J. A. Thomson, M.A., LL.D.
Prof. Patrick Geddes, M.A.
Prof. J. H. Muirhead, M.A., LL.D.
Prof. J. S. Mackenzie, Litt.D.
A. Newsholme, C.H., M.D.
W. Leslie Mackenzie, LL.D.
His Worship G. F. Armita-e, J.P. M.D.
C. W. Saleeby, M.D., F.R.S., Ed.
John Murray, Esq., C.V.O., D.L.
Wm. Baker, Esq., M.A., LL.B.
Alderman B. Broadbent, M.A., J.P.
Howard Williams, Esq.
George Cadbury, Esq.
Arnold Butler, Esq., J.P.
Percy Alden, Esq., M.A., M.P.
J. Ramsay Macdonald, Esq., M.P.

Ladies' Advisory Council:

The Dowager Countess of Chichester
Viscountess Falmouth
Lady Willoughby de Broke
Lady Butlin
Lady Godlee
Lady Pearce Gould
Lady Procter
Lady Barrett, M.D.
Hon. E. Kinnaird
Mrs. Bisseker
Mrs. Bramwell Booth
Mrs. Burgwin
Mrs. George Cadbury
Miss Curtis
Miss Dugdale
Mrs. Gollancz
Mrs. J. H. Hertz
Mrs. Macnamara
Mrs. F. B. Meyer
Mrs. George Morgan
Mrs. Rutter
Mrs. Spender

Headquarters: 20 BEDFORD SQUARE, LONDON, W.C. 1.

PRINTED IN GREAT BRITAIN BY
RICHARD CLAY & SONS, LIMITED,
BRUNSWICK ST., STAMFORD ST., S.E. 1,
AND BUNGAY, SUFFOLK.